THE ASHGATE RESEARCH COMPANION
TO QUEER THEORY

Queer Interventions

Series editors:
Noreen Giffney
University of Limerick, Ireland
and Michael O'Rourke

Queer Interventions is an exciting, fresh and unique new series designed to publish innovative, experimental and theoretically engaged work in the burgeoning field of queer studies.

The aim of the series is to interrogate, develop and challenge queer theory, publishing queer work which intersects with other theoretical schools and is accessible whilst valuing difficulty; empirical work which is metatheoretical in focus; ethical and political projects and most importantly work which is self-reflexive about methodological and geographical location.

The series is interdisciplinary in focus and publishes monographs and collections of essays by new and established scholars. The editors intend the series to promote and maintain high scholarly standards of research and to be attentive to queer theory's shortcomings, silences, hegemonies and exclusions. They aim to encourage independence, creativity and experimentation: to make a queer theory that matters and to recreate it as something important; a space where new and exciting things can happen.

The Ashgate Research Companion to Queer Theory

Edited by

NOREEN GIFFNEY
University of Limerick, Ireland

MICHAEL O'ROURKE

Routledge
Taylor & Francis Group

LONDON AND NEW YORK

First published in paperback 2018

First published 2009
by Routledge
2 Park Square, Milton Park, Abingdon, Oxon OX14 4RN

and by Routledge
711 Third Avenue, New York, NY 10017

Routledge is an imprint of the Taylor & Francis Group, an informa business

British Library Cataloguing-in-Publication Data
A catalogue record for this book is available from the British Library

Library of Congress Cataloging-in-Publication Data
The Ashgate research companion to queer theory / [edited by] by Noreen Giffney
    and Michael O'Rourke.
      p. cm. — (Queer interventions)
    Includes bibliographical references and index.
    ISBN 978-0-7546-7135-0 (hardback) — ISBN 978-0-7546-9057-3 (ebook)
1. Queer theory. 2. Homosexuality—Philosophy. 3. Gender identity—Philosophy.
I. Giffney, Noreen. II. O'Rourke, Michael, 1976– III. Title: Research companion
to queer theory.
    HQ76.25.A83 2009
    306.76'601—dc22

ISBN: 978-0-7546-7135-0 (hbk)
ISBN: 978-1-138-50583-4 (pbk)
ISBN: 978-1-315-61348-2 (ebk)

Typeset in Palatino Linotype
by Apex CoVantage, LLC

Contents

For Nicole, my *editor*

For John, folk devil, I miss you

List of Contributors

Jonathan Alexander is Professor of English and Campus Writing Director at the University of California, Irvine. He is the author or editor of six books, including: *Literacy, Sexuality, Pedagogy: Theory and Practice for Composition Studies*; *Digital Youth: Emerging Literacies on the World Wide Web*; *Finding Out: An Introduction to LGBT Studies* (with Deb Meem and Michelle Gibson); *Argument Now: A Brief Rhetoric* (with Margaret Barber); *Role Play: Distance Learning and the Teaching of Writing* (edited with Marcia Dickson); and *Bisexuality and Transgenderism: InterSEXions of the Others* (edited with Karen Yescavage). For more information visit https://webfiles.uci.edu/jfalexan/pubweb/index.html.

Margot Gayle Backus is Associate Professor of English at the University of Houston, where she teaches modern and contemporary Irish literature and literary modernism. She has published articles in journals including *Signs, Cultural Critique, American Imago* and *Interventions*. Her study, *The Gothic Family Romance: Heterosexuality, Child Sacrifice and the Anglo-Irish Colonial Order* (Duke University Press 1999), won the 2001 American Conference for Irish Studies' prize for an outstanding first book. With Joseph Valente, she has completed forthcoming articles on sexual initiation in *Dubliners* and *A Portrait of the Artist as a Young Man*, and on the politics of shame in 'An Encounter' and *Ulysses*. Her long essay tracing James Joyce's allusions to the Oscar Wilde Trial throughout *Ulysses* is forthcoming in the *Joyce Studies Annual*, and she is currently completing work on an article tracing changing representations of children in the Irish nationalist press. She was the Irish American Cultural Institute's 2007–2008 Research Fellow at the National University of Ireland, Galway, and is writing a book tentatively entitled *Odd Jobs: James Joyce and the Cultural Logic of Scandal*.

Jon Binnie is Reader in Human Geography at Manchester Metropolitan University. He is the author of *The Globalization of Sexuality* (Sage 2004), co-author of *The Sexual Citizen: Queer Politics and Beyond* (Polity 2000) and *Pleasure Zones: Bodies, Cities, Spaces*, and co-editor of *Cosmopolitan Urbanism* (Routledge 2006).

Jayne Caudwell is Senior Lecturer in the sociology of sport and leisure cultures at the University of Brighton, UK. Her research tends to focus on gender and sexuality, more specifically ongoing debate surrounding social theories of sexuality and women's experiences of sport. She is the editor of *Sport, Sexualities and Queer/Theory* (Routledge 2006). Her most recent publications include '*Girlfight*: Boxing Women', *Sport in Society* 11:2–3, 2008; and '*Girlfight* and *Bend it Like Beckham*: Screening Sport, Sexuality and Women', *The Journal of Lesbian Studies* (forthcoming).

Kathryn Conrad is Associate Professor of English and Honors Faculty Fellow at the University of Kansas. She has published widely on Irish and Northern Irish culture and politics, particularly with regard to gender and sexuality. Her book *Locked in the Family Cell: Gender, Sexuality, and Political Agency in Irish National Discourse* (University of Wisconsin Press 2004) explores the relationship between constructions of gender and national identity. Her most recent work focuses on the changing political landscape in Northern Ireland, especially the relationship between the public sphere and public space.

Thomas A. Dowson is an independent scholar now living and working in France. He trained as an archaeologist in South Africa, specialising in the field of prehistoric art, and taught archaeology at the Universities of Southampton and Manchester. He has published widely on the rock arts of southern Africa and Western Europe, including *Images of Power: Understanding San Rock Art* (with David Lewis-Williams) and *Rock Engravings in Southern Africa*. In a number of published articles and conference presentations over the last decade he has developed a uniquely queer critique of archaeological practice. In 2000 he edited 'Queer Archaeologies' (volume 32.2 of *World Archaeology*).

Garrett P.J. Epp is Professor and Chair of the Department of English and Film Studies at the University of Alberta. He specialises and has published widely in the fields of early English drama, medieval English literature and queer theory. He is also interested in the practical aspects of theatre performance: his company, the *Lewditores*, has performed both in Edmonton and Toronto; productions include *Youth* (1992), *Mankind* (1995) and *The York Temptation and Fall* (1998).

Linda Garber directs the Women's and Gender Studies Program at Santa Clara University in California, where she teaches courses in queer studies. She is the author of *Identity Poetics: Race, Class, and the Lesbian-Feminist Roots of Queer Theory* and *Lesbian Sources: A Bibliography*, and editor of *Tilting the Tower: Lesbians/Teaching/ Queer Subjects*. She is currently working on a new book titled '*Failing That, Invent*': *Lesbian Historical Fictions*.

Noreen Giffney is a lecturer in women's studies in the Department of Sociology at the University of Limerick, Ireland. She is the co-editor of *Twenty-First Century Lesbian Studies* (2007), *Queering the Non/Human* (2008), *The Lesbian Premodern* (2010) and *Theory on the Edge: Irish Studies and the Politics of Sexual Difference* (2010). She has just completed a monograph on key concepts in queer theory and is currently co-editing a book entitled *Clinical Encounters: Psychoanalytic Practice and Queer Theory*. She is in clinical training in psychoanalysis at the University of Dublin, Trinity College.

Peter Hegarty is Senior Lecturer in Psychology at the University of Surrey. He has published widely on lesbian and gay psychology and queer theory in journals, such as, *Social Cognition, Review of General Psychology, Group Processes and Intergroup Relations, Journal of Personality and Social Psychology, Journal of Applied Social Psychology, Journal of Community and Applied Social Psychology, Journal of Homosexuality, Feminism and Psychology, History of Psychology, History of the Human Sciences, Journal of the History of Sexuality, International Journal of Critical Psychology* and *The Psychologist.*

Myra J. Hird is Professor and Queen's National Scholar at Queen's University, Canada and the author of *Sociology of Science* (Oxford University Press forthcoming), *The Science of Social Relating* (Palgrave Press forthcoming), *Sex, Gender and Science* (2004) and *Engendering Violence* (Ashgate 2002). She is the co-editor of *Queering the Non/Human* (with Noreen Giffney, Ashgate 2008), *Questioning Sociology* (with George Pavlich, 2006) and *Sociology for the Asking* (with George Pavlich, 2003) and the author of over forty articles and book chapters on gender, sexuality and science studies.

Song Hwee Lim is Senior Lecturer in Film Studies at the University of Exeter. He is the author of *Celluloid Comrades: Representations of Male Homosexuality in Contemporary Chinese Cinemas* (University of Hawaii Press 2006), co-editor of *Remapping World Cinema: Identity, Culture and Politics in Film* (Wallflower Press 2006) and founding editor of the *Journal of Chinese Cinemas.*

E. Patrick Johnson is Professor, Chair and Director of Graduate Studies in the Department of Performance Studies and Professor in the Department of African American Studies at Northwestern University. A scholar/artist, Johnson has performed nationally and internationally and has published widely in the area of race, gender, sexuality and performance. He is author of *Appropriating Blackness: Performance and the Politics of Authenticity* (Duke University Press 2003) and the editor (with Mae G. Henderson) of *Black Queer Studies: A Critical Anthology* (Duke University Press 2005). His most recent book, *Sweet Tea: Black Gay Men of the South – An Oral History* (2008), is published by the University of North Carolina Press.

Steven F. Kruger is Professor of English at Queens College and The Graduate Center, CUNY and is currently Executive Officer of the PhD Program in English at The Graduate Center. He is author of *Dreaming in the Middle Ages* (Cambridge University Press 1992), *AIDS Narratives: Gender and Sexuality, Fiction and Science* (Garland 1996) and *The Spectral Jew: Conversion and Embodiment in Medieval Europe* (University of Minnesota Press 2006). He has co-edited *Approaching the Millennium: Essays on* Angels in America (with Deborah R. Geis, University of Michigan Press 1997) and *Queering the Middle Ages* (with Glenn Burger, University of Minnesota Press 2001).

Patricia MacCormack is Senior Lecturer in Communication and Film at Anglia Ruskin University, Cambridge. She has published extensively in the areas of the visceral dimension of cinema, corporeality, the post-human, queer theory, feminism, ethics and continental philosophy. Her particular interests lie in the work of Guattari, Deleuze, Lyotard, Foucault, Blanchot, Irigaray, Rancière and Serres. Recent work on perversion, masochism, body modification, non-huMan rights, Polysexuality and the ethics of becomings have appeared in *Body and Society, Women: A Cultural Review, Thirdspace, Rhizomes* and *Theory, Culture and Society*. She is the co-editor with Ian Buchanan of *The Schizoanalysis of Cinema* (Continuum 2008). Her book *Cinesexuality* was published by Ashgate in 2008. She is currently planning a book on post-human ethics.

Leslie J. Moran is Professor of Law at Birkbeck College, University of London. He has published widely in areas relating to sexuality and law including *Sexuality, Identity and Law* (2006), *Sexuality and the Politics of Violence and Safety* written with Beverley Skeggs (2004), *Legal Queeries* (1998) and *The Homosexual(ity) of Law* (1996). He has also published work on hate crime, *Critical Reflections on Hate Crime* (2001 published as a special edition of *Law and Critique*, Kluwer), and in the area of law and visual culture. His edited collection, *Law's Moving Image* (2004) is about law and film. His current research is on the sexual diversity of the judiciary and includes a study of the cultural lives of the judiciary for example in biography and autobiography, film and television, photojournalism and portraiture.

Iain Morland is a Lecturer in Cultural Criticism at Cardiff University, where he teaches critical theory, gender studies and queer theory. He has published widely on the ethics, theory and psychology of intersexuality in interdisciplinary journals such as *Textual Practice, Continuum, Feminist Theory* and *The Psychologist*. In addition to gender and sexuality studies, Iain's research interests include critical science studies, narratives of health and illness, and Freudian and Lacanian psychoanalysis. He is editor (with Annabelle Willox) of *Queer Theory* (Palgrave 2005), and guest editor of an issue of *GLQ* (2009) about the intersex treatment controversy.

J. Bobby Noble is an Assistant Professor in the Sexuality Studies Program, housed in the School of Women's Studies, at York University, Toronto. He is the author of *Sons of the Movement: FtMs Risking Incoherence in a Post-Queer Cultural Landscape* (Women's Press 2006) and *Masculinities Without Men?* (University of British Columbia Press 2004), listed as a Choice Outstanding Title, 2004, and is the co-editor of *The Drag King Anthology* (Harrington Park Press 2003), a 2004 Lambda Literary Finalist.

Michael O'Rourke is the co-editor of *Love, Sex, Intimacy and Friendship between Men, 1550–1800* (Palgrave Macmillan 2003), *Queer Masculinities, 1550–1800: Siting Same-Sex Desire in the Early Modern World* (Palgrave Macmillan 2006) and special issues of the journals, *Romanticism on the Net* (Queer Romanticisms) and *Borderlands* (Jacques Rancière on the Shores of Queer Theory), and the editor of *Derrida and Queer Theory* (Palgrave Macmillan forthcoming) and special issues of the journals, *Rhizomes: Cultural Studies in Emerging Knowledge* (The Becoming-Deleuzoguattarian of Queer

Studies) and *Medieval Feminist Review* (Queer Methodologies and/or Queers in Medieval Studies). He is (with Noreen Giffney) the series co-editor of two queer theory book series: Queer Interventions at Ashgate and Cultural Connections: Key Thinkers and Queer Theory at the University of Wales Press.

Meredith Raimondo is an Assistant Professor of Queer Studies in the Comparative American Studies Program at Oberlin College. Her work has appeared in *Environment and Planning D* and *Gender, Place and Culture* as well as anthologies such as *Just Advocacy: Women's Human Rights, Transnational Feminisms, and the Politics of Representation*, (ed.) Wendy Hesford and Wendy Kozol (Rutgers University Press 2005) and *Carryin' On in the Lesbian and Gay South* (New York University Press 1997). She is working on a book about US media representation of the geography of HIV/AIDS.

Todd R. Ramlow is Adjunct Professor of Women's Studies and English at George Washington University. His recent publications have appeared in *GLQ: A Journal of Gay and Lesbian Studies* and *MELUS*. His current research focuses on the intersections of queer theory and disability studies in popular culture and film. He is the Associate Film and Television Editor and a regular contributor to PopMatters.com.

Mair Rigby gained her PhD from Cardiff University, where she has also worked as an Associate Tutor in English Literature. Her thesis explores the extent to which queer theory and gothic fiction can be considered mutually illuminating fields of enquiry, focusing particularly on Mary Shelley and her novel *Frankenstein*. She has published an essay on John Polidori *in Romanticism on the Net* and has essays on queer theory and the gothic forthcoming in an edited collection and the journal *Gothic Studies*.

Sasha Roseneil is Professor of Sociology and Social Theory and Director of the Birkbeck Institute for Social Research at Birkbeck College, University of London. She is also Professor II of Sociology in the Centre for Women's Studies and Gender Research at the University of Oslo. She is one of the founding editors of the journal *Feminist Theory*, and is the author of *Disarming Patriarchy* (Open University Press 1995), and *Common Women, Uncommon Practices: The Queer Feminisms of Greenham* (Cassell 2000). She is editor or co-editor of *Stirring It: Challenges for Feminism* (Taylor and Francis 1994), *Practising Identities* (Macmillan 1999), *Consuming Cultures* (Macmillan 1999), *Globalization and Social Movements* (Palgrave 2000), and special issues of *Citizenship Studies* (2000), *Feminist Theory* (2001, 2003), *Current Sociology* (2004) and *Social Politics* (2004). Her latest books are *Sociability, Sexuality, Self: Relationality and Individualization* (Routledge forthcoming), and *Social Research after the Cultural Turn* (edited with Stephen Frosh, Palgrave forthcoming).

David V. Ruffolo teaches in the Department of Theory and Policy Studies in Education at the Ontario Institute for Studies in Education of the University of Toronto with the Higher Education Group. He received the 2008 Scholar-

Activist Dissertation Award from the Queer Studies Special Interest Group of the American Educational Research Association for his work on post-queer bodies. His publications in the areas of queer studies and education include 'Giving an Account of Queer: Why Straight Teachers Can Become Queerly Intelligible' (Peter Lang 2007), as well as articles in *Higher Education Perspectives* and *The Canadian Online Journal of Queer Studies in Education*. His book, *Post-Queer Politics*, is published in the Queer Interventions series from Ashgate.

Nikki Sullivan is Associate Professor of Critical and Cultural Studies at Macquarie University, and Director of the Somatechnics Research Centre (also at Macquarie). Nikki is the author of *Tattooed Bodies: Subjectivity, Textuality, Ethics and Pleasure* (Praeger 2001), *A Critical Introduction to Queer Theory* (Edinburgh University Press/ New York University Press 2003), and numerous articles on sexuality and/or body modification published in book collections and international journals. She is the editor (with Samantha Murray) of *Somatechnics: Queering the Technologisation of Bodies* (Ashgate 2009).

Yvette Taylor is a Lecturer in the School of Geography, Politics and Sociology, University of Newcastle. Her publications include *Working-class Lesbian Life Experiences: Classed Outsiders* (Palgrave Macmillan 2007) and 'Brushed Behind the Bike Shed: Class and Sexuality in School', *BJSE* 28:3, 2007. She is currently working on a British Academy funded project 'What Would the Parents Say? Lesbian and Gay Parents, Social and Educational Capitals'.

Calvin Thomas is Associate Professor and Director of Graduate Studies in the Department of English at Georgia State University. He is the author of *Masculinity, Psychoanalysis, Straight Queer Theory: Essays on Abjection in Literature, Mass Culture and Film* (Palgrave Macmillan 2008), *Male Matters: Masculinity, Anxiety and the Male Body on the Line* (University of Illinois Press 1996) and the editor of *Straight with a Twist: Queer Theory and the Subject of Heterosexuality* (University of Illinois Press 2000). He serves as the English Language Book Review Editor for *South Atlantic Review*.

Annabelle Willox holds degrees in philosophy, sexual politics, and critical and cultural theory from Cardiff University. She is the editor (with Iain Morland) of *Queer Theory* [Readers in Cultural Criticism series] (Palgrave Macmillan 2004), and has published articles on sexuality, gender and media representation. Having taught at Cardiff and Glamorgan Universities and presented papers at conferences throughout the UK and Europe, she now works at the University of Strathclyde where she is the Faculty Officer for Strathclyde Business School. She has an ongoing keen interest in queer theory and/as politics, transgender sexuality and pornography, and continues to believe that theory is nothing without practice. In her spare time she is an international field hockey umpire representing Wales and Great Britain at European and World level events.

Tamsin Wilton was the UK's first Professor of Human Sexuality. With a first degree in English Literature and Fine Art, a Master's degree in Gender and Social Policy and a doctorate in the Social Organisation of Sexualities, her approach to the study of sexuality was multi-disciplinary. She worked in lesbian and queer studies from 1988 as well as on the social and cultural aspects of the HIV/AIDS pandemic. Her books include *Lesbian Studies: Setting an Agenda*, *En/Gendering AIDS*, *Sexualities in Health and Social Care*, *Antibody Politic*, *Finger-Licking Good: The Ins and Outs of Lesbian Sex* and *Sexual (Dis)Orientation*. She died on 30 April 2006.

Dinesh Joseph Wadiwel is an independent scholar based in Sydney, with research interests in sovereignty, sexual and political power, race and human/animal relationships. He has completed a doctorate at the Centre for Cultural Research, University of Western Sydney and has taught social and political theory. Dinesh is Director of a national non-government peak representative organisation.

Karen Yescavage is an Associate Professor of Psychology at Colorado State University, Pueblo. She is a sex researcher and activist, writing on a variety of topics such as queer values, attitudes toward transpeople and women's reasons for faking orgasms. She is currently co-writing with Jonathan Alexander an interdisciplinary book on the future of sex, analysing both the science and science fiction literatures. Karen and Jonathan are professional (poly) life mates, joined together in scholarship and friendship.

Acknowledgements

Firstly, our thanks go to the contributors for their chapters and patience while we brought this book to fruition. We hope you are as proud of it as we are. Lisa Fingleton generously allowed us to use her image, *Flying Lesson*, for the front cover, for which we are profoundly grateful. Lisa's image and her artistic efforts more generally exemplify queer as process for us: the urgency, the movement, the elusiveness, the drama, the excitement, the joy. If the term queer signifies a moment in time, always a retrospective capturing of what has already taken place, Lisa's image expresses what language cannot: the experiencing of such a state as it happens. We appreciate the energy and enthusiasm of Mary Savigar, with whom we began this project at Ashgate, and the support and dedication of Neil Jordan, who saw the book through to publication. Anne Mulhall has been a valued friend and steadfast supporter of our work. Her welcome presence in academia has helped us to feel less alone. Ailbhe Smyth has been both a formidable influence on our intellectual development and unrelenting in her belief in the quality and integrity of our work. An innovator and uncompromising *enfant terrible*, we have learned much from her refusal to be constrained by academic norms and have been inspired by her dedication to the furtherance of knowledge for its own sake. We are indebted to all those who have taken part in The(e)ories: Critical Theory and Sexuality Studies, which we have convened since 2002. The events forming part of The(e)ories, their intellectual collegiality and theoretical energy have been integral to our theoretical development and a constant reminder of why we wanted to be part of academia in the first place. Michael would like to express his thanks to Diarmuid Hester, Deirdre Daly and Graham Price. In recognition of the fact that no scholarly work is possible without the support of friends and intimates, Noreen is indebted to everyone whose love and friendship help her to live a queer life, especially Nicole Murray, Gillian Downes, Aoife Kavanagh and Onslow.

ASHGATE
RESEARCH
COMPANION

The *Ashgate Research Companions* are designed to offer scholars and graduate students a comprehensive and authoritative state-of-the-art review of current research in a particular area. The companions' editors bring together a team of respected and experienced experts to write chapters on the key issues in their speciality, providing a comprehensive reference to the field.

Introduction:
The 'q' Word

Noreen Giffney

The title of this chapter raises more questions than it answers. What does 'The "q" Word' refer to? Why use 'q', which is more properly a letter, rather than spell out the word in full? Is there a reason for employing a lower case 'q' rather than a capital letter to represent this particular word? Are the quotation marks significant? Does the appearance of the term 'the' and the singular form 'word' mean that 'q' refers to one and only one term? Is 'q' operating here as an adjective (is there something 'q' about 'the word'?) or a noun (is 'q' *the* word that we should take note of?)? If I am to offer the information that I intend for 'q' in this instance to stand in for 'queer', are we any closer to discovering what 'The "q" Word' signifies? Let us focus more closely on 'The "queer" Word' for a moment: am I intending for queer to represent a noun ('x' is queer, queerness), adjective (queer 'x'), verb (to queer 'x', queering 'x') or adverb ('x-ing' queerly)? Each question leads, not to a resolution, but to another series of questions, thus continually frustrating our will to know, opening up a space of and for desire:

> The minute you say 'queer' … you are necessarily calling into question exactly what you mean when you say it … Queer includes within it a necessarily expansive impulse that allows us to think about potential differences within that rubric. (Harper, White and Cerullo 1990, 30)

This mode of questioning while simultaneously interrogating the structural formation of such questions, at the same time as being self-reflexive about the process of interrogative thinking, is a central tenet of queer theory (Butler 2004 [1991], 122–4; Giffney and O'Rourke 2007, 7–11). It is an attempt to resist being made a slave to the discourses one is operating within at any one moment by peeling back the multitudinous layers of meaning contained within each and every pronouncement. 'The "q" Word' is neither a statement nor a question yet it functions metonymically as both because its opacity encourages us to search for possible meanings within it, prompts us to ask questions about what those meanings might be and compels us to reflect on why we are driven to conduct a search for such meanings in the first place. When Lee Edelman remarks that 'queerness can never define an identity; it can only ever disturb one' (2004, 17), he could very well be writing about what I will refer to here as the 'queer statement', which may or may not (in the case of this chapter's title) be a grammatically-defined statement. The queer statement creates a space for reflection. It demands self-reflexivity and personal engagement. It refers beyond and outside of itself. It is a question without a question mark. As Thomas Dowson reminds us: 'Queer theory does not provide a positivity, rather it is a way of producing reflection, a way of taking a stand *vis à vis* the authoritative standard' (2000, 163).

Queer is a contentious term and one that encompasses defiance, celebration and refusal within its remit. It is, according to Mary McIntosh, 'defined more by what it is not than what it is for' (1997, 365). Genealogies of its academic manifestation can be identified in psychoanalysis, sexology, feminism, lesbian and gay studies, postmodernism and poststructuralism, HIV/AIDS activism and the black civil rights movement. Queer loosely describes a diverse, often conflicting set of interdisciplinary approaches to desire, subjectivity, identity, relationality, ethics and norms:

> ... it is not useful to consider queer theory a thing, especially one dignified by capital letters. We wonder whether queer commentary might not more accurately describe the things linked by a rubric, most of which are not theory ... It cannot be assimilated to a single discourse, let alone a propositional program. (Berlant and Warner 1995, 343)

Debates continue between practitioners about the extent to which queer signifies an identity category, an anti-identitarian position, a politics, a methodology and an academic discipline, prompting Donald Hall to insist that 'there is no "queer theory" in the singular, only many different voices and sometimes overlapping, sometimes divergent perspectives that can loosely be called "queer theories"' (2003, 5). Originally adopted to mark the appearance of something or someone 'odd' or 'strange' and later exercised as a slur predominantly for gay men, queer has been reclaimed in recent decades with anger and pride to signal an activist insurgence against homophobia and other forms of oppression, especially those relating to gender and sexuality. In fact, Judith Butler argues that queer 'derives its force precisely through the repeated invocation by which it has become linked to accusation, pathologization, insult' (1993, 226).

Queer can function as a synonym for 'lesbian and gay' or as shorthand for members of the lesbian, gay, bisexual and transgender (LGBT) community more generally; what Gloria Anzaldúa refers to as a needed but 'false unifying umbrella' (1991, 250). Queer is more often embraced to point to fluidity in identity, recognising identity as a historically-contingent and socially-constructed fiction that prescribes and proscribes against certain feelings and actions. It signifies the messiness of identity, the fact that desire and thus desiring subjects cannot be placed into discrete identity categories, which remain static for the duration of people's lives. Queer thus denotes a resistance to identity categories or easy categorisation, marking a disidentification from the rigidity with which identity categories continue to be enforced and from beliefs that such categories are immovable. Queer is championed by people both to reveal and revel in their differences in, what Cherry Smyth terms, its 'potential for radical pluralism' (1992, 25). It functions to designate a political persuasion, which aggressively challenges hegemonies, exclusions, norms and assumptions. In the words of David Halperin:

> ... 'queer' does not name some natural kind or refer to some determinate object; it acquires its meaning from its oppositional relation to the norm. Queer is by definition whatever is at odds with the normal, the legitimate, the dominant. There is nothing in particular to which it necessarily refers. (1995, 62)

When signalling an unapologetic, anti-assimilationist stance, queer champions those who refuse to be defined in the terms of, and by the (moral) codes of behaviour and identification set down by, the dominant society.[1]

While many queer theorists forward a fluid definition for queer and boast a capacious understanding of its epistemological and methodological potential, all too often the term is collapsed in its praxis into a synonym for lesbian and gay studies (Giffney 2004). In addition, a growing body of criticism has developed around the 'arrogant certainty' of queer (Khayatt 2002, 499) and the misrepresentation or silencing of lesbian, gay, bisexual or transgender issues and viewpoints by certain queer theorists. Many point to queer theorists' failure to deal adequately with how sexuality and gender intersect with other facets of our identities: race, ethnicity, nationality, (dis)ability, age, class and religious affiliation. This has had the positive effect of spurring on intersectional analyses, which attempt to answer E. Patrick Johnson's call for 'an epistemology of the body' (2005 [2001]). A variety of people within the university, in addition to activists and members of the LGBT community, have levelled charges of elitism at some queer theorists who bear the hallmarks of poststructuralism by employing jargon-laden prose in their explication of ideas. Despite the proliferation of queer theoretical work in locations as diverse as Ireland, Poland, the Netherlands, Germany, Russia, Africa, New Zealand and India, an unvoiced assumption circulates within LGBT studies that queer theory is produced in North America and to a lesser extent Britain, and then exported as a form of neo-imperialist rhetoric to other parts of the world. A 'star system' continues to underpin many queer writings, with the result that certain individuals, locations and disciplines have become conflated with producing theory while others are seen as simply applying it, as if colonised by its ideological effects.[2]

This interdisciplinary volume of 30 original essays provides an up-to-the-minute snapshot of queer scholarship from the past two decades, identifies many current directions queer theorising is taking, while also signposting several fruitful

---

1   An earlier version of this paragraph and the one preceding it appeared in Giffney and O'Rourke (2007).

2   An earlier version of this paragraph appeared in Giffney (2007a).

avenues for future research. The contributors, all specially commissioned, explain, develop, celebrate and criticise queer theoretical efforts as they engage with key concepts and debates within the field. In their chapters, the authors reflect on their personal, political and theoretical motivations while undertaking pioneering work in their individual areas of specialisation. The chapters gathered together here, by distinguished and emerging scholars who are based in a wide range of international locations, put the terms 'queer' and 'theory' under interrogation in an effort to map the relations and disjunctions between them. The contributors are especially attendant to the many theoretical discourses intersecting with queer theory: feminist theory, LGBT studies, postcolonial theory, psychoanalysis, disability studies, Marxism, poststructuralism, critical race studies and posthumanism to name a few. This research companion engages with four key concerns of queer theoretical work: identity, discourse, normativity and relationality. Although there is considerable overlap between the chapters in each part, we have grouped together essays which speak (sometimes at cross purposes) to one another across a range of disciplines and from a variety of personal, political and theoretical positions. Every chapter includes five suggested readings because this book is intended to facilitate discussion, debate and further study rather than acting as a so-called 'authoritative' endpoint in itself.

Identity and Normativity

> *I worry when 'queer' becomes an identity. It was never an identity. It was always a critique of identity. I think if it ceases to be a critique of identity, it's lost its critical edge. (Butler 2008, 32)*

Queer theory began with a concern for identity. Coined by Teresa de Lauretis at a conference at the University of California, Santa Cruz in 1990, queer theory was used there for 'theorizing lesbian and gay sexualities' (1991, iii).[3] According to de Lauretis, its coinage 'convey[ed] a double emphasis – on the conceptual and speculative work involved in discourse production, and on the necessary critical work of deconstructing our own [lesbian and gay] discourses and their constructed silences' (1991, iv). Thus, queer theory has functioned as an analytical tool for unpacking the ways in which the identities lesbian and gay are formed both from the (sometimes hostile) discourses propounded by people not aligned with those categories while also being constructed by self-identified lesbians and gays themselves. This linking of queer theory with lesbian and gay was (and continues to be) considered by many to be self-evident and unquestionable because, as Eve Kosofsky Sedgwick pointed out: 'given the historical and contemporary force of the prohibitions against *every* same-sex sexual expression, for anyone to disavow

---

3   De Lauretis distanced herself from the term shortly after, labelling it 'a vacuous creature of the publishing industry' (1997, 316).

those meanings, or to displace them from the term's definitional center, would be to dematerialize any possibility of queerness itself' (1993, 8). In this, queer theory has become somewhat of an epistemological extension of an ontological position, with queer theory a theory for, about and by 'queers'. Queers' theory in other words. Queers have pitted themselves against heteronormativity, a broad-based system privileging heterosexuality and the main benefactors of that system – straights – on the one hand (Anonymous 1997 [1990]), while critiquing homonormativity, lesbian and gay assimilationism to the so-called heteronorm on the other; what Gay Shame activist Mattilda calls 'the violence of a monolithic gay identity' (Bernstein Sycamore 2008, 238).

The critique of lesbian and gay discourses came from pressure within lesbian and gay circles but also from bisexuals and transgender people who were often denigrated when not elided altogether by lesbian and gay communities. The oppositional stance of lesbians and gays, enacted by their concentration on the homo/hetero binary (Roseneil 2002) left little room for identities, desires, practices and relationships that fell in between or outside of such categories, or challenged the premise upon which those identities were formulated. Bisexual theorists, such as Clare Hemmings, saw the bisexual as 'a figure of subversion and disruption' and argued for 'the need for a bisexual theory, which not only sheds new light on bisexual behaviour, but also has the potential for challenging the traditional boundaries of heterosexual and homosexual relations' (1993, 118).[4] Thus, bisexuality was posited as central to the deconstructive enterprise being forwarded by some lesbian and gay theorists and activists at that time. De Lauretis' sentiment of a critical practice for 'another discursive horizon, another way of thinking the sexual' (1991, iv), was echoed by Diana Fuss who urged:

> Perhaps what we need most urgently in gay and lesbian theory right now is a theory of marginality, subversion, dissidence, and othering. What we need is a theory of sexual borders that will help us to come to terms with and to organize around the new cultural and sexual arrangements occasioned by the movements and transmutations of pleasure in the social field. (1991, 5)

A desire for inclusivity and the move towards issue-based coalitional activism rather than identity politics has led practitioners of queer theory to concentrate on the exclusions through which identity-based movements come into being while endeavouring to keep the category queer provisional enough to allow for the inclusion of anyone who wants or needs it: 'Queer is not an "instead of", it's an "inclusive of"' (Adele Morrison, quoted in Duggan 1995, 165). This has led to the criticism that while trying to be all things to all people, queer actually elides differences and becomes a meaningless melange of competing aims and beliefs in the process. It is more usual to read queer writings with the underlying philosophy,

---

4   The so-called transgressive and subversive potential foisted upon transgender people in some quarters of queer theory has led to the exploitation of transgender as another meaning-laden category that polices those who can occupy it (Stryker 2004).

expounded by Lee Edelman, that 'queerness can never define an identity; it can only ever disturb one' (2004, 17). Queer is set up here as something, a tool perhaps, that produces self-reflection and feelings of uncomfortability; a troublesome agent of rebellion (Butler 2004 [1991], 121). Queer has, for some theorists, provided a framework for approaching, what Tim Dean terms, 'the radical impersonality of desire' and for thinking about 'sexuality outside the realm of individuals – indeed, outside, the realm of persons' (2000, 17).[5] 'Becoming', a concept borrowed from the lexicon of Gilles Deleuze and Félix Guattari, has become useful for facilitating an exploration of desire outside of identity categories. Becoming signifies not the movement through identification from one category to another – being via becoming to being – but the understanding that change is all there is. Becoming involves the shedding of the chimera of stability and certainty wrought through our attachments to objects towards an awareness and acceptance of the unrelenting dynamism that underpins the act of living itself (see Giffney and O'Rourke 2008, viii).

Identity persists because of a will to meaning. The 'will to meaning' is, according to Victor Frankl, 'the primary motivation in [a person's] life' (1959 [1946]: 121). I have experienced this will to meaning that Frankl talks about in my own life. The drive towards trying to make sense of my desires has led me to fixate on certain discursive categories at different times; terms such as 'heterosexual', 'bisexual' or 'lesbian', which I thought, in the past, facilitated me in understanding why I was drawn to particular people while assisting me in accessing other individuals clustering around such identities (O'Rourke 2005; Giffney 2007b). The sporting of identities always entails acts of faith; ones that have left me sorely disappointed for a set of linguistic signs can never exemplify that which is unrepresentable. Guy Hocquenghem's words are particularly pertinent here: 'Properly speaking, desire is no more homosexual than heterosexual. Desire emerges in a multiple form, whose components are only divisable *a posteriori*, according to how we manipulate it' (1993 [1972], 49). This is because desire is, as James Penney reminds us, 'essentially perverse' (2006: 1). It is here between desire and discourse that queer theory is situated, not to reveal desire so much as to revel in its extra-discursive leakages. Gloria Anzaldúa's words are instructive: 'Identity is not a bunch of little cubbyholes stuffed respectively with intellect, race, sex, class, vocation, gender. Identity flows between, over, aspects of a person. Identity is a river – a process' (1991, 252–3). This is not to suggest that the queer project's aim is to rid the world of identity, rather queer theory seeks ways in which to think about the following question posed by Judith Butler: 'how to use [the identity-sign] in such a way that its futural significations are not *foreclosed*?' (2004 [1991], 126).[6] There is something intensely personal in the queer project because of its imbrication in the mores of identity, braided as it is into the crevices of desire and its objects. Identities become not so

---

5   Dean (2000) turns to the work of Jacques Lacan, while Patricia MacCormack (2008) draws on the theories of Gilles Deleuze and Félix Guattari. See also Giffney and Hird (2008) and O'Rourke (2005/2006).

6   Butler is writing here with reference to the category lesbian.

much categories to be occupied, owned, protected or rejected, but spaces to be navigated, revisited, revised and elided on a moment-to-moment basis.

Discourse and Relationality

> ... how we talk about sex profoundly affects how we experience it. We live in a world of sexually transmitted diseases, a viral world where sexual intercourse can be lethal; but we also live in a symbolic world, where words can be medicinal as they can be deadly. (Dean 2000, 20)

Queer theory is an exercise in discourse analysis. It takes very seriously the significance of words and the power of language. If we take a look at some of, what have become enshrined later as, the earliest queer theoretical writings – *Gender Trouble* (1990), *Epistemology of the Closet* (1990), *Making Things Perfectly Queer* (1993), *Homographesis* (1994), *Fear of a Queer Planet* (1993), *Inside/Out* (1991), *Saint Foucault* (1995) – we witness close readings of literary, cultural, philosophical and political texts.[7] There is a careful attention to detail, not just to what is being said, but also to the context within which narratives unfold. Queer becomes, in these works, either a tool to decipher texts, a facilitative environment within which the reader's relationship with a text develops or an ontological property waiting to be uncovered within the text itself. It is here that queer theory's investment in the ideas of Sigmund Freud, Jacques Lacan, Jacques Derrida and Michel Foucault and the broader areas of psychoanalysis, poststructuralism and literary theory becomes most evident. Theorists seek out the ways in which texts are constructed by interrogating and denaturalising the text's manifold assumptions, and exposing the text's internal contradictions and reliance upon excluded properties to evoke a sense of unity. What is not said – slips, silences and unfinished thoughts – garner as much interest as that which is verbalised; unpicking the latent content becomes as important a task as understanding that which is stated directly. A good deal of queer research has been dedicated to silences and secrets for, as Michel Foucault put it, 'There is not one but many silences, and they are an integral part of the strategies that underlie and permeate discourses' (1978 [1976], 27).

'Queer theory' is a misnomer. It is more properly 'queer theories' rather than 'queer theory'; pluralities rather than singularity. As Donald Hall puts it:

> ... the concept 'queer' emphasizes the disruptive, the fractured, the tactical and contingent ... any implication that queer theorization is itself a simple monolith would be hypocritical. Simply put there is no 'queer' theory in the

---

7   The term 'text' can refer here to, for example, fictional or non-fictional writings, films, artworks, performance pieces, situations, verbal or non-verbal communications. This list is not exhaustive.

> *singular, only many different voices and sometimes overlapping, sometimes divergent perspectives that can loosely be called 'queer theories'. (2003: 5)*

While sympathising with Hall, I like the term 'queer theory'. It is precisely its inaccuracy that attracts me. Queer is all about excess, pushing the boundaries of the possible, showing up language and discursive categories more specifically for their inadequacies. Queer theory exposes in its very figuration the way in which discourse flattens out phenomena in an attempt to make them into palatable, digestible sound bites. It exemplifies the contradictions nestling within concepts, the way in which meanings proliferate and spill out of terms the more we try to contain them; the impossibility of owning, or securing so-called proper definitions for, words and phrases. While being interested in both what is and is not said, queer theorists are also excited by what cannot be said. There is an unremitting emphasis in queer theoretical work on fluidity, über-inclusivity, indeterminacy, indefinability, unknowability, the preposterous, impossibility, unthinkability, unintelligibility, meaninglessness and that which is unrepresentable or uncommunicable.[8] This theoretical emphasis points to the excess which cannot be categorised, that which is not or cannot be expressed through language; the queer remainder. There is an underlying belief permeating the field that sometimes things cannot be explained and that is okay. In this, queer theory seeks to allow for complexity and the holding of uncertainties by encouraging the experiencing of states without necessarily trying to understand, dissect or categorise them. Queer's 'strategic usefulness' rests, according to Carla Freccero, in its slipperiness and ability to 'elude definition' (2006, 5). Thus, queer itself becomes, in some writings, a signifier for that which cannot be clearly or concisely defined, or for that which resists definition altogether.

Despite its slipperiness, its unremitting resistance to categorisation and theorists' insistence that queer is a 'doing' rather than a 'being', queer theory has been described recently as 'a tradition that has managed somehow to have acquired a past' (Halley and Parker 2007, 428). While there may be a reluctance to say what queer 'is', there are assuredly assumptions circulating about what queer 'does'. These concern genealogies, aims, priorities, interconnections with activism and other theories and fields, and the thorny issue of who gets to decide on all of this.[9] As queer has developed into a field, however resistant practitioners might be about its institutionalisation – through university programmes, courses, book series, journals, conferences and so on – a number of beliefs (we might even say assumptions) have begun to circulate in writings aligning themselves with queer. These include a focus on transgression, radicalism, inclusion and difference. A number of streams have become identifiable within queer theory as people present intersectional work, which draws on other fields and theoretical discourses (McRuer 2006; Johnson and Henderson 2005; Boyarin, Itzkovitz and Pellegrini 2004). This

---

8   See Epps (2001); Smyth (1992); Freccero (2006, 6); Stacey and Street (2007, 1); Morland and Willox (2005, 5); Burger and Kruger (2001); Edelman (2004); Dowson (2000, 165); Haver (1997); Winnubst (2007); Noble (2006, 3); MacCormack (2008) respectively.

9   The early part of this paragraph appeared in Giffney and Hird (2008).

has meant that queer theory has become, not just a subject which speaks, but an object that is spoken about, evaluated and critiqued. The slipperiness so celebrated by queer theory – which Brad Epps (2001) has labelled its fetish – is sometimes lost in meta-theoretical analyses that seek to pin queer theory down as it were and examine the exclusions through which it comes into being. A queering of queer theory we might say. There have been stirrings in recent years towards a discussion of what it might mean to inaugurate the term 'postqueer' (Noble 2006; Giffney and Hird 2008, 5–6), and the impact such a move might have on queer theory. Talk of postqueer brings back memories of what now seem like prophetic words enunciated by Judith Butler in the early 1990s when urging that 'queer must remain that which it is, in the present, never fully owned', which 'also means that it will doubtless have to be yielded in favor of terms that do that political work more effectively' (1993, 228).

Queer discourses touch us, move us and leave us unsettled, troubled, confused. In an essay on Gilles Deleuze and Félix Guattari's approach to subjectivity, Paul Bains writes: 'What is disturbing about their endeavour is that it attempts to think that which cannot be thought and to write the unreadable' (2002, 102). There is something of this sentiment evident within queer writings, some of which aim, in William Haver's estimation, 'to practise invention to the brink of intelligibility'. Queer theory is often difficult to read (and write). There is a valuing of difficulty because of the concerted effort made by theorists not to make things easy or palatable but to challenge the reader to work through concepts with the same expenditure of energy exerted by the writer; to use the text as a tool to open up and provoke further thinking about the theme in question. This process is not without its pleasures. Haver asks: 'what if, indeed, thinking were always also the surplus or supplement of conceptuality – an erotics, for example?' (1997, 278). The erotics of thinking, speaking, writing, listening and reading is a chief concern for those of us who engage in an intensely personal and self-reflexive relationship with the discourses we (en)counter and (re)produce. The *jouissance* we achieve from the effort we exert in establishing and disentangling relationships with texts is a momentary gesture of liberation from discourse: it entails a loss of the self we think we know (Barthes 1990 [1973]; MacCormack 2008; Thomas 2008). This is why we keep returning again and again to queer theory: for the promise of a future not defined in terms of the past, for the possibility of becoming other to ourselves.

Acknowledgement

I am indebted to Nicole Murray for her careful reading of an earlier draft.

Suggested Further Reading

Garber, L. (2001), *Identity Poetics: Race, Class and the Lesbian-Feminist Roots of Queer Theory* (New York: Columbia University Press).

Hall, D.E. (2003), *Queer Theories* (New York: Palgrave Macmillan).

Jagose, A. (1996), *Queer Theory: An Introduction* (New York: New York University Press).

Sullivan, N. (2003), *A Critical Introduction to Queer Theory* (Edinburgh: Edinburgh University Press).

Wilchins, R. (2004), *Gender Theory, Queer Theory: An Instant Primer* (Los Angeles, CA: Alyson Books).

Useful Reference Texts

Eadie, J. (ed.) (2004), *Sexuality: The Essential Glossary* (London: Arnold).

Haggerty, G.E. and Zimmerman, B. (eds) (2000), *Encyclopedia of Lesbian and Gay Histories and Cultures* (London and New York: Taylor and Francis).

Johnson, E.P. and Henderson, M.G. (eds) (2005), *Black Queer Studies: A Critical Anthology* (Durham, NC: Duke University Press).

Storr, M. (ed.) (1999), *Bisexuality: A Critical Reader* (New York and London: Routledge).

Stryker, S. and Whittle, S. (eds) (2006), *The Transgender Studies Reader* (New York and London: Routledge).

References

Anonymous (1997 [1990]), 'Queers Read This; I Hate Straights', in M. Blasius and S. Phelan (eds), *We Are Everywhere: A Historical Sourcebook of Gay and Lesbian Politics* (New York and London: Routledge).

Anzaldúa, G. (1991), 'To(o) Queer the Writer – *Loca, escritora y chicana*', in B. Warland (ed.), *InVersions: Writings by Dykes, Queers and Lesbians* (Vancouver: Press Gang Publishers).

Bains, P. (2002), 'Subjectless Subjectivities', in B. Massumi (ed.), *A Shock to Thought: Expression after Deleuze and Guattari* (New York and London: Routledge).

Barthes, R. (1990 [1973]), *The Pleasure of the Text*, trans. R. Miller (Oxford and Cambridge, MA: Blackwell).

Berlant, L. and Warner, M. (1995), 'What Does Queer Theory Teach Us about X?', *PMLA* 110:3, 343–9.

Bernstein Sycamore, M. (aka Mattilda) (2008), 'The Violence of Assimilation', an interview with J. Ruiz, *Radical History Review* 100, 237–47.

Boyarin, D., Itzkovitz, D. and Pellegrini, A. (eds) (2004), *Queer Theory and the Jewish Question* (New York: Columbia University Press).

Burger, G. and Kruger, S.F. (2001), 'Introduction', in G. Burger and S.F. Kruger (eds), *Queering the Middle Ages* (Minneapolis, MN and London: University of Minnesota Press).

Butler, J. (1990), *Gender Trouble: Feminism and the Subversion of Identity* (New York and London: Routledge).

—— (1993), 'Critically Queer', in *Bodies That Matter: On the Discursive Limits of 'Sex'* (New York and London: Routledge).

—— (2004 [1991]), 'Imitation and Gender Insubordination', in S. Salih with J. Butler (eds), *The Judith Butler Reader* (Oxford: Blackwell).

—— (2008), '*Gender Trouble*: Still Revolutionary or Obsolete?', an interview with Aurore (Bang Bang), *Avonden van Sophia/Soirées de Sophia 2006–2007* (Brussels: Sophia), 29–38.

De Lauretis, T. (1991), 'Queer Theory: Lesbian and Gay Sexualities. An Introduction', *differences: A Journal of Feminist Cultural Studies* 3:2, iii–xviii.

—— (1997), 'Habit Changes. *Response*', in E. Weed and N. Schor (eds), *Feminism Meets Queer Theory* (Bloomington and Indianapolis, IN: Indiana University Press).

Dean, T. (2000), *Beyond Sexuality* (Chicago, IL and London: University of Chicago Press).

Dowson, T.A. (2000), 'Why Queer Archaeology? An Introduction', *World Archaeology* 32:2, 161–5.

Duggan, L. (1995), 'Making It Perfectly Queer', in L. Duggan and N.D. Hunter, *Sex Wars: Sexual Dissent and Political Culture* (New York and London: Routledge).

Edelman, L. (2004), *No Future: Queer Theory and the Death Drive* (Durham, NC: Duke University Press).

Epps, B. (2001), 'The Fetish of Fluidity', in T. Dean and C. Lane (eds), *Homosexuality and Psychoanalysis* (Chicago, IL and London: University of Chicago Press).

Foucault, M. (1978 [1976]), *The History of Sexuality. Volume 1: An Introduction*, trans. R. Hurley (New York: Pantheon).

Frankl, Viktor E. (1959 [1946]), 'Logotherapy in a Nutshell', in *Man's Search for Meaning* (London and New York: Washington Square Press).

Freccero, C. (2006), *Queer/Early/Modern* (Durham, NC: Duke University Press).

Fuss, D. (1991), 'Inside/Out', in D. Fuss (ed.), *Inside/Out: Lesbian Theories, Gay Theories* (London and New York: Routledge).

Giffney, N. (2004), 'Denormatizing Queer Theory: More than (Simply) Lesbian and Gay Studies', *Feminist Theory* 5:1, 73–8.

—— (2007a), 'Quare Theory', in W. Balzano, M. Sullivan and A. Mulhall (eds), *Irish Postmodernisms and Popular Culture* (Basingstoke: Palgrave Macmillan).

—— (2007b), 'Quare Éire', in N. Giffney and K. O'Donnell (eds), *Twenty-First Century Lesbian Studies* (Binghampton, NY: Harrington Park Press/Taylor and Francis).

—— and Hird, M.J. (eds) (2008), *Queering the Non/Human* (Aldershot: Ashgate).

Giffney, N. and O'Rourke, M. (2007), 'The "E(ve)" in The(e)ories: Dreamreading Sedgwick in Retrospective Time', *The Irish Feminist Review* 3, 6–21.
—— (2008), 'For the Love of Cinema', series editors' preface to P. MacCormack, *Cinesexuality* (Aldershot: Ashgate).
Hall, D.E. (2003), *Queer Theories* (New York: Palgrave Macmillan).
Halley, J. and Parker, A. (2007), 'Introduction', *The South Atlantic Quarterly* 106:3. 421–32.
Halperin, D.M. (1995), *Saint Foucault: Towards a Gay Hagiography* (New York: Oxford University Press).
Harper, P.B., White, E.F. and Cerullo, M. (1990), 'Multi/Queer/Culture', *Radical America* 24:4, 27–37.
Haver, W. (1997), 'Queer Research; Or, How to Practise Invention to the Brink of Intelligibility', in S. Golding (ed.), *Eight Technologies of Otherness* (London and New York: Routledge).
Hemmings, C. (1993), 'Resituating the Bisexual Body: From Identity to Difference', in J. Bristow and A.R. Wilson (eds), *Activating Theory: Lesbian, Gay, Bisexual Politics* (London: Lawrence and Wishart).
Hocquenghem, G. (1993 [1972]), *Homosexual Desire*, trans. D. Dangoor (Durham, NC: Duke University Press).
Johnson, E.P. (2005 [2001]), '"Quare" Studies, or (Almost) Everything I Know about Queer Studies I Learned from My Grandmother', in E.P. Johnson and M.G. Henderson (eds), *Black Queer Studies: A Critical Anthology* (Durham, NC: Duke University Press).
—— and Henderson, M.G. (eds) (2005), *Black Queer Studies: A Critical Anthology* (Durham, NC: Duke University Press).
Khayatt, D. (2002), 'Toward a Queer Identity', *Sexualities* 5:4, 487–501.
MacCormack, P. (2008), *Cinesexuality* (Aldershot: Ashgate).
McIntosh, M. (1997), 'Queer Theory and the War of the Sexes', in S. Kemp and J. Squires (eds), *Feminisms* (Oxford: Oxford University Press).
McRuer, R. (2006), *Crip Theory: Cultural Signs of Queerness and Disability* (New York and London: New York University Press).
Morland, I. and Willox, A. (2005), 'Introduction', in I. Morland and A. Willox (eds), *Queer Theory* (Basingstoke: Palgrave Macmillan).
Noble, J.B. (2006), *Sons of the Movement: FtMs Risking Incoherence on a Post-Queer Cultural Landscape* (Toronto: Women's Press).
O'Rourke, M. (2005), 'On the Eve of a Queer-Straight Future: Notes Toward an Antinormative Heteroerotic', *Feminism and Psychology* 15:1, 111–16.
—— (ed.) (2005/2006), 'The Becoming-DeleuzoGuattarian of Queer Studies', a special issue of *Rhizomes: Cultural Studies in Emerging Knowledge*, 11/12, http://www.rhizomes.net/issue11/hurley/index/html (accessed 30 August 2008).
Penney, J. (2006), *The World of Perversion: Psychoanalysis and the Impossible Absolute of Desire* (Albany, NY: State University of New York Press).
Roseneil, S. (2002), 'The Heterosexual/Homosexual Binary: Past, Present and Future', in D. Richardson and S. Seidman (eds), *Handbook of Lesbian and Gay Studies* (London: Sage).

Sedgwick, E.K. (1993), *Tendencies* (Durham, NC: Duke University Press).

Smyth, C. (1992), *Lesbians Talk Queer Notions* (London: Scarlet Press).

Stacey, J. and Street, S. (2007), 'Introduction: Queering *Screen*', in J. Stacey and S. Street (eds), *Queer Screen* (New York and London).

Stryker, S. (2004), 'Transgender Studies: Queer Theory's Evil Twin', *GLQ: A Journal of Lesbian and Gay Studies* 10:2, 212–15.

Thomas, C. (2008 [2002]), 'Must Desire Be Taken Literally?', in *Masculinity, Psychoanalysis, Straight Queer Theory: Essays on Abjection in Literature, Mass Culture, and Film* (New York: Palgrave Macmillan).

Winnubst, S. (2007), 'Bataille's Queer Pleasures: The Universe as Spider or Spit', in S. Winnubst (ed.), *Reading Bataille Now* (Bloomington, IN: Indiana University Press).

PART I

IDENTITY

On Being Post-Normal:
Heterosexuality after Queer Theory

Calvin Thomas

Unwelcome Excesses

You probably already know the story: in the early 1990s, academic and activist lesbian and gay studies had become co-implicated with (or, some would say, co-opted by) poststructuralist analysis and radical social constructionism; 'identity politics' takes it on the chin; the word 'queer', which has 'torque' and 'twist' in its etymological background, is itself torqued and twisted, promoted from slur to affirmation, productively reworked into a transitive, transformative verb, and the infinitive phrase 'to queer' emerges to take on a newly performative 'labor of ambiguating categories of identity' (Berlant and Warner 1995, 345). Thus 'queer' gets queered into 'theory'.

But in what ways could 'theory' itself – as a disparate set of denaturalising, defamiliarising, or otherwise identity-disturbing discourses loosely gathered into a general 'project of creative abrasion' (Hall 2003, 71) – be considered queer or queering? Was 'theory' itself already *implicitly* queer, desedimenting – 'recurrent, eddying, *troublant* … relational and strange' (Sedgwick 1993a, xii) – even before being *explicitly* queered by queer theory? Was 'theory itself' already not exactly itself, not exactly identical with itself, even before 'queer' – taken as 'an identity category that has no interest in consolidating or even stabilising itself', taken as 'less an identity than a *critique* of identity', taken as 'a site of permanent becoming: utopic in its negativity … curv[ing] endlessly toward a realisation that its realisation remains impossible' (Jagose 1996, 131; Edelman 1995, 345) – brought out the specifically sexual dimensions of theory's anti-identitarian tendencies? In terms of their mutual hostility to identity, their joint strategies of de-naturalisation, their persistent 'questionings and abrasions of normality' (Hall 2003, 54), could 'theorising' and 'queering' not be considered roughly analogous or coaxial activities? So that 'the challenge of queer theorisation … [would be] to return to those "sites of becoming", and more importantly *un*becoming, wherein identity is temporarily constructed, solidified, and then threatened or rendered inadequate in its explanatory power' (Hall 2003, 109)?

If your answer to this thick swarm of questions is even a provisional 'well, yes, maybe ... sort of', then another, perhaps more pesky query may light upon you: to wit, can simply *reading* (queer) theory turn a reader who isn't lesbian, gay, bisexual or transgendered into some 'sort of' a 'queer'? Assuming the possibility of juicing up the erotic acts of reading and writing with a sufficient charge of creatively abrasive energy, can merely *reading* (queerly written) theory – as opposed to actually *f***ing* 'queerly' – transform or provoke an otherwise heterosexual or 'straight' subject, who has never come with, into, onto or even in the vicinity of a person of his or her own sex, into becoming what Eve Sedgwick might call one of 'those other people who vibrate to the chord of queer without having much same-sex eroticism' (1993b, 13)? Can the *jouissance* of reading theory itself, by itself, beside itself, catch the otherwise straight reader up in what Sedgwick calls 'the open mesh of possibilities, gaps, overlaps, dissonances and resonances, lapses and excesses of meaning where the constituent elements of anyone's gender, of anyone's sexuality aren't made (or *can't* be made) to signify monolithically' (1993a, 8)?[1] And has theory not performed this miraculous excess of meaning by virally spreading the good news that no one's sexuality or gender can be made to signify monolithically because *signification itself* cannot be monolithically made, because signification itself is never exactly itself – thanks to what Jacques Derrida calls the 'non-self-identity' (1978, 297) of the sign, the irreducible difference between the sign and the referent, the word and the thing – and because of the radical unavailability of any such 'thing' as sexuality or gender or selfhood outside of signification, the constitutive failure of any such supports as centre, nature or essence at all?[2]

In my own work I have attempted, admittedly without much success, to bring these queries to bear on the question of how and why a 'straight intellectual', thinly disguised as myself, might engage with, relate to or otherwise end up (upended) in queer theory (Thomas 2000; 2002; 2008). I will attempt to address that question again here, again without much hope of success, without even a clue as to what 'success' in regard to *this* topic – the essence-free but norm-laden identity of something like the 'straight queer', the straight queered in and by theory, a figure at once 'at odds' and inevitably 'at evens' with the normal – could possibly mean. For what could critical 'success' amount to here, given, on the one hand, the inadequate explanatory power of even an oppositional identity (at, one hoped, politically useful, anti-homophobic odds), and, on the other, the very real possibility that any attempt to subversively resignify the figure of the straight (as) queer will only

---

1   The word *jouissance* means 'enjoyment' – from *jouir*, which in French means both 'to play' and 'to come'. In Lacanese, however, *jouissance* entails no simple pleasure but rather an excessive 'form of enjoyment so intense as to be barely distinguishable from suffering and pain' (Dean 2000, 271).

2   In the essay 'Ellipsis' in *Writing and Difference*, Derrida writes, 'As soon as a sign emerges, it begins by repeating itself. Without this, it would not be a sign, it would not be what it is, that is to say, the non-self-identity which regularly refers to the same. That is to say, to another sign, which will itself be born of having been divided. The grapheme, repeating itself in this fashion, thus has neither natural site nor natural center' (1978, 297).

reinscribe and reinforce the very 'regimes of the normal' (Warner 1993, xxvi) that the resignified straight had aspired to join 'really queer' queers in resisting (back again at seemingly futile evens)?[3] And yet, even with the odds so heavily against ever finally fatally dislevelling the even plane of straight regimentation, much less one's own apparently undisownable place of privilege within it, this straight will continue, here, again, along these recursive lines, perhaps utopically, certainly negatively, realising only the impossibility of realisation, hoping this time not to succeed but, in Samuel Beckett's worstward words, only to 'fail again', though perhaps this time to 'fail better' (1983, 7).

For, shameful truth be told, I am actually far less interested in participating in the 'success' of meaning than I am in proliferating its dissonant resonances, its abject lapses and excess, its figurative abortion. And given this preference – an oddly *sexual* preference – kindly allow me to describe an odd (and perhaps also oddly sexual) thing that happened recently when I was reading Annette Schlichter's essay 'Queer At Last? Straight Intellectuals and the Desire for Transgression', which critiques my own less than successful efforts at becoming uneven. At one adumbrating juncture in this essay, before pointing out the 'insufficiency' of my 'textual performance of twisted straightness' (2004, 553), Schlichter refers to 'the specter of the queer heterosexual (especially in its male version) as an indication of the queer project's perversion [sic] of social and political identities and their relations to power' (2004, 547). Schlichter cites Suzanna Danuta Walters, who 'reads the straight male sexual radical affiliated with queer discourse as a symptom of "the problematic implication of a queer theory dissociated from a gay and lesbian

---

3   If 'queer is by definition *whatever* is at odds with the normal, the legitimate, the dominant' (Halperin 1995, 62), can the 'straight intellectual' ever be at effectively critical odds with that position? Is he in any position to do any political good whatsoever? Or is it not the case that the straight intellectual, whatever his odd critical inclination, can barely even gargle or clear his throat, much less think, speak, write, teach or publish, without reconsolidating the privileged identity position he claims he desires to disturb? What I think I can safely say is that whatever the straight intellectual says about queer theory he says less queerly than safely because he actually risks very little with his (merely) discursive performance. No matter how passionately the straight intellectual who engages with queer theory may desire to disturb identity, no matter how deliberately the straight intellectual may attempt to sever himself from himself with the help of queer theory's cutting edge, such deliberation will neither free him from nor divest him of his deeply sedimented position of privilege. For the sedimentary structure of privilege is such that no subject can simply renounce it or voluntaristically dis-interpellate himself out of it. The straight intellectual can be 'critically queer' to his own heart's content without ever having to suffer the heartbreaking and ass-kicking consequences of being really queer in a murderously homophobic world. After all, at the end of the day, it isn't likely that anyone will kill, assault, disown or deny human rights to a straight intellectual simply because he has read a bit of Judith Butler. So what *good* does a straight intellectual's engagement with queer theory do? What *justifies* such engagement? Not much, I have to say. Or, perhaps even 'better' – and alluding here to the identity-disturbing words in the above epigraph from Lee Edelman's *No Future* (2004) – I might say that *absolutely nothing* justifies such engagement.

identity"' and who thinks that the '"deconstruction of identity politics ... might have some merit, but it can also, in the world of academia as well as in other social spaces, become the vehicle for co-optation: the radical queer theorist as married heterosexual"' (Walters 1996, 842, cited in Schlichter 2004, 547). Schlichter then cites Teresa de Lauretis, who 'mockingly evokes the straight queer to describe the *unwelcome excesses* of a postmodern critical project' (2004, 547, emphasis added). Here's De Lauretis (who first coined the term 'queer theory' in the feminist journal *differences* in 1991 and then denounced it in the same journal three years later as 'a conceptually vacuous creature of the publishing industry' [De Lauretis 1994, 297]):

> *The discourse on sexuality has moved from the impossibility of a feminine identity theorised by feminists since the late 1970s, to the alleged 'subversion' of gender identity in queer/lesbian studies, to the literal becoming-male of lesbian PoMo. An announced collection of essays on 'queer theory and the subject of heterosexuality' declares itself 'straight with a twist'. Who knows, by next year's [1995] MLA, we may be reading something like 'Lesbian Heterosexuality: The Last Frontier'. (De Lauretis 1997, 47, cited in Schlichter 2004, 547)*

Never mind for the moment the 'contempt-prior-to-investigation' that animates dismissing an intellectual endeavour for its *title* rather than for its then yet to be published content (I suppose that once you've decided in advance on the conceptual vacuity of a creature still slouching to be born there's no need to delay judgement upon reading). And never mind the hindsight that the editor of the announced collection (yours untruly) would have been wise to place a cautious question-mark at the end of the first part of its title to indicate the intended interrogative possibility rather than the perceived flat declaration. No, the odd thing, the funny thing – maybe the queer thing, maybe not (who am I to say?) – occurred when I beheld the words *unwelcome excesses* in Schlichter's lead-in to De Lauretis and realised that I am not only more interested in excess than 'success': I am also, perhaps perversely, more invested in excess than I am in being welcomed.[4]

Brief History of a Faint Spectre

My own perverse cathexes notwithstanding, note that in the history of queer theory the unwelcome 'specter of the queer heterosexual' sprang up, at least as a conjectural figure, pretty much from the get-go – that is, at the very historical moment when

---

4   I don't mean that I am interested in being excessive to the *exclusion* of ever being welcomed: I am in fact grateful for whatever welcome I receive, and I would like to thank Noreen Giffney and Michael O'Rourke for welcoming me into this volume, for inviting me to participate in their seminar on queer heterosexuality at University College Dublin in June 2006 and for their generous hospitality during my stay.

queer theory first began to dissociate itself from lesbian and gay identity politics. Having noted that De Lauretis first high-profiled the term 'queer theory' in 1991, we can also acknowledge the somewhat lower-profiled circulation in London in the same year of an anonymously authored pamphlet called 'Queer Power No', which declares that 'Queer means to f*** with gender. There are straight queers, bi-queers, tranny queers, lez queers, fag queers, SM queers, fisting queers' (cited in Sullivan 2003, 44). In 1992, San Francisco Queer Nation activist Karl Knapper opines that 'queerness is about acknowledging and celebrating difference, embracing what sets you apart. A straight person can't be gay, but a straight person can be queer' (cited in Kauffmann 1992, 20). In 1993, Eve Sedgwick, 'herself a straight writer of queer scholarship' (Schlichter 2004, 548) publishes *Tendencies*, from which I have already quoted. Also in 1993, in *Making Things Perfectly Queer*, Alexander Doty mentions 'cases of straight queerness, and of other forms of queerness that might not be contained within existing categories' (1993, xvii). In (again) 1993, Judith Butler brings out *Bodies That Matter*, which in the chapter called 'Critically Queer' offers the phrasing that first (or 'at last') activated my own impulse toward 'straight-queer' affiliation: here Butler writes of the word 'queer' as a 'discursive rallying point' for a number of socio-political sexual subjects, including, last and least, 'straights for whom the term expresses an affiliation with antihomophobic politics' (1993, 230).

Still again in 1993 (it was a very queer year), Michael Warner, introducing *Fear of a Queer Planet*, writes that 'The preference for "queer" represents, among other things, an aggressive impulse of generalisation; it rejects a minoritising logic of toleration or simple political interest-representation in favour of a more thorough resistance to regimes of the normal' (1993 xxvi). In their 1998 essay 'Sex in Public', Lauren Berlant joins Warner to suggest that some varieties of heteroerotics may resist normative regimentation. The authors distinguish, that is, between, on the one hand, heterosexuality as a loosely lubricated set of interactions among bodies and pleasures and, on the other, and more dryly, heteronormativity as 'the institution, structures of understanding, and practical orientations that make heterosexuality not only coherent – that is, organised as a sexuality – but also privileged'. If heteronormativity thus defined is 'a concept distinct from heterosexuality', then some 'forms of sex between men and women might not be heteronormative' (1998, 565 n. 2). In a somewhat similar vein, Leo Bersani, in his 1995 book *Homos*, writes not of queerness but of what he calls 'homo-ness' as an 'anti-identitarian identity' (1995, 101) and as 'a mode of connectedness to the world that it would be absurd to reduce to sexual preference' (1995, 10). Though Bersani considers homosexuality to be a 'privileged vehicle' for homo-ness, he considers the latter to be 'relevant to love between the sexes' (1995, 147), involving a 'mobility' that 'should create a kind of community … that can never be settled, whose membership is always shifting … a community in which many straights should be able to find a place' (1995, 9).

In the essay 'Straight with a Twist' (first published in *Genders* in 1997) I suggest as provisional participants in this shifting community the non-breeding or child-free heterosexual married couple who conscientiously object not to children as such but rather to what Lee Edelman, in *No Future*, calls the ideological figure of 'the Child'.

For Edelman, 'The Child … marks the fetishistic fixation of heteronormativity: an erotically charged investment in the rigid sameness of identity that is central to the compulsory narrative of reproductive futurism' (2004, 21). Back in 1995, however, David Halperin had already suggested in *Saint Foucault* that the queer aegis could conceivably cover the non-conceiving, could include 'some married couples without children … or even (who knows?) some married couples *with* children – with, perhaps, *very naughty* children' (1995, 62). Highlighting critical efforts to distinguish naughty heterosexuality from haughty heteronormativity, Nikki Sullivan, in the chapter of her *A Critical Introduction to Queer Theory* called 'Queering "Straight" Sex', does me the honour of citing *Straight with a Twist*. She writes (and please forgive this self-reflexively citational pastiche):

> *Calvin Thomas … suggests that '[h]eteronormative sex is teleologically narrativised sex: sex with a goal, purpose, and a product' … The product that must be (re)produced, argues Thomas, is 'the person', and this can be understood in terms of 'the child', 'the ego', or both. Given this, one could propose that heteronormativity is anti-sexual insofar as its primary aim is in direct contradistinction with what [Lynne] Segal, Bersani, [Catherine] Waldby and others have claimed is the fundamental characteristic of sex, that is, the (at least momentary) loss or destruction of the self and the boundaries that constitute it. Ironically, then, perhaps, as Thomas suggests, 'people who f*** in the name of identity … who make an identity out of who they f***, who f*** to reproduce 'the person', are f***ing heteronormatively … even if 'the person' or 'identity' thereby reproduced is 'homosexual'. (2003, 133)*

In *No Future*, Edelman further ironises the *telos* of heteronormative (anti)sex when he writes of 'the necessity of translating the corrupt, unregenerate vulgate of f***ing into the infinitely tonier, indeed sacramental, Latin of procreation' (2004, 40). As Edelman continues: 'No f***ing could ever effect such creation: all sensory experience, all pleasure of the flesh, must be borne away from this fantasy of futurity secured, eternity's plan fulfilled, as "a new generation is carried forward". Paradoxically, the child of two-parent families proves that its parents *don't* f***' (2004, 41).

Who Knows?

My purposes in rehearsing these moments in which the spectral possibility of something like 'queer heterosexuality' was first raised are several. First, I would point out that, with the notable exception of the 'straight writer' Sedgwick, most if not all of those theorists who initially opened the borders to thinking about straight participation in/proliferation of queer theory were not flippant, trend-savvy heterosexual academic consumers eager to appropriate the latest intellectual commodity but seriously queer writers of seriously (i.e. not vacuously) queer scholarship. Second, I would point out that, in fact, when 'straight queer' did appear as a small swatch of not particularly brilliant colour on the flag that queer theory had run up its pole, not many straight intellectuals even noticed, much less raised their hands in salute. Correspondingly, and to shift metaphors, I would suggest that perhaps what Schlichter calls 'particularly urgent' concerns about 'the representatives of the dominant sexuality who migrate into queer territory' (2004, 554) shouldn't really be considered all that urgent given the other and more serious challenges that transformative queer politics faces, and given that, after all, not *that* many straight birds actually flapped their way into queer territory ravening to wet their beaks.

Finally, I would submit that the most salient question raised in the preceding spectral history may be the one that emerges parenthetically, and which I happily tear out of its context, in the quotation from David Halperin – to wit: *who knows?* Sue-Ellen Case has suggested that queer theory 'works not at the site of gender, but at the site of ontology, to shift the ground of being itself' (1991, 3), and her suggestion allows us to focus on the shifting ground underlying the 'who' in the question 'who knows?' Queer theory also works at the site of epistemology, to shift the grounds of knowledge itself, allowing us to appreciate the fluid ambiguities of the object as well as the subject of possible knowledge in the open question 'who *knows?*' But queer theory also works, or plays, at the infinitely various sites of eroticism, allowing us to open further the question, and ourselves, and perhaps even some of our orifices, and wonder 'Who *the f*** knows?* Queer theory ultimately asks: who the f*** knows who or what one *is* in relation to the question of whom or how or what or when or even if one f***s? Who (besides some version of a fundamentalist) knows a stable, definitive answer to the question of how ontological questions (of being, of identity) and epistemological questions (of how one knows) circulate intricately in the territory of erotic questions (of bodies and pleasures, of power and the drives, of language and desire) – questions that are all as inexorably *political* as they are preeminently *textual*?

Who knows? And what are the social, cultural and political imperatives that attempt to implant within us, to impose upon us, this anxious desire to know and be able to say exactly who and what (we think) we are? Conversely, or perhaps perversely, to what extent can one resist – or, if the verb 'resist' seems too heroically voluntaristic, then maladroitly flop at following – these implanted, imposed and ultimately normalising imperatives? Refuse or fail to know who one is? Refuse or fail to say what one is? Refuse or fail to *be* what one (is told one) is? Or perhaps refuse or fail *not* to be what one (has been told and even has told oneself one) isn't? Perhaps this refusal/failure can be animated by what Leo Bersani calls 'a desire to be with an intensity that cannot be contained – held in or defined – by a self' (1990, 101). Or perhaps we desire to 'refuse what we are', as Michel Foucault puts it, in order 'to promote new forms of subjectivity through the refusal of this kind of individuality that has been imposed on us for several centuries' (1994, 336).

I should point out that Bersani is in the above writing about Friedrich Nietzsche, the 'proto-postmodernist' and (as Donald Hall calls him) 'proto-queer' philosopher 'who took up most intensely the late nineteenth century challenge to received notions of normality (2003, 56, 58). Proto-pomo-homo or no, Nietzsche was indeed one of the first Western thinkers to alert us to the way 'regimes of the normal' operate in the imperatives of knowledge, particularly self-knowledge. In Nietzsche's interpretation, the desire of the Western project of knowledge, from Socrates to Georg Wilhelm Friedrich Hegel, is *orthopaedic*: such knowledge is driven by 'the unshakeable belief that, by following the guiding thread of causality, thought reaches into the deepest abysses of being and is capable not only of knowing but also even of *correcting* being' (2006 [1872], 71). Self-knowledge, then, though arguably indispensable to any ethical critical project, can just as arguably also work as an orthopaedic correction or normative regimentation of the self: to 'know oneself' can mean little more than to familiarise oneself, to domesticate oneself, to recognise in oneself (and in self-mirroring others) only 'what everybody already knows' (Jagose 1996, 102): that is, only those aspects of subjectivity that conform to dominant, institutionalised regimes of truth, knowledge and power. 'Consequently', writes Nietzsche in *The Gay Science*:

> ... *given the best will in the world to understand ourselves as individually as possible, 'to know ourselves', each of us will always succeed in becoming conscious only of what is not individual but 'average'. Our thoughts themselves are continually governed by the character of [herd] consciousness – by the 'genius of the species' that commands it – and translated back into the perspective of the herd.* (2006 [1882], 368)

We are herded into knowing ourselves by being made afraid not to, by learning to fear being unfamiliar (to) ourselves – not to fear ignorance but rather to fear our own inner strangeness. Though as a social constructionist I might substitute the word 'institution' for 'instinct' in the following, here is Nietzsche in a formulation I consider indispensable for queer theory as a project of creative abrasion: 'Is it not the *instinct of fear* that bids us to know? And is the jubilation of those who attain knowledge not the jubilation over the restoration of a sense of security?' (2006 [1882], 368).

Michel Foucault, of course, knew his Nietzsche well. But Foucault was also a student of Louis Althusser, the structuralist Marxist philosopher influenced by Lacanian psychoanalysis, whose influential theories of ideological 'interpellation' suggest that 'we are constructed ... through pre-existing categories and imposed definitions of self-hood' (Hall 2003, 181). For Althusser, ideology brings us into being as subjects not only by imposing definitions of self-hood but by imposing as 'obvious' or natural the very notion that 'selves' must be (or just are) clearly and identifiably defined. Ideology, insists Althusser, works by imposing 'obviousnesses as obviousnesses'. He writes that 'the category of the subject is constitutive of all ideology' but adds that '*the category of the subject is only constitutive of all ideology insofar as all ideology has the function (which defines it) of "constituting" concrete individuals as subjects*':

It follows that, for you and for me, the category of the subject is a primary 'obviousness' (obviousnesses are always primary): it is clear that you and I are subjects (free, ethical, etc. ...). Like all obviousnesses, including those that make a word 'name a thing' or 'have a meaning' (therefore including the obviousness of the 'transparency' of language), the 'obviousness' that you and I are subjects – and that that does not cause any problems – is an ideological effect, the elementary ideological effect. It is indeed a peculiarity of ideology that it imposes (without appearing to do so, since these are 'obviousnesses') obviousnesses as obviousnesses, which we cannot fail to recognise and before which we have the inevitable reaction of crying out ...: 'That's obvious! That's right! That's true!'

At work in this reaction is the ideological recognition function .... (1971, 171–2)

Foucault develops (or queers) Althusser's argument by historicising the received and naturalised notion of '*sexuality*' as the 'truth' of one's 'personage'. Foucault, that is, exposes 'sexual identity' as a 'primary obviousness' and as an 'elementary ideological effect', perhaps *the* elementary ideological effect of the modern *episteme*. Thus, after our exposure to Nietzsche, Althusser, Foucault and others, it is no longer 'obvious' that eroticism of any sort must be routed through the regulatory fiction of identity. Nor is it any longer obvious or right or true that any *ethical* speaking, reading or writing subject should 'know' and be able coherently and successfully to articulate or self-identically repeat exactly what sort of erotic being she or he 'truly' or 'naturally' is. Indeed, after queer theory, *ethics* may involve a sort of disturbance or breakdown in the ideological recognition function, a strategic *failure* to recognise 'what we cannot fail to recognise', an inaptitude for assuming identity and a failure to repeat its obvious lessons, 'including [to repeat Althusser's words and *interpolate* a few of my own] those that make a word [like straight or gay or queer] "name a thing" or "have a meaning" (therefore including the obviousness of the "transparency" of language), [and including] the "obviousness" that you and I are subjects [with transparently readable sexual identities] – and that that does not cause any problems' (1971, 171–2). As arch problem-causer Judith Butler writes: 'Such a failure of interpellation may well undermine the capacity of the subject to "be" in a self-identical sense, but it may also mark the path toward a more open, even more ethical kind of being, one of or for the future' (1997, 131).

On the other hand, for Lee Edelman in *No Future*, queerness as interpellative failure or at least as 'what chafes against "normalisation"' (2004, 6) may open up a mode of being that is altogether indifferent – and not even 'benignly' – to an ethics of futurity. Linking even the most politically progressive ethics 'of or for the future' to heteronormative 'reproductive futurism', Edelman writes that queerness:

... finds its value not in a good susceptible to generalisation, but only in the stubborn particularity that voids every notion of a general good. The embrace of queer negativity, then, can have no justification if justification requires it to reinforce some positive social value; its value, instead, resides in its challenge

> to value as defined by the social, and thus in its radical challenge to the very
> value of the social itself ... [its] refusal of the coercive belief in the paramount
> value of futurity. (2004, 6)

Always the Last to Know

I will return to Edelman in the very near future. Here I must linger with Althusser, and with his word 'interpellation', which he uses to describe the way ideology (the social itself) calls to or 'hails' an individual and thereby 'recruits' that individual as a 'subject'. Althusser writes:

> I shall then suggest that ideology 'acts' or 'functions' in such a way that it
> 'recruits' subjects among the individuals (it recruits them all), or 'transforms'
> the individuals into subjects (it transforms them all) by that very precise
> operation which I have called interpellation or hailing, and which can be
> imagined along the lines of the most commonplace everyday police (or other)
> hailing: 'Hey, you there!'
>
> Assuming that the theoretical scene I have imagined takes place in the street,
> the hailed individual will turn round. By this mere one-hundred-and-eighty-
> degree physical conversion, he becomes a subject. Why? Because he has
> recognised that 'it was really him who was hailed' (and not someone else).
> (1971, 174)

I re-rehearse Althusser's famous 'theoretical scene' here because of the way I employed it in *Straight with a Twist* to narrate a bit of interpellative theatre from my own history that I want now briefly to revisit. Before returning, however, to my little scenario, which did in fact take place in the street, I will cite that of another, which took place in a high-school classroom.

In his book *Queer Theories*, Hall writes of his high-school experiences in 'rural Alabama in 1975'. A fellow student named Joan has turned 'the identity spotlight directly' on the 15-year-old Hall by asking him in front of a classroom if he were a queer, and even though Hall 'knew all too well that [he] desired other boys ... had recently "come out" to a couple of close friends, and even had a small stash of gay rights material hidden in [his] bedroom closet', Hall's 'well-honed survivor's instinct' compels him to answer 'no':

> I felt awful. Not particularly threatened or physically unsafe. Unlike many
> schools, my school was not a very violent place ... though certainly it was no
> place to celebrate difference. No, I felt awful because of the lie. I knew what
> I 'was' (confusion only came much later), was even comfortable with what
> I 'was', but also knew better than ever to turn around in the hallway when
> someone yelled, 'Hey, queer!' To be sure I always wanted to turn around and

say something smart and sarcastic. After all, I was not-so-secretly proud of being abnormal – bookish, ambitious, self-aware – in that bunch of losers (which, more than anything specifically sexual, may have been what they were calling me on). 'Hey, queer!' No response. (2003, 17)

My own interpellative 'scene', as related in *Straight with a Twist*, takes place around 1980 in midtown Atlanta. I am walking alone, apparently looking like a young male homosexual, or perhaps seeming only abnormally bookish, ambitious and self-aware, but in any case showing up as a blip on some loser's gaydar, for a car slows up and an unfriendly voice calls out: 'Hey, queer!' Unlike Hall, however, I *did* respond. In fact:

I turned. Perhaps not in the full 'one-hundred-and-eighty-degree physical conversion' described by Althusser in his example of interpellation as turning in response to being hailed by the policeman who says: 'Hey, you there!' But I did turn ... Fortunately for me, the car sped on ... and I was left only with the knowledge that I had turned – a vague knowledge, a recognition, with which I did not exactly know what to do. (2000, 33–4)

I guess I still don't know 'exactly what to do' with this 'knowledge'. But I would say that my desire in comparing these two scenes is to re-raise (and suggest again the im-possible queerness of) the question: who knows? After all, both scenes involve knowledge, recognition, address, interpellation, articulation, normalisation. Both imply the possibility of orthopaedic violence. But in one scene the 'really' queer one, the one who *did* know what he 'was', did know that he was 'really' queer, also instinctively knew better than ever to say so or ever to *turn* in the punitive, interpellative glare of the identity spotlight, while in the other scene the 'straight' one (always the last to know), who didn't yet know that he wasn't or isn't exactly *not* 'really' queer, didn't know better than *not* to turn in response to an urban redneck's menacing hail. But in bringing the Althusserian 'theoretical scene' down into the real streets and hallways of two different men's inverse but somehow contiguous (and not just because Alabama abuts Georgia) personal, political and historical memories, I also want to suggest that all the world's dramas of recognition and identification, big and little, high and low – from Hegel's master–slave dialectic and Jacques Lacan's mirror–stage and Althusser's theatre of ideology to the most quotidian of moments in the most banal of settings – inevitably take place in the context of the threat of alterity-phobic violence. It is, as Nietzsche tells us, truly the instinct and the institution of fear that bids us to know exactly who and what we are.

But perhaps it is something else, something other than the institution of fear – possibly the defamiliarising institution of *letters* – that can bid or invite us not to *know* (ourselves) but to *read* and *write* (ourselves) in ways that fail recognition, that f*** up self-knowledge, that do not define identity but more fundamentally disturb it. If 'the jubilation of those who attain knowledge' is in fact 'the jubilation over the restoration of a sense of security' (Nietzsche 2006 [1882], 368), then the abject jubilation of those who 'play without security' (Derrida 1978, 292), who read and write queerly, deconstructively, in a non-dialectically self-alienating spirit of creative abrasion, may be something else again. 'Our eyes can remain open' to this extimate alterity, to the estrangingness of the letter, 'provided we recognise ourselves as always already altered by the symbolic – by language. Provided we hear in language … that basic incompleteness that conditions the indefinite quest of signifying concatenations. That amounts to joying in the truth of self-division' (Kristeva 1982, 89).

Who knows this joy, this truth, any better or worse than 'I' who can 'identify myself in language, but only by losing myself in it like an object' (Lacan 2002, 84)? And what is it, after all, that (not exactly) 'one' such as (not completely) 'myself' *enjoys* about reading queer theory and attempting to write theory queerly? Is it, as Schlichter suggests, the narcissistic, egotistical thrill of puffing up my own 'seminal' (2004, 551) critical authority and my overarching 'need to be recognised as transgressive' (2004, 553)? I wouldn't deny myself or anyone else narcissistic pleasure or the desire for recognition: that is, I doubt the possibility of anyone's engaging in an utterly egoless critical writing that completely escapes a narcissistic economy, mainly because I doubt that anyone ever writes anything without being on some level motivated by the desire to be recognised as something or another by someone (if not by the Other).[5] And yet, without for a moment denying the yolky enjoyment of my own critical self-absorption, I would insist that there's also something more and other than ostentatious narcissism involved in my involvement with this *jouissance* of queer *écriture* – namely, the more masochistic money-shot of the encounter with the strangeness of language, with the extimate *ébranlement* or self-shattering that is inscribed therein (and disseminated thereout), with what Sedgwick (again) calls the 'open mesh of possibilities, gaps, overlaps, dissonances and resonances, lapses and excesses' (1993a, 8) of non-monolithic erotic signification. I think – it pleases/pains me to think – of reading and writing as erotic relationships (autoerotic, homoerotic and heteroerotic) with *the art of the sentence;* I think in and of language (in which every sentence is a death sentence) as the very enactment of the death drive and of desire; and I rightly or wrongly associate this self-divisive, basically incomplete, open mesh of thanatical dissonance and erotic excess both with *queerness* as what chafes against necrotic, normalised ego coherence and with *textuality* as the vital site of defamiliarisation and identity-disturbance. In other words, I am erotically thrilled not only by what Edelman refers to as 'the vicissitudes of the sign' (2004, 7) but by the devastating way a writer like Edelman *works* those vicissitudes.

---

5   Lacan, following a line of thought that leads through Alexander Kojève back to Hegel, suggests that what initially and constitutively separates specifically human desire from animal need is nothing other than desire for the other's recognition. Lacan writes that 'Man's desire finds its meaning in the other's desire, not so much because the other holds the keys to the desired object, as because his first object(ive) is to be recognized by the other' (2002, 58).

Queerness, however, is supposed (by some) to be a primarily *political* socio-sexual reality or disposition, and by associating it with *aesthetic* experience I leave myself open to the accusation not only of appropriation but of apolitical literary formalism. Thus Schlichter, an academic writer who apparently believes that academic writing (or at least *my* academic writing) has little interventional use-value, charges me with 'taking the textual for the political' (2004, 552). This charge, however, is yet another that I would not deny, a 'taking' that I would not withhold from anyone else and that in fact I could not take away from anyone or avoid myself even if I so wanted. For this textual-political confusion is both as old as *polis* and papyrus and as new as Derrida's 'there is nothing outside of the text' (1997, 158). In other words, it has always been and, as far as I can tell, will never *not* be radically constitutive of social reality itself. Far from wanting to deny 'taking the textual for the political', then, I desire (textually, politically, and, if possible, hell yes, transgressively) to participate in and exacerbate their confusion as much as possible because one possible way of helping to make social reality or 'the world queerer than ever' (Warner 1993, xxvii) is to insist on the *insistence of the letter* rather than on its *consistency*, to insist that social reality or 'the world' is always (disturbingly and disturbably) textually construed, to insist, as does Lacan, that 'reality, the whole of human reality, is nothing other than a *montage* of the symbolic and the imaginary' (1966/1967, unpublished manuscript).

If I do take the textual for the political, I want to 'take it' literally, that is, to the letter, *in writing*, and I want to 'take it' like a queer, like any other queer who somehow manages to fail to be. For this taking, this *writing* – if I take Edelman's meaning correctly – can be queerly (which is to say, ironically) interventional. Arguing, as I take it, *for* an anti-identitarian textual/political confusion, and *against* the covert 'reproductive futurism' (and hence heteronormativity) of stable identity politics (for him 'the future is kid stuff'), Edelman, in a book that bears the subtitle *Queer Theory and the Death Drive* (and this long passage will bear me to my conclusion, if not to my end), writes:

> By figuring a refusal of the coercive belief in the paramount value of futurity, while refusing as well any backdoor hope for dialectical access to meaning, the queer dispossesses the social order of the ground on which it rests: a faith in the consistent reality of the social – and by extension of the social subject ... [T]he queer insists that politics is always a politics of the signifier, or even of what Lacan will often refer to as 'the letter'. It serves to shore up a reality always unmoored by signification and lacking any guarantee ... [Q]ueerness exposes the obliquity of our relation to what we experience in and as social reality, alerting us to the fantasies structurally necessary in order to sustain it and engaging those fantasies through the figural logics, the linguistic structures, that shape them. If it aims effectively to intervene in the reproduction of such a reality ... then queer theory must always insist on its connection to the vicissitudes of the sign, to the tension between the signifier's collapse into the letter's cadaverous materiality and its participation in a system of reference wherein it generates meaning itself. As a particular story ... of why

storytelling fails, one that takes both the value and the burden of that failure upon itself, queer theory … marks the 'other' side of politics. (2004, 6–7)

I began this writing with reference to a particular story, the one about how 'queer' got queered into 'theory', and proceeded to attempt to narrate another story of particularly stubborn particularity, a story of how queer theory dis-positions one of its readers and writers who – thanks to a 'theory' that is always already 'queer' (and that transports him to the 'other' side of more than politics) – cannot '"be" in a self-identical sense' (Butler 1997, 131), who remains at chafing odds and yet privileged evens with the normal, who can no longer be and yet still cannot *not* be a representative of the dominant sexuality, and who apparently still doesn't know better than to accept (un)certain invitations, doesn't know better than not to turn in response to a hailing call that was clearly obliquely not 'really' meant for him. If I have not failed better this time in telling the story of why this storytelling fails, I hope at least to have failed no worse, though perhaps I should hope to have failed worse than ever, or, as Beckett dared put it, 'as no other dare fail' (1984, 145). In any case, this telling will of course take the burden of its failure, its *durchfall*, upon itself. As for its 'success', its possible interventional or transgressive intellectual, ethical or political usefulness, its 'positive social value', I'm sure there are those who know, and can say. No doubt *they* know exactly who they are. As for myself, my engagement with queer theory, my 'embrace of queer negativity', has no justification that I know of – and that's just the way I want to let things lie.

Suggested Further Reading

Dean, T. (2000), *Beyond Sexuality* (Chicago, IL: University of Chicago Press).

Fantina, R. (ed.) (2006), *Straight Writ Queer: Non-Normative Representations of Heterosexuality in Literature* (Jefferson, NC: McFarland).

Katz, J.N. (1995), *The Invention of Heterosexuality* (New York: Dutton).

Segal, L. (1994), *Straight Sex: Rethinking the Politics of Pleasure* (Berkeley, CA: University of California Press).

Waldby, C. (1995), 'Destruction: Boundary Erotics and the Refigurations of the Heterosexual Male Body', in E. Grosz. and E. Probyn (eds), *Sexy Bodies: The Strange Carnalities of Feminism* (New York and London: Routledge).

References

Althusser, L. (1971), *Lenin and Philosophy and Other Essays*, trans. B. Brewster (New York: Monthly Review).

Beckett, S. (1983), *Worstward Ho* (New York: Grove Press).

—— (1984), *Disjecta: Miscellaneous Writings and a Dramatic Fragment*, (ed.) R. Cohn (New York: Grove).

Berlant, L. and Warner, M. (1995), 'What Does Queer Theory Teach Us About X?', *PMLA* 110:3, 343–9.

—— (1998), 'Sex in Public', *Critical Inquiry* 24:2, 547–66.

Bersani, L. (1990), *The Culture of Redemption* (Cambridge, MA: Harvard University Press).

—— (1995), *Homos* (Cambridge, MA: Harvard University Press).

Butler, J. (1993), *Bodies That Matter: On the Discursive Limits of 'Sex'* (New York and London: Routledge).

—— (1997), *The Psychic Life of Power: Theories in Subjection* (Stanford, CA: Stanford University Press).

Case, S.-E. (1991), 'Tracking the Vampire', *differences: A Journal of Feminist Cultural Studies* 3:2, 1–20.

Dean, T. (2000), *Beyond Sexuality* (Chicago, IL: University of Chicago Press).

De Lauretis, T. (1991), 'Queer Theory: Lesbian and Gay Sexualities', *differences: A Journal of Feminist Cultural Studies* 3:2, iii–xviii.

—— (1994), 'Habit Changes', *differences: A Journal of Feminist Cultural Studies* 6:2/3, 296–313.

—— (1997), 'Fem/Les Scramble', in D. Heller (ed.), *Cross-Purposes: Lesbians, Feminists, and the Limits of Alliance* (Bloomington, IN: Indiana University Press).

Derrida, J. (1978), *Writing and Difference*, trans. A. Bass (Chicago, IL: University of Chicago Press).

—— (1997), *Of Grammatology*, corrected edition, trans. G. Spivak (Baltimore, MD: Johns Hopkins University Press).

Doty, A. (1993), *Making Things Perfectly Queer: Interpreting Mass Culture* (Minneapolis, MN: University of Minnesota Press).

Edelman, L. (1995), 'Queer Theory: Unstating Desire', *GLQ: A Journal of Lesbian and Gay Studies* 2:4, 343–6.

—— (2004), *No Future: Queer Theory and the Death Drive* (Durham, NC: Duke University Press).

Foucault, M. (1994), 'The Subject and Power', in *The Essential Works of Foucault, 1954–1984, Volume III: Power*, (ed.) J.D. Faubion and trans. R. Hurley (New York: The New Press).

Hall, D.E. (2003), *Queer Theories* (New York: Palgrave).

Halperin, D. (1995), *Saint Foucault: Towards a Gay Hagiography* (New York and Oxford: Oxford University Press).

Jagose, A. (1996), *Queer Theory: An Introduction* (New York: New York University Press).

Kauffmann, L.A. (1992), 'Radical Change: The Left Attacks Identity Politics', *Village Voice*, 30 June.

Kristeva, J. (1982), *Powers of Horror: An Essay on Abjection*, trans. L.S. Roudiez (New York: Columbia University Press).

Lacan, J. (1966/1967), *The Seminar of Jacques Lacan. Book XIV, The Logic of Fantasy 1966–1967* (unpublished manuscript).

—— (2002), *Écrits: A Selection*, trans. B. Fink (New York: Norton).

Nietzsche, F. (2006 [1872]), *The Birth of Tragedy*, in K.A. Pearson and D. Large (ed.), *The Nietzsche Reader* (Malden, MA and Oxford: Blackwell).

—— (2006 [1882]), *The Gay Science*, in Pearson and Large (ed.), *The Nietzsche Reader* (Malden, MA and Oxford: Blackwell).

Schlichter, A. (2004), 'Queer at Last? Straight Intellectuals and the Desire for Transgression', *GLQ: A Journal of Lesbian and Gay Studies* 10:4, 543–64.

Sedgwick, E.K. (1993a), *Tendencies* (Durham, NC: Duke University Press).

—— (1993b), 'Queer Performativity: Henry James's *The Art of the Novel*', *GLQ: A Journal of Lesbian and Gay Studies* 1:1, 1–16.

Sullivan, N. (2003), *A Critical Introduction to Queer Theory* (Edinburgh: Edinburgh University Press).

Thomas, C. (2000), 'Straight with a Twist: Queer Theory and the Subject of Heterosexuality', in C. Thomas with J.O. Aimone and C.A.F. MacGillivray (eds), *Straight with a Twist: Queer Theory and the Subject of Heterosexuality* (Urbana, IL: University of Illinois Press).

—— (2002), 'Is Straight Self-Understanding Possible?', *Transformations: The Journal of Inclusive Scholarship and Pedagogy* 13:2, 17–24.

—— (2008), *Masculinity, Psychoanalysis, Straight Queer Theory: Essays on Abjection in Literature, Mass Culture, and Film* (New York: Palgrave Macmillan).

Walters, S.D. (1996), 'From Here to Queer: Radical Feminism, Postmodernism, and the Lesbian Menace (Or, Why Can't a Woman Be More like a Fag?)', *Signs: Journal of Women in Culture and Society* 21:4, 830–69.

Warner, M. (1993), 'Introduction', in M. Warner (ed.), *Fear of a Queer Planet: Queer Politics and Social Theory* (Minneapolis, MN: University of Minnesota Press.

Why Five Sexes Are Not Enough

Iain Morland

Do intersexed individuals – those of us born with 'ambiguous' sexual characteristics – have a political obligation to identify as members of a third, or even a fourth or fifth, sex? It would seem that the unwilling recipients of medical treatment for bodies that cannot be easily described as either male or female must decide whether to identify as intersexed, even after the body parts that medicine calls intersexed have been removed in childhood. This is because for some patients, the suggestion that genital surgery in infancy has successfully eliminated their intersexuality constitutes an unacceptable capitulation to medical normalisation. 'I was not born with the genitalia of both *men* and *women*; I was born with *child-sized* intersexed genitals', insists gender theorist Morgan Holmes (2000, 99). Seen in this way, a baby that has (for instance) testes and a small phallus without a urethra does not have an 'ambiguous' combination of male and female genitalia – male gonads and a clitoris, one might say – but rather a perfect, and perfectly comprehensible, set of intersexed genitals. Therefore in Holmes's view, genital surgery cannot clarify one's sex as either male or female; it simply injures one's intersexed genitalia. Accordingly, an identity other than male or female seems to be the most politically appropriate response to injurious genital surgery. In other words, only by refusing to identify as female or male can a post-surgical individual counter surgery's claim to make a patient readily determinable as either one sex or the other.

In a pertinent essay on queer theory, transgender performance artist Kate Bornstein has contested what s/he calls 'the problem of suffocating identity politics' (1997, 16). Building on Bornstein, my starting point in this chapter is that the medical management of intersexuality, when experienced by patients as morally and physically injurious, creates as one of its negative effects precisely the 'suffocating identity politics' that Bornstein criticises. For example, when surgery is performed on an infant to reduce a clitoris that is perceived by clinicians and parents to be overly 'masculine' for a genetic 'female', and when that infant grows up to resent the surgery which has impaired clitoral sensation, a dilemma of identity politics seems to consume the post-surgical individual: ought they to identify, as a point of political principle, as 'intersexed' not 'female'? 'If I label my postsurgical anatomy female, I ascribe to surgeons the power to create a *woman* by *removing* body parts', states leading patient activist Cheryl Chase (1998, 214). In this way, it seems that if one wishes to voice objections to surgery performed for an intersex condition, then it's necessary to identify as 'intersexed', in order for one's objections to be politically cogent.

I take very seriously the statements by Chase and Holmes as symptomatic of the problem of genital surgery. Such surgery puts them (and me) in the suffocating position of apparently needing *either* to align one's identity with one's sexual politics (by identifying as intersexed), *or* conversely to relinquish the political critique of intersex medicine by docilely passing as female or male. To dismantle this unreasonable opposition, I want to follow Bornstein in advocating 'the abandonment of politicised identities in favour of the politics of values' (1997, 16). Therefore in this chapter I will use insights from queer theory's interrogation of identity politics to argue that a queer 'politics of values' offers a better way of understanding the identities claimed by individuals with atypical genitals – those of us who have received surgery, as well as those who have not. I will argue that the sex that one claims as an identity is a matter of the politics of values, not of a person's descriptively apprehensible anatomy, or of one's identity *as* a description of one's anatomy. In addition, I'll advance a polemical recommendation regarding the identities that ought to be claimed by those *without* atypical genitals.

I am going to begin by critically analysing an influential and controversial intervention into the identity politics of intersex. In the course of my analysis, I'll also explain the intellectual context of that intervention in early-1990s queer theory.

Biology through History

In 1993, feminist and biologist Anne Fausto-Sterling published an article in the prestigious organ of the New York Academy of Sciences, the *Sciences*. Titled 'The Five Sexes: Why Male and Female are Not Enough' (1993a), her essay was the cover story of the journal's March/April edition. It was also printed in the *New York Times* on 12 March (1993b). The problem posited by the essay's title is simply one of finding enough terms to describe five sexes, rather than the current terms that represent only two – and hence, it would seem, the identification as intersexed of those who have such atypical body parts. However, Fausto-Sterling advances her argument about the number of sexes not from the starting point of anatomy, the language and numeration of body parts, but interestingly from the starting point of history.

The 'Five Sexes' begins by telling the story of Levi Suydam. In 1843 Suydam, who was reportedly reputed to be 'more female than male', was examined by a physician in order to confirm whether he was entitled to vote in a Connecticut election (Fausto-Sterling 1993a, 20). Although the presence of a phallus vouched, to the physician's eyes, for Suydam's maleness and hence for his right to suffrage, it was discovered after the election that Suydam regularly menstruated. The puzzled physician later noted that not only was Levi Suydam's body atypical (for it transpired to feature a vaginal opening in addition to a phallus) but also that

Suydam had 'feminine propensities': for example, a fondness 'for pieces of calico' (1993a, 20). In particular, Suydam enjoyed 'comparing and placing … together' the pieces of cloth, wrote the doctor (Epstein 1990, 119). These revelations lead Fausto-Sterling to comment of Suydam that: 'Both his/her physique and his/her mental predispositions were more complex than was first suspected' (1993a, 20). As we will discover, this emphasis on complexity – specifically sexual complexity that requires valuation beyond what has 'first' been perceived – will become critical to her essay's argument.

It is not until after Suydam, and a brief discussion about the legal accommodation in Western cultures of only two sexes, that Fausto-Sterling introduces the biology of intersex. Testes, ovaries and the medical terms 'female pseudohermaphrodite', 'true hermaphrodite' and 'male pseudohermaphrodite' – terms to which I will return to below – make their first appearance at this point. And this structure, of turning to biology through history, is repeated shortly afterwards, which suggests that it has a significance beyond the stylistic: Fausto-Sterling's detailed exposition of embryological sexual differentiation also begins surprisingly with the narrative of Hermaphroditus. 'According to Greek mythology', she recounts, Hermes and Aphrodite 'parented Hermaphroditus, who at age fifteen became half male and half female when his body fused with the body of a nymph he fell in love with' (1993a, 22). The text then moves without segue to the observation that 'In some true hermaphrodites the testis and the ovary grow separately but bilaterally; in others, they grow together within the same organ, forming an ovo-testis' (1993a, 22). There follows a substantial discussion of sexual development in embryos. To be sure, the tale of Hermaphroditus has nominal relevance to true hermaphrodites. But Hermaphroditus's transformation is a love story, not a lesson in gonads – which weren't understood in ancient Greece to determine sexual differentiation anyway (Laqueur 1990, 4–5, 26).

I propose a better way of understanding the mythic story's placement. Structurally, the Greek myth's appearance repeats Fausto-Sterling's earlier manoeuvre during the Suydam story from history to biology. And later, the manoeuvre is performed once again in the slightly different form of a turn from history to biomedicine (1993a, 23). I argue that Fausto-Sterling uses history to introduce biology for two interrelated political purposes: to make intersexuality familiar, and to de-familiarise contemporary approaches to intersex. Hence, on the one hand, she states reassuringly that 'Intersexuality itself is old news. Hermaphrodites … are often featured in stories about human origins', before attending to recent developments in biomedicine (1993a, 23). On the other hand, Fausto-Sterling also observes that 'Ironically, a more sophisticated knowledge of the complexity of sexual systems [by medicine] has led to the repression of such [sexual] intricacy' (1993a, 23). The submerged foil to this key sentence is its implicit claim that a more sophisticated knowledge of history *will* allow recognition of precisely the sexual intricacy that current medical knowledge and practice fails to recognise. By means of this rhetorical strategy, she claims, 'medical accomplishments [in "biochemistry, embryology, endocrinology, psychology and surgery"] can be read not as progress but as a mode of discipline' (1993a, 24).

It appears, then, that describing intersex is a political act. By striving to make intersexuality familiar – located at the very root of the story of humanity – while concurrently making the contemporary medical treatment of intersex unfamiliar, Fausto-Sterling indicates that our acknowledgement of sexual diversity in history will illuminate the objectionable treatment in the present of individuals with atypical sex characteristics. The personalisation of this axiom is that if only it were possible for an individual to identify conclusively as 'intersexed', then a particular political standpoint regarding the appropriateness of one's medical treatment would follow from that identification – namely that treatment is a 'mode of discipline', which disregards (or 'represses') the sexual intricacy denoted by the identity 'intersexed.'

On Difference

In addition to making medical treatment unfamiliar, Fausto-Sterling's recurrent structural prioritisation over the discourse of biology of an eclectic range of intersex histories – ancient Greece, nineteenth-century America, early Biblical scholarship, Plato, the Jewish books of law and Europe in the Middle Ages are all mentioned – serves to emphasise the irreducible influence of culture on the perception and classification of sexual biology itself (1993a, 20–23). This was a principal insight of Thomas Laqueur's historical monograph *Making Sex*, published three years before the 'Five Sexes', and it is a concern that animates Judith Butler's *Bodies That Matter* (1993), which appeared in the same year as Fausto-Sterling's paper.

In this regard, the 'Five Sexes' essay not only follows Laqueur's contention that 'Two sexes are not the necessary, natural consequence of corporeal difference' (1990, 243) but also enacts an essential tenet of feminist science studies (on which Fausto-Sterling had previously published widely): the body can be described or accessed only through its non-biological social context. As feminist scientists Suzanne Kessler and Wendy McKenna had put it in 1978, 'Our seeing of two genders leads to the "discovery" of biological, psychological, and social differences' (1978, 163). Moreover, as Butler would say in *Bodies* nine months after the publication of the 'Five Sexes', 'what constitutes the fixity of the body, its contours, its movements, will be fully material, but materiality will be rethought as the effect of power, as power's most productive effect' (1993, 2). This reformulation by Butler and others of materiality would rapidly become a central topic for debate in queer theory during the 1990s; in brief, queer theory's denaturalisation of the body would take place by the exposé that the sexed body is, in fact, always different from itself, from its own effected appearance of naturalisation. For some commentators, like Butler in much of *Bodies*, the locus of such difference is power; for others, like Fausto-Sterling repeatedly in the 'Five Sexes', it is history.

So in one sense, when biology is read through history, the gendered body is 'seen' differently, to use Kessler and McKenna's terms. The shortcomings of a two-sex system are exposed. Such is Fausto-Sterling's hope. Her essay has this revelatory aim in common with Gilbert Herdt's innovative historical and anthropological anthology *Third Sex, Third Gender*, which too was completed in 1993. In his preface and introduction to that volume, Herdt laments that people who do not fit 'the sex/gender categories male and female' have been 'marginalised, stigmatised and persecuted' in Western cultures even though 'sexual dimorphism is not inevitable, a universal structure' (1996, 11, 80). In consonance with Herdt's anthology, Fausto-Sterling employs history to disclose that dimorphism is neither inevitable nor universal: in this fashion, in the 'Five Sexes', history is difference.

Fausto-Sterling's Herminology

Yet Fausto-Sterling also posits a kind of difference, a sexual complexity, which is distinct from history – in the case of Suydam, such complexity takes the form of 'physique' and 'mental predispositions'. Similarly, she reports 'contrasts and subtleties' between and within intersex conditions, which are 'so diverse' that they are detectible only through exploratory surgery (1993a, 22). Correspondingly, Fausto-Sterling hopes that in an ideal future, sexuality would be 'celebrated for its subtleties' (1993a, 24). It is perhaps, therefore, on the level of biology that the intricate sexual characteristics, for which the terms male and female 'are not enough', are located after all. Consider then Fausto-Sterling's central claim about the creation of categories to accommodate this sexual complexity:

> ... the standard medical literature uses the term intersex as a catch-all for three major subgroups with some mixture of male and female characteristics: the so-called true hermaphrodites, whom I call herms, who possess one testis and one ovary ...; the male pseudohermaphrodites (the 'merms'), who have testes and some aspects of the female genitalia but no ovaries; and the female pseudohermaphrodites (the 'ferms'), who have ovaries and some aspects of the male genitalia but lack testes. (1993a, 21)

There are no new sexes yet. The tone is taxonomic, the discourse anatomical. In this excerpt, Fausto-Sterling's language employs the conventions of biology instruction in order to fold together knowledge of the names for features (taxonomy) with knowledge of the features themselves (anatomy). As if it were a biology textbook, the article introduces readers to an umbrella term, intersex, and then identifies the term's 'three major subgroups'. The strategy is remarkable because it mimes orthodox biological accounts of sexual difference (which it calls 'the standard medical literature') in order to borrow their rhetoric of incontestability, but then adds, initially through abbreviation ('true hermaphrodites' is innocuously compressed to 'herms'), two adventurous new labels – 'merms' and 'ferms'.

Proof positive that for Fausto-Sterling describing intersex is a political pursuit, the proposed subgroups proved to be as contentious as they were audacious. Denounced as 'maddening' in the *New York Times* by the Catholic League for

Religious and Civil Rights (1995), Fausto-Sterling's terminology – a herminology – was adapted by writer Melissa Scott to become 'mems', 'herms' and 'fems' in her 1995 novel, *Shadow Man*, which won a queer science fiction award from the Lambda Literary Foundation. Nevertheless, one correspondent to the *Sciences*, R.P. Bird, savaged Fausto-Sterling's proposals as 'deranged' (1993, 3).

Next, in a manoeuvre that Bird calls 'truly bizarre', and which Fausto-Sterling later conceded 'clearly … struck a nerve', she proposes that the merms, ferms and herms are themselves sexes (2000b, 79). This proposition of five sexes emerges only after the authority of biology, which readers might have imagined to vouch for the existence of just two sexes, has been unravelled by history. I argue that this is because the proposition of five sexes requires language that is not simply biological; in making the controversial leap from the identification of 'three major subgroups' to the proposal that there are in reality five sexes, the tenor of Fausto-Sterling's argument strikingly departs from biological description: 'I suggest that the three intersexes, herm, merm and ferm, deserve to be considered individual sexes each in its own right' (1993a, 21). This assertion, in marked contrast to its taxonomic precursor concerning sexual subgroups, is put forward in the language of values. Herms, merms and ferms here *deserve* to be considered sexes, each *in its own right*. A two-sex system is therefore berated by Fausto-Sterling as not merely factually erroneous, but as a schema 'in *defiance* of nature' (1993a, 21; my italics).

I am suggesting that the essay's critical move to a five-sex system is notable for its consubstantiality with a move to the rhetoric of values. Whereas a subgroup ought to be acknowledged for the sake of scholarly completeness and scientific rigour, a sex, on the other hand, apparently deserves the *right* to acknowledgement. Because of this right, it would be politically wrong not to acknowledge a sex. This is significantly different to Fausto-Sterling's assumption, which I have explored above, that describing intersex biology is an inherently political project. The difference is that at precisely the point where she proposes five sexes, Fausto-Sterling's rhetoric of values indicates that the description of intersex biology is political only because non-binary sexes have an intrinsic right to be recognised. This right motivates, but also exceeds, the sexes' accommodation in the descriptive language of biology.

Moreover, for Fausto-Sterling the extent and variety of sexual difference in general, beyond intersexuality, warrants similar credit. 'I would argue further that sex is a vast, infinitely malleable continuum that defies the constraints of even five categories', she continues (1993a, 21). Although the declaration that sex is a continuum might seem initially to be descriptive, her statement's force is not situated in the continuum's facticity – because no direct evidence is presented of this inexpressibly 'infinitely malleable' array – but instead is located again in the language of rights. The proposal of a sexual continuum is a call for the valuation of a sexual diversity radically resistant to the biological taxonomy of categories and subgroups. 'No classification scheme could more than suggest the variety of sexual anatomy encountered in clinical practice', Fausto-Sterling cautions later in the essay (1993a, 22). Expressed in the vocabulary of values rather than the language of anatomy, this continuum is said to *defy* the *constraints* of even a five-sex system from which it *deserves* the *right* to be free.

To recapitulate, Fausto-Sterling is doing more than pointing out factual errors in embryology and sexology. She is using exhortative language to contest the enforced containment within *any* taxonomic discourse of sexual diversity. So, in addition to what Fausto-Sterling's pivotal essay says about the need for a five-sex system, it also demonstrates intriguingly such a system's redundancy.

Politics of Passing

To explain why the project of articulating why 'male and female are not enough' would dovetail with the redundancy of descriptive language about intersex (in the form of an admission that five sexes too are repressively taxonomic), we need to revisit the story of a person who did *not* describe himself as a member of a non-binary sex: Levi Suydam.

Immediately following the story of Suydam in the 'Five Sexes' is an assertion by Fausto-Sterling that 'Western culture is deeply committed to the idea that there are only two sexes' (1993a, 20). The statement frames Suydam's story as notable for the reason that it demonstrates the unfairness of a commitment to two sexes. The crudeness of the binary sex 'idea' is hereby set up in opposition to the complexity of Suydam's physique and mental disposition. However it is not obvious that Suydam's story should bear upon Fausto-Sterling's call for the recognition of five sexes. Actually, the story shows that Suydam accomplished his aim – of casting a Whig vote – by finding politico-legal accommodation within a two-sex system.

Certainly the question that seems to be raised by the historical story is whether Suydam simply allowed the Connecticut physician to make a mistake, in order to pass as male and to obtain male privilege. I want to argue, though, that this is the wrong kind of question to ask, because it presumes the possibility of a descriptive correspondence between the identification of one's genitalia (penis, vagina, clitoris, etc.), and one's identity as a member of a sex (male, female, hermaphrodite, 'merm', etc.). If one understands Suydam's passing as merely an instance of a discrepancy between a person's intersex biology, and the way that person's biology is described (in a two-sex system that is 'not enough' to permit an accurate description), then there are two mutually exclusive ways of characterising the significance of an intersexed person's passing.

On the one hand, 'When someone is discredited, a degree of hiding is always required', Herdt writes in *Third Sex*, 'and the fact that passing occurs in many instances of third sex and gender suggests that power commonly sanctions reproductive ideas and dimorphic roles' (1996, 79). In this view, an intersexed person passes because their intersexuality is neither socially nor economically sanctioned. Not to pass would be to put oneself at a social and economic disadvantage. In Suydam's case, it would have placed him at a political disadvantage too, for he would not have been allowed to vote. On the other hand, according to Julia Epstein's 1990 commentary on sexual ambiguity in the journal *Genders*, 'To marry, to vote, to teach, to love: the activities of ordinary social relations involve boundary crossing when practiced by these [intersexed] individuals.' This is because, as Epstein continues, 'Social boundaries depend on difference and hierarchy'; therefore 'Hermaphrodites highlight the privilege differential between male and female precisely because they cannot participate neatly in it' (1990, 124). In this latter view, the intersexed person who passes is a transgressive hero, illuminating and subverting sexual power relations by even their smallest act of passing.

Both these views are reductive. To live in a body that cannot be adequately described by the labels 'male' and 'female' is neither necessarily subversive, nor does it automatically lead an individual to identify as a member of a third, fourth or fifth sex. For example, just as it is often sensible for gay individuals to avoid drawing attention to their sexuality in non-gay public spaces, in order to avoid homophobic violence, so too are transgendered individuals in transphobic environments usually safer if perceived by others to be non-transgendered. As Leslie Feinberg showed in hir novel *Stone Butch Blues* (2003) – published, like the 'Five Sexes', in 1993 – this is not a matter of capitulation to dominant prescriptions concerning sexuality and gender. When sexually dissident individuals pass as non-gay or non-transgendered, they do not robotically become apolitical and acquiescent. In the face of the threat of violence, they are often being simply canny. Similarly, Suydam was, it seems, content to be identified as a man. 'With Suydam safely in their column the Whigs won the election by a majority of one', records Fausto-Sterling (1993a, 20). That Suydam was classed male by the local physician made possible nothing less than his political participation in nineteenth-century history.

My analysis shows that Suydam's story thematises a crucial distinction which Fausto-Sterling does not make: the difference between describing the existence of more than two sexes, and identifying *as* a member of a non-binary sex category. It is arguably the case that, on an individualistic level, the two-sex system worked in Suydam's favour, because it enabled him to claim the male right to suffrage, and to be recognised as a man within the public sphere, while simultaneously embodying certain 'feminine propensities' and enjoying calico.

Having made explicit this difference between identifying intersex and identifying *as* intersexed, I think we can appreciate the curious way in which Fausto-Sterling both advances and retracts the proposal of five sexes. That curious turnaround is not a contradiction in her argument, but a measure of the contradictory cultural position of intersexuality – subversive and subverted, transgressive and regulated, hidden and yet strenuously searched for, all at the same time. If identifying as a member of a third, fourth or fifth sex can lead to disenfranchisement, then a five-sex system is not an escape from, but a symptom of, the 'suffocating identity politics' precipitated by the social (in Suydam's time) and medical (in the late twentieth century) 'disciplining' of intersexed bodies.

To draw together the threads of my analysis so far, it might be true that Suydam's anatomy could be described as neither female nor male but as something else; indeed, Suydam may have referred to it thus in private. Likewise, when sexual dissidents pass in public, they do not automatically negate the sexualities and sexes that they claim within their communities, or privately among their families and lovers. Therefore it is not the case that the physician just used the wrong term

– 'male' – to identify publicly Suydam's sex. Rather, my contention in the next part of this chapter will be that the sex that one claims as an identity is not a matter of description at all, but of socially situated values.

Identities as Evaluative

In an important paper, titled 'Identity Judgements, Queer Politics', Mark Norris Lance and Alessandra Tanesini have argued for a non-descriptive understanding of identity claims. Along with other queer theorists such as Alan Sinfield and Judith Butler, Lance and Tanesini reject 'the tired, and by now tiresome, argument that identities presuppose essences' (2000, 42). Essentialism presumes that a person's social identity correlates with, and is motivated by, some fixed aspect of a person's character or body. For instance, feminists like Germaine Greer and Janice Raymond have proposed that male-to-female transsexuals are not women because for Greer and Raymond the identity 'woman' is necessarily and essentially linked to certain experiences and body parts, such as a girl's childhood, and the possession of XX chromosomes (Greer 1999, 64–74; Raymond 1979). In this essentialist view, an identity is a description. Consequently, a correctly claimed identity is neither more nor less than the attributes and experiences to which it refers; if the latter are not present in an individual, then the former is false, because the individual does not match the criteria (such as the possession of XX chromosomes) described by the identity (such as woman). Lance and Tanesini note that the reasons for the rejection by queer theorists of essentialist models of identity have centred upon the perceived limitations on sexuality and pleasure that essentialism entails (2000, 42). For example, essentialism can't explain the significance of cross-gender identification in sexual fantasies; in an essentialist account, such fantasies are simply descriptively incorrect.

In like manner, as we have seen, Fausto-Sterling objects to the reining in by medicine of sexual diversity. Her concerns are borne out by Chase's follow-up letter to the *Sciences*, wherein Chase boldly founded the Intersex Society of North America (ISNA), which has become the foremost intersex patient advocacy group (1993, 3). In her letter, Chase discloses, 'Unfortunately, the surgery [for intersex] is immensely destructive of sexual sensation as well as one's sense of bodily integrity.' For many post-surgical patients, left 'wishing vainly for the return of body parts' – as Chase puts it – an identity that presupposes a sexed bodily essence is a bitter impossibility. In its removal of body parts such as the clitoris, genital surgery tampers with the descriptive correlation that essentialism presupposes between an individual's attributes and identity.

For instance, intersex surgery raises for essentialism the question of how many of the body parts described by the essentialist identity 'man' would need to be surgically removed before an individual ceased to be describable as a man. But Chase's point in her letter, with which I agree, is that the issue faced by post-surgical intersexed individuals is one of identifying as a sex even without meeting essentialism's descriptive criteria. 'I get a kick out of it', intersexual Hale Hawbecker has written, 'when a male friend says, "Hale, you have balls". I have been tempted to laugh and tell him, "No I don't, actually, but then I have not really missed them much either"' (Hawbecker 1999, 113). Essentialism cannot explain Hawbecker's wry and robust male identity, other than to say that it is descriptively wrong. And this is essentialism's problem, not Hawbecker's.

By understanding identity as a matter of the politics of values, we can formulate a better account of the identities asserted by individuals with atypical sex anatomies. This will be, moreover, a queerer account in its refusal of essentialism. It is apt for intersexuality, then, that Lance and Tanesini refrain from asking 'what sexual identities might be' (2000, 42). Instead, they hold 'that questions about the importance of identity *claims* offer a better starting point' (2000, 42). Their queer distinction regarding sexual identities (such as straight and gay) maps onto the analytic shift that I've advocated in my discussion of the 'Five Sexes' from the description of intersex to the significance of identifying as a particular sex. What is one doing – socially, politically – when one makes such a claim?

The key idea put forward by Lance and Tanesini is that an identity claim is evaluative. In other words, such a claim is principally and actively an instance of the politics of values. 'In our view to claim an identity for oneself is to endorse a cluster of attitudes, behaviours and judgements on the part of oneself and of society, and to undertake a commitment to defend their appropriateness', Lance and Tanesini submit (2000, 47). Put another way, one's identity can be described – in terms of attitudes, behaviours and judgements – but when one *claims* that identity, one is offering to others not a description of the identity, but rather actively making a particular evaluative commitment, which in turn places a demand upon others.

To explain this, consider a vignette offered by Lance and Tanesini: 'There is a world of difference in the significance of knowingly serving pork to someone who dislikes it and to a practising Muslim' (2000, 44).[1] To understand the relevance of this example, let us imagine that pork is being offered to guests at the dinner table. The guest who says, 'I'm a Muslim' when the pork arrives from the kitchen is claiming the identity 'Muslim'. In so doing, he is neither indicating that he physically cannot eat pork, nor that he happens to dislike its flavour. In this way, an identity claim, such as 'Muslim', describes neither an aspect of an individual's biological constitution, nor a character trait produced by social construction (2000, 42–3). The claim is not a description.

Whilst the Muslim who refuses pork at the dinner table makes an identity claim, a woman who declines pork because she does not like its flavour is not making any such claim. Moreover, even if the dislike of pork that she describes is biological, its biological aetiology does not make her refusal a matter of identity. Conversely, 'I'm a Muslim' is an evaluative statement that *commits* its speaker to certain behaviours and attitudes (including, of course, not eating pork), and, crucially, also invites respect from others for the speaker's attitudinal and behavioural commitment.

---

1   The following discussion also adapts Lance and Tanesini's examples of ice cream, socialism and motherhood.

This example shows that although an identity claim can of course be described (otherwise the vignette of the Muslim could not be offered), an identity claim is not itself descriptive, but actively evaluative.

In exactly the same way, a moral code is eminently describable, even though the code itself is not a description of behaviour, but an exhortation to behave in a certain fashion. My comparison of an identity claim with a moral code is not arbitrarily chosen, because I am suggesting that an identity claim *is* a type of moral code. Hence, where the identity Muslim is claimed but Muslim attitudes, behaviours and judgements are wholly absent from the identity's claimant, the identity has been claimed erroneously, *and for specifically moral reasons.* That this error of identification is not merely a matter of an individual's failure to match a given description is shown by the fact that, in contrast, although we might be surprised to learn that the woman who dislikes roast pork loves gammon, we would not expect her to defend her tastes, because the public expression of her tastes does not constitute an identity claim. But to act counter to the commitments that one endorses when one claims the identity 'Muslim' would mean quite simply that one was not a Muslim. The deficiency in that scenario is thus not descriptive but moral – even spiritual. An identity claim in this way constitutes a commitment, so the measure of its accuracy is the evaluation of its claimant's integrity, not the determination of whether their language about identity is properly descriptive.

Counterintuitive as it may seem, I say that identity claims about one's sex work in the same manner. Levi Suydam sought legal recognition for his male identity – not for his genitalia, or for his liking of calico. Similarly, the social, legal and medical endorsement pursued by pre-operative transsexual individuals illustrates how claims to be of a particular sex are not descriptive of one's anatomy. A pre-operative transsexual woman, for instance, does not seek the social recognition of her pre-operative biology, but rather of the female identity that she claims. On this basis, I suggest that the claim to be a particular sex functions as an endorsement of sex-specific treatment by others, and symmetrically, that by identifying as a member of a sex, one places oneself under the obligation to act in a manner consonant with the behaviours associated with that identity claim. This is how a person passes. Divergence from such behavioural and attitudinal values is possible, but tends to necessitate an explanation – sometimes under threat of violence. And that is why a person passes.

What I'm arguing, then, is that the relation between one's identity and one's politics is, through and through, a matter of values – both personal and social – not of descriptive correspondence. This 'politics of values' offers a way forward from Fausto-Sterling's faltering descriptivism, because it opens a route to a discussion of *why* people would identify publicly as belonging to a sexual minority – whether gay, lesbian, or a third, fourth or fifth sex. Corroborating this, when in 2000 Fausto-Sterling would return to the idea of five sexes in the *Sciences*, she would begin with neither history nor biology but with Cheryl Chase and ISNA, commenting that 'Intersexuals are materialising before our very eyes' (2000a, 19). So although identification as a member of a sexual minority could lead to childhood genital surgery, it could also enable participation in a subculture (such as a patient advocacy group) organised around the goal of claiming rights for one's minority. Significantly, and contrary to Greer and Raymond, that goal does not depend on everyone in the subculture having the same biology or essence. Because identity claims do not merely reflect but *are* what Kate Bornstein calls the politics of values, I will conclude by contending that for political and moral reasons, even non-intersexed individuals should claim the identity 'intersexed'.

Descriptivism as Privilege

At the start of this chapter, I suggested that to identify as either 'female' or 'male' seems politically inadequate for those of us who object to our surgical management, because such identities appear tacitly to endorse the normalising surgery (which Fausto-Sterling has called a 'mode of discipline') that we have received. Yet my analysis has shown that this problem is not caused by a descriptive shortcoming in the use of the terms 'female' or 'male' to name unusual bodies – instead, it's because of the particular values that the identities 'female' and 'male' actively endorse. I want to propose that the burden of this problem ought to be borne not by people with atypical sex anatomies, but by the non-intersexed majority. Their refusal to identify as male or female would change the values associated with those identities by unfixing the terms' descriptive force.

My proposal may seem akin to literary and film theorist Judith Halberstam's argument that the postmodern fictitiousness of gender makes everyone transsexual, because genders and sexes are always already transposable, transitional and strange (1994, 226). But I am advocating a deliberate repudiation on moral grounds of male and female identities, not simply an awareness of how postmodernity allegedly destabilises essentialist notions of gender and sex. For comparable reasons, Lance and Tanesini argue that because 'The primary social markers of a positioning as straight are the trappings of privilege', people who are not gay, and who have a commitment to sexual diversity, should refuse the identity 'straight' (2000, 49–51). To the extent that an identity claim to be of a particular sex is an evaluative endorsement of a way of being treated, and of one's entitlement to behave in certain ways, the identity claims 'male' and 'female' cannot be appropriate, because they endorse and perpetuate one's access to unjust privileges. One of these privileges is descriptivism itself.

I argue that descriptivism, far from standing in value-free opposition to evaluative language about identity, is itself a value system. And it is morally deficient. In underpinning the essentialist accounts of identity that I criticised above, descriptivism disenfranchises intersexed individuals. Further, as my discussion of Suydam and Fausto-Sterling indicated, such disenfranchisement does not occur just because there aren't enough terms to denote intersexed anatomies. If that were the case, then intersex would remain in principle describable, requiring only additional sex categories for its accommodation. That would mistake part of the problem for the solution. Rather, it is specifically unwanted genital surgery

– with its aim of making genitals describable – that causes the cultural dominance of descriptivist accounts of identity to be agonisingly disenfranchising for people with unusual sex anatomies. This is because post-surgical individuals, as I stated at the beginning, find ourselves in the unreasonable position where *no* description of one's surgically modified sexual anatomy seems right, even though a description of one's pre-surgical sex seems politically necessary.

It is this dilemmatic position that fundamentally distinguishes intersex politics from transgender and transsexual politics, because the ability to identify one's sex has been fractured by surgery in a morally and physically injurious way that is irreparably prior to the desires and identifications of the individual in the present. In contrast, trans politics tends to centre on the realisation of desires and identifications that are knowable to the trans individual, and which require merely social acknowledgement. The problem of intersex surgery is that it can render an individual irrevocably uncertain over how to describe their desires and identifications in the first place; any description seems perilous, because it is an unwitting reiteration of the descriptivism that has been so objectionably inscribed into one's body by genital surgery.

Consequently, the identity claims 'male' and 'female', when made by people with non-intersexed anatomies, are morally indefensible because they constitute a commitment to the descriptivism that disenfranchises intersexed individuals. Now, this is different from Bornstein's point, made in the year following the 'Five Sexes', that a person who identifies as 'male' or 'female' perpetuates 'the violence of male privilege' (1994, 74). I appreciate the feminist value of Bornstein's insight, but as the writings of Greer and Raymond demonstrate, there is no necessary overlap between feminist and intersex politics. Indeed, some feminists regard intersex politics as anti-feminist, because they consider the description of individuals as either male or female to be prerequisite to social justice. For the purposes of distinguishing intersex politics from feminism, my recommendation that non-intersex individuals should relinquish the identity claims 'male' and 'female' shifts focus from the inequalities between men and women (critiqued by feminism) to the injustice of descriptivism that is peculiar to intersex treatment. Descriptivism devalues intersex, so descriptivism should be devalued, via the repudiation of those identity claims that reinforce it.

Finally, if my suggestion seems impractical, consider Suzanne Kessler's letter to the *Sciences*, written in response to Fausto-Sterling (1993, 3). Kessler agrees with Fausto-Sterling that the positive valuation of intersex is a worthwhile goal, but she argues importantly for its achievement by means that are directly converse to Fausto-Sterling's proposal of five sexes. Fausto-Sterling's project 'ignores that in the everyday world gender attributions are made without access to genital inspection'. According to Kessler, in a remark that captures queer theory's dramaturgic *zeitgeist* during the first half of the 1990s, it is 'the gender that is *performed*, regardless of the configuration of the flesh under the clothes' that takes precedence in everyday life. Writing again in the *Sciences* in 2000, Fausto-Sterling would agree with Kessler that 'It would be better for intersexuals and their supporters to turn everyone's focus away from genitals' (2000a, 22). If Kessler is correct that in everyday life the emphasis is on gender performance, not genitalia, then this certainly means that intersexed people (like Suydam) can pass as 'male' or 'female'. But it means equally that people who identify currently as 'male' or 'female' can – and I think, should – pass as intersexed.

Suggested Further Reading

Chase, C. and Hegarty, P. (2005), 'Intersex Activism, Feminism and Psychology', in I. Morland and A. Willox (eds), *Queer Theory* (Basingstoke: Palgrave).

Fausto-Sterling, A. (2000), *Sexing the Body: Gender Politics and the Construction of Sexuality* (New York: Basic).

Kessler, S.J. (1998), *Lessons from the Intersexed* (New Brunswick, NJ: Rutgers University Press).

Morland, I. (2005), 'The Injustice of Intersex: Feminist Science Studies and the Writing of a Wrong', *Studies in Law, Politics, and Society* 36, 53–75.

Preves, S.E. (2003), *Intersex and Identity: The Contested Self* (New Brunswick, NJ: Rutgers University Press).

References

Bird, R.P. (1993), Letter, *Sciences* July–August, 3.

Bornstein, K. (1994), *Gender Outlaw: On Men, Women and the Rest of Us* (London: Routledge).

—— (1997), 'Queer Theory and Shopping: Dichotomy or Symbionts?', in C. Queen and L. Schimel (eds), *PoMoSexuals: Challenging Assumptions about Gender and Sexuality* (San Francisco, CA: Cleis).

Butler, J. (1993), *Bodies That Matter: On the Discursive Limits of 'Sex'* (London: Routledge).

Catholic League for Religious and Civil Rights (1995), Advertisement, *New York Times* 3 September, D11.

Chase, C. (1993), Letter, *Sciences* July–August, 3.

—— (1998), 'Affronting Reason', in D. Atkins (ed.), *Looking Queer: Body Image and Identity in Lesbian, Bisexual, Gay, and Transgender Communities* (New York: Harrington Park Press).

Epstein, J. (1990), 'Either/Or – Neither/Both: Sexual Ambiguity and the Ideology of Gender', *Genders* 7, 99–142.

Fausto-Sterling, A. (1993a), 'The Five Sexes: Why Male and Female Are Not Enough', *Sciences* March–April, 20–25.

—— (1993b), 'How Many Sexes Are There?', *New York Times* 12 March, A29.

—— (2000a), 'The Five Sexes, Revisited', *Sciences* July–August 2000: 18–23.

—— (2000b), *Sexing the Body: Gender Politics and the Construction of Sexuality* (New York: Basic).

Feinberg, L. (2003), *Stone Butch Blues* (Los Angeles, CA: Alyson).

Greer, G. (1999), *The Whole Woman* (London: Doubleday).

Halberstam, J. (1994), 'F2M: The Making of Female Masculinity', in L. Doan (ed.), *The Lesbian Postmodern* (New York: Columbia University Press).

Hawbecker, H. (1999), '"Who Did This to You?"', in A. Domurat Dreger (ed.), *Intersex in the Age of Ethics* (Hagerstown, MD: University Publishing Group).

Herdt, G. (1996), 'Preface' and 'Introduction', in G. Herdt (ed.), *Third Sex, Third Gender: Beyond Sexual Dimorphism in Culture and History* (New York: Zone).

Holmes, M. (2000), 'Queer Cut Bodies', in J.A. Boone, M. Dupuis and M. Meeker (eds), *Queer Frontiers: Millennial Geographies, Genders, and Generations* (Madison, WI: University of Wisconsin Press).

Kessler, S.J. (1993), Letter, *Sciences* July–August, 3.

—— and McKenna, W. (1978), *Gender: An Ethnomethodological Approach* (New York: Wiley-Interscience).

Lance, M.N. and Tanesini, A. (2000), 'Identity Judgements, Queer Politics', *Radical Philosophy* 100, 42–51.

Laqueur, T. (1990), *Making Sex: Body and Gender from the Greeks to Freud* (Cambridge, MA: Harvard University Press).

Raymond, J. (1979), *The Transsexual Empire: The Making of the She-Male* (Boston, MA: Beacon).

Scott, M. (1995), *Shadow Man* (New York: Tom Doherty)

'The Scholars Formerly Known as …': Bisexuality, Queerness and Identity Politics

Jonathan Alexander and Karen Yescavage

As bi/queer activists and scholar-teachers, we have been thinking, teaching and writing for several years now about how sexual identity, as both a social construction and a deeply felt sense of self, simultaneously opens up and delimits possibilities of pleasure, intimacy and even community building. In particular, we have felt that bisexuality – the conscious choice to be open to loving and being intimate with partners, regardless of sex or gender – seems to challenge the limits that are placed on desire and question normalising (monosexual) identities into which so many fold their lives. At the same time, sexual identity is only so effective in challenging homophobic social norms; because of heteronormativity, for instance, bisexuality itself frequently disappears into the dominant (straight) cultural field of vision as many focus on the normative 'straight' relationship while thinking of same-gendered attractions and intimacies as simply 'experimentations' or 'erotic excursions'. As such, bisexual sexual identity can be observed being simultaneously shoved into and out of both gay and straight communities.

Reflecting on our lived experience as queers with bi-erotic feelings, emotions and investments that we wish to maintain and nurture, in this chapter we explore ways in which we have variously experimented with identity and sexual identity labels. Such 'experimentation' has arisen out of a desire both to find a queer community *and* to challenge exclusionary impulses within the LGBT community and the larger 'straight' world. As such, we have found ourselves shifting and playing with identity labels (from non-heterosexual to bi to gay to queer to bi/queer to queer to …) all to keep alive what we see as a productive friction between claiming an identity (and community) and 'getting stuck' in an exclusionary identity (and community). To unpack our reflections, this chapter combines narrative, self-reflection, critique of the available literature and a critical re-consideration and re-assessment of our thinking about queerness, our scholarly work in sexuality studies and our strangely wonderful queer lives.

In the Beginning ...

'Oh shit! I've done it now!': Karen's Story

Growing up in the early 1970s in Kansas City, Missouri, I never really considered my exploratory actions as indicative of any enduring personality attribute. Playing with the girl next door was hidden just like playing with the boy next door was. I never really thought much about it. Fast forward 20 years: my life was forever changed when the first real love of my life laid her beautiful head in my lap under the light of the moon. Oh shit! I've done it now! What does this desire mean, to me, to her, to those in my immediate world, to society at large? Will I still be attracted to men? Or, will I begin to weave the same story as so many others who said they never really were 'into' the opposite sex, but were simply expected to be?

It is a unique experience – to say the least – to wake up one day and be a part of a negatively portrayed group in society. I was somewhat prepared, having been engaged with issues of marginalisation in both Black Studies and Women's Studies. However, it was disheartening to find no real solace amongst my supposed comrades in the lesbian community. I quickly came to realise I was not 'one of them'. There were similarities, but clearly my expanded desire was not the same; further, for a few, it seemed to be a threat or worse, an outright offence. I wasn't sure what to make of it all at the time, being so new to the whole 'gay thing'. All I did know was that the moment we kissed, my life would be forever changed ... and with pride, I say, for the better.

My desires for the other sex were validated and reinforced, while my same-sex attractions were described at best as exploratory. I guess I didn't really take them seriously – or as a threat to my status as 'normal'. After all, I did have crushes on boys. (Could this be an example of female privilege? Are women allowed to explore bi-erotic possibilities, even just affection with one another, a bit more than men without the risk of being 'marked' as queer?)

'But I like it': Jonathan's Story

High school in the deep south of the United States in the 1980s was a nightmare, an all-boys Catholic school hell in which I was immediately identified as the 'class fag'. I was tall for my age, so I was not frequently assaulted physically, but the verbal taunts were a daily occurrence, and even some faculty, if my friends are to be believed, would refer to me as fag or queer. Though attending a Catholic school, I worshipped with my family in a Southern Baptist church, where I heard on numerous occasions that homosexuals, the preferred term for god-fearing Baptists (since 'gay' is man's term to put a smiley face on sin), were doomed to AIDS, neuroses and eternal hellfire. Not a pretty picture. Whatever fags and homosexuals were, I most definitely did not want to be one of them. In so many ways, my immersion in this intense pool of homophobia predated any conscious sexual feelings that I had. Before I knew that I wanted to kiss another boy (or tie him up and spank him – another queer perversion), I was baptised into self-hatred.

Still, despite this abuse, I had a crush on a boy, a young Latino named Domingo. I plotted and planned how to become friends with him, and though we never 'did' anything, I suspected that my interest in him (and his khaki-clad bottom, his hot pink undershirt, his luxuriant Navy pea coat) was bringing me perilously close to the forbidden realm of faggotry. My internal confusion, my soul-searching cognitive dissonance was intense: could something I want so much really be so evil? Imagine my confusion when I left the all-boy environment of high school to attend university and finding myself interested in some of the young women in my classes. (I might be safe after all!) I developed a crush on a classmate, Laura, and I eventually married another fellow student, Tara, some years later. Still, my interest in men continued, and I felt buffeted back and forth – a buffeting that ended my marriage.

I eventually 'came out' as bisexual, thinking that's the term that best describes my 'condition'. I developed a primary relationship with another man (with whom I still live), but my interest in women – as intimate friends and even subjects of desire – continues. Many of my gay friends scoff at this, wondering how I could 'stand' vaginal sex. But I like it. And I've come to see this plurality of desires as something that enriches me, that speaks to the complexity of connections I want to create with people. And I like it.

The Name Game

As we reflect on these opening stories, at least one striking commonality emerges for us: how do we identify the matrix of feelings, impulses and desires that prompt us to connect with others, intimately, emotionally, sexually? We are called by our society to self-identify, and self-identification in terms of sexuality is a crucial social category right now. Michel Foucault famously noted in *The History of Sexuality* the connection in the West between identity and sexuality; since the end of the nineteenth century, we *are* what we *desire*, not just what we *do* sexually or intimately. In the labelling systems created by sexologists and other members of the medical profession in the late 1800s, intimate and sexual practices began to be read as indicators of innate predispositions or proclivities. Our interests in engaging in certain erotic behaviours became signs of who we actually are as people – signs of our *identity*. If you're a man and want to have sex with men, you are 'homosexual'. That is who you *are*, not just something you do.

As our stories might suggest, however, we are interested in the desires that seem to resist labelling, or movements of the heart that prompt us to question the labels available to us. For instance, Karen was inaugurated into adult love by a woman's kiss; while her desires seem to be ever expanding, she has opted to commit to a monogamous relationship with a man. Jonathan lives with and loves a man, but he is attracted also to women and cherishes his memories of sexual encounters and lives with women. Is Karen straight, Jonathan gay, both bi, or just messed up? Many, including a good number of straights *and* gays, might vote for the 'messed up' option. Others would claim us as bi, but what does that mean? We're not (at the moment) each involved in erotic relationships outside our primary relationships, so are we bi just by virtue of our internal interests, our past experiences, our *possibility* for furthering 'messing up' the otherwise clear-cut division between gay and straight?

This is what we call the 'name game', the parsing of terms to identify what we do, how we feel, what we *are*. It's a game we are often called to play as we discuss our lives with others, with others who want to 'know' who we are. And it's a game with an interesting history, one revealed by the academic field of queer theory, which, in the last two decades, has exploded our notions of identity and allowed us to see more clearly how sexuality has emerged in the West as an important marker of who we are. Queer theory has also pointed out some of the limitations of identity, particularly as identity has the potential to 'lock' us into place, and trouble the possibility of connecting with others across identities.

Foucault, Queer Theory and the Limits of Identity

In *Saint Foucault, Towards a Gay Hagiography* (1995), David Halperin claims Foucault as the most important intellectual progenitor of 'queer theory', which emerged as a provocative academic field in the late 1980s and early 1990s. Numerous prominent queer theorists (for example, Eve Kosofsky Sedgwick, Judith Butler, Michael Warner, Lee Edelman and Teresa de Lauretis among others) rely heavily on Foucault for theoretical underpinnings in their critique of sexual identity. Specifically, they use Foucault's analyses in *The History of Sexuality* (1990/1976) to demonstrate that sexual identities – such as homosexual and heterosexual – have histories that are traceable, and that such identities are grounded in complex socio-political, ideological, cultural and even economic matrices. The rise of the terms 'homosexual' and 'heterosexual', for instance, can be traced to changes in the medical and emerging psychiatric professions that sought to categorise people's behaviour and understand such behaviour as symptomatic of innate identities. In other words, the psychologisation of identity at the end of the nineteenth century shifted identity from what you *did* to what you *desired*. You *are* your desires, in other words.

Interestingly, Foucault's late work on sexuality in general and gay identity in particular is very critical of how gay identity has itself become a form of power/ knowledge – in other words, an identity which could become every bit as restrictive and limiting to one's freedom as laws forbidding homoerotic sex. For instance, in contemporary urban gay ghettos, it certainly seems as though gay men are supposed to look and act and think a certain way. A limited number of fashion and behavioural styles are acceptable, resulting in the frequently remarked phenomenon of 'clones', or gay men who are mirror images of one another, reinforcing their gay identity by multiplying their numbers. In areas such as the Castro or West Hollywood, particular stores and clothing brands are clearly privileged over others, as are hairstyles and even underwear brands. While subcultural gay male venues will vary in their preferences for particular fashions or styles of representations

– bears and leathermen are noticeably different than club boys and twinks – each variation promotes its own 'uniform'; bears buy flannel while club kids purchase nylon. Certainly fashions change, but dress codes help individuals identify with their particular subgroups.

Commenting about such conformity to styles Foucault himself, while visiting San Francisco, is reported to have said, 'I am a homosexual in a city full of gays'. While past generations of homosexuals migrated to major urban centres to escape anti-gay mainstream America and learn how to become part of a gay community, queer activists critique and rebel against the ways in which such communities replicate themselves by reproducing gay clones and recognisable 'faggots' who buy the same t-shirts, eat the same vegetarian foods and read the same books on how to be good gay clones and recognisable faggots. We all want to feel as though we belong, but we should also be aware of what kinds of conformities we perform and enact in the service of such belonging and identity construction – particularly if they seem market driven.

Further, Foucault argues that an 'essentialist' understanding of sexual orientation, which suggests that our sexual identity is innately 'fixed' and must be 'discovered' as the truth of who we are, could have some unforeseen consequences. Jonathan distinctly remembers a sympathetic friend discussing homosexuality and saying, 'People need to realise that you people just can't help yourselves'. Foucault sees such essentialism as potentially limiting to our own – and others' – understanding of ourselves in that it belittles us and the choices we make about our lives. It's also potentially limiting to our freedom. After all, if we can't 'help ourselves', then someone might feel they need to 'help' us – such as some Christian counsellors engaging in reparative therapy for gays and lesbians. More radically, the search for a gay gene – the biological 'secret of desire' – might be used to 'correct' a biological mistake.

Here is another example: many queer activists and theorists have been critical of the push among many gays and lesbians for the right to be legally married and thus to assimilate into the mainstream of Western society; they feel that strategising for the right to marry, while laudable in many ways, may detract us from questioning the institution of marriage itself. In other words, queer activists feel we should be questioning why our society values marriage so highly and what restrictions marital relations place on people. For instance, marriage honours commitments between two people, but what about intimate commitments and arrangements between three (or more) people? Some bisexuals pursuing, developing and maintaining relations with both men and women are not served by marriages limited to two people. Marital rights extended to gays and lesbians might honour some relationships then, but would most likely still be limited in significant ways. Put another way, extending the rights of marriage to queers would most likely extend them – and thus extend socio-cultural and political validation – only to monosexual, not polyamorous relations. Thus it is important, according to queer activists and theorists, to question such 'bigger pictures' and institutional systems, asking who is served and excluded by them (Warner 1999). As such, the term 'queer', particularly in the 1990s, became transformed from a bigoted taunt into a rallying cry for those who resist any form of categorisation and normalisation, whether from homophobic straights or conforming and assimilationist lesbians and gays (as well as assimilationist bis and trans folk). Foucault's work was used by queer theorists and activists to critique proponents of both assimilationist and identity politics.[1] As David Halperin puts it, 'Queer is by definition whatever is at odds with the normal, the legitimate, the dominant' (1995, 62).[2]

Foucault himself spent much time before his death in 1984 trying to figure out how our lives are created and maintained as subjects so we could know better how to *de-subjectify* ourselves. Foucault may have always felt that power is here to stay, but he also expressed much hope for the future – especially if we learn to use the power surrounding us more effectively to expand and explore new possibilities of freedom. In fact, this upbeat belief permeates many of Foucault's last essays and interviews. One of the first things the reader notices about this work is how incredibly accessible it is; Foucault very much wanted his work to excite people into thinking – and acting – critically about their lives. With a very real interest in impacting individual existences, Foucault turns much of his attention to the problem, and possibility, of ethics, which Foucault defines as the 'conscious practice of freedom' (1997, 284). Specifically, Foucault wants to move us away from a movement based around an identity, which, using his analysis of power/ knowledge, can become every bit as constraining and imprisoning as legislation against homosexuals. Having to conform to the dictates of any kind of identity, even a gay one, was too constraining for Foucault, and, in his view, works against what he saw to be the primary responsibility of a philosophy of life:

---

1   Foucault's detractors are many, including the very articulate and formidable Richard Mohr who has soundly critiqued Foucault in particular and postmodernism in general. Mohr's primary complaint with Foucault is the French philosopher's heavy reliance on social constructionism and moral relativism, which, in Mohr's view, complicate the establishment of a sound, stable, demonstrable and sharable ethics out of which to articulate and defend gay rights to privacy, equality and freedom of speech. Calling Foucault the 'central saint and hero, archangel and evangelist' of postmodernism, Mohr describes how the French philosopher 'held to the cultural or social origins and nature of meaning, values, identities, knowledge and power'. Ultimately, for Mohr, the problem with Foucault is his belief that 'Nothing has meaning or value in itself, and the meaning of no "thing" – be it a text, individual or institution – is stable. Everything is both socially constructed and yet also self-deconstructing' (1995, 9–13). Mohr is an intelligent and powerful critic, and he is right, I think, to attack the postmodernist thinkers who promote belief (if that's the right word) in the nihilistic valuelessness of everything. But Foucault is not one of those thinkers, even if some might claim him as such, and much of his work demonstrates his commitment to human freedom, potential and possibility.

2   So along such lines, what if diversity, in this case, homosexuality, were the 'norm'? Would there be such a thing as a queer identity – or even the need for a queer identity? While Amsterdam, for instance, isn't only populated by gays, lesbians, and bis, the city is certainly seemingly very 'gay friendly', and the Netherlands is among a scant few countries that allows gays and lesbians to marry. Is queerness needed there as a strategic identity?

... one detaches oneself from what is accepted as true and seeks other rules – that is philosophy. The displacement and transformation of frameworks of thinking, the changing of received values and all the work that has been done to think otherwise, to do something else, to become other than what one is – that, too, is philosophy. (1997, 327)

Thinking about such a philosophy, Foucault's work strives to shift our conception of ourselves away from identity and toward *possibility*: 'The transformation of one's self by one's own knowledge is, I think, something rather close to the aesthetic experience' (1997, 131). Even more provocatively, he argues that 'the experience of the self is not a discovering of a truth hidden inside the self but an attempt to determine what one can and cannot do with one's available freedom' (1997, 276). For Foucault, the practice of homosexuality (his word) or queerness (our word) is liberating primarily because it 'seeks other rules', it has not and does not accept the heterosexual norm, but instead has the potential to challenge received values – values about who we go to bed with, what kind of pleasure we bring each other, what kind of relationships we form, and what kind of lives we will lead.[3] While Foucault does not discuss bisexuality at any significant point in his work, we still take critical energy from his critiques of sexual identity regimes, and we have sought to think of our bisexuality and bi-erotic interests as a way to 'seek other rules' outside of the heterosexual – or even homosexual – norm. As Foucault says in an interview, 'Sexual Choice, Sexual Act', 'There is no question that a society without restrictions is inconceivable, but I can only repeat myself in saying that these restrictions have to be within the reach of those affected by them so that they at least have the possibility of altering them' (1997, 148).

One of the primary questions we have faced – personally, professionally and politically – is how do we go about altering those restrictions productively, both for ourselves and others? How do we explore our available freedom? If we, like Foucault, have found identity to be more restricting than not, then what guides our exploration? What are *our* values? In *Queer Theory and Social Change*, Max H. Kirsch asks, 'If our goal, then, is to create a society that accepts difference, welcomes diversity, and champions human rights, how do we get there?' (2001, 9). More

---

3   Foucault is willing to admit that a 'homosexual consciousness certainly goes beyond one's individual experience and includes an awareness of being a member of a particular social group' (1997, 142–3). However, he is sceptical about the ability of late-twentieth-century gay groups to forge a 'class consciousness': 'homosexuals do not constitute a social class. This is not to say that one can't imagine a society in which homosexuals would constitute a social class. But in our present economic and social mode of organisation, I don't see this coming to pass' (1997, 143). Foucault suggests the following two 'goals of the homosexual movement': 'First, there is the question of freedom of sexual choice which must be faced.' Foucault distinguishes between 'freedom of sexual choice' and 'freedom of sexual acts'; and 'Second, a homosexual movement could adopt the objective of posing the question of the place in a given society which sexual choice, sexual behaviour, and the effects of sexual relations between people could have with regard to the individual' (1997, 143). We believe this is the personal, political and even *ethical* work of queerness.

specifically, we might add, what does it mean – *really* – to accept difference and welcome diversity? What does that look like in real life? Kirsch worries that the heady academic heights of queer theory in particular (and post-structuralist theories in general) might offer us interesting critiques but not always useful strategies for articulating and affirming our values, our vision of the world. What *is* that vision?

Beyond Identity: Personally, Professionally and Politically

When speaking personally, we frequently refer to ourselves as queer, with Karen usually offering a quick follow-up: 'Specifically, bisexual'. This prioritises our need for identifying *politically* first: we are queers, going against the norm, unwilling to be pigeon-holed into others' (often stereotypical) notions of what it means to be 'gay', 'straight' or even 'bi'. More recently, however, as we have delved into transgender issues, we struggle to continue using the term bisexual. For Karen, it feels a bit too restrictive considering her expansive taste for gender diversity as well. As Karen moves away from binary definitions of gender, she finds it more fitting to simply consider herself a curious explorer. Conversely, Jonathan has recently switched, in certain contexts, from identifying as queer/bi to queer/gay; in calling himself 'gay' and then speaking openly about his sexual interest (and past) with women, he hopes to destabilise notions of what 'gay' is, or could be. Context here is crucial, though. For instance, Jonathan has noticed that, sometimes, when he is becoming acquainted with a group of gay friends, some gay men might attempt to create bonds of friendship and camaraderie by joking about lesbians ('carpet munchers') or expressing distaste about vaginal sex. Jonathan, troubled by such sexism, attempts to affirm a gay identity that does *not* rest on excluding or showing contempt for women and that does not invalidate his past bi-erotic experiences. Jonathan wants to affirm rather the value of *choosing* to be with a man, of continuing in long-term relationships with a male partner, as opposed to feeling that other options are somehow 'disgusting'.

Interestingly, both of us perceive our identities as open to revision, not as something fixed. We have in the past struggled with how to 'identify', having bought into the socio-cultural pressure to 'have' an identity. More recently, though, we have enjoyed the *play* of identities, seeing identity as something 'under construction'. But we also recognise that our perception of identity and our desire to play with it have both professional and political ramifications, particularly as the personal and the political are so intimately tied together.

First, Karen reflects on her experience as a teacher:

Initially, in my professional life (i.e., in the classroom), I utilised the term 'non-heterosexual' to zero in on what I thought was the most pertinent issue, namely, not being of the norm, but rather, 'Other'. It wasn't until a little later that I began utilising the label bisexual. This first evolution occurred in order to add to the issues; specifically, I wanted to clarify what bisexuality was and draw attention to how biphobia is evident in both the straight and the gay/lesbian community.

It wasn't until I was exposed to queer theory that I really seemed to critically examine the broader issues involved in identity politics. Identifying as queer was a better signifier of my political interest with sexual orientation. I have often explained this to my students by comparing my identifying as queer with choosing to identify as Chicana as opposed to Hispanic. For those who are politically identified as well, they understand this power to name and reclaim an identity of one's own. For those who have little understanding of identity politics, they have more difficulty with the idea of choosing to identify with a pejorative term. Identifying as queer has served to reinforce my sense of agency as well as my choice of a label that openly, politically calls into question established ideas of what (or who) is normal. For example, when I wear my t-shirt that says, 'Queer as Apple Pie', I frequently get a confused look followed by the question, 'What does THAT mean?' Challenging normalcy, it seems, is a novel concept for some.

We also hunger for other people's stories, for others' lived experiences, for touching and connecting with how others perceive and live through the world. And this desire – this value – is reflected in our scholarly work together. Our first book, the edited collection *Bisexuality and Transgenderism: InterSEXions of the Others* (2004) was conceived out of this desire – to make connection with others, to show fruitful intersections between different sets of experiences, and even to confuse the labels we use to describe that experience.

Professionally, this is tough turf – for a number of reasons. Jonathan reflects on his experiences with 'trans'gressing identity boundaries to make connections:

I clearly remember speaking – and inciting some consternation – at a Feminisms and Rhetorics Conference in Columbus, Ohio about how Patrick Califia, the female-to-male author and activist, attempted to negotiate between his emerging self-understanding as a man and his desire to maintain ties with the lesbian community that nurtured him and had been his home earlier in his life. Califia's experiences are, granted, difficult for some to accept, and while some lesbians want to acknowledge his right to transition and explore new identities, they are also troubled by his continued identification with lesbianism. After all, he's a man.

But it wasn't just this challenging material that raised eyebrows during my presentation. In the words of one of the participants in the audience, it was my positioning myself as an 'authority' and claiming the right to talk about these issues that was troubling. I am neither a lesbian nor a transsexual, so how can I, a 'gay man', talk knowledgeably about such subjects. Most of the question-and-answer session following the presentation was taken up with this issue – which, interestingly, parallels and is at the heart of Califia's continued interest in lesbian community: how can a man identify with lesbian experience?

I can only answer such a question as I did during the discussion session after my presentation: no, I am not a lesbian and I am not transsexual, but why wouldn't I be interested in lesbian and trans lives? Does one have to be lesbian or trans to be moved by, compelled by, inspired by the stories of lesbians and trans individuals? I am not claiming to know what it's like to be lesbian or trans. But I am claiming the right to care about those lives, to want to know more about them, to want to understand them in as much as I can and understand myself better in the process of such reaching out. I claim the right to make connections – connections that may be mutually useful. I do not need to be something in order to reach out.

The question of disciplinarity also raises its strange head at times. We come from different disciplinary backgrounds: Karen is a social psychologist with a long-standing interest in race and sexuality issues, and Jonathan teaches writing and is interested in how new communication technologies shape and extend our understanding of what it means to be literate. When we met at the University of Southern Colorado in 1995, we were both just coming to terms with what our queerness might mean for our work, and we immediately began thinking and writing together, beginning a collaboration not only of scholarship but of friendship in which we inspire and challenge each other's notions about identity, community and love.

Many of our colleagues celebrated with us. Others were much more sceptical. After all, Jonathan was supposed to focus his scholarly attention on understanding how 'texts' move in the world, whereas Karen was supposed to direct her energies to understanding how people move in the world. Jonathan was immersed in the world of theory and interpretation; Karen in the seemingly very distant world of empirical studies. Some of our colleagues wondered what these two very different ways of understanding (and constructing) the world might have to say to each other. We distinctly remember one of our very first presentations, a queer critique of Ellen Degeneres's rather essentialist construction of lesbianism in the famous 'coming out' episode of her sitcom, *Ellen*. Our title quipped our critique: 'What do you call a lesbian who has never slept with a woman? Answer: Ellen Morgan' (1999), the name of Degeneres's character on the show. After we made our presentation, commenting on scenes in the show, reviews of the sitcom and a variety of magazine articles about Degeneres and her character, one of Karen's colleagues in the Psychology Department asked us how we could *know*, empirically, that what we were saying was valid. Where was our *data*? Apparently, textual interpretation was insufficient 'proof' that our critique had merit, and we ran up against a major assumption of empirically-driven psychological approaches: we can't make knowledge claims without controlled studies.

While we deny that we had nothing useful to say about Ellen, we nonetheless began thinking about how we could use empirical studies in our work. Our first major attempt was an article about the film *Chasing Amy*, entitled 'The Pleasure and Pain of *Chasing Amy*: Analysing Reactions to Blurred Identities and Sexualities' (2001), in which we combined interpretation of the film with analysis of viewer responses to and perceptions of the characters' sexual identities. We collected data about their responses, asking them if they thought the characters in the film were gay, straight, bi or 'other'. This blended approach allowed us to investigate how people with different identities perceived and even judged characters; for instance, bi-women were likely to see Alyssa, the initially gay-identified character who falls in love with a man, in a very positive light, while more 'traditionally'-identified gays and lesbians figured her as a 'traitor'. This is not information that we could have deduced had we only examined and interpreted the film. At the same time, our interpretation of the film allowed us to think critically about exactly what in the representation of the Alyssa character might have prompted such divergent reactions. We have since become advocates for this kind of inter-disciplinary work – work that challenges assumptions about methodology and knowledge production in all fields involved.

On a more personal note, we have often felt as we have collaborated that our actual writing is a form of bi-erotic or bi-intimate expression. While we have never been sexually involved with each other, our friendship is intensely intimate, and we have thought of our lives as densely intertwined, both professionally and personally. Our various partners over the last few years have had to acknowledge this friendship as vitally important to our work together and to our growth as individuals. As we have moved into publishing together, it is difficult not to think of our writing as anything but an extension of our friendship, one of its most important expressions and articulations. In this way, particularly when we write about intimacy, love and sex, we are writing both as bisexual people and as two intimate friends, creating work out of love. At the very least, our work together articulates our belief that we find nurturing, encouragement and love by sharing deeply with one another, by honouring our friendship, and by honestly acknowledging to others – even our sexual partners – that we hold deep places in one another's lives. One might call this a polyamory of souls, if not of the flesh. It has also been nicely bi-intimate when we have found ourselves in relationships at times with members of the same sex; our cross-gender friendship keeps multiple lines of intimacy open.

Beyond working and writing together, we have each been actively involved in a number of overtly political pursuits, serving as directors on boards for local and national organisations dealing with queer/bi issues. There are several levels of analysis here that are pertinent in terms of the name game. For instance, as a political community of queers, 'we' (whoever we is) should be asking, what is it we want to emphasise? What information do we consider valuable and pertinent? One path we have found is to continue to work the name game, continually modifying our organisations' names to reflect our growing community. In the beginning there was the homosexual; then gay; then gay and lesbian; then gay, lesbian, bisexual; then gay, lesbian, bisexual, transgendered; now most recently gay, lesbian, bisexual, transgendered, intersexed … and lastly there's the move toward Q or 'queer' that supposedly will traverse that entire landscape and then some.[4] In addition to these linguistic callisthenics, we see sexuality and gender activists continuing to challenge essentialist notions of sexuality and gender. With the burgeoning trans movement, for instance, activists are in the position to ask the public, what do you care more about? Someone's biological plumbing – past or present? Their socialised gender identity – past or present? Their actual sexual behaviours? Or desires, regardless of behaviour? Such questions challenge us to consider critically how sexuality, gender, and desire itself comes into being and is articulated – how it is *named*.

---

4   It should be noted, though, that not all members of the LGBT community are accepting of the term 'queer'. Some feminists, for instance, have argued that 'queer' still seems male-focused and, as such, is not sufficiently inclusive of women's concerns or issues.

From Names to Values

As we have lived and worked – personally, professionally and politically – we have come to see our concern with the limitations of identity (and identity politics) as inciting us to clarify our *values*. If our approach to queerness, to life, to political activism isn't rooted in an identity, then in what is it grounded? For us, it is rooted in our values, in the ways in which we want to question the rules, trouble the labels and open up new possibilities of freedom in the process. Remember what Foucault says is the aim of philosophy: 'the changing of received values and all the work that has been done to think otherwise, to do something else …' (1997, 327). *This* is what we value – to do 'something else', to push ourselves (and others, if they are willing) to think differently about who we are and what we might become. And this is a value that moves us to work with, live with and love other people.

These are values, though, that have at times put us in uncomfortable places. Our students, for instance, continue to remind us of just how disconcerting it can be to pull at their essentialist notions of gender and sexuality, thus reminding us of the importance of our work. For example, on Karen's campus, Dr Marci Bowers came to speak about her professional position as the new sex-change doctor in Trinidad, Colorado. She also personalised her presentation by speaking of her own transformation from man to woman. Student reactions were – to say the least – mixed. While some were inspired by her story, others seemed quite disturbed. Students' gender seemed to account for most of the variation in response. Many female students and a few male students saw Bowers as courageous and perhaps even a good role model for self-actualisation. One female student writes, 'I feel Dr Bowers is one of the bravest people I know. I am all for standing up and doing what you believe, but she has brought it to a new level for me … She is an inspiration.' Another reiterates, 'I admire her courage to speak so openly as well as work so openly with a subject which obviously carries the very real threat of discrimination, hatred and violence attached to it.'

Some male students tended to see Marci's life not as one of triumph, but rather as selfish and disrespectful of others. It was interesting to note that several male responses referred to Marci using male pronouns, refusing to recognise (validate?) her 'constructed gender'. Further, they seemed to question her right to become a woman. For example, one male student writes, 'What right do you have to change yourself from one sex to the other. My thought is all it helps is yourself.' Another male student contradicts himself while perhaps struggling to comprehend the impact of gender on our lives:

> *I see no reason for him [sic] to put himself through what he went through. Life is hard as it is and we don't need little things like that in our way. All in all I have nothing against it, I just don't agree with it in any way, shape, or form.*

Earlier in his reaction paper, this student summarises what he sees as perhaps the 'major needs' in life, namely, 'health, sex, and work'. So, is gender identity a 'little thing' we need not worry about, or is it incredibly influential? One more male student's comments shed light on just how important gender can be for some:

> Wouldn't there be a kind of false advertising thing going on? ... I wouldn't like the fact of dating a woman that used to be a man even if she looked, sounded, and acted like a woman in every way ... I guess I think it is a really selfish thing to do.

What is most disturbing about this student's response is his elaboration of the potential consequences of this presumed 'false advertising'. The trouble in his eyes begins by allowing birth certificates to be changed post-surgically:

> This is what gets people killed. If a straight man that hated to even be around gays slept with a woman and later found out that the woman was really [sic] a man, it could traumatise him and even drive him to murder that person.

The conclusion we draw from this is that people still see homophobia as a justifiable cause for homicide, and that a shift in a 'little thing' called gender can get you killed.

Clearly, what is needed here is an ethics or a value system that will allow others to explore lives and loves that are meaningful to them, even if they make us uncomfortable. In our book, *Bisexuality and Transgenderism: InterSEXions of the Others* (2004), we emphasise the importance of valuing diversity without perhaps first understanding the myriad ways in which we express that diversity. Such an approach actually allowed us to study trans lives and experiences; we had to be open to stories about gender, sex and sexuality that often diverged significantly from our own experiences – and that sometimes called our interpretations of our experiences into question. So, while we have found ourselves swept up with the changing tides of identity signifiers, we have tried to anchor ourselves to more fundamental or core concerns about how we can treat one another civilly and go about living peacefully with one another in a very diverse world, whether that diversity is expressed via the material body (for example, gender, race/ethnicity, sexuality) or the mind in terms of values, ethics or spiritual beliefs.

What we are arguing for ultimately is a relationship with life and existence, born not out of a sense of self, but out of an *engagement* with the world, *recognising its messy complexity and the call to experience the messiness of intimacy*. Ethics, what we call values, become the quality of that engagement – the ever-changing and provisional rules through which we consciously 'craft' relationships and, in the process, ourselves. The process is conscious – having become aware of our subjectivity, of what we are subject to, we move to transgress and recreate ourselves as an expression of freedom and becoming. At the same time, as we explore our own possibilities for becoming, we need to recognise that others are on different parts of this journey, even on different paths. We will not always understand where the 'others' are and we may not agree with what they say or do, but we must respect their right to pursue their own paths, their own visions, even as we seek to challenge them (gently, productively) and are in turn challenged by them.

Think of Karen's transphobic students, for instance. Respecting others becomes extremely difficult when such students contemplate murder, even if only hypothetically. Obviously, we want to respect where these students are as they grapple with the challenges that transgenderism is posing to their own values and identities. Obviously, though, we can't condone their impulses to lash out because they are being challenged – and we can't leave such impulses unchecked. So, how can we respect *and* challenge such students? Firstly, we can recognise their lashing out as *fear* – the fear of being challenged, of having their self-understanding as straight men questioned. In light of such challenges and fear, we can encourage self-reflection, a pausing before taking action. Secondly, we can see such fear and have compassion for it – if only because such men are themselves trapped in very limiting notions of gender, of what it means to be a man. In their view, men can only be and behave in certain ways. Again, prompting and encouraging reflection on the limits of identity is crucial. Such reflection may lead to not only greater self-understanding but also a greater respect for the struggles that others have as they work with gender and sexuality.

Do we really care if the majority of society will engage in the same reflective process of self-evaluation as those pushed to the margins, that is, those marked as 'other'? Absolutely. Some lives may depend upon it. At one point, the strategy of turning the tables – for example, asking others when *they* first knew they were heterosexual, or if they have tried to 'change' – was important to raise basic awareness that the issues gays and lesbians face are the same as those encountered by heterosexuals. And further, the same questions regarding origins of desire can be applied to straight society as well. In this day of shifting genders, however, perhaps we are *all* better off asking what exactly it is about another that I desire. Is it their personality, their physical characteristics, their pheromones? Do I desire to be loved by one gender and have sex with any? Do I desire to be loved by any and have sex with only one type? Can I be bold, courageous and respectful enough to allow others to question, pursue and love in ways that are meaningful to them?

Of course, we can't claim that bisexuality and queerness are 'cure alls' in and of themselves, or that they will necessarily lead to greater freedom from the constraints of identity or systems of gender and sexual oppression. For instance, some critics warn that we should not claim too much potential lying inherently in bisexuality or bi-eroticism. For instance, Clare Hemmings argues that bisexuality can be perceived both as 'subversive of gender norms' *and* as a 'reinscription of dominant (i.e. heterosexist) gender and/or sexual discourse' (2002, 117). That is, people engaging in bi-erotic behaviour *can* at times prompt us to question what a real 'man' or 'woman' should do; at the same time, other versions of bisexuality practised by some people might allow men and women to maintain dominant heterosexual relationships while 'playing around' with homo-eroticism in the privacy of a bedroom – without having really to confront what it means to be openly queer. At the same time, we hope with black poet and activist June Jordan, arguing for a 'New Politics of Sexuality', that 'Bisexuality invalidates either/or formulation, either/or analysis. Bisexuality means I am free and I am as likely to want and to love a woman as I am likely to want and to love a man, and what about that? Isn't that what freedom implies?' (1996, 14–15). Certainly, writers like Jordan see the potential in bisexuality to contribute to our sense of freedom; we need to continue thinking about and working toward a fuller understanding of how that freedom takes shape in the real world. Indeed, as Foucault ultimately argues:

> *Sexuality is something that we ourselves create – it is our own creation, and much more than the discovery of a secret side of our desire. We have to understand that with our desires, through our desires, go new forms of relationships, new forms of love, and new forms of creation. Sex is not a fatality: it's a possibility for creative life. (1997, 163)*

We believe in – and try to live – that 'creative life'.

Suggested Further Reading

Alexander, J. (ed.) (1999), 'Queer Values, Beyond Identity', a special issue of *The Journal of Gay, Lesbian and Bisexual Identity* 4:4.
Garber, M. (1995), *Vice Versa: Bisexuality and the Eroticism of Everyday Life* (New York: Simon and Schuster).
Hemmings, C. (2002), *Bisexual Spaces: A Geography of Sexuality and Gender* (New York and London: Routledge).
Rust, P. (1996), *Bisexuality and the Challenge to Lesbian Politics* (New York: New York University Press).
Storr, M. (ed.) (1999), *Bisexuality: A Critical Reader* (London and New York: Routledge).

References

Alexander, J. and Yescavage, K. (2001), 'The Pleasure and Pain of *Chasing Amy*: Analysing Reactions to Blurred Identities and Sexualities', *The Journal of Bisexuality* 1:1, 117–35.
—— (eds) (2004) *Bisexuality and Transgenderism: InterSEXions of the Others* (Binghamton, NY: Harrington Park Press).
Foucault, M. (1977), *Discipline and Punish: The Birth of the Prison*, trans. A. Sheridan (London: Penguin Books).
—— (1990/1976), *The History of Sexuality, Volume 1: An Introduction*, trans. R. Hurley (London: Penguin Books).
—— (1997), *Ethics: Subjectivity and Truth*, Volume 1 of *Essential Works of Foucault*, (ed.) P. Rabinow (New York: The New Press).

Halperin, D.M. (1995), *Saint Foucault: Towards a Gay Hagiography* (New York: Oxford University Press).

Hemmings, C. (2002), *Bisexual Spaces: A Geography of Sexuality and Gender* (New York: Routledge).

Jordan, J. (1996), 'A New Politics of Sexuality', in S. Rose, C. Stevens et al. (eds), *Bisexual Horizons: Politics, Histories, Lives* (London: Lawrence and Wishart).

Katz, J.N. (1995), *The Invention of Heterosexuality* (New York: Dutton).

Kirsch, M.H. (2001), *Queer Theory and Social Change* (London and New York: Routledge).

Mohr, R.D. (1995), 'The Perils of Postmodernism', *Harvard Gay and Lesbian Review* 2:4, 9–13.

Rose, S. et al. (eds) (1996), *Bisexual Horizons: Politics, Histories, Lives* (London: Lawrence and Wishart).

Warner, M. (1999), *The Trouble with Normal: Sex Politics and the Ethics of Queer Life* (Cambridge, MA: Harvard University Press).

Yescavage, K. and Alexander, J. (1999), 'What Do You Call a Lesbian Who Has Never Slept with a Woman? Answer: Ellen Morgan. Deconstructing the Lesbian Identities of Ellen Morgan and Ellen DeGeneres', *The Journal of Lesbian Studies* 3:3, 21–32.

The Curious Persistence
of Lesbian Studies

Linda Garber

In this queer (studies) age, lesbian studies emerges as the Curiously Strong Movement. The Unsinkable Molly Bolt. The little *vagin* that could.[1] We are supposed to be in a post-lesbian age; certainly post-structuralism deemed all identity-based movements and studies *passé*, if not actually *mort*, quite some time ago. So what gives? How is it possible to subscribe to both *GLQ* and *The Journal of Lesbian Studies* in the twenty-first century? How come I keep getting invited to represent lesbian studies at queer conferences and in queer volumes like this one?

The genealogy of lesbian studies has been discussed productively, and often enough, elsewhere.[2] What I aim to do in this chapter, instead, is to trace the justification lesbian studies has provided for its own existence over the years, and also to explore the method by which lesbian studies has survived in the face of the queer discourse juggernaut. Over the same 35 or so years that lesbian studies has persevered, a vast array of post-structuralist and queer critiques across many disciplines have proclaimed the death of identity – which, to put it mildly, complicates a straightforward lesbian studies approach. Judith Butler's refusal of identity politics is among the most authoritative in the queer studies context; in her 1991 essay 'Imitation and Gender Insubordination', Butler argues that 'identity categories tend to be instruments of regulatory regimes, whether as the normalising categories of oppressive structures or as the rallying points for a liberatory contestation of that very oppression' (1991, 13–14). Despite the wide influence of Butler and others, in the quarter-century since Margaret Cruikshank's

---

1   'The Curiously Strong Mint' was a ubiquitous, and funny, advertising campaign in the United States for a breath mint called Altoids; the 'Unsinkable Molly Bolt' is a reference to the main character of Rita Mae Brown's lesbian-feminist novel *Rubyfruit Jungle* and the Broadway show *The Unsinkable Molly Brown*, about a women's rights activist who survived the sinking of the Titanic; *The Little Engine that Could* is a classic children's story about self-esteem and perseverance.

2   Several compelling genealogies of lesbian studies are published, including Doan (2007); Zimmerman (2007).

groundbreaking book *Lesbian Studies: Present and Future* (1982) was published in the United States, countless essays and at least a half-dozen volumes have asserted the importance of lesbian studies as its own, if some might say complementary, field (Garber 1994; Wilton 1995; Zimmerman and McNaron 1996; Giffney and O'Donnell 2007a). Why? One reason too obvious to ignore is that many of these publications coincide with the birth and growth of queer studies in the 1990s; they were pushing back against a new discourse that seemed to threaten the existence of lesbian studies by calling into question its basic ideological assumption. But the pushback was never mere defensiveness; lesbian feminists saw (and continue to see) a pernicious problem in queer studies. The core reason why lesbian studies needs to survive was, and remains, sexism.

Sexism was a problem in the male-dominated Gay Academic Union, probably the first gay/lesbian studies organisation in the United States, founded in 1973 in New York City (D'Emilio 1992/1973, 121–5). Sexism was a problem in the beginning of queer theory, queer feminist designs to the contrary. (Teresa de Lauretis had argued hopefully in the 1991 'Queer Theory' issue of the journal *differences* that 'queer' could 'problematise' [1991, iii] the terms 'gay and lesbian' in such a way that gender differences – that is, lesbians – would no longer be 'covered over' [1991, vi].) Sexism, among other problems, was pointed out both times the Modern Language Association's Gay and Lesbian Caucus considered changing its name from 'Gay and Lesbian' to 'Queer' – perhaps one reason why the eventual switch, in 2005, was to the more ambivalent 'GL/Q Caucus'. The term was suggested, and adopted, as a 'compromise' between those who preferred 'queer', those who preferred a more inclusive list of initials, and those who found 'queer' objectionable either because of its history as a homophobic slur or its erasure of lesbians.[3] The decades-old problem of sexism haunts newer movements of 'GL/Q' studies, such as global and postcolonial queer studies (Garber 2005). Sexism remains such a problem in American academia generally that the field of women's studies is flourishing across the Unites States.[4]

So, in the first instance, lesbian studies remains necessary and relevant in order to combat lesbian invisibility. As Tamsin Wilton wrote in *Lesbian Studies: Setting*

---

3   My thanks to Harriette Andreadis, past president of the GL/Q Caucus for the Modern Languages, who gave me access to the archived Caucus discussion of the name change in 2005. I participated in the discussion as a member (and past president) of the Caucus; Harriette is the person who suggested the 'compromise' name that was adopted by a vote of the membership. Bonnie Zimmerman (1996) writes about earlier struggles in the MLA caucus.

4   By the generic term 'women's studies' I mean to include programmes that are variously named 'women's studies', 'women's and gender studies', 'feminist studies' or 'gender studies'. According to the National Women's Studies Association, at this writing there are 11 US institutions offering doctoral degrees and 20 offering master's degrees in women's studies; a large number of US institutions also offer graduate degrees in women's studies combined with another field (http://www.nwsa.org). Bachelor's degrees in women's studies, or in women's studies combined with another field, are very common in the United States.

an Agenda, 'lesbians – after all the deconstructing … – *are*, in the material here and now, *women*' (1995, viii). Although identity politics developed a bad name in the 1990s, its impulse, as explained by the Black feminist Combahee River Collective in 1977, still resonates, despite and alongside Butler's persuasive argument *contra* 'regulatory regimes'. The Combahee 'Black Feminist Statement' explains why the group embraced identity politics in the first place:

> *We realise that the only people who care enough about us to work consistently for our liberation is us. Our politics evolve from a healthy love for ourselves, our sisters, and our community which allows us to continue our struggle and work. This focusing upon our own oppression is embodied in the concept of identity politics. (1982/1977, 66)*

Watching the very name 'lesbian' disappear under the rubric 'queer', many lesbian activists and academics understandably have felt compelled to labour on under the banner of identity, even though such enterprises are now routinely dismissed as 'essentialist'. In the words of Toni A.H. McNaron:

> *… acknowledging myself as a lesbian was one of the most empowering acts of my adult life, allowing me to find my voice as a critic and memoirist even as it clarified my sense of the source of many of my academic approaches to literature and other art forms as well as the national news. (2007, 147)*

Why, McNaron wonders, would she want to give up that name?

Although I have been rehearsing in brief some of the lesbian studies complaints against gay studies and queer studies, the initial salvo from Cruikshank in *Lesbian Studies* was aimed at women's studies, the field out of which lesbian studies grew. Presumably, the lesbian-feminist (and some separatist) architects of lesbian studies in the 1970s took for granted that gay men's studies and the mainstream academy were too sexist to take lesbians seriously. They had higher hopes for, and perhaps experienced more bitter disappointment about, the field of women's studies. In a sort of manifesto with which she closed the introduction to *Lesbian Studies*, Cruikshank wrote,

> *Lesbians have come a long way since the first years of women's studies, but until the elimination of heterosexist bias is a widely accepted goal of our courses and programs, we will not have come far enough. If Lesbian Studies challenges academic feminists to re-examine their teaching and research and provides them with new material for their classrooms, it will achieve its purpose. (1982, xvi–xvii)*

This, I think, is an aim that lesbian studies has by and large reached; women's studies courses and texts today rarely ignore lesbians altogether. (I say this notwithstanding Wilton's far-reaching critique [citing Sheila Jeffreys] that 'historically … feminism has served lesbians poorly and reluctantly, and feminist scholarship reinforces the unquestioned hegemony of heteropatriarchy by refusing to reflect on its own practice and, hence, colluding with the invisibility of lesbians' [1995, 15]). Cruikshank makes only passing reference to the exclusion of lesbians from 'books purporting to treat homosexuality' (1982, xi), apparently considering gay studies beyond reform. Thirteen years later Wilton concurred, explaining on the first page of *Lesbian Studies: Setting an Agenda* that 'Lesbian studies has always occupied a precarious position on the cusp of [not only] women's studies [but also] lesbian and gay/queer studies' (1995, 1).

Cruikshank wrote the introduction to *Lesbian Studies: Present and Future* at a time when it was still deeply meaningful to understand lesbian studies in the United States as part of a lesbian-feminist grassroots movement that existed outside the academy. She explained that 'lesbian studies is essentially a grassroots movement' (1982, xiv), and while she noted the toehold lesbian studies had gained in the academy, she asserted:

> ... our integrity, in the root meaning of wholeness, would be lost if we followed the example of some women's studies coordinators and shaped our goals on the need to win approval from male administrators. (1982, xiv)

She noted that 'some individuals will choose to become fully integrated into the academic system', but exhorted readers that 'as practitioners of lesbian studies, we must remain apart; our scholarship cannot flourish in isolation from our communities' (1982, xiv). At the same time, Cruikshank asserted the importance of lesbian studies within the academy, and not only to women's studies. One of the book's stated purposes is to 'explore the consequences of our exclusion for the university curriculum' as a whole (1982, xi), in fact for the goals of education overall: 'The contributors to *Lesbian Studies* believe that our past invisibility has been harmful not only to us, but to all students and teachers, to anyone, in fact, who trusts education to "lead out" to comprehensive views and a tolerance for diversity' (1982, xi). Wilton makes the same point from her vantage in British academia: 'The academy needs lesbian studies if anything rather *more* than lesbian studies needs the academy' (1995, 24). By 1982 Cruikshank could say of the amount and variety of work going on under the rubric 'lesbian studies' that 'a new educational movement exists which ought now to be formally documented' (1982, xi), a movement that was both community oriented and profoundly lesbian-feminist. Cruikshank's notion of who should do lesbian studies, how and why was deeply informed by lesbian-feminist identity politics, but by 1982 things were already changing.

In the United States, the lesbian 1980s were informed by discord over major issues such as racism, sexual practices and common cause with gay men. Fewer lesbians identified with the term 'lesbian feminist' by the end of the decade. By the early 1990s, AIDS had ravaged gay men's communities, the religious right had been in power on the national level for more than a decade, and the homophobic pressure on gay men and lesbians alike had led to closer ties between the two groups in most communities. For many people, and especially for young ones, it became less meaningful to speak of 'the lesbian community'; the activist group

Queer Nation came and went in a blaze at the beginning of the decade, but its postmodern queer sensibility made an indelible mark, not least on theorists in the US academy.

Nevertheless, a lot of the lesbians on any given scene, activist or academic, had come of age when 'queer' was an epithet rather than a political stance, and when the brief experiment of working in coalition with gay men had faltered over sexism the first time around, in the early 1970s. Because a meaningful contribution had been made under the sign 'lesbian studies', there remained partisans. The 1990s saw the launch of the refereed *Journal of Lesbian Studies* as well as the publication of no fewer than three books about the interdisciplinary field of lesbian studies (Garber 1994; Wilton 1995; Zimmerman and McNaron 1996).[5] Caught, myself, in between what have been described as two lesbian 'generations', when I edited the lesbian studies/lesbian pedagogy anthology *Tilting the Tower*, I placed both names in the subtitle, in what I hoped was creative tension with one another: *Lesbians/ Teaching/Queer Subjects*.

By the mid-1990s, heterosexism in women's studies was no longer perceived to be the only or the main problem faced by lesbian studies. Tamsin Wilton captured the sense of the transitional era in the context of British (and US) national politics when she wrote:

> *Neither women's studies nor lesbian and gay studies have yet been able to offer an adequate theoretical or political framework for lesbians and lesbianism. Yet such a matrix is urgently needed, because the political and social position of lesbians is increasingly complex, especially in the light of the rise of the New Right and the new queer activism. (1995, frontispiece)*

In the introduction to *Tilting the Tower*, I positioned lesbian studies' predicament squarely within the academy: 'Lesbian studies grew out of women's studies and feminist activism, and it appears in danger, now, of being subsumed under the banner of queer studies' (Garber 1994, ix). As Cruikshank could take for granted, and barely mention, the sexism of gay men's studies in the early 1980s, my own assessment was that the caustic blend of sexism and homophobia that targets and dismisses lesbians in the larger society was understood – that our struggle as academics for representation and influence was with the growing enterprises of queer studies and queer theory, whose post-structuralist, post-identity stance threatened to bury lesbian, lesbian-feminist and perhaps even feminist studies under a landslide of what we then called 'high theory'. I was not alone when I wondered aloud, at the end of the decade:

> *... whether queer theory comprises a set of 'master's tools' as it straps on the master's theories, whether or not (or to what extent) queer theory opposes 'the*

---

5   I do not include two other, very influential anthologies (Munt 1992; Doan 1994) because they focus on literature and literary criticism and my concern here is the larger interdisciplinary field of lesbian studies.

> master's house' – and at what point queer theory itself becomes the house that
> screams for dismantling. (Garber 2001, 4)[6]

I have remained ambivalent about queer theory over the course of nearly 15 years of writing about its relationship to lesbian studies and lesbian feminism. When I edited *Tilting the Tower*, I was particularly interested in watching how contributors to the anthology were juggling theories and politics. Several contributors grappled with the inclusivity or exclusivity of terminology.[7] Some named themselves queer subjects, others claimed to teach queer subjects, some wanted nothing to do with a term they felt put lesbians, and particularly lesbian existence, under erasure all over again. Jacquelyn Zita's essay 'Gay and Lesbian Studies: Yet Another Unhappy Marriage?' closes *Tilting the Tower* with an interrogation into 'the nature of the marriage hidden behind the veil of queerness' (1994, 258), summing up some of the collective anxiety in lesbian studies about the still new queer academic movement. 'As a lesbian', Zita explained, 'I may understand the need for queer inquiry. As a feminist, I understand the need to maintain feminist subjectivity and autonomy in alliances with men' (1994, 259).

Without venturing into the more complicated, inclusive terrain of a queer studies that includes bisexual, trans and queer straight enquiry, Zita expressed scepticism at the wisdom of wholeheartedly adopting a lesbian-and-gay agenda, admitting to her 'anger and bitterness' over the subject (1994, 267). Zita was careful to articulate her concern that 'a new field of queer studies' was being developed 'without addressing misogyny, gender, male supremacy, race, and class as these are differently experienced by a wide diversity of female and male queers' (1994, 271). At issue for lesbian studies as a whole at that time was the sexism (that is, the neglect of lesbians) in the new queer theory, as much as it was the theoreticisation of a field that had been profoundly imbued with the importance of representing actual, diverse people's lives. In other words, to paraphrase Queer Nation, if we were here, and we were queer, where were the lesbians?

Tilting the Tower's answer, in part, was that we were in classrooms, and it mattered what we (thought we) were doing there, as one version of the 'future' contemplated by the contributors to *Lesbian Studies: Present and Future*. For example, Barbara Blinick explains her decision to teach LGBT content in her high school classes:

> *The inclusion of lesbian, gay, and bisexual material is crucial in letting our students know that there were others before us, and there will be others after us; we have always been in their lives. (1994, 146)*

---

6   With apologies to Audre Lorde, whose influential essay 'The Master's Tools Will Never Dismantle the Master's House' (1984/1979) formed the basis of my critique.

7   For some examples in *Tilting the Tower*, see González (1994) for a discussion of the political valences of terminology used by and for Mexican-Americans; Pellegrini (1994) for a discussion of the anachronism in the application of terms for sexual identity; or Pagenhart (1994) for a gloss on choosing the term 'queer studies' as characteristic of the 1990s.

She describes the importance for young people of seeing her in the classroom as 'another healthy, happy, and productive lesbian' (1994, 143). Cynthia D. Nieb writes about how her inclusion of lesbian subject matter in the college classroom elicits 'changes in attitude from homophobic resistance and curiosity to in-your-face militant activism and empathy', as proof that she is 'providing a worthwhile service' as an instructor (1994, 64). Kate Adams and Kim Emery make perhaps the boldest claim when they describe being out in the classroom as 'a disenfranchised group [taking] the Constitution literally and agitat[ing] for its civil and human rights' (1994, 33–4).

Two years after the publication of *Tilting the Tower*, Bonnie Zimmerman's and Toni A.H. McNaron's update of Cruikshank's volume, titled *The New Lesbian Studies: Into the Twenty-First Century* (1996), included a 'classroom' section but focused more broadly on lesbian studies as an enterprise. The volume is anchored in history, beginning with a foreword by Cruikshank and 'Part One: Remembering Our Roots', in which nine essays are reprinted from *Lesbian Studies: Present and Future*, 'in order to demonstrate that the present is never divorced from the past' (Zimmerman and McNaron 1996, xvi). As Zimmerman and McNaron report in their introduction, the authors of the nine essays 'declined [the] request to update their content or bibliographies, preferring to let the work stand not as a present-day report or study but as a pebble whose concentric reverberations still have significance to current researchers and activists' (1996, xvi). *The New Lesbian Studies* thus provides a testament to the history of lesbian studies and activism, but its main thrust is signalled by the word 'new' in the title, and by the subtitle 'Into the Twenty-First Century'. This future-directed project, edited by two stalwarts of lesbian-feminist studies, provides important clues to not only *why* but also *how* lesbian studies has persisted, through the twin forces of diligence (even doggedness) and adaptability.

It is a measure of the dedication of the field's founders that Cruikshank, McNaron and Zimmerman are represented in *Lesbian Studies: Present and Future* (1982), *The New Lesbian Studies* (1996) and *Twenty-First Century Lesbian Studies* (2007a),[8] over the course of whose publications the field has shifted, stretched, grown and fundamentally changed in certain ways. Of the three authors, Bonnie Zimmerman's is the voice most recognisably associated with lesbian studies, because of her prolific publishing in and about the field, and her leadership in women's and lesbian studies within the National Women's Studies Association and the Modern Language Association. For Cruikshank's anthology, Zimmerman contributed a review essay called 'One Out of Thirty: Lesbianism in Women's Studies Textbooks', in which she reported that in the 1970s 'heterosexism [was] alive and well in the women's studies textbook market' (1982, 130). Just a year earlier, Zimmerman had published her best known and most-reprinted piece, 'What Has Never Been: An Overview of Lesbian Feminist Criticism' in which she asserted that 'the questions' posed by lesbian critics 'are important not only to lesbians but to all feminists' (1993/1981, 33).

---

8   This book was published simultaneously as volume 11:1–4 of the *Journal of Lesbian Studies* (2007).

'Lesbian literary criticism', she concluded, 'simply restates what feminists already know, that one group cannot name itself "humanity" or even "woman"'(1993/1981, 53). 'What Has Never Been', became 'a part of the canon', as Zimmerman notes in her chapter in *Twenty-First Century Lesbian Studies*, in part because it laid out the positions and stakes in the debate 'over the meaning of the word "lesbian"'; this was the central (nearly obsessive) question of early lesbian literary criticism and activism alike, and it is still a relevant 'intellectual and ontological' starting point for lesbians in a queer era (2007, 42–3).

In a 1997 essay titled '"Confessions" of a Lesbian Feminist', Zimmerman's diligence was evident in her choice 'to "defend" lesbian feminism through a deliberately, unabashedly subjective revelation of individual history', confessing that 'lesbianism and feminism never have been separate or unconnected in my life' (1997, 158). She 'defends' lesbian studies by striking similar notes in her works spanning many years. In 'Placing Lesbians', an essay that appears near the end of *The New Lesbian Studies*, Zimmerman asks, 'What is the unregenerate lesbian feminist scholar to do in this brave new world?' 'This', she explains, is a world in which 'an identity hard fought for in the 1970s can be calmly deconstructed in the 1990s'; in which 'lesbian feminism gives way to gay and lesbian studies, which in turn is challenged by queer theory' (1996, 271). The reason Zimmerman's work – and by extension the enterprise of lesbian studies – remains relevant and vital is her answer to her own query. She concludes that the lesbian-feminist scholar can work 'anywhere and everywhere', but she recognises the cost of doing so:

> It means maintaining a multiple subject position that is neither comfortable, coherent, nor easy. It means being a gadfly everywhere ... It means constantly inspecting one's options and choices for complex and conflicting consequences. It means agonising over which principled position to take ... It means ... living always with contradictions. (1996, 272–3)

Which brings us to the most recent exhibit of lesbian studies' curious persistence, the volume *Twenty-First Century Lesbian Studies*, in which Zimmerman's essay 'A Lesbian-Feminist Journey through Queer Nation' is published alongside chapters by and about a former lesbian-feminist transman, lesbian/bisexual femmes and queer straights – all jockeying for position, amazingly, under the rubric of 'lesbian studies'.

While this may not be what Cruikshank envisioned when she invoked 'we ourselves' as the proper agents of lesbian studies in 1982, it is indeed a lesbian studies that helps to '[tell] us who we are' (1982, ix) at this juncture, insofar as 'we' are a much more diversely self-identified group than we were 25 years ago. It is potentially a lesbian studies that, as Cruikshank hoped, 'can help all women in the academy recover a sense of the deep bonds among us' (1982, xvi) – even though the category 'women' as queerly construed today would have been unrecognisable in 1982. The strange bedfellows published together in *Twenty-First Century Lesbian Studies* may neither be what Zimmerman means, exactly, when she calls for continuing study of the 'particularity of lesbian histories, perspectives, subjectivities and identities' (2007, 49). One could argue whether the 'value' of 'the specificity of lesbianism' that Zimmerman invokes is reflected by *Twenty-First Century Lesbian Studies*; certainly, it is included, but its boundaries are also stretched, some might say to the breaking point. McNaron's vehement partisan argument for retaining the term 'lesbian' – 'What we call the courses we offer, the articles and books we write, the research we do and the conferences we organise and attend reflect deeply held values' (2007, 150) – does not seem to be contradicted by editors Noreen Giffney and Katherine O'Donnell, nor really by the anthology's other contributors, but that doesn't mean the 'values' they hold are exactly the same. The editors' introduction to *Twenty-First Century Lesbian Studies* begins by juxtaposing the materialist lesbian pronouncement of Charlotte Bunch from 1975 and the anti-identity queer salvo of Judith Butler from 1991 (2007b, 1); Giffney and O'Donnell clearly state their goal to 'widen the contours of lesbian studies' with the selections they made for the book (2007b, 8).

Zimmerman's and McNaron's eloquent defences of lesbian-feminist studies across the decades notwithstanding, their own anthology began the widening of lesbian studies' parameters some years before Giffney and O'Donnell proclaimed it as the goal of their project. The selfsame Zimmerman/McNaron anthology that begins with Cruikshank protesting, 'I have fought too hard for the psychic freedom to name myself a lesbian to disappear now under the queer rubric' (1996, xii), ends with Zimmerman's essay acknowledging that the lesbian-feminist scholar must now accustom herself to 'living always with contradictions' (1996, 273).[9] Just before the closing essay, Zimmerman and McNaron placed 'Queering Lesbian Studies', in which Judith Halberstam (by now an acknowledged champion of transgender studies) seeks to emphasise both 'the fragility and the persistence of concepts of lesbian identity. I believe that this is the postmodern condition – a simultaneous disavowal and confirmation of desires, bodies and identities, and the pleasure that comes from holding onto identity in the face of radical uncertainty and letting go of it even if this entails considerable risk' (1996, 257).

Earlier in *The New Lesbian Studies*, Ann Pellegrini and Paul B. Franklin's essay, 'Queer Collaborations: Feminist Pedagogy' rues 'the abject status of feminism among queers on college campuses today', even though the authors understand this as one among many 'generational differences' (1996, 120). Like Pellegrini and Franklin, Halberstam is acutely aware of the problem of 'opposition ... from white gay men in the [queer] classroom' (1996, 259). In that context she says she understands the separatist tendency of an earlier lesbian studies, even though she disavows it herself. I would argue that Halberstam's experiences of sexism, tied to her recognition of the importance of lesbian-feminist communities to today's queer cultures, is an example of the reason that lesbian studies remains relevant today. For Halberstam, though, it is indeed a 'new' lesbian studies:

---

9   Zimmerman wittily alludes to the lesbian-feminist and separatist singer Alix Dobkin (1980): 'Living with contradictions/Going against the grain/It's not easy!'

> *Rather than a separatist lesbian culture or pedagogy … I would argue*
> *for a 'queer lesbian studies'. 'Queer' in this context performs the work*
> *of destabilising the assumed identity in 'identity politics'. However, by*
> *continuing to use and rely upon the term 'lesbian', we acknowledge that*
> *identity is a useful strategy for political and cultural organising. 'Lesbian'*
> *is a term that modifies and qualifies 'queer', and 'queer' is a term capable of*
> *challenging the stability of identities subsumed by the label 'lesbian'. (1996,*
> *259)*

If 'opposition … from white gay men in the classroom' made even so thoroughly a queer- and trans-identified scholar as Halberstam 'acutely aware of the pedagogical imperative for a separate space for lesbian history and culture' (1996, 259), then perhaps it is no wonder that a wide array of feminist/lesbian/queer/bi/straight/trans/gender-queer scholars and educators stake a place, or at least one of their places, within a redefined, twenty-first-century lesbian studies.

With the anthology *Twenty-First Century Lesbian Studies*, Giffney and O'Donnell present, via the work of 27 contributors hailing from five continents, a 'field of knowledge-production loosely referred to as Lesbian Studies' (2007b, 7). The editors take care in their introduction to 'point to the important ways in which the authors' concerns converge', though they admit they also revel 'in the many unresolved (perhaps irreconcilable) disjunctions between them' (2007b, 7). Maybe this, really, is the difference between the lesbian-feminist and queer generations in lesbian studies: Zimmerman is made anxious by the postmodern contradictions in which Giffney and O'Donnell delight. And maybe the most important thing is that they see each other as colleagues and allies even across that fundamental divide. The continuity is evident at least in one way, in that Giffney and O'Donnell name the sexism that I have pointed to as the *raison d'être* for lesbian studies' persistence, its least common denominator. 'All of the pieces' in the anthology, they explain, 'have one striking thing in common: their oppositional relation to heteropatriarchy' (2007b, 13).

The elasticity of the term 'lesbian studies' as defined by Giffney and O'Donnell goes a long way toward explaining the staying power of lesbian studies. One could argue that they breathe new life into the field through their time-honoured 'insisten[ce] that authors put the shifting boundaries of the term "lesbian" under interrogation' combined with their more contemporary conscious inclusion of 'pieces by people whose main research interests lie in areas such as bisexuality, transsexuality and transgender, intersex and queer in an effort to facilitate dialogue about "lesbians" and "Lesbian Studies" between members of the LGBTTIQQA alphabet' (2007b, 8).[10] Certainly, the doggedness of the remaining lesbian-feminist cohort alone could not sustain the field if it were not also stretched and reshaped

---

10   Even Giffney and O'Donnell feel compelled to provide a definitional footnote to this longest-ever iteration of the movement's alphabet soup. They explain that LGBTTIQQA stands for 'Lesbian, Gay, Bisexual, Transgender, Transsexual, Intersex, Queer, Questioning, Affiliated' (2007b, 15 n. 7).

by new practitioners; on the other hand, neither could lesbian studies survive if its basic premises had become entirely obsolete.

Instead of seeing the current concatenation of queer theories and theorists as comprising a worrisome contradiction, Michèle Aina Barale sees exuberant excess. She draws a clever parallel between her approach to the abundant LGBTQ studies output and the early lesbian-feminist value of non-monogamy. 'What seems most wonderful to me about the past decade of LGBTQ writing', she gushes, 'is that it is so luxuriously, lusciously, *there*. I don't have to take a vow of intellectual monogamy; I can fall in love with every single thing I read. I can also walk away, especially when it treats me wrong' (2007, 132). Her statement of joyful infidelity helps me, caught as I am between the lesbian-feminist and queer moments of our movement, to make peace with the fact that I feel sympathetic to lesbian-feminist Toni McNaron's impassioned polemic 'Post-Lesbian? Not Yet' (2007, 145–51), as well as to former lesbian-feminist FTM J. Bobby Noble's equally heartfelt advocacy of 'Lesbian-Trans Studies' (2007, 167–75), which confronts 'universalised heterosexualities and … supposedly naturalised bodies as socially-produced and socially-reinforced imperatives' (2007, 174). I suppose we have always said that 'We are everywhere', and now 'we' (always a problematic construct) are going in more and different directions than we could have foreseen.

I'll close by quoting Cruikshank, without whose groundbreaking activist scholarship and abiding friendship I'm sure I would have no academic career. I may temper her witty bitterness with a bit more optimism about our shared field, but I take to heart the closing lines of her essay in *Twenty-First Century Lesbian Studies*:

> With intermittent respect for queer theory laced with misgivings, with an uneasy sadness that my cohort of lesbian-feminist pioneers is waning, and with a sardonic sense that in time, queer theory will be supplanted by something else, I wish young lesbian scholars well. May this choice not obliterate the struggles and contributions of their foremothers. (2007, 157)

Suggested Further Reading

Garber, L. (ed.) (1994), *Tilting the Tower* (London and New York: Routledge, 1994).

—— (2001), *Identity Poetics: Race, Class and the Lesbian-Feminist Roots of Queer Theory* (New York: Columbia University Press).

Giffney, N. and O'Donnell, K. (eds) (2007), *Twenty-First Century Lesbian Studies* (Binghamton, NY: Harrington Park Press/Taylor and Francis).

Wilton, T. (1995), *Lesbian Studies: Setting an Agenda* (London and New York: Routledge).

Zimmerman, B. and McNaron, T.A.H. (eds) (1996), *The New Lesbian Studies: Into the Twenty-First Century* (New York: The Feminist Press).

References

Adams, K. and Emery, K. (1994), 'Classroom Coming Out Stories: Practical Strategies for Productive Self-Disclosure', in L. Garber (ed.), *Tilting the Tower*.

Barale, M.A. (2007), 'Of Hyacinths', in N. Giffney and K. O'Donnell, *Twenty-First Century Lesbian Studies* (Binghamton, NY: Harrington Park Press/Taylor and Francis).

Blinick, B. (1994), 'Out in the Curriculum, Out in the Classroom', in L. Garber (ed.), *Tilting the Tower*.

Butler, J. (1991), 'Imitation and Gender Insubordination', in D. Fuss (ed.), *Inside/Out: Lesbian Theories, Gay Theories* (New York and London: Routledge).

Combahee River Collective (1982/1977), 'A Black Feminist Statement', in G.T. Hull, P. Bell Scott and B. Smith (eds), *All the Women Are White, All the Blacks Are Men, But Some of Us Are Brave: Black Women's Studies* (New York: The Feminist Press).

Cruikshank, M. (ed.) (1982), *Lesbian Studies: Present and Future* (Old Westbury, NY: The Feminist Press).

—— (1996), Foreword to B. Zimmerman and T.A.H. McNaron (eds), *The New Lesbian Studies: Into the Twenty-First Century* (New York: The Feminist Press).

—— (2007), 'Through the Looking Glass: A '70s Lesbian Feminist Considers Queer Theory', in N. Giffney and K. O'Donnell, *Twenty-First Century Lesbian Studies* (Binghamton, NY: Harrington Park Press/Taylor and Francis).

De Lauretis, T. (1991), 'Queer Theory: Lesbian and Gay Sexualities: An Introduction', *differences: A Journal of Feminist Cultural Studies* 3:2, iii–xviii.

D'Emilio, J. (1992/1973), 'The Universities and the Gay Experience', in *Making Trouble: Essays on Gay History, Politics, and the University* (New York and London: Routledge).

Doan, L. (ed.) (1994), *The Lesbian Postmodern* (New York: Columbia University Press).

—— (2007), 'Lesbian Studies after *The Lesbian Postmodern*: Toward a New Genealogy', in N. Giffney and K. O'Donnell (eds), *Twenty-First Century Lesbian Studies*.

Dobkin, A. (1980) 'Living with Contradictions', *xxAlix* [music album].

Garber, L. (ed.) (1994), *Tilting the Tower: Lesbians/Teaching/Queer Subjects* (New York: Routledge).

—— (2001), *Identity Poetics: Race, Class, and the Lesbian-Feminist Roots of Queer Theory* (New York: Columbia University Press).

—— (2005), 'Where in the World Are the Lesbians?', *Journal of the History of Sexuality* 14:1–2, 28–50.

Giffney, N. and O'Donnell, K. (eds) (2007a), *Twenty-First Century Lesbian Studies* (Binghamton, NY: Harrington Park Press/Taylor and Francis).

—— (2007b), 'Introduction', in *Twenty-First Century Lesbian Studies*.

González, M.C. (1994), 'Cultural Conflict: Introducing the Queer in Mexican-American Literature Classes', in L. Garber (ed.), *Tilting the Tower*.

Halberstam, J. (1996), 'Queering Lesbian Studies', in B. Zimmerman and T.A.H. McNaron (eds), *The New Lesbian Studies*.

Lorde, A. (1984/1979), 'The Master's Tools Will Never Dismantle the Master's House', in *Sister Outsider: Essays and Speeches* (Freedom, CA: Crossing Press).

McNaron, T.A.H. (2007), 'Post-Lesbian? Not Yet', in N. Giffney and K. O'Donnell (eds), *Twenty-First Century Lesbian Studies*.

Munt, S.R. (ed.) (1992), *New Lesbian Criticism: Literary and Cultural Readings* (New York: Columbia University Press).

Nieb, C.D. (1994), 'Collaborating with Clio: Teaching Lesbian History', in L. Garber (ed.) *Tilting the Tower*.

Noble, J.B. (2007), 'Refusing to Make Sense: Mapping the In-Coherences of "Trans"', in N. Giffney and K. O'Donnell (eds), *Twenty-First Century Lesbian Studies*.

Pagenhart, P. (1994), '"The Very House of Difference": Toward a More Queerly Defined Multiculturalism', in L. Garber (ed.), *Tilting the Tower*.

Pellegrini, A. (1994), 'There's No Place Like Home? Lesbian Studies and the Classics', in L. Garber (ed.), *Tilting the Tower*.

—— and Franklin, P.B. (1996), 'Queer Collaborations: Feminist Pedagogy', in B. Zimmerman and T.A.H. McNaron (eds), *The New Lesbian Studies*.

Wilton, T. (1995), *Lesbian Studies: Setting an Agenda* (London and New York: Routledge).

Zimmerman, B. (1982), 'One Out of Thirty: Lesbianism in Women's Studies Textbooks', in M. Cruikshank (ed.), *Lesbian Studies: Present and Future*.

—— (1993/1981), 'What Has Never Been: An Overview of Lesbian Feminist Criticism', in S.J. Wolfe and J. Penelope (eds), *Sexual Practice, Textual Theory: Lesbian Cultural Criticism* (Cambridge, MA and Oxford: Blackwell).

—— (1996), 'Placing Lesbians', in B. Zimmerman and T.A.H. McNaron (eds), *The New Lesbian Studies*.

—— (1997), '"Confessions" of a Lesbian Feminist', in D. Heller (ed.), *Cross Purposes: Lesbians, Feminists, and the Limits of Alliance* (Bloomington and Indianapolis, IN: Indiana University Press).

—— (2007), 'A Lesbian-Feminist Journey through Queer Nation', in N. Giffney and K. O'Donnell (eds), *Twenty-First Century Lesbian Studies*.

—— and McNaron, T.A.H. (eds) (1996), *The New Lesbian Studies: Into the Twenty-First Century* (New York: The Feminist Press).

Zita, J.N. (1994), 'Gay and Lesbian Studies: Yet Another Unhappy Marriage?', in L. Garber (ed.) *Tilting the Tower*.

Making it Like a Drag King:
Female-to-Male Masculinity
and the Trans Culture of Boyhood

Bobby Noble

The emerging field of masculinity studies in Canada, as evidenced by the series of intriguing papers presented at the 'Making it Like a Man: Masculinities in Canadian Arts and Cultures' conference, is a fascinating site of complexity, interdisciplinarity and queerness.[1] Topics covered at the conference ranged from narratives of nation through the trope of the lumberjack and canoeist, to masculinity in Canadian hockey culture, to depictions of the 'geek' in film; each of the papers sought to challenge heteronormative and hegemonic ideas about masculinity and many accomplished this goal. But what intrigued me, as a female-to-male transsexual man sitting in the audience, was the one singular, essentialist thread that ran through each session I attended: that is, of course, that 'man' as a cultural description, even while it was being deconstructed as a heteronormative gender, was assumed to be secured or guaranteed by the supposedly self-evident body (read: the penis). This chapter seeks to deconstruct that assumption and offer instead one intersecting site of masculinity in Canadian cultural production where that assumption is directly challenged: that site is, of course, female and transsexual masculinities.[2] This is part of two larger projects which are investigating the existence of a paradigm shift in thinking sex

---

1   10–12 June 2004, Regina, Saskatchewan. Acknowledgements and thanks are due to David Garneau, Stephen McClatchie, Christine Ramsay and Angela Stukator, for a truly successful and memorable event.

2   While sometimes looking similar as cross-identified gender embodiments, there are important differences between female and transsexual masculinity. Female to male transsexual masculinity (often known as FtM) usually connotes body modification (hormones and surgical procedures) and a sexed identity that is understood as masculine regardless of the degree of changes to the body. Female masculinity connotes a complex gender identification, although in this case female sexed embodiment is often read as the backdrop or ground of the masculine even as it may well signal an ambivalence at the core of what that embodiment means or how it is or is not communicated. As a concept, the phrase 'female masculinity' comes into existence with the work of Judith

as the ground of gender difference (Noble 2006). Where the essentialist belief in unique and biologically distinct sexes, evidenced by sexed genitals, has been used to organise gender systems, many theorists, including Anne Fausto-Sterling and Judith Butler, are suggesting that how we define the ground of gender, that is, how we define and categorise sex itself, may well be within the realm of the social, cultural, discursive and hence, political (Fausto-Sterling 2000; Butler 1993). Such reconceptualisations of sex then force us to ask different kinds of questions about the mechanisms we use to secure gender.

This chapter offers the concept of post-queer genders – genders without genitals, to borrow a phrase (Jones 2003) – as one possible means by which we might conceive of genders differently. By post-queer I do not necessarily refer to a time beyond or after the end of queer social locations. Western cultures remain deeply entrenched within heteronormativity and its need for essentialised gender. Instead, I query the political utility of the concept of queer with its attendant histories associating it with 'gay and lesbian'. The advent of queer theory attempted to circumvent the normativities and stabilities of 'gay and lesbian' identity by tracking queer anti-identity locations instead (De Lauretis 1991). Queer, however, has not strayed far enough off that course to be functional with precision. Moreover, with the advent of transsexual, intersexual and transgender (where each of these have to be understood as different from one another) activism and now scholarship, queer's connotative work as lesbian and gay seems all the more limited. Instead, the idea of post-queer incoherence marks the ways that gender and sex are now so permanently ruptured that one can no longer be the guarantee or conveyor of the other. These genders, defined outside of the terms of essentialist sexed embodiment, then, are genders that not only matter in the larger scheme of things; but they are genders which defy the categorical and determinist imperatives of matter. That is, such imperatives classify sexed bodies as he, she or it. To matter as a human being, then, means occupying one of only two pronouns that delimit sex as a condition of human-ness.

To illustrate that argument I look at the paradoxes and incoherences in embodiment for female-to-male transsexual masculinity, some drag king performances, but I also offer a reading of each through a Canadian film screened at the conference, Ileana Pietrobruno's queer, sexy romp through female and female-to-male transsexual masculinities, *Girl King* (2003), which I also locate in this de-phallicised space of No Man's Land. By using the term 'de-phallicised' I want to suggest that *Girl King*, and the drag king as well as transsexual cultures it both evokes and parodies, points towards a significant re-conceptualisation of masculinity as no longer overdetermined by the penis as the privileged phallic signifier or ground of power. While the penis and the phallus are to be considered as two separate things, where the phallus functions as a cultural icon sometimes signalled by the penis, but not always, then FtM trans bodies have the potential to undo both. They answer two different kinds of articulations associated with the

---

Halberstam and replaces the term 'butch' in academic discourse but not always in everyday systems of speech and identification.

phallic mapping of gender difference as sex difference: does thinking differently about difference increase discursive visibility for both drag kings and transsexual masculinity within fields such masculinity studies, but also, ironically enough, how might it contest the hypervisibility of these same subjects in queer contexts as the privileged trope of gender queerness? Pietrobruno's pastiche, *Girl King*, intervenes in both articulations with a post-queer sexual romp, hailing the arrival of new gender and sexual vocabularies and yet de-phallicising the boy (drag) king[3] at the same time. In many ways, the curious silence surrounding this film at the conference was indicative of its success and yet unintelligibility in this context still grounded in essentialised grammars.

The scholarship presented at the 'Making it Like a Man' conference was groundbreaking and absolutely vital to the continuing deconstruction of conservative gender systems in a Canadian context. Central to any social constructionist reading of masculinity in the late twentieth century lies a pernicious and yet very productive contradiction: to render masculinity as a self-conscious and mediated subjectivity is to call the naturalised heteronormativity of that identification into question. This contradiction requires an equally tenacious remedy. Homi Bhabha begins to map that remedy when he writes:

> *To speak of masculinity in general must be avoided at all costs. It is as a discourse of self-generation, reproduced over the generations in patrilineal perpetuity, that masculinity [has always sought] to make a name for itself.* (1995, 58)

That name, he suggests along with Butler, is one that exceeds its referent and yet is a name that is bound up with the fictionality of that referent in the same moment. By articulating this contradiction, Bhabha rehearses the two primary axioms which have conditioned the problematics of masculinity studies: the masculine is itself a highly mediated social product; and the pronoun of this new invisible man, what Bhabha calls the masculinist signature of 'He', remain a free floating signifier with no stable referent or fixed content. Configurations of masculinity at the conference responded brilliantly to the first; but completely forgot, or else disavowed, socially produced corporeality as the ground of the second.

Even so, the remedy to this forgetting is equally always already dependent upon this larger problematic for its condition of possibility. 'The "I" who would oppose its construction', Butler told us in *Gender Trouble*:

> *... is always in some sense drawing from that construction to articulate its opposition; further, the 'I' draws what is called its agency in part through*

---

3   Drag kings are performers who stage imitations of masculinity and are mostly 'female' embodied although more recently, female-to-male transsexual and transgendered men can also be counted amongst performing kings. Like male-to-female drag cultures, 'male impersonation' has a uniquely queer and theatrical history with origins in butch-femme sub-cultural settings.

> *being implicated in the very relations of power that it seeks to oppose. To be implicated in the relations of power, indeed, enabled by the relations of power that 'I' opposes is not, as a consequence, to be reducible to their existing forms. (1990, 123)*

She reminds us that thinking in excess of social construction renders any subject, and masculinity in particular, incommensurate with self-knowledge or unable to know that which makes it it/self. Self-consciousness, in other words, is not in and of itself the remedy, as consciousness is conditioned by language and is a product of language all at the same time. Curiously, then, it is often what the subject cannot know just yet that conditions what it can know. Two points here: these reconfigurations of our 'I's' are always already ambivalent; and truer knowledge of self exists in excess of what we think we know for sure. Sedgwick puts this in a much simpler way: sometimes, masculinity has nothing to do with men (1995, 12).

The work I want to do in this chapter is located at the meeting point of these ambivalent contradictions and paradoxes – a space I am hailing as yet another No Man's Land. To ignore Sedgwick's axiom is to give credence to the argument that the contours of the body are determined by flesh rather than by discourse and signification, again something that the simile in the title of the 'Making it *Like* a Man' conference invited even as it was refused by the assumptions of many of the papers. If we cannot deny or disavow masculinity, as Bhabha suggests we cannot, then what we can do, within the larger ideological and discursive economies of essentialism, racism and heteronormativity, is disturb, or trouble its manifest destiny, deny, at the very least, its invisibility. By drawing attention to masculinity as a free-floating signifier we rearticulate it, again to quote Bhabha as a prosthetic subject. Bhabha uses the notion of masculinity as prosthesis – a 'prefixing' of the rules of gender and sexuality to cloak or hide a lack-in-being – to denaturalise masculine and to frustrate its articulations. Thus, the topic of this chapter is not necessarily masculinity as we have known it, but instead it is masculinity as we often cannot know, that is away from the conventionally defined male body (Halberstam 1998, 1). I suggest that we will find masculinity where it exists in excess of its essentialised materiality, as the (female to male transsexual) FtM boy, or the lesbian butch boy, or the tranny boy; these are, in fact, troubling prosthetic-boys indeed.

This subject has been the topic of a particularly heated border war in feminism and queer theory for some time. That there are triangulated border wars between feminism, lesbian masculinity and female to male transsexual masculinity (FtMs) is by now almost cliché. Such a belief – that thinking masculinity (trans or otherwise) in the context of feminism is its undoing – is the grammar of some continued feminist scholarship, for instance Tania Modleski's book, *Feminism Without Women* (1991) as well as those within queer theory. Where feminism has been slow to take up trans issues, queer theory has almost made them a fetish. There are some exceptions in feminist theory: queer theorist Robyn Wiegman (2006), Jay Sennett's new collection (2006) and, in a Canadian context, feminist work by theorists such as Eleanor MacDonald (1998) and Krista Scott-Dixon (2006) have each, from different disciplines, articulated the necessity of taking up queer theory, transsexuality and feminist theory as vital to the accomplishment of the other. Queer theorist Judith Halberstam and trans theorist C. Jacob Hale document similar border skirmishes in their collaboratively produced essay, 'Butch/FtM Border Wars' (1998), only they examine these border wars as they emerge between transsexual/transgender politics and queer theory. Halberstam, in particular, queried the space between lesbian masculinity and transsexual men in an earlier essay, 'F2M: The Making of Female Masculinity' (1994), and generated a great deal of debate when she argued that within postmodern economies of gender, all genders are 'fictions of a body talking its own shape ... for some an outfit can be changed; for others skin must be resewn. There are no transsexuals' (1994, 212). What Halberstam accomplished in the early work – suggesting that what has been at stake in the border wars are the terms of gendered embodiment itself – is undone by her later work where she resorts to categorical determinism and taxonomies when coining the phrase 'female masculinity'.

Clearly, what interests me about these debates is less the veracity or authenticity of these conversations (presuming such things are even possible or valued) but rather the way that these terms flag shared histories of resisting hegemonic ideas about gender and sexuality. That is, these movements – feminism, gay, lesbian, bisexual movements, the pro-feminist men's movement, anti-racism movements and trans movements – each remind us that becoming a self is a socially and discursively overdetermined process that is on-going, contingent, non-foundational and self-regenerating but always already in conversation with representation, language being one of the first representational systems. Articulating one's self as a subject (engendered, racialised, sexed, nationed, classed and so on) is the process through which we learn to identify our 'I' relative to bodies, power grids, as well as culturally available discursive and representational categories, like pronouns, and then always already attempt to become that configuration. Bound within this process are, of course, two axioms which are coterminous with those of feminism, queer theory and masculinity studies: first, not all 'selves' are commensurate with, and reducible to, hegemonically intelligible bodies, categories, pronouns and, indeed, bodies; and second, not all incongruities are equal and although we cannot always know in advance how they will be different, we certainly need to anticipate and correct for the work these differences are doing within our social justice movements (Sedgwick 1990, 27).

These incongruities amongst the subjects flagged by the phrase female masculinity are radically de-emphasised in Halberstam's extremely important book *Female Masculinity* (1998). *FM* makes several important interventions in sexuality and gender studies. First, after coining the phrase female masculinity, which works through juxtaposition – in other words through categorical indeterminacy – Halberstam's work theorises female masculinity as distinct from male masculinity, or as she says in an oft-quoted expression, 'conceptualising masculinity without men' (1998, 2). In the end, she wants to make masculinity safe for women and girls, even heterosexual women, so that with more gender freedom, perhaps even men will be able to re-create masculinity using her model of female masculinity.

Halberstam's work seems to be predicated upon a rupture or distinction between 'masculinity' and 'men' although she certainly promises more than she provides. For instance, in wanting to make masculinity workable for women and girls, and while only theorising female embodied masculinity, Halberstam generates a categorical imperative by taxonomising female masculinities. What Halberstam's categorical imperative inevitably accomplishes is that it produces an odd alignment of sex and gender which should be most powerful when it refuses such alignments altogether. Such conceptual oddities continue in her recent book. In a *Queer Time and Place: Transgender Bodies, Subcultural Lives* (2005), such categorical determinism, while spun around concepts of space and temporality, continues to fold transgendered bodies into queer paradigms. Post-queer logics, like those I'm advocating here, would query such analytical moves. On the one hand, Halberstam produces fascinating and important readings of transgender figures like Brandon Teena and Billy Tipton. But on the other, her use of queer continues to align its work with that accomplished by 'lesbian and gay' albeit with transgender stirred into the mix. Such operations of 'add and stir queer theory' – illustrated textually in Halberstam's work through an insistence on proximity of queerness rather than trans rupture of categorical paradigms – outs and stabilises that transgendered body through regimes of normative essentialisms. One example suffices here: if the transgendered body, as Halberstam wants to claim, can mark the limits of queer spatiality, then why undo such work by claiming someone like Brandon Teena as 'a young woman who passed successfully as a man' (2005, 48). Again, Halberstam offers vital caveats about the kinds of work accomplished when transgendered folks can no longer self-narrate. Brandon's self-identifications within trans paradigms remain unknowable. But writing the same identification of Brandon, for instance, as a 'young transgendered person' instead of 'young woman who passed a man' would clearly signal a willingness to read beyond binarised configurations of sex. If, as Halberstam goes on to argue, transgender as a term is used to 'account for the cross-identification experiences' of folks who 'choose among the options of body modification, social presentation, and legal recognition available to them' (2005, 53), then why gender Brandon, or any FtM transgendered person according to the body? Does a man only become a man if he acquires a surgically produced penis at exorbitant cost and guaranteed failure even where such surgeries exist? Does a transgendered woman who has not had male to female reassignment surgery, but who 'passes' in every other way, continue to be a man within these frameworks? Could she be described as a man passing as a woman? What's at stake in such categorical reductions? To phrase this differently, such categorical imperatives and deployments of transgendered as queer do similar kinds of work that 'men' does within discourses of essentialism. That is, it is successful as both an ideology and as a signifier, when the referent it imagines itself marking is the male body, complete with penis as supposedly self-evident referent. If, however, the term 'masculinity' accomplishes its work, then 'men' no longer must reference a self-evident penis. 'Men' collapses the distinction between gender and sex whereas 'masculinity' not only reasserts it (arguing that one does not cause the other), but suggests that the possession of a conventionally defined penis has nothing to do with securing manhood. Masculinity is detached from categorical economies. So, when we posit that sometimes masculinity has nothing to do with men, we are not necessarily arguing literally: 'that female masculinity isn't related to male masculinity'. Instead, the argument is that since masculinity now has nothing to do with the male body as it has been conventionally defined, both trans and female masculinity are each non-derivative forms of manhood where that subject is no longer secured or privileged by the body as it has been conventionally mapped. But neither is synonymous with nor reducible to the other.

Trans and female masculinities are not the only subjects seeking to destabilise phallic power that secures manhood. There are plenty of moments in mainstream North American popular culture where we see a masculinity rewriting itself through the trope of the boy. Two scholarly texts detail the emerging discourses – both popular and literary – shaping the constructions of boyhood.

In the chapter, 'Why Boys are Not Men', from his book *Masked Men: Masculinity and the Movies in the Fifties* (1997), Steven Cohan looks at the history of boys and men in Hollywood, suggesting that the boy first appeared in the films and film cultures surrounding the new 1950s boys of Hollywood. Tracing the emergence of what tough-guy John Wayne dubbed the 'trembling, torn T-shirt types' – Marlon Brando, Montgomery Clift, James Dean, Sal Mineo, Paul Newman – through the postwar era, Cohan posits that Hollywood crystallised a new boy-man. 'One has only to recall', argues Cohan:

> ... *the galvanising early screen appearances of the young Clift and Brando to see how readily imagery of a youthful male body, not only beautiful to behold but also highly theatricalised, marked out the erotic appeal of these new young actors within the star system, underscoring their alienation from the screen's more traditional representations of masculinity.* (1997, 203)

What appealed to mainstream American culture then was precisely this notion of boyishness. Such a new look challenged the conflation of sexuality and gender that supported a symbolic economy in which 'boys' were made legible and thinkable opposites of 'men'. The result of this open rejection of the imperatives of masculinity (grow up and be a 'real' man) was an erotic performance or impersonation which productively always fell short of the original. In falling short, that is, in refusing to be all that a man was supposed to be, the boy becomes a viable male subject.

What was moreover particularly compelling about the boy was signalled by Wayne's adjective 'trembling'. The term rightly suggested a conflation of that new look with an emotionality and vulnerability. Where old-guard actors like Wayne embodied virility and hyper-manhood, stars like Brando and Dean interiorised masculinity, converting social nonconformity and rebelliousness into inner torment and emotional excess. Where Wayne-esque Hollywood he-men wore masculinity on the outside as action, toughness and phallic power, the Brando and Dean types resisted such exteriorisations of masculinity in favour of a look synonymous with failed manhood: perpetual boyhood. The boy, then, became a positively gender-conflicted concept that at once signified failed masculinity and an excess of masculinity, disturbing the ease with which Hollywood's men equated sexual potency with hypermasculinity.

But most relevant for those of us studying drag king cultures is Cohan's assertion that these new boys of Hollywood were far more theatrical and theatricalised than their predecessors. If we agree that this boy is theatricalised, and by implication, denaturalised, soft, always already stylised, anti-heteronormative in his orientation to the imperatives of masculinity (that is, signalling their ideological work), then could we also agree, perhaps, that whether he appears on stage in a lesbian bar, or appears in a fag bathhouse, or in a (bio-)boy band, that this subject is always already trans-gendered? That is, I want to claim him as trans because of the way in which he is working his gender identity against the imperatives and expectations overdetermined by his body (sex); is this thinkable at all within the context of masculinity studies to date? Rather than suggest that the boy has simply failed in his gender, it is much more productive to suggest that these failures, in fact, are evidence of the theatricalisation, and hence denaturalisation, of the boy. Isn't part of the appeal of boyishness precisely masculine feminisation? In other words, part of the appeal of boyishness is its promise of phallic power and its resistance of masculinist heteronormative imperatives.

This was something articulated in the early days of the feminist men's movement by John Stoltenberg in his book called *Refusing to Be a Man* (1990). But it continues to be articulated through more recent work on the boy as well. For instance, Kenneth B. Kidd's book *Making American Boys: Boyology and the Feral Tale* (2004) makes significant discursive delineations between the cultures of boyhood (preoccupations he identifies as 'boyology'), articulations of 'effeminacy' and non-normative masculinities. Kidd's work argues that the figure of the boy itself has always functioned as a prototype of adult masculinity, all the more so when that boy is foiled in narrative by his feral other or the mythological wild boy (2004, 6). The lessons of this creature, Kidd argues, are significant to mark culture's transformation of this potentiality from 'nature to culture, from bestiality to humanity, from homosocial pack life to individual self-reliance and heterosexual prowess – that is, from boyhood to manhood' (2004, 7). Moreover, Kidd cites the work of Eve Kosofsky Sedgwick in 'How to Bring Your Kids Up Gay: The War on Effeminate Boys' (1993) to map the moral panics overdetermining gender conformity for the heterosexual as well as the gay boy: 'The sissy boy ... serves as the haunting object, not only of heteronormative masculinity but also of some gay-affirmative, gender-separatist discourse (in which the gay man is a "man's man")' (1993, 187). One only need notice the scorn and ridicule meted out to the admittedly complicated engendering of the metrosexual as a figure of failed normativity to take the measure of such gender panics. All the more potent, then, is the figure of the boy that resists such teleologies, as a boy. The appeal of the boy is not necessarily a confusion of gender imperatives but the potential for their refusal. And this is precisely where this instance of masculine feminisation overlaps with female masculinity: boys paradoxically threaten to become men while categorically rarely materialising, and more often than not, refusing that identity outright.

One other subject who resides in No Man's Land – or, one marked by the potential at least to refuse to become a man – has to be, of course, female to male transsexual men. This group of 'men' share with lesbian 'bois', bio-boys and drag kings an identity which I'm calling post-queer – that is, trans-gendered and/or trans-sexual but not gay and/or lesbian subjects who are, by definition, newly configured masculine subjects and bodies who deconstruct – in the flesh – the terms of hegemonic gendered embodiment. The subjects I'm theorising in No Man's Land are subjects who find power not by feigning indifference but rather by cultivating proximity, identification and similarity with other subjects of masculinity. The argument that female masculinity does not notice, or is not influenced by, or does not reciprocate or return the gaze to male masculinity cannot be supported.[4] As evident in the independent short film *Straight Boy Lessons* (2000), for example, almost each instance of transsexual masculinity is unquestioningly informed, influenced, mentored and otherwise shaped to become itself from other men in shared social, economic or racialised spaces. *Straight Boy Lessons* is a short film which details the top ten lessons given to a newly transitioned FtM by his mentor, Bo, a middle-aged, working-class trucker. The lessons instruct the young FtM Ray on what to expect now that he's stepped into spaces of masculine embodiment. The visual images accompanying the list include tips on shaving and tying ties, which link the behavioural lessons with the visualities of masculinity. Such visual economies remind us that the reading of a body as gendered involves presenting gender signifiers or cues within these particular economies where those signs accumulate toward the appearance of a precisely articulated and coherently gendered body. Suzanna J. Kessler and Wendy McKenna suggest something similar about gender in their early work, *Gender: An Ethnomethodological Approach* (1978). They argue that the perception of a fixed gender role is just that: an ideological perception interactionally coded by the external and hegemonic signifiers of gender. 'Gender attribution of a complex, interactive process', they write, 'involving the person making the attribution and the person she/he is making the attribution about' (1978, 6).

If Kessler and McKenna are right, then developing a critical practice as a transsexual man, however, means learning to read for those signifiers and then duplicating many of them to create an illusion of a gendered body. It also means occupying the permanent space of not just becoming but failing to become; that is, it is a permanent place of modulation of what came before by what comes after, never fully accomplishing either as an essentialist stable 'reality' but also of permanently destabilising that fiction. For me, as a transsexual man with a long history as a lesbian activist, this permanent state of becoming means also failing to become the kind of hegemonic man privileged in our culture. I have lived for almost 30-some years as a lesbian feminist first and this training ground has made

---

4   'Such affirmations [of female masculinity] begin not by subverting masculine power or taking up a position against masculine power but by turning a blind eye to conventional masculinities and refusing to engage … power may inhere within different forms of refusal: "Well, I do not care"' (Halberstam 1998, 9).

me, in some ways, a strategically failed heterosexual man. Along with many other very political pro-feminist men, I've refused, and continue to refuse, the privileges of becoming a man in the hegemonic ways this category is constructed. Instead, I've opted to occupy the pre-man space of boy/boi, a space of productive failure. I've done this by, among other things, maintaining the discursive space of 'F' on my driver's license, living and working in lesbian and queer circles, and working against white supremacy, capitalism and so on. These juxtapositions between presentation and that 'F', along with a categorical refusal to be fully 'manned' either in language (for me, in a refusal to be named Bob or Robert versus my boi name of Bobby), or in body, signal the critical, political but also discursive space of transsexual masculinity for many guys outside of the clinical and medicalised treatment of transsexual bodies. This often puts me, in daily practice, into some very interesting positions where my presentation trumps the 'F' but my political refusal of manhood allows me a daily deconstructive practice that aggressively refuses the hegemonic fantasy of white 'manhood'. There are many different ways of being masculine; there are many different subject positions available for men, some of which have more power than others. If this is true, then there are many different subject positions for FtMs to transition into (masculinity as modulated by power). As a tranny-boi it is my constant practice to refuse that hegemonic bargain. What I seek as a trans-man is categorical indeterminacy or in-coherence rather than categorical privilege.

One of the crucial triangulations that I'm seeking here is the way in which the figure of the boy/boi functions as a hybrid, anti-essentialist hinge point between three different kinds of resisting masculinities: lesbian boy, transsexual boy, drag king boy. This figure remakes manhood and gives us new vocabularies which are not just anti-essentialising but, simultaneously, a-essentialist; that is, they draw our attention to the ways that we remake gender everyday as fiction through our reading practices and our desires. Each of these is put on display in Ileana Pietrobruno's film *Girl King* (2002). One of the ways of accounting for the silence about this film is the fact that it is, deliberately and productively so, confusing in its gender politics. Written and directed by a female film-maker, the film's primary narrative tension spins around a quest by drag king pirates for their queen's Koilos, or source of all pleasures and harmony on her island. The main character is named, of course, Butch, who must, if he fails to recover the Koilos, give up his own stone butch virginity to Queen as his punishment. If that wasn't incentive enough, Queen is holding hostage Butch's love interest, the feisty femme Claudia, who herself decides not to wait for rescue. Claudia herself dons pirate garb and passes as one of Butch's sexy shipmates sailing with Captain Candy in search of Queen's Koilos. In the end, her Koilos is retrieved from the king who stole it; the king is himself, or so we discover through a series of turns, a drag king who actually gave birth to but eventually abandoned Butch who was washed ashore, as an infant, in a treasure chest. If we can assume a film has two audiences (one *to whom* it is directed, one *for whom* it is made), then *Girl King* is *directed at* female masculinity, trans masculinity and drag kings, but *for* a queer femme audience. That is to say, the film parodies a culture of female and trans masculinities, and sometimes, even queers gay masculinities (within each of which I am placing drag king cultures) but for the pleasures, and from the point of view, of queer femininities. The primary cultures parodied though are drag king cultures and female masculinities. But like any parody, it has much to tell us about each.

Playing on several different narratives, including the boy's swashbuckling pirate adventure narrative, the quest motif and a search-for-origins story, *Girl King* situates the drag king himself as a central element of each of these narrative structures. Central to the work that drag king cultures do to and through masculinity are three crucial processes: recognition and misrecognition, identification but simultaneous disidentification, and the queering of heteronormative sexual systems through gender play. What such queerings do is trouble heteronormativity by working gender against compulsory heterosexuality in the first place. Queering heteronormativity means, in some senses, destabilising presumptions of naturally occurring gendered essences. The effect is a dis-orienting visual space where trans-sexed bodies and gendered desire no longer register within a simplistic dichotomous gay versus straight economy. Let me take each of these in turn. First, recognition and misrecognition. One of the key pleasures of drag king performances depends upon recognition of the contradiction at their source: that is, the recognition of a supposedly stable sexed body in distinction with the performance of masculinity written on to it. Part of this pleasure is irony, yes, but so too are the pleasures of the incongruousness of the spectacle itself. The performances of drag kings permanently rupture masculinity from the male body and reconfigure masculinity as a series of signifiers performable by anyone who can get the arrangement right. We see this in *Girl King*, for instance, when Claudia cross-dresses as a boy or when Captain Candy teaches Butch how to *make it more like a man*: prosthetics such as clothing, the appearance of facial hair, the swagger, facial expressions and so on each together accrue toward a masculine persona so that the fictional 'truth' of the performance outweighs its supposedly authentic fictionality. The pleasures of drag kinging, indeed, of female masculinity writ large, lie somewhere between each pole. This is precisely what is so acutely ironic about *Girl King*; that is, its clever overlapping of form and content. Drag kings themselves perform a *pirated* version of masculinity, one plundered and, to pun on the term pirate itself, 'stolen' and used without authorisation. Pirating is such a powerful trope in postmodernity that theorists such as Jean Baudrillard (1995) have suggested that we've pirated so much, so thoroughly, that 'originals' are no longer discernable or even knowable. We use the trope of pirating in so many places; why not use it as a trope of masculinity? Why cling so tenaciously to the idea of an essential (read biological) masculinity if not only to maintain hegemonic power, albeit unconsciously? Pirating occurs as the narrative structure of *Girl King*, yes, as well as in the centralising of a drag king as the main character. But the formal visual structure itself is a performative pastiche of pirating. A multitude of images, motifs and tropes are sutured together, with sutures in full sight, from many different sources, including lesbian scenes from heterosexual male porn, to recontextualise and by implication remake their now irreverent and tenacious meaning.

Similarly, the pleasures involved in performing masculinity lie in their ambivalent positionings between two further poles: identification and disidentification. Numerous drag kings have detailed the degree to which they both identify with masculinity as a gender which hails them far more than conventional femininity does. At the same time, those hailings take place with a critical distance from conventionally defined male bodies (Noble et al. 2003; Halberstam and Volcano 1999). So, in the same way that boy cultures threaten to emerge with phallic failure, the difference between 'boy' and 'man' spins around the degree to which each materialises that power as potentiality. Similarly, female to male transsexual men also productively *become* that phallic male body even as they, at the same time, fully inhabit the fictional performance of that body (the way we see Butch, Captain Candy and even Claudia perform truthful lies about their bodies in *Girl King*). More than these examples, though, drag kings have as a goal the manipulation of the illusion of embodiment, a prosthetic illusion which, as we have seen already, tells a more interesting truth about the complexities of identification and disidentification than do supposedly 'actual' bodies.

Sailor is a fascinating example of the type of corporeal destabilisations that I'm drawing out in this chapter. One of the curious things about these destabilisations – that is, of masculinity from the essentialised male body – is that they are launched – and, by implication, can be restabilised – by desire. In many ways, the entire plot of *Girl King* is about desire but also about fantasy as the scene of those desires. Both the form and content stage fantasy for us: it takes place on a nowhere beach, its characters have names like 'Butch' and 'Sailor', spliced in to this swashbuckling, dress-up fantasy are queer appropriations from heterosexual 'lesbian' porn mixed with scenes from gender play in lesbian porn, and the narrative crisis itself spins around whether or not Butch can retrieve Queen's Koilos or else give up his stone, impenetrable virginity to (femme top) Queen as punishment for failing in his quest. Moreover, we see gay male desire equally parodied here as Butch and Claudia (passing as a boy) also flirt with phallic objects and eventually have sex dressed as two male shipmates, having both gay sex and lesbian sex at exactly the same moment. These are indeed scenes of queer(ed) desire. But it isn't until the very butch Captain Candy hooks up with Sailor, unbeknownst to Captain Candy, a male-to-female trans-femme (in this context, Sailor is passing as a woman but also as a lesbian femme sharing the quest for Queen's Koilos) that desire here is what I'm calling post-queer, that is, literally, off the gender maps as we currently know them.

Captain Candy is drawn to a kind of softness in Sailor which he mistakes for biological femininity. Sailor seems also drawn to Captain Candy's gender and it is this mutuality that makes their desires heterogendered but not heteronormative. That is, they each desire that their respective object choices be of a different gender even as the supposed 'sex' of that gender no longer matters. But this form of 'hetero-gender-sexuality' does not add up to anything 'normative', hetero- or otherwise. For example, it isn't until after they've made initial sexual and physical contact with each other that Captain Candy eventually discovers what seems to be a 'real' penis attached to Sailor's otherwise very feminine body. Of course, Candy disavows his attraction but after some convincing, Candy resigns himself to its presence and asks, 'Ok, how does this thing work?' The fascinating thing here, of course, is the queerness but also the post-queerness of this scene of desire. Each partner is performing a gender opposite to that dictated by their respective body parts, but the presence of these supposedly self-evidently sexed bodies does not in any way undo their genders. In fact, the illogical contradictions are quickly forgotten and almost virtually impossible to reconcile even in language. For instance, notice the way that the logic underwriting the relation between bodies and genders is thoroughly undone in the question that begs to be asked about their off-screen genital sexual contact: if his (Captain Candy's) vagina has contact with her (Sailor's) penis, does that contact make this heterosexual sex? If so, is every instance of 'heterosexual' sex heteronormative? Clearly, the answer has to be no, not at all. The gendered meanings of each character trumps what the sex/gender system wants to inscribe onto their bodies. In fact, we could push this question even further: which words and/or categories are we going to use to describe this sexual scene: two men? Two women? A man and a woman? Which one is which? This is a scene of what I call post-queer trans desire. As a descriptor, 'queer' cannot quite hold the complexity of these bodies, genders and desires working the way they do. Each seems to be undone by the destabilisation of the other. For instance, 'lesbian' and 'gay' may well be secured by the supposed self-evidence of the sexed bodies of both partners. Similarly, 'heterosexuality' is secured by the opposite sexed bodies of the partners. But in this scene, bodies, genders and sex acts do not map neatly onto each other. They are instead incoherent and post-queer where the logic defies even a simple queering of their attraction for each other. These are desires that defy logic, bodies and the grammars of both the sex/gender system and even many of the attempts, well-meaning as they are, to deconstruct 'gender' difference. What we are left with, then, is a completely new relation between bodies and identities, one that I referred to earlier as genders without genitals, or, to quote the title of my book, *Masculinities without Men* (2004). In that book, I mapped a genealogy of contemporary female and transsexual masculinity through early twentieth century and late nineteenth century discourse and fiction. In *Sons of the Movement* (2006), I argue that these new ways of thinking productively about bodies, sexualities and genders pose interesting and exciting challenges for feminist practices seeking to keep up with the politics and proliferation of incoherent forms of embodiment, including the reconceptualisations of masculinity. Future research will need to account in much more focused and nuanced ways for the particular challenges posed by and through these bodies for our paradigms of sexuality and pleasure. These new trans-genders, I suggest, will continue to mark an important paradigm shift and it is that shift we need to map if we want to re-make a masculinity that can really matter.

Suggested Further Reading

Fausto-Sterling, A. (2000), *Sexing the Body: Gender Politics and the Construction of Sexuality* (New York: Basic Books).
Green, J. (2004), *Becoming a Visible Man* (Nashville, TN: Vanderbilt University Press).
LeBesco, K., Troka, D. and Noble, J.B. (eds) (2002), *The Drag King Anthology* (New York: Harrington Park Press).
Scott-Dixon, K. (ed.) (2006), *Trans/Forming Feminisms: Transfeminist Voices Speak Out* (Vancouver: Sumach Press).
Sennett, J. (ed.) (2006), *Self-Organizing Men: Conscious Masculinities in Time and Space* (Ypsilanti, MI: Homofactus Press).

References

Baudrillard, J. (1995), *Simulacra and Simulation*, trans. S. Glaser (Ann Arbor, MI: University of Michigan Press).
Bhabha, H. (1995), 'Are You a Man or a Mouse', in M. Berger, B. Wallis and S. Watson (eds), *Constructing Masculinity* (New York and London: Routledge).
Butler, J. (1990), *Gender Trouble: Feminism and the Subversion of Identity* (New York: Routledge).
—— (1993), *Bodies That Matter: On the Discursive Limits of 'Sex'* (New York: Routledge).
Cohan, S. (1997), *Masked Men: Masculinity and the Movies in the Fifties* (Bloomington and Indianapolis, IN: Indiana University Press).
De Lauretis, T. (ed.) (1991), 'Queer Theory: Lesbian and Gay Sexualities: An Introduction', *differences: A Journal of Feminist Cultural Studies* 3:2, iii–xviii.
Fausto-Sterling, A. (2000), *Sexing the Body: Gender Politics and the Construction of Sexuality* (New York: Basic Books).
Girl King (2003), dir. I. Pietrobruno [feature film].
Halberstam, J. (1994), 'F2M: The Making of Female Masculinity', in L. Doan (ed.) (1994), *The Lesbian Premodern* (New York: Columbia University Press).
—— (1998), *Female Masculinity* (Durham, NC and London: Duke University Press).
—— (2005), *In a Queer Time and Place: Transgender Subjectivities, Subcultural Lives* (New York: New York University Press).
—— and Hale, C.J. (1998), 'Butch/FtM Border Wars: A Note on Collaboration', *GLQ: A Journal of Lesbian and Gay Studies* 4:2, 283–5.
—— and LaGrace Volcano, D. (1999), *The Drag King Book* (London: Serpent's Tail).
Jones, J. (2003), '"Hedwig's Six Inches: Gender Without Genitals" Other: Pop Culture and Politics for the New Outcasts', http://www.othermag.org/content/hedwig.php (accessed 17 March 2008).

Kessler, S.J. and McKenna, W. (1978), *Gender: An Ethnomethodological Approach* (Chicago, IL: University of Chicago Press).

Kidd, K.B. (2004), *Making American Boys: Boyology and the Feral Tale* (Minneapolis, MN and London: University of Minnesota Press).

MacDonald, E. (1998), 'Critical Identities: Rethinking Feminism through Transgender Politics', *Atlantis* 23:1, 3–12.

Modleski, T. (1991), *Feminism without Women* (New York and London: Routledge).

Noble, J.B. (2004), *Masculinities without Men? Female Masculinity in Twentieth-Century Fictions* (Toronto: University of British Columbia Press).

—— (2006), *Sons of the Movement: FtMs Risking Incoherence on a Post-Queer Cultural Landscape* (Toronto: Women's Press of Canada).

—— Troka, D.J. and LeBesco, K. (2003), *The Drag King Anthology* (New York: Harrington Park Press).

Scott-Dixon, K. (ed.) (2006), *Trans-Forming Feminisms: Trans-Feminist Voices Speak Out* (Vancouver: Sumach Press).

Sedgwick, E.K. (1990), *Epistemology of the Closet* (Berkeley, CA: University of California Press).

—— (1993), 'How to Bring Your Kids Up Gay: The War on Effeminate Boys', in *Tendencies* (Durham, NC and London: Duke University Press).

—— (1995), 'Gosh, Boy George, You Must Be Awfully Secure in Your Masculinity!' in M. Berger, B. Wallis and S. Watson (eds), *Constructing Masculinity* (New York and London: Routledge).

Sennett, J. (ed.) (2006), *Self-Organizing Men: Conscious Masculinities in Time and Space* (Ypsilanti, MI: Homofactus Press).

Stoltenberg, J. (1990), *Refusing to Be a Man* (New York: Penguin).

Straight Boy Lessons (1999), dir. Ray Rea [feature film].

Wiegman, R. (2006), 'Heteronormativity and the Desire for Gender', *Feminist Theory* 7, 80–103.

Phenomenology, Embodiment and the Political Efficacy of Contingent Identity Claims

Annabelle Willox

Our clothed body is constantly and inevitably being read and interpreted by those around us, who subsequently reach a conclusion about our gendered, and sometimes sexual, identity. I have frequently found myself in situations where the conclusions reached by other people about my gender, and my sexuality, do not align with my identity claims or the experience I have of my embodiment. Furthermore, when I have undertaken online or electronic gender and sexuality tests for fun I repeatedly confuse and confound the programs, obtaining a variety of error messages along the way.

While this is often amusing, in effect what is happening is that people (or computer programs) are translating their perceptions of me into a categorisation of my identity that is assumed to be 'true': my identity is defined by and through the perceptions of other people. The resulting categorisation and identification of me often has nothing to do with my embodied experience, and at times results in the need for me to defend my own identity claim(s) where there is disagreement. My identity, it seems, can be legitimately challenged by other people based on nothing more than *their* interpretation of *their* perception: this challenge can be, and often is, made regardless of *my* experience of embodiment.

Over the course of my life my embodiment has been read as that of a boy, a transsexual woman, a gay man, a trans person, a lesbian, a bisexual person: sometimes in accordance with my desire to be read as such, sometimes at odds with my experience of being embodied and my subsequent identity claims. In all of these situations, however, I have had to negotiate my identity and explain the experience that I had of being embodied within such a context before I have been afforded legitimacy by those reading me. These situations have concluded in a variety of ways from hilarity to anger: thankfully none have ended in physical violence. My experiences, however, expose the difficulty inherent in being read as a given gender identity based on assumptions about biology coupled with an ideology of gender identity. The issue that is exposed through my experiences is of how to deal effectively and productively with situations where gender identities and presentations do not fit standard normative expectations.

This chapter, therefore, will examine the experience of being embodied and the ideology attached to that embodiment, and how gender identity and embodiments might be understood differently in order to challenge those situations where embarrassment or violence function to constrain gender identity and deny the embodied experience of transgender people. I shall critically engage with and challenge theorisations of the body, gender and embodiment proposed by Judith Butler, Maurice Merleau-Ponty and Elizabeth Grosz. I will show how phenomenological methods, when properly applied, can provide a theoretical basis through which to understand gendered embodiment without relying upon binary thought, or by assuming an incontrovertible relation between body, body image and the lived experience of embodied subjects. Such a theory will not presume that a given biology necessarily results in a given gendered presentation or a specific embodiment. Rather, as I will show, because the relationships between these phenomena are contingent, such a theory will be based on the lived experience of being embodied, and on the political efficacy of gendered identity claims.

The most important issues are subjectivity and the *lived* experience of individuals, whether they are transsexual, transgendered, biologically male or female, or any other gendered combination. In other words, with such a diverse and precarious ground on which to base a theory of gender, one simply cannot apply a readymade theory *to* gender, but rather theory must come *from* the lived experience of gendered embodiment. 'The power of the appeal to what feels essential, to *what gender feels like*, in effecting changes in cultural representation and legal rights ... should not be underestimated' (Prosser 1997, 319; emphasis in original). I suggest, therefore, that a theoretical and political approach to gender based on phenomenology will allow a greater understanding of the actual lived experiences of gendered bodies, and will provide a theory that fits bodies, rather than trying to fit bodies into theories.

Phenomenology takes as its foundation the experiences that we have of the world – our subjective perceptual experience – and provides a foundation for knowledge understood and made meaningful through active and interactive perception. Phenomenology began as a movement with the works of Edmund Husserl, who wished to return epistemology to a foundation that could not be doubted. Husserl suggested that, while we could not be certain of the existence of objects in the world, nonetheless we could be certain of our perception of phenomena. Importantly, the subject is not passive in this process of perception. It is the interaction between the consciousness of the subject and the perceived object or phenomena that constitutes the phenomenological basis for knowledge. Perception within phenomenology is an act that constitutes both the object of perception and the subject perceiving. In this way, phenomenology steers a middle course between empiricism and rationalism where neither the object nor the subject is privileged. For empiricism, knowledge comes from the sense data that the subject passively receives from the object, whereas in rationalism, or intellectualism, knowledge comes from the intellectual capacities of the subject alone. Phenomenology, on the other hand, suggests a mutually constitutive relationship between the subject and the object, where neither has any epistemological or ontological meaning without the necessary and simultaneous existence of the other.

While there are numerous forms of phenomenology, I believe that the most productive method for queer theory is one that focuses on the lived body and embodiment such as that of Maurice Merleau-Ponty. For Merleau-Ponty, the most important aspect of phenomenology was the centrality of the body and as such he not only extended phenomenology in an existentialist direction, in line with Jean-Paul Sartre, but also introduced corporeal and historical situatedness into the field of phenomenological cognisance. It is the importance of the corporeal and situated body in Merleau-Ponty that leads to a productive form of phenomenology that is invaluable when dealing with issues of gender, sex and sexuality. For Merleau-Ponty the body is never explored in abstraction as the body can never exist apart from its situation: there is no isolated, self contained or non-situated body and he 'attacked what he called the "hypothesis of sensation", the empiricist claim that all knowledge is composed out of a bedrock of simple sensations … [F]or Merleau-Ponty there are no isolated sensations; all sensations are already drawn up into a world of particular significance for us' (Moran 2000, 415).

The body, for Merleau-Ponty, is at one and the same time both subject and object as not only does the body allow us to perceive objects, but 'I regard my body, which is my point of view upon the world, as one of the objects of that world' (Merleau-Ponty 1999, 70). Therefore the body allows us to comprehend the objective world by being at one time both object in the world, and subject perceiving the world. This is not to say that the body is simply an object, as the body is constantly perceived, thereby differentiating it from ordinary objects that can, at certain points, be removed from our field of vision. The body, due to the fact that it is always perceivable and can be perceived as phenomena, can be, and is, both the subject and object of perception.

It is important to clarify that the body is not an object in the same manner as ordinary objects. The body can never be removed from the experience of the perceiving subject; the body can never be absent in the way that objects can be. This links to the notion of perception being based on the first person perspective where the body of the subject is always already present in the act of perceiving. Further to this, Merleau-Ponty explains that '[w]hat prevents its ever being an object, ever being "completely constituted" is that it is that by which there are objects' (1999, 92). In other words, the body is that through which other objects have meaning, as the embodiment of the subject within the object-body allows the perception of objects to take place.

There have been feminist objections to the work of Merleau-Ponty, most notably, in the context of this chapter, from Judith Butler. Butler explains that 'Merleau-Ponty's conception of the "subject" is … problematic in virtue of its abstract and anonymous status, as if the subject described were a universal subject … Devoid of gender, this subject is presumed to characterize all genders' (1989, 98), and the assumption made at the time was that this universal gender was male. When Butler points out the 'lamentable naiveté concerning the anthropological diversity of sexual expressions and the linguistic and psychosomatic origins of human sexuality' (1989,

98), one must agree. However, one must also agree that the principle of exploring the lived experiences of gender and sexuality is a groundbreaking and important one on which more enlightened theorising may take place. While it is true that Butler does not totally deny the possibilities within Merleau-Ponty's work, nonetheless her critique of him seems to obfuscate the productive aspects, burying them under technicalities that, it could be argued, are founded on the historical and cultural assumptions of the era in which Merleau-Ponty was writing.[1] Butler's critique of the master/slave dialectic, coupled with Merleau-Ponty's apparent assumption of the heterosexual male as the universal subject, becomes the basis for her simplistic rejection of Merleau-Ponty as a foundation for a philosophy of sexuality and/or gender.

Conversely, in her analysis of feminine bodily comportment, motility and spatiality, Iris Marion Young points out Merleau-Ponty's inherent misogyny, but unlike Butler does not use this as a reason to ignore the productive possibilities in his writings.[2] Young points out that he assumes the body to be the same body regardless of sex, and she explains that this ignores 'woman's experience of her body as a *thing* at the same time that she experiences it as a capacity' (1989, 58; emphasis in original). Young applies the lived bodily experience of feminine comportment to Merleau-Ponty's limited theoretical understanding of human bodily comportment, and thereby extends his philosophy beyond the apparent misogynist barrier that Butler uses to discredit it. Young shows that the experience of being embodied as a girl, or as a boy, has repercussions for how one experiences one's body and spatial mobility. Furthermore, if the body is always situated and habitually comprehended, then this experience of the body can change due to different relations with other bodies in given situations.

It is this understanding of phenomenology that I wish to use to consider the embodied experience of subjects in queer sexual situations in order to examine the political efficacy of contingent identity claims. In order to achieve this, I will provide a critical exposition of Jacob Hale's article 'Leatherdyke Boys and Their

---

1   While the examples used by Merleau-Ponty in 'The Body in its Sexual Being' (1999) tend towards homophobic and misogynistic assumptions, his description of the master/slave dialectic could be read productively as an example of a theory of the gaze that does not deny the possibility of a continuing dialectic relationship between subjects. The slave, or object of desire, in Merleau-Ponty's description can turn the gaze onto the master, thereby giving subject making powers to the desired object-body and reducing the master to the status of object-body. Furthermore, it is possible to use Merleau-Ponty to explore productively stone butch sexuality, although this is beyond the scope of this chapter.

2   It is worth noting that Young's use of the term 'feminine' does not designate a modality exclusive to women, rather it is 'a set of structures and conditions which delimit the typical *situation* of being a woman in a particular society, as well as the typical way in which this situation is lived by the women themselves ... This understanding of "feminine" existence makes it possible to say that some women escape or transcend the typical situation and definition of women in various degrees' (1989, 54; emphasis in original).

Daddies' (1997) to further develop the political possibility inherent in his thinking. Hale's paper has weaknesses, but more importantly, it also has intriguing and underdeveloped phenomenological foundations that I shall expand. He sets out to explore the multiple gender statuses available within certain American communities as a means of interrogating, destabilising and recodifying gender. In other words, by exploring the current practices of certain gendered subcultures – specifically those of leatherdyke boys and their leatherdyke daddies – Hale intends to question the assumptions made by academics and non-academics alike concerning gender and gender limitations. Hale explains that leatherdyke boys are 'adult lesbian (dyke) females who embody a specific range of masculinities intelligible within queer leather (SM) communities; their "daddies" may be butch leatherdykes or, less frequently, gay leathermen' (1997, 224).

The gender play that Hale considers as a basis for his theorisation centres primarily on the clothing, presentations and mental attitudes of two or more biological females, although Hale explains from the outset that the delineation of gender within these scenarios is often vague (1997, 224). My reading of Hale will focus on interactions between those who live their bodies as female. As Hale underlines, 'masculine gender performatives, in conjunction with female embodiment, are given a wider range of expression within leatherdyke contexts than in many other lesbian or dyke settings' (1997, 226). Leatherdyke gender-play, therefore, would seem to disrupt traditional assumptions about gender and the body, allowing the presentation of a greater number of gendered embodiments than is assumed to be culturally available. The suggestion is that, by focusing on the genders that exist within these contexts, Hale can interrogate gender and point towards a theory of gender that is less restrictive.

Hale's methodology, however, seems to be based on a theoretical adherence to performativity, rather than on a genuine exploration of gender through phenomenological description of gender-play. This is apparent in his rhetoric where, before Hale has explored the lived experiences of leatherdykes, and before he has explained the intricacies of their gender-play, he implies a performative framework through his use of performative terminology (1997, 230). Hale's argument itself flounders on this central tenet of performativity theory – that one's words inevitably evoke their previous usages – because the use of the terms of performativity foreclose our reading of gender play before any phenomenological description can begin.

I would suggest, therefore, the use of an alternative term such as 'presentation', rather than 'performance' or 'perform', which would affiliate Hale's proposed theory with the phenomenological tradition that he claims as his basis. 'Presentation' still conveys the need for perception by another being for such a presentation to be understood. Further, it allows for slippage at the moment of presentation between the intention of the subject and the perceiver. Consider Hale's statement that 'Daddy, of course, could not have read my gender performativity as a boy's gender performativity if there had not been culturally available constructs of *boy* into which she could fit it' (1997, 229; emphasis in original). By replacing the occurrences of 'performativity' with 'presentation', no meaning is lost apart from the unnecessary invocation of performative gender theory. Using a term such as 'presentation' would allow the reader to comprehend that there is a presentation of a gender expression without leading them into the theoretical problems of performativity.

In order to understand why phenomenology would be a better methodological basis for Hale's discussion, it is necessary to turn briefly to the fundamental differences between performativity and a phenomenological approach to gendered embodiment. Butler's theory of performativity states that gender is an imitation for which there is no original. Because the performance that constitutes gender is bound to fail – due to this lack of original – the performance must be endlessly repeated in an attempt to substantiate the identity. Thus gender is performative in that the performance, which is necessarily and continuously repeated, constitutes the gender itself; the performance performatively creates the gender. This repetition produces a coherence of identity that constitutes the subject, so there can be no ungendered subject; gender becomes a truth of personal identity. This performative gender is further constituted through and by the dominant discourse, the heterosexual matrix, which produces a domain of 'unthinkability and unnameability' at its borders. Therefore, for Butler, we cannot escape the gender system; we can only subvert it through visible transgression (1993a, 312).[3]

This reliance on the visibility of cross-gendered identifications as a way of exposing the apparent mis-matching of bodies and gendered presentations is problematic. It is suggested that the butch in particular visibly crosses, subverts and exposes the inadequacies of the gender binary. As Judith Halberstam puts it:

> Butchness ... performs both female masculinity and a rejection of enforced anatomical femininity ... This imperfect performance reveals ... that gender is always a rough match between bodies and subjectivities. (1998, 126)

I would claim, however, that the butch does not in fact perform masculinity, nor does she pastiche or parody maleness; she embodies a female masculinity that is culturally understood as 'butch'. It is a misreading to understand butches and their relationships to femmes simply as performative performances of pre-existing masculine and feminine categories. They are specific embodied gendered subjects who warrant phenomenological description in and of themselves.

Unlike Butler's description of the butch, a theory of gender based on phenomenological description and embodiment understands such apparent juxtaposition and transgression as a *different* embodiment. There is no necessary crossing, no incongruity between identifications and bodies. Butler's theory relies on this crossing to exemplify the construction and performative nature of gender, yet her reliance upon crossing implicitly relies upon a binary structure that denies

---

3   The use of drag as the exemplar of performativity has lead to misreadings of Butler's theory not as performativity but as mere performance; the basis of this misreading being the definition of drag. Butler states, 'I do not mean to suggest that drag is a "role" that can be taken on or taken off at will' (1993a, 314), however I would contend that this is precisely the point of drag. For further discussion on these points, see Willox (2002).

the autonomy of the identity 'butch'. In contrast to this, a theory of gender that uses a phenomenological approach would account for the identity 'butch' not as an example of cross-gendered identification, but as a specific embodiment and gendered presentation. The experience of *being* butch should form the basis of the theory, rather than a theorisation of how to account for the apparent 'cross-gendered' identification and presentation of the butch. It is the very notion of a 'rough match between bodies and subjectivities', to use Halberstam's phrase, that a theory of embodiment based on phenomenological description seeks to overcome by attempting to break out of the traditional binary framework. This allows identifications such as 'butch' to become embodiments in their own right. Consequently the butch does not simply 'perform' masculinity, but rather this presentation is created through her embodiment of 'butch'.

Within his article 'Phenomenology as Method in Trans Studies' (1998), Henry Rubin examines the productive possibilities of using a phenomenological method. Rubin explains that phenomenology 'assumes the necessity of being a body in order for the world to exist for oneself', and that the body 'as it exists for oneself is the point of reference by which the whole world unfolds' (1998, 270, 268). By focusing on the primacy of trans lived experience – on those embodied experiences that question our assumptions of the body – not only is it possible to theorise about those bodies that challenge our understandings of embodied subjectivity, but this approach could also form the basis of theorising about the subject, body and body image as a whole.

Rubin takes forward the phenomenological method of Jean-Paul Sartre and Merleau-Ponty and attempts to show how their productive possibilities can be adapted and applied to trans theory. While he acknowledges the issue of assumptions and problems within Merleau-Ponty, he nonetheless suggests that this should not lead to the dismissal of Merleau-Ponty's method:

> Assuming, however, that the insights of discursive analysis can correct for the absolutism of Sartre and Merleau-Ponty, a phenomenological method can return legitimacy to the knowledges generated by the experiencing 'I'. This I confronts the world as a series of essences contingent upon an embodied location. (1998, 267)

In this way, Rubin indirectly challenges Butler for dismissing Merleau-Ponty on the basis of Merleau-Ponty's assumption of a universal male subject, and suggests that the issue of primary importance is the method that Merleau-Ponty proposes, rather than the examples that he provides.

Rubin proposes to use phenomenology both within trans studies and beyond. He begins by explaining the historical relevance of the theoretical battle between Foucauldian discursive analysis and phenomenology, explaining how and why the issue of transsexual subject positions becomes problematic for Foucauldian-based feminist analysis of the subject. Rubin suggests, however, that Foucauldian analysis is not incompatible with phenomenology simply because of their historical divergence. He proposes, rather, a phenomenology 'informed by Foucault's critique of its central claims for the authority of subjects and the significance of lived experience' (1998, 267). Rubin suggests a combination of phenomenological agency and Foucauldian discursive constitution that allows an amount of agency on the part of the subject, but not so much as to deny the limitations of self-presentation. He explains that his goal 'is to get us out of some sticky impasses in feminist and queer studies where the brazen critiques or appropriations of transsexual practices are a result of the rejection of (transsexual) subjectivity as a source of legitimate knowledge' (1998, 268).

Rubin explains that his version of phenomenology takes on the Sartrean notion of the body as 'fundamentally fragmented, containing radically distinct and permanently irreconcilable ontological levels' (1998, 268), these levels being the body-for-itself, the body-for-others and, finally, the alienated body. The body-for-itself is the body as the individual's point of view, the body that is lived by the 'I' that exists. This body is absolute – in that the 'I' cannot exist apart from it – lived and not known as an object, but rather experienced as that which exists in order that the world exists. The body-for-others, on the other hand, is the body as touched, viewed, perceived by others; '[t]his is the body as flesh, as corporeal reality' (1998, 269). Importantly, however, the body-for-itself and the body-for-others do not claim corporeal reality apart from their perceived state; these bodies only exist in that they are experienced (each for itself) or perceived (for others). The third level of bodily ontology, for Sartre, is the alienated body where the body-for-itself takes a view of itself as the body-for-others; when the subject perceives its own body as an object rather than as its viewpoint. This alienated body is the point of departure from Sartre and the point of intersection with Merleau-Ponty within Rubin's reformation of phenomenology.

Rubin uses the situation of transsexual people where the body image of the subject may appear to be at odds with the body-for-others, or the perceived body. He explains that there is no need for the physical body to correspond to the body image under Merleau-Ponty's explanation of the body image as the body image simply refers to our experience of the body-for-itself, rather than the perception of the body-for-others by other subjects. Rubin explains that, while phantom limb and agnosia sufferers:

> ... do not consciously call into being a body image that, through the addition or subtraction of psychical parts, mobilises their will, they do, however, use that body image to live in the world as embodied, active agents. The body image, often configured differently from the corporeal body, enables a continued engagement between the subject and the world. (1998, 270)

By suggesting that the body is only ever experienced or perceived, and by explaining that there is no incongruity in a body image that does not correspond to the body-for-others – due to the fact that the body image only need be concerned with the experience of the body-for-itself – Rubin manages to get out of the binary that feminist philosophers find insurmountable: the material body and the socially constituted body. Rubin's phenomenology assumes the necessity of the body-for-itself, but also recognises that the body-for-others may be perceived differently to the body image of the subject; the experience of the body-for-itself. Rubin explains that transsexual people may be described as failing to recognise their own body parts in the same way as those agnostics that Merleau-Ponty studied, but this does not negate the subject position of transsexual people, nor does it deny the lived experience of transsexual embodiment. Furthermore, Rubin suggests that transsexual people understood in this manner are not classified as psychotic, but rather '[a]gnostic transsexuals have a kind of embodied knowledge that resists the terms of sickness and health, absence and presence, real and unreal' (1998, 271).

If we return to the gender play outlined in Hale's paper and apply Rubin's phenomenological understanding of embodiment, it seems obvious that Hale could suggest a method of moving beyond the limits of intelligibility with regard to gender. His exploration of gender play could provide a different understanding of embodiment, gender and sexuality, yet with his reliance on performativity, he fails to do so. Within daddy-boy gender play, there is the possibility of confusing and subverting the gender matrix through the use of the gendered category 'boy' by a female-bodied person. Such an embodied subject position could re-define the category itself not by exposing this position as contradictory, as Butler would claim, but rather by questioning the very notion that there is a contradiction between body and presentation.

I am suggesting that the identity 'boy', when ascribed to a body that would seem to contradict that identity, is not contradictory. The embodiment and experience of being a boy with a lived female body is a different embodiment to that of a boy with a lived male body. They are distinct embodiments based on the experience that the subject has of their body, gender presentation, body image and identity, which are made meaningful and understood through phenomenological methods. By questioning the apparent subversion of cross-gendered identification, and by claiming that such an embodiment is not contradictory, a new gendered category could be produced that questions the intelligibility and logic of the matrix itself. The cultural assumption that the term 'boy' can only be ascribed to a male body can be undermined through the use of 'boy' to re-codify the body. In this way, the terms available to describe one's gendered presentation can be used in a subversive manner that questions any notion of a 'natural' link between biology and gendered presentation. Crucially, performativity is unnecessary for this manoeuvre.

If we return to the centre of Hale's discussion, it seems obvious that a phenomenological approach to gender is necessary. During an account of gender play Hale explains that certain inanimate objects may be able to be re-signified and imbued with meaning through such practices (1997, 233). An example is when one leatherdyke enters a play party and, over a period of time, the gender of the protagonist alters to encompass the identity 'Daddy'. Daddy's body is imbued with different cultural meanings through this diachronic gender change, but changes also occur which affect and effect the bodily perception that Daddy has of himself. Hale writes: '[o]nce Daddy's dick has become a *sensate* dick in Daddy's phenomenological experience of his own embodiment and in Daddy's boy's phenomenological experience of Daddy's embodiment, Daddy may be simply a very butch gay male leather bear-daddy' (1997, 233; my emphasis). The most important point here is that a phenomenological approach to this gendered experience allows us to understand the semiotic shift that takes place within an embodied subject's self-perception. The subject perceives no incongruity. The gender of Daddy changes in this context due to the embodied experience of being a daddy; the subsequent experience of a sensate dick is therefore not contradictory to the biology of Daddy. The suggestion here is that it is possible for inanimate objects to be imbued with phenomenological significance through extension of the body image.

How then can an inanimate object be imbued with semiotic and sensate meaning? How can a female-bodied person embody and experience their body as that of a daddy or a boy? My suggestion is that, following on from Rubin, a phenomenological understanding of the form and function of body image can show how this process is possible. Elizabeth Grosz, following Paul Schilder, explains:

> ... the body image cannot be simply and unequivocally identified with the sensations provided by a purely anatomical body. The body image is as much a function of the subject's psychology and sociohistorical context as of anatomy. The limits or borders of the body image are not fixed by nature or confined to the anatomical 'container', the skin. (1994, 79)

Therefore, through a comprehension of the form and function of the body image we can rethink the borders of the body, as well as the meaning of bodily parts. This is not to deny the importance of obtaining harmony between body image and anatomy where there is a real and tangible need to do so, for example where body and body image must be aligned for the continued health and wellbeing of transsexual people. This theory does not undermine such alignments; it merely points to other possibilities of signification of the body.

There are, however, two theoretical issues within Grosz's comprehension of body image, as illustrated through her description of driving a car, which must be critically appraised. For Grosz, the body image is not only extended to the interactive surroundings of the vehicle but to its entirety which 'becomes part of the body image, a body shell for the subject; its perils and breakdowns, chasing another car or trying to fit into a small parking spot, are all experienced in the body image of the driver' (1994, 80). Two remarks here. First, the use of the term 'shell' to describe the car itself as part of the body image re-creates a dualism of subject and body image that casts the latter as supplementary. I would argue, however, that the body image is necessary for the subject and cannot be described as housing, or housed by, another entity.

Second, according to Grosz, the only thing that is necessary for an inanimate object to become imbued with sensate and experiential meaning via extension of the body image is that such an object 'comes into contact with the surface of the body and remains there long enough' (1994, 80). Yet this would allow an inordinate quantity of objects to be incorporated into the body image, even when it is obvious that they cannot. For example, sitting on a sofa, walking on a carpet or leaning on a lamp-post could be argued to be all that is necessary for such objects to be incorporated into one's body image. I think that Grosz's analogy simply takes the limits of the body image too far. It is the interaction with, and through, an inanimate object that allows the body image to extend beyond the corporeal body to encompass a non-corporeal attachment to the body, not just proximity. There must be a use made of the object in order for it to be imbued with meaning.

I believe that it is a desire to effect, rather than a desire to move, that enables an object to become incorporated into the body image. In order to achieve a desired effect, I learn how to inhabit and use my corporeal body through experience of my body image and use of the spatial awareness that this provides. As Merleau-Ponty explains, 'when I move towards a world I bury my perceptual and practical *intentions* in objects which ultimately appear prior to and external to those intentions' (1999, 82; my emphasis). Therefore when *intention* effects one's interaction with objects they take on a different meaning and significance to ordinary objects; they become part of the subject. The difference between the body and an object is the ever-present immanence of the body versus possible absence of object. As Merleau-Ponty explains:

> *I move external objects with the aid of my body, which takes hold of them in one place and shifts them to another. But my body itself I move directly, I do not find it at one point of objective space and transfer it to another, I have no need to look for it, it is already with me. (1999, 94; my emphasis)*

It is the intention and desire to effect that drives the movement of the body and delimits the scope of the body image. In this way, then, purpose becomes the important factor.

To clarify the possibilities of such an understanding of the development of the body image, and to explain how such embodiments can be understood through phenomenology, it is worth looking at a representation of gender-play. My intention here is not to fictionalise the lived embodied experiences of protagonists involved in gender-play, but rather to show how the lived experience of engaging in such play can affect the consciousness that one has of one's own body, experience and identity. Such representation allows a method of imparting such experiential understandings in a traditional and widely understood format. My intention, therefore, is to allow people who have never engaged in gender-play to understand how such an experience could alter their body image and subsequently their identity, even if only temporarily. The example that I will provide is a detailed description of the processes through which the lived experience of an embodied subject changes via gender-play found in Patrick Califia-Rice's collection of essays, *Public Sex: The Culture of Radical Sex* (1994).

Written in 1983, 'Genderbending: Playing with Roles and Reversals' provides an autobiographical account of one of Califia's sexual encounters with a woman, before providing a thought-provoking article on the issues of gender, butch and femme, and sexuality. The sexual encounter involves Califia, who was presenting as biologically female at the time, donning a strap-on and other associated accoutrements in order to 'play' at being a boy. Importantly, the description takes the reader through the stages of buying, donning and using the inanimate objects, thereby giving us an almost real-time appreciation of the experiential and semantic changes that take place in gender-play of this sort. After getting dressed to play, Califia explains that 'I don't feel like a woman anymore. The semiotics have shifted ... And there's my c**k. I can grab it, stroke it – and it feels good' (1994, 175). The meanings of Califia's body have changed as a direct result of his change in presentation, and therefore his experience of his lived body is radically different now. In this context, he no longer embodies the gendered position of 'woman', and for the moment at least his body image, and therefore his body, possesses a c**k.

Throughout the subsequent description of the sexual encounter between Califia and his female-bodied partner, the c**k that Califia possesses provides him with the sexual stimuli that results in his orgasm: his c**k *feels*. Furthermore, the temporality of this experience is underlined when Califia states that 'next time we see each other, I will probably be the one on my knees. Her c**k is longer than mine' (1994, 176). Again we are told that the c**k in question is real, and belongs to the female-bodied person that Califia has just f****d. This allows an understanding of how a theory of gender based on phenomenology can allow multiple gendered possibilities without any apparent contradiction with either ideology or biology.

In other words, the protagonists of the text above do not alter their biology, yet their experience of their embodiment changes through gender-play. For the specific interactive event recounted in the excerpt above, the protagonists experience their bodies and their body images differently to how they would in other situations; this does not irreversibly alter their identities. The implication here is that, as with language and meaning, there is an expectation that the rules of gender, embodiment and experience are always constrained by dominant culture. Yet these extracts, and the concept of gender-play generally, suggest that these rules can be changed. Califia's subsequent transition to male makes this encounter all the more significant, although I would contend that transition is not the logical conclusion of all sexual gender-play, just one possible option.

It is also important to point out that these embodied experiences are *not the same as* some ephemeral or universal 'male' experience, rather these experiences are specific to context, subject(s), situation, embodiment, biology, habit body and interaction with others. This is not to say that they are unique – and therefore un-representable – indeed the fact that biographical and fictional representations are readily available indicates that these experiences are both representable and comprehensible beyond the individual. These experiences and embodiments do not fit unequivocally into ideological expectations of 'male' or 'female' experience, rather they disrupt the notion of such a binary, which is based on implicit assumptions of a 'correct' correlation between gender, sex, sexuality, experience and identity. These experiences disrupt the ideological apparatus of gender precisely because the embodied experience *seems* to contradict the biology of the protagonist, when phenomenologically speaking there is no contradiction.

This account, therefore, highlights and exemplifies the issues of temporality, lived experience and the re-signification of bodily and non-bodily parts that form the basis of a theory of gendered embodiment, which can be understood through a phenomenological approach, and an understanding of the body image. Furthermore, the temporary nature of such a change in embodiment and identity is underscored, while showing that, if the situation is understood phenomenologically, there is no contradiction between biology and embodiment over the timeframe of the gender-play.

Such a phenomenologically understood body image and embodiment allows an understanding of the transformation and re-codification of the body itself that current theories of gender fail to provide. It is this creative and volitional aspect that makes a theory of gender based on phenomenology and embodiment both insightful and productive. The forms of gender play outlined within Hale's paper and Califia's account allow just such a re-mapping of the meanings of bodies. As Hale notes, 'many transpeople must remap the sexualized zones of our bodies if we are to be sexually active' (1997, 230). Therefore the re-coding of existing body parts is essential for, and made possible by, subcultural discourses. Through transgender and transgendered experiences of embodiment and the body, bodies themselves become culturally unstable, thereby transgressing and confusing the assumption of biology as a site of truth. As Hale explains 'some leatherdyke daddies and boys are women, some are not, and ... in many cases *there is no fact of the matter*' (1997, 231; my emphasis).

This repudiation of the necessity of a 'truth' to gender is a fundamental issue, and deserves more explanation. To claim that there is no truth to gendered identifications allows for embodiments to be comprehensible regardless of any apparent contradictions over time; there is no contradiction where there is no assumption of a fixed or constant identity. The political possibility of such a theory of embodiment that allows us out of the constraints of performativity – which does not allow roles or identifications to be changed through personal agency – is that of temporary specificity based on politically defined situations. If, as my theory of embodiment has attempted to show, bodies are mutable and recodifiable both physically and phenomenologically, and gender claims are temporary political assertions based on these embodiments, then the political implications are diverse and numerous, because they are not grounded on a constant 'fact' or 'truth' to self-identity. One's identity, rather, has meaning depending on the individual social and cultural situation that the subject is in, such as during gender-play. The identity of a subject is contingent on the context that necessitates the attribution of an identity.

The idea of lived experience being fundamental to the comprehension of gender is similar to the approach that Alcoff takes with regard to race in her article, 'Towards a Phenomenology of Racial Embodiment' (1999). Alcoff's suggestion is for the contextualisation of race based on a subjectivist approach where the starting point for critical theory is the lived experience of racialisation, which itself reveals how race is itself constitutive of bodily experience. This is the same starting point Hale attempts to make within his article, where the subcultural practices that already exist inform subsequent theory; 'we must familiarise ourselves and others with the multiplicity of genders already available in the curvatures of gendered spaces' (1997, 235).

To illustrate this position, it is worth contemplating a final example provided by Hale. His driving licence and birth certificate bear seemingly contradictory sex/gender designations. He explains that he does not have a unitary or fixed gender identity as his driving license 'bears the sex/gender designation "M"' while his birth certificate 'bears the sex/gender designation "F"' (1997, 232). These designations, Hale says, rely on the legal requirements that must be met to be designated 'M' or 'F'. He explains further that his 'sex/gender status is specific to state interests and purposes … [and thus] is, in part, a juridical construction that falls apart on some transsexed (and intersexed) bodies … [Therefore] there is absolutely no discrepancy [between the two designations]' (1997, 232). Hale, by virtue of existing within such social and legal institutional regimes, exposes the contextual relevance of gendered identifications and underlines the idea that one need not have a fixed and continuous gendered identity. To identify as a 'woman' (or any other designation, such as 'F' or 'M') in any given context does not mean that one must always identify as a 'woman' in all contexts or situations; there is no contradiction between given gendered identifications under such a theory of embodiment. Certain contexts demand politically strategic gendered identification claims that may be different in other contexts. In this way, the idea of a fixed, continuous identity is false. Identity is based on context, political efficacy and legal requirement, and can be different depending on these constitutive demands.

The similarity between phenomenology and performativity is that, for both theoretical approaches, embodiments must be presented and read in order for them to be culturally intelligible. In other words, the presentation of one's gendered embodiment always already relies on current practices and institutions that constrain the ranges of meaning and significance of intelligible gendered presentations. One cannot simply invent a new gendered embodiment without adhering to certain contemporary constraints of intelligibility. The important difference, however, is that for phenomenology an embodiment it is not simply a matter of 'performance' or presentation but involves interactions between the body image, the body as lived, and the re-codification of the body itself.

While performativity provides a description of the function of gender within the heterosexual matrix, it fails to provide any subversive agency beyond visible subversion; and such visible subversion seems to me to be self-defeating, as it seems to recapitulate the 'naturalness' of the underlying binary structure. Embodiment, however, facilitates more than a mere play-acting; it allows the presentation of genders to be phenomenologically real. With phenomenology, there are interactions and creations, not contradictions and crossings. What is needed now is further exploration of how, why and where such temporary and politically contingent multiple identifications can be of paramount politically subversive value.

My suggestion would be to deliberately claim apparently contradictory identities in different situations, subverting notions of identity by demonstrating that claims are contingent political assertions rather than any description of 'truth'. In the same way that we all have several valid non-gender related identities – friend, manager, co-worker, umpire, partner – my suggestion is to extend this understanding of co-existent context dependant identity claims through a phenomenological understanding of embodiment as explained within this chapter to enable multiple sexual and gendered identity claims. This would enable the assumptions made about my sexual and gender identity highlighted at the outset of this chapter to all be equally valid: I am a boy, a transsexual woman, a gay man, a trans person, a lesbian, a bisexual person because all of these claims are valid contingent political assertions.

I believe that it is the effect of these contingent political assertions that matters, and the effect should be to confuse, subvert and undermine the notion of 'truth' regarding gender or sexual identity. In this way, the act of claiming a gender or sexual identity should become a politically motivated desire to effect rather than any description of 'truth', and should be actively used to deliberately challenge notions of gendered identity that constrain and limit people. Such understandings of gender and sexual identity claims as contingent political assertions will better serve queer theory/politics by enabling the spurious assumption of biology as the foundation of gendered and sexual identities to be confounded by severing the notion of gender/sexual identity from any stable reference point. My suggestion, essentially, is that deliberately proliferating and asserting multiple, apparently incongruent, contingent political identities actively subverts any notion of identity as 'truth', thereby undermining and destabilising the ideological (fictional) foundations of normative identity categories.

Suggested Further Reading

Ahmed, S. (2006), *Queer Phenomenology: Orientations, Objects, Others* (Durham, NC and London: Duke University Press).

Alcoff, L.M. (1999), 'Towards a Phenomenology of Racial Embodiment', *Radical Philosophy* 95, 15–26.

Hale, J. (1997), 'Leatherdyke Boys and Their Daddies: How to Have Sex Without Women or Men', *Social Text* 52–3, 223–36.

Moran, D. (2000), *Introduction to Phenomenology* (London and New York: Routledge).

Rubin, H. (1998), 'Phenomenology as a Method in Trans Studies', *GLQ: A Journal of Lesbian and Gay Studies* 4:2, 263–81.

References

Alcoff, L.M. (1999), 'Towards a Phenomenology of Racial Embodiment', *Radical Philosophy* 95, 15–26.

Butler, J. (1989), 'Sexual Ideology and Phenomenological Description: A Feminist Critique of Merleau-Ponty's *Phenomenology of Perception*', in J. Allen and I.M.

Young (eds), *The Thinking Muse: Feminism and Modern French Philosophy* (Bloomington and Indianapolis, IN: Indiana University Press).

—— (1993a), 'Imitation and Gender Insubordination', in H. Abelove, M.A. Barale and D.M. Halperin (eds), *The Lesbian and Gay Studies Reader* (London and New York: Routledge).

—— (1993b), *Bodies That Matter: On The Discursive Limits of 'Sex'* (London and New York: Routledge).

Califia-Rice, P. (1994), 'Genderbending: Playing with Roles and Reversals', in *Public Sex: The Culture of Radical Sex* (Pittsburgh, PA and San Francisco, CA: Cleis Press).

Grosz, E. (1994), *Volatile Bodies: Towards a Corporeal Feminism* (Bloomington and Indianapolis, IN: Indiana University Press, 1994).

Halberstam, J. (1998), *Female Masculinity* (Durham, NC and London: Duke University Press).

Hale, J. (1997), 'Leatherdyke Boys and Their Daddies: How to Have Sex Without Women or Men', *Social Text* 52–3, 223–36.

Martin, B. (1998), 'Sexualities Without Genders and Other Queer Utopias', in M. Merck, N. Segal and E. Wright (eds), *Coming Out of Feminism?* (Oxford and Malden, MA: Blackwell).

Merleau-Ponty, M. (1999), *Phenomenology of Perception*, trans. C. Smith (London and New York: Routledge).

Moran, D. (2000), *Introduction to Phenomenology* (London and New York: Routledge).

Prosser, J. (1997), 'Transgender', in A. Medhurst and S. Munt (eds), *Lesbian and Gay Studies: A Critical Introduction* (London and Washington, DC: Cassell).

—— (1998), *Second Skins: The Body Narratives of Transsexuality* (New York: Columbia University Press).

Rubin, H. (1998), 'Phenomenology as a Method in Trans Studies', *GLQ: A Journal of Lesbian and Gay Studies* 4:2, 263–81.

Willox, A. (2002), 'Whose Drag Is It Anyway? Drag Kings and Monarchy in the UK', in K. LeBesco, D.J. Troka and J.B. Noble (eds), *The Drag King Anthology* (New York: Harrington Park Press).

Young, I.M. (1989), 'Throwing Like a Girl: A Phenomenology of Feminine Body Comportment, Motility, and Spatiality', in J. Allen, and I.M. Young (eds), *The Thinking Muse: Feminism and Modern French Philosophy* (Bloomington and Indianapolis, IN: Indiana University Press).

Queer Posthumanism: Cyborgs, Animals, Monsters, Perverts

Patricia MacCormack

Queer theory works not to exchange binaries of masculinity/femininity, hetero/homo or even human/non-human but to theorise the spaces between and the mobilisation of categories of identity through desire. In order to interrogate the role of sexuality in the formation and reification of subjectivity one must presume the consistency of all subjects as first belonging to a hermeneutic ontological system – the human. Certain categories oppose or extend the concept of the human through the creation of hybrid desires extending in both directions of the evolutionary trajectory – the pre-human (animal, monster, molecule) and the posthuman (cyborg, body-modifier, surgically altered). These hybrid formations are the results of what Gilles Deleuze and Félix Guattari call an 'unnatural' alliance of desire.

This chapter will begin with an overview of the various structures of knowledge and power which invest in the notion of the human – at base level zero a white heterosexual man. The posthuman through queer emerged as a reaction to humanism and traditional sexuality studies, from psychoanalysis to philosophy. It will show certain examples of non- and posthuman challenges to the closing off of identity and sexuality studies which premise themselves on the stability of the base level zero 'human'. The creative, aesthetic, philosophical and ethical implications of these burgeoning fields will be addressed. One aspect of queer theory was initially a response from lesbian theorists to interrogate the presumed masculinity in gay studies which remains binarised by suffixing the methodology with 'and lesbian', affirming woman as both outside of and less than human – humanity as default masculine, white and so forth. Extending the field to address not only sex, gender and identity but also the category of human can be seen in the writings of, among others, Rosi Braidotti's work on monsters and Elizabeth Grosz's questioning of ontologies which includes resonances of subject positions, using queer theory and 'animal' sexuality. Posthuman studies problematise humanism and psychoanalytic sexuality studies founded on a series of isomorphic binary selections (what Deleuze and Guattari would call signified subjectification). Perversion studies – both through technological and masochistic autoerotics and through unnatural participations – question both sexual dialectics and the compulsion for traditional 'gay and lesbian' studies to affirm binarised relations between same sex partners.

Deleuze and Guattari's becomings will be read into modern examples of perverse sexuality. The posthuman is a direct challenge, not to the former human, but what it means corporeally and discursively to be, or more correctly to count as, human. Posthumanism refuses the coalescence of seemingly disparate discursive systems such as science, sexuality and social subjectivity into an essentially unified conflation of logic, phallicism, equivalence to whiteness and maleness. Like queer, the posthuman does not seek to exchange or go beyond toward a set goal. Both interrogate the arbitrary nature of systems of power masquerading as truth. Through a negotiation of alterity within self and an address to oppressed entities, queer theory and the posthuman mobilise and radicalise the here and now through desire, pleasure and pure potentiality. Although I have chosen to focus on the work of Deleuze and Guattari, theorists such as Tim Dean, Michael Warner, Steve Seidman, Cindy Patton, Leo Bersani and Vicki Kirby have used Jacques Derrida's work to explore the encounter between flesh and discourse in their various work on queer theory, while others such as Luciana Parisi explore through the bioscience work of Eric Whitehead. Perhaps the most prevalent theorist to influence queer theory across all works, including Judith Butler's, is Michel Foucault, whose writings on sexuality explore both its historical construction and the potential for future possibilities of sexual thought.

The posthuman, although also an America-coined theory, comes more as a symptom of Continental philosophy, particularly for feminism difference theory and, for humanism, the anti-transcendentalism of Deleuze, Guattari, Jean-François Lyotard and Michel Foucault. Extending the work of Benedictus De Spinoza and Gottfried Wilhelm Leibniz, many of these theorists collapse binary mechanisms which create the human in opposition to the non-human, living entity against inorganic matter and life against death. As humans and society become increasingly technological and virtual, is life itself able to be understood independent of the apparatuses and concepts which bring it into being and extend it, and through which it is negotiated? How do we – or even can we – define what constitutes the human as a dividuated entity, or human life as a consistency unique from other life forms?

Posthumanism acknowledges there is viable life in non-human entities, and that the human itself is not easily defined as living organic matter separate to the inorganic or discursive philosophical. Braidotti defines life as *zoe* which describes any entity that has a generative power. 'Life is half animal, non-human (*zoe*) and half political and discursive (*bios*)' (2005, 37). Non-human does not mean outside the human, but the collapse of a purity in defining the human as necessarily and irreducibly separate from anything else. *Bios* is human life as always and already discursive, *zoe* that which has life but is other and thus can only be understood to live through our discourse – an address to difference which must acknowledge its own flaws as subjective and coming from a dominant (the human) to a non-dominant, often marginalised or oppressed (the non-human).

Posthumanism collapses the human with the non-human and thus modes of address must change. Anthropocentrism 'breeds a kind of solidarity between the human dwellers of the planet' (Braidotti 2005, 108), making things viable by humanising them. Accountable address emphasises that discourse creates reality, that to 'know' things is to know them only insofar as they are created through discourse. Posthuman life collapses demarcated entities and refuses the compulsion to know in order to master rather than create. The creations of connections – life as relation not dividuation – is posthuman living. Desire is, put most simply, the need to create connections with other things, not to have or know but collapse the self with other(s). In this sense posthumanism is a form of queer desire, or queer 'life'.

Posthumanism celebrates the connectivity between incidents of *zoe* – living matter(s) – creating new configurations which are unique and generate subsequent unique assemblages – *bios*. One could argue this is modern ethics in the face of a refusal of rights through equivalence to the human as a different or better form of life, and the belief that human life is separate to other forms. Judith Butler's suggestion in *Precarious Life* (2004), that life is that which can be a grievable death, is deeply anthropocentric by demanding it be grievable, an explicitly 'human' compulsion. Lyotard, who both laments and celebrates the possibilities and effects of post-modernity, emphasises in his work the differend that life is simply the right to be and the responsibility of other lives to acknowledge any life's existence as viable enough simply by existing. Things not considered human are not considerable because we say they are, but because they are: 'A wrong ... [places] the defender of the animal [or any wronged entity] before a dilemma. This is why the animal is a paradigm of the victim' (Lyotard 1988, 28). Posthumanism thus demands a rethinking of the primacy of the human in humanism as an object of study and the zenith of an example of life. Posthumanism also questions the possibility of thinking the human as separate in post-modernity by acknowledging the materiality of discourse in that it constructs life, including the human, and the collapse of the human/non-human animal and the organic/inorganic.

Humanism, Bodies, Desire, Discourse

The posthuman, like the queer, is the materially incarnated agency emergent from an alteration of paradigms of humanism. Certain dominant templates by which thought emerges in humanism rely on logic, truth, the possibility of the absolute, the myth of objectivity, chronology and the triumph of the human precisely through *his* ability to know himself. His – because the human is always primarily male. This differentiates him from the animal (and indeed woman, sexual others, racial others), incorrectly defined as without logical objective self-reflexivity. His logic also extends his existence through science and technology toward a form of more-than-human, a God-Man who can both reflect upon and control the conditions of his existence. Here the structure of chronology is important, as existence from the devolved animal to the evolved God-Man is equivalent to thought from the logical or mechanical to the techno-logical, materially from (furred) flesh to intellect to virtual or machinic, economically from the primitive or poor to the capitally successful. Sexually the God-Man is economically a re-producer not simply of offspring but of a repeated ideology, and increasingly reproduction is man-made, in a test tube rather than a womb, synthetically rather than corporeally. Posthumanism is a remapping of reified systems and structures of knowledge toward thought, existence toward becomings, sexuality toward undifferentiated desire and power toward ethical mediation. The God-Man is a kind of posthuman in that humanism no longer simply reflects and questions the conditions and nature of its existence but seeks to control and extend that existence, what I would call 'posthuman-humanism'. These posthuman philosophies are not utopian thoughts for the future but, like queer thought, are available here and now as techniques of existence *within* modern culture.

Queering gender and desire emphasises the socially, culturally and individually arbitrary nature of categories and their maintenance as key for systems of power. If queer goes both beyond the gendered binary of lesbian or gay then we need a term which goes beyond systems of male/female, and even further trans-, inter- or other gendered. Structural and post-structural repudiations of oppressive techniques of power have incarnated as feminism, post-colonial or anti-racist studies, lesbian/gay studies, animal rights and diffability (formerly disability) studies among others. Each discourse emerges directly as a response to difference defined isomorphically. Isomorphism is the system of logic which defines alterity purely through failure to be the default human. After Jacques Derrida and Luce Irigaray, isomorphism excavates the myth of oppositional categories. For example, there is no male and its opposite female, there is only male and a failure to be such. Hence 'less-than-men' – queers, gay men, child men, disabled men – are not quite men. Expletives in modern culture prove this. Men are insulted by being called 'pussies' and 'girls' – toward what is considered the extreme end of profane insults. Another example is found in race, which is essentially colour alterity. White people, even those who speak different languages in another white culture, are rarely asked where they come from. Racial alterity is found in the skin. Black is not white, but so too is 'dark' – Hispanic, Asian, Indian, native American or Australian, Polynesian and so forth. 'Where do you come from?' is usually an abstracted way of asking 'why is your skin not white?'

The way in which alterity through isomorphism coalesces is what Deleuze and Guattari call biunivocalisation – each identity is a selection from these possible failures unified into one individual – black woman, white gay disabled man. This signification through failure is *signifiance*. After signifiance each individual is placed at a level within the hierarchical strata, which is their place of *subjectification* – the subject signified by the powers of those who create meaning. We must remember however that these overarching structures are both externally enforced and internalised as finite possibilities of identity. Powers of signification are given rather than taken. In reference to feminism Irigaray states:

Women's social inferiority is reinforced and complicated by the fact that woman does not have access to language except through recourse to 'masculine' systems of representation which disappropriate her from herself and to other women. The 'feminine' is never to be identified except by and for the masculine. (1985, 85)

Here the crucial role of identity is invoked. I-dentity, the I which is first the white male human, is discursively and actually the singular, phallic and unified subject. Biunivocalisation articulates in the face.

The face is the pure surface of signification where flesh and materiality is colonised by discourse and meaning. Sexuality is formed in positioning two faces in a dialectic encounter. Signifiance creates mythical guarantees of anatomical gender truth. A female face guarantees female genitalia, a male face a penis. The dialectic of same faces forms homosexuality, of different faces heterosexuality. The rest of the flesh is subsumed by the identity-forming face and its phantasmatic corresponding genitalia. Foucault states:

... nothing other than bodies with which combinations, fabrications of pleasure will be possible. You cease to be imprisoned by your own face, in your own past, by your own identity ... it's not the affirmation of identity that's important, it's the affirmation of non-identity. (2000, 243)

Loss of face is a form of de-humanisation but only of that humanisation found in narratives of identity, facialisation and the human emergent through signifiance rather than bodies as zones of possibility, connectivity and intensity. Bringing this into a sexual discourse, Jean Baudrillard defining seduction states:

The perverse is that which perverts the order of terms. But here there are no longer any terms to pervert: There are only signs to be seduced ... everything calls into question the very hypothesis of a secret and determinate sexual instance. (1990, 135)

By exploring the pure possibility of bodies, always in excess of what non-perverts are allowed to do, we can be seduced by the risks and delights of not knowing what will happen, not by the promise of a pay-off object such as an orgasm or partner. Becoming shares with seduction the entering into an alliance with an entity by which we are seduced because it is other, because it is strange and not us. Seduction is not a desire to know or assimilate the other, it wants the other to change us and us to change the quality of the other to create a unique hybrid beyond any sexual narrative. Seduction is a sexual technique of queer becomings.

Queer literally celebrates its deviant status, a deviation from the imperative oppressive dominant, not a new nomenclaturing of how to be. Resonant with the phallus, science is the study of solids. Fluids and fluidity resist the spatial and temporal nature of existence. The posthuman is continuum, mobile, transforming itself and that which it encounters. 'The object of desire itself ... would be the transformation of fluid to solid? Which seals – this is well worth repeating – the triumph of rationality' (Irigaray 1985, 113). Two important elements are mentioned here, the role of desire and the relationship between rationality and the solidification and immobilisation of identity, truth, power and discourse. Scientific discourses address 'truth' which is always associated with rationality, where the interests of the subject disappear in the face of the object of study.

Involution challenges the separation between object and subject, knowledge as reflection and creation – the involvement and inextricability of more than one entity. The invocation of science as the new religion is important for two reasons. Where the primacy of the white male as human used to be God's will, by claiming it is the will of nature takes the responsibility and thus the accountability and ethics of access to defining reality away from those who maintain their power. Unsurprisingly, where God looked like man, the new sciences study that which doesn't. The human is now a copyrighted genome, too tiny for ordinary humans to see. Access to defining self and other is invisible, another language whose dictionary and grammar are clandestine.

Two paradigms are essential for science, rationality and the new God of humanism. The first is the spatial immobility of the human which is physical identity, the second the temporal maintenance of that identity, reflecting the temporal maintenance of scientific discourses (science seems to conveniently forget some of its historically ridiculous claims, as, presumably current claims will in the future be considered ridiculous). Spatially to think any 'thing', human or not, is to observe its 'it-ness', its defined outline, its ability to be re-cognised. Thus a thing is singular, solid, demarcated and understood not through its immanent incarnation but its capacity to be inserted into an already established taxonomy of what things are possible. Temporally a thing does not change, but occurs as a stable thing within explicitly demarcated phases. Things are not transforming or metamorphosing in-betweens, they are moments or stages: the sphinx's riddle to Oedipus – young man, middle age man, old man; Aristotle's taxonomy of living things – animal, woman, man; the persistent misreading of Darwinian evolution – invertebrate, vertebrate, mammal, human; racist studies of human development – the primitive, the civilised, the technological adept. Sexually women are defined through their reproductive capacity rather than their desire – sexually immature, fertile, infertile. Things come in incarnations rather than consistencies. The posthuman is the moment of the in-between spatially and of the permanently mobile, not yet and never arrived becoming which occurs through the unnatural alliances formed through a repudiation of one's nomenclatured, sacred 'thingness'. Scientifically these are considered aberrations or deformities of human evolution – monsters, hybrids. Religiously these are daemonic legions – feminism, animal rights activists, other political terrorists of alterity, politics as creating 'packs' and other maligned entities.

Other Non-Humans

The posthuman does not stand alone in troubling the human. Many theorists who could be considered posthuman navigate concepts such as the inhuman, nonhuman, subhuman and future human or alien. Neil Badmington analyses the fetishisation of the alien as a symptom of posthumanism. Where once the alien was fiercely repelled to maintain the integrity of the human, Badmington suggests 'what was once repelled is now embraced, what was once "them" is now "us"' (2004, 43). The alien is loved and hated, fetishised and feared, enigmatic and infective. This is seen in the post-modern phenomenon of alien abduction, which itself emphasises certain binary collapses – the alien is smarter and more technologically advanced (instead of the 'primitive' other) and the alien is increasingly sexless and devoid of emotion, represented frequently as a giant vacant-eyed head on a shiny infantile body. Aliens here are both dehumanised as intellectual machines beyond flesh and superhuman by being compellingly advanced.

Tim Dean takes the relation of viable humanity into the biosexual arena, where modern disease, particularly AIDS, has made certain humans obsessive objects of study named 'subhuman' and, similar to Badmington's alien, subjects which constantly threaten to infect the 'pure' human. The purity and normality of heterosexuality as a socio-cultural enactment of one's life (or lifestyle) is refined to a molecular level, by shifting from sex to cells. The relationship between life and humanity is here made explicit – the 'sick' human is treated as the subhuman, aligning the AIDS sufferer with physically defined subhumanities such as the racial or gendered other. An anthropomorphic ethic would attempt to bring the nonhuman up to the level of the human – equality feminism, animal rights based on how animals are 'like us', the validation in all politics of similarity over difference and reification over transformation. Posthuman ethics makes everything nonhuman by troubling the very viability of the term itself.

Vicki Kirby explores what Braidotti would call *bios*, which is *zoe* being life as a discursive incarnation. The human is organic and inextricable from our compulsion to create the category by a desire to know it. Posthumanism critiques humanism's claim that objects exist *a priori* and are objects to be studied, hence known. Posthumanism points to knowledge as an act, not of reflection, but creation. Kirby describes flesh itself as a textual inscription. The compulsion to know categorises hierarchically. Her criticism comes as the scriptural body (surfaces) arouses interest (knowledge) not concern (thought – the collapse of subject/object) (1997, 57). While it is clear that surface creates women, racial others and animals as objects, sexuality is a little more difficult as a surface. Desire as intensity and sex as acts are made surface through sexuality become identity. Our sexual identity and talking about sex virtualise the bodies, acts and effects of desire and pleasure. Thus our sexuality is inscribed as an object available for analysis.

The Posthuman

Post-modernity knells both death and birth. According to feminist ethicist Seyla Benhabib, post-modernity involved *The Death of Man*, the excavation of the 'truth' of history or *The Death of History* and the death of the desire to master the self and the world by knowing everything, *The Death of Metaphysics* (1992, 211). The death of the primacy of the male necessarily coincides with a claim to that male's universal and universalising perception of the past – history – thus unravelling predicted patterns of the future, where knowledge of the now – metaphysics – acts as a guarantee for that future. The posthuman is thus inherently involuted with postmodernity. The great philosopher of post-modernity, Lyotard, emphasises that humanism was not a system of reflection on reality but its own form of postmodernity in that its discourses *produced* reality: 'knowledge has become the principle force of production over the last few decades' (1989, 15). Postmodernity acknowledges that all reflection is creation and thus for every reiteration of information which allows tradition to accumulate, there is a possibility for a resistant move in this 'game' of discourse. The posthuman requires an intervention in the game, active but not necessarily with predicted outcomes. Queer is sexuality which resists but seeks neither to predict nor legitimate its effects and creative turns as a new form of sexuality to add to the current systems of narrativised sexuality.

There has been an alternate, less celebratory definition of the posthuman. Certain hybrids are held up as icons of posthumanity, but are more usually examples of extending the human rather than creating hybrids. Extending the human forms hybrids as a necessary evil of creating the human as infinite. Two examples are the desire for animal organ transplantation to harvest other sentient beings so we can live longer as we used to plough the land to eat in order to survive. Beasts of burden are within our bodies rather than at the end of ploughs. Because animals are positioned before us in the evolutionary narrative they are perceived as without rights in the face of the human as zenith of life (itself a contentious term in postmodernity). Salient to the plough which connected the beast of burden to the human is the machinic or cyborg hybrid, again involving the intervention of apparatus within rather than annexed to the body.

Donna Haraway's discussion of the organic in extension with the machinic leads to a sexualisation of cyborgism: 'Mind, body and tool are on very intimate terms' (1991, 165). Haraway's discussion of bioscience as cyborg emphasises the breakdown of the flesh/inorganic divide which is also a breakdown of the extrication of man from the destiny of his own flesh, be it through God or the natural elements which destroy us – illness and so forth. The human is able to create their own subjectivity at an organic and physiological level which goes deeper than subjectivity as performativity. This is why, according to Haraway 'a cyborg is a cybernetic organism, a hybrid of machine and organism, a creature of social reality as well as of fiction' (1991, 149). Where animals are regressive within the humanist narrative, the machine is seen as more-human, as pure decorporealised inorganic technology, although machines as digital means the future cyborg is not analogous to anything but creates its own form, self and thus destiny – the pure virtual which ablates or colonises rather than extends the flesh – hence the cyborg gone haywire obsession in many films such as *2001* (Stanley Kubrick 1968) and *The Terminator* (James Cameron 1984). In *Westworld* (Michael Crichton 1973) and *Blade Runner* (Ridley Scott 1982) the virtual and the actual, the represented and real also go haywire because of cyborgism. In modernity such films as *Metropolis* (Fritz Lang 1927) and *Modern Times* (Charlie Chaplin 1936) represented the human physically consumed as a cog needed by the larger structure machine.

In their introduction to the important anthology *Posthuman Bodies*, Judith Halberstam and Ira Livingstone state: 'The posthuman does not necessitate the obsolescence of the human: it does not represent an evolution or devolution of the human. Rather it participates in re-distribution of difference and identity' (1995, 10). Creative posthuman hybrids resist narrativisation in two ways: first, they exist as multi-connective nodes, spatial immanent interstitials. Just as activated effectuations are non-causal effects, the interstitial is not about thinking what a hybrid has been or will be (history ensuring causality) but thinking it in the moment and within the in-between – what elements connect the entities rather than their relationship to each other as two separate entities. Second, hybrids do not know their own future(s) and thus cannot seek to preserve or extend their present, nor sacrifice other entities in order to affirm their current form or identity. Hybrid posthumans celebrate the sacrifice of self, but theirs is not a death sacrifice, theirs is a queer sacrifice because reproduction does not map sexual acts and indeed is not possible. While science has created reproduction in Petri dishes and virtual wombs, sexuality and sexual acts in society ironically continue to mimic what was, pre- sexual 'revolution' reproductive acts. The invention of the pill was simply a way to continue sexual acts more beneficial for men without reproduction – the results changed but the acts and thus the sexualities did not transform.

Non-Perverted Perverts, Unsexy Sex

Care should be taken in celebrating uncritically queer posthuman trajectories, particularly in reference to sexual acts which are considered beyond traditional human desire in the same way that a becoming-machinic risks both challenging and reaffirming paradigms of power. They should not be mistakenly undertaken within economies of exchange of the normal for the perverted. Both Foucault and Deleuze share a horror of the sexually transgressive subject who is transgressive for its own sake, because it creates *the* transgressive subject, another form of identity available for subjectification albeit placed on the fringe. In 1981 Lotringer lamented the lack of sex in 'free' sexuality: 'Our society is saturated with sex, but is our sex really sexual?' (1981, 272). Lotringer sees the representation and articulation of sex and sexuality as a draining or sucking out of flesh and pleasure, desire, fluidity and ambiguity toward a series of images of and discourses on. We can be free to be any form of sexuality we want, to get off on anything, because everything is a 'natural' part of 'human sexuality'.

Even the most 'perverted' sexual subject is only so through the enunciation of a series of acts or evidences which affirms/forms that sexual subjectivity to another. Gender and perceived taste may be fluid but the subject nonetheless coalesces into an enunciated identity. Transgressives 'don't explore sexuality, they exchange recipes' (1981, 276). Lotringer emphasises that sexual radicalism is a kind of new Victorianism. Modern Victorians are not prevented from sex but refuse it. They cause the most problems for modern perceptions of sexuality. *Not* doing it, *not* having enough, *not* being 'free', and most importantly, *not* talking about it are the new sexual pathologies. Enunciating one's sexuality has nothing to do with sex but with the possibility, even inevitability, of sex.

We no longer confess our sexual transgressions, we are transgressive if we don't, so we have to make up the wicked sexual things we *don't* do. Catholic guilt for what we have done is now capitalist guilt for the not-done.

> *Fear and mystery doesn't mean going places – erotic travelogue – but becoming out of place, collapsing individual time [sexual history and projected future] and space [signified/subjectified identity] in the vector of movement. (Lotringer 1981, 274)*

Any catalogue of perversions remains reliant on description. For example, an anal obsessive may be naughty or dirty, gender ambiguous, but the body must nonetheless have an ass in its signified place. If it is not the place of shit and denigrated by the sacred genitals then it is not naughty. A designified patch of flesh cannot be a fetish because it cannot be signified. So an ass obsessive's fascination may be considered unpalatable but it is nonetheless a fetish – a 'thing' no different to shoes or cars. Queer was a direct response to the refusal to speak and thus to signify, but remains a mode of unspeech speech. Posthuman queer involves entering into alliances with things that cannot speak and with one's own silence, entering into alliances with inhumans or less-than-humans. Refusing identity is identity.

Becomings

Becoming is a project of entering into the zones or affects of another(s) and thus challenging and irreversibly transforming the singular self from a subjectified relationship with self and striated within society to a unique and permanently mobilised singularity. As queer encourages sexual selves to create relations with objects of desire which challenge and deterritorialise the self, becomings use non-human terms to encourage these deterritorialisations. To deterritorialise means to change the territories that create the meaning of certain identities – the map occupied by the identity. If the structure changes, so do the meanings of those within the territory. For this reason I will argue that the posthuman as represented in Deleuze and Guattari is queer – queer because the unpredictable relationship deterritorialises, posthuman because becomings take another human for the minoritarian aspect which excludes them from striation. Sexually this could be the masochist, who confounds pain and pleasure and is relatively de-gendered, and the woman, who, devoid of the phallus is more than and less than able to conform to heterosexual paradigms.

What elements of a subject make them a minority which creates their minoritarianism? Where does that put them in the hierarchy of which subjects are better than others? More so becomings take inhuman terms – the animal and eventually the abstract (music). Deleuze and Guattari's first example is becoming-animal. But they warn against a becoming-dog, as dogs are Oedipal (the little child in the family) or Jungian symbols (the dog as anthropomorphised metaphor of human qualities). A becoming-wolf includes the (wild) animal, the traditionally monstrous hybrid (werewolf) and the wolf as a pack animal. Becoming is not a metaphor, nor is it an acting 'like' or a turning into. One selects an intensity from the alliance term – in the case of a wolf, an unbearable hunger, a need rather than want to eat, so one becomes a hungry thing, destroying all food as capitalist symbol for an undifferentiated want which collapses Sigmund Freud's division between want (*trieb*) and need (*instink*). A pack is a collective in which the subject is both part of a greater affective assemblage and is itself a colony of disparate particles and zones.

> *Among the characteristics of a pack are small or restricted numbers, dispersion, noncomposable variable distances, qualitative metamorphoses, inequalities as remainders or crossings, impossibility of a fixed totalisation or hierarchisation. (Deleuze and Guattari 1987, 33)*

Immediately the resonances with queer become apparent – collective numbers over dialectics or binaries, the body as dehierarchised so its totality is available libidinally, desire as moving and metamorphic in itself and through the bodies and intensities it affects. A frequent response to the work of Deleuze and Guattari asks for concrete examples of experimental becomings. Because becomings are ceaseless and alter their incarnations as they transform, it is inherently impossible to offer an example in a traditional sense. But we can seek alliance terms which relate and respond directly to issues in modern culture – sexually, politically and ethically. The point is not what should we do, what is sexy, cool or queer, but what alliances would best alter trajectories and paradigms which reiterate the huMan as dominant and oppressive. Each suggestion for alliance is contingent on the human of each era and culture. Precisely for this reason there are no narratives which create truths, no techniques which perpetuate dominant power. Proliferative entities colonise the singular subject, incarnated in the Devil's annunciation that 'I am legion for we are many'. The viruses which infect our computers and we ingest through animals traverse kingdoms. The entering of the individual into an assemblage occurs in political movements where individuals share nothing else except a desire to alter a collective oppression by mobilising themselves into a pack as ideological infection, or mobilising themselves in the interests of those which they are not (such as male feminists, animal rights activists and breeder queers. Not, however, anti-abortionists, as they fight for the potential that will 'be like me').

Similarly any becoming makes of the individual a unique entity, a specific instance of a hybrid identity. This means that any situation of desire within which two becoming entities are positioned is inherently queer. If the identities of the subjects are amorphous, unique and mobile then their possible sexual relations are limitless and unpredictable. The conflation of animals and machines in these examples is clear – familiars and demons as hybrids, and a pack of hairy feminists like wolves. Each demonised person, be they individual in an assemblage with an unpalatable other, or part of a pack as a political collective, is always more than and less than one. This matrix shares elements with Irigaray's critique of phallologocentrism, an inherent system describing the relationship between humanism as a sexual politic – the logic founded on the signifier of the phallus as masculine, solid, singular, hermeneutic and so forth. Irigaray describes woman within phallologocentrism as castrated – less than one – and unreliably fluid – more than one.

Whence the mystery that woman represents in a culture claiming to count everything, to number everything by units, to inventory everything as individualities. *She is neither one nor two.* Irigaray's exploration of the formless form of femininity is appropriately descriptive of female morphology but also of pack collectives such as political movements and non-dialectic queer desire. The secret is not one to be revealed but that which resists the ability to be known. Above I describe the non-reproductive hybrid, unable to be known because always a non-repeatable singularity. Certain feminists have picked up on the connection between Irigaray's feminism and Deleuze and Guattari's becomings to form what is loosely known as corporeal feminism. Braidotti, Grosz, Moira Gatens, Elspeth Probyn, Zoe Sofoulis, Rosalyn Diprose (all incidentally Australian) have explored this connection and its implications in posthuman technology and queer. Grosz asks how ethics of difference can offer political change which, rather than including the other through equality by resembling the huMan, a politics of becoming

> ... involve[s] the more disconcerting idea of unpredictable transformation – mutation, metamorphosis – upheaval in directions and arenas with implications or consequences that cannot be known in advance. (1999, 17)

Politics, like all experiments in existence (creative or reiterative of traditional paradigms), relies on desire. Because desire in posthumanism is not a dialectic desire, through Deleuze and Guattari we can suggest that a politics of posthumanism, be it political, gendered, racial, animal or sexual, is always a queer politics. Posthumanism extends queer from the realm of the social-sexual to infect and inflect all systems of transformation. Philosophers, queers and all subjects do not classify their moments of action or thought. We are not sexual in a timetabled way, thinkers or political activists at certain times of the day, in segments which begin and end. We are already and always such.

Some alliance terms which are currently being suggested as effective for transforming the human and responsive to ethical inequality include alliances with animals, machines and the invocation of monsters. The animal is less-than-human, machines inorganic and other monsters include the disabled (a wheelchair bound person for example is a machinic hybrid, a blind person with a guide dog a becoming-animal through animal-human proprioception, both are considered 'less' abled), and the homeless, where poverty makes people not count. Welcomed poverty makes us one of 'them' and ablates our worth. These few examples are modern monstrosities – the interstitial, the in-between, the germinal. In pre-modernity becomings would be considered demonic, in modernity pathology. Madness is simply a failure to navigate society within this system of logic and value.

We are always more than one – not just queer, not only political, not exclusively thinkers – but each as inflected together and as singularities. Our becoming-animal is neither acting like nor pretending to be, but an entering into particular affects shared with animals that join us into hybrid formations which transform the animal concept with our becoming. Animal rights should not be based on their similarity or equivalence to the human, but our ability to become unhuman, unlike ourselves, existent through our irredeemable divergence from the human rather than animal becoming-human. What zones do we share with animals? The point is that, for Deleuze, animals are neither functional to teleological systems of classification, nor about metaphors:

> They are rather about metamorphosis … Writers, like animals, are committed creatures who live on full alert, constantly tensed up in the effort of captivating and sustaining the signals that come from their plane of immanent contact with other forces. (Braidotti 2002, 126)

Similarly, like animals, women are at permanent and actual physical risk from violence perpetuated not simply by 'men' but by the systems that preserve sexual oppression, from desire to the legal and scientific structures which maintain these systems. Becoming-woman is not a metaphor, not transvestitism which can be put on and taken off. But a man in a skirt, a man neither woman nor man, creates a hybrid that may indeed put him at risk of violence in everyday situations and it is this zone, rather than an equivalent sexual violence, which is his becoming woman because first it is a becoming not-man, an inhuman. The cyborg self, the self with machinic substitutes for organs, the self on a computer, must use that self differently to negotiate the situation. Certain cyborg selves represent an enforced teratology borne of the pathological technological compulsion in scientific institutions to extend the human. Nonetheless monsters are being created in excess of science's ability to predict or control them. The extreme body modifier, which fashion has attempted to assimilate, still represents the monstrous, part of a demonic pack (think of a facial tattoo, or penile bifurcation, both examples of unaccepted modification).

The body modifier surgically interrogates and transforms volitionally, transgressing the body as a sacred site with which only medicine should intervene. Body modifiers are termed 'modern primitives', encompassing the valuation of the de-civilised (the association of the primitive with the animal, while problematic, is persistent). They are described collectively, what Alphonso Lingis would call a community of those who may have nothing else in common:

> *The aliens on other continents, encountered as the European Enlightenment*
> *[humanism] extended its scientio-technological and political institutions*
> *across the planet, were conceptualised as barbarians, animals without*
> *language ... animals with different bodies. (1994, 144)*

A posthuman interpretation of Lingis's anthropological work would acknowledge an uncommon community – political collectives of feminists who are all women in unique and incommensurable ways, queers who desire uniquely but nonetheless seek queer mobilisations, animal rights activists who in every other respect are divergent from each other. Unsurprisingly human culture often conflates these disparate dividuations into a singular 'threat' – the vegan animal rights activist who is also a queer feminist communist. All are different but all share the desire to redistribute power relations and so all are posthuman. These activists frequently have their political activism, their becomings, described as a form of madness. Strong or resistant women, racial others, homosexuals historically have had their difference classified as forms of madness, analysed and 'cured' psycho-medically. Activists are the madness which virally infect 'normal' society, as posthuman as any computer virus or animal borne infection. The 1980s AIDS panic was the physiological transformation of the former panic of 'catching' homosexuality. Madness is always infective, a modern Faustian temptation of the human individual into the pack. Feminists, ecologists, anti-capitalists and animal rights activists are seen to brainwash in order to recruit. The collective and the hybrid are thus always challenges to what it means to be human, indeed what it means to be organic and alive, just as postmodernity challenges truth and existence, knowledge and power:

> *There is no need to begin with transgression, we must go to the very limits ...*
> *spread out the immense body of the libidinal 'body' which is quite different to*
> *the frame. It is made from the most heterogeneous textures, bone, epithelium,*
> *sheets to write on, charged atmospheres, swords, glass cases, people, grasses.*
> *(Lyotard 1993, 2)*

Feminism, animal rights, racial studies and gay and lesbian studies are postmodern incommensurable but nonetheless co-present challenges to modernity. Becomings are borne of undifferentiated desire, to open oneself through a materialist, discursive, corporeal metamorphosis. The posthuman marks an end to exclusionary politics and reified knowledge, and is defined not by its limits but moments of plastic liminality created as various hybrid and pack encounters, always libidinal, always political and because it demands entering into irreducible alliances with alterity, offers what we could call a queer ethics.

Suggested Further Reading

Braidotti, R. (2002), *Metamorphoses: Toward a Materialist Theory of Becoming* (Cambridge: Polity).

Deleuze, G. and Guattari, F. (1987), *A Thousand Plateaus: Capitalism and Schizophrenia*, trans. B. Massumi (London: Athlone).

Giffney, N. and Hird, M.J. (eds) (2008), *Queering the Non/Human* (Aldershot: Ashgate).

Halberstam, J. and Livingston, I. (eds) (1995), *Posthuman Bodies* (Bloomington and Indianapolis, IN: Indiana University Press).

MacCormack, P. (2008), *Cinesexuality* (Aldershot: Ashgate).

References

2001 (1968), dir. S. Kubrick [feature film].

Badmington, N. (2004), *Alien Chic: Posthumanism and the Other Within* (London: Routledge).

Baudrillard, J. (1990), *Seduction*, trans. B. Singer (New York: St Martin's Press).

Benhabib, S. (1992), *The Situated Self* (Cambridge: Polity).

Blade Runner (1982), dir. R. Scott [feature film].

Braidotti, R. (2002), *Metamorphoses: Toward a Materialist Theory of Becoming* (Cambridge: Polity).

—— (2005), *Transpositions* (Cambridge: Polity).

Butler, J. (2004), *Precarious Life: Powers of Violence and Mourning* (New York: Verso).

Dean, T. (2000), *Beyond Sexuality* (Chicago, IL: University of Chicago Press).

Deleuze, G. and Guattari, F. (1987), *A Thousand Plateaus: Capitalism and Schizophrenia*, trans. B. Massumi (London: Athlone).

Foucault, M. (2000), 'Bodies and Pleasure', trans. J. Steintrager, in S. Lotringer (ed.), *More and Less* (New York: Semiotext(e)).

Grosz, E. (1995), *Space, Time and Perversion: The Politics of Bodies* (Sydney: Allen and Unwin).

—— (1999), 'Introduction', in E. Grosz (ed.), *Becomings: Explorations in Time, Memory and Future* (Ithaca, NY: Cornell University Press).

Halberstam, J. and Livingston, I. (eds) (1995), *Posthuman Bodies* (Bloomington and Indianapolis, IN: Indiana University Press).

Haraway, D. (1991), *Simians, Cyborgs and Women: The Reinvention of Nature* (New York: Routledge).

Irigaray, L. (1985), *This Sex Which Is Not One*, trans. C. Porter (Ithaca, NY and New York: Cornell University Press).

Kirby, V. (1997), *Telling Flesh: The Substance of the Corporeal* (London and New York: Routledge).

Lingis, A. (1994), *The Community of Those Who Have Nothing in Common* (London and New York: Routledge).

Lotringer, S. (1981), 'Defunkt Sex' in Lotringer, S. (ed.), *Polysexuality* (New York: Semiotext(e)).

Lyotard, J.F. (1988), *The Differend: Phrases in Dispute*, trans. G. Van den Abeele (Manchester: Manchester University Press).

—— (1989) *The PostModern Condition: A Report on Knowledge*, trans. G. Bennington and B. Massumi (Minneapolis, MN: University of Minnesota Press).

—— (1993), *Libidinal Economy*, trans. I. Hamilton Grant (Bloomington and Indianapolis, IN: Indiana University Press).

MacCormack, P. (2004), 'Perversion: Transgressive Sexuality and Becoming-Monster', *Thirdspace: A Journal of Feminist Theory and Culture* 3:2, http://www.thirdspace.ca/journal.

May, T. (2005), *Gilles Deleuze: An Introduction* (Cambridge: Cambridge University Press).

Metropolis (1927), dir. F. Lang [feature film].

Modern Times (1936), dir. C. Chaplin [feature film].

Nelkin, D. and Lindee, M.S. (1995), 'The Media-ted Gene', in J. Terry and S. Urla (eds), *Deviant Bodies: Critical Perspectives on Difference in Science and Popular Culture* (Bloomington and Indianapolis, IN: Indiana University Press).

Terminator, The (1984), dir. J. Cameron [feature film].

Westworld (1973), dir. M. Crichton [feature film].

PART II

DISCOURSE

Queering, Cripping

Todd R. Ramlow

In her early, important elaboration on the politics and continued efficacy of queer theory and politics, Judith Butler asserts: 'If the term queer is to be a site of collective contestations, the point of departure for a set of historical reflections and futural imaginings, it will have to remain that which is, in the present, never fully owned, but always and only redeployed, twisted, queered from a prior usage and in the direction of urgent and expanding political purposes' (1993, 228). Similarly, a decade later, Robert McRuer and Abby Wilkerson, in their elaboration of a queer influenced and inflected disability studies and politics, argue that 'suggesting that "in a free society everyone will be disabled," is not necessarily universalizing dismissal, fetishistic appropriation, or exploitative truth of the system; it is instead a recognition that another world can exist in which an incredible variety of bodies and minds are valued and identities are shaped, where crips and queers have effectively (because repeatedly) displaced the able-bodied/disabled binary' (McRuer and Wilkerson 2003, 14).

I begin with this queercrip[1] alliance among Butler–McRuer–Wilkerson as these two works seem to precisely mark the terrain through which the possibility of a progressive cripqueer politics and theoretical methodology has been articulated. For Butler, as well as for McRuer and Wilkerson, the radical possibility of queer theory (in the former) and an allied queer theory–disability studies (in the latter)[2] is that such theorisings and methodologies point the way to material practices that might shape reality in new ways. As McRuer and Wilkerson assert, 'another

---

1   Throughout I will use 'cripqueer' and 'queercrip' interchangeably (though McRuer and Wilkerson [2003] use the latter consistently in their introduction to the special volume of *GLQ* dedicated to the intersections of queer theory and disability studies). This is to foreground the non-hierarchical aims of both, in theory and in practice, so that neither the crip nor the queer occupy a privileged site of critique or dissent.

2   Though Butler is directly concerned with sexual politics, queer theory and queer practices in *Bodies That Matter* (1993), her recent work has begun to include questions of disability embodiment and performativity in her ongoing interrogation of gender, subjectivity and power. See Butler (2004a; 2004b) in which she briefly considers how disability as well as race, gender and sexuality work to define and shore up the very limits of the human.

world can exist'.[3] Butler's similar observation in *Bodies That Matter* informs McRuer and Wilkerson's own queercrip theorising: Queer, as Butler's epigraph demands, is a methodological and political tool which must always be queered/twisted/redeployed 'in order to accommodate – without domesticating – democratizing contestations that have and will redraw the contours of the movement in ways that can never be fully anticipated in advance' (1993, 228).

Queer theory and crip theory, then, as I understand and deploy them, are world-(re)making, they are, individually and together, both methodologies and shifting sets of practices, they are coalitional, creating ever new alliances across fields of difference in the construction of queercrip consciousness and societies. Cripqueer theory is, to risk a kind of essentialism, anti-normative in all regards (and so anti-racist, anti-homophobic, anti-neoliberalism, anti-ableist and on and on), out of the recognition that universalising discourses and normative societies have only produced violence and hostility towards difference.[4] As well, universals and their discourses flatten out differences through idealisms deployed through naturalised power relations that homogenise human life.[5] The anti-normativity of cripqueer theory then is to be understood, following Zillah Eisenstein, as 'polyversal' (2004, 29), in the sense that it is only in and through our differences that any provisional or coalitional unity may be claimed: if we are all somehow the same, our sameness lies only in our varying conditions of difference.[6] Queercrip theory offers one site for drafting not universalising but polyversalising discourses and politics.[7]

While queer and crip theory offer simultaneously methodology and ontology,[8] I will focus here on the methodological practices, though always with the understanding that the methods are reciprocally and mutually constitutive with the practices. In what follows I will survey the general scholarly terrain of

---

3   McRuer and Wilkerson are perhaps more direct when they assert: 'Another world is possible, but we need to be vigilant, since we are already being asked to consent to worlds that would short-circuit our public dissent. Cripping the (queer) nation or, for that matter, queering the (crip) nation entails, instead, claiming our dissent and locating disability and queerness at the center of the world that movements for social and global justice more broadly are working to effect' (2003, 10).

4   This is of course one of the main thrusts of Jean François Lyotard's (1984; 1992) elaboration on the postmodern.

5   In *Precarious Life* (2004a) Butler demonstrates how human rights discourse is precisely this kind of homogenising universal that hides its own investments in power (see in particular the chapter 'Violence, Mourning, Politics'), and in *What is Philosophy?* Deleuze and Guattari caution us that universals are not transparent categories, despite the fact that dominant ideologies encourage us to conceive of them as such (1994, 7).

6   This 'essential' anti-normativity is a kind of 'strategic essentialism' as suggested by scholars such as Stephen Heath (1978) and Diana Fuss (1989).

7   'Humanity transcends and articulates polyversality simultaneously because no individual is ever completely different or totally the same as another' (Eisenstein 2004, 61).

8   This is not, of course, the constitution of an ontological state that is ever fully totalised or closed. Cripqueer theory is, perhaps more properly, deontological.

'queering' as a primary mode of queer critique as well as 'cripping' in relation to crip/disability studies, and to how both ally to form a cripqueer theoretical project. In this I will look at two kinds of text that offer or open themselves to a queercrip consciousness and critique. I will consider the work of cripqueer performer and activist Greg Walloch, whose film *F**K the Disabled: The Surprising Adventures of Greg Walloch* (2001)[9] consciously erodes, through parody and camp aesthetics, the medical/charity models of ableist culture and its desexualisation of cripqueers. Lastly, I will show how we might apply a cripqueering methodology to popular culture texts that seem to have little to say about either queerness or disability. Despite the fact that the *X-Men* films (2000; 2003; 2006) are regularly read as allegories of race and racism (indeed, these topics are written into the structure of the narratives), these films can be (and are being) read as allegories of queercrip embodiment (McRuer 2006). I will demonstrate how we might undo the liberal humanist logic of these immensely popular films and offer a cripqueer destabilisation and reclamation of the bodily differences of the superhero; perhaps 'supercripping' the superhero.

Queering

Judith Butler's assertion of the necessary fluidity of queer is, as I have suggested above, integral to understanding queering as a methodological tool, but certainly she is not alone in her own queering of queer. The foundational texts of queer theory have insisted on as much from the beginning. In *Saint Foucault: Towards a Gay Hagiography*, David M. Halperin defines queer 'as an identity without an essence, not a given condition but a horizon of possibility' (1995, 79). Halperin continues: '[Q]ueerness constitutes not just a resistance to social norms or a negation of established values but a positive and creative construction of different ways of life' (1995, 81). Queering denotes a queer becoming in excess of totalised identity categories (and identity politics); it is a critical practice of reading that points to new ways of being (or of always becoming), new social arrangements and distributions of power.

Accordingly, queering poses a challenge to cultures of normativity and is deeply threatening to the *status quo*; the new worlds it calls into being upset the norms and forms of heteronormative society. As Robert McRuer has noted, queers and queering represent a 'critical perversion that continuously forges unexpected alliances and gives voice to identities our heteronormative culture would like to, and cannot, silence' (1997, 5). Similarly, Cindy Patton asserts that '"Queer," if it is to have any utility, is best understood, not as a model of identity and practice that can be imitated or molded to a local setting, but as evidence of a kind of

---

9   Co-written with Eli Kabillio, and directed by Kabillio, *F**K the Disabled* (2001) is based on Walloch's original performance piece, *White Disabled Talent*.

unstoppable alterity' (2002, 210).[10] Queering is mobile critique; it creates alliances, ever-changing modes of embodiment and embodied practices. As a methodological practice queering is relational in its political aims just as it resists universalising gestures within and without. Not all queers are queer in the same ways. Not all queerings read culture in the same modes. Queering, then, is a methodology that is continually renewing and reinventing itself in response to changing social and political climates.

So queering is a practice of reading culture to resist heteronormativity, but how might it proceed (and how has it proceeded)? In terms of critical work, queering sets out by reading against the grain of a wide variety of cultural texts in order to expose the normative logic, ideology and injunctions at work underneath. Queer critical interventions offer alternative readings and significations of those textual practices to demonstrate the necessary instability of such 'natural', 'fixed' or 'stable' discourses.[11] Lisa Duggan's article 'Holy Matrimony!' which appeared in *The Nation* in March 2004, exemplifies this mode of queering as a critical practice and its efficacy within the public sphere. Here, Duggan takes on the ongoing lesbian and gay marriage controversies in the United States, and refuses to acquiesce to the call for 'mainstream' (really, very traditional and conservative) social and political values demanded by dominant, national LGBT advocacy groups like the HRC.[12] Instead, Duggan queers the whole debate by uncovering the social and political implications of the push for state sanctioned lesbian and gay marriage.

Duggan demonstrates how calls for lesbian and gay marriage dovetail with much less 'progressive' politics, such as the 'Marriage Promotion' programme appended to the reauthorisation of TANF.[13] Marriage Promotion 'rewards' women on welfare with better benefits if they stay or become married. Obviously this government coercion of some of its citizens further disadvantages already disadvantaged women, 'encouraging' them to stay in potentially abusive and dangerous relationships in order to claim governmental 'benefits'. LGBT calls for federally recognised marriage, Duggan asserts, implicitly get in bed with

---

10 In 'How to Bring Your Kids Up Gay: The War on Effeminate Boys', Eve Sedgwick asserts that 'something about *queer* is inextinguishable. Queer is a continuing moment, movement, motive – recurrent, eddying, *troublant* ... The immemorial current that *queer* represents is as antiseparatist as it is antiassimilationist' (1993, xii).

11 It is to Michel Foucault that queer theory is most indebted, and in particular his multi-volume *History of Sexuality* (1990; 1986a; 1986b), especially *Volume I* (1990), which demonstrated that sexuality is not something 'natural', that homo- and hetero- sexuality (and everything in between and elsewhere) has a history, and that if sexualities, as they are currently constituted, have not always been the same, then they can be changed in response to urgent and emergent social and political conditions.

12 The Human Rights Campaign is the United States' largest, most visible, influential and best funded LGBT political action organisation, as revered for its political clout as it is criticised for its assimilationist strategies.

13 TANF is the current incarnation of US federal welfare. 'Temporary Aid to Needy Families' replaced the older 'Aid to Families with Dependant Children' under Bill Clinton's 1996 Welfare Reform Act.

Republican and Right edifications of the 'sanctity of marriage'. Ultimately Duggan radicalises the question of the legal status of marriage, and imagines a queer new world in which all sorts of relationships, romantic or otherwise, are valued and offered governmental benefits:

> What if there were a way to separate the tax advantages of joint household recognition, or the responsibilities of joint parenting, from the next-of-kin recognition so that such rights might go to a non-co-resident relative, a friend or a lover? And what if many benefits, such as health insurance, could be available to all without regard for household or partnership status? The moral conservative's nightmare vision of a flexible menu of options might become a route to progressive equality! (2004)

Duggan's queering of the lesbian and gay marriage debates opens the door to a radical new vision of social equality and the ethical terms of state sanctioning of private relationships and arrangements.

In a similar vein, Eve Sedgwick queered dominant cultural trends of the late 1980s in her essay 'How to Bring Your Kids Up Gay: The War on Effeminate Boys' (1993). The essay is a response to the 1989 US Department of Health and Human Services 'Report on the Secretary's Task Force on Youth Suicide', which infamously purged research detailing the much higher rate at which LGBT teens kill themselves. Sedgwick asserts that '[i]t's always open season on gay kids' (1993, 155), and locates the national antipathy towards gay teens in the 1980 revised DSM-III: 'The same DSM-III that ... was the first that did not contain an entry for "homosexuality", was also the first that *did* contain a new diagnosis ... "Gender Identity Disorder of Childhood"' (1993, 156). The implication is clear for Sedgwick. If gay and lesbian adults must be 'tolerated', proto-gay sissy boys and proto-lesbian butch girls must be medicalised out of existence. Sedgwick's provocative title also plays on dominant fears and anxieties about 'proper' parenting and the production of 'normal' children, and queers then current parenting bestsellers with titles like *Why Good Parents Have Bad Kids: How to Make Sure That Your Child Grows Up Right* (1988) by E. Kent Hayes and Tipper Gore's infamous *Raising PG Kids in an X-Rated Society* (1987). Sedgwick's and Duggan's essays demonstrate the social and political potential of queering as methodology and point to new, queer ways of seeing and being in the world. To return to McRuer and Wilkerson's assertion, queering shows that 'another world is possible'.

Cripping

Just as queer theory and queering have been indebted to Michel Foucault's genealogy of sexuality, so too are disability studies and cripping as methods of enquiry. Disability studies is often more directly engaged with Foucault's work in *The Birth of the Clinic: An Archaeology of Medical Perception* (1973) and *Discipline and*

Punish: The Birth of the Prison (1979), insofar as these two works elaborate on how the body is produced via empiricism as a type of object, schematised within the ideology of the 'norm', and subject to the disciplinary regimentations that pervade society.[14] Bodily differences are not 'natural' (though they are material) facts, but rather reflect socially constructed norms and values that uphold existing ideological practices, extend the grasp of normativity and organise (heteronormative and compulsorily able-bodied) societies.[15] Mark Jeffreys makes the contributions of Foucauldian notions of discursive constructivism to disability studies clear:

> *Constructivism opens up the study of disability, previously the exclusive domain of the biological, medical, and rehabilitative professions, as a new field of cultural studies. In particular, constructivism makes possible the argument that disability is itself not so much a pathological or even biological condition as it is a cultural condition, a marginalized group identity that has a history of oppression and exclusion, a stigmatized category created to serve the interests of the dominant ideology. (2002, 32)*

If disability is 'the most labile and pliable of categories' and 'a category whose constituency is contingency itself' (Bérubé 1998), then these constructions and contingencies can be de-naturalised, opened up to interventions so that a new or different 'order of things' (which might be against all such 'orderings') can emerge. This is the work of cripqueer consciousness and critical methodology.

Foucault's three-volume *The History of Sexuality* (1990; 1986a; 1986b) has also been integral to the evolution of disability studies and many foundational scholars in the field have limned disability methodology in relation to sexuality studies and queer theory. Robert McRuer has made the connection of queer theory and disability studies most clear in his neologism 'compulsory able-bodiedness' (2002). Taking off from Adrienne Rich's notion of compulsory heterosexuality, which denotes the

---

14   Of course, all of Foucault's major works are relevant to disability studies and queer theory in that they demonstrate the far-reaching effects of the regime of the 'norm' and how the norm's various discourses have real effects on bodily life. *Madness and Civilization: A History of Insanity in the Age of Reason* (1988) has clear implications for the experiences of mentally and cognitively disabled individuals, and *The Order of Things: An Archaeology of the Human Sciences* (1994) demonstrates how norms, bodily and otherwise, structure discursive fields as diverse as artistic representation, linguistics and economics. The recent publication of Foucault's *Abnormal: Lectures at the Collège de France, 1974–1975* (2004) further clarifies these imbrications of power, norms and the body. By extension, disability studies and queer theory are also linked to Georges Canguilhem's *The Normal and the Pathological* (1989), which directly and widely influenced Foucault's work (especially as Canguilhem was Foucault's doctoral supervisor). Recently, as an example of the fluid utility of the critique of the norm that Canguilhem and Foucault instituted, Lennard J. Davis (2002) has considered the imbrications of the norm, disability and political enfranchisement, as Catherine J. Kudlick (2005) has similarly shown, and Margrit Shildrick (2005) offers a genealogical critique of norms and disability.

15   As Simi Linton remarks: 'disability is socially constructed to serve certain ends' (1998, 4).

sets of practices by which occupation of spaces of privilege and normalcy within patriarchal cultures are determined by a disciplinary heterosexuality, McRuer asserts the same of able-bodied norms. Heterosexuality and able-bodiedness function as ideological ideals and normative injunctions that (re)produce and privilege the dominance of what Rosemarie Garland-Thomson has called the 'normate', 'the veiled subject position of cultural self, the figure outlined by the array of deviant others whose marked bodies shore up the normate's boundaries' (1997, 8).

A further alliance of disability studies with queer theory has been the way in which disability scholars have sought to describe the cultural conditioning of disability within the rhetoric of 'coming out' narratives. Simi Linton invokes this rhetorical gesture in the opening pages of *Claiming Disability* (1998, 3). This coming out may seem unnecessary or repetitive, as dominant ableist understandings of physical difference regularly conceive of disability as that mark of difference or Otherness that is always already eminently visible. However, dominant notions of social propriety and comportment for the normate dictate that disability is that which must never be directly addressed or spoken about.[16] Greg Walloch, a performance artist whose work I will consider in more detail shortly, tells an anecdote in *F**K the Disabled* about a little girl on the street who can't stop staring at his disabled body, and the mother who vocally and loudly remonstrates her to stop staring, a performance on the mother's part that draws much more attention to his physical difference than the little girl's stares.[17]

Rosemarie Garland-Thomson complicates dominant understandings of disability and makes the coming out connection stronger in her focus on the complication and potential subversion of able-bodied norms figured in invisible disabilities:

A disability's degree of visibility also affects social relations. An invisible disability, much like a homosexual identity, always presents the dilemma of whether or when to come out or to pass. One must always anticipate the risk of tainting a new relationship by announcing an invisible impairment or the equal hazard of surprising someone by revealing a previously undisclosed disability. (1997, 14)

---

16   Or at least social decorum demands that disability not be openly discussed in mixed gatherings of disabled and normate, and if it must be addressed, it is the obligation of the person with disability/ies to assuage normate anxieties, to make sure that social contact will be managed and boundaries maintained: 'In other words, disabled people must use charm, intimidation, ardor, deference, humor, or entertainment to relieve nondisabled people of their discomfort' (Garland-Thomson 1997, 13).

17   Of course, the power of the gaze to mark disability, to interpellate it as such and reinscribe normative hierarchies has been a major theme in much disability studies scholarship, most directly in the several essays by Rosemarie Garland-Thomson (2002; 2005a; 2005b) addressing the function of the stare, and in Eli Clare's essay 'Gawking, Gaping, Staring' (2003). Nonetheless, in dominant modes of social perception disability is that which we must never 'see' even while we stare directly at it. Tobin Siebers has complicated these dynamics of seeing and not-seeing, and theorised through queer theory and disability studies the implications and politics of 'passing' and 'coming out' for people with disabilities in 'Disability as Masquerade' (2004).

Coming out as disabled or queer or both carries more with it than risk, it also carries with it the possible subversion of dominant ideals of bodily norms and social decorum; the 'surprise' of disability as of queerness, whether 'visible' or 'invisible' prior to the moment of coming out, challenges currently constituted social orders and presumptions of bodily life.[18]

As Garland-Thomson's invocation of 'passing' indicates, disability studies has also drawn for its methodologies on other 'minority studies' frameworks, particularly those of critical race studies. David Mitchell and Sharon Snyder assert, in *Narrative Prosthesis: Disability and the Dependencies of Discourse*, that 'disability, like gender, sexuality, and race' are constructed categories of 'discursive investment' (2000, 2). Garland-Thomson's work in *Extraordinary Bodies* details the imbrications of these in the history of US popular cultural spectacles like the freak show and in canonical American literature by white and black women writers. This is not to say that the experience of disability is directly correlative to those of race or sexuality, but rather, as I have remarked in another essay, that 'queerness and disability intersect with gender, race, and class to compose a hegemonic formation of cultural aberrancy and social exclusion' (Ramlow 2003, 108). In its attentive detailing of these intersections, disability studies points to the kind of coalitional politics necessary for the construction of 'another world'.

'Cripping' has been a recent refinement of disability methodology and rhetoric that most precisely articulates these possibilities. Similar to the queering of queer, cripping reframes, reinterprets and resignifies multiple representations of disability in the service of urgent and emerging social and political contexts. In *Narrative Prosthesis*, Mitchell and Snyder anticipate the reclaiming of 'cripple' as a methodological tool in what they term 'transgressive reappropriation': 'Rather than rail against the unjust social exclusion of cripples, scholars have begun to attend to the subversive potential of the hyperbolic meanings invested in disabled figures' (2000, 35). Cripping, in these terms, recasts 'deviance as value' (2000, 35). Mitchell and Snyder invoke Leonard Kriegel's 'identification with [Shakespeare's] Richard III's antipathy toward the incomprehension of an able-ist world' (2000, 21), and question 'the pleasure that audiences, disabled and nondisabled alike, continue to find in the performance of the play' (2000, 114). In their 'transgressive reappropriation', or cripping, of *The Tragedy of King Richard the Third*, Mitchell and Snyder read agency into the character. Cripping Richard III shows him to be a powerful figure 'disabled' only by the society and environment in which he lives. Richard III is only normatively an object of sentimentality or pity, and cripping can reclaim one of Anglophone literature's most toxic stereotypes for disability agency.

Another type of agency is claimed in Robert McRuer's 'Crip Eye for the Normate Guy: Queer Theory and the Disciplining of Disability Studies' (2005). McRuer plays on the implications of the title of Bravo's surprise smash-hit reality show *Queer Eye for the Straight Guy* for a crip perspective and crip politics. *Queer Eye* is, of course,

---

18 This is also the potential of what Siebers calls 'unconventional uses of disability identity' (2004, 4).

premised on the belief that gay men are 'naturally' more stylish and sophisticated than their straight male counterparts, and that if only the straight guys could get a little advice from the queers, things could, as the title song goes, 'only get better'. Presumably 'better' for straight guys and, more important to the show, for their female wives, girlfriends and partners. Playing on the show's title, McRuer implicitly claims a valuation of crip identity and imagines a world in which a crip eye might teach normate guys more than a thing or two about embodiment and 'normalcy'. Of course, McRuer isn't easily celebratory of Bravo's show, and critiques its normalising rhetoric. McRuer's crip eye is not at all the same as Bravo's *Queer Eye*, which skips happily along with mainstream LGBT assimilationist politics and neoliberal market economics. Rather, for McRuer, a crip eye is, as he remarks of queer elsewhere, a 'critical perversion' (1997, 5) of dominant modes of seeing and being, and which is resistant to and transgressive of discourses of normativity. Seeing with a crip eye would mark the 'capacity for recognizing and withstanding the vicissitudes of compulsory able-bodiedness' (2005, 591) in order to undermine those norms and 'demand access to a world shaped otherwise' (2005, 592). Cripping, then, looks to revitalise the past, as in Mitchell and Snyder's re-reading of *Richard III*, but also to reimagine the future as in McRuer's rhetoric of the crip eye, which is really, as his essay demonstrates, a cripqueer eye.

We can see this coalitional methodology in action by applying a queercrip eye to a variety of cultural objects. I will focus in the next sections on a few examples from contemporary visual culture, Greg Walloch and Eli Kabillio's *F**k the Disabled* and the *X-Men* films.

Cripqueering/Queercripping

Based on his live performance piece 'White Disabled Talent', Gregg Walloch's film *F**k the Disabled* is a series of connected monologues, interspersed with skit comic vignettes and interviews with the performer, his family and peers, that chronicles Walloch's various experiences onstage and off with disability and queerness; it is a kind of cripqueer testimonial and a critique of normativity. The film, like the original performance text, opens with Walloch taking the stage, manoeuvring up the few steps with his crutches and declaring, 'I'm gay, I'm disabled, and I am living in Harlem. Because I like keeping it real.' Here Walloch directly and immediately invokes several taboos of bourgeois social norms. His opening is, of course, a coming out performance, but this 'coming out' is complicated by the visuality of his disabled body. When Walloch takes the stage his body disrupts the normative visual field of the comedy/performance art space.[19] His direct address acknowledges this

---

19 This notion of the presence of physical disability and how it disrupts the normative visual field is, of course, Lennard Davis's, from *Enforcing Normalcy* (1995), especially in Chapter 6, 'Visualizing the Disabled Body: The Classical Nude and the Fragmented Torso'.

disruption, but only secondarily. His first assertion is of his queerness, up until this moment his invisible difference. His subordinating disability to queerness is not a performance dismissing or trivialising his disability, as if it were of lesser concern, thematically, personally. Rather, his primary declarative performance of queerness undermines what the audience presumably 'knows' when he takes the stage, his physical disability, and furthermore, what the audience presumably 'knows' about the sexuality of people with disabilities. As many disability scholars and activists have noted, sexuality is routinely that which is denied to people with disabilities, and compulsory heterosexuality is perhaps even more impacted in the disabled body (Shakespeare, Gillespie-Sells and Davies 2006). Walloch's declarative opening undermines the presumed stability of these sexual and bodily norms.

Furthermore, Walloch's invocation of his 'living in Harlem' because he likes 'keeping it real' connects his own body and identity to the marginalisations of race and bourgeois norms of occupying 'appropriate' space. What would a gay, white, disabled boy be doing living in historically black Harlem? In response, in one of the documentary style interview clips interspersed throughout the film Walloch quips, 'It's amazing what an artist will do for cheap rent.' Here, Walloch invokes the stereotype of the 'starving artist', but more subtly indexes the economic vulnerability of people with disabilities, who are unemployed and underprivileged at rates far higher than their normate counterparts, regardless of race, gender or class position. But his invocation of economic necessity is not the disavowal of a connection between disabled, homophobic, and racist marginalisation. Rather, Walloch asserts these as mutually constituting and reinforcing structures of oppression, and his parody and playfulness point to possible alliances among marginalised groups.

In the bit that gives the film its title, Walloch more directly takes on the disciplining and proscriptions of the queercrip body, and demonstrates exactly how compulsory heterosexuality is intimately bound to compulsory able-bodiedness. Walloch tells a story of how at brunch one day a friend asked 'Is the reason that you're gay due to the fact that you're crippled and you can't get lucky with women? So, you know, you had no choice but to sleep with men for sex?' The friend's query raises common normate prejudices and the belief that both homosexuality and disability are pathological conditions. Homosexuality is seen as a kind of disability and disabled people are undesirable as hetero sex partners. Walloch takes the homo/dis-phobia at work in this perception and parodies it to the extreme. He declares: 'Because of my unfortunate, grotesque disfigurement I was shunned by women and polite society, and forced into the underground world of man-to-man sex.' In a skit immediately following, which evokes 'ex-gay' testimonials, Walloch camps up the implications and 'tragedies' of being forced into homosexuality by disability. This 'tragedy' has led him to create the non-profit foundation, 'F*** the Disabled'. This imaginary foundation elicits pity sex from properly liberal (and 'perverse') heterosexuals. Their motto: 'F*** the disabled. To keep the disabled from turning gay'. In this skit Walloch turns the tables on heteronormative and normate presumptions, exposing the ridiculousness of both homophobia and liberal sentimentality and pity.

In what is perhaps Walloch's most famous bit he further queercrips the socially sanctioned relationship of dominant culture to disability in the form of public service/charity advertisements. Walloch performs a kind of Sally Struthers/ Jerry Lewis PSA about a 'crisis facing gay men in our community', and solicits contributions to the 'Chelsea Gay Men's Literacy Project', quipping at the end of this bit: '[R]emember, if you don't care about an illiterate Chelsea boy, who will?'

As Carrie Sandahl has noted, here Walloch 'critiques gay men's gym culture by positioning the inhabitants of these hyperperfect bodies as defective, as "cute" charity children in need of a cure' (2003, 38). But Walloch's critique obviously goes further, and queercrips the 'proper' charitable model and patronising attitude of normate, heteronormative culture to difference. Here and throughout *F**k the Disabled* Walloch deploys a cripqueer consciousness and playful performativity in order to undermine dominant social and political relations among queers, crips and 'normals'.

Following the example of Walloch (and many other cripqueer artists), we might look to popular culture and media artefacts that seem, on a surface level, to have little or nothing to say about disability, or that represent disability in 'normal' or 'proper' ways, as the site of critical queercrip interventions, and how we might engage in a methodological cripqueering of these texts. I will, as a way of ending and of pointing toward work that has only begun to be done in relation to visual culture, briefly examine the *X-Men* films as one possible site of such cripqueer work.

Supercripping the Superhero?

Earlier in this chapter I raised the possibility of a cripqueer reading of the *X-Men* films as a potential 'supercripping' of the superhero. This should not be confused with what disability studies scholar Rosemarie Garland-Thomson has identified as the 'supercrip' mode of visual representation. For Garland-Thomson the supercrip is the modern instance of the visual rhetoric of the 'wondrous', which elicits 'amazement and admiration' from a presumed normatively bodied audience' (2002, 59). In its modern form, the wondrous has become secularised in 'the stereotype of the supercrip, who amazes and inspires the viewer by performing feats that the nondisabled viewer cannot imagine doing' (2002, 60–61). The supercrip model here represents an overcoming frame that celebrates the determination of the disabled individual *despite* their disability.

The 'supercripping' I have in mind here is closer in politics and practice to what Tobin Siebers has termed disability 'masquerade'. For Siebers disability masquerade is marked by 'unconventional uses of disability identity' that 'disguise one kind of disability with another or display … disability by exaggerating it' (2004, 4). This masquerade is a negotiation and rejection of norms, expectations and stereotypes of disability embodiment that I would align with a critical cripping. Socially and politically, disability masquerade 'track[s] … examples, descriptions, and narratives that establish greater awareness about the everyday existence of people with disabilities as well as attack the history of their misrepresentation' (2004, 7).

139

While Siebers focuses on the strategic masquerades of people with disabilities in daily life and the productions of disabled performers, I would suggest that critically engaged, mainstream popular culture might also offer such masquerade.[20] This is the cripqueer space opened by the *X-Men* films.[21]

The *X-Men* comic series is, of course, one of, if not the, most popular super-hero comic series published, and the first to critically and continually attend to the multiple determinants and intersections of marginalised identities, as Bradford Wright observes of the comic series' 'multiculturalism' (2001, 263).[22]

Both Bryan Singer's and Brent Ratner's film treatments of the franchise make much of the multicultural aspects and implications of the superheroes. *X-Men* opens with the genesis of Magneto/Eric Lensherr, the leader of the 'bad' mutants. Magneto's powers first manifest themselves as his family is torn asunder during the Nazi takeover of Poland during the Second World War. When separated from his parents the young Lensherr struggles to get back to them. As more and more Nazi guards attempt to restrain him, metal objects in the vicinity like gates and wire fences bend towards him (Magneto's power being the manipulation of magnetic fields), stopping only when a guard knocks the boy unconscious.

In this opening scene, Singer connects the anti-mutant propaganda and politics that are to come to the ongoing modern history of genocide, racism and eugenics. The Nazis were of course not just concerned with the extermination of the Jews, but of all undesirable 'stock' according to eugenic principles, such as queers and people

---

20   Siebers takes mainstream representation largely to task, asserting that they often 'masquerade disability for the benefit of the able-bodied public' (2004, 13), and he invokes the normative figure of the 'supercripple'. He is particularly disparaging of the common Hollywood employment of normatively bodied actors to portray characters with disabilities, even while he admits that it is not the actor alone who bears responsibility for the political implications of these types of representation but that 'disability accuracy' depends also on 'the overall narrative structure and plot of the films' (2004, 17). This dual orientation is important for the *X-Men* films in that they feature normatively bodied actors in 'disabled' roles (rather progressively performed I would argue), as well as a critical consciousness of disability 'accuracy' and history within the narrative structures.

21   Another potential siting of disability masquerade connecting the superhero and 'supercrip' is M. Night Shyamalan's *Unbreakable* (2000), which establishes a kind of disability continuum between the villain Elijah Price/Mr Glass, who lives with osteogenesis imperfecta, and the hero David Dunn, who is seemingly impervious to physical harm. The argument could be forwarded that this continuum of bodily differences implicitly 'supercrips' the superhero, denying any constitutive, essential or natural difference between bodily pathology, norm and ideal. However, the evaluative associations of Elijah Price with villainy, racial disadvantage and moral corruption, and David Dunn with altruism and the heteronormative family (however fractured) simultaneously undoes the film's potential progressivism, and realigns supercrip/superhero along socially and politically negative/positive poles.

22   Wright (2001) offers a concise and impressively documented history of the comic industry and its engagement (or eschewal) of surrounding social and political conditions in America.

with disabilities. In their study of the ongoing history of eugenic thinking, Snyder and Mitchell point to the *X-Men* films as an example of 'recent contemporary films that dramatize a canny awareness about a social model of disability' (2006, 167). *X-Men: The Last Stand* most overtly incorporates eugenic history as genetic engineering in its narrative of the 'cure' discovered for mutants. Much of the narrative of this, the third, film is centred on the moral and ethical implications of the 'mutant cure', and the internal struggles of the mutant community over the assimilated normativity of the 'cure' versus the radical rights and integrity of mutant embodiment. As Robert McRuer notes, in 'A "Last Stand" Against Cure' (2006), 'Challenging both the two-dimensional, able-bodied "cure or kill" mentality and a hard-line anti-cure activist position, *X-Men: The Last Stand*, from a disability perspective, is pretty complex.'

The connections forged in the films between racism and eugenics in the extermination of bodily differences are furthered in characters such as Storm/Ororo Munroe, one of the few central and regular black and female characters in the comic industry, who most consistently throughout the series rejects both assimilation and 'cure'. Additionally, we might read, with relative ease, the depictions of Mystique/Raven Darkholme (who asserts in *X2* that mutants shouldn't have to try to pass or subject themselves to normalisation) and Nightcrawler/Kurt Wagner, in all their blue-skinned, quasi-reptilian glory, as ciphers of racial difference just as much as their morphological differences are ciphers of disability.

The *X-Men* franchise isn't content to let the differences of the various mutants and their treatments within a culture of normativity symbolise racism and eugenics, but simultaneously connects the plight of the mutants to homophobia and sexism. There is a queer relationship between Magneto and Mystique, for instance, beyond comradeship or sexual attraction, which emerges in *X2* as a recognisable and campy relationship between a queer man and his best straight girl pal. At one point, after Magneto and Mystique whisper and giggle together, Magneto remarks to Rogue, in an eminently arch manner, 'we *love* what you've done with your hair' (a shock of which has turned white as a result of Magneto's attempt to take vengeance on the humans in the first film). There is, too, Rogue herself, whose power drains the life force of anyone with whom she comes into physical contact, reactions to which might be read as allegories of masculinist paranoia over unrestrained female sexual excess. Most pointedly in *X2* is the coming out scene in which Iceman/Bobby Drake, a teenaged mutant and student at Professor X's school, informs his family of his powers. His parents are confused, wondering aloud what they did to make Iceman/Bobby turn out the way he did, while his brother is resentful and silent. It's an all too familiar scene to queers, and when Iceman/Bobby's mother asks, 'Have you ever tried *not* being a mutant?', the connections forged between the mutants' difference and homophobic discourse are made transparent.

It is telling, then, in terms of dominant consciousness of disability social status, rights and politics, that despite the fact that physical differences are everywhere and interconnected within the films, popular discourses routinely index racism and homophobia as addressed within the film, but rarely raise issues of disability rights and awareness.[23] This is most obvious in Charles Xavier/Professor X, leader of the X-Men team, who is paraplegic (his wheelchairs in the films are sexy, stylish and high-tech), and his visible disability should be enough to direct our attention to the physical differences/disability of the other superheroes. Most reviews and popular critical commentary on the film ignore Professor X's disability, or contrast his physical immobility with the impressive fluidity of his psychic mind (as if, in Garland-Thomson's normative supercrip model, intellect were a superhuman achievement for the physically disabled). The fact that the films haven't produced larger cripqueer critical awareness in audiences suggests the ways in which disability continues to be ignored or elided by the dominant culture.

The films evoke disability politics in less obvious manners as well. There is the already mentioned political rhetoric in the films' world of the eugenicist movement, which sought, through 'science', to keep the nation's gene pool 'healthy' by identifying and isolating genetic 'undesirables', often through forced institutionalisation, sterilisation or extermination of people with disabilities, and which comes full circle in *X-Men: The Last Stand*'s 'cure'. The 'Mutant Registration Act', in *X-Men*, also raises the spectre of similar proposals in regard to people with HIV/AIDS in 1980s US politics, which further connects disability and queer sexuality.

Several of the characters, in their animal-like qualities and superpowers, extend these critiques of the limits of the human as promoted by empiricism and liberal humanism, much as people with disabilities have occupied a similar position within heteronormative/normate discourses as marking those limits. Sabretooth, Toad and Wolverine/Logan are the obvious examples. Cyclops's superpower is laser-beam eyes, but considering how he is never without protective eyewear/sunglasses, might he not more simply be blind? Furthermore, couldn't we read Cyclops's power as a kind of return of the disabled gaze? Lennard Davis (1995; 2002) has described the physical presence of disability in the social as a disruption of the visual field that must be managed, its unsettling threat defused by the normative gaze. There is a power in looking back, in returning the 'paralysing' gaze of the normative I/eye, as scholars in postcolonial theory, film/queer theory and critical race studies, among other critical fields, have shown. This return of, or challenge to the gaze, is also part of the political challenge of Siebers's disability masquerade as it 'claims disability as a version of itself rather than simply concealing it from view' (2004, 5), or overdetermining disability from the subject position of the norm. In this case Cyclops's return of the gaze literally blows 'normal' humans away.

The political differences between the 'good' mutants, represented by Professor X and the X-Men, and the 'bad' mutants, represented by Magneto and his Brotherhood, might be most progressively reclaimed for a cripqueer reading and politics. These two factions represent the two historical poles of minority political struggle in the United States, with Professor X representing the reformist, assimilationist model, and Magneto the revolutionary model of radical transformation. I would like to

---

23   See, for instance, reviews of the first film by O'Hehir (2000); Ebert (2000); Edelstein (2000); Mitchell (2000); Travers (2000).

suggest that though the films, unsurprisingly, come down on the side of Professor X and his 'we can all get along' conviction, we might queercrip the devalued and dismissed revolutionary politics of Magneto, similar to Mitchell and Snyder's 'transgressive reappropriation' of Richard III, as discussed earlier. In this cripqueer reading, Magneto and the 'bad' mutants might become figures of real power and revolutionary struggle representing the desires of cripqueers of all sorts. As Magneto tells Professor X near the beginning of the first film, 'The future is ours, Charles', and in so doing asserts that, to return to the quotation excerpted from McRuer and Wilkerson (2003) with which I began, 'another world is possible'. Only a cripqueering of *X-Men*, *X2* and *X-Men: The Last Stand* can expose the alternative worlds circulating underneath the seemingly normative presumptions and politics of those films and this is, finally, the productive and progressive potential of queercripping as a methodological tool.

Suggested Further Reading

Garland Thomson, R. (1997), *Extraordinary Bodies: Figuring Physical Disability in American Culture and Literature* (New York: Columbia University Press).

McRuer, R. (2006), *Crip Theory: Cultural Signs of Queerness and Disability* (New York: New York University Press).

——— and Wilkerson, A. (eds) (2003), *Desiring Disability: Queer Theory Meets Disability Studies*. Special Issue of *GLQ: A Journal of Lesbian and Gay Studies* 9:1–2, 1–23.

Snyder, S.L., Brueggemann, B.J. and Garland Thomson, R. (eds) (2002), *Disability Studies: Enabling the Humanities* (New York: MLA).

Snyder, S.L. and Mitchell, D.T. (2006), *Cultural Locations of Disability* (Chicago, IL: University of Chicago Press).

References

Bérubé, M. (1998), 'Foreword: Pressing the Claim', in S. Linton, *Claiming Disability: Knowledge and Identity* (New York: New York University Press).

Butler, J. (1993), *Bodies That Matter: On the Discursive Limits of 'Sex'* (New York and London: Routledge).

——— (2004a), *Precarious Life: The Powers of Mourning and Violence* (New York: Verso).

——— (2004b), *Undoing Gender* (New York and London: Routledge).

Canguilhem, G. (1989), *The Normal and the Pathological*, trans. C.R. Fawcett and R.S. Cohen (New York: Zone Books).

Clare, E. (2003), 'Gawking, Gaping, Staring', *GLQ: A Journal of Lesbian and Gay Studies* 9:1–2, 257–61.

Davis, L.J. (1995), *Enforcing Normalcy: Disability, Deafness, and the Body* (New York: Verso).

—— (2002), 'Bodies of Difference: Politics, Disability, and Representation', in S.L. Snyder, B.J. Brueggemann and R. Garland-Thomson (eds), *Disability Studies: Enabling the Humanities* (New York: MLA).

Deleuze, G. and Guattari, F. (1983), *Anti-Oedipus: Capitalism and Schizophrenia*, trans. R. Hurley, M. Seem and H.R. Lane (Minneapolis, MN: University Minnesota Press).

—— (1994), *What is Philosophy?*, trans. H. Tomlinson and G. Burchell (New York: Columbia University Press).

Duggan, L. (2004), 'Holy Matrimony!', *The Nation* 26 February 2004, http://www.thenation.com/doc/20040315/duggan (accessed 15 January 2006).

Ebert, R. (2000), Review of *X-Men*, dir. Bryan Singer, *RogerEbert.com* 14 July 2000, http://rogerebert.suntimes.com/apps/pbcs.dll/article?AID=/20000714/REVIEWS/7140304/1023 (accessed 23 September 2006).

Edelstein, D. (2000), 'The Grim Weeper: *The Eyes of Tammy Faye* Gives an Icon Her Due. *X-Men* Dares to have Gravitas', review of *X-Men*, *Slate* 28 July 2000, http://www.slate.com/id/87122 (accessed 23 September 2006).

Eisenstein, Z. (2004), *Against Empire: Feminisms, Racism, and the West* (New York: Zed Books).

Foucault, M. (1973), *The Birth of the Clinic: An Archaeology of Medical Perception*, trans. A.M. Sheridan Smith (New York: Vintage Books).

—— (1979), *Discipline and Punish: The Birth of the Prison*, trans. A. Sheridan (New York: Vintage Books).

—— (1986a), *The Use of Pleasure: The History of Sexuality, Volume Two*, trans. R. Hurley (New York: Vintage Books).

—— (1986b), *The Care of the Self: The History of Sexuality, Volume Three*, trans. R. Hurley (New York: Vintage Books).

—— (1988), *Madness and Civilization: A History of Insanity in the Age of Reason*, trans. R. Howard (New York: Vintage Books).

—— (1990), *The History of Sexuality, Volume One: An Introduction*, trans. R. Hurley (New York: Vintage Books).

—— (1994), *The Order of Things: An Archaeology of the Human Sciences* (New York: Vintage Books).

—— (2004), *Abnormal: Lectures at the Collège de France, 1974–1975*, (eds), V. Marchetti and A. Salomoni, trans. G. Burchell (New York: Picador).

*F**k the Disabled: The Surprising Adventures of Greg Walloch* (2001), dir. E. Kabillio [feature film].

Fuss, D. (1989), *Essentially Speaking: Feminism, Nature, and Difference* (New York and London: Routledge).

Garland-Thomson, R. (1997), *Extraordinary Bodies: Figuring Physical Disability in American Culture and Literature* (New York: Columbia University Press).

—— (2002), 'The Politics of Staring: Visual Rhetorics of Disability in Popular Photography', in S.L. Snyder, B.J. Brueggemann and R. Garland-Thomson (eds), *Disability Studies: Enabling the Humanities* (New York: MLA).

—— (2005a), 'Dares to Stares: Disabled Women Performance Artists and the Dynamics of Staring', in C. Sandahl and P. Auslander (eds), *Bodies in Commotion: Disability and Performance* (Ann Arbor, MI: University of Michigan Press).

—— (2005b), 'Disability and Representation', *PMLA* 120:2, 522–7.

Gore, T. (1987), *Raising PG Kids in an X-Rated Society* (Nashville, TN: Abingdon Press).

Halperin, D.M. (1995), *Saint Foucault: Towards a Gay Hagiography* (New York: Oxford University Press).

Hayes, E.K. (1988), *Why Good Parents Have Bad Kids: How to Make Sure That Your Child Grows Up Right* (New York: Doubleday).

Heath, S. (1978), 'Difference', *Screen* 19:3, 50–112.

Jeffreys, M. (2002), 'The Visible Cripple (Scars and Other Disfiguring Displays Included)', in S.L. Snyder, B.J. Brueggemann and R. Garland-Thomson (eds), *Disability Studies: Enabling the Humanities* (New York: MLA).

Kudlick, C.J. (2005), 'Disability History, Power, and Rethinking the Idea of "the Other"', *PMLA* 120:2, 557–61.

Linton, S. (1998), *Claiming Disability: Knowledge and Identity* (New York: New York University Press).

Lyotard, J.F. (1984), *The Postmodern Condition: A Report on Knowledge* (Minneapolis, MN: University of Minnesota Press).

—— (1992), *The Postmodern Explained: Correspondence, 1982–1985* (Minneapolis, MN: University of Minnesota Press).

McRuer, R. (1997), *The Queer Renaissance: Contemporary American Literature and the Reinvention of Lesbian and Gay Identities* (New York: New York University Press).

—— (2002), 'Compulsory Able-Bodiedness and Queer/Disabled Existence', in S.L. Snyder, B.J. Brueggemann and R. Garland-Thomson (eds), *Disability Studies: Enabling the Humanities* (New York: MLA).

—— (2005), 'Crip Eye for the Normate Guy: Queer Theory and the Disciplining of Disability Studies', *PMLA* 120:2, 586–92.

—— (2006), 'A "Last Stand" Against Cure', *Ragged Edge Online* 2 June, http://www. raggededgemagazine.com/departments/frontpgfeature/001144.html (accessed 16 September 2006).

—— and Wilkerson, A.L. (eds) (2003), *Desiring Disability: Queer Theory Meets Disability Studies*. Special Issue of *GLQ: A Journal of Lesbian and Gay Studies* 9:1–2, 1–23.

Mitchell, D.T. and Snyder, S.L. (2000), *Narrative Prosthesis: Disability and the Dependencies of Discourse* (Ann Arbor, MI: University of Michigan Press).

Mitchell, E. (2000), 'Pow! Misfit Heroes to the Rescue! Zap!', Review of *X-Men*, *The New York Times on the Web* 14 July, http://www.nytimes.com/library/film/071400xmen-film-review.html (accessed 23 September 2006).

O'Hehir, A. (2000), Review of *X-Men*, *Salon.com* 14 July, http://archive.salon.com/ent/movies/review/2000/07/14/x_men/index1.html (accessed 23 September 2006).

Patton, C. (2002), 'Stealth Bombers of Desire: The Globalization of "Alterity" in Emerging Democracies', in A. Cruz-Malavé and M.F. Manalansan IV (eds), *Queer Globalizations: Citizenship and the Afterlife of Colonialism* (New York: New York University Press).

Ramlow, T.R. (2003), 'Bad Boys: Abstractions of Difference and the Politics of Youth "Deviance"', *GLQ: A Journal of Lesbian and Gay Studies* 9:1–2, 107–32.

Sandahl, C. (2003), 'Queering the Crip or Cripping the Queer? Intersections of Queer and Crip Identities in Solo Autobiographical Performance', *GLQ: A Journal of Lesbian and Gay Studies* 9:1–2, 25–56.

Sedgwick, E.K. (1993), 'How to Bring Your Kids Up Gay: The War on Effeminate Boys', in *Tendencies* (Durham, NC: Duke University Press).

Shakespeare, T., Gillespie-Sells, K. and Davies, D. (1996), *The Sexual Politics of Disability: Untold Desires* (New York: Cassell).

Shildrick, M. (2005), 'The Disabled Body, Genealogy, and Undecidability', *Cultural Studies* 19:6, 755–70.

Siebers, T. (2004), 'Disability as Masquerade', *Literature and Medicine* 23:1, 1–22.

Snyder, S.L., Brueggemann, B.J. and Garland-Thomson, R. (eds) (2002), *Disability Studies: Enabling the Humanities* (New York: MLA).

Snyder, S.L. and Mitchell, D.T. (2006), *Cultural Locations of Disability* (Chicago, IL: University of Chicago Press).

Travers, P. (2000), Review of *X-Men*, *Rolling Stone Online* 10 December, http://www.rollingstone.com/reviews/movie/5949101/review/5949102/xmen (accessed 23 September 2006).

Unbreakable (2000), dir. M.N. Shyamalan [feature film].

Wright, B.W. (2001), *Comic Book Nation: The Transformation of Youth Culture in America* (Baltimore, MD: Johns Hopkins University Press).

X-Men (2000), dir. B. Singer [feature film].

X2 (2003), dir. B. Singer [feature film].

X-Men: The Last Stand (2006), dir. B. Ratner [feature film].

Generic Definitions: Taxonomies of Identity in AIDS Discourse

Meredith Raimondo

The Violence of Definition

The "Frequently Asked Questions on HIV and AIDS" page of the United States Centers for Disease Control (CDC) website offers the visitor a hyperlinked index to its content ("Frequently Asked Questions"). Its broad categories suggest the contested social process from which knowledge about HIV/AIDS emerges. For example, "transmission" – a category intended to offer transparently factual information about the science and epidemiology of HIV – is coupled with "rumors," those alternative theories that fail to meet scientific criteria for veracity.

The inclusion of "Men on the Down Low" among broad topics like "Prevention," "Definitions," and "Statistics" is indicative of both the level of media frenzy about this category and the instability of knowledge about it. The CDC begins its explanation with a definition:

> The most generic definition of the term down low, or DL, is "to keep something private," whether that refers to information or activity.
>
> The term is often used to describe the behavior of men who have sex with other men as well as women and who do not identify as gay or bisexual. These men may refer to themselves as being "on the down low," "on the DL," or "on the low low." The term has most often been associated with African American men. Although the term originated in the African American community, the behaviors associated with the term are not new and not specific to black men who have sex with men. ("Men on the Down Low")

The absence of agents underscores the contested meaning of this phrase. Who uses it to describe behavior? Who associates it with African American men? What is the difference between "originated in" and "specific to"? The passive voice contributes to the appearance that the information offered is indeed "generic," in contrast to forms of (proprietary?) knowledge emerging from specific social formations ("the African American community").[1]

This initial promise of usable information swiftly gives way to uncertainties and unknowns. "What are the sexual risk factors associated with being on the down low?" asks the imagined reader. "Many questions have not yet been answered," replies the FAQ. Five queries outlining specific areas of uncertainty follow. Three refer to "bisexual men," one uses the phrase "on the down low," and one uses the phrase "men who have sex with male and female partners." The reader is left to decide whether these terms are synonyms. On "the implications for HIV prevention," the FAQ can only report that "there are no data to confirm or refute publicized accounts of HIV risk behavior associated with these men." "What steps is CDC taking to address the down low?" asks the final section. "CDC and its many research partners have several projects in the field," the FAQ promises, but the assurance that "the results of these studies will be published in medical journals and circulated through press releases in the next few years" only underscores that knowledge is something yet to be realized.

***

As the AIDS epidemic entered its third decade, men on the down low joined diseased prostitutes, sex-mad gay men, animalistic biting school children, desperate Haitian refugees, and mindless drug addicts in the catalogue of the dangerous "AIDS carriers" who populate the national epidemiological imaginary. Although there are important differences between the narratives that accrue around these figures, they share the dilemma of hypervisibility. Their perverse desires are not life-affirming but murderous, and their emergence in popular debate is the result of a violent exposure on behalf of those who they are imagined to threaten. Rhetorics of race, class, gender, sexuality, and age mark them for an anxious public seeking to preserve its privileged safety.

"So how does a story based entirely on anecdotal and circumstantial evidence become a mainstream media sensation big enough to generate headlines in the *New York Times* and *Washington Post* and to be discussed on the nation's most respected daytime television talk show?" asks Keith Boykin in his thoughtful analysis of "America's recent obsession with the down low" (*Beyond the Down Low*, 130, 5). This controversy powerfully demonstrates that the proliferation of new sexual categories does not always challenge the malevolent disregard often glossed as invisibility, but rather reifies the very power relations that sustain variously distributed inequalities. In this case, debate about black male sexualities reinscribed

---

1   The word "originated" might be read here as a kind of uncanny doubling of the much contested "African origin" theory – once again, the threat of HIV emerges from a racialized context to affect the "general public."

the normativity of particular forms of gay identity. A queer reading of the down low controversy offers important insight into the politics of normalization that can play out even in well-intentioned efforts to acknowledge diversity.

Although this response to mass media and professional narratives about the down low emerges from an academic context, I would be remiss not to acknowledge the impact of this discourse in what is colloquially called "the real world." Keith Boykin offers an eloquent personal reflection on its oppressive consequences in the introduction to his critical investigation of constructions of the down low:

> *As I said, there is nothing worse than being blamed for something you have not done. And that is exactly why the public discussion about men on the down low is so dangerously wrong. Almost every time I hear talk about the down low, I remember the feeling being blamed for something I did not do. Facts are not important in this environment. Perception is reality. I live in a world that has already been trained to fear and despise me. It is not because of what I have done. I have never murdered anyone. I have never smoked crack. I have never been in prison. And I have never passed a deadly disease to anyone. But none of that matters. I am still guilty, and I will still be held accountable for the rest of my life. (Beyond the Down Low, 4)*

Boykin reminds me that representations of the down low are both an important site of critical intervention and a treacherous territory for the queer cultural critic. As I started to track the controversy, I found myself uncertain how to offer a meaningful critique that did not reproduce some of the most oppressive features of the mass media coverage. These narratives were preoccupied with the dangerous sexuality of black men, a familiar racist trope thinly authorized by an apparent concern with public health. Even the most sympathetic defined men on the down low as Other to both the author and the assumed audience. This distancing did not always employ the same rubrics – the constellation of gender, race, class, and sexuality positioned writers differently in relationship to men on the down low. But in all cases, they remained a troubling phenomenon to contemplate rather than a site of identification. To the extent that this chapter is "about" men on the down low, it replicates this problem.

In an essay on discourse about barebacking and bug chasing – terms central to another recent HIV transmission controversy – Gregory Tomso asks, "Can we speak of bug chasing and barebacking *at all* without perpetuating some form of homophobic violence? The answer is simple: there is no nonviolent articulation, nor can there be, of bug chasing or barebacking as such" (92). Eve Sedgwick described a similar problem in *Epistemology of the Closet* when she identified "the terrible one-directionality of the culture's spectacularizing of gay men, to which it seems almost impossible, in any powerful gay-related project, not to contribute" (60). Such concerns are equally relevant for a critical analysis of discourse about men on the down low. One of the obvious problems with this controversy is that the "debate" has been structured in such a way that the objects of these stories never became their subjects. Put another way, the material concern that seemed to animate this subject – the disproportionate impact of HIV on African Americans – did not open cultural space for those most affected to articulate their needs. Instead, mass media coverage of men on the down low was largely a spectacular drama directed at an audience understood to stand at some distance from the threat of HIV infection. In this way, it remained consistent with other mass media coverage of AIDS, speaking to a "general public" (Grover, 23) no longer imminently at risk but still curious about the nature of its safety.

Practices of representation – including those of the "queer theorist" – are fraught with relations of power. For Tomso, an engagement with the risk of representational violence is none the less useful:

> We might concentrate less on a politics of exposure than on a consideration of ethics: On a consideration of how one might best speak of and to the Other when all acts of speech seem destined to end in violence, and yet when speech is essential for care for survival. What makes sense, then in the contexts of popular and scientific writing is to build a movement toward a more responsible discourse, a more responsible question. (92)

Judith Butler makes a similar point when she argues that "if we engage the terms that these debates supply, then we ratify the frame at the moment in which we take our stand. And this signals a certain paralysis in the face of exercising power to change the terms by which such topics are rendered thinkable" (40). In this chapter, I take up this challenge by focusing on Boykin's invocation of accountability, which he uses to describe the discriminatory effects of well-entrenched tropes of blame. I propose shifting the locus of responsibility. Instead of measuring the accountability of social subject for HIV transmission, I hope to hold discourse accountable for its effects. In this sense, accountability suggests a condition of being answerable to and for.

Engaging accountability requires an understanding of how I enter this discourse in particular ways. I am not, like Keith Boykin, directly targeted by the racist homophobia of these discourses. And yet some of the urgency I bring to this project is attached to the ways in which I am yet interpolated by them. Reading various accounts of the down low and its purported relation to HIV transmission, I found myself uneasily aware of the ways in which I, as a white queer feminist academic, was not exactly their intended audience – but nor was I entirely outside of it. However I might understand myself, I was also the white, middle-class, educated reader hailed by newspapers and newsmagazines. And I could see myself in the experts called on to explain the cultural politics of sexuality, even if I disagreed with the particular conclusions they reached.

I offer this analysis as a necessary engagement with an oppressive discourse. Methodologically, it situates the analysis of media sources in a rich conversation among African American critics about sexuality, identity, and desire. In doing so, I hope to interrupt some of the increasingly naturalized ways of thinking that shape what can be said about AIDS in the hegemonic public spheres of mass media, public health, and public policy. The personal urgency I bring to this work is located in the ways in which race and class privilege structure what is said and what is heard, a larger context that must always remain in view if criticism is not to replicate the very power dynamics it hopes to interrupt.

Queer Aliases: Taxonomies of Identity and the Politics of "Risk"

The CDC's FAQ might be read simply as public health damage control, an attempt to employ scientific rationalism to interrupt escalating media panic. However, such an interpretation does not account for the ways in which the knowable functions not as an object waiting to be discovered but a site of political contest. In this sense, public health authorities and talk show hosts share the same investments in the down low – each wants to fix the boundaries of a porous category and explain what it "really" means.

The preoccupation with definition indicates a widespread normalization of an epidemiologic imaginary based in distinctly recognizable risk categories. AIDS cultural critic Thomas Yingling argued that "myths of identity *have framed* the interpretation of AIDS, and it remains a disease that attaches – rightly or wrongly – to identities: gay, IV-drug user, African, hemophiliac, infant, transfusion patient" (49–50). As Yingling suggests, early epidemiology suggested a correlation between identity, behavior, and illness. Although multiple groups were targets in this early surveillance, AIDS cultural critics point out that it was the visibility of AIDS in urban gay communities – and the homophobia it provoked – that most structured the early construction of epidemic in the United States. Nor were the effects of this homophobia felt only by gay men. As Cindy Patton argued, "the insistence that AIDS is somehow a mark of perversion transforms infected persons into 'queers,' regardless of their exposure route, a phenomenon I have called the 'queer paradigm'" (117). Paula Treichler pointed out that this reliance of identity distorted knowledge about AIDS. Gay men's intravenous drug use, for example, disappeared in a schema obsessed with sexuality. Thus, she argued, "the commitment to categories based on monolithic identity filtered out information" (19–20). Further, the assumed correspondence of identity and practice left no place for men who had sex with men but who did not identify as gay. Illegible in the available identity models for HIV surveillance, they simply fell through the cracks.

The shift from risk groups to risk behavior did not dislodge the logic of identity as fully as activists hoped. The problem is especially clear in the shift from the category of "homosexual" to "men who have sex with men (MSM)". The latter designation provided a solution to the methodological challenge of recording data about people who reported various kinds of same-gender sexual contact but did not identify as gay. While it represented a partial move towards a behavioral model, its reliance on the universality of gender identities left it a blunt instrument. As Plummer and Porter note, in cultural contexts in which social gender roles do not map clearly onto a binary construction of biological sex, the notion of "same-sex" or "same-gender" behavior is not immediately transparent (43). Nor did the focus on same-gender sexual behavior address a long-standing problem with "homosexual" as a risk category. Because it did not distinguish among sexual behaviors, it tended to collapse activities at very low and very high risk of transmission. "Sexual contact" – a commonly used phrase – could stand in for a wide range of possibilities. Even when used as a polite euphemism for anal intercourse, it did not necessarily illuminate the very different stakes for receptive and insertive partners (Young and Ilan, 1147). At its worst, Simon Watney argues, "the category of MSMs is little more than a reconceptualization of the earlier concept of the 'bridging group,' imagined as a Trojan horse full of 'AIDS carriers' inside 'the heterosexual community'" (75). Watney points here to the history of epidemiological concern with bisexual men as a vector of "heterosexual" transmission, bringing HIV from their male partners to unsuspecting wives (Rodriguez Rust, 537).

Epidemiology – in both its professional and popular forms – is certainly an example of what Eve Sedgwick calls "taxonomic discourses," invested in the production of categorical knowledge through the proliferation of ever more specific distinctions (2). But while sex is perhaps the most explicit concern in debates about men on the down low, race, gender and class also play key roles in articulating its meanings. These narratives are also examples of what Dwight McBride calls "racialized discourse." McBride explains,

> *They serve to make us think (if even for the moment and for the very sake of discourse itself) that "the black community" is knowable, totalizable, locatable, and certainly separate from or other than the speakers (black or non-black in some cases). The use of such terminology, then, represents not only a false will to power on the part of the speaker who appropriates such language, but carries with it extremely high political stakes as well. Such labels deny the heterogeneity among African Americans (class, gender, educational level, sexuality, etc.) and easily seduce us into the language of stereotypes by characterizing in a facile manner the entirety of the experiences of African American people. (172)*

Popular discourse about the down low used rhetorics of racial difference to homogenize meanings of sexual identity and represent "the black community" as the cause of HIV transmission. It did not represent a pluralist interest in the diverse ways in which people name themselves, but rather an anxious attempt to wrest a stable truth from the complexity of dimly perceived social worlds.

The trope of deception marked the racialized border between the down low and gay and/or bisexual. Consider, for example, a selection of definitions culled from mass media reports:

> *Many gay and bisexual black men – maybe most – keep their sexual orientation a secret. Some are living what they call the "down low" lifestyle. (Hollinshed, A1)*

DL gay subculture (men who deny their bisexuality despite frequent homosexual encounters). (Morris, H5)

Now the term is often used to characterize the bisexual double life led by some African-American men. (Hooper, B3)

Some men thought to be heterosexual are on the "down low." That is, they secretly have sex with infected men and spread the virus to women who didn't protect themselves because they were unaware of their male partner's activities. (Young, M1)

Bisexual black men who have sex on the sly with other men and may be – may be – infecting their wives or girlfriends with HIV/AIDS. The term for the behavior: Down Low, or DL. (Dorsey, E3)

In all of these examples, secrecy or deception was a more important behavioral marker of the down low than the gender(s) of sexual partners. In this sense, it represented the opposite of "gay," a concept associated with the visibility of "coming out." Bisexuality proved to be a more vexed term in these definitions. Sometimes, it functioned in a way consistent with its earlier representation as a form of dangerous duplicity. In other contexts, it was recuperated as a form of visible identity, acceptable to the extent it named itself clearly.

The shifting signification of bisexuality was particularly visible in the media frenzy that surrounded J.L. King, who attempted to represent the public voice of men on the down low on a much-reported visit to the Oprah Winfrey show and in his autobiographical books *On the Down Low* and *Coming Up from the Down Low*. In his conversation with Oprah, he resisted being scripted into a conventional sexual identity. "To be on the down low means to keep it hush-hush, to be unreadable, to be able to cover your tracks," he explained. When Oprah asked, "Do you then not consider yourself gay," King responded, "No, I don't," and then elaborated, "Why do I – and so why do I have to label myself?" (Oprah Winfrey Show). While this exchange seemed to offer a critique of the demand to identify in particular ways, King's larger investment in sexual normativities undermined his attempt to disaggregate desire and identity. By the time of his follow-up book *Coming Up from the Down Low*, he had reframed his self-narrative, describing identity as a form of freedom:

Now that I've opened myself up to a more complete and honest understanding of myself – helped by listening to the hundreds of men and women I've met over the last few years who are struggling with these issues themselves – I've come to this liberating truth: I'm not a straight man who has sex with men; I'm a bisexual man. (15)

In this statement, bisexual is aligned with other categories of sexual orientation. To that extent that bisexuality "comes out," it functions not as a threatening vector that bridges (or even undoes) gendered forms of desire but as a form of identity around which one can take the necessary precautions. King's narrative may particularly reinforce this construction of bisexuality because he offers it as an alternative to gay, a racialized construct whose normative whiteness he underscores again and again. He is vehement about his discomfort with what he characterized as the effeminacy of white gay identity: "To this day, even though I'm honest with those in my life about my sexual habits, I will not be labeled gay" (*On the Down Low*, 24). This representation of white gay men seems largely consistent with his broader tendency to treat social identities as homogenous and (stereo)typical. However, it seems potentially useful to consider how his resistance identification might also be taken as a partial challenge to some of the most hysterical elements of discourse about the down low's dangers, reframing the debate around the production of subjectivity.

In a Foucauldian framework, an investment in sexual honesty signals a context in which the disciplinary operations of power act in and through the production of knowledge, including self-knowledge: "Misunderstandings, avoidances, and evasions were only possible, and only had their effects, against the background of this strange endeavor: to tell the truth of sex" (57). Honesty is a moral term, constructed in a hierarchy in which a flawed dishonesty serves as its necessary Other. And yet, it is also possible that honesty also gestures towards something more radical, more akin to the models of communal care that invigorated early safe sex projects. King's formulation opens the possibility that the honest agent does not require gay identity to engage in transmission-interrupting sexual practices, only a commitment to the sociality of sex.

This interpretation is a generous reading of King – perhaps too generous in the larger context of the function he played in discourse about the down low. His wide media visibility served mostly to reinforce some of the most damaging aspects of dominant discourse about the down low. Keith Boykin suggests that racism and homophobia helped make King such a visible, reportable story: "J.L. King was proving a perfect iconic image for white America to understand. It was the stereotypical image of black men as pathological liars, surreptitiously satisfying their primitive sexual cravings by cheating on their wives" (*Beyond the Down Low*, 116). Certainly, King's formulations are often alarmist and sensational. Offering himself as an icon for the many men on the down low he assures his readership are out there, he does not, to use Bryant Keith Alexander's invocation of Chandra Mohanty, offer his "own 'dense particularity'" as a way to produce understandings attentive to the intersections of race, gender, class, and sexuality (Alexander, 1285). Instead, he engages in his own kind of taxonimical project, describing different types of men on the down low through categories such as the "thug brother" and the "professional brother" (*Beyond the Down Low*, 135). His investment in patriarchal heteronormativity makes him less a queer crusader against sexual fixity than a defender of gender norms.

The consistent return to practices of categorization reveals a deep attachment to the idea of identity-based surveillance. The down low is threatening because it confounds attempts to make sexual identities transparent in relation to HIV transmission. "The resulting permutations confounded just about everyone, black and white, straight and gay," wrote Benoit Denizet-Lewis, the white gay author of a major feature in the *New York Times* Sunday magazine (28). In this configuration, heteronormativity admits a necessary, even needed place for gay identity. The down low is textually relegated to the de-authorizing space of scare quotes rather than acknowledged as an agentive form of self-naming that enriches sexual understanding. It becomes the queer Other to the apparently universal forms of identity that construct boundaries around the risk of HIV transmission.

"Fear, Denial, and Rejection": Homophobia in Mass and Community Media

Men on the down low served a particular purpose in narratives about HIV/AIDS, providing an explanation for the disproportionately high rates of HIV transmission among particular populations, especially African Americans. Consider, for example, this quotation from Denizet-Lewis's *New York Times Magazine* article: "Today, while there are black men who are openly gay, it seems that the majority of those having sex with men still lead secret lives, products of a black culture that deems masculinity and fatherhood as a black man's primary responsibility – and homosexuality as a white man's perversion" (28). To the extent that secrecy and deception formed the core of this trope, reporters found themselves needing to explain the seeming racial disparity in practices of sexual disclosure. They turned to concepts of "community" and "culture." In the context of a popular construction of racism as judgmental statements or actions directed unfairly at individuals, "culture" seemed to provide a safe – or even sensitive – site to articulate notions of African American sexual difference.

In particular, reporters described the oppressive demands of black masculinity, which disallowed black men from adopting conventional forms of gay identity. As Denizet-Lewis argued in the *New York Times*, "Rejecting a gay culture they perceive as white and effeminate, many black men have settled on a new identity, with its own vocabulary and customs and its own name: Down Low." This practice does not prove to be neutral in Denizet-Lewis's assessment: "For all their supposed freedom, many men on the DL are as trapped – or more trapped – than their white counterparts in the closet." He tells the story of a source named Jigga to support the idea that the down low is a closet from which black men might be liberated into more appropriate forms of sexual identity. "Jigga says he has sex with both men and women, but mostly he doesn't label himself as bisexual," reports Denizet Lewis. "'I'm just freaky,' he says with a smile." Though this response might have opened the opportunity to consider the complexities of sexual subjectivities – and the very real possibility that freaky articulates a different notion of selfhood than bisexual – Denizet-Lewis uses Jigga's story to reinforce a developmental narrative. By the end of the story, Jigga "seems considerably more comfortable with his sexuality than he was the first time I met him, and I suspect that soon enough, he may be openly gay in all facets of his life without losing his much-coveted masculinity" (28).

The construction of African American communities as a site of homophobia illustrates the centrality of race to the construction of sexuality. As literary critic Roderick Ferguson argues,

> *The distinction between normative heterosexuality (as the evidence of progress and development) and non-normative gender and sexual practices and gender identities (as the woeful signs of social lag and dysfunction) has emerged historically from the field of racialized discourse. (6)*

In this case, reporters assumed that deformed African American notions of masculinity forced men who would be gay into dangerous practices of deception. For example, a *Times-Picayune* article claimed that "in the African-American community, the men are reluctant to come out as gay because of the fear of being ostracized" (Young, M1), while a front page feature in the *Post-Dispatch* noted that "homophobia – the irrational fear or hatred of homosexuals – has deep roots throughout the world. But in America, the fear of ostracism may be greatest in the black community, where masculinity is especially prized" (Hollinshed, A1). This apparent cultural relativism relies on an essentialized notion of racial difference, with no acknowledgement of the histories shaping African American gender and sexual politics. Instead, such "prejudice" appears to be a particular pathology of African American communities, a premodern remnant that they have yet to leave behind.

These narratives uphold heteronormativity not by linking gay identity with AIDS, but by defending it as a necessary requirement to AIDS prevention. Mass media narratives about the down low focused on the politics of masculinity not to understand the consequences of white supremacist heteropatriarchy, but rather to reanimate a familiar historical conversation about "the black community" as a site of national pathology. By focusing on social conditions, these narratives reconstituted homophobic African Americans as the dangerously queer subjects of this story about AIDS.

Similar narratives about African American homophobia appeared in the lesbian and gay commercial press. "The prevailing norms of black urban culture have made it incredibly difficult for a black man to come out of the closet and build a relationship with another man," explained *The Gay and Lesbian Review*. Identity was once again the underlying issue: "These men's unwillingness to address the fact that they may be gay or bisexual leads many to engage in unprotected sex on the DL" (Williams, 6). "Fearful of being shunned by their families, friends, and churches, men who desire other men sexually stay in the closet," agreed an *Advocate* article (Lisotta, 32). "More evolved humans see the down low for what it really is, a sad and compromised way of life for people facing multiple kinds of bigotry," reflected Bruch Vilanch in the punch line of his parodic consideration (46). Although the *Advocate* also published Keith Boykin's argument that "we find it much easier to continue using a racial typecast that confirms our preconceived beliefs about black male guilt" ("Not Just a Black Thing," 31), the magazine's apparent liberal inclusivity did not address the ways in which its presentation of multiple perspectives favored certain readings. With the exception of Boykin's, these stories did not consider the role of racism in shaping either media coverage or the material lives of the men they described. Boykin's was the only piece to ask consumers to consider their reading practices as the central issue. The others shared the assumption that gay identity was itself a protection against HIV transmission. This narrative tended to individualize and psychologize gay identity, constructing an appropriate and universal developmental process.

In the African American press, there was significant suspicion about media interest in men on the down low. These stories considered the larger historical context of mass media and public health racism as a way to make sense of the representation of race, sexuality, and gender. The *Sentinel* provides one articulate example:

> *America has been enamored with and simultaneously in fear of the Black man's mythical sexual prowess and reckless sexual behavior for ages ... The Down Low controversy is not very divergent, in that it proclaims that the Black man has such an insatiable appetite for sex, combined with irresponsible behavior to result in increasing HIV infection of his new victim – the Black woman. (Darryl, A6)*

Essence described the difficulty of making space for a public conversation about HIV prevention, noting "the challenges we face as Black women who are navigating the rocky – and now deadly – waters of relationships have become fodder for the American media to dissect and sensationalize" (Smith, 148). This last point illustrates the extent to which oppressive power relations shape the kinds of narratives available in what Cathy Cohen calls "indigenous sources of information" (*Boundaries of Blackness*, 231). As Darlene Clark Hine argues in her influential analysis of the historical development of a "culture of dissemblance" among middle-class African American women, conversations about oppression, HIV, and sexual politics take place in a context in which they may be exploited to cause harm (912).

Questions of community were central to African American media coverage of the down low. At times, these stories replicated key features of the mass media coverage. "More than just a fleeting, indulgent, freaky lifestyle choice, the insidious scourge that is brothers on the down low is making for a deadly and dismal state of affairs for Black's social and medical wellbeing" argued the Chicago-based *N'Digo* (Baker, 12). Cathy Cohen offers a tool for interpreting such narratives in the concept of "secondary marginalization," the process by which more privileged members of marginalized communities police more stigmatized members to protect their status (*Boundaries of Blackness*, 208). Roderick Ferguson links this process directly to processes of surveillance: "The terms for black middle-class subject and social formations demanded that black middle-class persons and those seeking middle-class status would make themselves, as well as queer and working-class blacks, available for surveillance and do so in the name of recognition and normativity" (76). Such processes of misattributed blame emerge from structures of inequality.

Other stories took up the concept of homophobia to explore the ways in which community might function as a site of liberation. For example, the *Sentinel* accepted the argument that men on the down low represented an important vector of HIV transmission, but also asked the reader to think about issues of power: "The most obvious reason men are living on the down low is the social stigma attached to homosexuality and the homophobic attitude many African Americans have in the black community" (Anderson, A1). The *Skanner* challenged readers to examine such strategies of blame: "The Black community's fear, denial and rejection of homosexuality must share responsibility for the proliferation of the 'down low' lifestyle, the families and marriages it destroys and the very real danger it poses to women" ("Book: A Guide for Women," 6). Such accounts raised homophobia in order to address the complexities of secondary marginalization and seek collective strategies for transformation and survival.

In some instances, transparent sexual identity seemed a solution to the gendered politics of HIV transmission (an effect not substantiated by epidemiological research, but well circulated in the media). This problem was especially pronounced in women's magazines. In a response to J.L. King, *Ebony* asked, "So the DL man is sleeping with his men and his women and not using protection with anybody, and putting the entire Black community at risk of AIDS, just because he can't face the fact that he is gay?" The magazine offered a seemingly obvious answer to this not-so-rhetorical question: "Come out of the closet, out of the basement, Down-low Brothers, face up to who you are, and let us live!" (Norment, 34). *Essence* offered this summation:

> I am incensed by the dramatic numbers of African-American women being infected with HIV, mainly from men who sleep around with other men. Now that the down low isn't such a secret anymore, I hope these brothers will find it in their hearts to be honest – if not for themselves, then for the sake of saving the lives of the women who love them. (Smith, 148)

In this instance, gay identity liberates not the individual man but also women who wish to be certain of their partners' sexual histories. Although the editorial refuses the demand that the women play "down low detective," a strategy both incited and denied by J.L. King, this framing ultimately protects heteronormativity by suggesting that the transparency of identity will interrupt HIV transmission, distinguishing "risky" bisexual partners from presumptively safe heterosexual ones.

In mass media accounts, rearticulating men on the down low as gay or bisexual provided a strategy to erase African American difference, a normalizing mechanism for producing unmarked and universal subjects. In the African American press, the demand to adopt gay identity served as a strategy to protect African American identity. In this sense, it is a complex example of secondary marginalization, disciplining the diversity of sexual expression in a way that admits a specific, though circumscribed, space for gay identity. What this tactic left unexplored was the ways in which a politics of sexual diversity might necessarily work against, rather than through, such modes of identification.

"Honest Bodies": The Limits of Homophobia

"The danger of current internal US epidemiological trends is that as HIV increasingly disproportionately affects communities of color, the 'identities' of people in relation to HIV risk will appear increasingly fixed," warned performance studies scholar Barbara Browning (137). The example of men on the down low seems an apt illustration of her concern, illuminating the assumption that fixity provides a necessary basis for HIV prevention. One strategy to challenge the racial essentialism of these representations was to claim the universality of sexual secrecy. Keith Boykin adopts this approach, pointing to the much-publicized revelation of married New Jersey governor James McGreevy's simultaneous relationship with a man: "We perpetuate a lie to ourselves if we believe that McGreevy is simply a rare exception. White men on the down low are everywhere" ("Not Just a Black Thing," 31). In 2005, the *Atlanta-Journal Constitution* reported that the CDC had reached a similar conclusion: "The slang phrase 'being on the down low' – applied to black men who conceal having sex with other men from their wives or girlfriends, and possibly spread HIV that way – should include other races and men without steady male partners, a new federal study suggests" (Wahlberg, E4). This reversal of terms puts pressure on the normative logic that constructs the down low as a form of racial perversity. Boykin pushes further, using the notion of a "white down low" to challenge the epidemiologic utility of this notion altogether (*Beyond the Down Low*, 74).

Using discourse about the down low to turn a critical lens on the public health practices has proved one meaningful form of resistance for health researchers. Mays, Cochran and Zamudio argue that the investment in logics of classification undermines efforts to serve those most affected by HIV infection:

> This need to categorize people is still, in view of the diversity of African American men who have sex with men (gay men, MSM, homo thugz, and men on the down low), a weakness in how we approach prevention. We classify people with labels that make sense from either a disease-transmission standpoint or from a sampling and recruitment need. We put people into discrete categories so that we can package programs for them. When programs do not work, we may blame the person rather than blame the categorization process. (93)

Physician David Malebranche situates research into sexual transmission of HIV in the larger context of the failure of health care to meet the needs of black men (Malebranche et al., 104). In particular, he draws attention to research challenging the assumption that visible gay identity leads to transmission-interrupting behavior:

> *If disclosure of one's sexuality is not necessarily associated with safer sexual behavior and decreased HIV risk for [black Men who have sex with men], pressuring these men to "come out of the closet" may be counterproductive, particularly with "down low" Black men who are secretly engaging in homosexual behavior while living "heterosexual" lives. (Malebranche, 863)*

Young and Meyer use the specificity of the down low, along with other expressions of sexual specificity, to argue that the categories "men who have sex with men" and "women who have sex with women" do not serve to illuminate the complexity and diversity of sexuality and thus serve to hinder rather than help the larger project of HIV prevention (1147).

Queer, wrote critic Michael Warner, is a political concept characterized by "resistance to regimes of the normal" (xxvi). For AIDS cultural critics in the 1980s, exposing homophobia represented an important strategy to challenge the sexual normativities of AIDS discourse (Crimp, Patton, Treichler). At the time, homophobia was a useful term to illuminate the centrality of gay identity to the intersecting domains of media, politics, medicine, and public health. The down low controversy suggests that this concept does not provide the necessary critical traction at this juncture to illuminate the processes of racialization central to AIDS discourse. In an influential critique, Cathy Cohen argued that a singular focus on sexuality delimited the potential of queer politics to challenge the ways in which normativity operates through the intersection of race, sexuality, gender, and class ("Punks," 203). The concept of homophobia may only reinforce this tendency, installing the hetero/homo binary as the foundation of oppression. But as Thomas Shevory argues, "HIV has been imbued with racial constructions since the beginnings of the epidemic" (11). I would extend his observation by suggesting that constructions of sexuality have also been racialized, even when their normative whiteness made them seem unmarked. For those interested in participating in progressive coalitions around HIV/AIDS, foregrounding the effects of racism – with a clear acknowledgement of its gender and sexual politics – may be a more productive response at this time than seeking to challenge a universalized homophobia.

If the taxonomical discourses of identity cannot meet the needs of the diverse men interpolated by the category of down low, what alternative might there be? Outlining the project of queer of color critique, Roderick Ferguson proposes that "instead of identity driving critical interventions, the heterogeneous formations that make up the social drive critical interventions" (143). Cohen suggests that queer theory can play an important role in such a project: "Through its conception of a wide continuum of sexual possibilities, queer theory stands in direct contrast to the normalizing tendencies of hegemonic sexuality rooted in ideas of static, stable sexual identities and behaviors" ("Punks," 201). Activist and research strategies that seek the proliferation of possibilities represent one important response to the normalizing logics of taxonomies of identity.

Clearly, there are pressing issues just barely visible through the obfuscating constructions of the down low. How might they be illuminated more effectively? Tricia Rose offers one alternative in her vision of a politics of "intimate justice"

(400). This notion offers a strategy for linking particular sexual encounters to the larger context of social inequality, thus challenging the "biomedical individualism" which focuses on individual risk and not structural conditions shaping HIV transmission (Lane et al., 321). Patricia Hill Collins uses June Jordan's concept of "honest bodies" to describe social change in the space of sexual encounter. This notion is not the compelled honesty of Foucauldian confession, but rather a shared process of decolonization that seeks to explore the way "power relations invade the body" (283). For Collins, such a process is critical in the context of HIV: "When individual African American women and men strive to develop honest bodies and to reclaim the erotic as a site of freedom, and love as a source of affirmation for self and others, they challenge the spread of HIV/AIDS" (290).

Unfortunately, Collins imagines the down low as the dangerous outside to this liberatory project (291). But what would happen if the Others she constructs were treated as honest bodies as well, with important knowledge of the complexities of negotiating the intersections of race, class, gender, and sexuality in the space of desire? Evelynn Hammonds suggests one way to imagine such a shift in her work on African American women in the context of AIDS: "I want [the epidemic] to be used to make visible black women's self-defined sexualities" ("Black (W)holes," 141). This project is not exactly an identity politics. She calls for a mode of representation that maps the heterogeneous social formations Ferguson described:

> In overturning the "politics of silence" the goal cannot be merely to be seen: visibility in and of itself does not erase a history of silence nor does it challenge the structure of power and domination, symbolic and material, that determines what can and cannot be seen. The goal should be to develop a "politics of articulation." This politics would build on the interrogation of what it makes possible for black women to speak and act. ("Black (W)holes," 141)

Without a commitment to such a politics of articulation, the deconstruction of dominant discourse can serve to reproduce the very dynamics it hopes to supplant. Instead of undermining what Foucault called "the 'political economy' of a will to knowledge" (73), such analysis may reproduce the power dynamics of dominant discourse. I end with this potentially sobering thought precisely for the challenge it makes to my own critical practice. Exposing its insufficiency is my own form of accountability.

Suggested Further Reading

Boykin, Keith. *Beyond the Down Low: Sex, Lies, and Denial in Black America*. New York: Carroll and Graf Publishers, 2005.

Cohen, Cathy. *The Boundaries of Blackness: AIDS and the Breakdown of the Black Community*. Chicago: University of Chicago Press, 1997.

Ferguson, Roderick. *Aberrations in Black: Toward a Queer of Color Critique*. Minneapolis: University of Minnesota Press, 2004.
Johnson, Patrick and Mae Henderson (ed.), *Black Queer Studies: A Critical Anthology*. Durham: Duke University Press, 2005.
McBride, Dwight. *Why I Hate Abercrombie and Fitch: Essays on Race and Sexuality*. New York: New York University Press, 2005.

References

Alexander, Bryant Keith. "Reflections, Riffs and Remembrances: The Black Queer Studies in the Millennium Conference (2000)." *Callaloo* 23.4 (2000): 1285–305.
Anderson, Makebra. "Undercover Brothers: Life on the 'Down Low.'" *Sentinel* 6 June 2002, A1. Proquest Ethnic Newswatch. Online Database. 7 September 2005.
Baker, Derrick. "'Down Low' Black Men Actually Low Down." *N'Digo* 1 April 2004, 12. Lexis Nexis Academic Universe. Online Database. 2 September 2005.
"Book: A Guide for Women Living with 'DL' Men." [Seattle] *The Skanner* 23 February 2005, 6. Proquest Ethnic Newswatch. Online Database. 7 September 2005.
Boykin, Keith. *Beyond the Down Low: Sex, Lies, and Denial in Black America*. New York: Carroll and Graf Publishers, 2005.
——— "Not Just a Black Thing." *Advocate* 18 January 2005, 31–3. Lexis Nexis Academic Universe. Online Database. 2 September 2005.
Browning, Barbara. *Infectious Rhythms: Metaphors of Contagion and the Spread of African Culture*. New York: Routledge, 1998.
Butler, Judith. "Is Kinship Always Already Heterosexual?" *differences: A Journal of Feminist Cultural Studies* 15.1 (2002): 14–44.
Campbell, James. "'Down Low' Has Victims: Black Women," *Houston Chronicle* 10 May 2004, A18. Lexis Nexis Academic Universe. Online Database. 2 September 2005.
Cohen, Cathy. *The Boundaries of Blackness: AIDS and the Breakdown of the Black Community*. Chicago: University of Chicago Press, 1997.
——— "Punks, Bulldaggers, and Welfare Queens: The Radical Potential of Queer Politics?" *Sexual Identities, Queer Politics* (ed.), Mark Blasius. Princeton: Princeton University Press, 2001. 200–227.
Collins, Patricia Hill. *Black Sexual Politics: African Americans, Gender, and the New Racism*. New York: Routledge, 2004.
Crimp, Douglas. "How to Have Promiscuity in an Epidemic." *AIDS: Cultural Analysis, Cultural Activism* (ed.), Douglas Crimp. Cambridge, MA: MIT Press, 1988. 237–70.
Darryl, James. "HIV on the Down Low." *The Sentinel* 24 June – 1 July 2004, A6. Proquest Ethnic Newswatch. Online Database. 7 September 2005.

Denizet-Lewis, Benoit. "Double Lives on the Down Low." *New York Times Magazine* 3 August 2003, 28. Lexis Nexis Academic Universe. Online Database. 2 September 2005.

Dorsey, Gary. "'Down Low' Author Talks About 'Straight' Black Men Who Are Gay." [Saint Louis] *Post-Dispatch* 9 June 2004, E3. Lexis Nexis Academic Universe. Online Database. 2 September 2005.

Ferguson, Roderick. *Aberrations in Black: Toward a Queer of Color Critique*. Minneapolis: University of Minnesota Press, 2004.

Foucault, Michel. *The History of Sexuality, Volume 1*. New York: Vintage Books, 1990 [1978].

"Frequently Asked Questions on HIV and AIDS." National Center for HIV, STD, and TB Prevention, Divisions of HIV/AIDS Prevention. 8 September 2005. Centers for Disease Control. 10 December 2005. <http://www.cdc.gov/hiv/pubs/faqs.htm>.

Grover, Jan Zita. "AIDS: Keywords." *AIDS: Cultural Analysis, Cultural Activism* (ed.), Douglas Crimp. Cambridge, MA: MIT Press, 1988. 17–30.

Hammonds, Evelynn. "Black (W)holes and the Geometry of Black Female Sexuality." *differences: A Journal of Feminist Cultural Studies* 6.2–3 (1994): 126–45.

—— "Missing Persons: Black Women and AIDS." *Radical America* 24.2 (1990): 7–24.

Hine, Darlene Clark. "Rape and the Inner Lives of Black Women in the Midwest: Preliminary Thoughts on the Culture of Dissemblance." *Signs* 14 (August 1988): 912–20.

Hollinshed, Denise. "Some Gay Black Men Are Keeping a Deadly Secret." [Saint Louis] *Post-Dispatch* 21 April 2002, A1. Lexis Nexis Academic Universe. Online Database. 2 September 2005.

Hooper, Ernest. "Black Men on 'the Down Low' and AIDS are Scary Trends." *St. Petersberg Times* 15 April 2004, B3.

King, J.L. *Coming Up from the Down Low: The Journey to Acceptance, Healing, and Honest Love*. New York: Crown, 2005.

—— *On the Down Low: A Journey into the Lives of "Straight" Black Men who Sleep with Men*. New York: Broadway, 2004.

Lane, Sandra et al. "Structural Violence and Racial Disparity in HIV Transmission." *Journal of Health Care for the Poor and Underserved* 15 (2004): 319–35.

Lisotta, Christopher. "Reaching Out to the Down Low." *Advocate* 17 August 2004, 32–3. Lexis Nexis Academic Universe. Online Database. 2 September 2005.

Malebranche, David. "Black Men Who Have Sex with Men and the HIV Epidemic: Next Steps for Public Health." *American Journal of Public Health* 93.6 (June 2003): 862–4.

—— et al. "Race and Sexual Identity: Perceptions about Medical Culture and Healthcare among Black Men Who Have Sex with Men." *Journal of the National Medical Association* 96.1 (January 2004): 97–107.

Mays, Vickie, Susan Cochran, and Anthony Zamudio. "HIV Prevention Research: Are We Meeting the Needs of African American Men Who Have Sex with Men?" *Journal of Black Psychology* 30.1 (February 2004): 78–105.

McBride, Dwight. *Why I Hate Abercrombie and Fitch: Essays on Race and Sexuality*. New York: New York University Press, 2005.

"Men on the Down Low." National Center for HIV, STD, and TB Prevention, Divisions of HIV/AIDS Prevention. 21 June 2005. Centers for Disease Control. 10 December 2005. <http://www.cdc.gov/hiv/pubs/faq/Downlow.htm#Q1>.

Morris, Phillip. "Advice, Wake-Up Signs from 'Slick Rick.'" [Cleveland] *Plain-Dealer* 7 March 2004, H5. Lexis Nexis Academic Universe. Online Database. 2 September 2005.

Norment, Lynn. "The Low-Down on the Down-Low." *Ebony* August 2004, 34. Lexis Nexis Academic Universe. Online Database. 2 September 2005.

Oprah Winfrey Show. "A Secret Sex World: Living on the Down Low." 7 July 2005. Transcript on line. Lexis Nexis Academic Universe. Online Database. 2 September 2005.

Patton, Cindy. *Inventing AIDS*. New York: Routledge, 1990.

Plummer, David and Doug Porter. "The Use and Misuse of Epidemiological Categories." *No Place for Borders: The HIV/AIDS Epidemic and Development in Asia and the Pacific* (ed.), Godfrey Linge and Doug Porter. New York: St. Martin's Press, 1997. 41–9.

Rodriguez Rust, Paula. "Popular Images and the Growth of Bisexual Community and Visibility." *Bisexuality in the United States: A Social Science Reader* (ed.), Pula Rodriguez Rust. New York: Columbia University Press, 2000. 537–53.

Rose, Tricia. *Longing to Tell: Black Women Talk about Sexuality and Intimacy*. New York: Picador, 2003.

Sedgwick, Eve Kosofsky. *Epistemology of the Closet*. Berkeley: University of California Press, 1990.

Shevory, Thomas. *Notorious H.I.V.: The Media Spectacle of Nushawn Williams*. Minneapolis: University of Minnesota Press, 2004.

Smith, Taigi. "Deadly Deception." *Essence* August 2004, 148. Lexis Nexis Academic Universe. Online Database. 2 September 2005.

Tomso, Gregory. "Bug Chasing, Barebacking, and the Risks of Care." *Literature and Medicine* 23.1 (Spring 2004): 88–111.

Treichler, Paula. "AIDS, Homophobia, and Biomedical Discourse: An Epidemic of Signification." *How to Have Theory in an Epidemic*. Durham: Duke University Press, 1999. 11–41.

Vilanch, Bruce. "Der Führer on the Down Low." *Advocate* 8 June 2004, 46. Lexis Nexis Academic Universe. Online Database. 2 September 2005.

Wahlberg, David. "Secret Sex, Drug Use Fuel Rise in AIDS." *Atlanta Journal-Constitution* 16 June 2005, E4. Lexis Nexis Academic Universe. Online Database. 2 September 2005.

Warner, Michael. "Introduction." *Fear of a Queer Planet: Queer Politics and Social Theory* (ed.), Michael Warner. Minneapolis: University of Minnesota Press, 1993. vii–xxxi.

Watney, Simon. *Imagine Hope: AIDS and Gay Identity*. New York: Routledge, 2000.

Williams, Jeffrey Lee. "The Low-Down on the Down Low." *The Gay and Lesbian Review* 11.6 (November–December 2004): 6.

Yingling, Thomas. *AIDS and the National Body* (ed.), Robyn Wiegman. Durham: Duke University Press, 1997.

Young, Rebecca and Ilan Meyer. "The Trouble with 'MSM' and 'WSW': Erasure of the Sexual-Minority Person in Public Health Discourse." *American Journal of Public Health* 95.7 (July 2005): 1144–9.

Young, Tara. "Black HIV Epidemic is Focus of Forum." [New Orleans] *Times-Picayune* 30 April 2004, M1. Lexis Nexis Academic Universe. Online Database. 2 September 2005.

Rethinking the Place
of Queer and the Erotic within
Geographies of Sexualities

Jon Binnie

Queering Geographies

In this chapter I will consider the place of sexuality, queer politics and the erotic within geographical knowledge. In doing so I want to revisit an earlier paper I wrote on this subject (Binnie 1997) that focused on the relationship of sexuality to 'the field' – the sexual and erotic politics of fieldwork and the sexualised construction of geographical knowledge. A rethinking of the reasons for the original paper and the re-evaluation of its main arguments are necessary for a number of reasons. There has been an explosion in work on sexuality and space within human geography in recent years. In this work one emerging line of enquiry and debate is the role of the erotic within geographies of sexualities. A second and related concern has been the place of queer politics and theory within geographical studies of sexuality. I will develop these concerns about queer and the erotic through an examination of the way they have been treated in discussions on the mundane and normativity. This chapter then considers the practical example of the undergraduate geography field trip which is reflective and illustrative of these more abstract theoretical concerns.

To say that queer is a contested term is something of an understatement. It is a sentiment and label that is often used to denote acts, effects, practices and (more contentiously) identities that claim or are claimed to run counter to heteronormativity and heterosexuality. As Browne (2006) finds in her recent essay on queer geographies, queer is a slippery term that can be very difficult to pin down. In an endnote to a recent paper, Jasbir Puar acknowledges that while queer is often used to denote differences from lesbian and gay, she 'suggest[s] that some queers are implicated in homonormative spaces and practices' (2006, 86). She notes, however:

> While I adhere to these contextual usages within rotating contexts, invariably there will be slippage. I note the inadequacy of all of these terms,

> *because they are overdetermined and vague, too specific yet too broad. It is precisely the attempt to mediate these tensions that is symptomatic of the problem. (2006, 86)*

It is in these slippages that exclusions are created, that problematic assumptions are revealed about who or what is seen as queer. In the introduction to a special issue of *Social Text* entitled 'What's Queer about Queer Studies Now?', David Eng, José Esteban Muñoz and Judith Halberstam argue:

> *Much of queer theory nowadays sounds like a metanarrative about the domestic affairs of white homosexuals. Surely, queer studies promises more than a history of gay men, a sociology of gay male sex clubs, an anthropology of gay male tourism, a survey of gay male aesthetics. (2005, 12)*

They are right that queer studies needs to be much more than these things, but I do think it is troubling that they pick on the study of gay male sex clubs as a target for their criticism. Surely a sociology of gay male sex clubs is something that is valuable and necessary, given current rates of HIV transmission and infection? We have yet to see many studies of gay male sex clubs in geography.[1]

In some discussions of the field of geographies of sexualities, there have been criticisms that work on geographies of sexualities in the early to mid-1990s uncritically studied homosexualities to the exclusion of other sexual practices and had an exclusive focus on urban communities. For instance Richard Phillips argues that the collection *Mapping Desire* was predominantly about geographies of homosexuality and left other sexualities largely ignored. In taking David Bell and Gill Valentine, he argues:

> *Their own influential edited volume on the subject did not quite fulfil the promise of its inclusive subtitle* Geographies of Sexualities. Mapping Desire *was concerned was less with sexualities than sexuality in the singular: homosexuality. Twelve out of eighteen chapters in the book were about gay men and/or lesbians. (2006, 165)*

This is an ungenerous argument for the authors' avowed intention was to make a collection that was not limited to homosexualities, or to urban areas (there was hardly an abundance of research on heterosexualities in the early 1990s), but this volume of essays, which is now 12 years old, was the first on the subject of sexualities within geography and omissions are inevitable in a volume that is seeking to open up a new field of enquiry. While attempts to queer geography have been contested within the discipline, there have been relatively few attempts to challenge the way in which the discipline has sought to control and regulate queer research. In this context I am primarily concerned with the notion of queer as an erotic potential

---

1   See Brown (2006) for an insightful essay on the scalar erotic politics of bathhouses and political obligation in Seattle.

and a deconstructive but sex-positive force. In the next section I argue that the erotic is still a marginal and neglected area within geographical research.

Sex and Geographical Knowledge

In 1997 I wrote a paper entitled 'Coming Out of Geography' which sought to examine how sexuality was implicated in the research process. This intervention examined the relation between the researcher and the researched in terms of desire, erotics, politics and knowledge. At the same time it attempted to challenge the various ways in which the geographical academy sought to limit what could and couldn't be spoken in terms of embodied sexual practices. David Bell's (1995a) paper '[Screwing] Geography' was another intervention that sought to make visible the institutional constraints on doing work on sexuality and the erotic in geography including the censoring of titles of conference papers. Central to both of these interventions was the call for geography to reflect on its own squeamishness when it comes to sex and bodily matters more generally. In my essay I argued that this squeamishness needed to be confronted if we were to produce more meaningful discussions about the relationships between erotics, communities and identities. I sought to make connections between how geographical knowledge was created and the exclusion of sexual dissidents. I argued therefore that epistemological and methodological issues could explain the marginalisation of sexual dissidents within human geography. In doing so I argued that the mainstream geographical community often displayed squeamishness about sex:

> Heterosexuals seem to cope with queer theory in its most abstract, intellectualised, disembodied form, but then to run scared when confronted with the materiality of lesbian, bisexual and gay lives, experiences and embodiments. (Binnie 1997, 227)

The striking essentialism within this statement makes me somewhat squeamish re-reading it in hindsight. Clearly the issue of squeamishness around embodiment is not simply a question of the homo/hetero divide. The notion of homosexual respectability is a theme that is increasingly being foregrounded within debates on homonormativity within lesbian and gay studies/queer theory.

Since the blossoming of work on sexuality within geography in the early 1990s we have witnessed many transformations in the sexual political landscape. These in turn have informed changes in the terrain of queer theory/sexuality studies. In the early 1990s there was a preoccupation with *transgressive* sexual practices and performativities – for instance the ICA conference 'Preaching to the Perverted' and the *New Formations* special issue on perversions (Squires 1993). In the UK this concern with transgressive sexual practice reflected specific events on the ground – for instance the effective criminalisation of sadomasochism following the Operation Spanner trial (Bell 1995b; Bibbings and Alldridge 1993). Since the mid-

1990s there has certainly been a turn away from this focus on transgression to a concentration on topics that are seen as being more worthy. Yet despite the fact that sadomasochism is no longer the focus of activist and critical attention it was in the mid-1990s, this does not mean that the criminalisation of sadomasochism is no longer a salient political issue as Darren Langdridge (2006) reminds us.

In critical human geography we have witnessed a non-representational turn, partly inspired by Judith Butler's work on performativity, to examine all manner of topics. As Butler's work on performativity has become assimilated within mainstream critical human geography, it would appear that the body has become more abstract than ever. We see for instance in the criticisms of Butler's work that it has rendered discussion of the physicality and guts of embodied sex as abstract and safe as ever. This is not to call for a deployment of the body in essentialist terms – the body is always social. Nor does this mean a simple celebration of embodiment in which we are obligated to provide confessional discussions of how our own bodies and sexual practices are implicated in our research. Kim England's (1994) essay is exemplary in this regard in providing a discussion of the limits and constraints of who does work on what group or identity. When I read it originally I felt a strong sense of relief that at last someone had the guts to confront these issues head on – and that straight researchers were at last admitting to some sense of humility in recognising the limits in their ability to represent the voice of the Other. Some years later I feel perhaps much more ambivalent in this regard. While researchers of sexuality should demonstrate sensitivity in discussing and researching sexuality this obligation should not lead to silences around awkward methodological issues to do with sex.

In the mid-1990s there were books that sought to foreground ethnographic accounts and examine the sexual politics of ethnography (Kulick and Willson 1995; Lewin and Leap 1996; Newton 1993). These interventions were significant in raising the issue of the connection between academic authority, status, power and sexuality. Discussion of power in the research process has to acknowledge the relationship between sexuality and power/knowledge. Has the prominence of discussions of desire rooted in psychoanalysis and the turn towards non-representational theory rendered the sexualised body more abstract than ever? The question of sex and the relationship between erotics, sex and sexuality remains troubled despite these earlier pioneering attempts to make the aforementioned visible as objects of study. To speak of sex acts can sometimes appear clumsy or awkward, embarrassing, painful or smutty.

Erotic Politics and Queer Practice

Politically we need to understand a complex shifting terrain and cartography of politicised acts and identities. Focusing on the erotic rather than the category of sexuality may be fruitful in helping us to get to the materiality and physicality of sex as opposed to identities and communities which have been much studied within human geography (though this is of course an artificial distinction as eroticism, connection may be seen as the foundation of sociality, even community within some sexual dissident communities). Thus far we have seen that a queer epistemology has to take on board the relationship between the erotic and knowledge.

Samuel Delaney's (1999) work on the purification of space in Times Square in Manhattan is one example of the way in which the erotic can be incorporated in the study of sexuality and space. His study examines the erotic politics of zoning legislation in New York (Dangerous Bedfellows 1996; Papayanis 2000) which has had the consequence of purifying the space and reducing the possibilities for the opportunities for eroticised contact and encounters with difference within this part of the city. Delaney's partly autobiographical account of the disappearing streetscape of porn cinemas and opportunities for erotic encounters on 42nd Street is marked by a matter-of-factness and candour in its discussions of sex that is far from voyeuristic. This comfort in discussing sex is refreshing but rare in academia. That such frankness is rare is unsurprising given the costs associated with discussing the erotic in such a direct manner in academic writing. As Ralph Bolton argues:

> The few who have written most explicitly about such matters are precisely those on the margins who, not by choice but because of discrimination, have been excluded from academically respectable positions in major universities – in other words, individuals with nothing to lose by being honest and forthcoming. (1995, 158)

In highlighting the work of Delaney I do not want to appear prescriptive in stating that some forms of methodology are preferable to others in terms of a progressive politics of sexuality. Can there be an essential queer method or technique? I think here we need to learn much from discussions of epistemology and methodology within feminism. The notion that some methods and techniques are more feminist than others seems to be increasingly questionable. In relation to matters queer, can a specific technique be deemed queerer than others? I am not so sure. Perhaps rather than articulating a queer standpoint theory we should more modestly pay attention to how the techniques are used and to what end? Stephen Valocchi (2005) suggests that ethnographic methods are best suited for advancing a queer understanding of identities and practices. While I would not necessarily share Valocchi's faith in ethnography, it is still the case that qualitative techniques may be more suitable for research in this area – though again it comes down to what is fit for which purpose.

In this section I have reflected on some ways in which the erotics of space have been explicitly studied as well as discussing more generally the relationship between erotics, sexuality and methodology. My interventions in this area have sought to resist attempts to deny the value of the erotic component of everyday life in research on sexuality and space. This has been in response to the institutional attempts to exclude frank examinations of the erotic that were discussed in Bell's '[Screwing] Geography' (1995a). Now that research on sexuality has proliferated, we are witnessing a lively discussion of the place of the erotic within geographical research on sexuality. Referring to the titles of sessions organised by the Sexuality and Space Speciality Group at the Association of American Geographers conference in 2005, Richard Phillips bemoans the phrases 'Sexy Spaces!', 'More Sex! More Gender!': 'both titles suggested an interest in erotic spaces in which sexuality – of whatever forms – is most overt' (2006, 167). Discussing these sessions, during which he praises the more inclusive and diverse range of themes and approaches taken by the presenters he notes disparagingly: 'Still, the dominant interest within the sessions and the field more generally remains with sexualised minorities and erotic locations' (2006, 167). This discussion of the place of the erotic within geographical research on sexuality can benefit from a consideration of how the erotic is treated and framed within debates on normativity and everyday life.

The Erotic, the Normative and the Mundane

As evident from the previous section, the erotic and its relationship to geographies of sexuality is a topic that has become rather fraught in recent years. There have been calls for geographers to refocus their critical attention away from the erotic, the sexy and to focus on so-called 'unsexy geographies'. This is partly inspired by Heidi Nast's paper 'Unsexy Geographies' (1998) in which she called for critical attention to be focused on the unsexy geographies of mainstream sexualities specifically 'normative heterosexuality'. In a similar vein Richard Phillips argues:

> *Geographical and historical research on sexualities, preoccupied with overtly sexualised minorities, has much to gain intellectually and politically from interrogating the hidden and apparently benign sexualities of the moral centre: people and places constructed as normal … it was (and is) not just in frank or dramatic moments of sexual expression or transgression that power is transferred, constructed, expressed and contested through sexuality; these things also happen in mundane moments of conformity and continuity.* (2006, 163)

While Phillips is right to argue for a broadening of the intellectual scope of geographies of sexualities, there is an interesting way in which the everyday is constructed in this argument. The implication is that the focus on transgression is about non-mundane, out of the ordinary, spectacular other spaces. There is subtle relocation of the erotic in the realm of the non-mundane as if somehow erotic desire is not a facet of mundane, everyday existence – that it can only be found in other spaces, elsewhere outside of the everyday. But, as Clare Hemmings and Felicity Grace (referring to Bell and Valentine's *Mapping Desire* and Ingram's *Queers in Space* (1997)) argue:

> *… sexual geographers have insisted on the materiality of the everyday negotiations that take place within particular spaces (sexual or otherwise) in*

the formation of conflicted, changing, uncomfortable as well as pleasurable sexual selves. (1999, 390)

In thinking through how questions of norms and normativity link to notions of the everyday, we need to keep in mind how the everyday is framed and whose conceptualisation of the everyday we are considering. The idea that sex is somehow not an ordinary part of mundane, everyday life is laughable yet the erotic and questions of desire are routinely marginalised within theoretical discussions of the everyday (Highmore 2002).

Phillips is right to argue that certain sexualities are seen as having an excess of sexuality – for instance gay men have been routinely pathologised as hypersexual and promiscuous. For instance, in her analysis of British parliamentary debates on Section 28 which became Section 28 of the Local Government Act 1988, Anna Marie Smith (1991) argued that gendered norms were reproduced in the rhetorical construction of gay men as hypersexual, promiscuous, irresponsible 'dangerous queers' while lesbians were constructed as restrained, responsible, asexual 'good homosexuals'. In this regard it is instructive to pay attention to Phillips's call to resist what he sees as the 'over-sexualisation' of some sexualities, and the invisibility of others within studies of sexuality and space in critical human geography:

It means contesting the over-sexualisation of those constructed as sexually deviant and exposing the taken-for-granted, hidden sexualisation of people and places constructed as normal. It means recognising the limits of sexual frankness, freedom and expression, the reality and social functions of celibacy, modesty and secrecy. (2006, 168)

However we should also recognise contemporary dominant media representations of gay men that configure them as de-sexualised and devoid of an erotic subjectivity. One current media trope is the focus on gay men as responsible, domesticated, model consumer citizens that provide a socially useful function as sources of fashion advice and reservoirs of taste.

The notion of heteronormativity is highly powerful rhetorically in challenging the way in which society is structured along the two gender model – norms that enshrine heterosexuality as normal and therefore lesbians and gay men, bisexuals and transgendered people as Other and marginal. However, I am not so sure about its usefulness now. The notion of heteronormativity tends to lump all heterosexuals together in the same box and can mask or obscure the differences between and within sexual dissident identities and communities. It can sometimes appear that heterosexual identities are uniformly normative and socially conservative, while non-heterosexuals or sexual dissidents are constructed as radical, progressive or outside of social norms. Are these norms as stable, immutable and static as these assumptions would uphold? As straight men are disciplined in their lifestyle choices by gay men in the television makeover programme *Queer Eye for the Straight Guy*, are we not witnessing subtle changes in the sexual landscape whereby what is valued as normal or normative is increasingly confused and up-for-grabs? Moreover, we witness the media attention devoted to pathologising and 'outing' non-normative heterosexual practices – for instance dogging, which involves straights meeting for public sex in car parks (Bell 2006).

At the same time there has been considerable discussion about the notion of homonormativity (Bell and Binnie 2004; Duggan 2002; 2003; Puar 2006) and the development of the Gay Right in the United States (Goldstein 2002). The notion of homonormativity refers to certain definitions of norms or mainstreaming within lesbian and gay communities associated with the consumption and the exclusion of others on the basis of race, class, gender and disability. This turn towards focusing on homonormativity is politically significant because it draws critical attention away from some simplistic rhetorical constructions of heterosexuality as a uniform, monolithic entity. In an essay on US homonormativities, Jasbir Puar insists that it can be dangerous to argue that heterosexuality is a stable, singular, monolithic identity arguing against the resurrection of 'feminist constructions of "patriarchy" which homogenise and universalise heteronormative and nuclear familial and sexual relations, inferring that heterosexuality is the same everywhere' (2006, 75).

This section has focused on the erotic, the mundane and the normal. We have seen that the erotic is commonly framed as existing outside of the everyday – a force located in the extraordinary, not the banal. Likewise we have witnessed debate on the desirability of studying erotic practises. For instance, does the focus on erstwhile transgressive sexual practices such as gay male SM reproduce a dominant representation of gay men as hypersexual and let heterosexuality off the hook, or does it contest the attempts to render these troublesome sexual practices invisible? I will now proceed to discuss one specifically geographical pedagogic practice where we see a constellation of these issues around the erotic, the mundane, heteronormativity and homonormativity: the undergraduate field trip.

Sexuality, Erotics and Power/Knowledge: The Disciplinary Specificity of Geography

One mundane example of the constellation of erotics, power and knowledge that is perhaps specific to geography is the undergraduate field trip. In any assessment of the relationship between sexuality, erotics and knowledge in geography we must not overlook pedagogical concerns. I think these are particularly significant in terms of the often considerable fracturing between, on the one hand, the way geography is taught, and on the other, how it is researched. There is still the particular socialisation of geographical knowledge that takes place via a field trip which is a particularly sexualised space. We are all meant to recognise the value of field trips within geography. They are a valuable recruitment tool – a way of branding the discipline, making it distinctive from other natural and social sciences. Field trips are also a significant way of distinguishing one geography degree programme from another. We all know the value of field trips on open days and the demand to offer ever more exotic destinations to prospective students as one means of differentiating our courses from those of our competitors.

The relationship between pedagogy and geographical research on sexuality is the key concern of Karen Nairn (2003) in her valuable and challenging paper on the sexual politics of field trips. Discussing the politics of gender, race and sexuality in the construction of geographical knowledge on field trips, she examines the geography of sleeping arrangements on such trips. Focusing on embodiment can fruitfully interrogate the way these are intertwined within notions of squeamishness and comfort. As Nairn argues, the discomfort felt by some of her informants reflects uneven power relations in terms of whose subjectivities are valued, and whose are rendered marginal.

> Hegemonic spaces and discourses favouring particular sexual and cultural identities have the potential to act as gatekeeping mechanisms to readily include geography students and staff most comfortable with those spaces and discourses while those who do not conform are implicitly provided with the message that their subjectivities and needs for particular kinds of spaces do not matter. (2003, 77)

In the conclusion to her article, Nairn goes on to question 'whether fieldwork needs to take place away from universities and schools to count as "real" fieldwork and whether indeed it offers the best means of relating theory and practice' (2003, 78). So perhaps it is the centrality of fieldwork within the discipline – or rather the specific privileged status accorded to it – that can explain the specific attitude towards sexuality within the discipline? Is there, however, not a certain essentialism being articulated here, too? Do all queer students and staff experience the kind of dislocation, marginalisation and sense of exclusion that Nairn speaks about? She makes the valid point that 'geographic knowledge is not only the formal and explicit curriculum but also the informal and implicit curriculum that is often referred to as the hidden curriculum' (2003, 69). So we are speaking about the values that are communicated down through fieldwork but also through the social environment, particularly on residential fieldtrips. Gill Valentine speaks of the blurring of home and work, public and private spheres that takes place on fieldtrips:

> Nowhere is this more so than in the ubiquitous geography field class, where part of the raison d'etre is often to encourage informality and a 'get to know you' relationship between staff and students ... Even if personal information is not volunteered, it is certainly sought out by students. (1999, 418)

As Nairn and Valentine argue, field trips can be sites of considerable anxiety and discomfort for both students and staff. While field trips may present specific challenges, what about the mundane space of the everyday geography classroom?

Valentine argues that because of the assumption that mundane environments are coded as straight, lesbian, gay and bisexual staff are faced with the issue of whether to be out with their students. There is a suspicion that simply teaching this material will lead students to make assumptions about a teacher's sexuality. I think this has certainly changed in my experience – with the mainstreaming of work on the geography of sexualities and the proliferation of undergraduate courses on which sexuality is taught this has now perhaps becoming less of an issue. Coming out is only the beginning, though, as there are many forms of coming out and many closets. For instance, Glen Elder, discussing coming out in the geography classroom, notes that 'the politics of nation, immigration, "race", and sexuality in contemporary US society require that as a white South African national I "come out" on several fronts: anti-racist, foreigner, African and gay' (1999, 87). Whatever form of closet or coming out, Valentine suggests that 'in the small and incestuous world of academia, once you are "out" there are few possibilities to retreat into the closet if the going gets tough' (1999, 421). The personal risks associated with coming out should be balanced against the notion that being a certain kind of gay or lesbian subject may be becoming fashionable – one which has cultural capital associated with it. In an era marked by subjects such as the metrosexual, can it always be seen as such a disadvantage? Perhaps we should examine the way in which professions are sexualised – that having the right kind of self-presentation, speech, clothing and performance matters. So rather than focusing on coming out *per se*, we should be more concerned with which public performances of queer sexuality are acceptable, and which are not. Which are acceptable within mainstream geography and which are not? We must of course still acknowledge the fact that there is an economic cost for people being out (Badgett 2001). That cost is not borne evenly – for instance financial/economic independence is often a prerequisite for coming out. Here I am thinking about class issues. So there may be significant differences in economic power and how this relates to performances of sexuality. While those with less may have less financial independence to be out; then others with more may also have more to lose by behaving inappropriately.

Valentine comments:

> *Visibility across the curriculum is important for dissident sexualities because it normalises them. Otherwise the danger is that lesbian, gay and bisexualities are missed out altogether or become relegated to the one-off 'exotic other' lecture, which only serves to reinforce stereotypes and perpetuate the taken-for-granted heterosexuality of the university environment. (1999, 421)*

But is this visibility always so desirable for all sexual dissidents? Can visibility do harm? Is it always a positive experience? Likewise, is *normalisation* so desirable either? For many, normalisation is preferable to enfreakment or being marked out as an exotic Other. The question is: whose kind of normal? I think what Valentine really means to emphasise here is actually the mundanising aspect of normal. There is also the embarrassment that queer students may feel about being lectured about queer sexuality by an older lecturer. The notion that neither student nor teacher may share very much other than a common disposition means that classes on sexuality and space might produce dis-identification as easily as identification (in the same way that students may be embarrassed by pedagogic attempts to relate to popular and youth culture).

Future Directions for Studying the Erotic in Geographies of Sexualities

In a paper on value and geographical knowledge, David Bell (2007) provocatively discusses the institutional politics of contemporary geographical research. Research has to demonstrate a use value to an institution otherwise it is seen as worthless and useless. The utility of research will obviously depend on the specific institutional context and matrix of power/knowledge. This question of utility and the value of research has been one that has mattered a lot to those researching sexuality – wanting to claim a place at the table of human geography. Research on sexuality, like any other within human geography, is seen as valid if it furthers the goals of the institution or discipline – in the UK context, how it contributes to the RAE (Research Assessment Exercise) which is the review of university research quality that determines government funding of university departments. The failure of an individual researcher to be entered into the RAE can lead towards redundancy and the poor performance of a department can contribute towards its closure, so the consequences of failure here can be immediate, dramatic and draconian. Is this always compatible with other goals such as the development of research on erotic practices that may be considered more risky in this context? Who is research on the geographies of sexualities for and to what purpose? Who should be the subject and object of such research and to what ends? Geographical research should make visible and challenge the shifting terrains of norms that regulate and control sexualities. In geographical studies of the everyday we must not overlook the erotic as a component of the mundane, while understanding how sexuality is deployed as a force, and to what ends.

Suggested Further Reading

Bell, D. (1995), '[Screwing] Geography: Censor's Version', *Environment and Planning D: Society and Space* 13, 127–32.

Binnie, J. (1997), 'Coming Out of Geography: Towards a Queer Epistemology?' *Environment and Planning D: Society and Space* 15, 223–37.

Nairn, K. (2003), 'What Has the Geography of Sleeping Arrangements Got to Do with the Geography of Our Teaching Spaces?' *Gender, Place and Culture* 10:1, 67–81.

Nast, H. (1998), 'Unsexy Geographies', *Gender, Place and Culture* 5:2, 191–206.

Phillips, R. (2006), 'Unsexy Geographies: Heterosexuality, Respectability and the Travellers' Aid Society', *ACME: An International E-Journal for Critical Geographies* 5:2, 163–90.

References

Badgett, L. (2001), *Money, Myths and Change: The Economic Lives of Lesbians and Gay Men* (Chicago, IL: University of Chicago Press).

Bell, D. (1995a), '[Screwing] Geography: Censor's Version', *Environment and Planning D: Society and Space* 13, 127–32.

—— (1995b), 'Perverse Dynamics, Sexual Citizenship, and the Transformation of Intimacy', in D. Bell and G. Valentine (eds), *Mapping Desire: Geographies of Sexualities* (London and New York: Routledge).

—— (2006) 'Bodies, Technologies, Spaces: On Dogging', *Sexualities* 9: 387–407.

—— (2007), 'Fade to Grey: Some Reflections on Policy and Mundanity', *Environment and Planning A* 39:3, 541–54.

—— and Binnie, J. (2004), 'Authenticating Queer Space: Citizenship, Urbanism and Governance', *Urban Studies* 41, 1807–20.

—— and Valentine, G. (eds) (1995), *Mapping Desire: Geographies of Sexualities* (London and New York: Routledge).

Berlant, L. and Warner, M. (1998), 'Sex in Public', *Critical Inquiry* 24, 547–66.

Bibbings, L. and Alldridge, P. (1993), 'Sexual Expression, Body Alteration and the Defence of Consent', *Journal of Law and Society* 20, 356–70.

Binnie, J. (1997), 'Coming Out of Geography: Towards a Queer Epistemology?' *Environment and Planning D: Society and Space* 15, 223–37.

Bolton, R. (1995), 'Tricks, Friends and Lovers: Erotic Encounters in the Field', in D. Kulick and M. Wilson (eds), *Taboo: Sex, Identity and Erotic Subjectivity in Anthropological Fieldwork* (London and New York: Routledge).

Brown, M. (2006), 'Sexual Citizenship, Political Obligation and Disease Ecology in Gay Seattle', *Political Geography* 25, 874–98.

Browne, K. (2006), 'Challenging Queer Geographies', *Antipode* 38, 885–93.

Dangerous Bedfellows (eds) (1996), *Policing Public Sex* (Boston, MA: South End Press).

Delaney, S. (1999), *Times Square Red, Times Square Blue* (New York: New York University Press).

Duggan, L. (2002), 'The New Homonormativity: The Sexual Politics of Neoliberalism', in R. Castronovo and D. Nelson (eds), *Materializing Democracy: Toward a Revitalized Cultural Politics* (Durham, NC: Duke University Press).

—— (2003), *The Twilight of Equality? Neoliberalism, Cultural Politics, and the Attack on Democracy* (Boston, MA: Beacon Press).

Elder, G. (1999), '"Queerying" Boundaries in the Geography Classroom', *Journal of Geography in Higher Education* 23:1, 86–93.

Eng, D. with Halberstam, J. and Muñoz, J.E. (2005), 'Introduction: What's Queer about Queer Studies Now?', *Social Text* 84–5, 23:3–4, 1–17.

England, K. (1994), 'Getting Personal: Reflexivity, Positionality and Feminist Research', *Professional Geographer* 46, 80–89.

Goldstein, R. (2002), *The Attack Queers: Liberal Society and the Gay Right* (London: Verso).

Hemmings, C. and Grace, F. (1999), 'Stretching Queer Boundaries: An Introduction', *Sexualities* 2.4 387–96.

Highmore, B. (2002), *Everyday Life and Cultural Theory* (London and New York: Routledge).

Kulick, D. and Willson, M. (eds) (1995), *Taboo: Sex, Identity and Erotic Subjectivity in Anthropological Fieldwork* (London and New York: Routledge).

Langdridge, D. (2006), 'Voices from the Margins: SM and Sexual Citizenship', *Citizenship Studies* 10:4, 373–89.

Lewin, E. and Leap, W. (eds) (1996), *Out in the Field: Reflections of Lesbian and Gay Anthropologists* (Champaign, IL: University of Illinois Press).

Nairn, K. (2003), 'What Has the Geography of Sleeping Arrangements Got to Do with the Geography of Our Teaching Spaces?' *Gender, Place and Culture* 10:1, 67–81.

Nast, H. (1998), 'Unsexy Geographies', *Gender, Place and Culture* 5:2, 191–206.

Newton, E. (1993), 'My Best Informant's Dress: The Erotic Equation in Fieldwork', *Cultural Anthropology* 8, 3–23.

Papayanis, M. (2000), 'Sex and the Revanchist City: Zoning Out Pornography in New York', *Environment and Planning D: Society and Space* 18, 341–53.

Phillips, R. (2006), 'Unsexy Geographies: Heterosexuality, Respectability and the Travellers' Aid Society', *ACME: An International E-Journal for Critical Geographies* 5:2, 163–90.

Puar, J. (2006), 'Mapping US Homonormativities', *Gender, Place and Culture* 13, 67–88.

Smith, A.M. (1991), 'Which One's the Pretender? Section 28 and Lesbian Representation', in T. Boffin and J. Fraser (eds), *Stolen Glances: Lesbians Take Photographs* (London: Pandora).

Squires, J. (ed.) (1993), 'Perversity', a special issue of *New Formations* 19.

Valentine, G. (1999), 'Ode to a Geography Teacher: Sexuality and the Classroom', *Journal of Geography in Higher Education* 23, 417–23.

Valocchi, S. (2005), 'Not Yet Queer Enough: The Lessons of Queer Theory for the Sociology of Gender and Sexuality', *Gender and Society* 19, 750–70.

To 'Play the Sodomits':
A Query in Five Actions

Garrett P.J. Epp

Prologue

Alan Bray has argued that the visible signs of male friendship and of sodomy in Elizabethan England were queerly similar, even though 'The reaction these two images prompted was wildly different; the one was universally admired, the other execrated and feared' (1994, 40). Mario DiGangi has countered 'that an historical analysis of early modern sexuality must distinguish between socially "orderly" and socially "disorderly" forms of male homoeroticism' (1997, ix), arguing that 'an emphasis on sodomy' on the part of Bray and others has prevented recognition of 'the pervasiveness of nonsodomitical or nonsubversive homoerotic relations' (1994, 9). Yet it is DiGangi, more than Bray, who succumbs to the negative force of what Michel Foucault famously termed 'that utterly confused category' (1990, 101), 'sodomy'. Like 'queer', the term is worthy of reclamation.

In Defence of the Offensive

Some of the best early modern English writing about the theatre condemns its subject, both as a physical place and as an artistic form. What is reborn in 'the English dramatic Renaissance' is less drama, which arguably just changes venue and subject matter, than an ancient antitheatrical tradition. Around the same time that the great biblical cycles of York (last performed in 1569) and Chester (1576) were actively suppressed, the first permanent public playhouses in London were built (the Red Lion in Stepney in 1567, and the Theatre in 1576 and the Curtain the following year, both in Shoreditch), and caused an immediate storm of criticism, both in sermons and in lengthy polemical works, such as *A Treatise wherein Dicing, Dauncing, Vaine playes, or Enterluds with other idle pastimes, &c. commonly vsed on the Sabboth day, are reproued by the Authoritie of the word of God and auntient writers. Made Dialoguewise by Iohn Northbrooke, Minister and Preacher of the word of God* (1577). When

Northbrooke's Youth asks about 'those places ... which are made vp and builded for suche Plaies and Enterludes, as the Theatre and Curtaine is', Age replies:

> ... I am persuaded that Satan hath not a more speedie way and fitter schoole to work and teach his desire, to bring men and women into his snare of concupiscence and filthie lustes of wicked whoredome, than those places and playes, and theaters are: And therefore necessarie that those places and Players shoulde be forbidden and dissolued and put downe by authoritie, as the Brothell houses and Stewes are. (1974, 59–60)

Stephen Gosson's better known contribution, *The Schoole of Abuse, Conteining a plesant inuectiue against Poets, Pipers, Plaiers, Iesters, and such like Caterpillers of a Commonwealth* (1579), was dedicated to Sir Philip Sidney, and provoked a swift *Reply ... in Defence of Poetry, Music, and Stage Plays* from playwright Thomas Lodge (1579), as well as opposition from others, which in turn prompted a hurried *Apologie of the Schoole of Abuse* from Gosson (1579). Sidney's own famous response, *The Defence of Poesie* (published in 1595), was written only after the publication of Gosson's more vehement *Playes confuted in five Actions* (1582).

Such works, most of which treated theatre as part of an axis of evil that included gambling, whoring and stylish clothing, found a ready audience. As Margaret Jane Kidnie notes, Philip Stubbes's massive and highly popular *Anatomie of Abuses*, which deals more with the evils of feminine fashion than with theatre, 'captured its readers' imaginations, going through four editions and two issues between 1583 and 1595' (2002, xi). It has also captured the imaginations of modern critics, mostly due to its evocative description of the social effects of theatre-going:

> ... marke the flocking and running to Theaters and Curtens, dayly & hourely, night and day, time and tyde, to see Playes and Enterludes, where such wanton gestures, such bawdy speeches, such laughing and flearing, such kissing and bussing, such clipping and culling, such wincking and glauncing of wanton eies, and the like, is vsed, as is woonderfull to beholde. Then these goodly Pageants being ended, euery mate sorts to his mate, euery one brings another homeward of their way very friendly, and in their secret conclaues (couertly) they play the Sodomits, or worse. And these be the fruits of plaies and Enterludes for the most part. (2002, 203–4)

Stubbes is right, at least within the cultural context of sixteenth-century England. Unlike their opponents, he and other antitheatrical writers deal specifically with theatrical performance, rather than with poetic fiction. And within the theoretical frameworks available to them, from the rhetorical to the metaphysical, theatrical performance is necessarily threatening and destabilising; drama is, and leads to, what in early modern England was termed sodomy.

The explicit connections made between theatre, effeminacy and sodomy in these antitheatrical polemics have been discussed at length by Lisa Jardine (1983), Laura Levine (1986; 1994) and Stephen Orgel (1989; 1996), among others, but specifically, and often misleadingly, within the context of the Elizabethan transvestite stage. As Jonathan Goldberg has pointed out, modern critical conflations of transvestism and homosexuality are too often informed by heterosexist presumptions (1992, 106ff.), and too seldom by a careful reading of the textual evidence. While the convention of male actors playing women's roles is a major concern for Gosson, Stubbes nowhere mentions it. As Margaret Jane Kidnie politely understates, this is 'a silence which sometimes seems overlooked or ignored in studies of Renaissance antitheatricality' (2002, 33). The crossdressing that most concerns Stubbes is that of fashionable women wearing masculine doublets, an issue that Laura Levine connects both to theatrical crossdressing and to playing 'the Sodomits, or worse'. As Kidnie explains, the connection is misleading:

> Claiming that the passage in question immediately follows Stubbes' description of [female] transvestites as hermaphroditic monsters, Levine silently elides more than fifty quarto pages of text, implying that the concept of sodomy in the Abuses is presented by the author itself as intimately tied up with fears of gender instability. (2002, 34 n. 44)

Yet even Kidnie wrongly asserts, following Levine, that Stubbes thinks that 'men risk degenerating into women' by wearing effeminately luxurious clothing, in the same way that 'women risk degenerating into hermaphrodites' by wearing masculine doublets with their skirts (2002, 33). For Stubbes, 'these women may not improperly bee called Hermaphroditi, that is Monsters of both kindes, halfe women, half men' (2002, 118), precisely because they are wearing both masculine and feminine garb. However, becoming effeminate is not the same as becoming a woman. Effeminacy constitutes, rather, a loss of masculine virtue (Latin *virtus*, from *vir*, 'man') to which both women and men should aspire.

Nor does Stubbes's reference to playing 'the Sodomits, or worse' imply any particular sexual act, position or partner, much less what they may or may not be wearing at the time. Stephen Orgel asks, 'what can be worse than playing the sodomite? If the sodomy were in fact homosexual, then it would be the sodomised who is worse than the sodomite, the passive partner in the act … Stubbes names the worst thing he can imagine, but leaves room for the unimaginable things that are worse' (1996, 159 n. 34). Yet Orgel also admits the unlikelihood of this same homosexual implication. As Goldberg had already pointed out:

> … the one other time Stubbes uses the same phrase, those 'playing the vile Sodomits together' (H6v) are an adulterous man and woman. So little can Stubbes imagine the possibility of members of the same sex having sex together, that he proposes, as a solution to the incitement to lust that dancing is said to offer, that men should dance with men, women with women (N8v–O1r). Sodomy, for Stubbes, is a debauched playing that knows no limit – that has violated the proprieties of male/female married sex – or whose limit can only be gestured toward in a supplementary addition, 'Sodomits, or worse'. (1992, 120–21; see also Kidnie 2002, 34–5)

Playing the sodomite need not even be sexual: in a later passage, Stubbes complains of holiday festivities as encouraging 'drunkennesse, Whoredome, gluttony, and other filthy Sodomiticall Exercises' (2002, 214).

In calling theatre sodomitical, I not only embrace semantic slippage, but also risk the charge that Goldberg directed against Lisa Jardine, of slipping 'perilously from explaining the attitudes of antitheatrical polemicists to adopting them' (1992, 112); I want to make use of the categorical confusion that affects both Stubbes and his readers, not simply explain it away. In the opening chapter of *Sodometries*, Goldberg discusses the 1986 Bowers *v*. Hardwick decision that was overturned in 2003 by the US Supreme Court. In the more recent case, Lawrence et al. *v*. Texas, categorical confusion worked in favour of equal rights to privacy and what Texas law had termed 'deviate sexual intercourse'. In the latter decision, a very brief historical survey served to prove that 'early American sodomy laws were not directed at homosexuals as such but instead sought to prohibit nonprocreative sexual activity more generally'. The *Bowers* Court, in contrast, had stated, 'Proscriptions against that conduct have ancient roots' (see Goldberg 1992, 7). My hope is to make productive use of such ancient and terminologically vague proscriptions, both to demonstrate a major source of antitheatrical anxiety, namely, a crucial breakdown in a gendered metaphysic of authority, and to defend the subversiveness of theatre, against detractors and defenders alike. I write in defence of sodomy, and of actors.

The Devil's Instrument

Sidney's *Defence of Poesie* has little to do with the theatre as such, and less that is positive. As an ostensible reply to Stephen Gosson, the *Defence* is both oblique and extremely partial. It refuses to consider what Gosson and others most blame for the abuses of drama, namely, the actor. This is hardly uncommon. In the words of Henry Phillips, describing theatre criticism in seventeenth-century France, 'The actor is seen as an instrument rather than as a creator; hence the emphasis in theoretical writings is on composition rather than on acting' (1980, 174). Yet Phillips sharply distinguishes these 'theoretical writings' from the polemics of theatre's detractors:

> *The religious moralists ... see the actor as directly responsible for what takes place on the stage; he is accused of moral irresponsibility for performing what is corrupt, and making corrupt by means of gesture and tone of voice plays or parts of plays which would otherwise be considered harmless. The actor thereby embodies, in the most literal sense of the word, the corruption of drama ... (1980, 174)*

In seventeenth-century France, transvestism is not an issue. These religious moralists, like their English counterparts, refer to acting in terms of unnatural sexuality, but most vehemently in regard to female actors (1980, 187–8). Still, it is the actor as actor that matters here, as for Gosson; it is the actor as actor that Sidney refuses to take into consideration.

Sometimes the refusal is especially pointed, and revealing. For instance, in opposition to the claim that Plato banished the poets, Sidney writes:

> ... a man need go no further then to Plato himselfe to knowe his meaning: who in his Dialogue called Ion, giveth high, and rightly, divine commendation unto Poetrie. So as Plato banisheth the abuse, not the thing, not banishing it, but giving due honour to it, shall be our Patron, and not our adversarie. For indeed, I had much rather ... shew their mistaking of Plato, under whose Lyons skinne, they would make an Aslike braying against Poesie, then go about to overthrow his authoritie ... (1995, I1v)

Yet the purpose of the *Ion* is not commendation of poetry or poets, but rather to deny them any claim to art or authority. Sidney's misappropriation of Plato establishes authority less for his own explicit view of poetry than for his implicit view of actors. In the dialogue, Socrates uses the metaphor of magnetic transference, from one magnetic stone through a series of iron rings, to explain his theory of divine inspiration to Ion, the performer:

> Then do you know that the member of the audience is the last of those rings which I described as getting power from each other through the magnet? You the reciter and the actor, are the middle ring, and the first is the poet himself; but God through all these draws the soul of men whithersoever he will, by running the power through them one after another. It's just like that magnet! And there is a great string of choristers and producers and under-producers all stuck to the sides of these hanging rings of the Muse. (1956, 20)

The actors and crew, like the audience, literally depend upon the divine inspiration granted first and foremost, if at all, to the poet. Poet, playwright and director Bertolt Brecht once commented, 'Not everything depends on the actor, even though nothing can be done without taking him into account' (1978, 202). However, Sidney the poet and aristocrat feels no need to take actors into account, much less defend them, because he considers them essentially irrelevant, a ring through which a more authoritative force is thrust.

A similar theory of inspiration proves useful to Sydney's opponent: in the 'first action' of his *Playes Confuted*, citing Tertullian, Gosson states 'That Stage Playes are the doctrine and inuention of the Deuill' (1974, 151), substituting the devil for God and poet in the chain of authority as the 'efficient cause' of drama in the Aristotelian terms that, according to editor Arthur Kinney, help define the structure of his treatise (1974, 59). Throughout the Middle Ages the efficient cause of a text is generally identified as the human author, except in the case of holy scripture, where God may be named 'principal efficient cause' as part of a multiple efficient cause (see Minnis 1987, 78ff.). In *The School of Abuse*, Gosson states that there are 'more causes in nature then Efficients. The Carpenter rayseth not his frame without tooles, nor the Deuill his woorke without instruments: were not Players the meane, to make these assemblyes, such multitudes wold hardly be drawne in so narowe room' (1974, 94). Here, too, the devil is identified as efficient cause, although Gosson does not specify which cause – material, formal or final – actors might represent. He does not see them as merely irrelevant, however, since the devil works through them: 'There is more in them then we perceiue, the Deuill standes at our elbow when we see not, speaks, when we heare him not, strikes when we feele not, and woundeth sore when he raseth no skinne, nor rentes the fleshe' (1974, 94). In *Playes Confuted* he goes further, deeming actors to be 'the worste, and the dangerousest people in the world' (1974, 130).

Sodomising Authority

Gosson condemns actors absolutely as a category, but admits 'that some of them are sober, discreete, properly learned honest householders and Citizens well thought on amonge their neighbours at home' (1974, 96). As Thomas Lodge notes in his *Reply* (1579), Gosson himself was once 'a professed play maker, & a paltry actor'. Gosson refers to his past as a learning experience: 'I haue bene matriculated my selfe in the schoole, where so many abuses florish' (1974, 81). There he learned that, while actors may 'seeke not to hurte, but desire too please (1974, 94), it is the nonetheless devil's work they do. In their effort to entertain, 'they abroche straunge consortes of melody, to tickle the eare; costly apparel, to flatter the sight, effeminate gesture, to rauish the sence; and wanton speache, to whet desire too inordinate lust' (1974, 89), thereby serving, however unintentionally, to 'effeminate the mind, as pricks vnto vice' (1974, 85). Thus Stubbes can call down upon actors God's wrath and 'eternall damnation' (2002, 199), then indicate willingness to welcome actors back into the fold of Christian men, if only they repent and leave behind 'so infamous an Arte' (2002, 205). It is a classic example of tolerating the sinner, but not the sin: actors, like any vile sodomites, can be fine persons, but what they do, and those they do it with, are effeminate and disgusting.

As Laura Levine points out, 'One could chart the development of anti-theatricality in terms of the increasing anxiety raised by the idea that there is no such thing as an essential gender' (1994, 19). Yet Levine, like others who deal with these works in terms of the transvestite stage, never explains why references to sodomy and effeminacy occur in contexts that do not mention cross-dressing. Goldberg criticises Levine's own essentialised distinctions between male and female, heterosexual and homosexual (1992, 109–11), and usefully recontextualises the issue through discussion of the 'sodomitical regime' of transgressed sexual and political hierarchies, as presented in Marlowe's *Edward II*. However, even Goldberg fails to explain why theatre itself – as opposed to cross-dressing, or a particular playtext – should be seen to trouble these hierarchies. The Platonic account of poetic inspiration itself offers a clue. In the *Ion*, Plato denies the actor's claim to authority over the performance – the dramatic text providing an interesting absence here

– while placing the actor below the poet/playwright in a hierarchy of dependence that implies gradations of authority. The metaphor itself, however, implies a lack of hierarchy; those magnetised rings should be interchangeable. Theatre allows such interchangeability and an undue measure of authority to the actor over the dramatic text.

A theory of authorship that allows a text multiple efficient causes might be thought capable of accommodating the actor as efficient cause alongside the playwright (and, optionally, God or a poetic Muse) without anxiety, or at least without sexual anxiety. However, medieval and early modern hierarchies were both rigid and rigidly gendered. Authority was singularly masculine. Even Queen Elizabeth, addressing her army in 1588, felt compelled to state, 'I know I have the body but of a weak and feeble woman, but I have the heart and stomach of a king' (Marcus et al. 2000, 326). As Thomas Laqueur has argued, sex itself was masculine: from antiquity through to the eighteenth century, 'men and women were arrayed according to their degree of metaphysical perfection, their vital heat, along an axis whose telos was male' (1990, 5). To have authority is to be masculine, to have a sex, to be at the top of a vertical axis.

The placement of the actor along this axis is problematic. Author and text are clearly at opposite ends: rhetoricians from Quintilian to Puttenham regularly code the writer as masculine and his text as feminine; as in the properly ordered patriarchal household, active masculine authority informs and controls passive feminine *materia*. Ancient and early modern theorists of the theatre agree that the actor cannot be placed at the top of any hierarchy, and thus cannot be perfectly masculine, if at all. Elizabethan law infamously classed itinerate actors with rogues and vagabonds as 'masterless men' dangerously outside the gendered, patriarchal system of government authority – a classification often informally extended to include all actors, or indeed all who enter a theatre. Gosson closes both *The Schoole of Abuse* and *Playes Confuted* with anxious appeals to actors to take their proper places in an ordered commonwealth (1974, 107, 195). Whatever threatens or remains outside the patriarchal system (rogues, whores, sodomites, actors) is coded as feminine, or effeminate, along with what properly stays at the bottom of the hierarchy (good women, children and servants). Anyone and anything under the control and authority of the effeminate actor must be more feminine still. To allow the actor any level of authority grants him an ostensible masculinity unwarranted by his social position, and dangerously destabilising of the whole gendered framework, or of gender itself.

Sidney and Gosson not only identify different efficient causes – divine or demonic – but do so in relation to different products. For Sidney, the poet, the authorised or inspired object is the poetic or dramatic text; for Gosson, former playwright and actor, it is the theatrical performance. Text and performance vie for position within the hierarchy: Sidney treats the actor, and the theatrical performance, as a neutral medium – the metaphorical iron ring – between divinely inspired text and audience; Gosson asserts that the demonic power of theatre is transferred to the audience even through 'good playes and sweet playes, and of al playes the best playes' (1974, 97), including those that he himself has written.

In her discussion of Gosson's attitude toward the play as text, Levine asserts that, 'To avoid the morally relativistic claim … that plays are sometimes good and sometimes evil, or the convention argument that the use of the play determines whether or not it is evil, Gosson is forced to break the term "play" itself into two ontological entities – plays-not-to-be-performed-but-read and plays-to-be-performed' (1994, 17–18). However, Gosson's attitude to his own dramatic work clearly indicates that the problem is performance – 'the use of the play'. In *Vagrant Writing*, Barry Taylor cites a 1597 letter to the Privy Council from the Lord Mayor and Aldermen of London that makes an explicit distinction:

> … *between the 'matter' of [theatrical] representation and the way it is 'framed' or 'set forth'. The distinction suggests that however dangerous the matter, there exists the possibility – which stage-plays evade – of framing it in a way that would make the whole representation – matter plus frame – acceptable to authority. That representation would be one which set forth the matter so as to move the spectator 'to the avoiding of those faults and vices which they represent'. (1991, 6)*

Gosson suggests, and the Lord Mayor would likely have agreed, that no such possibility exists. Performance is necessarily an 'abuse' because it destabilises hierarchical order, allowing the actor authority over the playtext equal to or greater than that of the legitimately masculine playwright.

Even playwrights without any known antitheatrical bias can reveal a similar anxiety over the potential subordination of the text to the actor. Shakespeare's Hamlet famously advises players not just to 'Suit the action to the word, the word to the action', but also to 'speak no more than is set down for them' (*Hamlet* 3.2). Earlier in the century, in his commentary on Aristotle's *Poetics* (1548), Francesco Robortello delineates some differences between the poet and the actor in terms of what they can represent to an audience, but quickly assures his readers that 'the actor's art is obviously dependent on poetry' (Sidnell 1991, 86). Efforts were and still are regularly made to keep it that way, as evident from the repeated refusals of Samuel Beckett and his estate to allow cross-gendered performances of *Waiting for Godot* (see Rimmer 2003), as well as from the sixteenth-century annotations in the official fifteenth-century Register of the York plays – the only complete script – recording discrepancies between the performance and the written text.

The text itself could serve as a form of control. Eugene O'Neill provided extensive stage directions that detailed his characters' offstage past as well as their onstage actions. Bertolt Brecht not only directed his own plays and created explicit production models for others to follow, but also attempted to encode the actor's movement, stance and intonation – all of what he termed 'Gestus' – through the dialogue itself. But this tactic is hardly a modern invention: Ann Slater and others have demonstrated how Shakespeare's dialogue directs performance; the anonymous playwrights responsible for the York plays similarly relied on 'gestic' writing, more than on civic authority, to control the mix of amateur and professional actors that staged their work (Epp 1991). For these earlier playwrights, at least, such control is necessarily bound up with the issue of masculinity. The (male) playwright inscribes within the text his own masculine authority over the (male) actor. But the actor in turn, in performance, enacts his own masculine authority over the text. The competing authorities of actor and playwright do not contest the same ground, the same position in the hierarchy of authority, so much as they contest the very concept of authority, and the masculinity it defines and grants. In effect, competing masculinities interpenetrate, and sodomise each other.

Even the most neutral performance of a text necessarily relies on and reveals the physical and sensual realm of the actor. In theatre, unlike criticism, flesh never quite disappears into discourse, but discourse can all too easily vanish into flesh. Even in the ostensibly positive Overburian characterisation of 'An Excellent Actor' attributed to playwright John Webster, what is deemed 'exquisitely perfect in him' is what Brecht attempts to avoid, and what Gosson and Stubbes abhor: 'for by a full and significant action of body he charms our attention. Sit in a full theatre and you will think you see so many lines drawn from the circumference of so many ears, whiles the actor is the center' (Overbury 2003, 277). Textual authority is displaced as the word becomes flesh.

While early English drama tends to emphasise its own theatricality in ways that Brecht would approve, it often does so at the expense of proper masculine authority. Actors in Tudor interludes often play both virtue and vice in the same play, collapsing opposing abstractions into one theatrical entity. Vicious characters in particular, from *Mankind*'s Mischief (1470) to Shakespeare's *Richard III* (1587), draw attention to themselves as actors, interacting with the audience and exposing the workings of the play, and leading others to damnation through association with vice – that is, themselves. Virtuous characters reiterate the dominant masculine ideal as end and origin, but the vices, some of which are explicitly sodomitical (Epp 1997; 1998), cite a demonic, theatrical origin that marks them all – vice and virtue alike – as feminised and perverse. The Excellent Actor may 'not strive to make Nature monstrous', but he does so all the same.

As a citation of the playtext, the actor's performance functions like Luce Irigaray's citations of Plato, as described by Judith Butler:

> ... the citations expose precisely what is excluded from them, and seek to show
> and to reintroduce the excluded into the system itself ... This is citation, not
> as enslavement or simple reiteration of the original, but as an insubordination
> that appears to take place within the very terms of the original, and which
> calls into question the power of origination ... [This] miming has the effect
> of repeating the origin only to displace that origin as an origin. (1993, 45;
> emphasis in original)

The actor, simply by acting, sodomises social and textual authority. In the process, he calls into question all that defines authority, and all that excludes him from it. 'The Actors Remonstrance' of 1643, written in protest to the closing of the theatres the year before, closes with a promise not to 'entertaine any Comedian that shall speake his part in a tone, as if hee did it in derision of some of the pious, but reforme all our disorders …'. Yet no conscious or audible derision is necessary to cause disorder. By claiming a voice, the actor claims authority; in the gendered terms of the Middle Ages and Renaissance, he claims a sex otherwise denied him, and uses it. Such use is sodomy.

Like Will to Like

Ulpian Fulwell's 1568 *Enterlude Intituled Like wil to like quod the Deuel to the Colier* does not centre on a generic Mankind figure but, atypically, on 'Nichol newfangle the vice'. Like *Mankind's* New Guise before him (see Epp 1997; Hayes 2004), he is a personification of effeminate fashion, as well as much else that contemporary moralists railed against, including theatre itself. Alan Somerset's introduction to the play allies it with antitheatrical writing: 'By its presentation of social groups, *Like Will to Like* impresses on us that social and moral evil are allied, the crimes being similar to those reprehended by Puritan moralists such as Philip Stubbes' (1974, 21). Nichol's companions engage not only in crimes such as theft, but also in card-playing and dancing – activities that Stubbes and others align with theatre. Yet dancing in particular is clearly used to entertain the audience, rather than held up as something to avoid; while there is no male–female pairing to worry Stubbes, he would hardly be charmed by the sight of Nichol dancing with devil and collier.

The plot consists of loosely connected episodes in which Nichol orchestrates the downfall of other rogues. He sends Rafe Roister and Tom Tosspot to lose their fortunes and clothes at dice, and carouses with Cutbert Cutpurse and Pierce Pickpurse before handing them over for hanging. As Somerset notes, 'Although Cutbert Cutpurse and Pierce Pickpurse call upon God at the last (1147ff.), there is no assurance that their prayer is answered. The social fable seems forbiddingly deterministic' (1974, 21). Yet Nichol himself receives nothing worse than a comic beating for his misdeeds, and the payment of a condemned man's coat from the hangman. Somerset writes, 'Remembering the traditionally seductive role of the vices, one wonders why the Vice is central in *Like Will*, where clearly the unregenerate have always been as we see them. Further, is the Vice a seducer at all, or just a master of ceremonies?' (1974, 22).

What he clearly is not is a suitable authority figure. Lucifer himself repeatedly calls him his 'boy'. Given the regular reference made to Nichol's youth, the role was likely meant to be acted by a prepubescent male, perhaps the apprentice in a troupe consisting of 'four men and a boy'. However, given the later onset of puberty prior to the last century, such a boy could be as old as 18 years (Rastall 1985, 29). An apprentice actor need not be prepubescent to be termed a boy; any apprentice would qualify as a boy in the sense of 'servant' (*OED* 3), and an actor of any age would qualify as a boy in the sense of 'knave, varlet, rogue' (*OED* 4), as all unlicensed actors were soon to be termed by law, or again as 'servant', under a noble patron.

But Nichol is apparently also Lucifer's boy in a sexual sense. In their first scene together, Nichol complains about the violent, apparently sexual relationship between his mother and his 'godfather' Lucifer. He then adds,

Dost thou not remember since thou didst bruise me behind?

This hole in thy fury didst thou disclose,

That now may a tent be put in, as big as thy nose.

This was when my dame called thee bottle-nosed knave;

But I am like to carry the mark to my grave (Somerset 1974, 86–90)

Nichol is clearly not referring to a hole in his clothing. It may be worth noting that the devil is conventionally large-nosed, but is commonly pictured as having another face and nose at his crotch (Hayes 2004, 49). While the sexual implication seems clear (if, like sodomy, invisible to many modern critics), the implied sexual hierarchy is unusually unstable. At the end of the play, Nichol makes his exit riding off to Spain on the back of his 'nag' (Somerset 1974, 1200) Lucifer, calling first for someone to 'hold my stirrup' (1206) and then for 'a pair of spurs …/To try whether this jade do amble or trot' (1210). His lines just prior to the devil's entrance are full of sexual innuendo directed at the audience, including both a 'good gentle boy' (1176) and 'little Meg' (1183). Nichol the boy, presumably visibly young and very much a rogue if no one's servant, is playing the man.

The only change normally allowed any character in a morality play is a fall from or return to a state of grace for a generic Mankind figure. If the personification of Virtuous Life ceased to be virtuous, it would cease to exist; Nichol Newfangle must continue to represent the fashionable and newfangled. The fictional world of *Like Will to Like* admits less abstract characters such as Tom Tosspot and his drunken 'Flemish servants' (Somerset 1974, 410), Hance and Philip Fleming; however, even those social types remain types, playing clearly defined roles: Tosspot exclaims of his pot tossing 'thus play I my part' (397), and Cutpurse, his knife and newly stolen purse in hand, cries 'it doth me good to the heart/To see how cleanly I played this part' (599–600). Despite the intrusion of the contemporary social realm, this is still an allegorical morality play, and any change in a character has moral and metaphysical implications. The implications of Nichol's change in status are partly hidden by association with the devil: the vicious and sodomitical hierarchy is, like theatre itself for Gosson, demonic in origin; a devil can shift his shape, but changes in accident only, rather than in essence. It could be argued that the alteration of Nichol is of this order, too, except that masculinity itself remains a moral category, aligned with all that is good and godly, in opposition to all that is vicious, including Nichol. This change, then, is essential, in the Platonic sense of the word.

Bruce R. Smith has pointed out that the statute through which Henry VIII first defined sodomy as a felony (25 Henry VIII 6) – the same statute to which the US

Supreme court referred both in the *Bowers* decision and in its reversal – rendered it a specifically political, rather than religious offence, despite a continuance of religious rhetoric. Its reenactments under both Edward VII and Elizabeth (Queen Mary having abolished the statute along with the surrounding anti-Catholic legislation) entailed revisions that emphasised the personal individuality of the offence. Most notably, the goods and property of a convicted sodomite's family and heirs were no longer materially affected. Blood lines constituted an essentialised category, transcending the individual; sodomy now legally constituted a mere accident, an individualised act or quality, but one deemed essentially opposed to masculinity. Unlike legal bloodlines, masculinity is undone by sodomy. Yet sodomy cannot exist without masculinity: legally it required an active, masculine party. The characterisation of Nichol in *Like Will to Like* depends on at least two contrary contemporary assumptions regarding sodomy. First, that the act of sodomy is an act, not an essential quality: hence Nichol can change places in the sexual hierarchy. Second, that sodomy affects, or effects, gender: he who penetrates, dominates, initiates is the man, whether or not he is a boy, or a woman.

It is worth remembering, too, that the latter categories were generally conflated. Shakespeare's Rosalind, playing the boy Ganymede about to 'play' Rosalind, explains: 'At which time would I, being but a moonish youth, grieve, be effeminate, changeable, longing and liking, proud, fantastical, apish, shallow, inconstant, full of tears, full of smiles; for every passion something and for no passion truly anything, as boys and women are for the most part cattle of this colour …' (*As You Like It* 3.2). Yet prepubescent males, unlike women, were expected to become men. Women could not – often still cannot – take on a dominant or active sexual role without transgressing their gendered role and thus upsetting the 'natural' order, whereas a boy was expected to take on such as role as he grew older; a man should not, could not play the boy.

Then again, many considered playing anything at all to be dangerous, a danger here flaunted. *Like Will to Like* draws attention to the vice as actor, skilled at manipulation and deception, exercising undue authority over his audience – both on and off the stage – and thus forcing them into the position of passive partner in a sodomitical game. The better the actor, the more seductive the performance, and the greater the threat to the stability of gendered hierarchies. Somerset argues that 'Nichol's survival, sardonic and victorious, is a final honest lesson' (1974, 22) in a deeply moral play. However, when Nichol rides triumphantly off to Spain, no longer the devil's instrument but authoritatively playing (with) the devil's part, sodomy evades moral closure. The play's virtues may then gather to denounce vice, singing praises to God and to the Queen, but all the virtues in the world cannot re-engender the oppositions that have collapsed around this newfangled sodomitical boy. When Nichol changes places, he reveals that these places are not real, not essential. Masculinity, like all the world, is a stage.

In the Flesh

'Then', according to Stubbes, 'these goodly Pageants being ended, euery mate sorts to his mate, euery one brings another homeward of their way very friendly, and in their secret conclaues (couertly) they play the Sodomits, or worse' (2002, 204). Stubbes likely thought that audiences went home and imitated the vicious activities and characters whose onstage representation had just afforded them ungodly pleasure. Plays do not merely 'nourish Idlenesse', which in turn 'doth minister vice' (2002, 203); rather, they directly 'maintaine Bawdry, insinuat foolery, & renue the remembrance of Heathen Idolatrie ... [and] induce to whoredom and vncleannesse' (2002, 203). However, Stubbes is not explicit as to how they manage all this. Indeed, it is doubtful that he ever saw a play himself. He makes no reference to specific plays or theatrical features of any kind, in stark contrast to the highly detailed denunciations of fashion trends and sinful activity that fill the rest of the treatise; all too much like the lively vices of morality plays, his 'lively accounts at times have the unintended effect of attracting readers to, rather than repelling them from, the focus of attack' (Kidnie 2002, 18). However, his brief description of 'the matter and ground' of comic drama, which he lifts almost verbatim from Gosson (1974, 160), includes 'Bawdrie, Cosonage, Flatterie, Whoredome, Adulterie' – the same sort of disorderly, pleasurable, fleshly, sodomitical activity that he expects of theatre patrons.

Gosson refers at length, repeatedly, to the problem of 'carnall delight' in theatrical performance, claiming:

> It whets vs to wantonnes: because it breedeth a hunger, & thirst, after pleasure. For when the thing which our appetite enioyeth cannot bee receued all at once, but by succession, or change, we gape after more, as hee that hearing one halfe of a sentence, & delighteth in that, is very desirous to haue the rest. So in Comedies delight beeing moued with varietie of shewes, of euents, of musicke, the longer we gaze, the more we craue, yea so forcible they are, that afterwards being but thought vpon, they make vs seeke for the like an other time. (1974, 186)

That is, such delights are addictive. For Gosson, the pleasure of theatrical performance 'is a blocke in the way of reason, because it locketh vp the powres of the minde from doing their duetie' (1974, 186). Brecht, for one, would have agreed. In one dialogue he states that 'it is the theatre's job to present the hero in such a way that he stimulates conscious rather than blind imitation'. In his *Short Organum for the Theatre*, he emphasises that this takes hard physical work on the part of the actor, and explains that the actor's 'feelings must not at bottom be those of the character, so that the audience's may not at bottom be those of the character either' (1978, 194).

Preventing audience empathy is rendered even more difficult if an actor is attractive. Attraction to a particular actor or character can lead an audience member to identify not just with that actor or character, but with anyone who demonstrates an enviable relation to that character. Desiring what Nichol Newfangle stands for – fashionable dress, or clever manipulation of others – could lead an audience member to identify with the character; desiring Nichol Newfangle, or the actor who plays him, could lead one to identify with any of his vicious companions, including – or especially – the devil. Depending on one's personal erotic proclivities, a preference to ride or to be ridden, one might identify more with Lucifer at the start of the play, or at the end. The actor playing Lucifer may indicate discomfort with his role as Nichol's 'jade', either by means of carefully produced Brechtian *Verfremdungseffekten* – explicit, intentional distancing of the audience – or through unconscious indications of personal distaste. However, he will still not prevent empathy if the role is one that we – male or female – would like to play.

We might be excited simply by the idea of changing places, altering seemingly immutable categories and hierarchies. One might imagine new sexual possibilities or partners, or new roles – sexual or otherwise. Tom Tosspot claims that he is:

> *... acquainted with many a woman*
>
> *That with me will sit in every house and place;*
>
> *But then their husbands had need fend their face,*
>
> *For when they come home they will not be afeard*
>
> *To shake the Goodman, and sometime shave his beard. (1974, 405–9)*

Within the sixteenth-century view of society and marriage, such wifely insubordination is likewise sodomitical. Likeness, in *Like Will to Like*, is radically, dangerously ungendered. When Newfangle introduces Tosspot to Rafe Roister, he claims 'for thee he is fit a mate/As Tom and Tib for Kit and Kate' (1974, 275–6). Somerset notes that 'Tom and Tib are the jack and ace of spades in the game of Gleek; hence the expression could mean "as women for card games". Alternatively, a "tib" was a loose woman, and "Kit" was another name for Katherine, so the line could be taken to allude to matching together men and loose women' (1974, 181). But 'Kit' is also short for 'Christopher' (as in 'Kit Marlowe'). Much like Stubbes, Somerset does not imagine pairings between men and men, or women and women, playing more than just card games.

Stephen Gosson feared that theatres served as 'snares vnto faire women' (1974, 194) at least in part because of the young men in the audience who would inevitably approach them there, '& eyther bring them home to theire houses on small acquaintance, or slip into tauerns when the plaies are done' (1974, 195) – a passage that might well have served as source for Stubbes's description of the sodomitical 'fruits of plaies and Enterludes'. Plays and players were clearly not the only potential source of sinful inspiration in the theatre. Gosson even blames audiences for their own corruption, deeming them incapable of the judgement required to understand any moral messages that plays might manage to present:

At Stage Plaies ... no indifferency of iudgement can be had, beecause the worste sort of people haue the hearing of it ... If the common people which resorte to theaters being but an assemblie of Tailers, Tinkers, Cordwayners, Saylers, olde Men, yong Men, women, Boyes, Girles, and such like, be the iudges of faultes there painted out, the rebuking of manners in that place, is neyther lawfull nor conuenient, but to be held for a kinde of libelling, and defaming. (1974, 164)

That is, the audience is already too much like, too empathetic with, what the plays condemn. Moreover, Gosson's list of 'the worst sorte of people' is highly inclusive: all humanity, young and old alike, is subject to the fleshly allure of theatre, easily seduced by the sensual display of actors doing things that no one in a properly ordered society ought to do, into thinking thoughts that no one in a properly ordered society ought to think.

In the end, all willing audiences are sodomitical. Now, as in the sixteenth century, we are eager to identify with or desire actors we do not know; we reimagine our own lives by living vicariously through the actions and desires of the characters that they play. Theatre presents us with endless opportunities, erotic and otherwise, that the playwright may never have imagined, through the intervention of the actor who makes the playwright's words become flesh. It remains up to us, the audience, to take that subversion and ostensible disorder to the streets, or simply 'homeward', to 'play the Sodomits, or worse'.

Suggested Further Reading

Dollimore, J. (1991), *Sexual Dissidence: Augustine to Wilde, Freud to Foucault* (New York: Oxford University Press).

Masten, J. (1997), *Textual Intercourse: Collaboration, Authorship, and Sexualities in Renaissance Drama* (Cambridge: Cambridge University Press).

Rambuss, R. (1998), *Closet Devotions* (Durham, NC: Duke University Press).

Sinfield, A. (2006), *Shakespeare, Authority, Sexuality: Unfinished Business in Cultural Materialism* (New York and London: Routledge).

Stewart A. (1997), *Close Readers: Humanism and Sodomy in Early Modern England* (Princeton, NJ: Princeton University Press).

References

'The Actors Remonstrance or Complaint, for the silencing of their *Profession*, and banishment from their severall PLAY-HOUSES' (London 1643), (ed.) R. Bear. Renascence Editions Online, http://darkwing.uoregon.edu/~rbear/actors1.html (accessed 20 May 2008).

[Bowers v. Hardwick], 478 U.S. 186. Bowers, Attorney General of Georgia v. Hardwick et al., certiorari to the United States Court of Appeals for the Eleventh Circuit. No. 85-140. Argued March 31, 1986, decided June 30, 1986. *FindLaw Online*, http://caselaw.lp.findlaw.com/cgibin/getcase.pl?navby=case&court=US &vol=478&invol=186 (accessed 20 May 2008).

Bray, A. (1994), 'Homosexuality and the Signs of Male Friendship in Elizabethan England', in J. Goldberg (ed.), *Queering the Renaissance* (Durham, NC: Duke University Press).

Brecht, B. (1978), *Brecht on Theatre: The Development of an Aesthetic*, ed. and trans. John Willett (London: Methuen).

Butler, J. (1993), *Bodies That Matter: On the Discursive Limits of 'Sex'* (New York and London: Routledge).

DiGangi, M. (1997), *The Homoerotics of Early Modern Drama* (Cambridge: Cambridge University Press).

Epp, G.P.J. (1991), 'Visible Words: The York Plays, Brecht, and Gestic Writing', *Comparative Drama* 24, 289–305.

—— (1997), 'The Vicious Guise: Effeminacy, Sodomy, and *Mankind*', in J.J. Cohen and B. Wheeler (eds), *Becoming Male in the Middle Ages* (New York: Garland).

—— (1998), '"Into a womannys lyckenes": Bale's Personification of Idolatry', *Medieval English Theatre* 18, 63–73.

—— (2001), 'Ecce Homo', in G. Burger and S. Kruger (eds), *Queering the Middle Ages* (Minneapolis, MN: University of Minnesota Press).

Foucault, M. (1990), *The History of Sexuality, Volume I: An Introduction*, trans. R. Hurley (New York: Vintage Books).

Goldberg, J. (1992), *Sodometries: Renaissance Texts, Modern Sexualities* (Stanford, CA: Stanford University Press).

Gosson, S. (1974), *Markets of Bawdrie: The Dramatic Criticism of Stephen Gosson*, (ed.) A.F. Kinney (Salzburg: Salzburg Studies in English Literature).

Hayes, D.W. (2004), *Rhetorical Subversion in Early English Drama* (New York: Peter Lang).

Jardine, L. (1983), *Still Harping on Daughters: Women and Drama in the Age of Shakespeare* (Sussex: Harvester Press).

Kidnie, M.J. [see Stubbes, below].

Laqueur, T. (1990), *Making Sex: Body and Gender from the Greeks to Freud* (Cambridge MA: Harvard University Press).

Lawrence et al. v. Texas, certiorari to the Court of Appeals of Texas, Fourteenth District. No. 02-102. Argued March 26, 2003, decided June 26, 2003. *FindLaw Online*, http://caselaw.lp.findlaw.com/scripts/getcase.pl?court=US&vol=000&in vol=02-102 (accessed 20 May 2008).

Levine, L. (1986), 'Men in Women's Clothing: Anti-Theatricality and Effeminization from 1579–1642', *Criticism* 28, 121–43.

—— (1994), *Men in Women's Clothing: Anti-theatricality and Effeminisation, 1579–1642* (Cambridge and New York: Cambridge University Press).

Lodge, T. *A Reply to Stephen Gosson's Schoole of Abuse in Defence of Poetry, Musick, and Stage Plays*. 1579, (ed.) Richard Bear. Renascence Editions Online [also known as *Honest Excuses*], http://darkwing.uoregon.edu/~rbear/lodge.html (accessed 20 May 2008).

Marcus, L., Mueller, J. and Rose, M.B. (eds) (2000), *Elizabeth I: Collected Works* (Chicago, IL: University of Chicago Press).

Minnis, A.J. (1987), *Medieval Theory of Authorship: Scholastic Literary Attitudes in the Later Middle Ages* (Philadelphia, PA: University of Pennsylvania Press).

Northbrooke, J. (1974), *A Treatise wherein Dicing, Dauncing, Vaine playes, or Enterluds with other idle pastimes, &c. commonly vsed on the Sabboth day, are reproued by the Authoritie of the word of God and auntient writers. Made Dialoguewise by Iohn Northbrooke, Minister and Preacher of the word of God*. 1577. Facsimile edition, with a preface by A. Freeman (New York: Garland).

Orgel, S. (1989), 'Nobody's Perfect: Or Why Did the English Stage Take Boys for Women?', *South Atlantic Quarterly* 88, 7–29.

—— (1996), *Impersonations: The Performance of Gender in Shakespeare's England* (Cambridge: Cambridge University Press).

Overbury, Sir T. et al. (2003), *Characters, together with Poems, News, Edicts, and Paradoxes, based on the eleventh edition of A Wife Now the Widow of Sir Thomas Overbury* [1622] (ed.), D. Beecher (Ottawa: Dovehouse Editions).

Phillips, H. (1980), *The Theatre and its Critics in Seventeenth-Century France* (Oxford and New York: Oxford University Press).

Plato (1956), *Great Dialogues*, trans. W.H.D. Rouse, (ed.) E.H. Warmington and P.G. Rouse (New York: New American Library).

Rastall, R. (1985), 'Female Roles in All-Male Casts', *Medieval English Theatre* 7:1, 25–51.

Rimmer, M. (2003), 'Damned to Fame: The Moral Rights of the Beckett Estate', *InCite* 24, http://www.alia.org.au/publishing/incite/2003/05/beckett.html (accessed 20 May 2008).

Shakespeare, W. (1997), *The Norton Shakespeare*, (ed.) S. Greenblatt et al. (New York and London: Norton).

Sidnell, M. (1991) (ed.), *Sources of Dramatic Theory* (Cambridge and New York: Cambridge University Press).

Sidney, P. (1995), *Defence of poesie* (Ponsonby edition, 1595), (ed.) R. Bear. Renascence Editions, http://darkwing.uoregon.edu/~rbear/defence.html (accessed 20 May 2008).

Smith, B.R. (1991), *Homosexual Desire in Shakespeare's England* (Chicago, IL: University of Chicago Press).

Somerset, J.A.B. (1974), *Four Tudor Interludes* (London: Athlone Press).

Stubbes, P. (2002), *The Anatomie of Abuses* (ed.), M.J. Kidnie. Medieval and Renaissance Texts and Studies v. 245; Renaissance English Text Society 27 (Tempe, AZ: Arizona Center for Medieval and Renaissance Studies, in conjunction with the Renaissance English Text Society).

Taylor, B. (1991), *Vagrant Writing: Social and Semiotic Disorders in the English Renaissance* (Toronto: University of Toronto Press).

Queer, but Classless?

Yvette Taylor

In an article entitled 'Deconstructing Queer Theory or the Under-Theorization of the Social and Ethical', Steven Seidman writes:

> *Queer theorists are positioned to become a substantial force in shaping lesbian and gay intellectual culture. Frequently unified by generation and by academic affiliation, sharing a culture based in common conceptual and linguistic practices, and capturing the spirit of discontent toward both the straight mainstream and the lesbian and gay mainstream, queer theory is an important social force in the making of gay intellectual culture and politics in the 1990s. (1995, 123)*

Among Tim Edwards's 'Queer Fears' (1998) in contrast, is a sense that in spite of the Seidman's sentiments of hope, momentum and change, a clear definition of what queer might mean is lacking (Richardson 2006). Queer critiques metanarratives, undermines sexual categorisation based upon a heterosexual–homosexual divide, and points towards the increasingly multiple, shifting and fragmented sexual identifications currently in existence. It brings into play a politics able to respond to such changes in lifestyles and identities, and champions an 'outness' or clarity about sexual identity in academic, personal and political terrains.

Nonetheless, the positioning of an alternative, subversive, cultural programme as anti-mainstream is itself problematic when considering the inclusions and exclusions such an agenda may foster, a point critiqued by materialist, sociological approaches which previously occupied the foreground in theories of sexuality, a position now mostly conceded to queer theory (Jackson 1999; 2006; Hennessy 2000; Jeffreys 1997; 2003). True to Seidman's positioning of queer theorists as cutting edge, this continues into the twenty-first century as queer continues to set much of the agenda in sexuality studies. Indeed, it is possible to argue that queer has moved into the academic mainstream, into the solid circles of respectability (McLaughlin 2006).

Rather than being the underground alternative, queer theory now extends across multiple disciplinary boundaries, fostering a sense of 'newness'. Indeed 'newness' seems to be the ever-present theme and driving force as new pleasures, new uncertainties, new risks, new families, new futures and new politics are announced (Epps 2001; Roseneil 2000; Taylor 2007a). This shiny, optimistic and at times overwhelming sense of newness, extending from intimacy to personal and political identifications, from home and workplace locations to sexual citizenship and scene spaces, also relies upon past debates, ongoing struggles and the ever-present potential for interruption, heightened moralism, restriction and regulation (Weeks 2003; Richardson et al. 2006). One of the most frequently voiced criticisms against queer theory comes from materialist approaches, notably from materialist feminist thinkers who, while noting that queer's social constructionist approach to sexualities is not that 'new' at all, point to the evacuation of the everyday, embodied materialities of negotiating (sexual) identities as they intersect with other social positions and identifications in *real* life (Hennessy 1995; 2000; Field 1996; Jackson 1999; 2006).

Few, if any of us, have the privilege of considering our sexuality alone and in taking sexuality as its primary focus via cultural texts, queer theory has been accused not only of sidelining materialities but also of separating out sexuality as the most significant, disruptive source of subversion (Edwards 1998; Jackson 1999; Hennessy 2000; 2006). This chapter explores the queer inattention to class inequality, drawing on empirical work on self-identified working-class lesbians. It will also explore some of the potentialities of queer theory, in connection with empirical, sociological approaches, while exercising a healthy scepticism toward academic and political 'respectability'.

Queer Exclusions

The relationship between sexuality and class has received little academic attention with queer theory, in particular, having been criticised for unhinging sexuality from the social structures that organise it, allowing only for a re-thinking of the culturally-constructed meanings of sexuality, rather than re-thinking social meanings and formations (Hennessy 2000; Jackson 2001; Jeffreys 2003; Taylor 2007a). Class may well be disappearing, lost as the 'invisible ghost' amidst a queer transgressive politics, situated mostly if not solely in the academy, in film, in the novel and in the market place (Mann 2000; McLaughlin 2006). Queer theory has been associated with the pursuit of a queer lifestyle, an 'aestheticization of daily life' constructed through a 'postmodern consumer ethic' (Fraser 1999; Hennessy 2000). The implied accusation is one of 'selling-out'; of compromising, spending and exhausting personal and political credentials. Becoming fashionable to fit-in rather than making subversive fall-outs is an accusation reaching across queer terrains (McLaughlin 2006). Queerness could be understood here as a niche market operating in the academy and beyond (Hennessy 2000; Jeffreys 2003).

In highlighting the social and economic organisation of sexuality, Chasin (2000) reveals links between the development of the lesbian and gay movement in the United States and the growth of lesbian and gay niche markets which promise inclusion into the marketplace and the nation itself – but at a price (Richardson

2004). *Selling Out* deals with the structuring of the 'proper', 'respectable' (middle-class, white and male) ways of being gay and the exclusions and limitations of this, which prevents radical social transformation, or as Chasin would say 'economic justice'. Within this account, social recognition becomes dependent on the ability to consume as identity is branded, commodified, consumed and, it would seem, depoliticised. Such an analysis links the cultural proliferation of queer items, lifestyles, spaces, visibilities and politics, with wider, interconnected socio-economic inequalities (D'Emilio 1996; Field 1996; Hennessy 2000; 2006; Taylor 2007a; 2007b).

Contrary to intended queer anti-mainstream pursuits, lesbians and gays may be integrated, even assimilated, as well-behaved, spending consumers rather than as citizens, subversive or otherwise, with money being the prerequisite for participation as well as the boundary dictating who is included (Richardson 2004). Significantly, activism and consumption are often collapsed in queer politics. Chasin (2000) and McLaughlin (2006) demonstrate this in relation to boycotting as a political strategy – the limitation of which lies in the fact that a consumer must be in a market in order to withdraw from it. Such scepticism resonates with well-established critiques offered by many other materialist accounts (Hennessy 2000; Evans 1993).

Theories of identity are increasingly preoccupied with the queer subject of desire, rather than with material needs and constraints. Queer opportunities may be available to middle-class urban dwellers but lesbians living on the breadline may well have few opportunities for engaging in subversive parodic practices. A queer identity, politics and even theory may in fact only be accessible to those materially placed to occupy such a position, in contrast to those excluded from both heterosexual privilege and the circles of the fashionably queer or 'lesbian chic' (Hennessy 2000; Taylor 2005a). As Hennessy argues the queer emphasis on identities as 'performative significations' rarely takes account of the material distribution of opportunities for such self-fashioning.

In 'Classing Queer', Mariam Fraser makes such a contention, arguing that queers' stance on visibility and recognition further marks a connection between identity and aesthetics, whereby queer becomes a brand name, an identity project assuming the form of aesthetic, consumer-based lifestyles (Fraser 1999; Featherstone 1991; Hennessy 1995). The queer body in displaying and signifying is, from a queer perspective, seen to convey a political value, drawing attention to the 'increasing politicisation of theatricality' (Butler 1993, 233). But within this are important ramifications for escalating class inequality given that appearance can be another signifier upon which to denigrate working-class bodies and tastes, in which they (again) become 'flawed consumers' who cannot pay and display in 'proper', 'tasteful' ways (Bauman 1998; Skeggs 1999; 2001). Aesthetics and identity constructed via the consumption of cultural goods may mark the self as tasteful, authentic and thus entitled (for example, to occupy queer space) or it may exclude and mark people as wrong, unentitled and inauthentic (Binnie 2004; Taylor 2007c). In such ways, sexuality *and* class are written on the body and cannot easily be discarded or refashioned at will: not so much performative subversions as entrenched material dispositions – signs to be read, understood (and misunderstood) by those in 'the know', those with the social, cultural and economic capital to decode and decipher and even degrade these appearances.

Queers' focus on representation, culture, aesthetics, visibility and recognition lies close to the heart of efforts – maybe failures – to class queer. These focal points often fail to address the ways in which working-class individuals have been positioned as being without cultural worth, as lacking and inherently flawed. Such spaces, venues and arenas are not always empowering places for working-class people to inhabit, 'come out', to re-appropriate and subvert (Skeggs 2004); such a 'cultural turn' literally cannot be capitalised upon. This debate has been covered in the discussions and disputes between Judith Butler (1997) and Nancy Fraser (1997) in the disputed shift from the 'politics of redistribution' to the 'politics of recognition': the former refers to injustices of class, the latter to injustices of status. Although Fraser contends that there is no hierarchy between these two injustices, and that issues of status are material, Butler objects to the distinction between 'redistribution' and 'recognition' on the grounds that it renders issues of sexuality as 'merely cultural' in contrast to the real, substantive and material issues of class. The challenge for queer activism, Mariam Fraser (1999) suggests, lies in addressing the politics of performativity and visibility, which queer advocates.

This view echoes Hennessy's (1995; 2000) critique of queer which, in promoting and marketing queer bodies, identities and lifestyles, disguises and simultaneously recreates a classed story, reducing the question of social change to cultural representation alone. Materialist accounts continue to highlight race, class and gender dynamics and inequalities as constituting and intersecting with sexuality but the connection between processes/structures (capitalism) and classed, gendered and racialised *individuals* is often not made explicit or visible. There is often little consideration of the meanings, strategies and refusals of sexual and classed individuals in 'buying into' or even 'selling-out'.[1]

The Sociology of Queer and Queer Sociology

The intention here is not to provide an extensive overview of all things queer but rather to provide some examples in order to demonstrate the potentialities of classing queer. Brekhaus (2003) speaks of the spatial aspects of negotiating, performing and contesting identity. Drawing upon theories of reflexivity, performativity and mobility, he makes clear his disappointment with mainstream social theory, arguing that it has tended to ghettoise queer theory into special, 'niche' enclaves. The identity strategies, or grammars, deployed by gay men across different times and places are examined, moving the focus on gay identity out of commercialised city scene space and into everyday, mundane suburban space. Yet this queer

---

1   The binary between materialist and queer thought is variously highlighted and challenged by Richardson et al. (2006) who tease out the similarities, compatibilities and intersections between feminist and queer theory.

framework of identity performances, within a highly specific 'local' context, gives little exploration of the subjective and material factors at play in such processes, sidelining the classed positions foregrounding movements and strategies across time and place (Halberstam 2005).

McLaughlin (2006) and Garber (2006) suggest that a potential crossover between feminist and queer theory lies in refocusing attention on transnational feminism and global queer studies, whereby the accusations against and binaries between queers' 'localisms', versus feminists' supposed grand 'universalisms', can be dropped (McLaughlin 2006, 75). Garber and McLaughlin pay homage to the work of Gloria Anzaldúa (1991) and her theorisations of intersectional and shifting political identity, poetically expressed and lived, potentially capturing the queer and the material, a 'theory in the flesh'. Such a material theorisation might be able to capture the embodied fleshiness of class and the ways that some become 'fixed' in space while others move across and in-between space.

Binnie (2004) untangles the links between sexuality, the nation state and globalisation critiquing previous studies for their heteronormative assumptions, by choosing to 'queer' globalisation. Binnie – like D'Emilio (1996) Field (1996) and Hennessy (1995; 2000) – links issues of sexuality and globalisation with class inequalities contesting the link between globalisation and inevitable mobility, movement and liberation. Instead such movements are seen to 'fix' classed 'others', highlighting the need to resist globalising discourses of sexuality and corresponding classed-based, cosmopolitan 'truth' claims. Hennessy's (1995; 2000) attention is on the 'political economy of sex' while Binnie's is on the 'economics of queer globalization'; both negotiate the connections between cultural, political and economic inequalities and the various Marxist, feminist and queer readings of such developments.

The idea of a universal gay rights discourse is widely problematised by both materialist and queer accounts, emphasised and overlapping in Chasin's (2000), Binnie's (2004) and Hennessy's (2000) discussion of, for example, international campaigning groups (Rahman 2004). The exclusion of working-class queers who cannot be rightfully included in the nation state is demonstrated, again responding to Mariam Fraser's (1999) concerns about queer activism, which relies so heavily upon 'outness', voice and recognition, with little sense of the multiple misrecognitions experienced by the working-class (Lawler 2002; Skeggs 1999; 2001). The idea of a universal closet may be explored, queered and challenged here; for so many this concept has little or no relevance. Many lesbians and gay men face a continual struggle to find a sense of home, place and identity (Binnie 2004; McLaughlin 2006; Garber 2006). Abiding distinctions between 'cosmopolitan', 'sophisticated' centres, of scene spaces and the 'provincial' 'unsophisticated' (working-class) towns, serves to further class queer space, consumptions and bodies who access and purchase. Where do we situate ourselves in the marketing and reproduction of our spaces and ourselves as un/sophisticated? One place may well be in the bedroom.

Weeks et al. (2001) identify a number of 'experiments in living', constituted through increased choice and reflexivity, and suggest that a transformation of intimacy is well underway signified by new 'families of choice' based on democratic, egalitarian personal relationships. There are many proponents who suggest that family formations are being increasingly queered representing a queering of traditional sociological areas of enquiry, or a shift towards a 'queer sociology' (Roseneil 2000). Roseneil suggests that there has been an erosion of the heterosexual/homosexual binary and that a greater fluidity in 'postmodern', reflexive sexual identities actively undermines heterosexuality as an organising principle of sexuality. Sociological depictions of actors jam-packed with choices, choosing to live the way they want to live, choosing to create autonomous, equal, 'pure' relationships, choosing to reallocate, move up and move out, if necessary, are widespread. Various sociological studies of lesbian relationships have pointed to evidence of 'sameness' and 'equality' (Dunne 1997) at times suggesting that this group most typically achieves the 'pure relationship' (Giddens 1992), exemplifying 'new' forms of intimacy whereby intimacy is not sought through couple relationships alone but rather through the 'family of friends' (Weston 1997; Heath and Cleaver 2003). These accounts reinforce the sense of the 'flexible', geographically and economically mobile chooser, deciding on and preferring certain ways of being. Although such portrayals give a clear sense of agency, from a more materialist perspective caution needs be voiced about the broader applicability of such depictions.

The argument for multiplicity and fluidity in intimate and familial relationships put forward by Giddens (1992) is differently positioned by Weeks (2003) in highlighting the greater tolerance and recognition, hence possibilities, of lesbian and gay lives. Nonetheless, 'liberalizing' discourses of sexuality and intimacy can co-exist with restrictive practices, and, importantly, with an actual reproduction of the homosexual/heterosexual binary (Richardson 2004). Thus, while the social and political climate of sexuality and intimacy may well have changed somewhat, the everyday experience of *doing* heterosexuality is still founded through, and reinvents, rigid boundaries and borders. Many have documented a re-orientation of lesbian and gay politics away from issues of sexual liberation and community building towards creating and protecting families (Weston 1997; Meeks and Stein 2006). At the same time as Hennessy critiques the commodification of queer and the steadfast incorporation of 'new families' into the marketplace, Meeks and Stein (2006) challenge feminist and queer accounts of same-sex marriage for their anti/assimilationist critiques, where same-sex marriage is a 'virtually normal' sell-out or a parodic re-signification (O'Brien 2007). Meeks and Stein (2006) see marriage as dynamic and changing rather than static, as potentially exemplary of the 'pure relationship' in which associations are entered into and exited from for their own sake. Yet the economic, moral and social 'binds' are still fully in place. Perhaps then the effects and consequences do not lie in the de-centring of heterosexuality, as Meeks and Stein hope for, but rather in renewed de-legitimisation (especially for those who cannot re-package as 'new families') (Breen 2005; Richardson 2004).

There has been an increasing recognition of same-sex relationships across Western Europe and elsewhere, such as Canada, Australia and New Zealand, with the introduction of the Civil Partnership in the UK in December 2005 effectively mainstreaming same-sex right. With this Act has come the proliferation of new sexual stories, taking up much coverage in the lesbian and gay press and international media (Plummer 1995). While some evangelical Christian groups have disapproved of civil partnerships, given that they supposedly parody and make a mockery of traditional heterosexual marriage, others question why lesbians and gays would want to adopt the conservative values of marriage in the first place, given that it places sexuality in its 'proper' place: within the private, monogamous (tax-paying, dual-income) household (Richardson 2004). There have been extensive feminist critiques of marriage as an institution which perpetuates gender and sexual inequalities (Jackson 2001), yet the Civil Partnership Act, in transferring this model of monogamous coupledom over to same-sex relationships, perhaps fails to 'undo' hierarchies of intimacy, thus aggravating the distinction between un/acceptable lifestyles.

Entering a civil partnership may not constitute a performative subversion, a queer erosion of the traditional version of coupledom but does the proliferation of commercial services, from 'bride and bride' attire to 'gay' wedding cake, represent what Roseneil (2000) describes as the cultural valorising of the queer in popular culture, fashion and magazines? It is important to remember who may be and who *is* excluded from such 'aspirational' markers of queerness and that not all heterosexualities are equally validated or legitimised (Head 2005; Kidger 2005). For example, for many working-class lesbians and gays, civil partnerships may mean little, given that extension of pension rights are less likely to apply; instead the implications and consequences of civil partnerships may actually be restrictive and penalising (Taylor 2007b).

In 'keeping it real' I would like to situate myself within such academic frameworks and positionings, to self-position with awareness of the privilege in claiming a reflexive self. Sullivan (2003) highlights the difference between queer as an identity and queer as a methodological framework, posing the question 'Queer: a question of being or doing?' Queer may simultaneously be about *being* and *doing* – but in order not to be un-done, deconstructed or totally disappeared (Jeffreys 2003), it is necessary to pay attention to intersecting identities and identifications as significant personally and politically. In moving on to discuss the 'Queer case of working-class lesbians' it can be noted that not one of my respondents identified as queer and whilst not wishing to dismiss the difference between queer theory and the use of queer as an identifier, that fact largely speaks for itself. Similarly, respondents' own self-identification as working-class can be seen as a challenge to notions that people do not identify in classed terms; respondents classed themselves and others daily, just as they were classed by others. Personal experience motivated my project on working-class lesbians' lives; stirrings which explain ongoing dis/affections.

As I have pointed out, both classed and sexualised identifications are greeted with a range of surprised, affirming or challenging responses and while 'queer' identification may be relatively unproblematic here my class identifications are up for debate, even dismissal: what right do I as an academic have to talk about class inequalities, to lay claim to a working-class identity? I situate myself and my easy and difficult dis/identifications in order to provide a sense of not only where I am coming from but also where I am going: I am taking both my classed and sexual identifications with me, rather than seeking to escape or trade in one, or both, for a 'new' improved, respectable academic identity. At the same time as 'setting the record straight', I also feel a slight ambiguity towards such a self-positioning; it may well bridge the hierarchy between the 'outness' sought from respondents and the potential silence on my part as researcher, but it may also serve to authorise my account as a reflexive, authoritative one. And simple snippets and glimpses of autobiography may only serve to individualise and personalise what are essentially social processes. One of my interviewees' powerful statements comes vividly to mind here when discussing the issue of self-definition: 'You can define it 'til you're blue in the face, I *am* working-class ...' (Michelle, 37, Edinburgh). Both class and sexuality can be endlessly named, interrogated, unpacked and deconstructed but I have found it more useful and important to think about how these intersect empirically in everyday lives.

My approach has favoured empirical investigation (Taylor 2004a) and in this respect I may be properly placed and recognised within a traditional sociological framework escaping the criticism often aired against queer theory's overly cultural focus sweeping across arts and humanities disciplines and into the social sciences (Jackson 1999). Previously I have been sceptical about a queer agenda and its ability to include material realities, intersections and inequalities, noting the gap between 'lives lived and books read', the mis/application of poststructuralist theory against the backdrop of continued socio-economic hardship (Taylor 2005a). My criticisms echoed those of materialist feminists and in fact mostly still do (Hennessy 2000; Jackson 1999; Richardson et al. 2006). There is, I feel, much to be gained by reminding ourselves of the origins of social constructionism, not solely recast as a new queer discovery and the inevitable interconnection between the material and the cultural, between things and words (Barrett 1992; Jackson 1999). In speaking of 'sticks and stones' McLaughlin (2006) emphasises real material hurts, while disputing the expectation that 'words will never hurt me', taking seriously queer arguments about the presence and importance of 'words' (discursive and linguistic processes) within the 'material'. Words are never just that, while action requires well chosen, disputed, words in order to say *something*.

Nonetheless, materialist agendas often also fail to capture the urgency of living out material structures, structures of class, in everyday lives: classed individuals are often absent from these accounts, even as materiality and sexuality are linked, for example, in the labour market (Dunne 1997; Chasin 2000; Hennessy 2000). Moreover, class is not 'just' about material inequality but also about a vast array of social and cultural inequalities, structures and subjectivities, which all contribute to its reproduction (Bourdieu 1984; Skeggs 1997). This shift away from, and return of, class analysis raises the question about the usefulness of the concept of class – should class itself be queered? Bradley and Hebson (1999) invoke the concept of 'class hybridity' as a strategy for renewed theorisation but care has to be taken in considering whether this is an attempt to make class more 'interesting' (to 'privileged' knowledge producers?). Class is variously produced through social, cultural and economic practises and attention to all these dimensions disrupts the straightforward polarisation between 'old' 'objectivist' approaches, which seek to precisely name, measure and define class, and 'new' culturalist class analysis models (Bottero 2004).

The cultural and embodied aspects of class have often been absent from traditional sociological agendas as well as queer ones, and following the arguments of Mariam Fraser (1999), who seeks to 'class queer', I see the benefit in engaging with queer theorisation (Richardson et al. 2006). I propose that sociology can contribute to queer theorisation and suggest that more materialist agendas could also benefit from theorising notions of 'performativity' and 'visibility' as relevant to classed individuals (Fraser 1999; Skeggs 2001). Such a process would halt the 'queer disappearance', to borrow from Jeffreys (1997), of working-class lesbians and provide a theoretical as well as empirically grounded model of the intersection between class and sexuality.

The Queer Case of Working-Class Lesbians

By including working-class lesbians'[2] views, experiences and exclusions from commercialised scene space the socio-economic inequalities operating there can be grasped: these have been given attention in terms of the structuring of scene space, via commercialism, regeneration and 'sophistication', serving to produce upmarket and 'classy' scene space. But while the general 'structural' forces defining the trend of commodification have been commented upon (Evans 1993; Morton 1996; Chasin 2000; Hennessy 2000), there has been virtually no attempt to understand the meanings that individual, classed, lesbians find in commercialised scene spaces. Working-class lesbians participated in scene space, felt excluded from it, criticised it as 'pretentious' and 'unreal' and overall expressed a sense of regret that despite its flaws something, some space, was 'better than nothing'. One interview alluded to the 'whole uniform thing' (Sukhjit, 29, Manchester) as an embodied, gendered, classed and sexualised performance and exclusion – the difference and distinction between wearing DKNY outfits as opposed to TK MAXX ensembles (Liz, 23, Manchester). Repeatedly the importance of having the 'right' appearance, the 'right' wardrobe was expressed, while Alice makes the straightforward and succinct point about classed discomfort in scene spaces: 'Unless you feel comfortable in middle-class surroundings then you're not going to go in there' (Alice, 25, Edinburgh) (see Taylor 2007c). These responses need to be included in conceptualisations of 'queer' scene space as reactions which can combine and advance Binnie's work on 'queer cosmopolitanism', Skeggs' work on the misrecognition of white working-class women in scene space, and Mariam Fraser's work on classing queer.

---

2   I asked the women to define class in relation to themselves. The women worked in low paid 'feminised' employment sectors. Fourteen women were unemployed. Fifteen women had children, ten were single-parents. In self-identifying as 'working-class', the women provide a challenge to the notion that working-class identities remain unnamed or are rejected.

Binnie (2004, 58) notes that 'without these commercialised territories, there would be far fewer possibilities for people to explore their sexuality and "come-out"', yet as he and Bell note, lesbians and gay men on low incomes are excluded from the 'urban commercial scenes that represent the most visible and intelligible manifestations of gay culture' (Bell and Binnie 2000, 71). In attempting to re-locate scene space within a class framework Binnie argues that 'queer cosmopolitanism' is based on knowingness and sophistication: 'knowingness about the hippest destinations and urban sites for queer consumption becomes a self-reflective marker of their own sophistication' (2000, 173). In contrast, working-class and 'provincial' sexualities are marked as being unsophisticated and 'less developed', outside of 'metronormativity' (Halberstam 2005). Similarly, Weston (1995) reveals the connection between 'coming-out', developing a gay identity, and becoming a 'sophisticated' city dweller, which ultimately requires access, both culturally and economically, to these spaces and positions. As such not having financial capital 'seriously compromises one's attempts to lead a 'modern gay lifestyle'. It directly impacts upon one's ability to take up space within the city' (Binnie 2000, 171).

Many women in my study did indeed know of gay spaces, including 'trendy' and 'cosmopolitan' ones but this knowledge was often unsupported by economic 'know how'. Similarly, they were often critical of commercialised scene spaces and unlikely to describe the space itself, or its inhabitants, as sophisticated. Alongside a critique of the pretentiousness of middle-class scene space there existed a realisation that an alternate working-class space is often not a viable substitute. The dichotomy that Binnie (2000) invokes comes to life in the women's choices of where to go and what to do. The spatial struggles and mis/placement of working-class lesbians as 'mis-fits', marginalised outsiders, can contribute to the recent theorisation of the processes of 'misrecognition' of working-class lesbians in queer consumer spaces (Skeggs 1999; 2001).

Research into lesbian and gay space has typically focused on scene spaces and although there have been proposals for a re-conceptualisation of where lesbians are, and therefore who and what they can be (Bell and Valentine 1995; Valentine 1995) these still overlook class as an important component of 'everyday space'. As such, the experiences of working-class lesbians, their relations to space and their identities are marginalised. There has been limited attention to the places that working-class people inhabit, places that are often socially, economically, aesthetically marginal, in comparison to 'trendy' and fashionable scene space (Howarth 2002). Interviewees were aware of the emotional and geographical distance between scene space and 'home' space, conscious of the ways working-class areas and their inhabitants may be read, devalued and further marginalised, something apparent in the demarcation of 'sink estates', delineating a spatialised 'underclass' (Taylor 2004b). The spatial intersection between class and sexuality becomes one of falling between these differently located, invested, consumed, valued and affirmed spaces. This is not just a material intersection but an embodied, emotive, cultural and social one, as class and sexuality are read from location, from the bodies of those within – and outwith – such zones of not/belonging.

Focusing mostly on issues of employment and finances, Dunne (1997) suggests that a lesbian lifestyle necessitates and facilitates access to higher female earnings: what then for working-class lesbians who may be excluded from such career strategies by virtue of their uneasy and unequal location in terms of both sexuality and class? My findings differ vastly from Dunne's as most of my interviewees worked in 'feminised' low paid sectors. In classing lesbians' material negotiations the importance of subjective workplace identities and dis/identifications should also be recognised. The work of materialist feminists (Dunne 1997; Hennessy 2000) can be combined with analyses provided by Adkins (2000) and Holliday (1999), who reveal the importance of appearance as constituting, identifying and making in/visible 'the lesbian' at work. Such a combination best explains interviewees' subjective and material journeys through classed and sexualised environments; classing the 'performative' and the 'material', through attention to the embodiment and mis/recognitions of class and sexuality and the economic and emotional consequences of these. The structural conditions of gendered labour markets, as emphasised by Hennessy (2000), are vividly highlighted in Sharon's embodied actions, cleaning buses in the 'black squad' and believing that her lesbian status protected her from 'performing' heterosexual femininity: 'I don't think if you wanted to wear make-up and put nail varnish on you would have fitted in too well!' (Sharon, 47, Glasgow).

Adkins (2000) examines whether the commodification aesthetic can be seen as making, or constituting sexual subjects at work, exploring how desires, sexualities, bodies and identities are figured through aesthetics. A warning is issued against the simple conflation of aesthetics and identity but Adkins (2000) looks at the examples of hairstyles, appearances and clothes to show how particular aesthetics ('lesbian hair', 'lesbian skirt') may constitute 'the lesbian' at work. Stylised workplace performances become potential workplace resources, linking cultural and economic capital as each works to enhance or indeed devalue the other: 'a new sovereignty of appearance, style and image is understood to be at play at work, where stylised workplace performances have emerged as key resources and increasingly secure workplace rewards' (Adkins 2000, 206). The link between aesthetics and resources points to another operation of sexuality in the workplace, while there remains an underlying question about who can appear, or perform, effectively. In noting that the aestheticisation of work allows for mobility and flexibility (McDowell 1997) a qualifier is given with regard to those workers with 'different ascribed identities' who are unable to capitalise upon such processes of aestheticisation.

The experiences of working-class lesbians suggest the worth in combining materialist and performative perspectives on sexuality, and indeed class, given that class and sexuality intersect aesthetically, emotionally and economically in the workplace. The performativity of identity is demonstrated in the appearance and embodiment of sexuality (Adkins 2000; Holliday 1999): it can be extended by classing workplace aesthetics, giving attention to the ways that bodies and identities are rendered un/entitled to occupy workspace though in/adequate 'performances'. To be recognised as something is often also to be in receipt of material resources (Fraser 1999; Skeggs 1999; 2001); systems of evaluation are deployed and these have real effects on material movements through space and for individual movers (Bourdieu 1984). There are material, embodied and subjective consequences to occupying both working-class and lesbian positions and identities, and sometimes these amount to subversions, sometimes to survivals: 'being on the dole is a survival thing, you don't live on the dole you just survive' (Jill, 28, Edinburgh).

The intersection of class and sexuality takes us beyond the politics of visibility and recognition to the significance and intersection of cultural and economic classed capital (Bourdieu 1984; Fraser 1999). The consideration of the ways that working-class lesbians are *misrecognised* illuminates the complex politics of recognition potentially classing queer (Fraser 1999). Working-class lesbians' political 'awareness' and activism is apparent even within a changing political climate that promotes notions of 'classlessness'. In looking at the legislation against the 'promotion of homosexuality' enforced in the UK's Section 28 as a particular site of contested *sexual* citizenship, it is possible to see the significance of class in many ways. The economic resources mobilised by pro- and anti-repeal protestors in the fight to repeal Section 28 were highly relevant, as was the ownership of social connections and forms of capital, which bestowed political confidence and entitlement (Taylor 2005d). These dispositions were utilised and actively mobilised by both pro- and anti-repeal protesters, whose members, as potential and actual sexual citizens, were able to occupy and argue for social positions legitimated as 'normal' and 'respectable' making their classed investments and forms of protest apparent (Richardson 2004). Interviewees were politically aware, they had opinions and beliefs to express, especially around 'past' and present class struggles but rarely did these achieve political credibility; rarely were their concerns easily assimilable or respectably mainstream and no queer agenda intervened in this sexualised and classed politics (Taylor 2005d). Rejecting mainstreamed 'rainbow coloured LGBT banner[s]' and 'Utopian cloud cuckoo land' (as a place only for middle-class lesbians) one interviewee argues that 'it's a very frustrating, unfocused time politically for lesbians just now' (Elaine, 37, Highlands).

Rahman (2004) and Burridge (2004) identify discourses of 'tolerance', innocence and contamination: the tolerant versus the tolerated, the innocent versus the perverse, the moral majority versus the campaigning crusaders, who are wrongly and worryingly preoccupied with fighting for their 'special rights'. The political experiences of working-class lesbians highlight processes of being included or excluded from sexual citizenship and the lived experiences of negotiating such discursive and, importantly, *material* conflicts (Taylor 2005b). Class is unavoidably 'added' to working-class lesbians' struggle for citizenship for they cannot afford to isolate or privilege their sexual identity over and above their class positions, experiences and identifications. In the intersection of class and sexuality I propose that class injuries, inequalities and subjectivities be considered alongside sexual ones. This would disrupt, challenge and expand – not blur, diffuse or distort – the queer focus on sexual matters.

Many working-class lesbians reflected on the classed politics of 'past' generations, which still firmly influenced their own political conceptions and attitudes, the erosion of which left them without the corresponding political weight

(Taylor 2005d). I would not want to romanticise past activism as a seamless fit as many women themselves pointed out. But, given the lack of political spaces to articulate enduring class concerns and identities, the working-classes are all too easily depicted as apolitical, or, as Lawler (2002) has shown, simply unable to articulate the right kinds of politics, the right kinds of protest (Fraser 1999).

As previously discussed, there is increasing recognition (and a potential misrecognition) of lesbian and gay partnerships at a national level in Europe, which has important implications for social and economic cohesion. There are important implications for the development of social policies that recognise the plurality of families, problematising both the sexual and *classed* aspects of constructed 'proper families'. Inclusion of class dynamics in intimacy offers a rather different picture painted by notions of lesbian 'sameness' as an equal, transformative force (Giddens 1992; Dunne 1997; Heath and Cleaver 2003) or by queer accounts of disruptive tendencies and increasing choice, reflexivity and disruptions to (hetero)normativity (Roseneil 2000). Johnson and Lawler (2005) explore how class can become an obstacle to successful heterosexual relationships and suggest that it is crucial in how people experience and enact intimacy. Within heterosexual relationships, class 'differences', unlike biological differences, are not viewed as positive, compatible forms of variation. While love may be thought of as authentically personal, once again the social organisation of who we love or feel 'at home' with, and the fact that love really cannot conquer all, is revealed. Working-class lesbians' experiences of intimacy also suggest new directions for unpacking and problematising conceptualisations of intimate transformations. In privileging accounts of 'reciprocity' and 'accountability' in lesbian relationships, inequalities and challenges within lesbian relationships are smoothed over (Weeks et al. 2001). While continued divisions are often theorised in relation to gender (Jamieson 1998), the influence of class on relationships is under-researched. 'Sameness' is highlighted with reference to shared gender but there is little attention to the 'differences' of class within this. While I argue that class can effect, enhance, disrupt and fracture the relationships of working-class lesbians (Taylor 2007b), the dominant academic position tends to emphasise individual agency, creativity, autonomy, choice and mutual responsibility; on establishing 'pick and mix' relationships, rather than being confined to traditional family ties.

However, factors such as poverty and unemployment have an impact on 'picking and choosing', affecting access to spaces and the possibility of meeting other people, having choices supported and confirmed versus one interviewees' articulated uncertainty: 'We didn't have many places to go. We didn't know of these gay pubs' (Sally, 37, Manchester). Another interviewee spoke of trying and 'failing' to match her girlfriend economically: 'I worked in a chip shop so as far as our kinda lifestyle together was that I was constantly having to match that and I couldn't you know, I couldn't match that' (Becky, 22, Edinburgh). As well as material, monetary divisions within intimate relationships there are boundaries around class identifications, experiences and empathies which can produce dis-identifications, disassociations and mis-understandings apparent in the following statement: 'My ex used to say she was working-class and she was so not, do you know what I mean. Em, 'cause she said she was working-class when I first met her and I thought, you so aren't' (Grace, 30, Edinburgh). There are continued tensions and withholding of important identifications as well as classed resentments where the material, cultural, social, embodied and emotive aspects of class and sexuality combine and intersect in intimacy as they do in a multiplicity of social spheres.

Further, not all interviewees' relationships were happy and/or healthy. Several women reported isolation, dependence and even abuse. Abuse within lesbian relationships is an under-researched area, the existence of which compromises the conceptualisation of lesbian relationships as alternative sites of equality (Dunne 1997; Giddens 1992; Weeks et al. 2001). The potential for and actuality of abuse present in lesbian relationships is perhaps heightened by the compelling grounds for silence, secrecy, non-disclosure and even erasure as Jeannette makes clear: 'She had been quite abusive and I told my mum because I was too upset all of the time really to hide it and she pretended that she thought we were just friends and I was like 'How could you?' (Jeannette, 39, Glasgow). Many have questioned the ability of a queer, transgressive politics to be able to respond to such 'sexual dangers', where there seem to be few possibilities to engage in subversion, pleasure and fun (Jackson 1999; McLaughlin 2006).

Conclusion

In this chapter I have explored criticisms of queer theory as being overly concerned with the academic, the textual, the cultural rather than with 'real' life and *material* reality. For more materialist approaches the 'cultural turn' represents a further turning away from more traditional sociological studies of sexuality, which aim to fully appreciate the material context in which we enact and live out our sexualities, as well as the everyday settings in which gender is enacted, even 'performed' (Jackson 1999). Such an approach differs from and yet resonates with Butler's (1990); it is not so much about creating subversive 'new' possibilities (simply demonstrating that gender is performative) but rather with undoing the unequal social relations, which may result in an undoing of the boundaries, binaries and inequalities through which gender exists. It appears more appropriate to adopt a materialist reading of performance and, in expanding Bourdieu's (1984) classed framework, Mariam Fraser (1999) and Skeggs (1999; 2001) may be seen to offer a more useful illumination of both classed and queer identity.

Class, as it applies to individual classed actors, as well as social structures, deserves more attention from materialist and queer directions. Attention to the ways that class operates in global and local, everyday settings may usefully combine materialist frameworks with those concerned with exploring class as a social process, embedded and embodied in everyday encounters. Bourdieu's (1984) model of cultural, social and economic capital has been widely utilised by feminist theorists and I would suggest that there is scope for utilising this model in order to theorise the intersection between class and sexuality. If queer, as Hennessy

(2000) suggests, is perpetuating the 'aestheticisation of everyday life' then attention needs to be given to those included in and those excluded by such a politically and culturally mainstreaming process.

Mariam Fraser's (1999) analysis pays attention to classed recognition and the classing of aesthetics, lifestyles and tastes: the re-appropriation of signifiers of difference may itself be a form and deployment of cultural capital, whereby positive identification and visibility manifests in a claim for the right to be recognised, a politics which working-class women may refuse (Skeggs 1997; Taylor 2005d). Working-class lesbians are also political, even 'subversive', yet are often excluded from much queer activism and consumption. If our everyday, material, social and cultural spaces are being suffused with 'queer tendencies' then they are also being negotiated and played out in various classed contexts. The interconnection between class and sexuality could usefully be developed in queer and feminist theorisation (Richardson et al. 2006) with attention to often absent classed structures, subjectivities and in/visibilities.

Suggested Further Reading

Butler, J. (1997), 'Merely Cultural', *Social Text* 52–3, 15:3–4, 265–77.

Chasin, A. (2000), *Selling Out: The Gay And Lesbian Movement Goes to Market* (Basingstoke: Palgrave).

Fraser, M. (1999), 'Classing Queer: Politics in Competition', *Theory, Culture and Society* 16:2, 107–31.

Fraser, N. (1997), 'Heterosexism, Misrecognition, and Capitalism: A Response to Judith Butler', *Social Text* 52–3, 15:3–4, 279–89.

Hennessy, R. (2000), *Profit and Pleasure: Sexual Identities in Late Capitalism* (London and New York: Routledge).

References

Adkins, L. (2000), 'Mobile Desire: Aesthetics, Sexuality and the "Lesbian" at Work', *Sexualities* 3:2, 201–18.

—— and Skeggs, B. (eds) (2005), *Feminism after Bourdieu: International Perspectives* (Oxford: Blackwell).

Anzaldúa, G. (1991), 'To(o) Queer the Writer – Loca, escritora, y chicana', in B. Warland (ed.), *Inversions: Writing by Dykes, Queers and Lesbians* (London: Open Letters).

Barrett, M. (1992), 'Words and Things: Materialism and Method in Contemporary Feminist Analysis', in M. Barrett and A. Phillips (eds), *Destabilizing Theory* (Cambridge: Polity).

Bauman, Z. (1998), *Work, Consumerism and the New Poor* (Buckingham: Open University Press).

Bell, D. and Binnie, J. (2000), *The Sexual Citizen: Queer Politics and Beyond* (Cambridge: Polity).

Bell, D. and Valentine, G. (eds) (1995), *Mapping Desires: Geographies of Sexualities* (London and New York: Routledge).

Binnie, J. (2000), 'Cosmopolitanism and the Sexed City', in D. Bell and A. Haddour (eds), *City Visions* (Harlow: Prentice Hall).

—— (2004), *The Globalization of Sexuality* (London: Sage).

Bottero, W. (2004), 'Class Identities and the Identity of Class', *Sociology* 38:5, 985–1003.

Bourdieu, P. (1984), *Distinction: A Social Critique of the Judgement of Taste*, trans. R. Nice (London and New York: Routledge).

Bradley, H. and Hebson, G. (1999), 'Breaking the Silence: The Need to Re-Articulate Class', *International Journal of Sociology and Social Policy* 19:9, 178–203.

Breen, M.S. (2005), 'The Evils of [Same] Sex: The U.S. Gay Marriage Debate', in M.S. Breen (ed.), *Minding Evil: Explorations of Human Iniquity* (Amsterdam: Rodopi).

Brekhaus, W.H. (2003), *Peacocks, Chameleons and Centaurs: Gay Suburbia and the Grammar of Social Identity* (Chicago, IL: University of Chicago Press).

Brickell, C. (2001), 'Whose "Special Treatment"? Heterosexism and the Problems with Liberalism', *Sexualities* 4:2, 211–35.

Bristow, J. and Wilson, A. (eds) (1993), *Activating Theory: Lesbian, Gay, Bisexual Politics* (London: Lawrence and Wishart).

Burridge, J. (2004), '"I Am not Homophobic but …": Disclaiming in Discourse Resisting Repeal of Section 28', *Sexualities* 7:3, 327–44.

Butler, J. (1990), *Gender Trouble: Feminism and the Subversion of Identity* (London and New York: Routledge).

—— (1993), *Bodies That Matter: On the Discursive Limits of 'Sex'* (London and New York: Routledge).

—— (1997), 'Merely Cultural', *Social Text* 52–3, 15:3–4, 265–77.

Cameron, D. and Kulick, D. (2003), *Language and Sexuality* (Cambridge: Cambridge University Press).

Chasin, A. (2000), *Selling Out: The Gay And Lesbian Movement Goes to Market* (Basingstoke: Palgrave).

Crompton, R., Devine, F., Savage, M. and Scott, J. (eds) (2000), *Renewing Class Analysis* (Oxford: Blackwell).

D'Emilio, J. (1996), 'Capitalism and Gay Identity', in D. Morton (ed.), *The Material Queer: A Lesbigay Cultural Studies Reader* (Boulder, CO: Westview Press).

Dollimore, J. (1991), *Sexual Dissidence: Augustine to Wilde, Freud to Foucault* (Oxford: Clarendon Press).

Dunne, G.A. (1997), *Lesbian Lifestyles: Women's Work and the Politics of Sexuality* (Basingstoke: Palgrave Macmillan).

Edwards, T. (1998), 'Queer Fears: Against the Cultural Turn' *Sexualities* 1:4, 471–84.

Epps, B. (2001), 'The Fetish of Fluidity', in T. Dean and C. Lane (eds), *Homosexuality and Psychoanalysis* (Chicago, IL: University of Chicago Press).

Evans, D. (1993), *Sexual Citizenship: The Material Construction of Sexualities* (London and New York: Routledge).

Eves, A. (2004), 'Queer Theory, Butch/Femme Identities and Lesbian Space', *Sexualities* 7:4.

Featherstone, M. (1991), *Consumer Culture and Postmodernism* (London: Sage).

Field, N. (1996), 'From Over the Rainbow: Money, Class and Homophobia', in D. Morton (ed.), *The Material Queer: A Lesbigay Cultural Studies Reader* (Boulder, CO: Westview Press).

Fraser, M. (1999), 'Classing Queer: Politics in Competition', *Theory, Culture and Society* 16:2, 107–31.

Fraser, N. (1997), 'Heterosexism, Misrecognition, and Capitalism: A Response to Judith Butler', *Social Text* 52–3, 15:3–4, 279–89.

Fuss, D. (ed.) (1991), *Inside/Out: Lesbian Theories, Gay Theories* (London and New York: Routledge).

Garber, L. (2006), 'On the Evolution of Queer Studies: Lesbian Feminism, Queer Theory and Globalization', in D. Richardson, J. McLaughlin and M. Casey (eds), *Intersections in Feminist and Queer Theory* (Basingstoke: Palgrave).

Giddens, A. (1992), *The Transformation of Intimacy: Sexuality, Love and Eroticism in Modern Societies* (Cambridge: Polity).

Halberstam, J. (2005), *In a Queer Time and Place: Transgender Subjectivities, Subcultural Lives* (New York: New York University Press).

Head, E. (2005), 'The Captive Mother? The Place of Home in the Lives of Lone Mother', *Sociological Research Online* 10:3, http://www.socresonline.org.uk/10/3/head.html (accessed 1 January 2008).

Heath, S. and Cleaver, E. (2003), *Young, Free and Single? Twenty-Somethings and Household Change* (Basingstoke: Palgrave Macmillan).

Hennessy, R. (1995), 'Queer Visibility in Commodity Culture', in L. Nicholson and S. Seidman (eds), *Social Postmodernism: Beyond Identity Politics* (Cambridge: Cambridge University Press).

—— (2000), *Profit and Pleasure: Sexual Identities in Late Capitalism* (London and New York: Routledge).

—— (2006), 'The Value of a Second Skin', in D. Richardson, J. McLaughlin and M.E. Casey (eds), *Intersections between Feminist and Queer Theory* (Basingstoke: Palgrave).

Hockey, J., Meah, A. and Robinson, V. (2007), *Mundane Heterosexualities: From Theory to Practices* (Basingstoke: Palgrave).

Holliday, R. (1999), 'The Comfort of Identity', *Sexualities* 2:4, 475–91.

Howarth, C. (2002), '"So You're from Brixton?" The Struggle for Recognition and Esteem in a Stigmatized Community', *Ethnicities* 2:2, 237–60.

Jackson, S. (1999), 'Feminist Sociology and Sociological Feminism: Recovering the Social in Feminist Thought', *Sociological Research Online* 4:3, http://www.socresonline.org.uk/socresonline/4/3/jackson.html (accessed 1 January 2008).

—— (2001), 'Why a Materialist Feminism is (Still) Possible – and Necessary', *Women's Studies International Forum* 24:3–4, 283–93.

—— (2006), 'Heterosexuality, Sexuality and Gender: Re-thinking the Intersections', in D. Richardson, J. McLaughlin and M.E. Casey (eds), *Intersections between Feminist and Queer Theory* (Basingstoke: Palgrave).

Jamieson, L. (1998), *Intimacy: Personal Relationships in Modern Societies* (Cambridge: Polity).

Jeffreys, S. (1997), 'The Queer Disappearance of Lesbians: Sexuality in the Academy', in B. Mintz and E. Rothblum (eds), *Lesbians in Academia: Degrees of Freedom* (New York and London: Routledge).

—— (2003), *Unpacking Queer Politics: A Lesbian Feminist Perspective* (Cambridge: Polity).

Johnson, P. and Lawler, S. (2005), 'Coming Home to Love and Class', *Sociological Research Online* 10:3, http://www.socresonline.org.uk/10/3/johnson.html (accessed 1 January 2008).

Kidger, J. (2005), 'Stories of Redemption? Teenage Mothers as the New Sex Educators', *Sexualities* 8:4, 481–96.

Lawler, S. (2002), 'Mobs and Monsters: Independent Man Meets Paulsgrove Woman', *Feminist Theory* 3:1, 103–13.

Lovell, T. (2000), 'Thinking Feminism with and against Bourdieu', *Feminist Theory* 1:1, 11–32.

Mann, S.A. (2000), 'The Scholarship of Difference: A Scholarship of Liberation?', *Sociological Inquiry* 70:4, 475–98.

McDowell, L. (1997), *Capital Culture: Gender at Work in the City* (Oxford: Blackwell).

McLaughlin, J. (2006), 'The Return of the Material: Cycles of Theoretical Fashion in Lesbian, Gay and Queer Studies', in D. Richardson, J. McLaughlin and M.E. Casey (eds), *Intersections between Feminist and Queer Theory* (Basingstoke: Palgrave).

Meeks, C. and Stein, A. (2006), 'Refiguring the Family: Towards a Post-Queer Politics of Gay and Lesbian Marriage', in D. Richardson, J. McLaughlin and M.E. Casey (eds), *Intersections between Feminist and Queer Theory* (Basingstoke: Palgrave).

Morton, D. (ed.) (1996), *The Material Queer: A Lesbigay Cultural Studies Reader* (Boulder, CO: Westview Press).

Nicholson, L. and Seidman, S. (eds) (1995), *Social Postmodernism: Beyond Identity Politics* (Cambridge: Cambridge University Press).

O'Brien, J. (2007), 'Queer Tensions: The Cultural Politics of Exclusion and Belonging in Same Gender Marriage Debates', in N. Rumens (ed.), *Sexual Politics, Desire, and Belonging* (Amsterdam: Rodopi).

Plummer, K. (1995), *Telling Sexual Stories: Power, Change and Social Worlds* (London and New York: Routledge).

Rahman, M. (2004), 'The Shape of Equality: Discursive Deployments during the Section 28 Repeal in Scotland', *Sexualities* 7:2, 150–66.

Reay, D. (2004a), '"It's All Becoming a Habitus": Beyond the Habitual Use of Habitus in Education Research', *British Journal of Sociology of Education* 25:4, 431–44.

—— (2004b), 'Gendering Bourdieu's Concept of Capitals? Emotional Capital, Women and Social Class', in L. Adkins and B. Skeggs (eds), *Feminism after Bourdieu* (Oxford: Blackwell).

Richardson, D. (2004), 'Locating Sexualities: From Here to Normality', *Sexualities* 7:4, 391–411.

—— (2006), 'Bordering Theory', in D. Richardson, J. McLaughlin and M.E. Casey (eds), *Intersections between Feminist and Queer Theory* (Basingstoke: Palgrave Macmillan).

—— McLaughlin, J. and Casey, M.E. (eds) (2006), *Intersections between Feminist and Queer Theory* (Basingstoke: Palgrave Macmillan).

Roseneil, S. (2000), 'Queer Frameworks and Queer Tendencies: Towards an Understanding of Postmodern Transformations of Sexuality', *Sociological Research Online* 5:3, http://www.socresonline.org.uk/5/3/roseneil.html (accessed 1 January 2008).

Seidman, S. (1995), 'Deconstructing Queer Theory or the Under-Theorization of the Social and Ethical', in L. Nicholson and S. Seidman (eds), *Social Postmodernism: Beyond Identity Politics* (Cambridge: Cambridge University Press).

Skeggs, B. (1995), 'Women's Studies in the 1990s: Entitlement Cultures and Institutional Constraints', *Women's Studies International Forum* 18:4, 475–85.

—— (1997), *Formations of Class and Gender* (London: Sage).

—— (1999), 'Matter Out of Place: Visibility and Sexualities in Leisure Spaces', *Leisure Studies* 18:3, 213–32.

—— (2001), 'The Toilet Paper: Femininity, Class and Mis-Recognition', *Women's Studies International Forum* 24:3–4, 295–307.

—— (2004), *Class, Self and Culture* (London and New York: Routledge).

Smith, A.-M. (1997), 'The Good Homosexual and the Dangerous Queer: Resisting the "New Homophobia"', in L. Segal (ed.), *New Sexual Agendas* (London: Macmillan).

Sullivan, N. (2003), *A Critical Introduction to Queer Theory* (Edinburgh: Edinburgh University Press).

Taylor, Y. (2004a), 'Working-Class Lesbians: Classed in a Classless Climate', unpublished PhD Diss., University of York.

—— (2004b), 'Negotiation and Navigation: An Exploration of the Spaces/Places of Working-Class Lesbians', *Sociological Research Online* 9:1, http://www.socresonline.org.uk/9/1/taylor.html (accessed 1 January 2008).

—— (2005a), 'The Gap and How to Mind It: Intersections of Class and Sexuality', *Sociological Research Online* 10:3, http://www.socresonline.org.uk/10/3/taylor.html (accessed 1 January 2008).

—— (2005b), 'Inclusion, Exclusion, Exclusive? Sexual Citizenship and the Repeal of Section 28/2a', *Sexualities* 8:3, 375–80.

—— (2005c), 'Classed in a Classless Climate', *Feminism and Psychology* 15:4, 491–500.

—— (2005d), 'Real Politik or Real Politics? Working-Class lesbians' Political "Awareness" and Activism', *Women's Studies International Forum* 28:6, 484–94.

—— (2007a), 'Sexuality', in D. Richardson and V. Robinson (eds), *Introducing Gender and Women's Studies*, 3rd edition (Basingstoke: Palgrave Macmillan).

—— (2007b), *Working-Class Lesbian Life Experiences: Classed Outsiders* (Basingstoke: Palgrave Macmillan).

—— (2007c), '"If Your Face Doesn't Fit ...": The Misrecognition of Working-Class Lesbians in Scene Space', *Leisure Studies* 27, 161–78.

Valentine, G. (1995), 'Out and About: Geographies of Lesbian Landscapes', *International Journal of Urban and Regional Research* 19:1, 96–111.

Weeks, J. (2003), *Sexuality* (London and New York: Routledge).

——, Heaphy, B. and Donovan, C. (2001), *Same Sex Intimacies: Families of Choice and Other Life Experiments* (London and New York: Routledge).

Weston, K. (1995), 'Get Thee to a Big City: Sexual Imaginary and the Great Gay Migration', *GLQ: A Journal of Lesbian and Gay Studies* 2:3, 253–77.

—— (1997), *Families We Choose: Lesbians, Gays, Kinship* (New York: Columbia University Press).

Queer-in the Sociology of Sport

Jayne Caudwell

Introduction

Sports studies has developed as a legitimate academic discipline within many institutions of higher education. Courses on offer tend to reflect either a 'scientific' engagement with the body and performance, for example, exercise physiology and sports biomechanics, or the social and cultural analysis of sport. Importantly, the 'social sciences', including history, sociology, politics and cultural studies, have helped to produce an understanding of sport, which goes beyond attempts to fulfil the Olympic ideal: *citius, attius, fortius* (higher, faster, stronger). The social and cultural dimensions of sport are far-reaching and it is easy to imagine the potential sport, as a social and cultural practice, provides for critical enquiry. This chapter offers a brief introduction to some existing critical discussion surrounding sport. It goes on to identify the emergence of queer and queer theory in sports studies. The title intends to capture how 'queer' has emerged as a way to understand sporting experiences, in other words, a look at how queer appears *in* the sociology of sport. In addition, *Queer-in*, suggests that queer, as a developing theoretical 'paradigm', challenges existing theorisations of sport, queering the sociology of sport. The aim of the discussion is to highlight contributions that help to forge new ways of explaining sport cultures, practices and rituals. Finally, the chapter considers future (im)possibilities for queer bodies in sport (studies), in particular transsexual bodies (Cavanagh and Sykes 2006) and compulsory able-bodiedness (McRuer 2006).

The Sociology of Sport

Many modern sports and sporting events were 'invented' in Western countries in the nineteenth century. During industrialisation and colonisation, games, including invasion games (based on scoring goals in the opposition's territory), racquet games and net games became codified and governed by rules. Similarly, sporting events such as the modern Olympics (re)entered the public forum as spectacles indicating stoicism and success. The social movements of Christian muscularity,[1] rational recreation and the protestant work ethic are all recognised as contributing to the formation of what can now be described as traditional sports (rugby, cricket, football, tennis, athletics).

Initially, sport sociology tended to reflect a Functionalist approach to understanding sport and society (Coakley and Dunning 2002). Critical writings emerged from Marxist analyses during the 1970s. Writers, mostly men, from North America and Europe documented the many ways sport produced and reproduced capitalist practices and ideologies. Brohm (1978) captures the essence of some Marxist sentiments in his aptly entitled book *Sport – A Prison of Measured Time*. Bound by rules, regulations of space and time, codes of conduct and an unfettered competitiveness, it is easy to see how sport reflects processes of industrialisation, Fordism and capitalism. In particular, the infamous slogan, first used by team coaches during the early and mid-1900s, 'winning isn't everything; it's the only thing' epitomises a sport culture, germinated in the mid- to late 1800s and evident today, that demands success. In addition to participation, spectatorship has also been considered a form of social control. Sport, like religion, has been described as the 'opiate of the masses'. In short, participants and spectators alike have been viewed as oppressed and alienated by those with economic power (Hoch 1972).

Despite the visible links between sport practices, ideology and capitalist modes of production, some Marxist writers, dissatisfied with classical Marxism, shifted analysis to include Antonio Gramsci's notion of hegemony. Hegemony describes the ways the dominant class or group achieve consensus through controlling the cultural, ideological and institutional production of common sense beliefs. Importantly, the move to consider the cultural opened the way for analyses of social divisions and power relations as complex and nuanced. Challenge, resistance and transformation, emerged as concepts to help explain the significance of sport in the everyday lives of people. It is at this juncture that sports feminism gained momentum and writers, mostly women, documented the many inequalities experienced by girls and women in sport.

Feminists (Hargreaves 1994) identified and defined sport as a hetero-patriarchal institution and the practices that took place within sport were regarded as upholding compulsory heterosexuality and compulsory heterosexual femininity. One of the earliest contributions to a critical understanding of women and/in sport is Helen Lenskyj's *tour de force*, *Out of Bounds* (1986). She exposes the male medical myths that operated to control women's participation *and* women's gendered bodies. In this book and her more recent compilation of essays written between 1989 and 2000, *Out on the Field: Gender, Sport and Sexualities* (2003), she unpicks patriarchal ideology

---

1   Christian muscularity or muscular Christianity refers to the coming together of religion and sport. It highlights shared values of disciplining the body through hard work, success through meritocracy and healthy lifestyle through exercise. The idea of Christian muscularity emerged from the boy's public school in England and was part of the Victorian ethic to control boys' and men's bodies. It was a way to train men for the military and regulate licentiousness.

surrounding menstruation and motherhood to expose medical surveillance that serves to establish a female frailty myth. Such gendered medical surveillance is evident within the practices of sexology and similar to sexology, working-class women, lesbians and black women received different treatment to their middle-class counterparts. Interestingly, it was middle-class women who were understood as most frail. The frailty myth intended to keep middle-class women out of sport but not working-class women or black women out of strenuous physical labour/employment. Being active was deemed damaging to reproduction, child birth and child care, and middle-class women were valued more highly in the reproduction stakes because their children were deemed more worthy.

Lenskyj's documentation of women's past experiences is supported by similar feminist accounts by Jennifer Hargreaves (UK), Susan Cahn (US) and Sheila Fletcher (UK). All identify as sports feminists and wrote during the late 1980s and early 1990s. Their accounts put women's experiences of sport on the sports studies agenda and challenge the existing analyses that favoured the economic focus of classical Marxism. In addition, the feminist intervention contested traditional sporting epistemologies and methodologies. The academic study of women and/in sport tended to be accompanied by either a liberal agenda for equal opportunity or a radical agenda for separatism. Susan Birrell (2002) plots this feminist intervention in sports studies and identifies it as a modernist project. Here, modernism is associated with identity politics, human rights, liberation, emancipation and empowerment. In contrast post-modernism criticises identity as stable, fixed and authentic, and calls into question grand narratives of progress and liberation (Sykes 2006).

The unfair/unequal treatment of women athletes continues to be important. However, after the initial focus on gender, sport and women, a pro-feminist movement emerged. Scholars, mainly men, developed a critical analysis of gender, men, masculinity and sport. To add to familiar concepts such as compulsory heterosexuality and compulsory heterosexual femininity, writers such as Michael Messner applied Robert W. Connell's (1995) concept of masculine hegemony. For Connell, there exist multiple masculinities, it is the most powerful that is hegemonic, however this is not fixed but exists in a given arrangement of gender relations. Domination relies on the subordination of women and 'other' men, such as gay men, black men and disabled men. The process involves both marginalisation and complicity, with the majority of men gaining from the hegemonic pattern. Connell's concept can be easily applied to sporting contexts. For example, studies of 'locker room' behaviour illustrate sexist, misogynist and homophobic language and practices that serve to mark men and their sports spaces as heterosexual, and hegemonic (Curry 1991). Men's relationship to their bodies highlights the use-value of their bodies as weapons and how violence on sports' fields determines privilege for some men. Building bulky bodies through extensive physical 'work out' (Klein 1993) and endeavouring to 'play on' (Messner 1990) despite injury also ensures men's bodies are read in relation to hegemonic masculinity.

It is these feminist and pro-feminist concerns that propelled gender theory in sport sociology. The emphasis on gender relations to power meant that sexuality and desire, and the sexed body and bodily performance, although implicit to gender relations theory, received less direct scrutiny. However, as a result of this work, fundamentally underpinned by identity politics, writing on gay men and/in sport appeared. Brian Pronger offers a detailed account of sexuality through his documentation of gay men's experiences. In his book *The Arena of Masculinity* (1990), informed by feminist perspectives, he illustrates the functioning of homophobia and heterosexism. In particular, his quest to make visible the homoerotic in sport illuminates desire and phallic sexual practice, which he argues dislocate assumed male heterosexuality. In an article entitled 'Outta My Endzone: Sport and the Territorial Anus' (1999), Pronger likens competitive sport, more specifically invasion games, the marked out pitch or field that usually contains these games and competition to win/score, to the spatial domination of the sexual/erotic:

> *Drawing parallels, the violating phallus with desire to win and the closed anus with desire not to lose, the article deconstructs the emotional logic of sport as a celebration of patriarchal violation and homophobic resistance to penetration. (1999, 373)*

Pronger's emphasis on desire and the erotic provides an important turn to sexuality and sport. Such an explicit engagement with desire and the (homo)erotic has not yet emerged in the literature on women. That said, lesbian experience of prejudice, harassment and abuse has received considerable coverage. Pat Griffin (1998) identifies the many ways homophobia and heterosexism, as sporting practice, are mobilised within gender relations to privilege heterosexuality. However, her account falls short of a consideration of desire and neglects the ways lesbian presence, whether imagined or actual, can undermine heterosexuality.

Queer-in Sport Studies

The modernist feminist agenda continues to be important to the study of sport, however, some sport feminists have shifted focus and recent work demonstrates an engagement with politics and theory associated with the queer movement. The early 1990s are often cited as the moment when queer theory entered the academy. In 1995, at the annual conference for the North American Society for the Sociology of Sport (NASSS), Messner, in his presidential address, mentioned queer theory in his call for a 'Studying Up On Sex'. He later argued that:

> *... the study of race, class and gender had become foundational in sports studies, whereas by contrast, we had barely scratched the surface of the study of sexualities – and particularly of heterosexuality, as a historically-formed social category, and a contextually-created identity and (or) performance. (1998, 367)*

Davidson and Shogan (1998), responding to his initial address (Messner 1996), criticised Messner for confusing aspects of poststructuralism, deconstruction, discourse analysis and queer theory. In addition, they claim that he remained unreflective about 'the position of power he inhabits within academic and straight masculinity discourse' (1998, 359). For instance in his retelling of his experiences as a heterosexual youth, his 'sexual story', Davidson and Shogan argue that he 'only gently pushes the "straight mind" (Wittig 1992) and overwhelmingly renaturalises heterosexuality, reproducing the assumption that understanding sexuality is bounded by the limits of the hetero-homo binary' (1998, 364). Davidson and Shogans's disappointment with Messner's attempt to promote a particular kind of analysis of sexuality and sport is the result of their belief that Messner merely reproduces 'the stable knowledge bases and political aims of a new hegemonic "critical" sports studies' (1998, 359). In other words, sexuality is examined via the same modernist project to unmask discrimination and seek change, which is used to explain class, gender and 'race'. Davidson and Shogan argue that queer theory offers something different and that this potential was missed by Messner.

To reiterate, sport as a popular cultural practice is socially significant not least of all because it valorises the body. The intention of sporting practices is to differentiate the sexed body (Hood-Williams 1995; Caudwell 2003; Cavanagh and Sykes 2006). Both sport and sport skills are socially constructed to regulate sporting bodies. It is apparent that bodily performance of movements and gestures, sport skills, are read as gendered, sexualised, raced and in terms of ability. The regulation of sporting bodies occurs within a context that is not pre-discursive. In other words, the codification of play, competition and 'skill' are all historically and culturally constructed. The categorisation of sport and athletes' bodies extends beyond sex *per se*, with sporting rituals and discourses also categorising gender, sexuality, 'race', ethnicity and (dis)ability.

Given that sport is premised on the idea of sexual difference and that as a popular cultural activity sex-gender-desire are perniciously regulated to produce a compulsory order, which upholds the idea of sexual difference, it is easy to see why and how queer theory has appeal. After all, only recently have gender verification or sex tests been suspended (International Association of Athletics Federation [IAAF] stopped testing in 1991/1992 and the International Olympic Committee [IOC] did not test at Sydney 2000 and Athens 2004) for elite women athletes, and transgendered people have only really been allowed to take part in recent Gay Games events (New York 1994; Amsterdam 1998; Sydney 2002; Chicago 2006). The uptake of a queer approach to sport lags behind debate that appears commonplace in the humanities. Sport, however, is being recognised as heteronormative and some writers are exploring the intricacies of this construct.

Existing Critical InQueery

If we accept that queer theory is concerned with sexuality and acknowledge that it is more complicated than a straightforward 'theory of sexuality', then it is possible to trace work in sports studies which explores sport and sexuality, as well as sport and gender, sport and desire, sport and 'race', and the future possibilities for queer bodies in sport.

Sport and Sexuality: The Closet and Pride and Shame

Heather Sykes was probably one of the first to apply queer to a sporting context in 'Turning the Closet Inside/Out: Towards a Queer-Feminist Theory in Women's Physical Education' (1998). She argues:

> One of the ways heterosexuality maintains its privileged status is through the discursive figure of 'the closet', where everyday speech normalizes heterosexuality while silencing lesbian sexuality. (1998, 154)

Her focus on the boundaries of the physical education (PE)-closet, the inside and the outside, the lesbian and the heterosexual, demonstrates the usefulness of the deconstruction of (heterosexual) identity. She explores the limits and maintenance of these boundaries and concludes that the sexual secrets and sexual silences surrounding women in PE 'foreclos(es) the very possibility of lesbian subjectivity within discourse, [and] stabilizes the rickety boundary between self-assured heteronormativity and obscured lesbian sexuality' (1998, 170). Her work is interesting because it signals a shift of emphasis from (lesbian) identity politics to a critique of heteronormative speech, discourses and scripts.

Judy Davidson in a more recent piece, 'The Necessity of Queer Shame for Gay Pride: The Gay Games and Cultural Events' (2006), continues this line of enquiry in her work on the Gay Games, Tom Waddell and juridical Olympic prohibitions. In 1982, the United States Olympic Committee (USOC) was given a court injunction to prevent Waddell and his co-workers from using 'Olympic' in their quest to establish a major international sporting event for 'gay' athletes. For Davidson, losing the name Gay Olympic Games and enduring the name Gay Games 'underpin and motivate the production of a frenzied athletic event of urgent gay pride' (2006, 91). Her archival research, exploring the documentation of the loss by those involved in the struggle for Olympism, reveals fictions of gay pride. She demonstrates how:

> ... shame cannot be expressed, only its corollary, gay pride is allowed to surface. The greater the expressions of pride, the more unacknowledged the loss is. The lost, shameful Olympics thus motivate and sustain this very successful gay pride event. (2006, 99)

Both Sykes and Davidson interrogate heteronormative binary discourses of inside/ outside and shame/pride. We see these familiar binaries re-appear in some of the work on sport and desire below. In the queer analyses of the PE-closet and Gay Games, we see how the social and psychic domains are linked and how speech and silence operate in complex ways to uphold heteronormativity. In these two accounts, sexuality is understood as central. For some writers gender has provided the site/sight for a queer analysis.

Sport and Gender – Female Masculinity and Femme-ininity

In 1974, in an article in *Quest*, a journal for physical educators, feminist Jan Felshin wrote about the 'gender apologetic' in sport. The gender apologetic describes the process women athletes go through in order to ensure and affirm their femininity and consequently their identity as 'woman'. Felshin understood the performance of femininity as a signal of apology for violating gender norms and an attempt to reaffirm womanhood. Sport was, and continues to be, understood as masculinising and therefore essential to the production of men and manliness. Obviously, women's active involvement disturbs this process and the production of femininity. Femininity is often used to encode 'woman' and/or recuperate the category 'woman'.

More recently, Kendal Broad (2001) re-coins the concept in 'The Gendered Unapologetic: Queer Resistance in Women's Sport'. Her participant observation research with women who play rugby in the United States, shows that the players present 'in your face' confrontation to the stigma attached to their 'masculine' and sexually explicit sport culture. The queer resistance is identified as a gendered one, which also tampers with the heterosexual–homosexual binary. Similar research conducted in England and with women who play football (Caudwell 2003) documents the significance of players' re-materialisation of the sexed body, gender and sexuality. Despite numerous practices that intend to produce normative sex-gender-desire, the arrangement is recognised as unstable (Butler 1993). In my own interview research some of the footballers talk about 'gendering the self':

> When I was younger, as a teenager, I looked very boyish and whatever ...
> and I think that not only did they assume sometimes that I was a boy. I
> would often get called 'sonny'. When they realised you was a woman, they
> assumed that you might be gay, because you look boyish. I think in the end
> my boyfriend was more embarrassed by that, you know we'd go somewhere
> and they'd say 'come in lads'. As you get older, perhaps a wedding ring, and
> with kids, it just don't become an issue any more. I would still describe myself
> as a tomboy erm ... and I don't have any problem with that. I mean I got
> called a man this morning and I just laughed ... it's not a problem. (extract
> from interview with football player)

My research suggests that female masculinity (Halberstam 1998) is embodied by women who identify as lesbian *and* women who identify as heterosexual. In addition, 'sexing others', the process of categorising into the binary system the sexed-body of 'others', suggests possibilities for new sex-gender-desire articulations:

> The women I first knew as a fourteen year old were very strong physically, these were big tough women, at one point when I walked into the changing room, I thought I'd walked into a man's football team, because everyone had hair, everyone didn't shave their armpits, everyone didn't shave their legs.
> (extract from interview with football player)

The focus on the materialisation of gender implicates sexuality and the sexed body. Clearly some women refuse the heteronormative arrangement and sportswomen's female masculinity offers challenge to the 'gender apologetic'. However, it might be that femme-ininity provides the most potent challenge to heteronormativity. Recent research on a lesbian-identified football team and the spatiality of sexuality on the field of play (Caudwell 2007) demonstrates how the femme-inine player/defender is materialised. Engaging with work that seeks to queer femininity (Brushwood Rose and Camilleri 2002; Gomez 1998; Harris and Crocker 1997; Nestle, Howel and Wilchins 2002), I demonstrate how (lesbian) sporting practice fails to recognise femme as a viable player/defender. An extract from my research field notes demonstrates how the femme is (mis)placed on the football pitch:

> During the brief moment of silence, a player suggested the team line up butch-femme-butch-femme and so on. The line up reflects the spatiality of the team within the boundaries of the pitch. Playing a competitive game involves specific spatialisation of playing positions. A team consists of players placed in defensive, midfield or striker/attacking positions. A team line up is usually read out as three rows (defense, midfield and attack). The suggestion of butch-femme-butch-femme, in this case illustrates a line of defending players and the assumed coupling of butch-femme. This coupling was contested when another player suggested that this might upset the cohesion of the butch back line, a suggestion that demonstrates the existence of an established defending line of players. The 'butch back line' refers to the four defenders that form the last line of defense in front of the goal keeper. Interestingly, the reference to a butch back line produces normative butch lesbian-gender on the football field. In this particular sport's space the butch is celebrated as a viable player/defender, which is unusual given practices that operate to socially construct sporting butch as abject and abhorrent (Caudwell 1999). In the changing rooms and during a pre-match team talk she is re-produced as a valuable member of the team; she is capable of protecting the goal and preventing the opposition from scoring and possibly winning. However at the same time the butch is celebrated, the femme and femme-ininity are dismissed and misplaced. The femme player is not recognised as a defender within the spatial arrangement of the team line up. In this way, team tactics privilege the butch

and marginalise the femme. The process also highlights assumptions made about physicality and femme-ininity in a lesbian-identified football team; the femme is viewed as fragile.

Analyses of femininity and women's active involvement in sports that are defined as male, such as boxing (Halbert 1997; Hargreaves 1997; Mennesson 2000), rugby (Carle and Nauright 1999; Howe 2001; Wright and Clarke 1999), ice hockey (Theberge 2000) and body building (Brace-Govan 2002; Holmlund 1997; Johnston 1996; Wesely 2001), focus on the many ways participants embody femininity. For example, Mennesson's research with women boxers found that:

> *All of the respondents were keen to confirm their feminine identities both in and out of the ring. This affirmation involved choosing appropriate attire for the ring ('something sexy'), wearing mini skirts after competition, and having long hair. (2000, 28)*

However analyses of such findings assume feminine display either functions to appease the male gaze or is the corollary of hetero-patriarchal regulation. Within sports studies femininity continues to be viewed pejoratively as patriarchally imposed. Sports researchers interested in engaging with queer theory have yet to engage fully with a re-reading of femme. If we take up Harris and Crockers's (1997) assertion that femme and femme-ininity can be understood as radical, critical, subversive, empowering, transgressive, disruptive and chosen, then concepts such as compulsory heterosexual femininity can be more fully interrogated, especially in relation to heteronormativity.

Sport and Desire – Doing Sex

Since Pronger's (1999) comparison between sporting endeavour and sexual practice very little has appeared that explicitly centres sexual activity in sporting contexts. That said, recent contributions consider sexual innuendo and flirting, sex acts and same-sex desire. Nigel Jarvis in his ethnographic study of softball, 'Ten Men Out: Gay Sporting Masculinities in Softball' (2006), shows how some players successfully challenge the heteronormative sexing of men's competitive sport. Speech in men's competitive sport usually indexes heterosexuality, however, Jarvis, through his detailed field notes, demonstrates how players use baseball-inflected language to reference gay sexual acts and desires:

> *Brian called to Steve to bend his legs more to stop some of the ground balls hit his way, 'Hey, I only bend down for a few things in life', Steve responded jokingly. Dennis said to another player who had just made a tough defensive catch in the outfield, 'Nice catch on your knees, but then again you're probably used to being on your knees'. Steve S., a part time player, commented during a pre-game warm-up, 'Alright these guys get hard on each other if they get*

> *behind and take it out on each other.' 'Oooh, we don't want that much detail',*
> *Paul joked as the rest of the team laughed. Craig, resting on the sidelines,*
> *and nearly hit by two stray balls joked, 'Balls coming from everywhere, now*
> *normally I wouldn't mind this' ... The team name provided an opportunity*
> *to link to sexual connotations. The team chant at the end of one game, 'Way*
> *to go Generals!' was subverted to 'Genitals!' by Les. 'Hey I like that cheer*
> *better', commented some other players ... Talk centred around expressions*
> *such as, 'Look at that ass' or 'crotch'. Many players from 5ive cheered on a*
> *team from Chicago, 'Oh my God, these guys are all gorgeous, they are the best*
> *looking team here', noted Chris. (2006, 67–8)*

Eng (2006), in her research with intermediate and elite Norwegian athletes, reminds us that the sporting context cannot be forgotten. The baseball players in Jarvis's study participate in competitive sport with other gay men. The athletes in Eng's research compete in spaces that are obdurately defined as heterosexual. She asked her research participants about the opportunities they experienced 'for *doing* sex/uality – that is how they were able to make visible, communicate and embody sex/uality through, for example, flirtation, falling in love, and sexual and erotic interaction' (2006, 52). As with previous work (Sykes 1998; Davidson 2006) it is 'silence itself – the things one declines to say, or is forbidden to name ... There is not one but many silences, and they are an integral part of the strategies that underlie and permeate discourses' (Foucault 1990, 27; quoted in Eng 2006, 52). Eng considers homoerotic desire and practice in the locker room and concludes:

> *... locker room culture is based on the view that homosocial spaces are*
> *nonsexual. For example, how the locker rooms as sex segregated – one for*
> *female athletes and one for male athletes – are supposed to eliminate sexual*
> *acts (such as voyeurism, sexual harassment, or sexual/erotic intercourse).*
> *This is a striking example of what is called heteronormative thinking, where*
> *homosexuality does not come to mind – or more precisely, exists as silences*
> *underlying and permeating discourses of normality. (2006, 53)*

During her research an athlete told her about sexual contact between men in the locker room/sauna after training. The athlete recounts the paradoxes surrounding being able to shower and masturbate with other men but not being permitted to touch the men, which appeared to be an unspoken agreement. For this athlete the homoerotic exists at the same time as homophobia. Touching signals the homosexual, which is forbidden in this case, however 'shared' sexual activity is permitted. Eng considers whether the acts are queer; she decides that despite the sexual activity between the men, 'those exploring their sexuality and those who might be closeted', the sex acts do not constitute queer because a 'non-romantic script is in use, hiding any homosexual desire under cover of secrecy, straightness and homophobia' (2006, 59). Therefore, there is no queering of this sporting context. The incident raises interesting issues for queer theorists and, for me, remains open for debate because the public engagement with sexual activity, which is shared, shatters illusions of homosocial and heterosexual sport spaces. Romantic scripts are not a perquisite of desire and/or queer, in fact it might be suggested that romantic scripts inform heteronormativity. In this way, I argue, the men's activity can be considered queer.

In a more overt acknowledgement of same-sex desire Gareth Owen (2006) deploys reflexive ethnography, to show how his body and emotions are inseparable from understanding gender and sexual identities in competitive rowing. As a member of a gay rowing club and 'out' men's crew (coxed eight) he uses his 'body as an instrument of data collection' (2006, 127) and explores the possibilities of sporting narrative. His recollection of the start of a two-lane regatta race highlights his main concerns:

> We now turn the boats and prepare to line up with our opponents. It's that same crew who we have raced twice before already this season. On both occasions we led until our chances were scuppered by catching a crab. I try hard not to look at my opposite number in seat 6, remembering him very well from our first meeting. In a show of cocksure bravado he had shouted over to us before the race, asking if we were their opponents. He had taken his shirt off to reveal an impressive physique of muscle and hairy chest, topped off by a crew cut. Snatching a quick look I experienced conflicting emotions. Part of me did feel intimidated by his confident display but this also made me more determined to win the race. But perhaps the most disconcerting feeling was that I desired his dominant beef-cake masculinity. This feeling had to be sublimated because we were about to go head to head, and this was the arena of competitive sport not the arena of homosexual desire. How do we negotiate masculine desire in competitive sport? (2006, 140)

Owen turns to the work of Bech (1997) to help understand his conflicting emotions as a gay man experiencing desire in competitive rowing. The incident provides a stark reminder of how, according to Bech, men gaze at each other as a way to assess masculinity and form a gauge of what constitutes the *ideal* man, which according to Owen and Bech is in fact a cultural fantasy. Via the gaze, identification and comparison Owen experiences 'a wish, a longing, a desire … to be like my opposite number in seat 6' (2006, 140). However, in a return to psychic domain of shame, too much pain is at stake; to lose the race symbolises a lack of masculinity and to acknowledge same-sex desire erodes gay pride. These dimensions of pain amount to heteronormative scripted feelings of shame:

> Some members of the crew took pleasure in subverting the masculine image of sport by imagining rowing in drag. It was a recurring conversation in the pub after training sessions. We had imagined ourselves rowing in hooped skirts, another time in tartish drag and another time in long white Audrey Hepburn gloves. However, these were private imagined moments of subversion, while in public we tended to conform to 'appropriate' masculine behavior which was ironically policed by reminders to 'butch it up'.

> *At one regatta, riding high after winning a race, we discussed how our opposing crew might have felt losing in a race against gay men. The drag fantasy appeared again, this time imagining the enhancing effect of a victory in pretty bonnets or 'big hair' wigs. We enjoyed the image until one of the group reminded us of how silly we would look if we had lost. We shared a shameful image of our wigged and vanquished crew returning to the pontoon, trying to vacate the water with dignity. (2006, 139)*

In Owen's work we are treated to the possibilities of desire and queerness. He does not interrogate the structures of sport that prevent articulations of sexualities but introduces the emotional dimensions of competition, desire, shame and pride. Again we witness the imbrications of the social and psychic domains.

Sport and 'Race' – Whiteness

To date, Mary McDonald is one of the few scholars to explicitly apply queer theory to whiteness in sport studies. For her, sporting bodies are given meaning through compounded normalising discourses of whiteness and heteronormativity. In her analysis of American basketball player Suzie McConnell Serio, 'Queering Whiteness: The Peculiar Case of the Women's National Basketball Association' (2002), she shows how the media help to produce an imagined or fictional sport's space. Her interrogation succeeds in making visible the processes that normalise heterosexuality and whiteness. Moreover, making the 'good white girl', Suzie McConnell Serio, the 'alleged obverse' of 'fatal women – that is, bodies marked as black and lesbian' (2002, 379). McDonald exposes heterosexual identity as unstable and in need of constant re-articulation.

In a more recent piece McDonald turns her attention to the academy. She presents criticism of accounts 'that reaffirm both whiteness and narrow understandings of sexuality' (2006, 35) and engages with the writings of José Esteban Muñoz (1999) to:

> *… make visible one existing queer of color analytic framework that he calls the practice of disidentification. Muñoz's insights offer queer sport scholars fresh ways of theorizing race, identity and resistance while exposing the complex cultural processes of normalization and difference. Thus the practice of disidentification or 'reformulating the world through the politics of performance' (Muñoz, 1999, xiv) is one way to help sport scholars reimagine what Somerville calls 'queer fictions of race.' In doing so, the practice of disidentification also provides another way to think differently about sport, the body, sexuality and the social. (2006, 35)*

McDonald references Muñoz's readings of Jean-Michel Basquiat's sport-inspired paintings *Famous Negro Athlete* and boxer *Sugar Ray Robinson*. The art work is deliberately incomplete with simple half-formed lines, crudely drawn. The reiteration of a call for 'queer fictions of race' demands a re-reading of these images, which ignores the 'white imaginary where black men are reduced to their physicality, as alluringly sensual, even hypersexual, and in the case of athletes, as naturally athletic' (2006, 42). Disidentification, therefore, involves a re-coding and re-ordering, and most importantly an acknowledgement that subjectivity is an incomplete process. Importantly, McDonald's concern with 'race' provides a timely contribution, which has great potential to change the focus of queer sports studies inquiry.

(Im)Possibilities for Queer Bodies in Sport

There are many ways queer theory can help to describe and explain sport. Some of these avenues have been highlighted above. I will now consider transsexual bodies and disabled bodies. Writers show how the presence of these bodies in sport demonstrates Butler's 'gender trouble' (Cavanagh and Sykes 2006) and what Robert McRuer has described as 'ability trouble' (2006, 29). To date, sport has not been critically assessed in relation to compulsory able-bodiedness despite the increasing popularity of the Paralympics and compilation of complex classification systems to categorise disabled athletes.

Transsexuality in sport devastates the entire arrangement of sporting competition. Interestingly, with the small strides in transsexual rights, governing bodies of sport have been pressed into producing rulings for transsexual participation. As Cavanagh and Sykes (2006) point out, recent changes in policy and legislation do not reflect a move to prevent discrimination, instead, they serve to further reify a two-sexed/gendered peremptory. In their analysis of the International Olympic Committee's endeavours to regulate transsexuality and sport, we are shown how the IOC formulates yet another disciplinary regime to contain bodies. Inability to imagine bodies and competition beyond notions of the 'natural', the 'fair' and 'the truth', by those involved in competitive sport, means that it is women's bodies that are tested and become the object of surveillance. For Cavanagh and Sykes such regulation of the social is connected to the psychic and involves anxiety to define bodies via neatly organised criteria. What we know is that bodies do not exist in this way and any attempts to materialise them, in the name of fair competition, produces a fiction or illusion, that of the sexed body.

Given that the Gay Games offers opportunity for previously marginalised athletes, it is interesting to see how the Games provide for transsexual and transgendered athletes. Caroline Symons and Dennis Hemphill (2006) trace the policy developments for inclusivity from the first event in 1982. The New York Gay Games (1994) appear to be the first international sports event to include transgender participants within policy and procedure. The Amsterdam Games (1998), despite having coherent transgender policy, are criticised for reliance on medical and psychological criteria leaving many dissatisfied with the outcome and the Sydney Gay Games (2002) are cited for improved practice in particular regarding the netball competition:

> Netball, along with volleyball, experienced the largest numbers of transgender participants during Gay Games VI. There were eight indigenous netball teams (representing 56% of all netball participants), of which seven identified as transgender (representing 44% of all netball participants). These players originated from Palm Island, Northern Queensland (Sistergirls), Samoa (fa'afafine), Tonga (fa'afafine) and Papua New Guinea. (2006, 122)

Sydney adopted a 'gender policy', which was based on social identity and not, as in the case of the Amsterdam Games, proof of sex/gender identity. Transgender lobbyists had protested the inadequacy of existing policy not least because it assumed a western medical model. Symons and Hemphill conclude that Sydney can claim some successes because: 'Indigenous Australian Sistergirls, Indonesian Waria, Thai Kathoey, South Asian Hijra and Samoan Faafafine were able to play the sport of their choice in the gender in which they lived' (2006, 123). However they remain cautious about policy and procedure given that there is 'an ever-expanding number of sexualities that have a stake in the Gay Games' (2006, 123), and that organisers of competitive sport are reluctant to give up systems of corporeal classification. Such reluctance is evident when we consider the treatment of disability.

In McRuer's study of the 'institutional sites where compulsory able-bodiedness and heterosexuality are produced and secured and where queerness and disability are contained' (2006, 3), he asks 'how many institutions in our culture are showcases for able-bodied performance?' (2006, 9). Sport, in particular the Paralympics, provides one example. As sports sociologists Howe and Jones (2006) point out, the categories used to arrange disability and sport reflect 'a cumbersome and complex classification system ... [which] is the result of the historical development of sport for the disabled' (2006, 31). The testing and indexing of athletes is based on functional ability. For example, in swimming the Integrated Functional Classification (IFC) involves swimmer's bodies being evaluated in relation to body position, technical skill and control (Jones and Howe 2005). We can take up McRuer's argument here that 'it is precisely the introduction of normalcy into the system that introduces compulsion' (2006, 7). The IFC is premised on able-bodiedness. In addition, the practice of engaging the 'functional' suggests disability can be transformed and improved and this reflects a developing neoliberalism. As McRuer concludes, there is an inevitable impossibility, even if made compulsory, of an able-bodied identity. His application of Butler's gender trouble to illustrate ability trouble reveals how able-bodiedness is a constant parody of itself, an elusive normalcy. The IFC and similar classification systems in athletics and basketball reveal practices that aim to achieve able-bodied identity. As with transsexuality, governing bodies of sport are anxious to 'normalise' bodies in order to sustain the fiction of fair competition.

Concluding Remarks

Sport has a tradition which is capitalist, conservative and competitive. This milieu encourages heteronormativity and, rather ironically, provides potential for queer possibilities. Queer sports theorists arrive on the back of a modernist project to expose inequality and given this starting place sport sociology has a tradition of identity politics and liberation. That said, it is becoming more accepted that 'identity' no longer holds the key to liberation and some are keen to explore the political consequences of operating outside the existing structures of identity. Identity politics, in relation to sexuality, gender, 'race' and ability for example, are more often recognised as strategic. Identity as a discreet and separate category is being acknowledged as an illusion that has momentary status. With this shift in emphasis sports sociologists, especially those interested in queerness, are grappling with how heteronormativity (re)produces itself. However, what might be more fruitful for those interested in exploring the potential for a queer theory of sport is how bodies are made to fit a sporting discourse that refuses to give up the belief that sporting competition is fair. The ways transsexual and disabled bodies are 'tested' reveals the frantic protection of sport as authentic and competition as imperative. Analyses that scrutinise the multilayered processes of disciplinary regimes, such as Sykes and Cavanagh's work on the IOC, are vital. In addition, 'new' work on disability, the body and sport that consider McRuer's call for a crip theory will help to unravel previously ignored aspects of heteronormativity in sporting contexts.

Suggested Further Reading

Caudwell, J. (ed.) (2006), *Sport, Sexualities and Queer/Theory* (London: Routledge).
Coakley, J. and Dunning, E. (eds) (2002), *Handbook of Sports Studies* (London: Sage).
King, S. (2008), 'What's Queer about (Queer) Sport Sociology Now?', *Sociology of Sport Journal* 25:4, 419–42.
Markula, P. and Pringle, R. (2006), *Foucault, Sport and Exercise: Power, Knowledge and Transforming the Self* (London: Routledge).
Rail, G. (1998), *Sport and Postmodern Times* (New York: SUNY Press).

References

Bech, H. (1997), *When Men Meet Men: Homosexuality and Modernity* (Cambridge: Polity).
Birrell, S. (2002), 'Feminist Theories for Sport', in J. Coakley and E. Dunning (eds), *Handbook of Sports Studies* (London: Sage).

Brace-Govan, J. (2002), 'Looking at Bodywork: Women and Three Physical Activities', *Journal of Sport and Social Issues* 26, 403–20.

Broad, K. (2001), 'The Gendered Unapologetic: Queer Resistance in Women's Sport', *Sociology of Sport* 18, 181–204.

Brohm, J.-M. (1978), *Sport – A Prison of Measured Time* (London: Ink Links).

Brushwood Rose, C. and Camilleri, A. (eds) (2002), *Brazen Femme: Queering Femininity* (Vancouver: Arsenal Pulp Press).

Butler, J. (1993), *Bodies That Matter: On the Discursive Limits of 'Sex'* (London: Routledge).

Carle, A. and Nauright, J. (1999), 'A Man's Game?: Women Playing Rugby Union in Australia', *Football Studies* 2, 55–73.

Caudwell, J. (1999), 'Women's Football in the United Kingdom: Theorising Gender and Unpacking the Butch Lesbian Image', *Journal of Sport and Social Issues* 23:4, 390–402.

—— (2003), 'Sporting Gender: Women's Footballing Bodies as Sites/Sights for the (Re)Articulation of Sex, Gender and Desire', *Sociology of Sport Journal* 20, 371–86.

—— (2007), 'Queering the Field? The Complexities of Sexuality within a Lesbian-Identified Football Team in England', *Gender, Place and Culture: A Journal of Feminist Geography* 14:2, 183–96.

Cavanagh, S.L. and Sykes, H. (2006), 'Transsexual Bodies at the Olympics: The International Olympic Committee's Policy on Transsexual Athletes at the 2004 Athens Summer Games', *Body and Society* 12, 75–102.

Coakley, J. and Dunning, E. (2002), *Handbook of Sports Studies* (London: Sage).

Connell, R.W. (1995), *Masculinities* (London: Polity Press).

Curry, T.J. (1991), 'Fraternal Bonding in the Locker Room: A Profeminist Analysis of Talk about Competition and Women', *Sociology of Sport Journal* 8, 119–35.

Davidson, J. (2006), 'The Necessity of Queer Shame for Gay Pride: The Gay Games and Cultural Events', in J. Caudwell (ed.), *Sport, Sexualities and Queer/Theory* (London: Routledge).

—— and Shogan, D. (1998), 'What's so Queer about Studying Up? A Response to Messner', *Sociology of Sport Journal* 15, 359–66.

Eng, H. (2006), 'Queer Athletes and Queering Sport', in J. Caudwell (ed.), *Sport, Sexualities and Queer/Theory* (London: Routledge).

Gomez, J. (1998), 'Femme Erotic Independence', in S.R. Munt (ed.), *Butch/Femme: Inside Lesbian Gender* (London: Cassell).

Griffin, P. (1998), *Strong Women, Deep Closets: Lesbians and Homophobia in Sport* (Champaign, IL: Human Kinetics).

Halberstam, J. (1998), *Female Masculinity* (Durham, NC: Duke University Press).

Halbert, C. (1997), 'Tough Enough and Woman Enough: Stereotypes, Discrimination, and Impression Management among Women Professional Boxers', *Journal of Sport and Social Issues* 21, 7–36.

Hargreaves, J. (1994), *Sporting Females* (London: Routledge).

—— (1997), 'Introducing Images and Meanings', *Body and Society* 3, 33–49.

Harris, L. and Crocker, E. (eds) (1997), *Femme: Feminists, Lesbians, and Bad Girls* (London: Routledge).

Hoch, P. (1972), *Rip Off the Big Game: The Exploitation of Sports by Power Elite* (New York: Anchor Doubleday).

Holmlund, C. (1997), 'Visible Difference and Flex Appeal: The Body, Sex, Sexuality and Race in "Pumping Iron" Films', in A. Baker and Y. Boyd (eds), *Out of Bounds: Sport, Media and the Politics of Identity* (Bloomington, IN: Indiana University Press).

Hood-Williams, J. (1995), 'Sexing the Athletes', *Sociology of Sport Journal* 12:3, 290–305.

Howe, P.D. (2001), 'Women's Rugby and the Nexus between Embodiment, Professionalism and Sexuality: An Ethnographic Account', *Football Studies* 4, 77–92.

—— and Jones, C. (2006), 'Classification of Disabled Athletes: (Dis)Empowering the Paralympic Practice Community', *Sociology of Sport Journal* 23, 29–46.

Jarvis, N. (2006), 'Ten Men Out: Gay Sporting Masculinities in Softball', in J. Caudwell (ed.), *Sport, Sexualities and Queer/Theory* (London: Routledge).

Johnston, L. (1996), 'Flexing Femininity, Female Body-Builders Refiguring "The Body"', *Gender, Place and Culture: A Journal of Feminist Geography* 3, 327–40.

Jones, C. and Howe, P.D. (2005), 'The Conceptual Boundaries of Sport for the Disabled: Classification and Athletic Performance', *Journal of Philosophy of Sport* 32, 133–46.

Klein, A. (1993), *Little Big Men: Bodybuilding Subculture and Gender Construction* (Albany, NY: SUNY Press).

Lenskyj, H. (1986), *Out of Bounds: Women, Sport and Sexuality* (Toronto: The Women's Press).

—— (2003), *Out on the Field: Gender, Sport and Sexualities* (Toronto: Women's Press).

McDonald, M. (2002), 'Queering Whiteness: The Peculiar Case of the Women's National Basketball Association', *Sociological Perspectives* 45:4, 379–96.

—— (2006), 'Beyond the Pale: The Whiteness of Sport Studies and Queer Scholarship', in J. Caudwell (ed.), *Sport, Sexualities and Queer/Theory* (London: Routledge).

McRuer, R. (2006), *Crip Theory: Cultural Signs of Queerness and Disability* (London: New York University Press).

Mennesson, C. (2000), '"Hard" Women and "Soft" Women: The Social Construction of Identities among Female Boxers', *International Review for the Sociology of Sport* 35, 21–33.

Messner, M. (1990), 'When Bodies are Weapons: Masculinity and Violence in Sport', *International Review for the Sociology of Sport* 25, 203–20.

—— (1996), 'Studying up on Sex', *Sociology of Sport Journal* 13, 221–37.

—— (1998), 'Our Queer Dilemma: Response to Davidson and Shogan', *Sociology of Sport Journal* 15, 367–71.

Muñoz, J.E. (1999), *Disidentifications: Queers of Color and the Performance of Politics* (Minneapolis, MN: University of Minnesota).

Nestle, J., Howell, C. and Wilchins, R. (2002), *Genderqueer: Voices from Beyond the Sexual Binary* (New York: Alison Books).

Owen, G. (2006), 'Catching Crabs: Bodies, Emotions and Gay Identities in Mainstream Competitive Rowing', in J. Caudwell (ed.), *Sport, Sexualities and Queer/Theory* (London: Routledge).

Pronger, B. (1990), *The Arena of Masculinity: Sports, Homosexuality and the Meaning of Sex* (New York: St Martin's Press).

—— (1999), 'Outta My End Zone: Sport and the Territorial Anus', *Journal of Sport and Social Issues* 23, 378–89.

Sykes, H. (1998), 'Turning the Closet Inside/Out: Towards a Queer-Feminist Theory in Women's Physical Education', *Sociology of Sport Journal* 15, 154–73.

—— (2006), 'Queering Theories of Sexuality in Sport Studies', in J. Caudwell (ed.), *Sport, Sexualities and Queer/Theory* (London: Routledge).

Symons, C. and Hemphill, D. (2006), 'Transgendering Sex and Sport in the Gay Games', in J. Caudwell (ed.), *Sport, Sexualities and Queer/Theory* (London: Routledge).

Theberge, N. (2000), *Higher Goals: Women's Ice Hockey and the Politics of Gender* (New York: SUNY Press).

Wesely, J. (2001), 'Negotiating Gender: Bodybuilding and the Natural/Unnatural Continuum', *Sociology of Sport Journal* 18, 162–80.

Wittig, M. (1992), *The Straight Mind and Other Essays* (Boston, MA: Beacon Press).

Wright, J. and Clarke, G. (1999), 'Sport, the Media and the Construction of Compulsory Heterosexuality: A Case Study of Women's Rugby Union', *International Review for the Sociology of Sport*, 34:1, 5–16.

'Things That Have the Potential to Go Terribly Wrong': Homosexuality, Paedophilia and the Kincora Boys' Home Scandal[1]

Margot Gayle Backus

Through the work of such scholars as James Kincaid (1998) and Lee Edelman (2004), queer studies has established a fairly detailed account of the logic by which homosexuality and paedophilia became ideologically entangled within Anglo-American modernity (Kincaid 1998; Edelman 2004, especially Chapter 1). The more recently-occurring conditions under which a similar entanglement between homosexuality and intergenerational sex occurred in Northern Ireland, however, have yet to be accounted for. In Northern Ireland, a stigmatising discourse equating child sexual abuse or, indeed, all child abuse, to homosexuality, came into being during the late 1970s and early 1980s, the period when homosexuality was first emerging as a public, contested discourse. The process by which this new discourse emerged represents an important test case for ongoing debates regarding paedophilia's status within queer theory. The 1981 Kincora scandal represents a well-documented case in which the entanglement of various forms of abuse and homosexuality in a public scandal vastly complicated the emergence of homosexuality into discourse in a particular society. The centrality of violence, coercion and the generalised abuse of power to the Kincora scandal thus allows for a re-examination of the relationship between child sexual abuse and the gay community as a whole, a matter that gay rights activists and queer theorists in various ways have routinely bracketed out.[2]

---

1   For Lillian Robinson, *in memoriam*.
2   One example of the bracketing out of age and power inequalities in queer theory exists in the vast scholarship on the Oscar Wilde Trials, which, by a sort of gentleman's agreement, routinely focuses exclusively on the homosexual character of Wilde's liaisons and on the homophobic elements of institutional and societal responses to

As I will argue, gay activists on the ground at the time of the Kincora scandal used a strategy similar to those that both queer theorists and contemporary gay activists have in different ways employed: to establish a clear and definitive boundary between criminality and queer sexuality. As Teresa de Lauretis has characterised Michel Foucault's position favouring the decriminalisation of rape, attempts to 'brea[k] the link between sexuality and crime' seek to 'free the sexual sphere from intervention by the state' (McNay 1992, 45). Such moves also, however, no matter how theoretically sophisticated they may be, inevitably mirror the logic by which heteronormativity seeks to project all shameful or criminal sexual behaviour onto the homosexual, by conversely defining all *legitimately* criminal sex acts as outside the realm of the homosexual, typically through a brief statement that only consensual sex falls within the purview of a given study, and, particularly in studies involving intergenerational sex, often followed up with a far longer critique of the very notion of consent.[3] It is my argument in this chapter that rather than distinguishing queer sexuality from any or all forms of violence and coercion, it is, instead, the obligation of queer theory to formulate a theory of queer sexual violence that allows for the possibility of sexual abuse – queer abuse – perpetrated both within and outside of the queer community, *by* those both nominally within and beyond that community.

Queer, intersubjective spaces defined by a shared knowledge of sexual 'practices … that run counter to the official version' (Sedgwick 1985, 90) are spaces one may well enter consensually, as one might voluntarily patronise Michael Warner's paradigmatically shameless:

> … *bars where hair of all kinds gets let down, … [where] everyone's a bottom, everyone's a slut, anyone who denies it is sure to meet justice at the hands of a bitter, shady queen, and if it's possible to be more exposed, more abject then it's sure to be only a matter of time before somebody gets there.* (1999, 34)

---

them. Jeff Dudgeon confirms the broad consensus that exists concerning the irrelevance of age, class and educational inequality to Wilde's sexual practices when he argues that 'like Oscar Wilde [Roger Casement's] interest was frequently angled toward youths. Yet nobody in Dublin would … dare say that Wilde should still have been jailed for his sexual acts' (2002, xix).

3   See, for instance, Steven Angelides (2004) in which he briefly concedes that 'adults must be accountable for their behavior towards children' (2004, 158). The majority of Angelides's argument, however, undermines the possibility of adult accountability from a range of angles, arguing, in effect, that children's consent to sex acts short of rape should be taken at face value, giving as evidence the view of a 1970 sex education text that Vladimir Nabokov's *Lolita* (1997/1959) represents a realistic portrayal of twelve-year-old psychology (2004, 144), the argument that among animals sex between mature and immature individuals is common (2004, 146), and the claim that Sigmund Freud found early childhood sex so common that he concluded that 'abusive encounters themselves had no etiological significance' (2004, 156).

On the other hand, and importantly, as Ann Cvetkovich has pointed out, one may enter such a space more or less involuntarily, for instance, through childhood sexual abuse (2003, 90). One might be tricked, seduced or initiated at gunpoint into the exposure and abjection that Warner celebrates, as Sedgwick acknowledges when she specifies the most typical practices defining gothic literary spaces running counter to the official version as incest and rape (1985, 90). While acknowledging the 'many strategic reasons there are to avoid the lure of trying to identify the causes of homosexuality and to ward off bad versions of the associations between incest and lesbianism' (2003, 91), Cvetkovich nonetheless begins, crucially, to map within the cultural terrain of the queer the complex interrelations that necessarily if often invisibly coexist within it, between the forcible and the consensual, the unconsciously or prematurely incorporated and the consciously chosen, the lacerated and the whole. The kinds of queer sex that happen in sites characterised by extreme, unaccountable power differentials, where there is no policing of sex *or* violence – that is, in prisons, families, boarding schools, the military and so on – can and often do foster both queer sex and sexual abuse, including the sorts of extreme abuse that may ultimately call public attention to homosexuality, so that the public discourse of homosexuality frequently emerges alongside abuse narratives. In *Gay New York*, for instance, George Chauncey notes that in the early twentieth century a steep rise in the numbers of prosecutions against men for sodomy stemmed primarily 'from the efforts of the Society for the Prevention of Cruelty to Children', which 'did not make homosexuals a special target', but rather brought homosexuality in general into the courts and into public discourse only incidentally, through their efforts to protect 'children in immigrant neighborhoods … in the poorest sections of the city' (1994, 90–91). This account reverses the standard assumption that the protection of children has always been merely a pretext for homophobic fishing expeditions. Instead, it suggests that now firmly-established discourses of child abuse that offer concern for the welfare of children as an alibi for attacks against queers originally emerged out of material conditions that placed the least socially-protected homosexuals and the least socially-protected children within abject economic/social spaces about which society at large claimed to know nothing but which could be configured, at the same time, so as to take the fall for more general failures on the part of the existing social order. The *de facto* spatial simultaneity of the consensual and the coercive within such queer lacunae within the larger society makes the special relationship between homosexuality and child sexual abuse something more than the product of an overheated heterosexual imagination, and has significant implications for the emergence of homosexuality into discourse.

Central to the question of the status of intergenerational sex within queer theory are the paired issues of empathy and culpability, questions that both turn on what, and to what extent, we are encouraged to think about the child in question's needs and experiences, and, as Judith Levine and Steven Angelides both remind us, the age we are tacitly encouraged to ascribe to the 'child' in a hypothetical intergenerational encounter (Angelides 2004, 149). Pervasively and influentially, stock images of child molestation of the most gruesome sort can be summoned in the collective imagination with the most economical of phrases. As Levine repeatedly shows in *Harmful to Children* (2002), the image of the monstrous paedophile has such cultural authority in the contemporary United States that virtually all stories involving children and sex may be inscribed, through a few well-worn phrases and the careful suppression of any details that might break the conventional frame, as representing unthinkable harm to children inflicted by nearly inhuman perpetrators. She writes of one adolescent, whose acts of dissent and rebellion were suppressed in news accounts that instead emphasised her youthful innocence, that 'the innocent child is defined by her very nullity, a template onto which others may inscribe passivity, naiveté, and desirelessness' (2002, 74–5). Queer theoretical attempts to break through this Manichean construction of all intergenerational sex acts as involving a victim and a perpetrator, on the other hand, typically counterbalance in the other direction, rendering children who have been exposed to behaviour that is, at minimum, heedless of their best interests, into ciphers of impassive resilience.[4]

Whether a minor is reduced to innocent nullity or resilient cipher, the discourse of paedophilia is shot through with what Lisa Ruddick terms, in her discussion of the inherent abusiveness of professor/student sex, 'trance logic', which operates through flawed syllogisms to rationalise the desires of individuals in positions of power, and to minimise or deny their actions' harmful effects on others (2000, 605). Both of these strategies – the one asserting youth's absolute vulnerability to sexual contamination, and the other, its absolute imperviousness – respond to the tendency that Kevin Ohi has elegantly summarised, that 'blame for the violation of childhood nearly always devolves onto the nearest deviant' (2000, 236). While one strategy denies that any violation has occurred, the other distances the speaker from such violations, asserting the speaker's conformity while firmly projecting deviance elsewhere. The flawed syllogisms at the core of most queer theoretical discussions of intergenerational sex tend toward the denial of damage, postulating first that intergenerational sex that *is* abusive is not queer, and second, that intergenerational sex that a minor enjoys or in any way participates in is *queer* and therefore *not* abusive.

The two finest critiques of the rationale that denies that more or less consensual sex across differentially empowered positions is potentially harmful are Lisa Ruddick's (2000) and Tania Modleski's (2000) responses to Jane Gallop's (2002), James Kincaid's (1998) and Ann Pellegrini's (2003) advocacy for the abolition of rules forbidding teacher–student sex. Responding to Pellegrini's complaint that we tend only to hear about professor–student sex when it has gone 'terribly wrong' (2003, 625; cited in Modleski 2000), Modleski points out that individuals in positions of authority over others, in this case, educators, 'have an obligation to take precautions against things that have the potential to go "terribly wrong"' (2000, 593). Modleski argues that in discussions of sex and power, it has become 'the norm to talk about

---

4   See, for instance, Foucault's account of Jouy (1990/1978, 31–2), which I have critiqued (1998, 164–5), or Gayle Rubin's account of the firing of a Cornell art professor for exhibiting photographs of her seven-year-old son masturbating (2004/1985, 310).

the exception and the exception to talk about the norm' in a manner that deploys legitimate concerns for sexual minorities so as to validate the age-old prerogatives of those in authority to exercise sexual power over those under them (2000, 597). While Modleski doesn't say so, the logic she is critiquing is the logic of queer theory, where the impulse to purge or at least rigorously question all libidinal prohibitions and to honour all sexual desires risks leaving the children whose queer desires it increasingly celebrates vulnerable to straightforward exploitation of their very real economic, emotional, intellectual and physical inferiority relative to adults.

Unfortunately, as a close study of discourses competing to make sense of the abuse of homeless adolescent boys 'in care' in a Belfast youth hostel demonstrates, there is a deeply ingrained tendency on the part of authorities embedded within power structures to evade any open-minded and scrupulous enquiry into the root causes of abuse. These evasions will first and most economically take the form of denial. This is a response that queer theorists replicate when we write, as the ordinarily judicious Ohi does, that 'it should go without saying that pedophilia ... is not the same thing as child abuse' (Ohi 2000, 195), thereby neatly if arbitrarily separating 'straight' sexual abuse from queer and hence presumably non-abusive paedophilia. However, as Judith Levine (2002) has shown through a staggering compendium of institutional over-reactions to mild or imagined sexual transgressions involving children, denial is often preferable to the form that authority's evasions, when pressed, will subsequently take. The tendency of power structures to turn stories of child abuse to their own account when they cannot suppress them altogether makes queer theory's current turn toward denial understandable, if still regrettable. Secondarily, and under duress, authorities, whether governmental, judicial or academic, will deploy uncontainable accounts of trauma so as to direct blame toward their group's political or cultural enemies or Others, typically, in Ohi's words, by means of 'the nearest deviant' (2000, 236). This pattern of avoiding genuine enquiry into the institutional causes of abuse is understandable: such enquiry almost inevitably would route accountability toward those with the resources to damage or destroy their accusers.

In this chapter, I will consider the redeployment of empathy and culpability that was accomplished through the work of Irish and Northern Irish journalists, activists and committees of enquiry as they struggled to maintain or improve their own constituency's moral position in the wake of a longstanding series of homosexual intergenerational sex acts that became public in 1981. Following initial revelations concerning sexual abuse at Belfast's Kincora Boys Home, long-suppressed transgressions fairly surged into discourse in a range of forums. Newspaper articles and courtroom testimony were succeeded by the findings of several panels of enquiry, extensive journalistic investigations by Chris Moore and Paul Foot, and *Resurrection Man* (1994), a novel by Eoin McNamee. Because abuse at Kincora involved sexual contact between adult men and underage boys, every representation of Kincora instantiates a theory concerning paedophilia and homosexuality. Official conceptions of homosexuality associated with the Unionists and the British state were so demonising that they virtually obscured the sense in which sex at Kincora was also intergenerational and abusive, both of which were treated as mere by-products of homosexuality. Significantly, in the wake of Kincora, those commentators who were best able to discuss homosexual, intergenerational sex, in the words of Gunter Schmidt, 'without any persecutory zeal and without defensively attempting to minimise [the complexities of paedophilic sex]'(1991, 3) were not gay rights activists, but political progressives like Paul Foot, Eoin McNamee and Chris Moore. Each of these commentators balanced empathy for abused minors with concern about Northern Irish society in general, which was, during this period, famously saturated with sectarian violence, by placing institutionalised child abuse and exploitation in the context of larger colonial power imbalances in Northern Ireland that were making violence and abuse inevitable at a range of levels.

Anatomy of a Scandal

The clandestine events known in Ireland as the Kincora Scandal, or simply 'Kincora', occurred between adult male staff members and 'working-age' or adolescent boys 'in care' at the Kincora Working Boys' Hostel during the years from 1958 to 1980. Located in a Protestant area of east Belfast, Kincora inmates would have been largely but not exclusively Protestant. Employment throughout the moribund Northern Irish economy in the mid-to-late twentieth century was awarded through a patronage system, based on religious and political affiliation. The hostel system in particular was a direct extension of the (Protestant, pro-British) Unionist government, and, after the fall of the Northern Irish Stormont government, of the British state. Positions at Kincora were awarded on the basis of sectarian loyalty; those who held them were Protestant, Unionist and politically connected. Self-evidently, the position of the boys as destitute and institutionalised heightened their vulnerability, while the position of the Kincora staff members within a Unionist patronage system enhanced both their real and perceived power over the boys. For the purposes of this analysis, I will define the events at Kincora as both queer and, even though accounts by a small number of Kincora survivors describe elements of mutuality, consent and pleasure as part of their experiences while at Kincora, abusive. Specifically owing to the overlap between homosexuality and abuse at Kincora, the staff members who had sex with inmates at Kincora, as well as the social workers, supervisors, police investigators and journalists who looked the other way, were engaging in acts that, not only for the inmates, but also the gay community and the whole of Northern Irish society, had the potential to go terribly wrong.

From the hostel's opening in 1958, sexual abuse by Joseph Mains, house warden, and Raymond Semple, his deputy, took the forms of seduction, bribery and harassment. Mains's and Semple's well-documented activities sometimes resembled courtship and sometimes entailed coercion. Mains and Semple focused their interest on older boys; indeed, in several cases relationships that started with boys who were in care at Kincora continued well into their adulthoods. Accounts by former inmates who were not abused indicate that some who put up resistance were able to fend off Mains's and Semple's advances. Starting in 1971, however, with the installation of a British intelligence agent – Orange Lodge Secretary William McGrath – as House Father, the climate at Kincora changed dramatically. What had been a climate of opportunistic harassment became one of outright sexual terrorism.

News of events at Kincora first came to light on 24 January 1980, in an article by Peter McKenna in the Dublin-based *Irish Independent*, under the headline 'Sex Racket at Children's Home'. The article alleged that starting in 1977 there had been an official cover up of the sexual abuse of hostel inmates and of a staff member's involvement in (pro-British) paramilitary activities, accompanied by state inaction in response to a police report and the destruction of reports on certain cases by the Social Services Department, all with the collusion of prominent Unionist businessmen and politicians. These allegations were later borne out in the accounts of former inmates and by evidence accumulated by the Royal Ulster Constabulary, a series of enquiries, and by journalists, particularly BBC reporter Chris Moore. The article led to the December 1981 conviction of all three senior members of the caring staff at Kincora 'for homosexual offenses'. As this charge already indicates, in the two years between the article's publication and the convictions that sent Joe Mains, Raymond Semple and William McGrath to prison for relatively brief stays, the explanatory context of the events that McKenna exposed to public scrutiny underwent a dramatic change. Throughout the investigation, trial and subsequent enquiries, a narrow-gauged focus on homosexuality served to re-contain the threat to state credibility and stability Kincora represented.

The Hughes Report: 'A minor breach ...'

Following the trial and conviction of Mains, Semple and McGrath, as well as the uncovering, investigation and prosecution of additional abuse at four other children's homes in Northern Ireland, a number of embarrassing questions remained unanswered. In 1984, the British Secretary of State James Prior announced a further enquiry to be chaired by Judge William Hughes 'to deal with the allegations of homosexual abuse which remained following the Terry Report' (Lynch 1986, 4). Prior's charging of the Hughes Committee to 'deal with allegations of homosexual abuse' is both odd and significant. It is odd because while many aspects of the Kincora scandal remained unexplained, the abuse itself was already documented extensively in the RUC's initial criminal investigations. It is significant because it so exhaustively delineates the parameters of the extensive report it initiated.

The *Report of the Committee of Inquiry into Children's Homes and Hostels* stands as a monument to the ideological usefulness of homosexuality as a talking point. In a manner that strikingly bears out the arguments of Foucault in *The History of Sexuality, Volume I* (1990/1978), homosexuality serves in this study as a usefully abstract range of identities and practices about which the Committee of Inquiry and the society it represents claim to know nothing and which must therefore be endlessly investigated, even as the investigation itself invents and re-invents the abstraction it explores out of the raw materials of children's suffering. Its 355 pages bear witness to the virtually endless permutations by which discussions of homosexuality can be used to take up virtually as much space as required in order to eclipse other less propitious topics. At the global level, virtually the entire report is taken up with discussions of whether or not a vast array of abuses were homosexual in nature, whether staff members could reasonably have detected the homosexuality motivating various acts of reported abuse, and the extent to which homosexuality in staff members found to be guilty of homosexual offenses could have been spotted and thus excluded from the children's homes under investigation. This obsessive, narrow-gauged focus on homosexuality has the effect of interrupting any narrative of causality that might be produced to explain the appalling instances of abuse upon which the report so diligently focuses.

An early and detailed written complaint against Kincora Warden Joseph Mains brought forward in 1967 by two Kincora inmates, the Unionist-dominated police force's loss of which was to become one of the key allegations in McKenna's *Irish Independent* article, was to become known to newspaper readers as the Mason file. This complaint's failure to elicit action constitutes one clear basis for accusations that abuse at Kincora was covered up. In the Mason file, inmates reported that Mains drank around the boys to the point of drunkenness, failed to stay with the boys on an overnight camping trip, asked them for kisses, put his hand down a boy's underpants, felt a boy's body under the covers as he lay in bed and entered a sleeping inmate's room to wake him while in his underpants. In an interview with Henry Mason, the Belfast City Welfare Officer, Mains claimed that he did not drink to excess, but admitted to the other charges, explaining them away as instances of caring for difficult and recalcitrant inmates who refused to bathe, cut their hair, change their underwear and get out of bed. He explained that he stuck his hands down their underpants and under their sheets in order to physically check their hygiene, and asked them to kiss him in order to shame them into cutting their hair. These explanations were satisfactory to Henry Mason, and they were equally satisfactory to the Hughes Committee, since they 'did not, for instance, refer to any interference with the boys' genitals' (1986, 65–8). Of a slightly later complaint, that Mains slapped an inmate on the buttocks, a similar argument is made. Mains' striking of an inmate is dismissed as 'a minor breach of the statutory regulations governing corporal punishment in children's homes', reasonably found by Mains' superiors to be of no concern because it 'contained no obvious homosexual colour' (1986, 75–6). The committee concludes, in effect, that it is acceptable to shame a child, but not to shame a child homosexually, to strike a child, but not to do so homosexually, and for an adult to physically invade a child's space without the child's consent so long as one's aim in so doing is not homosexual. The pattern that emerges in complaints concerning Mains is of an adult caregiver who is out of control, in various ways intimidating and mistreating the boys in his care as well as violating numerous rules. However, as the Hughes Committee, with its charge to 'deal with allegations of homosexual abuse', determined, nothing that Mains was doing was overtly homosexual, and thus his supervisors were faultless for failing to act on the complaints they received.

The Hughes Report is a patchwork of specifics such as these, in which episodes of abuse are recounted, usually in the passive voice, and then dismissed because they were not homosexual or perceptibly homosexual. Rather than emphasising the rape, compulsion, violation, threats and favouritism to which the Kincora staff members unquestionably subjected their charges, the *Report of the Committee of Inquiry into Children's Homes and Hostels* uses strangely passive and neutral constructions that (wherever possible) leave open the possibility of reciprocity, such as, 'Came into R14's bedroom about teatime and anal intercourse and masturbation occurred' (1986, 105), and 'Came into the hostel toilet … and intercourse took place' (1986, 105). Oddly, in one of the only active constructions in this catalogue of disembodied sexual events, the boy is made the agent: 'R14 masturbated him' (1986, 105). Even representations of extreme violence distance the rapist from his 'activities', as in the statement 'Mr. McGrath's activities caused anal bleeding on occasions' (1986, 108).

The Hughes Report is the least critical of any of the enquiries that have been made into events at Kincora. Even the sections of the Terry Report that were made public at least criticise the police for 'several occasions when, through inadequacy or inefficiency, insufficient cognisance [*sic*] was taken by supervisory officers of the implications of information' (Moore 1996, 222). The Hughes Report, on the other hand, 'is generally couched in mild and somewhat reassuring tones. Some of its harshest language is reserved for those who deigned to shout "cover-up"' (Lynch 1986, 5). True to its charge, the Hughes Committee's report documents in exhaustive, even encyclopaedic detail, precisely *what* kinds of things happened in Kincora during the two decades when public servants on the state payroll supplemented their meagre pay with the free use of the bodies of working-age youths in their care; however, it does virtually nothing to explain why boys who complained were unable to find institutional support short of going to a journalist in another country with their concerns. Exhibiting the trance logic visible throughout Kincora accounts, the more the Hughes Report talks about homosexuality, the less it talks about power differentials, including age, and hence the less it talks about causality.

Large, detailed and systematic as it is, the Hughes Report is at the same time radically internally contradictory. For while it expends nearly 400 pages ostensibly seeking out homosexuality at the heart of a scandal that, for all the ways it transcends and exceeds issues of sexual orientation, still turns upon male-on-male sexual transgressions, the committee ultimately fails to find discernible homosexuality in any of the three Kincora defendants, in their mistreatment of inmates or in the network of helpfully placed supervisors and city functionaries who hired them, excused their conduct and lost or neglected to bring forward complaints and evidence against them. Indeed, at the end of this strange trek through the world of institutional child abuse in Northern Ireland, the committee shows itself to be quite unexpectedly magnanimous, and, in a terse reversal, advises against withholding employment in social work to homosexual men, claiming that 'the weight of public opinion is against a policy of exclusion of homosexuals per se if it is only based on the misconduct of a minority', adding thoughtfully that 'the same criterion could be applied to heterosexuals' (1986, 294). Given the urgency and exhaustiveness with which the committee sought out homosexuality over the course of its deliberations, its ultimate dismissal of homosexuality as a decisive factor in the abuse of children actually reads as an astonishing show of bad faith. While earnest homophobes might understandably if deplorably have blamed the abuse at Kincora exclusively on the sexual orientation of the Kincora staff, the Hughes Committee and the British officials who dreamed it up evidently found homosexuality merely a convenient and always arresting topic of conversation in a situation where they had to be seen as diligently investigating *something* without actually finding anything out.

Jeff Dudgeon's 'Kincora Sentences': 'We can expect no mercy ...'

In a March 1982 article, 'Kincora Sentences', Northern Irish gay rights leader Jeff Dudgeon calls attention to the nearly unprecedented 'extent and length' of Kincora coverage on the part of liberal British and Northern Irish 'press and television' (1982, 8). The breadth of this coverage was, in Dudgeon's view, 'unequalled locally and parallels only the Profumo case, when a Tory War Minister was caught sharing the same mistress as a Soviet Diplomat' (1982, 8). Thus far I have argued that an obsession with Kincora's homosexual dimension in state administered investigations into the scandal shut down debates in the North concerning state power at the expense of homosexuality as a category and homosexuals as a group. Dudgeon, however, critiques an obsession with Kincora itself, rather than the particular juridical and common sense views of child abuse that shaped its ideological significance, for promoting the already existing conflation of child abuse and homosexuality in the public mind. Rather than critiquing specific analyses of the scandal, Dudgeon decries the overall extent of the coverage that Kincora was receiving, and gets especially huffy with liberal reporters and media sources whose 'insatiable appetite for new Kincora items' was putting homosexuals at risk while seeking to capitalise politically on 'the contradiction' within Northern Irish Unionism represented by 'the public persona of [House Father William] McGrath' (1982, 8).

Dudgeon's position was shaped by a complication that emerged as the Northern Irish press set about investigating those of McKenna's original allegations that remained unaddressed in the sentencing of Mains, Semple and McGrath. As coverage of the scandal unfolded, Kincora's shadowy links to specific Unionist leaders, and to the social work administrators, politicians and MI5 leaders who at times protected Kincora staff members, often led to insurmountable roadblocks. The scandal had gone on for so long that some of the Belfast bureaucrats who protected Mains and Semple in the early days were dead, and the one Unionist politician with clear links to the home eventually committed suicide rather than talk to the

RUC. As various lines of enquiry failed them, the tangential connection between Kincora and Ian Paisley, influential Free Presbyterian minister and leader of the ultra-conservative wing of Protestant Unionism, presented an increasingly inviting target for liberal journalists. While current or former state employees sometimes spoke off the record and in murky generalisations about state involvement, two former Free Presbyterian employees, one formerly of Paisley's camp, and one of McGrath's, eagerly came forward to testify that they had tried to talk to Paisley about McGrath's 'homosexuality' on several occasions (Moore 1996, 188–205). Since dislike for Paisley is far more widespread among Northern Irish and British liberals than is an outright rejection of the British presence in Northern Ireland, and since former church employees were willing to speak openly, Paisley's isolation as the sole documentable vestige of a Unionist cover-up became increasingly inevitable. Given the nature of the evidence supplied by conservative Christians disgusted because Paisley did not hound McGrath out of loyalist circles for his purported homosexuality, liberals zealous to implicate Paisley found themselves parroting their sources' common-sense assumption that queers should not be allowed near children. Thus, as Dudgeon points out, the use by liberals of McGrath's ties to Paisley to expose Unionist hypocrisy represented a bizarre and disastrous rapprochement between right-wing sexual views and left-wing political aspirations.

As Dudgeon argues, McGrath's rigidly conformist public identity as an 'Evangelical Protestant Orangemen [sic], paramilitary loyalist, friend of the DUP and the Free Presbyterians' conflicted radically with 'the reality of his personal life which included abuse of power and coercive sexual acts with teenagers in his care' (1982, 8). Dudgeon describes the contradiction between McGrath's public and private identities as 'a perfect vehicle to bring Dr Paisley into disrepute as a hypocrite, and ... the motivating force behind the radical journalists' (1982, 8). While Dudgeon's analysis of liberals' motives in connecting Paisley to Kincora is accurate, he responds to liberals' trafficking in homophobic stereotypes by insisting that Kincora is a relatively unimportant issue that has been blown up out of all proportion. His rationale for minimising Kincora's importance is ultimately based in his rejection of any clear sexual *or* political causality underlying the scandal; if the scandal was not brought about by either significant sexual or political dynamics within Northern Irish society, it is anomalous and unworthy of the extensive media attention it is receiving. The queer theory that results from this dual rejection is rife with its own contradictions.

Declaring that 'Kincora is not a homosexual scandal anymore than it is a Protestant scandal' (1982, 8), Dudgeon seeks to fend off two threats to Northern Ireland's emergent gay/lesbian community. To protect individual homosexuals, Dudgeon obviously must stand up and challenge the nearly ubiquitous depictions of the scandal as 'homosexual' in nature. On the other hand, Dudgeon must also protect himself and the organisation of which he was president – the Northern Ireland Gay Rights Association (NIGRA) – from being identified in any way with sectarian politics. Paradoxically, however, owing to this need for the Northern Irish gay/lesbian community to maintain a stance of radical neutrality concerning sectarian politics, Dudgeon finds himself and his community on the same side of this rhetorical conflict as the homophobic Paisley, who the previous year had launched the Save Ulster from Sodomy Campaign in direct response to NIGRA's increasingly effective calls for decriminalisation. It is, Dudgeon finds, in the best interests of gays, as well as of Paisley, to put a stop to further discussions of Kincora, and it is the left in particular who ought to shut up about it. The victims of the Kincora scandal, Dudgeon predicts, 'will be gay people in social work and the limited acceptability we have achieved elsewhere' (1982, 8). Already, in March 1982, Dudgeon argues that there have been 'four suspensions' of homosexual employees 'employed near young people', which are in two cases attributable 'to the individual's homosexual orientation alone' (1982, 8). Political radicals gunning for Paisley are in part responsible for this backlash, he argues, and since radicals, in whom gays would ordinarily expect to find allies 'ignore the consequences of their actions' then 'we can expect no mercy from the liberals or the conservatives' (1982, 8).

Chris Moore's *The Kincora Scandal*: 'I began to enjoy it …'

In a short prologue to his account of the material that he spent 17 years gathering on Kincora, Chris Moore attempts to depict rather than explain the complex mesh of thoughts and feelings that drew him into years of frustrating and often fruitless investigation by describing 'a cold night in January 1982' when he broke into the building that had once housed the staff and inmates of Kincora Boys' Home. He recalls that 'having spent thirteen years covering murder, bloodshed, hardship and grief, I, like so many other reporters, had developed a tough exterior. This was just another assignment' (1996, 20). While Moore works assiduously to make visible the connections between abuse at Kincora, Northern Irish Unionists and the British secret service, his explication of the complex web of causality that led to sexual abuse at Kincora is undermined by his insistent focus on the purported homosexuality of Semple, Mains and the married and homophobic McGrath. Uneducated about the moral necessity to separate rhetorically the terms 'homosexuality' and 'child abuse', Moore, in his account of the events at Kincora, made a number of 'mistakes' that initially enraged me, but which I now think may have provided a clearer account of what, exactly, went wrong at Kincora, and why.

At worst, homosexuality could be read as at the very core of Moore's crusade to 'expose the evil of Kincora' (1996, 20). A close reading of Moore's prologue, however, reveals a profoundly complex relationship between the common sense homophobia that was reinforced in virtually every account of the case other than those by gay rights campaigner Dudgeon (which would have been read predominantly by other gay activists and sympathisers, among whom Moore clearly did not number), and Moore's growing conviction that some factor other than 'homosexuality' is responsible for the extensive damage that had unquestionably been visited upon some of Kincora's former inmates. In effect, Moore's depiction of his physical exploration of Kincora's floor plan makes visible and tangible the profound moral and epistemological complexities inhering in attempts by numerous journalists and bureaucrats to tell the story of the abuse at Kincora.

Moore's movements in the dark, abandoned house chart the process by which Kincora became more than 'just another assignment'. They are interpolated first with the words of a particular former inmate whom Moore had interviewed in order to cover the trial of the Kincora three (1996, 15–16), who testified:

> I am a practicing homosexual at the present time and I think that I am the way I am as a result of what Joe Mains did with me when I lived in Kincora. I have a certain amount of resentment … but I have kept in touch with him because when you are an orphan you have no one other than the people who run the homes you have lived in. (1996, 16)

This assertion violates a powerful code of honour within the GLBT community: that no queer person ever state publicly that his or her adult sexual identity was significantly or substantially the product of sexual abuse. Ann Cvetkovich cites influential self-help writer Laura Davis explaining this code, which Davis's *The Courage to Heal* (1988) codifies, in the following way: 'saying sexual abuse causes homosexuality is making an assumption that there's something wrong with being lesbian or gay' (2003, 90). This powerful speech prohibition is unquestionably one of the central, if often tacit, structures underlying the theoretical separation of homosexuality and sexual abuse. In Moore's account, however, the inclusion of a former Kincora inmate's description of his adult homosexuality as the product of abuse productively points to the constructed and imposed nature of absolute divisions between the two.

This informant's attribution of his sexual orientation to his experience of abuse at Kincora, and, importantly, to his status as an orphan, lacking other defining ties, serves, in Moore's account, as evidence of the lasting effects of Kincora on the lives of its victims. The credibility of the informant's account of abuse, and, by implication, abuse's aftermath, is borne out through Moore's nocturnal investigations inside Kincora. Moore discovers a 'little mark on the wall where once the plaque hung for the "Best Boy of the Year" award', an award that was, his informant recalls, typically given to a particularly sexually compliant inmate (1996, 17–18). The mark is 'just where I was told it would be', and this visual corroboration of his informant's description of the internal workings of Kincora metonymically confirms both the inmate's account of abuse and, simultaneously, his account of its effects. The voice of this particular inmate, which testifies to the lasting damage the abuse has done to the lives of its victims through its imprint on their adult sexuality, modulates into a plethora of voices, emanating from 'the statements given to the police by some of the young men who had been sexually abused in this place' (1996, 19).

These statements are of three basic types, describing specific acts of sexual abuse, instances of subtle or explicit sexual and ideological manipulation of inmates by their supervisors, and House Father William McGrath's religious and political ideas and connections. The descriptions of actual sexual encounters are not particularly sensational; the passage below is representative in terms of tone, and it is the most sexually explicit of those Moore includes:

> *I had sex with McGrath at least three times a week. This always took place in the hostel in either the cloakroom on the ground floor, the sitting-room or in my bedroom. It was nearly always both of us riding each other and sometimes sucking and wanking. At first I did not like it but later I began to enjoy it. (1996, 18)*

Like most of the other quotations, this one is couched in a conversational tone, and the acts described are not overtly violent. A reader is left without clear guidance as to the impact these remembered quotations have on Moore as he moves around the darkened house.

In their very lack of sensationalism, these accounts suggest that something other than sex constitutes the core violation to which Moore is responding; conversely, however, they might also suggest that it is the more pleasurable rather than the most overtly violating of the encounters that trouble him and are meant to trouble us as readers. Disturbingly, Moore is an adult man wandering around a children's home that he has, symbolically and literally, violated, remembering accounts of sex with boys. These remembered accounts could be read as disturbing because the men who are speaking seem relatively at ease with the acts they describe. Memories such as those conveyed in the above quoted passage could readily alarm a man socialised in a highly homophobic society, particularly one who is physically occupying the precise spaces associated with specific, minutely documented acts of sexual transgression, with their frank (and perhaps obscurely appealing) eroticism, or with the open implication that prohibitions against homosexual desire might, over time, give way to active pleasure.

As James Kincaid has argued in *The Culture of Child-Molesting* (1998), it is the unconscious fear of such forbidden but culturally-hardwired pleasures that has propelled Western societies to embrace the trance logic of sexualised hate, to 'creat[e] a monster to hate, hunt down, and punish' (Levine 2002, 27). In addition to expressing paedophilic panic, however, Moore's evident refusal to pleasurably identify with the representations of queer abuse he includes also works to sustain empathy with the disempowered parties in these episodes by resisting the cultural tendency to transform the pain of the powerless into the sensationalised pleasure of moral outrage or pornographic fantasy. Moore's empathetic identification with the abuse survivors of Kincora, which he ultimately maintains without having to deny the ways in which the activities of closeted homosexuals, who might have risked death had they approached men over whom they wielded no power, shaped their experiences, ultimately affords an astonishing glimpse into the connections between private, sexual violations within Kincora and larger, society-wide inequalities.

Moore's reconstruction of power abuses at Kincora reads the sexual encroachments that occurred there as part of a larger affective and ideological system of penetration that constituted dependent minors as the vessels of not only erotic and individual but also political and collective desires. Counterposed against explicit accounts of sex between inmates and staff members are memories of other abuses of power, as when 'McGrath and me built up a friendship and used to talk a lot about religion and the Orange Order' (Moore 1996, 17), and 'McGrath boasted about his contacts high up in the Orange Order and loyalist paramilitaries such as the [paramilitary Ulster Defence Association]. He boasted of his contacts with top unionist politicians' (1996, 19). These accounts culminate in passages that position Kincora explicitly within a neo-imperial relationship between the intensively policed Catholic nationalists and the settler colonial Protestant Unionists and their allies in the British government:

> I always had the feeling McGrath was through his influence in the Orange Order … and in the group Tara,[5] prodding Northern Ireland as best he could towards the troubles he himself predicted, the blood on the streets and the holocaust which would accompany the fight for Protestant freedom. (1996, 20)

Together, these accounts build up a profile of the gross power inequalities characteristic of the colonial periphery, ranging from the most intimate and individual to the most far-reaching and collective, as they intermingled within a specific liminal and queer space in which the domestic and the state were coterminous, coalescing as an eroticised, threatening and all-pervasive web.

The desire on the part of queers, whether as theorists, activists or community members, to keep the state out of our bedrooms and our sites of socialisation through the creation of or gravitation toward spaces of opacity within the state, as well as through the maintenance of an absolute conceptual distinction between the sexual and the criminal, is understandable, perhaps even inevitable. As the Kincora case illustrates, however, such lawless spaces can become sites for the interpenetration of queer eroticism and abuse, while queer theories that deny the potential of queer eroticism to co-exist in the same space with abuse can be one factor contributing to the continued maintenance of such spaces as acceptably outside of accountability to the state and simultaneously central to its replication.

Acknowledgements

I owe an enormous debt of gratitude to the many colleagues who helped to guide my thinking, sort out my arguments and generally push me back into the thorny issues this chapter tackles. I wish to thank Declan Kiberd, Ann Cvetkovich, Kenneth

---

5   A secretive paramilitary group led by William McGrath, with ties to MI5, Tara was never intended for the kind of street violence favoured by, for instance, the Ulster Volunteer Force or the Ulster Defence Association (which McGrath helped to found), but rather it viewed itself, through the eyes of its MI5 handlers, as a 'doomsday organisation' that would help the British to keep control of the loyalist side in the event of a complete political meltdown in the North.

Kidd, Kathryn Conrad, Tramble Turner, David Lloyd, Michael O'Rourke, Noreen Giffney, David Mazella, Hosam Aboul-Ela, Maria Gonzalez, Helen Burke, Susan Harris, Sarah McKibben, Paige Reynolds, Mary Trotter, Elizabeth Cullingford and Jeff Dudgeon. Thanks also to Jeff Dudgeon and Chris Moore, both of whom generously granted extensive interviews and shared a great deal of otherwise unavailable archival material.

Suggested Further Reading

Bruhm, S. and Hurley, N. (eds) (2004), *Curiouser: On the Queerness of Children* (Minneapolis, MN: University of Minneapolis Press).

Cvetkovich, A. (2003), *An Archive of Feelings: Trauma, Sexuality, and Lesbian Public Cultures* (Durham, NC: Duke University Press).

Kincaid, J. (1998), *Erotic Innocence: The Culture of Child Molesting* (Durham, NC: Duke University Press).

Levine, J. (2002), *Harmful to Minors: The Perils of Protecting Children from Sex* (Minneapolis, MN: University of Minneapolis Press).

Ohi, K. (2000), 'Molestation 101: Child Abuse, Homophobia, and *The Boys of Saint Vincent*', *GLQ: A Journal of Lesbian and Gay Studies* 6:2, 195–248.

References

Angelides, S. (2004), 'Feminism, Child Sexual Abuse, and the Erasure of Child Sexuality', *GLQ: A Journal of Lesbian and Gay Studies* 10:2, 141–77.

Backus, M.G. (1998), 'Discourse and Silence in the Victorian Family Cell: Problems of Subjectivity in *The History of Sexuality: Volume I, Victorian Literature and Culture* 24, 159–74.

Bruhm, S. and Bruhm, N. (eds) (2004), *Curiouser: On the Queerness of Children* (Minneapolis, MN: University of Minneapolis Press).

Chauncey, G. (1994), *Gay New York: Gender, Urban Culture, and the Making of the Gay Male World, 1890–1940* (New York: Basic Books).

Cvetkovich, A. (2003), *An Archive of Feelings: Trauma, Sexuality, and Lesbian Public Cultures* (Durham, NC: Duke University Press).

Davis, L. (1988), *The Courage to Heal* (New York: Harper and Row).

Dudgeon, J. (1982), 'Kincora Sentences', *Scope* March, 8–9.

—— (2002), *Roger Casement: The Black Diaries, with a Study of his Background, Sexuality, and Irish Political Life* (Belfast: Belfast Press).

Edelman, L. (2004), *No Future: Queer Theory and the Death Drive* (Durham, NC: Duke University Press).

Foot, P. (1990), *Who Framed Colin Wallace?* (London, Pan Books).

Foucault, M. (1990/1978), *The History of Sexuality, Volume I: An Introduction*, trans. R. Hurley (New York: Vintage).

Gallop, J. (2002), *Anecdotal Theory* (Durham, NC: Duke University Press).

Kincaid, J. (1998), *Erotic Innocence: The Culture of Child Molesting* (Durham, NC: Duke University Press).

Levine, J. (2002), *Harmful to Minors: The Perils of Protecting Children from Sex* (Minneapolis, MN: University of Minneapolis Press).

Lynch, J. (1986), 'The Unanswered Questions that Continue to Haunt Kincora', *Fortnight: An Independent Review for Northern Ireland* 234: 24 February–9 March, 4–5.

McKenna, P. (1980), 'Sex Racket at Children's Home', *Irish Independent* 24 January.

McNamee, E. (1994), *Resurrection Man* (New York: Picador).

McNay, L. (1992), *Foucault and Feminism* (Boston, MA: Northeastern University Press).

Modleski, T. (2000), 'Fight the Power: A Response to Jane Gallop, James Kincaid, and Ann Pellegrini', *Critical Inquiry* 26, 591–600.

Moore, C. (1996), *The Kincora Scandal: Political Cover-Up and Intrigue in Northern Ireland* (Dublin: Marino Books).

Nabokov, V. (1997/1959), *Lolita* (London: Penguin).

Ohi, K. (2000), 'Molestation 101: Child Abuse, Homophobia, and *The Boys of Saint Vincent*', *GLQ: A Journal of Lesbian and Gay Studies* 6:2, 195–248.

Report of the Committee of Inquiry into Children's Homes and Hostels (1986) (Belfast: Her Majesty's Stationery Office).

Rubin, G.S. (2004/1985), 'Thinking Sex: Notes for a Radical Theory of the Politics of Sexuality', in D. Carlin and J. DiGrazia (eds), *Queer Cultures* (Upper Saddle River, NJ: Prentice Hall).

Ruddick, L. (2000), 'Professional Harassment', *Critical Inquiry* 26, 601–9.

Schmidt, G. (1991), 'The Debate on Pedophilia', in T. Sandfort, E. Brongersma and A. van Naerssen (eds), *Male Intergenerational Intimacy: Historical, Socio-Psychological and Legal Perspectives* (New York: Harrington Park Press).

Sedgwick, E.K. (1985), *Between Men: English Literature and Male Homosocial Desire* (New York: Columbia University Press).

Warner, M. (1999), *The Trouble With Normal: Sex, Politics, and the Ethics of Queer Life* (Cambridge, MA: Harvard University Press).

PART III

NORMATIVITY

Queer Theory Goes to Taiwan

Song Hwee Lim

In discussing the globalisation of 'alterity' in emerging democracies, including Taiwan, Cindy Patton suggests that, '"Queer", if it is to have any utility, is best understood, not as a model of identity and practice that can be imitated or molded to a local setting, but as evidence of a kind of unstoppable alterity that flies, like a stealth bomber, beneath the annihilating screen of nation' (2002, 210). This chapter studies the travel of queer theory, like a stealth bomber in Cindy Patton's quotation, to Taiwan from the mid-1990s. It begins by dealing with the translingual aspect of this transcultural flow, raising questions about translation and translatability while situating the discussion in the context of postcoloniality in Taiwan. It goes on to highlight the difficulties of delimiting the field of queer studies in Taiwan by providing an analysis of the issues of cultural production and institutional practices that have engendered queer theory's travel to Taiwan. By way of conclusion, it problematises the field of queer studies in and on Taiwan, foregrounds its own positionality in this circuit of production of cultural knowledge, and reflects on the tactics and politics of intervention in the field of queer studies.

Translation, Translatability, Postcoloniality

In his essay 'Travelling Theory', Edward Said identifies a recurrent pattern of stages common to the way any theory or idea travels. These are: a point of origin, a distance traversed, a set of conditions (of both acceptance and resistance) and the transformation of the theory or idea by its new uses and position in a new time and place (1991, 226–7). Using György Lukacs's *History and Class Consciousness* (1923) as an example, Said illustrates how it travelled from Budapest to Paris where it was put to use by Lucien Goldmann in his thesis *Le Dieu cache* (1955), and later to Cambridge where Raymond Williams discussed both Lukacs's text and Goldmann's reading. While I agree with Said that it seems perfectly possible to judge misreadings as 'part of a historical transfer of ideas and theories from one setting to another' (1991, 236), what is strangely, if (in)conspicuously, missing in his account of travelling theory is the question of translation, as if language has had no part to play in this transcultural flow.

For Lydia Liu, it has become unthinkable 'to continue treating the concrete language issue in cross-cultural scholarship as a superfluity or merely part of a critique of the effects of colonialism and imperialism' (1995, xv). Rather, she argues, difference 'cannot be conceived at the ontological level without first presenting itself at the constitutive level where the question of linguistic transaction must be brought in' (1995, 8). I contend that Liu's idea of 'translingual practice' must be foregrounded in the examination of any cross-cultural phenomenon, for the travel of a theory raises questions not only about translation but also about translatability, and thus about both ontology and epistemology. Moreover, while Said's essay does not deal with issues of translation, colonialism and imperialism presumably because Lukacs's thesis travels within a seemingly homogenous Europe, such issues cannot be ignored when we are dealing with the travelling of a theory from the West to the East given the legacies of European colonialism, cultural imperialism and Orientalist discourse.

My study of queer theory's travel to Taiwan demands a more complex framework for the power dynamics of this transcultural flow than the binary opposition of Self and Other allowed for in many postcolonial writings. This framework has implications for the issues of translation and translatability, for the practice of translation is premised on presumed linguistic and cultural differences between the guest language and the host language, and on the 'origins' of these languages being necessarily located in distinct geographical spaces.[1] However, precisely because of the legacies of imperialism, postcolonial spaces are invariably hybrid spaces that play host to a multiplicity of languages, often including the guest language by which a theory subsequently travels. That is, on the occasion of a travelling theory having arrived at a postcolonial, multilingual society, the guest (presumed foreign) language may have long existed in the space where it is now being translated into the host (presumed native) language. If the Other has become, via the experience of colonisation, an inextricable part of the Self, how does this state of embodied otherness alter our understanding of the issues of translation and translatability, and how does it impinge upon the terms of negotiation in the process of translation?[2]

What I am suggesting therefore is a framework based on the (already) *translated condition*. Within this framework, the terms of translation and the question of translatability have to be problematised as a *pre*condition of any travelling theory rather than as mere effects brought about by the transcultural exchange. This framework is also necessary for dealing with the messy historicity of Taiwan. It has

---

1   Here I follow Lydia Liu in replacing concepts of 'source language/target language' with those of 'guest language/host language' (1995, 381 n. 1) as it shifts the focus, balance and, most importantly, power to the autonomy and agency of the translator.

2   As Kwame Anthony Appiah argues in relation to postcolonial African culture, we are all 'already contaminated by each other', and the 'construction and celebration of oneself as Other' might be called 'alteritism' (1997, 67).

been proposed that because of the consecutive colonisation of Taiwan by various powers over the past centuries, and because of the absence of decolonisation processes in some instances owing partly to the fact that those ruling powers have never been acknowledged as colonial, it has become almost impossible to theorise Taiwan in postcolonial terms.[3] For example, Emma Jinhua Teng argues that the failure to acknowledge the very existence of Qing China's (1644–1911) imperialism renders it impossible to name the historical relation between China and Taiwan as 'colonial' (2004, 250). After the Qing regime ceded Taiwan to Japan in 1895 as a result of China's defeat in its war with the Japanese, and following Japan's surrender in 1945 at the end of the Second World War, Taiwan was 'returned' to a China under Nationalist (Kuomintang, or the KMT) rule. Thus, not only was Taiwan's rule by the Qing regime unacknowledged as colonial, but Taiwan's decolonisation from Japan was also immediately replaced with what can arguably be seen as re-colonisation by a mainland-Chinese regime that was the KMT. The seemingly seamless change of political power in both instances masks the 'double lack of decolonization (from Japan and China) [that] precludes the possibility of Taiwan's postcoloniality' (Teng 2004, 250).

To complicate matters, after the Second World War, a Cold War system dominated East Asia and effectively took over the structures of colonialism while foreclosing the decolonisation process that unfolded elsewhere in the world (Chen 2001, 82). In his study of Club 51, founded in Taiwan on the Fourth of July 1994 by 51 intellectuals and businessmen with American experience and with an aim for Taiwan to become the 51st state of the United States, Kuan-hsing Chen notes that 'a Cold War formation of subjectivity remains with us' and that the chain of cultural flows from America 'still traverses the social body' of East Asian denizens (2001, 73–4, 83, 85–6). According to Chen, not only is the post-war generation of Taiwanese intellectuals largely trained in the United States and currently in power to implement American-style modernisation in Taiwan, but US academic texts have also travelled to, and are actively read and taught in, East Asian universities, where intellectual trends largely reproduce 'fashions on American campuses' (2001, 83, 86–7).[4] Hence, the travel of queer theory to Taiwan has to be situated in the contexts of, on the one hand, the translated condition of Taiwan as a result of its colonial experiences while noting the impossibility of speaking of it in postcolonial terms and, on the other hand, Taiwan's *de facto* status as a sub-colony of the United States since the end of the Second World War, a status further complicated by its still

---

3   While Chinese immigrants had inhabited Taiwan since the seventeenth century, Taiwan was under the control of the Dutch until 1662, then taken by China's Koxinga (Zheng Chenggong) and ruled as a separate kingdom until 1683, before it was conquered by forces of the Qing, the Manchu dynasty that had taken over China in 1644 (Wachman 1994, 6).

4   An example in the opposite direction illustrating how easily Taiwanese could integrate into America is Shu-mei Shih's proposal in relation to the film director Ang Lee: 'Knowledge of American culture became a given for the educated Taiwanese to the extent that a national subject from Taiwan can be readily transformed into a minority subject in the US' (2000, 91).

unresolved political stalemate with the Chinese Communist Party (CCP) which continues to claim Taiwan as an indivisible part of the People's Republic of China (PRC).[5]

While it is undeniable that the flow of cultural influences has, since the Second World War, been for the most part in one direction only – from America to East Asia (Chen 2001, 86), I am less certain if Asia and the Third World are necessarily in the position to offer what Chen calls alternative sites of identification as 'part of a decolonization in motion' (2001, 87). Discourses on the decolonisation of the mind often presume a pre-colonial state to which postcolonial subjects can return to draw upon resources for identification and cultural production. However, as the problematic of Taiwan's (post)coloniality reveals, what if the processes of decolonisation have been repeatedly deferred so that postcoloniality has become almost impossible, and what if the histories of colonisation stretch so far back that a pre-colonial state cannot be unproblematically resuscitated because if it is, in the case of Taiwan, it does not belong to the current Han-Chinese claimants of postcoloniality but to the many tribes of aborigines who have been written out of the (de)colonisation narratives altogether?

The question of the aborigines in Taiwan is inextricably linked to Taiwan's postcoloniality, and this is reflected clearly in the issue of translation, for queer theory's travel to Taiwan has been mediated through translation into Chinese rather than the (recent) colonial language of Japanese or any of the aboriginal languages.[6] If translation is an activity that takes place between a guest language and a host language, the host language in this instance (Chinese) belongs to a settler community (Han Chinese) that has come to occupy, in both senses of the term, Taiwan first through waves of immigration dating back centuries, then through a militaristic process that established a new polity on the island. The travel of queer theory to Taiwan and its translation from English to Chinese can only be understood as an indigenisation from the point of view of the Han Chinese.[7] For the aborigines in Taiwan, queer theory's travel to Taiwan, while bearing little if no relation to them, is also in fact an instance of double neo-colonisation, as both

---

5   In 1949, the KMT lost its civil war with the CCP and retreated to the island of Taiwan where it established the Republic of China, a regime technically still at war with the PRC today.

6   The issue of language is a very thorny one in Taiwan. While the written form of the Chinese language is fairly standardised, there are at least three main spoken forms (Mandarin, Hoklo/Taiwanese and Hakka) in Taiwan. During the years of Japanese occupation and KMT rule, the Taiwanese were forced to learn Japanese and to speak Mandarin respectively. With the rise of Taiwan nationalism particularly since the lifting of the martial law in 1987, the Taiwanese dialect spoken by the majority of the population has reclaimed social respectability and even become fashionable (Wachman 1994, 109), and there are movements to develop a more standardised written form for the Taiwanese dialect.

7   Similarly, both Teng's claim about the impossibility of Taiwan's postcoloniality and Chen's analysis of the foreclosure of decolonisation for Taiwan seem to stem from the Han Chinese perspective.

English and Chinese are but colonial languages, with the latter playing host to the former guest while disguising its own status as (an albeit earlier) guest (or guest-turned-host).[8] Paradoxically, I believe this makes it all the more pertinent and imperative to emphasise Taiwan's state of postcoloniality from the perspective of the aborigines, rather than conflating postcoloniality with decolonisation and the establishment of an independent nation-state, the latter two of which tend to obscure the role, if not continue to inflict a violence by eradicating the voice, of the aborigines.

Given Taiwan's messy historicity and translated condition, to analyse queer theory's travel to Taiwan simply in terms of a US-style McDonaldisation of the rest of the world is not satisfactory.[9] Rather, in the context of the complexity of Taiwan's postcoloniality, this transcultural flow epitomises what Kwame Anthony Appiah calls a 'space-clearing gesture' that may or may not be sensitive to the issue of neo-colonialism or cultural imperialism (1997, 63). The question is, under what circumstances does one feel what Appiah describes as 'the need to clear oneself a space' (1997, 61), and who is this 'one' doing the clearing and what kind of space is being cleared? It is therefore important to scrutinise the role of the agents facilitating this transcultural flow and to ask the following: When was queer theory introduced to Taiwan, by whom, in whose name, and for what purpose? Under what institutional mechanisms did it travel and continue to operate? What use has it been put to and what kinds of research are carried out in its name? What is queer theory's position in the academic and intellectual fields, and how does it interact with other disciplinary practices? Does it promote or impede the careers of those who introduced and continue to practise queer theory in their research? Or, to borrow Pierre Bourdieu's concept of 'the field of cultural production', how is the cultural knowledge of queer theory imagined and (re)produced in Taiwan, and what are the eco-system and power dynamics of the field in which this knowledge production is carried out?

For my purpose here, I think it is equally important to note the postcolonial subject's *desire* for both the cultural commodities from the West and a role in facilitating the exchange. Taiwan's translated condition, I would argue, manifests not so much in its linguistic hybridity as in its *imperative* to translate. By this I do not mean that the Taiwanese necessarily occupy a passive position in which they are always at the receiving end of Western modernity through translation, though modernisation has indeed been the overriding discourse driving the translation of Western texts since the Meiji period (1868–1912) in Japan and from the late Qing (1644–1911) to the early Republican era in China (1912–49), both of which must

---

8   Of course, as James Clifford rightly questions in the context of 'Fourth world [indigenous] peoples' claiming 'first world sovereignty': 'How long does it take to become "indigenous"?' (1997, 288–9). In the case of queer theory's travel to Taiwan, however, the aborigines are a subaltern who cannot and do not speak, and thus the issue of 'indigenisation' should be highlighted.

9   For another study on the problems of translating queer theory into a non-American context, see Mizielinska (2006).

have had an impact on the continual practice of translation in postwar Taiwan. On the contrary, it can be argued that it is partly (if not largely) the translator's cultural imagination of the Other that determines what gets translated or what theory gets to travel to the host culture, thus underlining the agency of the translator. In her study on the Chinese translation of Western sexological terms in Republican China, Tze-lan Sang suggests that, while the Chinese translator's agency is never uncircumscribed, it is precisely 'in the moment of choice, when the translator has the freedom to cite and appropriate certain materials rather than others, that we witness the possibility of cross-cultural understanding and coalition, rather than bleak, wholesale Western cultural imperialism and imposition in the name of universality' (2003, 101). In this sense, translation is not so much cultural imperialism as cultural appropriation, with potential for the empowerment of agents in the host culture to subject the translated theory to their own purposes. Translation, particularly in a postcolonial context, must be seen as an exchange that is imbued with complex power relations, both historical and contemporary, but never one-way or merely imperialistic, involving agents, institutions, mechanisms and processes that demand careful delineation rather than ideological posturing.

Whither Queer Theory in Taiwan?

The very act of examining a theory's travel to another space, Said argues, betrays 'some fundamental uncertainty about specifying or delimiting the field to which any one theory or idea might belong' (1991, 227). While there are books that set out to introduce queer theory (Jagose 1996; Sullivan 2003) or trace its genealogy (Turner 2000), the demarcation of the field of queer studies and the definition of queer theory are far from clear-cut. For example, while queer theory is largely understood as a 'Western' theory, there has been contestation to (Kuzniar 2000), and disavowal of (Duyvendak 1996) the category of queer within Western societies, and also attempts to pluralise it (Hall 2003). A historical approach proposed by Said (1991, 230) can certainly identify specific instances and examples of theories having travelled from one place to another. In the context of this chapter, the only sure way of ascertaining that the theory that has travelled to another locale is indeed queer theory is for the translated text to possess unquestionable qualities of canonicity, authenticity and currency in both the guest and host cultures. This, however, has the effect of transplanting queer theory's hegemony from one context to another, and it may also foreclose queer theory's potential for change as a result of its travel to another culture.

To attempt to provide a critical enquiry into the state of the field of queer studies in Taiwan is difficult for several reasons. To begin with, there is the question of translation and translatability. Do we assume that all ideas and theories are translatable (both linguistically and culturally), and do we know that the idea or theory being mobilised is the translated one only if the agent indicates it as such? In

Taiwan, there have been three translations of the term 'queer' since the 1990s:[10] firstly, *'Tongzhi'* (literally 'same will'), itself a Chinese translation of the Soviet communist term 'comrade', was appropriated for a homosexual identity by the organisers of Hong Kong's inaugural lesbian and gay film festival in 1989, and introduced to Taiwan in 1992 as the translation for 'New Queer Cinema' at its Golden Horse international film festival.[11] Secondly, *'Ku'er'* (literally 'cool kid'), a transliteration of 'queer', made its debut in the January 1994 issue of the radical intellectual journal *Isle Margin*, with the cover bearing the title *'KU'ER QUEER'.*[12] Thirdly, *'Guaitai'* (literally 'strange foetus'), a colloquial term referring to people who are strange or eccentric, appeared as *'guaitai yizu'* (queer tribe) in the preface of the June 1994 issue of the lesbian journal *Ai Bao* (literally 'love paper'), which featured a special section entitled 'Queer Nation', translated as *tongzhi guo* in Chinese.[13]

The three Chinese/Mandarin translations of the term 'queer' highlight the question of translatability as 'queer' was simultaneously rendered as *guaitai* and *tongzhi* in the last example while *tongzhi* was used in the first example to refer to both 'lesbian and gay' and 'queer'. Unless the user explicitly indicates as such, it is almost impossible to determine in Taiwan whether any of the referents of these three Chinese terms is the translation for the English term 'queer'.[14] Of the three Chinese terms, *ku'er* presents the least potential for confusion as a transliteration of 'queer', though it is worth noting that *ku'er* is also the translation for Qoo, a soft drink manufactured by Coca Cola and promoted by McDonald's in Taiwan, with an eponymous mascot designed to be given away with the latter's kid's meal. For *guaitai*, it is only intelligible within the context of its use whether the referent is 'queer' or the colloquial 'weirdo'. As for *tongzhi*, most theorists concur that its referent is usually 'lesbian and gay' (Chi 1997, 38; Martin 2003, 3), though it can also refer to 'queer'.

The multiple translations of the term 'queer' into Chinese/Mandarin and thus the indeterminacy of its referents in the Taiwanese context are also reflected in the field of queer studies in Taiwan. For example, one of the main sites that queer theory has travelled to, the journal *Chung-Wai Literary Monthly* published by the Department of Foreign Languages and Literatures at National Taiwan University (NTU), devoted a few special issues to queer studies over a number of years. The journal mobilises various Chinese translations for the term 'queer' in these special

---

10   The problem of translation here should not obscure from us the multiplicity of meanings embedded in the etymology of the word 'queer' itself. As Eve Kosofsky Sedgwick points out, the word 'queer' means 'across' and comes from the Indo-European root *-twerkw*, which also yields the German *quer* (transverse), Latin *torquere* (to twist) and English *athwart* (1993, xii).

11   On the identity politics of the term *tongzhi*, see Chou (2000).

12   On the translation of 'queer' as *ku'er*, see Lim (2007).

13   On the translation of 'queer nation' as *guaitai yizu* in a different issue of *Ai Bao*, see Martin (2003, 2–5).

14   From her experience of teaching queer theory in Taiwan and encountering the problem of translation, Patton decided to 'stop searching for a Mandarin translation for what I meant to express by "queer"' (2002, 211–12 n. 4).

issues while featuring the original English term in its bilingual titles namely, 'Tongzhi lunshu/Queer Studies' (June 1996), 'Yanyi xing yu xingbie: ku'er xiaoshuo yu yanjiu/Proliferating Sexual and Gender Differences: Queer Study and Queer Fiction' (August 1997), 'Guaitai qingyu xue/Queer Sexuality' (May 1998) and 'Tongzhi zaixian/ Queer Re(-)presentation' (August 2003). In addition to the complications brought about by the multiple translations of the term 'queer' in Chinese, even with the bilingual titles indicating the marker of 'queer' in English, do the research papers contained in these special issues necessarily fall into the disciplinary practice that is queer studies?

The last question, of course, returns us to the issue of whether it is possible to delimit the field to which an idea or a theory might belong. Queer theory and queer studies developed in Anglo-American institutions partly as a reaction to the perceived hegemony and limits of lesbian and gay studies and its politics at the turn of the 1990s. However, it is not always possible to distinguish between research that can be best described as queer studies from those in lesbian and gay studies, and this impossibility of delimitation cannot but replicate itself in its transplantation to another locale.[15] In the case of Taiwan, prior to the lifting of martial law in 1987, lesbian and gay studies (and its politics) only had a negligible representation. In the new political climate since the 1990s which witnessed a proliferation of previously marginalised communities, including the aborigines, women and homosexuals, Taiwan also experienced an influx of fashionable theories amenable to identitarian politics. This wave of travelling theories to Taiwan, I would suggest, has had the effect of meshing queer theory with lesbian and gay studies to the extent that they have often become indistinguishable from each other in Taiwan.

Rather than attempting to identify or define what queer theory or queer studies is in Taiwan, the more important question for me is why did queer theory travel to Taiwan in the first place. That is, why did the agents facilitate such a transcultural flow and under what institutional mechanisms was this flow made possible? To recall my earlier argument about Taiwan's translated condition and its imperative to translate, the swift introduction of queer theory to Taiwan is not simply a one-way reception of, or response to, the latest trendy Western theory by Taiwanese academics. Rather, in the political climate of the post-martial-law era that has been marked by oppositional and 'a-statist' social movements, the arrival of queer theory can be seen as part of a greater development in Taiwanese academia that increasingly places emphasis on the marginal, the alternative and the contestatory – all hallmarks of queer theory and politics (Ka 1997, 238). In addition, the prominence of all forms of post-isms (postmodernism, postcolonialism, poststructuralism) circulating in certain quarters of Taiwanese academia and intellectual circles during

---

15 The impossibility of totally distinguishing queer from lesbian and gay, whether in terms of studies or politics, is evident in the title of the 1991 special issue of the feminist journal *differences*, 'Queer Theory: Lesbian and Gay Sexualities'. For Michael Warner, queer activists are also lesbians and gays in other contexts, and queer politics has not replaced, but rather exists alongside, other modes of lesbian and gay identity (1993, xxviii).

the same period makes the travel of queer theory (which 'essentially' is a form of poststructuralist thought; Hall 2003, 4; Martin 2003, 24–5) a corollary rather than an anomaly. In effect, queer theory has joined forces with other travelling theories in lending theoretical buttresses to oppositional and identitarian politics that range from debates about gender and sexuality to a turn to nativist nationalism in the guise of postcolonialism in late-twentieth-century Taiwan.

Taiwan's translated condition and its imperative to translate hence engendered a coevalness and homogeneity in queer theory's travel to Taiwan. By coevalness, I refer to the decade of the 1990s during which queer theory emerged in both Taiwan and the West; by homogeneity, I refer to the disciplines of English (or, as it is sometimes known in Taiwan, part of Foreign Languages) and cultural studies where queer theorists are based in both locales.[16] I should qualify that here I am taking a decade as a unit of time, and the concept of coevalness is dependent upon, among other factors, one's perception of time and (im)patience with it. The launch of queer theory in the West can be marked with the 1991 special issue of the feminist journal *differences* (Jagose 1996, 127), while the introduction of the idea of queer theory in Taiwan can be traced to the 1994 special issue of *Isle Margin*. As the editors of the Taiwanese journal state clearly in the foreword that the special issue hopes to address the 'lack of a queer discourse' in Taiwan (1994, 5), does this perceived lack not betray an anxiety brought about by a sense of belated (post)modernity owing to the three year time-lag between queer theory's emergence in the West and its travel to Taiwan? On the other hand, the forewords of the special issues on queer studies in *Chung-Wai Literary Monthly* (from 1996 to 2003) merely note, matter-of-factly, the journal's intention to present the research output in queer studies and to deepen it in Taiwan, with no discernable (post)colonial hang-ups to 'catch up with the West'. The contrast between the two can be explained as follows. The editors of the special issue of *Isle Margin* were then students at the abovementioned Department of Foreign Languages and Literatures at NTU, whereas the editors of *Chung-Wai Literary Monthly* are their professors in the same department. If one's perception of time does expand with age, the young turks' impatience with the late arrival of queer theory and their professors' quiet confidence in practising it can be attributed to the possession of academic and cultural capital (or the relative lack thereof in the former case) and also to the nature of publications (the former intellectually radical, the latter institutionally academic).

In terms of homogeneity, what are the implications for queer theory to reside primarily in the disciplines of English and cultural studies in Taiwan? Not unlike their counterparts in the Anglo-American context where they are often perceived as the progressive engine in academia, English departments in Taiwan represent both modernity and alterity in literary and cultural terms. For example, in the 1960s, students at the abovementioned NTU department not only founded the most acclaimed modernist literary journal, *Modern Literature*, but also became the most important modernist writers in Taiwan, though these writers and their

---

16　On the 'burst' of queer theory onto the disciplines of English and cultural studies in Anglo-American academia, see Hall (2003, 54).

literary works were labelled 'Western' in a heated debate with the nativist camp in the 1970s.[17] The department's in-house journal, *Chung-Wai Literary Monthly* ('Chung' refers to Chinese and 'Wai' denotes foreign), has been the vanguard of both literary writing in the modernist mode and scholarly research on it. Despite being published by a foreign languages department, the journal is, as is clear from its title, also devoted to the study of Chinese literature, albeit that with a decidedly modern and modernist bent. On the contrary, Chinese departments in Taiwan are usually perceived as the fortress of traditional literature and anathema to both the production and the study of modern Chinese literature.[18] Insofar as queer theory resides mainly in foreign languages departments rather than in the 'native' language departments in Taiwan, it is likely to be confined to a tightly-knit circle of US-trained academics and their *protégés* and can also be easily dismissed as 'Western'.[19] Rather than unsettle cultural hegemonies and orthodox ideologies in Taiwan's 'native' culture, queer theory's image of foreignness and alterity, coupled with its poststructuralist epistemological grounding, while amenable to English and cultural studies departments, may become a hindrance to queer theory's access to other academic disciplines. That said, because queer theory's travel to Taiwan has invariably been mediated by translation into Chinese, it still has the potential to reach a wider audience beyond its more hospitable constituencies.

Unlike in the United States, where queer theory emerged partly as a result of political activism surrounding the issue of AIDS (which gave birth to the organisation of Queer Nation), queer theory's travel to Taiwan does not so much engender a new identity category in reaction to the perceived complacency of lesbian and gay politics as to function as a sign under which a particular form of institutional practice and cultural production can come into being.[20] That is, queer theory grants legitimacy to certain kinds of intellectual inquiry that might otherwise be dismissed as deviant and academic capital to its theoreticians and practitioners. This is evident in the most prominent institution devoted to queer studies in Taiwan,

---

17   On modernist literature in Taiwan and its debate with the nativist camp, see Chang (1993).

18   For an example of the vicissitudes of offering courses on gender and sexuality in Chinese departments, see Jen-peng Liu (2001).

19   Most of the authors published in *Chung-Wai Literary Monthly*'s queer studies special issues are US- and UK-trained scholars and their postgraduate students. On the issues of African writing in Western languages and the exhibiting of contemporary African art in the West, Appiah (1997, 62) argues that postcoloniality is the condition of 'what we might ungenerously call a *comprador* intelligentsia: a relatively small, Western-style, Western-trained group of writers and thinkers, who mediate the trade in cultural commodities of world capitalism at the periphery' (emphasis in original). This seems to me a rather harsh accusation, and I am not sure to what extent those responsible for queer theory's travel to Taiwan might stand accused of the same charge.

20   As Patton notes: 'Jet-lagged and, having crossed the international dateline, confused even about what day it is, American-style queer theory does not know how to behave: it arrived [in Taiwan] not to harass extant, but in advance of, mainstreamed gay civil rights discourse' (2002, 199).

the Centre for the Study of Sexualities in the Department of English at the National Central University. The Centre not only holds regular conferences in which the doyennes of queer theory, including Eve Sedgwick, have been invited to speak, but also publishes a journal entitled *Working Papers in Gender/Sexuality Studies*, which devoted a special issue to 'Queer Politics and Queer Theory' in September 1998.[21] By declaring queer theory/studies an 'established field' in the disciplines of the arts and humanities (*Working Papers* 1998, 9), queer theorists in Taiwan have been able to legitimise their own disciplinary practices within academia, produce cultural knowledge about queer sexuality through publications and conferences, participate in wider debates and social movements related to issues of gender and sexuality, and establish a centre that has become a focal point for an imagined community of queer scholars, students and activists. Indeed, queer theory's travel to Taiwan can be said to have created a cottage industry of queer studies-related academic (sub)disciplines, teaching programmes and courses, careers for scholars, educational opportunities for students and a host of publications and activities, all of which contribute to a broader understanding and acceptance of queer sexualities within Taiwanese society and the greater Chinese-speaking world.[22]

Re(:)Searching Queer Studies in/on Taiwan

By way of conclusion, I would like to problematise the field of queer studies in and on Taiwan, foreground my own positionality in this circuit of cultural production, and reflect on the tactics and politics of intervention in this field. As demonstrated above, beyond certain identifiable academic institutions, publications and individual scholars, given the indeterminacy of the referents of 'queer' and 'queer studies' in the guise of their multiple Chinese translations, delineating the state of the field of queer studies in Taiwan as such is an almost impossible mission. My account of queer theory's travel to Taiwan has thus far focused on its facilitation by scholars based in English departments. Besides the journals mentioned above, there have also been publications devoted to queer subjects ranging from special issues in literary magazines (*Unitas, eslitebookreview*) and community-based journals (*Ai Bao*) to research articles from the disciplines of architecture (*Newsletter of the Research Center of Gender and Space*) and sociology (Chu 1996). In addition, a distinction

---

21 Of course, it could equally be argued that North American-based queer theorists such as Sedgwick and Cindy Patton also gained credibility in their home countries by having given guest lectures in Taiwan and thus demonstrating the reach of queer theory. The publication of the journal was terminated in 1999 and replaced with a book form. For more information on the Centre, see http://sex.ncu.edu.tw.

22 An example of queer theory's reach, via Taiwan, to another Chinese-speaking world is mainland-Chinese sociologist Yinhe Li's adoption of the term 'ku'er' in her publication on queer studies, in which she notes the translated term's origin from Taiwan (and, erroneously, Hong Kong). See Li (2003).

has to be made between queer studies conducted *in* Taiwan aimed at a Chinese-reading, local audience and those conducted outside of but *on* Taiwan targeted at an English-reading, *glocal* audience.[23] For my purposes here, I will focus on the latter since a discussion of the former will not be meaningful to the target audience of this book.[24]

I must begin by stating that the little English-language research done to date on Taiwanese queer matters hardly constitutes a field. More importantly, the very act of surveying the state of a particular field, as Gail Hershatter suggests in her survey of the study of women in twentieth-century China, presents some 'not-so-innocent taxonomical choices' (2004, 992).[25] Searching for research in queer studies (which is necessarily interdisciplinary) among various disciplinary practices throws up specific questions in each instance. While queer work exists mainly in English and cultural studies departments in Taiwan, the two most obvious disciplines in Anglophone academia for the study of queer cultures and sexualities of Taiwan are East Asian/Chinese studies and gender/sexuality/queer studies. However, as key members of AsiaPacifiQueer (APQ), a network of scholars researching Asian same-sex and transgender cultures and histories, point out, established Asian area studies departments are 'often unsympathetic, if not hostile, towards critical theory and research on homosexuality and transgenderism' whereas Anglophone queer studies has generally overlooked 'issues of linguistic, discursive and theoretical translation at the heart of the practices of Asian queer studies'. The 'imbricated networks of professional homophobia and Eurocentrism' have implications for institutional practices ranging from difficulties in finding sympathetic MA and PhD supervisors and limited access to research funding to restricted employment opportunities and the failure of libraries to collect relevant research materials (Jackson, Martin and McLelland 2005, 299). If academic institutions are in the business of knowledge production, we have to ask what kinds of knowledge are variously sponsored and censored by current institutional practices. Do institutional disciplinary practices ultimately serve to discipline the production of knowledge itself?

In addition to these practical problems facing scholars and students working on queer cultures in Taiwan, the disciplinary location of such work also poses other, more theoretical, questions. As Hershatter argues, to draw on categories of

---

23 I do not wish to frame this distinction in the binary opposition of local versus global, with its assumption of cultural specificity versus universality. Rather, by replacing global with *glocal*, I highlight the consumption and production of English-language scholarship in queer studies on Taiwan within the local, thus reinforcing my broader argument about Taiwan's translated condition and its access to global discourses as a precondition for their travel. In this process, I invariably betray my own (and Taiwan's?) limitation in accessing global discourses only through the English language, though this arguably reflects the hegemony of the English language in the field of queer studies in the world. On the problematic of the global/local dyad, see Lee (2004).

24 For those who read Chinese, see Chao (2001) for a survey of queer studies in Taiwan.

25 For a different attempt at capturing the state of a field, this time that of 'queer Japan', see the special issue in *Intersections* edited by Mark McLelland (2006), especially his introduction.

analysis developed in non-Chinese contexts, including the categories of 'woman' and 'gender' themselves, risks 'analytical imperialism' (2004, 992), and this is the particular risk of studying Taiwanese queer subjects within Anglophone queer studies disciplines if sensitivity is not applied to historical, cultural, linguistic and discursive differences. On the other hand, researching Taiwanese queer subjects within so-called area studies disciplines cannot be divorced from the internal logic of their own *raison d'être* which has historically enabled scholars to, following Benjamin Disraeli's famous phrase, build the East as a career (Chow 1993, 1–15). The tendency in area studies scholarship to prioritise ethnic or cultural differences over any other differences may also result in a (mis)appropriation of the 'area' and its 'indigenousness' simply for the purpose of undermining Anglo-US hegemony, an act which paradoxically colludes to serve reactionary ends in the politics of gender and sexuality within the area itself (Shimizu 2005, 302–3).

At this juncture I must foreground my own positionality in this circuit of knowledge production. At the time of writing an earlier draft of this chapter, I was based at an East Asian studies department of a university that boasts a Centre for Interdisciplinary Gender Studies. When I presented a talk on the translation of the term 'queer' into '*ku'er*' in Taiwanese publications to a postgraduate seminar group in Taiwan in 2003, their professor asked me how I position my queer work on Taiwan within UK academia. This question highlights the problematic issue of representation, and though I certainly do not wish to play the role of a native informant of Taiwan/East Asia to an Anglophone queer audience or of a queer subject to scholars of East Asian studies, the burden (and curse) of representation, unfortunately, cannot be transcended by individuals at will.[26] I must also qualify here that my research often gives the impression that I am Taiwanese whereas I am originally from Singapore but completed my undergraduate education in Taiwan. I can at best attempt to be self-reflexive about the institutional dynamics that engenders my research practices, but I must stress that the interdisciplinarity of queer studies should not be taken for granted and demands institutional commitment at all levels. While current institutional practices have made possible my research and publication on Taiwanese queer subjects, it remains the case that wider mechanisms of multiple exclusions are still at work. Were it not for the efforts of APQ in organising themed panels to queer an Asian studies conference in 2003 in Singapore and to Asianise a queer studies conference in London in 2004 (Jackson, Martin and McLelland 2005, 299), both occasions in which I participated, I often find myself, especially within the UK and Europe, in the position of being the sole 'queer' representative in Chinese/Taiwan/East Asian studies disciplines and the lone 'Asian/Chinese/Taiwanese' voice in queer studies circles.

My experience of straddling the two, often mutually exclusive, disciplines has led me to reflect upon the tactics and politics of intervention. It seems strange to me that in writing about queer sexualities, we almost always emphasise diversity and hybridity, but in que(e)rying East Asia, notions of the nation-state and transnationalism are often left nicely intact. For example, by celebrating the

---

26   On the burden of representation, see Mercer (1990) and Fung (1995).

multifarious representations of queer cultures in certain societies, queer becomes the problematic and discursive subject in ways that the 'area' within East Asia simply is not. As a result, we have neglected to queer the very notions of the nation-state and East Asia, and to ask how these national and supranational constructions delimit the expression of queer sexualities.[27] Posed as practical research problematics, do we confine our interest to expressions of queer sexualities within the nation-state or look out for transnational cultural flows and community links? Do we see subjects in each country as exhibiting a unique expression of queer sexualities or seek to promote a pan-ethnic (say, 'Chinese') sexual identity that exists not only within East Asia but also beyond, both moves risking essentialisms of different kinds? Do we see ourselves primarily as a national subject or a transnational (say, East Asian) subject, and what are the relative advantages and disadvantages in assuming each of these subject positions? These are questions that should inform our critical inque(e)ry.

Though I have not encountered any incident of homophobia towards my work within East Asian studies disciplines, I regrettably experienced the US-centrism displayed at the Queer Matters conference in London in May 2004 and the Theorising Queer Visualities conference in Manchester in April 2005.[28] On both occasions, there was a distinct refusal to confront issues of race and class within queer studies. This, I believe, is symptomatic of the dominance of Anglo-American scholarship in queer studies and of an 'outmoded postcolonial ethnography that posits the West as "global" and non-Western regions as "local"' (Berry 2005, 307). For example, a collection of essays focusing mainly on queer Anglophone films

---

27   For an attempt to queer the notion of 'Chineseness', see Lim (2007).

28   I highlight US-centrism, rather than, say, Eurocentrism, precisely because the hegemony of US-based scholars has been keenly felt (and at times resented?) in so-called Western academia. For example, a British scholar said to me at the Queer Matters conference in a knowingly ironic way: 'Haven't you noticed? This conference is taking place in New York'. See a special section devoted to responses to the Queer Matters conference in the journal *Inter-Asia Cultural Studies*. Another evidence of US-centrism in queer theory is the Fall-Winter 2005 special issue on 'What's Queer about Queer Studies Now?' of the journal *Social Text*, in which all 16 articles deal with nothing but queer theory, representation and politics within the United States, with any attention to race/ethnicity framed within the context of hyphenated-American identities. The editors ask in their introduction, 'What does queer theory have to say about empire, globalization, neoliberalism, sovereignty, and terrorism?' (Eng, Halberstam and Muñoz 2005, 2). The answer is 'very little' given the parochialism of the articles and it is clear that those questions of empire and terrorism relate only to the United States anyway. The conclusion of the introduction rehearses the rhetoric of humility – 'We propose epistemological humility as one form of knowledge production that recognizes these dangers' [of queer scholarship replicating the rise and consolidation of US empire] (2005, 15) – first heard at the Queer Matters conference, despite no evidence of such humility in the selection (or invitation?) of contributions for the special issue. This rhetoric of humility was met with cynicism at the Queer Matters conference as one audience member quipped: 'We don't want your humility, just your resources' (Leung 2005, 304).

presumes universality in its title of *New Queer Cinema* (Aaron 2004), whereas region-focused studies indicate their cultural/geographical specificities with titles such as *Queer Asian Cinema* (Grossman 2000) and *The Queer German Cinema* (Kuzniar 2000). Admittedly, 'new queer cinema' also refers to a short-lived movement encompassing films made mainly in the UK and the United States at the turn of the 1990s, and the book edited by Michele Aaron might have set out to review this specific movement. However, with its token inclusion of an article on 'New Queer Cinema and Third Cinema', one could argue, along with Chris Berry's critique of the Queer Matters conference, that in its original design to take stock only of Anglo-American queer representations more than a decade after the emergence of queer theory, the book (and the conference) is misconceived and betrays its own 'blind spot' (Berry 2005, 305–6). It cannot be over-emphasised that Anglo-American representations are no less culturally-specific than non-Anglo-American ones, and the persistent assumption of universality by the former, even within the confines of Anglo-American scholarship, is increasingly untenable in this globalised age.

To recall the title of an essay by Lauren Berlant and Michael Warner, 'What Does Queer Theory Teach Us About "X"?' (1995), the travel of queer theory to Taiwan should teach us to be attentive to the material conditions for travel (thus the issue of class) and, if the travel traverses countries and continents, the complications of race. In the case of Taiwan, the study of its queer sexualities can no longer disregard the aborigines and non-Mandarin-speaking subjects who may not have access to the cultural resources afforded by queer theory that is located in the cosmopolitan capital of Taipei (Tan 2001, 132; Martin 2003, 14). It also has to confront the elitism that engenders its own institutional disciplinary practices. Having stealthily travelled to Taiwan, queer theory must yield further mileage for the denizens of Taiwan and, in return, offer lessons for the field of queer studies in the world.

Acknowledgements

I wish to thank the editors of the volume, as well as Chris Berry and James St. André, for their insightful comments and suggestions on an earlier version of the chapter.

Suggested Further Reading

Lim, S.H. (2008), 'How to be Queer in Taiwan: Translation, Appropriation and the Construction of a Queer Identity in Taiwan', in P.A. Jackson, M. McLelland, F. Martin and A. Yue (eds), *AsiaPacifiQueer: Rethinking Gender and Sexuality in the Asia-Pacific* (Champaign, IL: University of Illinois Press).

Martin, F. (2003), *Situating Sexualities: Queer Representation in Taiwanese Fiction, Film and Public Culture* (Hong Kong: Hong Kong University Press).

Patton, C. (2002), 'Stealth Bombers of Desire: The Globalization of "Alterity" in Emerging Democracies', in A. Cruz-Malave and M.F. Manalansan IV (eds), *Queer Globalizations: Citizenship and the Afterlife of Colonialism* (New York: New York University Press).

Sang, T.D. (2003), *The Emerging Lesbian: Female Same-Sex Desire in Modern China* (Chicago, IL and London: University of Chicago Press).

Tan, C.K. (2001), 'Transcending Sexual Nationalism and Colonialism: Cultural Hybridization as Process of Sexual Politics in '90s Taiwan', in J.C. Hawley (ed.), *Postcolonial, Queer: Theoretical Intersections* (Albany, NY: State University of New York Press).

References

Aaron, M. (ed.) (2004), *New Queer Cinema: A Critical Reader* (Edinburgh: Edinburgh University Press).

Ai Bao (June 1994), special section on 'Queer Nation'.

Appiah, K.A. (1997), 'Is the Post- in Postmodernism the Post- in Postcolonial?', in P. Mongia (ed.), *Contemporary Postcolonial Theory: A Reader* (London: Arnold).

Berlant, L. and Warner, M. (1995), 'What Does Queer Theory Teach Us About "X"?', *PMLA* 110:3, 343–9.

Berry, C. (2005), 'Coalition Politics, or, Queer Matters Today', *Inter-Asia Cultural Studies* 6:2, 305–7.

Bourdieu, P. (1993), *The Field of Cultural Production: Essays on Art and Literature*, (ed.) R. Johnson (Cambridge: Polity Press).

Chang, S.-S.Y. (1993), *Modernism and the Nativist Resistance: Contemporary Chinese Fiction from Taiwan* (Durham, NC and London: Duke University Press).

Chao, Y.-N.A. (2001), 'Taiwan tongzhi yanjiu de huigu yu zhanwang: yige guanyu wenhua shengchan de fenxi' [Looking Back at and Looking Ahead of Taiwan's Tongzhi Studies: An Analysis on Cultural Production], in Kuan-hsing Chen (ed.), *Wenhua yanjiu zai Taiwan* [*Cultural Studies in Taiwan*] (Taipei: Juliu).

Chen, K.-H. (2001), 'America in East Asia: The Club 51 Syndrome', *New Left Review* 12, 73–87.

Chi, T.-W. (1997), 'Ku'er lun: sikao dangdai Taiwan ku'er yu ku'er wenxue' [On Queer: Reflections on Contemporary Taiwan Queer and Queer Literature], in Ta-wei Chi (ed.), *Ku'er qishilu: dangdai Taiwan Queer lunshu duben* [*Queer Archipelago: A Reader of the Queer Discourses in Taiwan*] (Taipei: Yuanzun Wenhua).

Chou, W.-S. (2000), *Tongzhi: Politics of Same-sex Eroticism in Chinese Societies* (New York: The Haworth Press).

Chow, R. (1993), *Writing Diaspora: Tactics of Intervention in Contemporary Cultural Studies* (Bloomington and Indianapolis, IN: Indiana University Press).

Chu, Y.-H. (1996), 'Cong bingli dao zhenglüe: Gaowai yige shehuixue dianfan' [From Pathology to Politics: Queering a Sociological Paradigm], *Taiwan shehui yanjiu jikan* [*Taiwan: A Radical Quarterly in Social Studies*] 24,109–41.

Chung-Wai Literary Monthly [Zhongwai wenxue] (June 1996), special issue on 'Tongzhi lunshu/Queer Studies'.

—— (August 1997), special issue on 'Yanyi xing yu xingbie: ku'er xiaoshuo yu yanjiu/Proliferating Sexual and Gender Differences: Queer Study and Queer Fiction'.

—— (May 1998), special issue on 'Guaitai qingyuxue/Queer Sexuality'.

—— (August 2003), special issue on 'Tongzhi zaixian/Queer Re(-)presentation'.

Clifford, J. (1997), 'Diasporas', in M. Guibernau and J. Rex (eds), *The Ethnicity Reader: Nationalism, Multiculturalism and Migration* (Cambridge: Polity).

De Lauretis, T. (ed.), 'Queer Theory: Lesbian and Gay Sexualities', a special issue of *differences: A Journal of Feminist Cultural Studies* 3:2.

Duyvendak, J.W. (1996), 'The Depoliticization of the Dutch Gay Identity, or Why Dutch Gays Aren't Queer', in S. Seidman (ed.), *Queer Theory/Sociology* (Cambridge, MA and Oxford: Blackwell).

Eng, D.L., Halberstam, J. and Muñoz, J.E. (2005), 'What's Queer about Queer Studies Now?', a special issue of *Social Text* 84–5, 1–17.

eslitebookreview (Chengpin yuedu) (October 1994), a special issue on 'Tongxinglian' [Homosexuality].

Fung, R. (1995), 'The Trouble with "Asians"', in M. Dorenkamp and R. Henke (eds), *Negotiating Lesbian and Gay Subjects* (New York and London).

Grossman, A. (ed.) (2000), *Queer Asian Cinema: Shadows in the Shade* (New York: Harrington Park Press).

Hall, D.E. (2003), *Queer Theories* (Basingstoke: Palgrave Macmillan).

Hershatter, G. (2004), 'State of the Field: Women in China's Long Twentieth Century', *The Journal of Asian Studies* 63:4, 991–1065.

Inter-Asia Cultural Studies (2005), special section on 'Re-placing Queer Studies: Reflections on the Queer Matters Conference (King's College, London, May 2004)', 6:2, 299–311.

Intersections: Gender, History and Culture in the Asian Context (2006), special issue on 'Queer Japan', 12.

Isle Margin [Daoyu bianyuan] (January 1994), special issue on 'KU'ER QUEER'.

Jackson, P.A., Martin, F. and McLelland, M. (2005), 'AsiaPacifiQueer: An Introduction', *Inter-Asia Cultural Studies* 6:2, 299–301.

Jagose, A. (1996), *Queer Theory* (Victoria: Melbourne University Press).

Ka, W.-B. (1997), 'Shenme shi ku'er? Seqing guozu' [What is Queer? Erotic Nation], in T.-W. Chi (ed.), *Ku'er qishilu: dangdai Taiwan Queer lunshu duben* [*Queer Archipelago: A Reader of the Queer Discourses in Taiwan*] (Taipei: Yuanzun Wenhua).

Kuzniar, A. (2000), *The Queer German Cinema* (Stanford, CA: Stanford University Press).

Lee, W.C. (2004), 'Just What Is It That Makes the Term "Global-Local" So Widely Cited, Yet So Annoying?', in G. Mosquera and J. Fisher (eds), *Over There: International Perspectives on Art and Culture* (New York: New Museum of Contemporary Art, and Cambridge, MA and London: MIT Press).

Leung, H.H.-S. (2005), 'Queer Matters, What Else Matters?', *Inter-Asia Cultural Studies*, 6:2, 303–5.

Li, Y. (trans.) (2003) *Ku'er lilun* [Queer Theory] (Beijing: Wenhua yishu shubanshe).

Lim, S.H. (2007), 'Queering Chineseness: Searching for Roots and the Politics of Shame in (Post)Colonial Singapore', in E. Jurriens and J. de Kloet (eds), *Cosmopatriots: On Distant Belongings and Close Encounters* (Amsterdam and New York: Rodopi).

—— (2008), 'How to be Queer in Taiwan: Translation, Appropriation and the Construction of a Queer Identity in Taiwan', in P.A. Jackson, M. McLelland, F. Martin and A. Yue (eds), *AsiaPacifiQueer: Rethinking Gender and Sexuality in the Asia-Pacific* (Urbana and Chicago, IL: University of Illinois Press).

Liu, H.-L. (1995), *Translingual Practice: Literature, National Culture and Translated Modernity – China 1900–1937* (Stanford, CA: Stanford University Press).

Liu, J.-P. (2001), 'Cong "dianwu" tanqi: zai "Zhongwenxi" shang xing/bie yanjiu xiangguan kecheng' [Speaking of 'Contamination': Offering Gender and Sexuality Studies-related Courses in 'Chinese Department'], in K.-H. Chen (ed.), *Wenhua yanjiu zai Taiwan* [Cultural Studies in Taiwan] (Taipei: Juliu).

Martin, F. (2003), *Situating Sexualities: Queer Representation in Taiwanese Fiction, Film and Public Culture* (Hong Kong: Hong Kong University Press).

Mercer, K. (1990), 'Black Art and the Burden of Representation', *Third Text* 10, 61–78.

Mizielinska, J. (2006), 'Queering Moominland: The Problems of Translating Queer Theory into a Non-American Context', *SQS: The International Journal of Queer Studies in Finland* 1, 87–104.

Newsletter of the Research Center of Gender and Space [Xingbie yu kongjian yanjiu tongxun] (July 1998), special issue on 'Tongzhi kongjian' [Tongzhi Space].

Patton, C. (2002), 'Stealth Bombers of Desire: The Globalization of "Alterity" in Emerging Democracies', in A. Cruz-Malave and M.F. Manalansan IV (eds), *Queer Globalizations: Citizenship and the Afterlife of Colonialism* (New York: New York University Press).

Said, E.W. (1991), 'Travelling Theory', *The World, the Text, and the Critic* (London: Vintage).

Sang, T.-L.D. (2003), *The Emerging Lesbian: Female Same-Sex Desire in Modern China* (Chicago, IL and London: University of Chicago Press).

Sedgwick, E.K. (1993), *Tendencies* (Durham, NC: Duke University Press).

Shih, S.-M. (2000), 'Globalisation and Minoritisation: Ang Lee and the Politics of Flexibility', *New Formations* 40, 86–101.

Shimizu, A. (2005), 'The Catch in Indigenousness, or What is Wrong with "Asian Queers"', *Inter-Asia Cultural Studies* 6:2, 301–3.

Sullivan, N. (2003), *A Critical Introduction to Queer Theory* (Edinburgh: Edinburgh University Press).

Tan, C.K. (2001), 'Transcending Sexual Nationalism and Colonialism: Cultural Hybridization as Process of Sexual Politics in '90s Taiwan', in J.C. Hawley (ed.), *Postcolonial, Queer: Theoretical Intersections* (Albany, NY: State University of New York Press).

Teng, J.E. (2004), *Taiwan's Imagined Geography: Chinese Colonial Travel Writing and Pictures, 1683–1895* (Cambridge, MA and London: Harvard University Asia Center).

Turner, W.B. (2000), *A Genealogy of Queer Theory* (Philadelphia, PA: Temple University Press).

Unitas [Lianhe wenxue] (February 1997), special issue on 'Tongzhi xue, tongzhi wenxue' [Tongzhi studies, tongzhi literature].

Wachman, A.M. (1994), *Taiwan: National Identity and Democratization* (Armonk, NY and London: M.E. Sharpe).

Warner, M. (1993), 'Introduction', in M. Warner (ed.), *Fear of a Queer Planet: Queer Politics and Social Theory* (Minneapolis, MN and London: University of Minnesota Press).

Working Papers in Gender/Sexuality Studies [Xing/bie yanjiu] (September 1998), special issue on 'Ku'er: Lilun yu zhengzhi' [Queer Politics and Queer Theory].

Queer Theory Meets Archaeology: Disrupting Epistemological Privilege and Heteronormativity in Constructing the Past

Thomas A. Dowson

Introduction

The title of this contribution, as I am sure most readers will be aware, is an overt reference to what for me was an influential set of essays edited by Elizabeth Weed and Naomi Schor entitled *Feminism meets Queer Theory* and published in 1997. Although the relationship between queer theory and archaeology is not, and can never be, anything like that of feminism to queer theory, I think the inclusion of this chapter in this research companion does present an opportunity to be grasped. So, rather than choosing to connote 'a staging of strangeness and unpredictability' as Weed and Schor have done, I use this chapter to stage an introduction of the sexual politics of the past, or more accurately those of the past in the present, in an arena where the past often serves as little more than a handmaiden to the history of the West.

As with many other academic disciplines there have been a few young and ambitious archaeologists who have used queer theory to offer new insights to our interpretation of the past and/or the practice of archaeology. In 2004 queer theory's potential was seized upon by the student organisers of the annual Chacmool conference hosted by the Archaeology Department of the University of Calgary, Canada. For nearly forty years now a group of students each year organises a conference with a specific theme that reflects emerging and influential trends in archaeology; in 2004 the conference was called 'Que(e)rying Archaeology'. Not surprisingly, not all members of the academic staff were supportive of the idea when it was initially proposed. But the department and its students went on to produce a conference that provided a safe academic environment for a number of 'queer' students and scholars from all over the world to meet and share ideas about the past that up until then at least would have been either not permissible in other contexts or simply ridiculed.

Chacmool 2004 was an important conference for gender studies in archaeology. In a sense it marked queer theory's broader acceptance in the discipline. But, the many and varied papers that were presented at the conference also demonstrated how *queer* was being negotiated by archaeologists. It was abundantly clear that 'queer' was being seen as an umbrella term that encompasses a wide variety of sexual identities. And it felt as if it was the task of queer archaeologists to demonstrate that sexual 'deviants' did in fact exist in the past. While there is certainly political mileage to such a project, there is more to queering archaeology than identifying all manner of fags, dykes, bis and trannies in past communities. Archaeology can do so much more than provide (pre)historic precedents for contemporary sexual politics.

For many archaeologists and non-archaeologists alike the discipline of archaeology is the 'scientific' recovery of *the past* – there is only one past and it awaits the 'scientifically' trained archaeologist to unearth it and all its glories. One only has to think of the mythology that surrounds the discovery of Tutankhamen's tomb in 1922, and the enormous interest his 'treasure' still attracts today. Archaeologists all over the world are labouring away at a common goal, the complete *reconstruction* of that past. This project is so obvious in so many ways, but most noticeable in the countless and varied discoveries of 'missing links'. Humanity is conceived of as everything human beings and their communities could be, a compendium of social rules and values, and humanity's history is a progressive unfolding and realisation of these rules and values. Archaeology still comes across as being an exercise in charting the unfolding of that history. Christopher Tilley suggested that archaeology 'is a form of social practice which helps, in however minor a way, to sustain, justify and legitimate the values of a capitalist society' (1989, 107). While readily acknowledging and accepting Tilley's caveat, I do not believe much has changed since 1989. Archaeology as a disciplinary culture continues to maintain rather than challenge a Western social order. And, as Engels argued over a century ago (1884 [1972]), the family, like private property and the State, is a basic institution of capitalist society. Not surprisingly then, the family features prominently, and unquestioningly, in archaeological constructions, both popular and academic, of past communities. But, the family, like private property or the state, is not a 'natural' entity; they are all products of a historically specific set of economic and social conditions. With this emphasis on constructions of the family, I argue that one of archaeology's overall strategies has been to construct and maintain a heterosexual history of humanity. This is achieved by manipulating all aspects of archaeological practice. Queer theory, I believe, offers a set of unique positions from which to challenge such practice. Queer archaeologists must not only attempt to fill in the 'sexual' missing links, but rather also challenge all aspects of epistemological privilege founded on the heterosexual authority of archaeology.

Just as archaeologists are now sensitive to the way in which the past has been, and continues to be used to legitimise political regimes, so too they need to be sensitive to the way in which their pasts are perceived as showing the modern family to be timeless and culturally universal, and thus sanctioning a heterosexual hegemony that justifies and legitimises some of the most bigoted thinking about sexual identities; a thinking that often leads to horrific and premature endings. As archaeology underpins the heterosexual history of humanity, archaeologists need to be mindful of the discipline's complicity in Western society's institutionalised homophobia.

Autoarchaeology

On the evening of Thursday 8 October 1998 Matthew Shepard, a young gay student from the University of Wyoming in Laramie, USA, was lured out of a student bar. Two men, who led him to believe they were also gay, took him to a remote spot on a country road on the outskirts of town. As they drove him away they hit him on the head with a pistol. Matthew was then dragged from their truck, tied spread-eagle to a fence, beaten over the head with a baseball bat, burned and robbed, and finally left to die in near freezing temperatures.

Some twenty hours later Matthew was found by passing cyclists, who at first mistook his body for a scarecrow. His face was caked in blood, except for streaks that had been washed clean by his tears. He arrived at hospital in a critical condition having sustained severe head injuries; his skull was so badly fractured doctors were unable to operate. He lay on a life support system in a coma while news of this brutal attack spread around the world.

On Monday 12 October at 12:53 am Matthew Wayne Shepard died.

Beth Loffreda (2000) offers a reasoned and moving account of life and politics in the days and months following Matthew Shepard's murder. No one could have predicted the profound impact the murder of a young gay student would have nationally and internationally, let alone on the town where this awful chain of events began. When I heard the news various thoughts tumbled about in my mind: gay-bashing – fear – Laramie – archaeology. I suppose initially I silently uttered the phrase, perhaps along with other gay men and women, 'there but for the grace of God go I'. Despite the rhetoric of liberal politicians, gay and straight, homophobia is as rife and as violent now as it has ever been, perhaps more so. And yes, there are times when I feel threatened and scared. I remember thinking of two archaeology students who had 'come out' to me in confidence. I was reminded of their fears and anxieties, and the burden of ignorance they carried for their peers and family. I was reminded of my attempts to alleviate their fears. But in the face of such a gruesome tragedy my words could never be reassuring; they rang hollow and meaningless in my own ears. My heart went out to them, and the many other people negotiating the minefield of coming out. I knew only too well how trapped and even desperate some of them must have been feeling. I thought also it was inconceivable that such a savage assault could have taken place in that town, a town that, up until then, had such pleasant memories for me.

In 1992 and 1993 I visited Laramie a few times while on research leave from a post I held at the University of the Witwatersrand, South Africa. As an archaeologist I visited the Department of Anthropology at the University of Wyoming. In 1993 I gave the banquet address at the Wyoming Archaeological Society's annual conference. I met a number of friendly and interesting archaeologists in Wyoming, and I was made to feel very welcome there. In October 1998 I wondered what they were thinking. To them and the world, I was sure, archaeology seemed so far removed from the events surrounding Matthew's death that no one could possibly imagine a connection. Slowly but surely I began to realise there was indeed a connection.

During October 1998 I was writing an article for a Catalan archaeological journal, *Cota Zero*, in which I was exploring the relationship between archaeology and homosexuality (Dowson 1998). More specifically, I was reading David Halperin's *Saint Foucault: Towards a Gay Hagiography* (1995) when I heard the news of Matthew's death. It was, I believe, simultaneously hearing the news from the United States and my reading of Halperin's book that caused two aspects of my life to collide. At once, I was fearful of and angry at the homophobia that resulted specifically in Matthew's death and the homophobia we all confront regularly. But also I was reading Halperin's account of his experiences as a 'gay' academic. It was then that I started to question my responsibilities as an archaeologist in the light of my sexuality. Something I had not allowed myself to do in any way previously.

In fact, for some time after 'coming out' I emphatically believed my sexuality had absolutely nothing to do with my being an archaeologist. And with the growing interest in gender studies in archaeology then, I was determined not to get involved. I know a number of lesbian, gay, bisexual and transgendered colleagues, in various disciplines, who have had, and still have, similar reactions. This sort of reaction does not result from being unsympathetic towards issues of gender. Rather, it derives from an unspoken social rule whereby academic men and women are forced to maintain an authority to act by denying or downplaying their 'deviant' sexuality. Although writing specifically of himself and his intellectual and political relationship to Foucault, but acknowledging a much wider social relevance, Halperin explicitly expresses the *status quo* many if not all of us gay, lesbian and bisexual academics find ourselves in. We all share the problem of how to:

> ... *acquire and maintain the authority to speak, to be heard, and to be taken seriously without denying or bracketing [our] gayness. It's not just a matter of being publicly or visibly out; it's a matter of being able to devise and to preserve a positive, undemonised connection between [our] gayness and [our] scholarly or critical authority. That problem of authorisation ... dramatises the more general social and discursive predicament of lesbians and gay men in a world where a claimed homosexual identity operates as an instant disqualification, exposes you to accusations of pathology and partisanship ... and grants everyone else an absolute epistemological privilege over you.* (Halperin 1995, 8)

Here Halperin is drawing on Eve Kosofsky Sedgwick's analysis of the *Epistemology of the Closet* (1990). Sedgwick explores the consequences of the binary distinction between heterosexuality and homosexuality that began to be the primary defining characteristic of men and women from the end of the nineteenth century onwards. Sedgwick argues that the distinction resulted from a homophobic desire to devalue one of those oppositions. Consequently, homosexuality is not symmetrically related to heterosexuality – it is subordinate and marginal, but necessary to construct meaning and value in heterosexuality (1990, 9–10). In her ground-breaking study Sedgwick argues this asymmetrical relationship between homosexuality and heterosexuality has been at the heart of every form of representation since the start of the twentieth century, and the disciplinary culture of archaeology is not immune from such social pressures.

My strategy to preserve a positive connection between my scholarly authority and my sexuality, like so many other academics, was to distance my research from dealing with issues of gender. I was under the impression that my explicit researching of gender relations in archaeology would only serve to draw attention to my sexuality, and reinforce my colleagues' (misguided) sense of epistemological privilege. I was explicitly, and in some cases gently, told by some very liberal-minded archaeologists not to be 'too vocal' about my sexuality. While I was prepared to 'come out', it seemed obvious to me that I could only do so by downplaying my sexuality.

When homosexual men and women 'come out' of the 'closet' there is the widely held view they are emerging into a world of unfettered liberty. Sadly, as Sedgwick, Halperin and many others have shown, this is not the case; 'the closet' is not some personally perceived space; it is a product of complex power relations. And one cannot magically emerge from those power relations: 'To come out is precisely to expose oneself to a different set of dangers and constraints' (Halperin 1995, 30). In archaeology those dangers and constraints manifest themselves in a powerfully and universally masculinist disciplinary culture that is repeatedly negotiated in all aspects of professional archaeological practice, not just the popular representations of the discipline one encounters in such fictional characters as Indiana Jones and Lara Croft. I now appreciate I did not need to specifically address issues of gender to be dismissed – whatever I wrote or said was easily dismissed because of an authority based on the superiority of heterosexuality. And again from Halperin:

> … as I discovered to my cost … if you are known to be lesbian or gay your very openness, far from pre-empting malicious gossip about your sexuality, simply exposes you to the possibility that, no matter what you actually do, people can say absolutely whatever they like about you in the well-grounded confidence that it will be credited. (And since there is very little you can do about it, you might as well not try and ingratiate yourself by means of 'good behaviour'.) (1995, 13)

So, just as I was once no longer prepared to deny my sexuality, by the end of 1998 I was no longer prepared to compromise it either. I am now comfortable with my sexuality, and clear about how it influences my lifestyle as well as the way in which I think about and construct the past. I am proud of who I am and what I produce. But more importantly, because epistemological privilege in archaeology is unequivocally related to homophobia (see also She 2000; Claassen 2000), I now actively challenge the manner in which epistemological privilege is negotiated in archaeology. Not just as it affects me, or other supposedly sexually deviant archaeologists, but also the way in which the very practice of archaeology authorises an entirely heterosexual history of humanity.

To mount such a challenge I draw on that diverse body of critical thinking we know of as queer theory. I adopt, like scholars such as Sedgwick and Halperin, a Foucauldian analysis, by refusing to engage with the content of archaeological discourse. If I can not succeed with 'good behaviour' (good = heterosexual) I am going to be as queer as I possibly can. I analyse the homophobic/heteronormative discourse of archaeology in terms of its overall strategies. Instead of trying to play the game of archaeology harder, better, more intelligently or more truthfully (the way in which the discipline has developed until now), I look at the rules of archaeology to find out 'how the game is set up, on what terms most favourable to whom, with what consequences for which of its players' (Halperin 1995, 38).

I deconstruct the way in which epistemological privilege is produced and recursively re-produced, and therefore constantly maintained in archaeology. I recognise its control in three crucial aspects of the disciplinary culture. First, the game of archaeological discourse, to develop Halperin's metaphor, is set up by determining who has the authority to act and speak. Secondly, those authoritative voices require their own favourable terms and methods, the rules of the game, by which to act in an authoritative manner. And finally, those authoritative actions produce restricted constructions of the past.

A number of archaeologists are indeed committed to socio-political critique of the disciplinary culture of archaeology; what Wylie (1999, 555) has identified as 'equity' and 'content' critiques. Studies of equity issues include analyses of the status of women within the discipline, but also the analysis of the impact of class, race and nationalism on archaeological practice. Content critiques on the other hand expose bias founded on sex, race, class and nationality in our constructions of the past; how men's activities such as hunting are privileged over those of women for example. But, as Wylie (1999, 555) points out, 'sociopolitical critics in archaeology have tended to side-step explanatory questions about how the silences and stereotypes [that these critiques] delineate are produced or why they persist.' Equity critiques have rarely been deployed to show how the content of archaeological knowledge is produced, and, *vice versa*, content critiques rarely make a connection between the content of archaeological knowledge and specific equity issues. By attending to the overall strategies of archaeological discourse in the manner outlined above we are able to reveal why and how at least some of those silences and stereotypes persist. I begin my queering of archaeology by examining each of the three aspects of disciplinary authority in turn.

Authoritative Actors

In a recent book that offers a 'new' interpretation of European Palaeolithic cave art, Guthrie (2005) produces what must surely be the most obvious example in archaeology of the way in which someone's intellectual authority is judged on the basis of their sexuality. Guthrie draws to our attention the anatomical representations of female genitalia on carved statuettes of the female body from the European Stone Age. The artists of these statuettes 'incorrectly' represented the vulva pointing forward. We are asked to compare these images with Leonardo da Vinci's well-known sketch that depicts a cross-section through the bodies of a male and female couple engaged in sexual intercourse. Despite the fact that Leonardo's woman is reclining backwards, Guthrie maintains that Leonardo da Vinci's drawing of the female body is anatomically incorrect in the same way as the statuettes of the Stone Age artists. He suggests that Stone Age artists got the anatomy of the female form wrong because they were inexperienced, adolescent boys.

We are told, 'Leonardo da Vinci made the same mistake in adulthood, but perhaps for the same reason of inexperience' (Guthrie 2005, 358). There is surely no need to explain that what Guthrie means by Leonardo's 'inexperience' is his homosexuality. Because da Vinci is generally thought to have been homosexual it is assumed he would not have had accurate knowledge of female anatomy. Leonardo's 'inexperience' is then used to challenge his claims to knowledge. That the artist conducted numerous dissections of the human body is not important; the fact that he had what most think of as a deviant sexuality is. As obvious and blatant as this example may be, Guthrie can only really get away with it because Leonardo da Vinci is far removed and somewhat distant from the day-to-day practice of archaeology. Dismissing the claims to knowledge on the basis of their sexuality, as overtly as Guthrie's example, is only one way in which epistemological privilege is negotiated in archaeology. Epistemological privilege is more frequently exercised in much more subtle, but no less harmful, ways: homosexual men and women are treated less favourably in comparison to their heterosexual colleagues.

One moving and powerful autobiographical testimony that demonstrates how a homosexual identity has impacted on the life of one professional female archaeologist is provided in a recent anonymous contribution (She 2000). No one can dismiss this account. She gives us an immediate and contemporary account of how being an 'out' lesbian has affected her education and training as an archaeologist, and her subsequent career in archaeology. Being open about her sexuality did not stop the homophobia, from both men and women, and has denied her access to certain opportunities, such as candidacy for professional office. She's account is not an isolated one; there are many more – all either anecdotal or anonymous.

In my own experience as an 'out' queer academic I identify with much of what She has experienced. When applying for promotion, for example, I have been denied support required from senior male colleagues because these men were more concerned with how their supporting a gay man would appear to the overt masculinist culture of the faculty. These men were not merely judgemental about any impact my use of queer theory may or may not have had in archaeology; they simply denied any knowledge of my publications. And of course this was not thought unusual, why should it be? After all, they were heterosexual men. For these men, that my editing an issue of one of the world's leading archaeology journals, *World Archaeology*, and calling that issue *Queer Archaeologies* (Dowson 2000) (which provided a source of inspiration for the internationally-renowned

Chacmool Conference) had no bearing on my abilities as an archaeologist. Also, when suffering from depression this was dismissed as a result of my being HIV+ (I am in fact HIV-, but as a gay man rumours about my HIV status were unquestioned – it is after all not that surprising for a gay man to be HIV+, in fact a lot of bigoted individuals expect it), and had nothing to do with the fact (acknowledged in writing by the Dean) that I was teaching significantly more and undertaking more administrative duties than any of my colleagues. That this workload had a negative effect on my personal life was dismissed because, as the Head of Department exclaimed 'I cannot be expected to help you there!' And yet allowances are always being made for married and unmarried heterosexual staff when their workloads affect their domestic situations.

It is also painfully clear in She's account that 'out' academics are not the only persons to be affected by the openness of their sexuality: 'The knowledge of my sexuality has charted who constitutes my professional network, and what professionals my students have immediate access to' (2000, 172). Homophobia, of both homosexual men and women, is as obvious in archaeology as it is in any other aspect of society, and it continues to play a significant role in shaping the character of archaeology by influencing who gets to practice and succeed in archaeology (Claassen 2000).

Authoritative Methods

Feminist theorists have convincingly demonstrated that the normative and objectivist nature of scientific methods are the result of masculinist practice (Harding 1986; 1987; Longino 1987; 1990). A number of feminist archaeologists have similarly related normative practice in archaeology with masculinist practice within the discipline (Wylie 1999; 2002). It is this masculinist practice that dictates how the rules of the archaeological game are set up and maintained. But I argue that it is not only masculinist, it is heterosexist.

The study of prehistoric rock art, those images painted and/or engraved on cave walls, rock shelters or on rocks in boulder fields the world over, has always occupied a somewhat marginal role in archaeology (Dowson 1993; Lewis-Williams 1993; Whitley 1997). In Palaeolithic archaeologies, for instance, the excavation and analysis of stone tool assemblages and the bones of animals is the dominant focus of attention, while the images painted and engraved on the rock shelters from which these remains are recovered receive little or no attention. Rock art is simply not something mainstream archaeologists study. Part of the reason may lie in the way in which artists and art are stereotypically perceived in Western society today. Artists are thought to be eccentric individuals, whose work is inspired by some form of divine inspiration and has no significant impact on our lives (Wolff 1981). Such misconceptions of artists and their work have strongly influenced archaeological constructions of prehistoric and ancient artistic practices and traditions. And the study of rock art is no different. The images painted onto and engraved into rock surfaces are perceived to be snapshots of prehistoric artists spiriting away idle hours. These images, then, can have little value. They may offer insights into how artefacts might have been used in the past, such is the techno-centric nature of much archaeological research, Palaeolithic archaeology in particular, but nothing more.

This misconception of artists and their work is, however, not sufficient to explain why archaeologists have ignored rock art. Despite a growing body of theoretically and methodologically sophisticated research on rock art traditions around the world (for three exceptional introductions, see Chippindale and Taçon 1998; Whitley 2001; Helskog 2001), prehistoric imagery still remains irrelevant for most mainstream archaeologists. Most if not all archaeologists and rock art researchers accept there are numerous methodological problems in any attempt at incorporating rock art imagery in our efforts to develop our understandings of prehistoric communities. But there is one specific problem that is cited again and again as the final blow:

> *Numerous difficulties beset viewing rock art as the key to constructing San history, but the one which particularly concerns my research programme is the lack of a firm chronological context for the majority of the Natal Drakensberg paintings. Nonetheless, I would like to make it clear that I believe that the paintings form part of the San historical process, and that if, or more positively when, we are able to date them, they will be an important component in constructing these historical processes. (Mazel 1993, 890)*

Rock art, as data for constructing the past, is not afforded the same status as other excavated materials, because it 'lacks a firm chronological framework'. (This statement does beg the question: where in archaeology is there a firm chronological framework?) The chronocentrism that underwrites this dismissive view derives, I argue, from the very core of masculinist practice in archaeology. Dating is a key component of most archaeological narratives, particularly those narratives associated with origins – which are decidedly masculinist in character (Conkey and Williams 1991).

In Western society, the male body is the desirable norm, and the woman's lack of the phallus is the key factor determining their intellectual and moral difference from men. The patriarchal order is structured around the primacy of the phallus as the signifier of difference. This allows men to misidentify their status and position in terms of women. Lack of the phallus is equated with a lack of power and control in our phallocentric world. Similarly, in archaeology, chronology is of paramount importance. But crucially for this discussion about the marginalisation of rock art chronology is the primary signifier of difference between mainstream archaeology and rock art. In no way am I suggesting that dating is unimportant. Rather, I challenge the normative view, widely held in archaeology, that without a 'firm chronological framework', constructions of the past are at best, and only for a few scholars, inferior and meaningless, or, worse still and this applies to most archaeologists, entirely impossible.

Archaeologists have power and control over the past because it is they who decide what constitute acceptable methodologies. Artefact assemblages, stone tools and animal bones for example, are excavated from different archaeological deposits one on top of the other. As a result, it is possible to construct from these stratified relationships a chronological framework: artefact Y is older than artefact X because Y was found in a deposit underneath X, and with highly sophisticated (but not free of controversy) scientific techniques these deposits and artefacts can be dated with varying degrees of precision. Unfortunately, the situation I have just very simply, but not inaccurately, outlined, does not pertain to rock art imagery. And where scholars have attempted to construct a chronological framework, these have been highly contentious, and often easily dismissed. So, without a chronology rock art research is rendered irrelevant and powerless. Chronocentrism is, I argue, as one of the rules that determine how the past is constructed, indicative of the phallocentric nature of heterosexist archaeology.[1]

Authoritative Constructions

I introduce this section by briefly returning to Guthrie's reference to Leonardo da Vinci's sexuality discussed above, if only to demonstrate the obviousness of the point I wish to make here. Remember Guthrie argues that images of women in the cave art of prehistoric Europe are anatomically incorrect – showing the artist has a lack of experience with the female body. He draws an analogy with Leonardo da Vinci's anatomical drawing of a male and female engaged in sexual intercourse – in which the female body is anatomically inaccurate. Guthrie implies this inexperience is a result of da Vinci's homosexuality and lack of first-hand experience with women. Palaeolithic artists' lack of experience of the female body (and of animals, etc), on the other hand, is a result of their immaturity: cave artists were adolescent boys fantasising about women and the hunt. Nowhere is it even considered that perhaps these artists were like da Vinci – homosexual – not even to dismiss the idea. Although such a suggestion is almost certainly wildly incorrect, the argument would in fact be more logical than that of Guthrie's. What this example shows is that the past is *always already heterosexual*. But there are more serious, less absurd, examples than this.

In 1964 a Fifth Dynasty tomb built for two men was discovered in Lower Egypt (Basta 1979; Moussa and Altenmüller 1977; Baines 1985; Reeder 1993; 2000). In the bas reliefs of the tomb Niankhkhnum and Khnumhotep are often depicted in intimate postures (Figure 16.1). But nowhere are there any inscriptions that reveal the exact nature of their relationship. The 'exaggerated affection' these two men display was not considered normal by archaeologists, and therefore required explanation. Various suggestions were proposed. For instance, they were thought

---

1   For a discussion of phallocentricism in other aspects of archaeological practice see Baker 1997.

Figure 16.1 Niankhkhnum and Khnumhotep in an intimate embrace

Source: Photograph by Greg Reeder, reproduced here with permission.

to depict twin brothers, or perhaps two men who were on an equal footing with one another, sharing similar values and holding the same power. The representation of intimacy between the two men was thought to be symbolic of their closeness during their time together on earth. The questionable becomes acceptable – the unspeakable is neatly avoided.

Representations of intimacy between men and women also exist in other Fourth, Fifth and Sixth Dynasty tombs. But these are acceptable and require no explanation. Obviously they represent males and females in marital relationships. Archaeologists then identify an iconographic canon, and suggest it was deployed by dynastic artists to represent husbands and wives (Cherpion 1995). But, by analysing the iconography used to portray Niankhkhnum and Khnumhotep, rather than making judgemental observations, Greg Reeder (2000), an independent, gay writer (i.e. not a normatively trained archaeologist), has shown that the same canon was used to depict these two men as was used supposedly to represent husband and wife at the same time. But, the idea that Niankhkhnum and Khnumhotep might have been a same-sex couple has never been entertained until now, not even in very recent studies of homosexuality in Ancient Egypt (Parkinson 1995). Given the overt display of their relationship in their tomb, and the lack of any other evidence that might have revealed the nature of their relationship, we can only speculate as to the nature of that relationship.

Critiques such as Reeder's are often dismissed as being political correctness run riot. In referring to Reeder's research Lyn Meskell (2002, 145) rather gratuitously asserted that 'there has been a tendency to push the ancient data in the service of contemporary sexual politics, irrespective of the evidence (e.g. Reeder 2000)'. There is no reasoned critique of Reeder's analysis; such a critique is indeed unnecessary. Reeder and others are required to produce closely argued analyses for why a particular relationship should be seen as homosexual, whereas heterosexual identities are merely and credibly presumed. The rules of the game of archaeology, and who plays the game, are predetermined. It is enough to dismiss Reeder as gay to belittle and ignore what he has to contribute.

The point I would now make in response to Meskell's offhand dismissal of Reeder's critique is similar if not identical to a point Meskell herself has already made. In an earlier publication responding to critics of those authors whose research of ancient peoples was influenced by Foucault, Meskell (1999, 92–3) writes:

> ... *personal motivations have been called into question and fingers have been pointed at various groups in the gay, feminist and other radical social movements who have appropriated elements of Foucault's theory or historical research in order to advance their respective political struggles (Lamour et al 1998a, 12). Why such subjectivities should be singled out against other political positions surprises me, as if we can ever be objective in our interests or arguments, and at least in this case feminists and queer theorists have been up front in their politics.*

In her later publication Meskell (2002) does not offer the same support to Reeder; in fact, she becomes one of those pointing the fingers at a gay writer, accusing him of using archaeology to service contemporary sexual politics. There is no clue to the apparent change of heart. But, because the heterosexual authority of archaeology protects her, Meskell is not required to explain herself. The reason for the difference is that Reeder is not an archaeologist, and he does not play the game of archaeology as Meskell would. Contrary to what Meskell says about the paper, Reeder's analysis of the tomb is thorough in its attention to detail; he presents us with a straightforward challenge to Egyptian archaeology.

In the context of this discussion of the way in which archaeology maintains a heterosexual authority, whether or not the representations of intimacy between Niankhkhnum and Khnumhotep are evidence for some form of same-sex desire or sexuality is of secondary unimportance. What Meskell and others fail to accept is that Reeder's study shows there exists an unequivocal heterosexist bias in archaeological interpretation of this particular tomb. Either, the two men did have an intimate, perhaps accepted, sexual relationship, in which case archaeologists would need to rethink the nature of marital relationships in Ancient Egypt at this time. Or, Niankhkhnum's and Khnumhotep's relationship was not sexual, in which case the accepted iconographic analysis that reveals a heterosexual, marital relationship is flawed and misleading. Reeder does not provide the answer to this dilemma; he does not claim to do so. But he does draw attention to what is an obvious problem in Egyptology specifically, but archaeology more generally.

The discourse surrounding the archaeology of these tombs (one depicting intimate scenes between two men, and others depicting identical scenes between men and women) from ancient Egypt provides evidence for one of archaeology's overall strategies: to construct and maintain unquestioningly a heterosexual history of humanity. The Reeder–Meskell interchange shows quite succinctly how epistemological privilege is produced and recursively reproduced in archaeology (see also Dowson 2008). And because of the presumption of heterosexuality, the elaborate and unsubstantiated hypotheses of 'twinship' or 'metaphorical brothers' are permissible – more palatable is perhaps more accurate. And, it is the epistemological privilege in archaeology that enables Reeder's research to be simply dismissed as being in the service of contemporary sexual politics. The superficial dismissal of Reeder's work shows that the rules of the archaeological game are stacked in favour of maintaining the heterosexual bias.

Challenging Epistemological Privilege and Heteronormativity

The three aspects of archaeological practice I have discussed comprise the overall strategies of a normative archaeology that is not only masculinist in character but also heterosexist. These are the authoritative standards by which all archaeological research is measured, and they constitute the normative basis on which the practice of much archaeology continues to be conducted, and on which all archaeology is judged. In fact 'normativity' has had a long and entrenched position in archaeological thinking. The poststructuralist trends of the 1980s may have introduced a more critical and self-reflexive approach to archaeology, but none of those critiques managed to step away from the heteronormative. An entirely new attitude in archaeology is required, for which I believe queer theory provides some direction.

Queer theory actively and explicitly disrupts the heteronormativity of scientific practice. 'Queer' began as a challenge to essentialist constructions of a 'gay' identity. In contrast to gay and lesbian identity, queer identity is not based on a notion of a stable truth or reality. As Halperin explains '"queer" does not name some natural kind or refer to some determinate object; it acquires its meaning from its oppositional relation to the norm. Queer is by definition *whatever is at odds* with the normal, the legitimate, the dominant. *There is nothing in particular to which it necessarily refers*' (1995, 62; emphasis in original). Queer theory is not like a theory in the scientific use of the word in that it does not provide a system of ideas used to explain something, as in Marxist theory or Einstein's theory of relativity. Queer theory does not provide a positivity, rather 'a positionality *vis-à-vis* the normative' (Halperin 1995, 62), a way of producing reflection, a way of taking a stand *vis-à-vis* an authoritative standard.

To affect that positionality queer theory 'takes on various shapes, risks, ambitions and ambivalences in various contexts' (Berlant and Warner 1995, 343). In so doing, it allows for a 'reordering [of] the relations among sexual behaviours, erotic identities, constructions of gender, forms of knowledge, regimes of enunciation, logics of representation, modes of self-constitution, and practices of community – for restructuring, that is, the relations among power, truth, and desire' (Halperin 1995, 62; see also de Lauretis 1991). Queer theory is thus very definitely not restricted to homosexual men and women, but to anyone who feels their position (sexual, intellectual or cultural) to be marginalised. The queer position then is no longer a marginal one considered deviant or pathological; but rather multiple positions within many more possible positions – all equally valid.

These brief comments inform my use of queer in the context of my attempts to construct the past. Queering archaeology does not involve looking for homosexuals, or any other supposed sexual deviant for that matter, in the past. Nor is it concerned with the origins of homosexuality. Queering archaeology is actively engaged in moving away from essentialist and normative constructions of presumed and compulsory heterosexuality (male: female – deviant third sex), but also the normative character of archaeological discourse. It necessarily has to confront and disrupt the presumption of heterosexuality as the norm inherent in archaeological interpretation. Queer archaeologies are not better, more intelligent or more truthful than what has gone before – they are different – neither judgemental nor heteronormative. They are queer. As Sandra Harding points out, experiences of 'marginalised peoples are not the *answers* to questions arising either inside or outside those lives, though they are necessary to asking the best questions' (1993: 78, original emphasis). While queer archaeologies adopt what the establishment might regard as deviant practice, these constructions are no less valid and can stand up to the same close scrutiny as any other construction of the past.

Guarding Against the Normalisation of Queer Archaeology

It has often been remarked that theoretical developments come late to the discipline of archaeology. I am not so sure that this applies to the way in which 'queer theory' has been taken up by archaeologists. Queer archaeologists have been quick to recognise the potential of queer agendas and their relevance to the construction of the past as well as the contribution archaeology can provide to the continued development of these agendas. Archaeology no longer simply provides the illustrations for the covers of monographs in this field (Butler 1993). On the contrary, the way in which archaeologists have explored the embodied lives of prehistoric and ancient peoples from all corners of the world has added significantly to our understanding of the diversity of the human experience, and provided theoretical insights into cultural comparisons in terms of presenting lived experiences within the context of cultural difference (Meskell and Joyce 2003). But where to next?

Queer archaeology has provided a forceful and compelling challenge to the presumption of heterosexuality – but queering archaeology must be so much more than identifying the diversity of human sexual experience. In his critique of attempts to display queer histories and public culture, Robert Mills rightly points out that 'the still nascent field of queer archaeology has barely even begun to attend to the complexity of locating queerness in material culture' (2006, 260). Archaeologists are now starting to explore materiality in ways that make the old school sit back and shake their head; and certainly queer theory has the potential to inform that discussion. As much as I agree with Mills, to identify specific areas to be queered in an attempt to provide a direction for the future of queer archaeology runs counter to the queer agenda. Just as queer theory has become comfortably institutionalised within the academy, it is not surprising that queer archaeology is similarly accepted by archaeologists. We need no longer worry that queer sessions at conferences will not be accepted; in fact they are now becoming an essential ingredient. While 'queer' is a harmless qualifier of 'theory' (Halperin 2003), so too in archaeology 'queer' is little more than a harmless addition to gender archaeology. By focusing on sex and sexuality, at the expense of broader issues of archaeological practice, queer archaeology has become an obvious extension of gender/feminist archaeology. As crucial as challenging the heterosexual history of humanity is (see Schmidt and Voss 2000) we are failing to challenge the very practices in archaeology that produced that heterosexual history of humanity in the first place, and maintain that history even when it is challenged. The normalisation of 'queer archaeology' merely serves to provide *deviance* with a (pre)history. If queer archaeology:

> ... is going to have the sort of future worth cherishing, we will have to find ways of renewing its radical potential – and by that I mean not devising some new and more avant-garde theoretical formulation of it but quite concretely, reinventing its capacity to startle, to surprise, to help us think what has not yet been thought. (Halperin 2003, 343)

Suggested Further Reading

Dowson, T.A. (ed.) (2000), 'Queer Archaeologies', special issue of *World Archaeology* 32:2.

——(2006), 'Archaeologists, Feminists and Queers: Sexual Politics in the Construction of the Past', in P.L. Geller and M.K. Stockett (eds), *Feminist Anthropology: Past, Present, and Future* (Philadelphia, PA: University of Pennsylvania Press).

Perry, E.M. and Joyce, R.A. (2001), 'Providing a Past for "Bodies that Matter": Judith Butler's Impact on the Archaeology of Gender', *International Journal of Sexuality and Gender Studies* 6:1–2, 63–76.

Schmidt, R.A. (2002), 'The Iceman Cometh: Queering the Archaeological Past', in E. Lewin and W.L. Leap (eds), *Out in Theory: The Emergence of Lesbian and Gay Anthropology* (Urbana, IL: University of Illinois Press).

Terendy, S.A., Lyons, N. and Kelley, J. (eds) (2008), *Que(e)rying Archaeology* (Calgary: Calgary University Press).

References

Baines, J. (1985), 'Egyptian Twins', *Orientalia* 54, 461–82.

Baker, M. (1997), 'Invisibility as a Symptom of Gender Categories in Archaeology', in J. Moore and E. Scott (eds), *Invisible People and Processes: Writing Gender and Childhood into European Archaeology* (London: Leicester University Press).

Basta, M. (1979), 'Preliminary Report on the Excavation at Saqqara (1964) and the Discovery of a Tomb from the 5th Dynasty', *Annales du Service des Antiquités de l'Égypt* 63, 1–50.

Berlant, L. and Warner, M. (1995), 'What Does Queer Theory Teach Us About "X"?', *PMLA* 110:3, 343–9.

Butler, J. (1993), *Bodies That Matter: On the Discursive Limits of 'Sex'* (New York: Routledge).

Cherpion, N. (1995), 'Sentiment Conjugal et Figuration à l'Ancien Empire', in *Kunst des Alten Reiches (Symposium im Deutschen Archäologischen Institut, Kairo, Oktober 1991)* (Mainz am Rhein: Verlag Phillipp von Zabern).

Chippindale, C. and Taçon, P.S.C. (eds) (1998), *Archaeology of Rock Art* (Cambridge: Cambridge University Press).

Claassen, C. (2000), 'Homophobia and Women Archaeologists', *World Archaeology* 32:2, 173–9.

Conkey, M.W. and Williams, S.H. (1991), 'Original Narratives: The Political Economy of Gender in Archaeology', in M. di Leonardo (ed.), *Gender at the Crossroads of Knowledge: Feminist Anthropology in the Postmodern Era* (Berkeley, CA: University of California Press).

De Lauretis, T. (1991), 'Queer Theory: Lesbian and Gay Sexualities, An Introduction', *differences: A Journal of Feminist Cultural Studies* 3:2, iii–xviii.

Dowson, T.A. (1993), 'Changing Fortunes of Southern African Archaeology: Comment on A.D. Mazel's "History"', *Antiquity* 67, 641–4.

—— (1998), 'Teoria Queer i Arqueologia', *Cota Zero* 14, 81–7.

—— (ed.) (2000), 'Queer Archaeologies', *World Archaeology* 32:2, 161–274.

—— (2008), 'Queering Sex and Gender in Ancient Egypt', in C. Graves-Brown (ed.), *Sex and Gender in Ancient Egypt: 'Don Your Wig for a Joyful Hour'* (Swansea: Classical Press of Wales).

Engels, F. (1972 [1884]), *The Origin of the Family, Private Property, and the State* (New York: Pathfinder Press).

Guthrie, R.D. (2005), *The Nature of Paleolithic Art* (Chicago, IL: The University of Chicago Press).

Halperin, D.M. (1995), *Saint Foucault: Towards a Gay Hagiography* (New York: Oxford University Press).

—— (2003), 'The Normalisation of Queer Theory', *Journal of Homosexuality* 45: 2–4, 339–43.

Harding, S. (1986), *The Science Question in Feminism* (Ithaca, NY: Cornell University Press).

—— (ed.) (1987), *Feminism and Methodology: Social Sciences Issues* (Bloomington, IN: Indiana University Press).

—— (1993), 'Rethinking Standpoint Epistemology: What is "Strong Objectivity"?', in L. Alcoff and E. Potter (eds), *Feminist Epistemologies* (New York: Routledge).

Helskog, K. (ed.) (2001), *Theoretical Perspectives in Rock Art Research* (Oslo: Novus Forlag).

Lewis-Williams, J.D. (1993), 'Southern African Archaeology in the 1990s', *South African Archaeological Bulletin* 48, 45–50.

Loffreda, B. (2000), *Losing Matt Shepard: Life and Politics in the Aftermath of Anti-Gay Murder* (New York: Columbia University Press).

Longino, H.E. (1987), 'Can There Be a Feminist Science?', *Hypatia* 2, 51–64.

—— (ed.) (1990), *Science as Social Knowledge: Values and Objectivity in Scientific Enquiry* (Princeton, NJ: Princeton University Press).

Mazel, A.D. (1993), 'Rock Art and Natal Drakensberg Hunter-Gatherer History: A Reply to Dowson', *Antiquity* 67, 889–92.

Meskell, L.M. (1999), *Archaeologies of Social Life: Age, Sex, Class et cetera in Ancient Egypt* (Oxford: Blackwell).

—— (2002), *Private Life in New Kingdom Egypt* (Princeton, NJ: Princeton University Press).

—— and Joyce, R.A. (2003), *Embodied Lives: Figuring Ancient Maya and Egyptian Experience* (London: Routledge).

Mills, R. (2006), 'History at Large: Queer is Here? Lesbian, Gay, Bisexual and Transgender Histories and Public Culture', *History Workshop Journal* 62, 253–63.

Moussa, A. and Altenmüller, H. (1977), *Das grab des Nianchchnum und Chnumhotep* (Mainz: Deutches Archäologisches Institut).

Parkinson, R.B. (1995), '"Homosexual" Desire and Middle Kingdom Literature', *The Journal of Egyptian Archaeology* 81, 57–76.

Reeder, G. (1993), 'United for Eternity', *KMT, A Modern Journal of Ancient Egypt* 4:1, 22–31.

—— (2000), 'Same-Sex Desire, Conjugal Constructs, and the Tomb of Niankhknum and Khnumhotep', *World Archaeology* 32:2, 193–208.

Schmidt, R. and Voss, B. (2000), *Archaeologies of Sexuality* (London: Routledge).

Sedgwick, E.K. (1990), *Epistemology of the Closet* (Berkeley, CA: University of California Press).

She (2000), 'Sex and a Career', *World Archaeology* 32:2, 166–72.

Tilley, C. (1989), 'Archaeology as Socio-Political Action in the Present', in V. Pinsky and A. Wylie (eds), *Critical Traditions in Contemporary Archaeology* (Cambridge: Cambridge University Press).

Weed, E. and N. Schor (eds) (1997), *Feminism Meets Queer Theory* (Bloomington, IN: Indiana University Press).

Whitly, D.S. (1997), 'Rock Art in the US: The State of the States', *International Newsletter of Rock Art* 1, 21–7.

—— (ed.) (2001), *Handbook of Rock Art Research* (Walnut Creek, CA: Altamira Press).

Wolff, J. (1981), *The Social Production of Art* (London: Macmillan).

Wylie, A. (1999), 'The Engendering of Archaeology: Refiguring Feminist Science Studies', in M. Biagioli (ed.), *The Science Studies Reader* (New York: Routledge).

—— (2002), *Thinking from Things: Essays in the Philosophy of Archaeology* (Berkeley, CA: University of California Press).

A Queer Case of Judicial Diversity: Sexuality, Law and Judicial Studies

Leslie J. Moran

Introduction

Within legal scholarship there are many different approaches to the study of law. To those legal scholars (known as black letter lawyers), dedicated to studying the meaning of statutes and judicial decisions by reference to nothing more than the words found in statutes and the judgements of the higher courts, an engagement with identity politics, social and cultural theory in general and queer theory in particular would be scholarly heresy. Other approaches to the study of law, that seek to examine the day to day operation of law, or examine its role in society more generally, or seek to understand the impact and operation of the wider political, social and cultural forces in and upon the law, are more open to the use of political, social and cultural theory in a variety of ways. It is in this context that queer has been influential. Most legal scholarship that has engaged with queer is to be found in law and society scholarship and critical legal studies.

The title of Lisa Bower's essay, 'Queer Acts and the Politics of "Direct Address": Rethinking Law, Culture and Community' (1994), captures perhaps the most important feature of queer in legal scholarship; its capacity to challenge and disrupt (or rethink) the *status quo*, be it the nature of 'law' or 'culture' or 'community' or the links between them. While the exuberance of queer activism fuelled Bower's analysis and critique of lesbian and gay civil rights identity politics in the United States, the activist inspired use of queer had a short life in legal studies. Queer's more sustained presence and impact in legal scholarship has drawn upon queer theory's close association with poststructuralism and deconstruction. Queer has provided a set of tools to refocus the agenda of critical scholarship on sexuality in law. US legal scholar Janet Halley (1991; 1993a; 1993b) was one of the first to effectively deploy deconstruction to analyse the operation of the hetero/homo binary. In this respect her major work focuses upon the infamous US Supreme Court decision of *Bowers v Hardwick* (1986) [478 US 186], in which the court refused to accept the argument that the total prohibition of sexual relations between men in private was in violation of a US citizen's constitutional rights. Carl Stychin developed a more overt and sustained queer theory analysis of US law in his monograph, *Law's Desire* (1995). By the time Australian legal scholar, Margaret Davies was publishing her brilliant analysis of property relations, 'Queer Property, Queer Persons: Self-Ownership and Beyond' (1999; on property and sexual identity, see also Moran et al. [2004]), she noted that 'queer' had lost its critical dynamic and in many respects had become just another identity category both in society in general and in legal scholarship in particular. Not defeated by this degradation she offers a dazzling analysis of the capacity of a queer critique to reveal the impact of sexuality on core legal themes and key social values of 'personality' and 'property'. Her work exemplifies queer theory's ability to expose the fundamental instability of what appear to be fixed categories and to challenge and disrupt the sexual and gender hierarchies through which heterosexuality is given shape and form though legal concepts. Finally, the substantive themes of queer inspired work in law range across the spectrum of legal issues from criminal law to civil law, human rights, to kinship and the workplace.

Further than this very brief introduction it is not my intention to proceed in this chapter by way of a more detailed analysis of the significance and use of queer theory within the wider body of existing legal scholarship. Instead I want to explore and exemplify the contribution that queer theory might make to legal studies by way of a case study. The case I have chosen is contemporary debates on judicial diversity and sexual diversity in the judiciary in particular. After a brief introduction to the judicial diversity debates I turn to explore the significance of queer theory to a study of the sexual diversity of the judiciary. Thereafter I offer an analysis of some existing data and some new data on sexuality in the judiciary generated by way of interviews I have been conducting with lawyers and judges in several legal systems. I explore two issues: first, I examine some existing data on the sexual make up of the judiciary and second, I consider the visibility and invisibility of sexuality in judicial settings.

Judicial Diversity Debates

Judicial diversity debates and reform initiatives have been a feature of several jurisdictions, such as Australia, Canada, England and Wales, Ireland, Northern Ireland, Scotland, South Africa and the United States, over many years. These debates seem to have had the highest profile and been most prolific, and the problem most intractable, in those nation states that draw upon the political/legal model of Western liberal constitutional democracy, share a legal heritage that has its origins in the English legal tradition, the Common Law, and draw their judiciary from those who practise the law. Two strands of diversity, gender and ethnicity, have dominated these debates. More recently the diversity agenda has been expanding to include disability and faith. One dimension of diversity notable by its absence is sexuality. Nothing in the general arguments used to rationalise judicial diversity, that judicial appointments should comply with equalities legislation, that the judiciary needs to be sensitive to the needs and experiences of the diverse users of the legal system, that the judiciary should be reflective of the diversity of the nation that it serves, that a diverse judiciary is a more accountable judiciary in Western legal democracies, precludes the incorporation of sexuality as a dimension of judicial diversity. One reason given for the absence of debate and initiatives relating to sexual diversity is the lack of qualitative and quantitative data on experiences and perceptions of sexuality bias in the judiciary.

It is the case that data and scholarship relating to sexuality in the context of the judiciary is very limited. No jurisdiction has official data on the sexual diversity of the judiciary and none have plans to change this state of affairs. Studies collecting and analysing experiences and perceptions of sexual orientation bias in court systems in general and the judiciary in particular are rare. However there is lots of scholarship mapping bias and inequality in law, much of which shows the role of the judiciary in generating and perpetuating bias across a wide spectrum of laws and judicial acts of interpretation. Todd Brower (2006; see Brower [2004] for information about his English studies) has identified four studies that focus on sexual orientation bias in the courts. Brower argues that these studies tell us that once sexual orientation becomes visible in courts, experiences of hostility multiply. Bias mainly takes the form of the use of derogatory terms, ridicule, snickering and jokes. A small amount of data explores the impact of sexuality upon the experiences and perceptions of those who hold judicial office. Three short autobiographical notes by gay men and lesbians, all holding judicial office in the United States, were published in Robin Buhrke's edited volume, *A Matter of Justice: Lesbians and Gay Men in Law Enforcement* (1997). Another more recent autobiographical account is to be found in the published memoirs of Edwin Cameron, a judge in the South African Supreme Court of Appeal. In *Witness to Aids* (2005), Cameron gives an account of his coming out as an HIV-positive gay man, his involvement with HIV/AIDS policy and activism and details the impact of these developments upon some of his experiences as a judge. These autobiographical works indicate the operation of a pervasive heterosexual assumption in the institution of the judiciary and the potential for bias and discrimination within that institution. Together these different sources of data offer some evidence of the impact of sexual orientation upon the courts and within the judiciary.

What Has Queer Got to Do with It?

Before proceeding further I want to reflect upon some of the general and theoretical challenges raised by an engagement with diversity politics in general and sexual diversity in particular. Queer theory has been an important influence challenging the identity politics associated with sexual diversity, problematising assumptions, exposing omissions that shape sexual identities. Steven Seidman has argued that queer theory demands that we question, 'what has been the dominant foundational concept of both homophobic and affirmative homosexual theory: the assumption of a homosexual subject or identity' (1994, 173). I want to highlight three connected aspects of this challenge. First, I want to examine assumptions of the singularity and cohesion of sexual identity categories such as 'lesbian' and 'gay'. Second, I want to develop a critique of the use of identity in relation to ideas of community. More specifically, I want to consider the use of a 'minority' and a 'minority community' model of individual and group identity, a model more commonly associated with racial and ethnic minority identities, in relation to sexuality. The third issue I want to address is the impact that assumptions about the sexual identity categories of 'lesbian' and 'gay' (and a critique of those assumptions) might have upon the way 'heterosexuality' is understood and addressed in judicial diversity settings. I want to use the data generated by way of interviews with lesbians and gay men who are members of the judiciary in a variety of legal systems to explore these issues.

The Challenge of Sexual Identity

Let me begin with assumptions about the singularity and cohesion of categories of sexual identity. Judge Katherine Satchwell sits as a judge in South Africa. She is a member of the bench of the High Court sitting in Johannesburg. While in this post she brought a successful case under the sexual orientation equality provisions of the South African Constitution before the Constitutional Court demanding the extension of judicial pension provisions to incorporate same-sex partners, including her own partner, *Satchwell v The President of the Republic of South Africa* (2002). When I interviewed her she told me that she had never experienced a problem being 'out' as a lesbian in the judiciary. She went on to explain that her sexual identity had to be understood in relation to many other factors such as her racial and ethnic background (she is a white British-born South African), her access to a liberal/radical education and her long political career within the anti-apartheid movement. All played a part in her identity. Other judges drew attention to the impact and importance of gender and faith upon their experiences of identity. Location is another important influence. Justice Satchwell suggested that the specific social, political and cultural conditions in South Africa will impact upon the way sexual identity is performed and constituted and upon its meaning. Thus the sexual politics of identity will be different in different national settings (Stychin 1998; 2003). Institutional settings, in this instance the institutions of judgement and justice, are also an important context, which needs to be taken into account in understanding the operation of sexual identity. Comparative studies of law and legal institutions draw attention to the need to be sensitive to the impact of different structural influences in each legal system such as the different modes of judicial appointment (election in contrast to the appointment by government or a commission of various stakeholders), the size and composition of the legal profession, different judicial work practices, the size and degree of autonomy or inter-dependence of a legal system, the impact of different degrees of juridification of everyday relations. Sexual diversity in the context of the courts and the judiciary will not only be subject to the complexities of sexual identity but also affected by the idiosyncrasies and peculiarities of each legal setting.

As a symbol of community, sexual identity categories suggest that people who identify with a particular sexuality have things in common. Seidman suggests that the model of community imagined by reference to 'lesbian' and 'gay' identity tends to adopt a 'minority' and 'minority community' model that is most commonly associated with racial and minority ethnic identities (1994, 171). The 'minority community' model assumes that the identity category gives a coherence, a homogeneity, a shared singularity to all those who resort to that identity category. In turn these different communities, when conjoined, make up the diversity that the nation now represents. This logic of communities (multiple minority communities) making up the larger community informs the wider characterisation of contemporary democracy as a multi-cultural, cosmopolitan polity.[1] Applied to lesbians and gay men, the logic of the minority model suggests that 'lesbians-and-gay-men' may be identified collectively as a single community. This assumes that the lesbian and gay community can be singled out and differentiated, as a relatively coherent, homogenous, socially, culturally and spatially distinct and separable entity. Furthermore, in that form it becomes one of the pieces of the community jigsaw, of a multi-cultural or cosmopolitan whole.

My research data illustrates some of the problems with the idea of sexual communities and the minority model. For example Justice Satchwell commented that she felt that she had very little in common with a fellow lesbian, Justice de Vos who also brought and won a constitutional case about lesbian rights (rights of adoption). Justice Satchwell explained that Justice de Vos had a very different ethnic background, (white Afrikaner) and a very different political background. Justice Satchwell identified her privileged left liberal background and engagement in the anti-apartheid 'struggle' as central to her politics, her position on the bench and her sense of community, which she defined as a community made up of 'struggle people'. This she suggested is very different from the social, cultural and political background of Justice de Vos. The being in common that 'lesbian' provides is described here as in part serendipitous, being something that arises out of coincidence (the litigation), in part it is imposed externally, by the media, and in part it is a conscious choice of individuals deciding to act in common. Sexual commonality is not so much something that is merely brought into being by a name, uniformly applicable, taken for granted or enduring but may be an alien and alienating, a qualified, partial and fleeting experience.

The insights offered by queer theory and the observations made by interviewees suggest that merely adding lesbian and gay sexualities to the agenda of judicial diversity is problematic. Furthermore, queer theory also suggests that to expose, problematise and critique assumptions about lesbian and gay identity is also

---

1   I have explored some of the problems, challenges and uses of the minority idea of sexual identities in the context of homophobic violence and hate crime reform. See Moran et al. (2004).

insufficient. In short, one effect of such a critique may be to reinforce already commonplace associations and assumptions about 'lesbian' and 'gay' as identities, that they are social fabrications, unstable, incoherent, while leaving the positive attributes and qualities already commonly associated with heterosexuality, such as coherence, stability and homogeneity, unchallenged. This is particularly problematic as this distribution of differences between on the one hand lesbian/gay and on the other, heterosexual, can readily be accommodated within an existing logic that positions heterosexuality as the positive (the superior, the norm, the natural, the civilised, the good and the healthy) over against 'lesbian' and 'gay' which are associated with the negative. As Seidman notes, this threatens to reproduce not only the hetero/homo binary (1994, 174), but also the values that secure the status and privilege associated with heterosexuality. Clearly this is problematic and needs to be challenged.

Queer theory, Seidman argues is not of relevance only to the sexual identities of gay men or lesbians but of significance to all sexual identity categories. It aspires to transform homosexual theory into a general social theory from which to analyse whole societies thereby bringing heterosexuality into the frame of critical analysis (1994, 174). How do you examine heterosexuality without bringing into play all of the problematic assumptions about the nature of sexual identities already identified?

An important tool in achieving this objective is the concept of heteronormativity. Heteronormativity focuses not on sexual identities, such as 'heterosexuality', but on the 'sexual regime' which Seidman describes as, 'a field of sexual meanings, discourses and practices that are interlaced with social institutions and movements' (1994, 169). In their seminal essay, 'Sex in Public' (1998), Lauren Berlant and Michael Warner explain that, 'heteronormativity' offers a way of understanding the fabrication and reproduction of the homo/hetero binary and the fabrication of the hetero as norm (1998, 547). But it does not itself work within that binary relation. It offers a general social theory of the sexual order of whole societies. Heteronormativity requires a shift in approach; from identity to culture. It requires that we turn our attention to the institutions, structures of understanding, and practical orientations that not only bring heterosexuality into being but make that sexuality seem not only coherent – that is, organised as a sexuality – but also privileged. Its privilege, they suggest, can take several (sometimes contradictory) forms. One is manifest in the way heterosexuality works as the 'unmarked', as the basic idiom of the personal and the social. A second manifestation is in heterosexuality's manifestation as a natural state. A third form of privilege is in the way heterosexuality is projected as an ideal or moral accomplishment. Heteronormativity consists less of norms that could be summarised as a body of doctrine and more a diffuse sense of rightness produced in contradictory manifestations – often unconscious, immanent to practice or to institutions. Another objective of this cultural turn is to expose the provisional nature of the apparent coherence of heterosexuality. Heterosexuality, Berlant and Warner suggest, is always provisional. This is based upon a conclusion that it is difficult to imagine any culture and more specifically to imagine heterosexuality as a culture that is so one dimensional, or that is reduced to a single ideology, or a unified set of shared beliefs. Where such displays of singularity and coherence are offered, they argue, they are never more than a provisional unity. The purported totality of heterosexuality, displays of its cohesion and singularity, not only mask but also expose the fragility of 'heterosexuality'. A heteronormative approach requires that these conflicts no longer go unrecognised. Thinking sexuality as a sexual regime or culture, rather than an identity requires us to recognise the diffusion of heterosexuality. While heterosexual culture is the central organising index of social membership, it has no centre, no singular moment of operation or final moment of realisation. But its temporal and spatial diffusion potentially makes it much more difficult to recognise its forms of operation. Because of its diffuse nature, Berlant and Warner suggest that, 'It involves so many practices that are not sex that a world in which this hegemonic cluster would not be dominant is, at this point, unimaginable' (1998, 558).

Shifting the Frame of Enquiry

How does heteronormativity shift the frame of enquiry into sexual diversity in the judiciary? One key insight is that as a 'regime' and a pervasive culture, sexuality is not so much absent, rarely spoken of or predominantly missing from the data or the agenda but, as Berlant and Warner explain, it is always in play and always in public. Thus, the perceived absence of sexuality from judicial diversity debates and judicial studies more generally needs to be treated with caution. Queer theory points out that a requirement to be silent about sexuality does not so much lead to the disappearance of sexuality but informs its mode of appearance. Silence is a device by which sexuality appears in public and more specifically it is one of the devices through which heterosexuality as the norm is (re)produced in society in general and queer theory would suggest in the institution of the judiciary in particular. Heteronormativity suggests that the absence of references to sexuality in current judicial studies is nothing more than the public display of the sexuality of the judiciary, as exclusively heterosexual. The appearance of references to same-sex behaviour and same-sex relations of intimacy in judicial settings is not so much an invasion of something that is alien to judicial settings but perhaps more a shift or a disruption of the existing public sexual culture of that institution. Another important insight offered by queer theory is that there is a need to be cautious about any alignments between sexuality, privacy and the private. As Eve Kosofsky Sedgwick (1990) has noted, the public/private divide has played a major role in the public management and display of sexuality in general and the generation and display of the homo/hetero binary as a violent hierarchy, structuring and framing the appearance and representation of sexuality in a particular way, requiring conformity with a particular pattern and performance of intimacy. Attempts to confine sexuality to the private and domestic sphere do not take sexuality out of the public realm; rather, they are central to its public performance. Through heteronormativity various research questions emerge. For example, what public form does sexuality take under the experienced effects of this 'disappearance'? How does the particular ideal or moral model of intimacy associated with heterosexuality, as the unmarked, in-distinctive, in-different, and as a partisan position that takes on the form of being quintessentially the non-partisan, come into being in a judicial setting? How does the economy of prohibitions work in the generation and reproduction of the current public sexual culture of the judiciary?

Sexual Diversity in the Judiciary: Institutions of Intimacy

I begin my analysis of the sexual diversity of the judiciary with a study of the judges of Britain's highest judicial body, the House of Lords. Maxwell Barrett's (2001) study of the Law Lords includes a brief biographical note on each of the judges who have been in post between 1876, when the current court was established, and 2000, when his study ended. I have extended Barrett's research adding information about the judges appointed between 2000 and 2006. One aspect of the biographical data is of particular interest here: the marital status of the judges. Between 1876 and 2006 there have been 104 appointments, 103 men and one woman (the first woman, Baroness Brenda Hale, was appointed in 2004). Ninety-seven judges were 'married' and six 'never married'.[2] The marital status of the current court (as of 1 April 2006) is as follows: of the 12 Law Lords, 11 are 'married' and one 'never married'.

What relevance is this to a study of sexual diversity in the judiciary? Throughout the period covered by this data 'marriage' has been and remains an intimate and domestic relationship and institution that can only be formally entered into and officially recognised by two people who are respectively a man and a woman. When read through sexuality, marriage is one institution that can be read not only as heterosexual but also as a particularly privileged, state sanctioned ideal of sexual intimacy and sexual identity. The social, political and moral superiority of this form of intimacy is amplified when account is taken of the criminal and civil prohibitions circumscribing other relations of intimacy in general and same-sex relations in particular during the period. Barrett's distinction between 'married' and 'never married' echoes the privilege associated with 'marriage'. Marriage (and thereby heterosexuality) provides the overarching frame of understanding and the basic personal and social idiom against which all is measured and made sense of.[3] Based upon Barrett's research of the judges who have made up the UK's highest court, the evidence suggests that it is a judicial institution that may best be characterised as exclusively heterosexual.

---

2   The term 'never married' is Barrett's category.

3   The distinction between 'married' and 'never married' is also used to accommodate those who have been married but are now divorced and single. It has the effect of bringing them back within the marital institution. It also has the effect of potentially erasing their sexual difference; they might have been divorced subsequent to coming out as lesbian or gay but remain 'married' according to this distinction.

How are we to make sense of the marital profile of this judicial institution? Is it right to conclude that a particular marital status and thereby a particular sexuality has been a requirement for judicial office? Writing in response to an announcement in 1991 that henceforth homosexuality would no longer be a bar to judicial office, English journalist Colin Richardson revealed that in the past, at least under the Lord Chancellor, Lord Hailsham (Conservative Lord Chancellor from 1970 to 1974 and 1979 to 1987), a policy only to appoint people who were married was in operation. This policy was avowedly to ensure that there would be no 'homosexual controversy' in the judiciary. As such, the marital policy operated as a sexuality policy: dedicated to achieving a heterosexual judiciary. Anthony Scrivener QC, a senior barrister, interviewed at the time of this revelation explained to Colin Richardson that it was an 'open secret', that candidates for most judicial appointments were rigorously vetted and that this procedure included their private lives (Richardson 1992, 130–31). While the paucity of 'never married' Law Lords (and with one recent exception they have all been male Law Lords) is not confined to this period, the marital profile of the Law Lords over the 130-year duration of that institution may suggest that a marital requirement was, if not at all times explicitly, then at least implicitly, a policy which had the objective, if not the effect, of securing a uniform (male) heterosexual judiciary, at least in that institution. Returning briefly to queer theory, its insights also suggest that the absence of an explicit sexuality policy is not indicative of the absence of sexual prerequisites. Silence, queer theory shows us, is one manifestation of the privileged status associated with the forms of sexual intimacy and identity that is heterosexuality. Being unmarked is the way heterosexuality as the 'ideal' and the 'natural' is manifest. Heterosexuality in its absence is not so much a missing requirement but a pervasive and compulsory one.

How might the removal of prohibitions on the appointment of those who have different relations of intimacy work to produce a more sexually diverse judiciary? One interviewee, a senior barrister, pointed to the potential contribution that legal recognition of same-sex marriage, or, in the case of the UK, civil partnerships, might make. He suggested that while the new institution of civil partnership may be something of a radical departure, broadening the parameters of intimate relations that are given state recognition and approval, it may also work to facilitate a change in reactions to lesbians and gay men by way of its close proximity to the institution of (heterosexual) intimacy that has long occupied the moral high ground, 'marriage'.

If the expansion of state recognition to patterns of same-sex intimacy has the effect of facilitating the greater sexual diversity of the judiciary, does it also impose new limits? The same senior barrister suggested that it might strengthen the resolve to exclude relations of intimacy that do not follow the heterosexual pattern given legitimacy via marriage and now civil partnership. In order to sustain the illusion of perfection and the ideal associated with these privileged categories of intimacy, much work has to be done to exclude other possible relations of intimacy from the realms of morally privileged intimate relations. Different patterns of intimacy, which are equally capable of moral worth – being caring, nurturing, respectful acts and relationships – will have to be devalued and degraded. The greater sexual diversity of the judiciary may come at the price of the reinforcement of the existing parameters of respectable intimacy and thereby do little to achieve a deeper substantive diversity within the judiciary.

(In)visibility

Todd Brower (2006), in his analysis of the four existing studies of sexual orientation bias in courtroom settings as noted above, has highlighted the importance of invisibility and visibility in the experiences and perceptions of bias. Most lesbians and gay men he suggests are not visibly identifiable either in courtroom settings or more generally. While invisibility is not a phenomenon that is exclusive to 'sexual minorities', it can for example also have significance in the context of disability and faith. It is, Brower concluded, 'particularly significant' in relation to sexual diversity. Non-heterosexual identity, which Brower describes as 'minority sexual identity' in general, involves ongoing conduct dedicated to negotiating and managing the boundary between invisibility and visibility. Crossing the boundary from invisibility to visibility, he suggests, may be a fraught and dangerous activity. In this section I will use the interview data from lesbians and gay men who are members of the judiciary to pursue two objectives: first, to explore how these men and women experience and manage their sexual invisibility and their sexual visibility; second, to identify some of the factors that appear to influence and inform the generation of the boundary between visibility and invisibility in this context.

In my interview with Justice Cameron, a judge in the Supreme Court of Appeal in South Africa, he offered the following example of his experiences of the boundary between invisibility and visibility. Justice Cameron has been 'out' for over 20 years, as an activist, a scholar with an extensive body of writings relating to lesbian and gay human rights and HIV/AIDS, including the publication of his memoirs in 2005, and since 1995 as a prominent judge in South Africa. The incident he described occurred during the course of his visit to London in July 2006. At the end of a meeting with three members of the English Court of Appeal as they were going to lunch, the presiding judge asked 'Is your wife here with you?' Justice Cameron explained that for him this question was an example of both the assumption of heterosexuality, an instance of its visibility, which in turn is the moment of the invisibility of other sexual possibilities. It was also an example of the (ongoing) requirement for an act to break the assumption. When I asked him how he dealt with 'invisibility' more generally in judicial settings he explained that his approach was to be 'very obtrusive' about being gay, taking male partners to judicial functions and talking a lot about being gay with other judges. Justice Kirby, a judge sitting in the highest court in Australia explained, 'I think it is important … for me to confront those who have a stereotyped image of the judiciary, not in an aggressive or in an irrelevant way'. He does this through his extra-judicial activities such as his scholarly writing and giving public lectures attended by senior members of the judiciary. But Justice Kirby also indicated that the movement from invisibility to visibility may have certain limits. What factors might facilitate and motivate such a movement and what might inform their limit?

The interview with Justice Kirby offers numerous examples of factors that might have informed his decisions to become visible. In the specific context of his decision in 1999 to announce his relationship with a man in the pages of the Australian edition of *Who's Who*, he identified three factors that influenced the event. The first was his professional position and more specifically his elevation in 1996 to the most senior court in Australia, the High Court of Australia. A second factor was the impact of the Royal Commission in New South Wales into the Police Service, which in the mid- to late 1990s generated hysteria in Australia about gay men on the bench.[4] The Royal Commission investigated and made links between 'gay judges', 'rent boys' and 'police corruption'. To begin 'out' would reduce the potential of any future allegations of hidden intrigue or 'conspiracy' to damage a person's career. The third factor might be described as a combination of social justice and sexual politics. Justice Kirby explained that Johan, his partner of 37 years, 'said that we owed it to the next generation to do something that would make their journey a little easier than ours had sometimes been'. The reference to 'Johan', I'd suggest points to a fourth factor, the particular relations of intimacy Justice Kirby inhabits. In the light of my earlier analysis of the way particular relations of intimacy might be either an explicit or implicit factor in the disclosure or non-disclosure of sexuality in a judicial setting, it is important to note that Justice Kirby's 'coming out' in *Who's Who* takes place in the context of an announcement of his long-term domestic partnership with Johan. As an enduring, stable, loving relationship this has some of the key characteristics associated with those intimate relations that have long been privileged in and through heterosexuality as the basic idiom of personal and social respectability within the judiciary and elsewhere. Domestic respectability may be an important social and cultural value enabling an individual to redraw the boundary between invisibility and visibility. The interview data also suggests another significant factor. It appears in the context of a reflection about the unwillingness of other gay people in different prominent positions who have partners, long-term partners, to disclose their relationship in their entry in *Who's Who*. Job security, which Justice Kirby described in terms of his own constitutionally protected position, is another important factor.

It is also important to note the institutional and social settings in which these instances of visibility take place. Some occur in what might be described as informal judicial settings, such as business meetings and judicial social events. Another context is in extra-judicial settings, sometimes those settings might be the wider legal community, such as a lecture to members of the profession including judges,

---

4   In December 1994, the Royal Commission into the New South Wales police service (the Wood Commission) extended its investigations into the existence and extent of corruption in the police service into a new area: the sexual behaviour of members of the judiciary in New South Wales. This investigation arose in relation to allegations of police protection of paedophiles.

sometimes they might be more popular locations. *Who's Who* is a publication that falls within the wider parameters of the mass media. All are out of the courtroom. So what about visibility in relation to the official role of the judge and in the courtroom?

An interview with Justice Adrian Fulford, a judge appointed to the High Court of England and Wales in 2002 sitting as a judge in the criminal division, offers data on experiences and perceptions of invisibility/visibility in the context of judicial office and in relation to the judicial role. Justice Fulford explained his understanding of the relationship between sexual orientation and the role of the judge when he explained, 'I don't think that the fact that I am a gay man has very much, if anything, to do with the way I perform my job as a judge. It is almost entirely irrelevant.' Justice Fulford's comments about the irrelevance of sexual orientation need to be put into the context of his pre-judicial career. Called to the bar in 1978, he was one of the first 'out' gay men working as a barrister in the UK who did a lot of work relating to gay men. A desire to change attitudes, promote social justice, generate an income and develop a career appear here to have been factors influencing this decision to be 'out'. He described a key characteristic of this phase of his career, as working in 'a partisan way'. How does his portrait of being a lawyer differ from his portrait of being a judge? His portrait of the role of a judge is in stark contrast to the portrait he paints of being a lawyer. Justice Fulford's characterisation of his practice as a lawyer is one of sexual visibility, both in the performance of himself and his professional role. Sexuality was visible in his 'partisan' work for particular clients. The judicial role is radically different: it is characterised by sexual invisibility in the erasure of his sexual identity, which is conjoined with the performance of an official role that is 'non-partisan'. This seems to point to a rather rigid boundary between sexual invisibility and sexual visibility in the context of the judicial role. How might this be explained and understood?

Justice Cameron offers an insight. In his memoirs he describes the 'resplendent robes' of judicial office, the bib, sash, waistband and flowing scarlet robes that English judges imported into South Africa in the early nineteenth century as 'a full-body disguise' (Cameron 2005, 31). In his memoirs he mentions the disguise not in relation to making his sexuality *per se* invisible but making his ill health, his status as HIV positive, invisible. But does 'the disguise' have significance in relation to sexuality? We explored this during the course of my interview with him. He explained his position on the function of court dress, and also the spatial arrangements of the court, in terms of the role of the judge. He suggested that judicial dress and the staging are concerned with the performance of distance that is understood to be a key feature of impartiality. Distance, Justice Cameron suggested, is functional to the work of the judge: both necessary and unavoidable. This suggests that in a courtroom setting the visibility of a judge's sexuality may break the magic otherwise produced by the paraphernalia that stages distance.

In the context of the social and cultural forces that make non-heterosexual sexualities invisible, the paraphernalia and staging of the judicial role as non-partisan may make it easier for a lesbian or a gay man (as already invisible) to achieve that required performance. At the same time, this 'necessary and unavoidable' performance may make it more difficult for a lesbian or gay man to, 'affirmatively break the assumption of heterosexuality that silence often brings'. Feminist scholars have noted the dangers women on the bench face when they attempt to break gender assumptions. In some instances invisibility may either not be an option or be more difficult to achieve. The visibility of a woman's performance of gender and the visibility of some ethnic minorities may make the visual performance of judicial impartiality even more challenging and more difficult for women and ethnic minorities on the bench. Nor are the challenges of gender, colour and ethnicity remote from sexuality. In some instances they may work to enhance the difficulties facing individuals, for example gender may impact differently on lesbians than gay men, colour and ethnicity may generate more challenges for gay Muslims who wish to pursue a judicial career. The combination of these different hierarchies of difference may also facilitate visibility. For example, returning to Justice Satchwell, she explained that she had never had any problems being a lesbian on the bench. As noted earlier a number of factors were at work in the generation of this experience including, ethnicity and race, social class, education and political beliefs. Finally, the adoption of invisibility may at best leave unquestioned and unproblematised the nature and meaning of 'distance' and 'impartiality', and at worst may reproduce the hierarchy of social distinctions that have in the past made a group of white, middle-aged, upper-middle-class, privately educated men the embodiment of 'impartiality'.

Does this mean that the sexuality of, for example, Justice Kirby or Justice Cameron never appears in the official setting of the court? The short answer, my research suggests, is no. It does appear. But both Justice Kirby and Justice Cameron suggested that the appearance of their sexuality is not so much the result of an overt or conscious performance in the courtroom by these judges but more as something that others in the court, the lawyers presenting the argument and fellow judges might read into the proceedings due to performances of sexual visibility that have occurred elsewhere.

In 2004 Anna Marie de Vos, who was then a judge sitting on the bench of the South African High Court in Pretoria, appeared with her partner and their two children in a South African television documentary, *Two Moms* (2004). *Two Moms* profiles Justice de Vos, her partner Suzanne Du Toit and their two adopted children. The filming took place during the judicial recess. The production crew spent four days shooting in Pretoria and Johannesburg, two days travelling down to the coast and a further four days at the family farm near Plattenberg Bay, on the Cape coast. The production company, Underdog, describes the film as, 'a revealing multifaceted portrait of an extraordinary, yet very normal family'. The film's director, Luiz Debarros, explained the film focused 'on the human stories we found within the family, and not on the issues themselves, although these invariably came to the fore in a natural way'. The screening of the documentary, Justice de Vos explained to me, was something of a turning point in her relations with her fellow judges. As a result of the hostility shown to her by some of her fellow judges she felt that she had crossed a boundary. What is the nature of the boundary? Justice de Vos describes it in part as an issue of visibility in contrast to invisibility, a boundary between the private and the public.

Is this a breach pure and simple of an unspoken rule that prohibits the representation of family life, or the intimate life of judges in South Africa? The short answer is no. The judicial biographies on the website of the Constitutional Court of South Africa give details of the family lives of the judges of that court, present and past. There have also been instances where details of the intimate lives of senior judges in South Africa have been made public with little or no hostile reaction (Sachs 2000 and Cameron 2005). How are we to make sense of Justice de Vos's experiences? There is some evidence here of a common denominator between the various judges who have made the 'private', 'public'; all the disclosures referred to above are framed by reference to important political and moral causes and objectives informing the uses of publicity/visibility and an awareness of the dangers that might flow from the loss of privacy. However, the different reaction to Justice de Vos's eminently respectable family life offers some evidence in support of a conclusion that gay men and lesbian women may be differently positioned both with respect to privacy and publicity and in relation to invisibility and visibility. There is some evidence here of the gendered character of these boundaries and their deployment. Men appear to be able to exercise more control over boundary formation and boundary maintenance. This draws our attention to the way the formation and management of the boundary between invisibility and visibility and between privacy and publicity is informed by a hierarchy of power (Fraser 1992, 595).

Conclusion

While the excitement generated by association with the public theatre and spectacle of queer may have long faded and the proliferating references to 'queer' in studies of law lost much of their challenging critical edge, queer's potential and in particular the insights offered by queer theory have not faded or diminished. Not only the progressive reforms that promote increasing respect of sexual difference but also continuing resistance to change and the reinvigoration and retrenchment of reactionary sexual politics still demand critical analysis which the best of queer theory can facilitate.

My case study, of a potentially progressive policy of judicial diversity, illustrates the ability of queer theory to make sense of the still prevalent assumption that lesbian and gay sexualities in particular and sexuality more generally are and ought to be largely unspoken and unspeakable subjects. One key insight arising out of the research and analysis offered here is that sexuality is not so much absent or rarely spoken, or predominantly missing from the judicial institution and the lives of the judiciary, but is always present and, more specifically, always in public. Silences and the formation and maintenance of boundaries of visibility and invisibility are central to its pervasive operation. Sexuality is already a part, and a very public part of judicial institutions, judicial roles and judicial cultures.

It may however, still be the case that putting sexual diversity on the legal agenda will be experienced by government officials, key legal actors, fellow academics and researchers, and the public at large as a vertiginous journey across a boundary that is fraught with danger. It is likely to remain a hotly contested and highly controversial issue. These responses are not so much a reaction to violating social taboos associated with the preservation of an institution or a culture that is free from sexuality, which effectively confines and preserves sexuality to places beyond the public gaze, but are more a reaction that reveals the nature and operation of the existing public sexual culture we occupy, dedicated to the pursuit of a dream of a sexually homogenous social order. Research focusing on the legal experiences of gay men and lesbians provides a unique opportunity to analyse not particular identities but provides an opportunity to examine and critically explore the whole of that public sex culture in law.

Suggested Further Reading

Bower, L. (1994), 'Queer Acts and the Politics of "Direct Address": Rethinking Law, Culture and Community', *Law and Society Review* 28:5, 1009–33.
Davies, M. (1999), 'Queer Property, Queer Persons: Self-Ownership and Beyond', *Social and Legal Studies* 8:3, 327–52.
McGhee, D. (2001), *Homosexuality, Law and Resistance* (London and New York: Routledge).
Moran L.J. (2002), 'Lesbian and Gay Bodies of Law', in D. Richardson and S. Seidman (eds), *Handbook of Lesbian and Gay Studies* (London: Sage).
—— (2006), *Sexuality Identity and Law* (Aldershot: Ashgate).

References

Barrett, M. (2001), *The Law Lords: An Account of the Workings of Britain's Highest Judicial Body and the Men who Preside over It* (Basingstoke: Macmillan).
Berlant, L. and Warner, M. (1998), 'Sex in Public', *Critical Inquiry* 24, 547–66.
Bower, L. (1994), 'Queer Acts and the Politics of "Direct Address": Rethinking Law, Culture and Community', *Law and Society Review* 28:5, 1009–33.
Brower, T. (2004), 'Pride and Prejudice: Results of an Empirical Study of Sexual Orientation Fairness in the Courts of England and Wales', *Buffalo Women's Law Journal* 13, 17–96.
—— (2006), *Multistable Figures: Sexual Orientation Visibility and its Effects on Experiences of Sexual Minorities in the Court* (Berkeley, CA: The Berkeley Electronic Press), http://law.com.expresso/eps/1519 (accessed 26 April 2008).
Buhrke, R. (ed.) (1997), *A Matter of Justice: Lesbians and Gay Men in Law Enforcement* (New York and London: Routledge).

Cameron, E. (2005), *Witness to AIDS* (South Africa: Tafelberg).

Davies, M. (1999), 'Queer Property, Queer Persons: Self-Ownership and Beyond', *Social and Legal Studies* 8:3, 327–52.

Fraser, N. (1992), 'Sex, Lies and the Public Sphere: Some Reflections on the Confirmation of Clarence Thomas', *Critical Inquiry* 18, 595–612.

Halley, J.E. (1991), 'Misreading Sodomy: A Critique of the Classification of "Homosexuals" in Federal Equal Protection Law', in J. Epstein and K. Straub (eds), *Body Guards: The Cultural Politics of Gender Ambiguity* (London and New York: Routledge).

—— (1993a), 'The Construction of Heterosexuality', in M. Warner (ed.), *Fear of a Queer Planet: Queer Politics and Social Theory* (Minneapolis, MN and London: University of Minnesota Press).

—— (1993b) 'Reasoning about Sodomy: Act and Identity in and after *Bowers v Harwick*', *Virginia Law Review* 79, 1721–80.

Moran L.J. and Skeggs, B. with Tyrer, P. and Corteen, K. (2004), *Sexuality and the Politics of Violence and Safety* (London and New York: Routledge).

Richardson, C. (1992), 'Homosexuality and the Judiciary', *New Law Journal* 31 January, 130–31.

Sachs, A. (2000), *The Soft Vengeance of a freedom fighter*, 2nd edition (Cape Town: David Phillip).

Sedgwick, E.K. (1990), *Epistemology of the Closet* (Berkley, CA: University of California Press).

Seidman, S. (1994), 'Queer-ing Sociology, Sociologizing Queer Theory: An Introduction', *Sociological Theory* 12:2, 166–77.

Stychin, C.F. (1995), *Law's Desire: Sexuality and the Limits of Justice* (London and New York: Routledge).

—— (1998), *Nation by Rights* (Philadelphia, PA: Temple University Press).

—— (2003), *Governing Sexuality: The Changing Politics of Citizenship and Law Reform* (Oxford: Hart).

Two Moms (2004), dir. A. Genge L. DeBarros [documentary film].

Queerying Lesbian and Gay Psychology's 'Coming of Age': Was the Past Just Kids' Stuff?

Peter Hegarty

Coming of Age

The field of 'lesbian and gay psychology' – or 'lesbian and gay affirmative psychology' – came into being when lesbian and gay liberation movements of the late 1960s and early 1970s successfully challenged the definition of homosexuality as a mental illness, and the American Psychiatric Association voted to remove homosexuality from its *Diagnostic and Statistical Manual of Psychiatric Disorders* in 1973 (Bayer 1981). Prior to these events, psychologists had largely avoided affirmation of lesbian and gay identities. Since 1973, lesbian and gay psychology has both described those identities as legitimate, mature, adjusted, psychologically healthy ways of being in their own right, and theorised the psychological problems that lesbians and gay men face as consequences of social stigma rather than any inherent pathology. Research has shifted away from questions about the causation and mutability of sexual orientation towards a wider set of research questions which concern lesbians' and gay men's lives within sexual minority communities and larger heterosexist cultures (Morin 1977; Morin and Rothblum 1991).

Currently, this field is globalising and diversifying to a degree that troubles any attempt to definitively name it. 'Lesbian and gay psychology' is represented by professional organisations in such countries as Australia, Brazil, Britain, Colombia, the Netherlands and the United States. Furthermore, in some national contexts there have been moves beyond the narrow construction 'lesbian and gay'. For example, 'bisexual' was added to the name of Division 44 of the American Psychological Association in 1997 such that this organisation is now actioned to speak to 'lesbian, gay, and bisexual concerns'. The outcome of recent discussions within the Lesbian and Gay Psychology Section of the British Psychological Society about changing the name of this organisation are difficult to predict. The adjectives 'lesbian and gay' have often been read as indicating a psychologists' own sexuality, but many in the field point out that this is an error; 'a "lesbian and gay psychologist" can be heterosexual, just as a "social psychologist" can be anti-social, or a "sports psychologist" a couch potato' (Kitzinger 1997, 203).

However, the error of presuming to know the sexuality of a lesbian and gay psychologist reveals the historically recent, and contingent, possibility of being both a 'psychological expert' and openly lesbian or gay at all. A rhetoric of 'experiential authority', drawing on direct experience with lesbian or gay life, may characterise some post-1973 'affirmative' social science research (Kitzinger 1987, 29–31). In contrast, prior to 1973, psychological research on homosexuality was characterised by deliberate erasure of collaboration with lesbian and gay researchers; erasure that was required if such research was to appear 'objective' (Minton 2001). 'Dr Anonymous', a speaker at the 1973 American Psychiatric Association meetings where lesbian and gay affirmative perspectives were voiced for the first time, sits at the boundary of these two periods of psychology's history. His co-panellists were Barbara Gittings and Frank Kameny (who were openly lesbian and gay, but were not psychiatrists) and Judd Marmor (who was an openly straight psychiatrist). 'Dr Anonymous' who spoke as a gay psychiatrist, did so from behind a mask and through a machine that disguised his voice (Bayer 1981).[1] One of lesbian, gay and bisexual psychology's ongoing tasks is to continue to trouble the range of sexual subject positions that can overlap with the category of 'psychologists'.

The Trouble with Coming of Age

These historic shifts can warrant a celebratory mood. In landmark volumes of lesbian and gay psychology this celebration has been figured as a 'coming of age.' 'Lesbian and gay affirmative perspectives in psychology have come of age' wrote Gonsierek (1994, viii) in the preface to the American Psychological Association's first edited volume of work in this area. 'Publication of this book marks the "coming of age" of British lesbian and gay psychology' echoed Kitzinger and Coyle (2002, 1) some years later, marking a new national context for lesbian and gay psychology against the unmarked US norm. Here, I want to query my colleagues' 'coming of age' narratives, which tend to imply that the field has arrived at a 'mature' epistemological telos. I'm less sure that coming out of childhood and into adulthood – particularly as psychology's more senior discipline of 'child psychology' configures such transformations – is necessarily either grounds for a celebration, or the narrative needed to keep the impulse to queer psychology going. [2] According to canonical theories in child psychology, children take some time to get into the habit of labelling people in terms of their genders, often initially

---

1 For a photo of the panellists, including the masked Dr Anonymous, see Marcus (1992, 224).

2 See Kitzinger (1997) for a longer discussion of the politics of lesbian and gay psychology's complicity with psychology. For a critique of developmental psychology see Burman (1994) and Morss (1995).

disagree as to what makes someone a boy or a girl, and take longer still to alight on the belief that you've got your gender for life, or that gender is determined by your genitals (Kohlberg 1966; Bem 1989). Of course, ethnomethodology, feminist studies of science, and queer theory have all offered related challenges to the factual status of those trans-abjecting 'facts' that child psychologists celebrate as children's developmental milestones (Kessler and McKenna 1978; Fausto-Sterling 1993; Butler 1990). Indeed, the construction of these common changes in children's understandings of gender as normative development, rather than as particular forms of subjectification, contributes to their sedimentation as the 'natural facts' of gender more generally; only a child could believe anything different. Those of us trying to do translation work between psychology and queer theory experience strange kinship with children when we are similarly infantilised for insisting that there are more than two physical sexes, and that genitals do not automatically determine gender. ('Surely all of this talk of there being no absolute truth is just postmodernist word play?' 'You're not serious though, are you?')

The celebratory 'coming of age' narrative sometimes gets on the disciplinary bandwagon to make this translation work more difficult still. For example, Gonsierek continues by attributing the proper development of the field to 'critical thinking and arguments based on empirical information' which he contrasts with the 'politically correct foolishness' of lesbian and gay studies courses which are 'inward looking and self-absorbed with arcane academic debates' (Gonsierek 1994, viii–ix). In contrast, Kitzinger and Coyle's use of 'coming of age' does flag up the contingent and incomplete nature of British 'lesbian and gay psychology', particularly with regard to the underdeveloped state of bisexual and transgender psychology.[3] But LGBT psychology will require more than just a knowledge base about bisexuality and transgender if it is to do justice to the sexual and gender minorities that modern psychology has been complicit in abjecting. The 'development' of both children and academic fields of inquiry will have to be rethought at a more fundamental level.

Consider the current difficulties involved in putting 'bisexual psychology' on an equal status with 'lesbian and gay psychology' *without* rethinking the logic of development. Clare Hemmings argues that much lesbian, gay and queer theory is founded on a logic of repudiation, in which foreclosing the possibility of either homo- or hetero- sexuality is necessary for a sexual identity to be recognised as mature. Within such theories, bisexuality gets positioned as a phase, a middle-ground, or a polymorphously perverse origin point, but adult bisexual identities are rendered unthinkable (Hemmings 2002). Although her text is not aimed at

---

3   Kitzinger and Coyle 2002, 4. I follow the thread of this exclusion of bisexuality here, but this is not to suggest that inclusion of transgender psychologies would not require an equally fundamental rethinking. See Parlee (1996). Nor are these the only pieces of unfinished business in the field. Kitzinger and Coyle further note that the volume focuses on sexual *identity* to the exclusion of work on sexual *behaviour*. Elsewhere I examine how the construction of British lesbian and gay psychology between the spaces of positivist psychology and social constructionism can contribute to this retreat from sexual practice. See Hegarty (2007b).

psychologists, Hemmings' argument applies to such classic theories of coming out processes as counselling psychologist Vivienne Cass's model, which describes bisexuality only as an identity that is taken on temporarily when moving from closeted to openly lesbian or gay identities.[4] At the end point of the coming out process, as Cass envisaged it, the mature lesbian/gay person shuttles happily between the heterosexual mainstream and affirmative lesbian/gay subcultures at will, but their erotic orientation is maturely solidified around same-sex desire (Cass 1979, 219–21). Of course, this is too limited a scheme to make sense of life narratives, and Cass herself has moved beyond it (Cass 1999). [5]

Psychologists can also occlude the possibility of the conceptual rethinking necessary to put bisexuality on a more equal relationship with lesbian and gay when we celebrate the field's coming of age too. Social psychologist Gregory Herek adopted a celebratory tone about the field's development in the preface to his edited volume *Stigma and Sexual Orientation: Understanding Prejudice against Lesbians, Gay Men, and Bisexuals.*

> *The mainstreaming of research on antigay stigma is important not only because it offers the promise of finding better ways to combat prejudice, but also because studying homophobia will enrich the study of attitudes in general. (Herek 1998, viii)*

While the title of Herek's useful volume mentions bisexuality, none of the book's 11 chapters comparatively analyse homo- and bi-phobia, none are oriented more towards biphobia than homophobia, and several would not need substantive revision if bisexuality simply did not exist.

The 'mainstreamed' researcher that Herek celebrates here resembles the lesbian or gay subject at the end of Cass's coming out model; shuttling freely between engagement with lesbian and gay psychology and the more 'general' field of attitude science. Does bisexuality need to be undone for this mature professional identity to cohere, as in Cass's model? Sean Massey and I have recently argued that the mainstreaming of work on heterosexist prejudice involved the construction of lesbians and gay men as a distinct minority group, and by so doing occluded one possibility for theorising biphobia (Hegarty and Massey 2006). Early models of anti-gay prejudice borrowed from sexual liberationist thinking and understood homophobia to result from such factors as 'personal anxiety', 'sex guilt' or 'fear and denial of personal homosexual tendencies' (Dunbar, Brown and Amoroso 1973; Millham, San Miguel and Kellogg 1976; Mosher and O'Grady 1979). Assuming a bisexual potential for all, fears of homosexual feelings among the heterosexual-identified were understood as evidence of 'homophobia' and assessed with

---

4   My argument here is indebted to Kitzinger (1987), who similarly called attention to the limited utility of lesbian and gay psychology's identity models for radical lesbians. However, the version of feminism upon which Kitzinger alights is no more accepting of bisexuality than the lesbian and gay psychology is rejecting. See Hegarty (2005a).

5   See also Diamond (2008).

such questionnaire items as 'I am frightened that I might have homosexual tendencies'.[6] By so doing, these models allowed the possibility of conceptualising heterosexual-identified people's own *biphobia*, a possibility that was occluded in later minoritising work.

It is not always easy to shuttle between lesbian and gay psychology and mainstream psychology while keeping bisexuality on the table. I was reminded of this in 2005 when I was invited to supply a 50-word comment to the British journal *The Psychologist* on a study which had claimed (in typical bi-negating fashion) to have found new evidence for the biological basis of sexual orientation in men. Within these imposed limits, with the help of my friends, I managed to critique the study for media-baiting, exclusion of lesbian and bisexual people, and general irrelevance to lesbian, gay and bisexual people's lives.[7] The journal's editor subsequently allowed a full half page for a personalised response that impugned my credentials as both a psychological scientist and a historian of psychology (Dickens, Hardman and Sergeant 2005). My insistence on the need to study bisexual men was described as ill-informed and censorious of scientific writing, particularly as I had not accepted, without criticism, a soon-to-be-controversial unpublished study which denied that men could feel bisexual desire at all (Rieger, Chivers and Bailey 2005). Discussion of the limits of *that* work are far beyond the current discussion. However, both the personal public attack and the published defence of my 50-word commentary by a group of bisexual scholars (Barker, Iantaffi and Gupta 2005) were further evidence that a commitment to bisexuality limits the forms of easy movement between margin and centre for lesbian and gay psychologists that models of 'lesbian and gay' development describe.

Leaving Queer Children Behind

These limitations on the theorising of adult bisexualities, and the possibility that children might be better gender theorists than adults, both suggest that 'coming of age' might foreclose critical possibilities in psychology rather than open them up. My argument to centre children in this queer project seems at odds with the account of criticality in Lee Edelman's *No Future: Queer Theory and the Death Drive*. Here, Edelman rightly points to the problem of 'reproductive futurism' in which the welfare of an abstract figure of a future child is used to limit the rights and freedoms of adults in the here-and-now. For Edelman, queerness 'names the side of those *not* "fighting for the children," and is also that which "chafes against normalization"'(Edelman 2004, 3–6). Within the 'cult of the Child' that Edelman conjures up, the child is both innocent and straight, and 'no shrines to

---

6   This questionnaire item was used by Mosher and O'Grady (1979).

7   My comment was inserted into the following news item: 'How Messages Are Scent', *The Psychologist* 18, 399. The study critiqued was Savic, Berglund and Lindström (17 May 2005).

the queerness of boys and girls' are permitted. This last point was also made by Bruhm and Hurley who point out that queer children are up against a contradictory discourse in which they are paradoxically constructed as both innocent of desire and necessarily already heterosexual (Bruhm and Hurley 2004).

Edelman's critique pertains to psychology most obviously because it assumes a Lacanian ontology of what it means to be singularly human, to experience desire and to be motivated by a death drive. Given the breadth of application that Edelman claims for this critique, it is worth considering its relevance for hegemonic theories of child psychology which produce truth effects on the lives of queers of all ages (unlike the popular culture texts that Edelman subjects to Lacanian analysis). Consider the now-familiar arguments of lesbian and gay psychologists that children grow up equally 'well-adjusted' with same-sex and opposite-sex parents (Patterson 2006), arguments which have successfully compelled courts to consider lesbian (and less often gay) parents as valid custodians of their children. The politics of securing parenting rights by appeal to a reassuring developmental narrative that lesbians and gay men produce children that come of age quite normally are vexing indeed. Unlike the psychological literature which affirms ethnic or religious minority parents, lesbian and gay parents are rarely deemed successful when they pass on their minority identity to their children. Celia Kitzinger cites parenting research as supporting her argument that psychological knowledge ought to be used to secure lesbians' and gay men's civil rights (Kitzinger 1997). Her former student Victoria Clarke notes that the logic of parenting research is heteronormative for assuming heterosexual parents to be a useful standard of comparison and heterosexuality to be evidence of a 'well-adjusted' upbringing (Clarke 2000). Tellingly, it has been sociologists who have offered the most sustained critique of the psychological literature. Judith Stacey and Thomas Bilbarz conclude that, by some psychological measures, children of lesbian mothers have always been visibly more queer than psychologists dared to admit, being particularly more likely to break the rules of childhood gender conformity than children reared by heterosexuals (Stacey and Bilbarz 2001). 'Such evidence, albeit limited, implies that lesbian parenting may free daughters and sons from a broad but uneven range of traditional gender prescriptions' (Stacey and Bilbarz 2001, 169–70). Children of lesbian, gay and bisexual parents also often report that they value the greater affordance for their own genders of growing up in queer families (Goldberg 2007; Saffron 1998).

While the future rights of queer families are being worked out here with reference to fantasies about straight children, this debate troubles the terms of Edelman's critique, because the imagined heterosexual children of queer parents are being used to support the rights of queer adults in the here-and-now, and not to limit them. If Stacey, Bilbarz, and the children of LGB parents who talked to Goldberg and Saffron are right, then research on lesbian and gay parents has shied away from understanding the gender transgressive features of queer families to ensure that lesbians and gay men can continue to parent. Edelman's understanding of queer draws also on Warner's useful argument that to be queer is to be normalised. For Warner within queer subcultures – at their occasional best – '[t]he rule is: Get over yourself. Put a wig on before you judge. And the corollary is that you stand to learn most from the people you think are beneath you' (Warner 1999, 35). Yet Edelman's derogation of the future as just 'kids' stuff' seems to shame, in an infantalising manner, those who would see children as integral to their queer lives. In addition to Warner's suggested wigs, perhaps we need to draw on the best of kid culture including boys with Barbie dolls, ontologies that permit more than two genders, shitting at the dinner table, and possibilities for bi-friendly theory to challenge adults notions that children are only politically interesting as wards of their rights-bearing parents or future rights-bearing subject. The future is 'kids' stuff'? Bring it on! I can't imagine anything more queer.

If psychological research on lesbian and gay parents writes off children's queer possibilities, postmodern queer theory runs the risk of a fascination with *the figure* of the child in cultural texts. As Bruhm and Hurley note, there are long-standing, ongoing, contested translations between children's lives and psychological facts. For Foucault, 'all the sciences, analyses or practices employing the root "psycho-"' (Foucault 1977, 193) operate through individualisation by making their subjects visible, and children are more individualised than adults. In *The History of Sexuality: Volume 1*, Foucault also declared that 'silence … is less the absolute limit of discourse … than an element that functions alongside the things said' before going on to discuss how schoolchildren were taught to speak about sex (Foucault 1978, 27). The politics of individualising children while enforcing their silence has not gone unchallenged. Organisations such as the *Intersex Society of North America* and *Bastard Nation* have protested the keeping of those records *through* which individualising power operates *from* the subjects *on* which it operates.[8] Psychologists have long been pruriently interested in intersexed and adopted children as 'natural experiments' because of their rare locations within categories of gender, sexuality and kinship. Only rarely has psychology been understood as a practice that matches this prurience with concern to make those locations more inhabitable. All of these contested operations of power can be conveniently forgotten by adults in the habit of thinking of 'the figure' of the child as the focus of their politics and textual analysis as the primary strategy of political engagement.

One the most significant contributions of queer theory to developmental psychology to date has been Eve Kosofsky Sedgwick's important essay 'How to Bring Your Kids Up Gay' (1991). Sedgwick's title cleverly disappoints readers looking for self-help, and highlights the degree to which we look to developmental psychology to answers the question of whether a child is normal, or should be taken to the clinic. When published in 1980, the third edition of the *Diagnostic and Statistical Manual* did not list homosexuality as a categorical reason to go to the clinic, but 'Gender Identity Disorder in Childhood' appeared, bringing a new reason to bring your kids there.[9] This diagnosis was, and remains, based on children's expressed desire to be a member of the opposite sex, and the display of behaviour deemed

---

8   See www.isna.org and www.bastards.org. On the history of adoption see Ellen Herman, 'The Adoption History Project', http://darkwing.uoregon.edu/~adoption/.

9   American Psychiatric Association (1980). On the diagnosis of Gender Identity Disorder in Children see also Burke (1996) and Minter (1999).

appropriate for the 'opposite' sex (in such domains as clothing, play and gender of preferred playmates). Sedgwick notes the comparative silence that surrounded this pathologising of children's gender, in comparison to the much-celebrated removal of homosexuality from the *Diagnostic and Statistical Manual*, and pointed out that the repudiated figure of the effeminate boy could come to constitute 'a node of annihilating homophobic, gynophobic, and pedophobic hatred internalised and made central to gay-affirmative analysis' (Sedgwick 1991, 21). As Karl Bryant (2006) argues, the debates that lead to the formation of the GIDC (Gender Identity Disorder in Childhood) diagnosis show that the imperative to consider effeminate boys mentally ill involves many more motives than simply junior homophobia.

Queer psychology is not just 'junior queer theory' either. Rather, any analysis of how to live with queer children will involve thinking as a psychologist might about what methodologies do. To support her assumption that gay men have effeminate boyhoods, Sedgwick leaned on an empirical psychological study by Bell, Weinberg and Hammersmith, published in 1981, which she describes as 'the most credible of these studies [linking childhood gender with adult sexual orientation] from a gay-affirmative standpoint' (Sedgwick 1991, 27). Yet, by taking this study at face value, Sedgwick overlooked how the gynophobic impulse – that her essay otherwise exposes – operates within its methods. The data for Bell et al.'s study consists of thousands of interviews about childhood experiences with gay, lesbian, bisexual and heterosexual adults, conducted in the San Francisco area during 1969 and 1970. Bell et al. used these reports of childhood to construct statistical models of the developmental pathways to adult sexual orientation. This particular quantification of 'experience' constructed gender as a unidimensional personality trait anchored at 'masculine' and 'feminine' extremes. Where did this 'gender' come from? Participants answered such questions as 'to what extent did you enjoy specifically girls' activities (e.g. hopscotch, playing housejacks)' and 'did you ever dress in boys clothes and pretend to be a boy other than at Halloween or for school plays?' allowing the researchers to tie diverse childhood experiences to specific points on an M-to-F axis (Bell, Weinberg and Hammersmith 1981, 74). In other words, the 'gender' to which proto-lesbian, gay and bisexual people did not conform was skewed toward children's leisure, defined 'masculinity' and 'femininity' as logical opposites, and left no place for androgynous childhoods. Within these limits 'gender conformity' did indeed predict adult sexual orientation (but more for whites, more for men, more for monosexuals than bisexuals, and, among women, more for those who had been in psychotherapy). Thus all too familiar forms of normativity were conceded by Sedgwick's endorsement of the credibility of this study. Sedgwick was right to inquire, in kid-friendly fashion, after the effect of the haunting abject position of the effeminate boy. But might not a gynophobic impulse have lead white, male, heterosexual interviewees to repudiate the gender nonconformity of their childhoods more than any others?

The trick of reading this kind of empirical psychological work might lie in learning to live with 'the disjunction between historical subjects and constructed scientific objects'.[10] Raising such double-consciousness that looks both at the networks of natural and social actors that materialise scientific truths, and the promises of science to address where the natural ends and the social begins requires, as Bruno Latour reminds us, a rethinking of modernity itself (Latour 1993). I came to this conclusion since attempting to use the modernist method of social psychology experimentation to understand the constructedness of heterosexual people's recall of childhood experience. I hoped to demonstrate the constructedness of such reports, by showing that heterosexual people report more gender-conforming experiences if they are in conversation with an interviewer who believes that they might be lesbian or gay. In my experiments I first briefed individual heterosexual students that they were taking part in a study about 'personality and job choices', or a study about 'personality, job choices and sexual orientation'. I then left the room and a research assistant who was the same sex as the study participant interviewed them about childhood experiences. I returned at the end for a debriefing. I had predicted that informing the students that the study was about sexual orientation would render their recall of childhood more gender conforming.[11]

My modernist ideas were, as Sedgwick would have it, more concerned with undoing essentialist narratives linking the coming of age of adult gay men to effeminate boyhoods than with forwarding knowledge of how to care for effeminate boys themselves. Moreover, gender nonconformity became a haunting abject of my modernist methods. This experiment was necessarily social, not least because it required two people to interview each heterosexual participant; one to brief them, and another to interview them while unaware of the effects of that briefing. Lesbian and gay students were keenest to work with me as interviewers, but because the study aimed to manipulate participants' feelings of being perceived as lesbian or gay themselves, I wanted them to believe that the interviewers were straight. I selected students whom I, naively, guessed had 'gender conforming' presentations of self to play the part of the interviewer. I also began to scrutinise my own gender as a piece of unreliable scientific apparatus. Was I out to the participants or not? How could I check? The assumption that lesbian and gay psychologists are necessarily lesbian or gay also manifested itself in the experiment. One male heterosexual assistant was read as gay by some participants. The experiment did not yield publishable results, but did show how scientific cultures are sites where gender is 'in the making'. Indeed, as Latour would have it, the impulse behind the experiment was quintessentially modern for its attempt to purify 'gender nonconformity' into real and constructed parts, while the work of doing the experiment led to new investments in gender that worked against any such purification.

Happily, Sedgwick's argument that there has been no response from within the caring professions around the nurture of effeminate boys has been made somewhat outdated by the work of Edgardo Menvielle, Catherine Tuerk and their colleagues (e.g. Menvielle and Tuerk 2002). Their support group and self-help materials for

---

10   Here I borrow from Treichler's (1991) useful thinking about the politics of deconstructing AIDS science.

11   For a description of these experiments see Hegarty (2001).

the parents of children with gender-variant behaviours refute the homophobic and transphobic assumptions that underlie the pathologisation of children through the category of Gender Identity Disorder in Childhood. By so doing their work shows that the terror of individualised behaviour modification aimed at normalising children's gender is not the only response that the helping professions are capable of offering to parents whose children quite spontaneously reveal that adults' 'mature' way of thinking about gender is, after all, only a set of acculturated beliefs. Alternate forms of psychology can and do emerge, but are far from being commonly practised yet. Instead of a celebration of 'coming of age', lesbian and gay psychology's history needs a narrative about its present that recognises how important its contingent futures might be.

The Past is Kids' Stuff

There is a need to live with the disjunction that networks of psychological truths open up, to think of children, gender, sexuality and truth as 'simultaneously real, like nature, narrated, like discourse, and collective, like society' (Latour 1993, 6). Indeed, for Latour, 'the child' is one of the 'fuzzy areas' where moderns find it difficult to locate the boundaries of their cultural condition, and against which we 'believe it is our duty to extirpate ourselves from those horrible mixtures' to restore the apparent purity of modernity' (Latour 1993, 100). Neither modernist narratives of coming of age that forget the past, nor postmodern despair which writes of the future entirely are sufficient here. Both forget the normalised children still caught up in psychiatric, pediatric and social work disciplines. I have a completely unwarranted optimism that I might enrol some allies from queer theory into the project of rethinking psychology's past along these lines. Because I am not so optimistic as to be non-strategic, I will focus my attention on an activity that is real, narrated and social, and has become crucial in queer theory's understandings of its own project: *reading*. When children read they can stimulate their own disciplining and concerns about where their minds might go. What's queer about the way that children have read, and been read, through the lens of modern psychology?

Lesbian and gay psychologists typically know that lesbians and gay men are stereotyped as having 'gender inverted' personalities. Scholars familiar with queer theory are more likely to be familiar with Judith Butler's argument that the 'genders' which lesbians and gay men are said to invert are implicitly already heterosexual, and that heterosexuality is formed as much from its relationship to homosexuality as the reverse (Butler 1993). But almost no-one remembers that the earliest technologies for measuring 'gender' as a personality trait were targeted at children not adults, and were anxiously deployed at the haunting abject of the effeminate boy within the literature on high IQ children. Psychologists Terman and Miles' 1936 book *Sex and Personality* has been largely understood, since second-wave feminists, to be the foundational measure of masculinity and femininity in modern psychology.[12] The Masculinity–Femininity test developed there was first deployed in studies on the feminine psychologies of 'passive male homosexuals' in California prisons. Thus, normal gender has been, as Butler would have it, a regime of truth that results from the abjection of queerness from its putative origin. Yet this origin *is* putative, for years earlier Lewis Terman measured the gender of a cohort of high IQ children to negate the possibility that they could be considered psychologically maladjusted.[13] This move was rightly described by Andrew Elfenbein as carrying 'faint hints of the older association between genius and sex/gender deviance' (Elfenbein 1999, 211). A lofty literary canon is the means by which Terman and Miles materialise gender. A person scores more 'feminine' if he enjoys *Little Women* or Helen Keller's *Story of My Life*, but more 'masculine' if he has enjoyed *The Swiss Family Robinson* or *The Call of the Wild*. Indeed, Terman's utterly androcentric work on genius insisted on the masculinity of genius, rendering effeminate gifted boys anomalous, and gifted tomboys a more interesting curiosity than any genius manifested by adult women. In their 1936 book on the measurement of gender, Terman and Miles explain that their test would be useful for the normalisation of effeminate boys such as one from their gifted cohort that they identify only as X. They describe how he, at age 15, liked 'to dress himself as a stylish young woman, apply cosmetics liberally, and walk down the street to see how many men he could lure into flirtation' (Terman and Miles 1936, 14). As Bryant (2006) would have it, the impulse to normalise the effeminate boy in psychology exceeds the simple urge to inhibit the development of gay men.

Reading is not absent from contemporary regulations of children's leisure pursuits either. Psychiatrist Kenneth Zucker describes how boys with Gender Identity Disorder 'have greater interest in female heroines in children's books and on TV … In middle childhood, characters such as Wonder Woman, Bionic Woman and She-Ra become favourites' (Burke 1996, 62). This is not the first time that *Wonder Woman* has found a psychiatrist among her enemies, but she used to be feared for inducing queerness in girls as well as boys. *Wonder Woman* was originally co-authored by psychologist William Marston, who celebrated the rise of feminism, and argued that America's cultural prowess depended on the future leadership of women, who were understood to be morally superior to men (Marston 1928). For Marston, passion and captivation by the female body – itself a state of bondage – forestalls emotional suffering and creates a desirable state of normalcy in men. Unsurprisingly, Marston's theory of the emotions has never had a central place in the canon of Western psychology. Marston knew that his ideas would be more effectively distributed through the popular genre of comic books than any psychological prose. Wonder Woman, the comic book heroine that he created in 1941 was a response to both the androcentrism and the violence of the superhero genre. Like lie detection technologies, which Marston has dubiously

---

12   Terman and Miles (1936). For feminist and queer analysis of this study see Hegarty (2007b); Kline (2002); Lewin (1984); and Terry (1999).
13   Terman (1925).

been credited with inventing, Wonder Woman tends to vanquish the bad guys and gals by ensnaring them in her lasso of truth without recourse to the SMACK! and POW! of her male counterparts' third degree (Bunn 1997; 2007).

Marston located Wonder Woman's origins on Paradise Island, a land with no men. She comes into being through the intervention of the goddess Aphrodite and the craft of her mother Hippolyte. Thus, decades before Heather, Diana Prince was a subject of children's literature who already had two mommies (Robinson 2004, 28–32). As *Wonder Woman*'s focal points are all-female separatist societies removed from civilisation, the responsibilities of recognising female superiority, and an endlessly deferred romance with Steve Trevor, it is worth speculating, as Molly Rhodes does, how *Wonder Woman* opens up the historical category of the lesbian reader for Second World War and post-war times (Rhodes 2000). Historian of psychology Ellen Herman argues that second wave feminism borrowed largely from the humanistic discourse of post-war psychology (Herman 1995), but this may not have been the only form of pop-psychology from which American feminist notions of self were borrowed. Robinson cannot have been the only girl for whom *Wonder Woman* afforded possibilities of tomboy identification. (Nor I, the only proto-homo boy who found Diana Prince's TV adventures more inspiring than the male TV and film superheroes of the 1970s.) Did William Marston's comic serve as a similar conceptual resource for any radical lesbians who imagined feminism as the theory and lesbianism as the practice? As Rhodes notes, in classically Foucauldian fashion, Wonder Woman was explicitly named as 'lesbian' by psychoanalysts who opposed the comic and feared its effects on children's minds. *Wonder Woman*'s lesbian connotations were occluded when she was reclaimed as a feminist icon in the 1970s, and are not necessarily flagged up in the here-and-now either (Pereira 2006, 34–9). Nor does the recognition of the BDSM erotics of *Wonder Woman* always lead to clarifying interpretations. In an argument that conflates SM with nonconsensual violence, Robbins argues that Wonder Woman is *not* an SM text as 'rather than punching them out, she used her magic lasso to capture the bad guys and compel them to obey her. Compared to most male-oriented action comics, *Wonder Woman* was pretty nonviolent' (Robbins 1996, 12). Pereira recognises these pleasures more accurately when she writes that '[w]hether Wonder Woman is encouraging Marva to be strong and unafraid or trying to stop Marva from helping Dr. Psycho, the sub/dom vibe is surely meant to titillate' (Pereira 2006, 35). No wonder children are banished from the room before these conversations can take place.

Psychoanalytic fears about *Wonder Woman*'s ability to induce a wide range of desires in young girls are, of course, part of the history of post-war psychoanalysis which repeatedly promised to address fears about the impure development of children who might lapse into homosexuality. Not all forms of psychiatry were so uniformly negative about the power of children's same-sex affiliations. In contrast to the reassuring narratives of Freudian ego psychology, the interpersonal theories of American psychiatrist Harry Stack Sullivan understood personality development to be incomplete until children had experienced social dynamics located *outside* the heterosexual nuclear family. In pre-adolescence, every child needs a *chum* – a close, intimate, age mate of the same sex – who represents 'the quiet miracle of adolescence' (Sullivan 1947, 41). Sullivan's notion of chumship was homosocial, dependent on feelings of similarity, and could include, but did not require, genital sexuality. Chumships were often a route of entry into adult heterosexuality, but were also vital in their own right, representing 'the best grasp on the problems of life that some people ever manifest' (Sullivan 1954, 137).

Sullivan's notion of chumship was formed through clinical work conducted in the 1920s with men institutionalised for schizophrenia. Naoko Wake's recent work on Sullivan has gone much further than that of previous scholars who have tended to balk at the erotics of Sullivan's clinical practices, through which these theories took shape (Wake 2006). Bruhm and Hurley (2004) have recently suggested that narratives which afford queerness in children on condition that it be 'just a phase' may be a resource for the development of queer cultures. This insight seemed to have shaped Sullivan's psychiatric practice also. As Wake's work shows, many of Sullivan's patients were troubled by homosexual yearnings, some saw these yearnings in Sullivan himself, and others found room in conferences with him to explore and problematise the sense of dread that those feelings engendered. Sullivan often appealed to the notion that homosexuality was 'only a phase' to encourage these men to engage in same-sex eroticism for the good of their mental health. Long before contemporary queer reading strategies, forms of therapeutic practice that defined themselves *against* psychoanalysis have deployed the affordances of considering that homosexuality might be 'just a phase'.

The *reading* of those chumships also became disciplined after Sullivan's death. Sullivan's lectures and writings were selectively published by the William Alanson White institute in the 1950s and 1960s. Biographical accounts of Sullivan appeared in the 1970s and 1980s, which tended to read the chums in his writings as coded references to his own childhood friendship with Clarence Bellinger. Without doubting the relevance of this friendship to Sullivan's understanding of personhood, the explanation of the presence of the chums in the theory as autobiography rehabilitates Sullivan's unique theory by moving it closer to Freud's. By writing the chums off as relevant to Sullivan, and Sullivan only, the narrative of development is rehabilitated as more similar to the Oedipally organised psychoanalytic one.[14] It is at least an interesting question why queer theory still prefers to traffic within the terms of those Oedipal narratives rather than the wider world of childhood affiliation that Sullivan's theory opens up.

Conclusions

According to Latour, we can only maintain the illusion that we are modern subjects by appealing to a break with our pre-modern past. In this chapter, I have argued that the possibility of creating a critically queer developmental psychology (both

---

14   Hegarty (2005b). On Sullivan's life and work see Allen (1995), Chatelaine (1981) and
     Perry (1982).

in theory and in practice) requires such a rethinking, and an ability to live with the uncomfortable impure disjunctures between ahistoricist psychology and genealogical histories of truth. In lesbian and gay psychology, modernism has taken the form of a break with the pathologising narratives of the past in coming of age narratives. Postmodern readings of the figuration of the future as 'the future of *the* child' have some accuracy, but critical children are needed, and not just adults' critique of childhood. Sedgwick is right that gay theory has seen the effeminate boy as a construction, while psychiatry has seen him as a too real figure who must be normalised away. Doing psychological science in this domain proves how unlikely we might be to contain this fuzzy creature within the modernist discourses of what is real and what is constructed. Rather, the existence of children with gender variant behaviours reminds us that we are less modern – and less grown up – than we think, and that 'lesbian and gay psychology' is not qualified to celebrate its maturity. Latour calls for an expansion of democracy to include those quasi-objects that are positioned as devoid of agency by the modernist split between the political representation of people and the scientific representation of things. Perhaps queer theory and lesbian and gay psychology can usefully pollute each other by affording the movement of queer children across this boundary.

Suggested Further Reading

Bruhm, S. and N. Hurley (eds) (2004), *Curiouser: On the Queerness of Children* (Minneapolis, MN: University of Minnesota Press).

Edelman, L. (2004), *No Future: Queer Theory and the Death Drive* (Durham, NC and London: Duke University Press).

Latour, B. (1993), *We Have Never Been Modern* (Cambridge, MA: Harvard University Press).

Sedgwick, E.K. (1991), 'How to Bring Your Kids Up Gay: The War on Effeminate Boys,' *Social Text* 29, 18–27.

Terry, J. (1999), *An American Obsession: Science, Medicine and Homosexuality in Modern Society* (Chicago, IL: University of Chicago Press).

References

Allen, M. (1995), 'Sullivan's Closet: A Reappraisal of Harry Stack Sullivan's Life and His Pioneering Role in American Psychiatry', *Journal of Homosexuality* 29: 1–18.

American Psychiatric Association (1980), *Diagnostic and Statistical Manual of Mental Disorders*, 3rd edition (Washington, DC: American Psychiatric Association).

Barker, M., Iantaffi, A. and Gupta, C. (2005), 'Countering Bi-invisibility', *The Psychologist* 18, 662–3.

Bayer, R. (1981), *Homosexuality and American Psychiatry: The Politics of Diagnosis* (New York: Basic Books).

Bell, A.P., Weinberg, M.S. and Hammersmith, S.K. (1981), *Sexual Preference: Its Development in Men and Women* (Bloomington, IN: Indiana University Press).

Bem, S.L. (1989), 'Genital Knowledge and Gender Constancy in Preschool Children', *Child Development* 60, 649–62.

Bruhm, S. and Hurley, N. (2004), 'Curiouser: On the Queerness of Children', in S. Bruhm and N. Hurley (eds), *Curiouser: On the Queerness of Children* (Minneapolis, MN: University of Minnesota Press).

Bryant, K. (2006), 'Making Gender Identity Disorder of Childhood: Historical Lessons for Contemporary Debates', *Sexuality Research and Social Policy* 3:3, 23–39.

Bunn, G.C. (1997), 'The Lie Detector, Wonder Woman and Liberty: The Life and Work of William Moulton Marsten', *History of the Human Sciences* 10, 91–119.

—— (2007), 'Spectacular Science: The Lie Detector's Ambivalent Powers', *History of Psychology* 10, 156–78.

Burke, P. (1996), *Gender Shock: Exploding the Myths of Male and Female* (New York: Anchor Books).

Burman, E. (1994), *Deconstructing Developmental Psychology* (London: Routledge).

Butler, J. (1990), *Gender Trouble: Feminism and the Subversion of Identity* (New York: Routledge).

—— (1993), *Bodies That Matter: On the Discursive Limits of 'Sex'* (New York: Routledge).

Cass, V. (1979), 'Homosexual Identity Formation: A Theoretical Model', *Journal of Homosexuality* 4, 219–21.

—— (1999), 'Bringing Psychology in from the Cold: Framing Psychological Theory and Research within a Social Constructionist Psychology Approach', in J.S. Bohan and G.M. Russell (eds), *Conversations about Psychology and Sexual Orientation* (New York: New York University Press).

Chatelaine, K. (1981), *Harry Stack Sullivan: The Formative Years* (Washington, DC: University Press of America).

Clarke, V. (2000), '"Stereotype, Attack and Stigmatize Those Who Disagree": Employing Scientific Rhetoric in Debates about Lesbian and Gay Parenting', *Feminism and Psychology* 10, 152–9.

Diamond, L.M. (2008), 'Female Bisexuality from Adolescence to Adulthood: Results from a 10-year Longitudinal Study', *Developmental Psychology* 44, 5–14.

Dickens, T., Hardman, D. and Sergeant, M. (2005), 'Nothing to Get Sniffy About', *The Psychologist* 18, 532.

Dunbar, J., Brown, M. and Amoroso, D.M. (1973), 'Some Correlates of Attitudes Toward Homosexuality', *The Journal of Social Psychology* 89, 271–9.

Edelman, L. (2004), *No Future: Queer Theory and the Death Drive* (Durham, NC: Duke University Press).

Elfenbein, A. (1999), *Romantic Genius: The Prehistory of a Homosexual Role* (New York: Columbia University Press).

Fausto-Sterling, A. (1993), 'The Five Sexes: Why Male and Female Are Not Enough', *The Sciences* 33, 20–25.

Foucault, M. (1977), *Discipline and Punish* (New York: Pantheon Books).

—— (1978), *The History of Sexuality: Volume 1, An Introduction* (New York: Vintage).

Goldberg, A.E. (2007), '(How) Does It Make a Difference? Perspectives of Adults with Lesbian, Gay, and Bisexual Parents', *American Journal of Orthopsychiatry* 77, 550–62.

Gonsierek, J.C. (1994), 'Foreword', in B. Greene and G.M. Herek (eds), *Lesbian and Gay Psychology: Theory, Research and Applications* (Thousand Oaks, CA: Sage).

Hegarty, P. (2001), '"Real Science", Deception Experiments and the Gender of My Lab Coat: Toward a New Laboratory Manual for Lesbian and Gay Psychology', *International Journal of Critical Psychology* 1:4, 91–108.

—— (2005a), 'Kitzinger's Irony: Then and Now', *Lesbian and Gay Psychology Review* 6, 114–16.

—— (2005b), 'Harry Stack Sullivan and His Chums: Archive Fever in American Psychiatry?', *History of the Human Sciences* 18:3, 35–53.

—— (2007a), 'From Genius Inverts to Gendered Intelligence: Lewis Terman and the Power of the Norm', *History of Psychology* 10, 132–55.

—— (2007b), 'What Comes after Discourse Analysis for LGBTQ Psychology?', in E.A. Peel and V.C. Clarke (eds), *Out in Psychology: LGBTQ Perspectives* (Chichester: Wiley and Sons).

—— and Massey, S. (2006), 'Anti-homosexual Prejudice … As Opposed to What?: Queer Theory and the Social Psychology of Anti-homosexual Prejudice', *Journal of Homosexuality* 52, 47–71.

—— and Pratto, F. (2001), 'The Effects of Category Norms and Stereotypes on Explanations of Intergroup Differences,' *Journal of Personality and Social Psychology* 80, 723–35.

Hemmings, C. (2002), *Bisexual Spaces: A Geography of Sexuality and Gender* (London: Routledge).

Herek, G.M. (1998), 'Preface', in G.M. Herek (ed.), *Stigma and Sexual Orientation: Understanding Prejudice against Lesbians, Gay Men, and Bisexuals* (Thousand Oaks, CA: Sage).

Herman, E. (1995), *The Romance of American Psychology: Political Culture in the Age of Experts* (Berkeley, CA: University of California Press).

Hill, D.B. and Willoughby, B.L.B. (2005), 'The Development and Validation of the Genderism and Transphobia Scale', *Sex Roles* 53, 531–44.

Kessler, S.J. and McKenna, W. (1978), *Gender: An Ethnomethodological Approach* (Chicago, IL: University of Chicago Press).

Kitzinger, C. (1987), *The Social Construction of Lesbianism* (London: Sage).

—— (1997), 'Lesbian and Gay Psychology: A Critical Analysis', in D. Fox and I. Prilleltensky (eds), *Critical Psychology: An Introduction* (London: Sage).

—— and Coyle, A. (2002), 'Introducing Lesbian and Gay Psychology', in A. Coyle and C. Kitzinger (eds), *Lesbian and Gay Psychology: New Perspectives* (Oxford: BPS Blackwell).

Kline, W. (2002), *Building a Better Race: Gender, Sexuality, and Eugenics from the Turn of the Century to the Baby Boom* (Berkeley, CA: University of California Press).

Kohlberg, L. (1966), 'A Cognitive-developmental Analysis of Children's Sex-role Concepts and Attitudes', in Eleanor E. Maccoby (ed.), *The Development of Sex Differences* (Stanford, CA: Stanford University Press).

Latour, B. (1993), *We Have Never Been Modern* (Cambridge, MA: Harvard University Press).

Lewin, M. (1984), '"Rather Worse than Folly?" Psychology Measures Femininity and Masculinity, 1: From Terman and Miles to the Guildfords', in M. Lewin (ed.), *In the Shadow of the Past* (New York: Columbia University Press).

Marcus, E. (1992), *Making History: The Struggle for Gay and Lesbian Equal Rights, An Oral History* (New York: HarperCollins).

Marston, W.M. (1928), *Emotions of Normal People* (New York).

Menvielle, E. and Tuerk, C. (2002), 'A Support Group for Parents of Gender Non-conforming Boys', *Journal of the American Academy of Child and Adolescent Psychiatry* 41, 1010–13.

Millham, J., San Miguel, C.L. and Kellogg, R. (1976), 'A Factor-analytic Conceptualization of Attitudes toward Male and Female Homosexuals', *Journal of Homosexuality* 2, 3–10.

Minter, S. (1999), 'Diagnosis and Treatment of Gender Identity Disorder in Children', in M. Rottnek (ed.), *Sissies and Tomboys: Gender Nonconformity and Homosexual Childhood* (New York: New York University Press).

Minton, H. (2001), *Departing from Deviance: A History of Homosexual Rights and Emancipatory Science in America* (Chicago, IL: Chicago University Press).

Morin, S.F. (1977), 'Heterosexual Bias in Psychological Research on Lesbianism and Male Homosexuality', *American Psychologist* 32, 329–67.

—— and Rothblum, E.D. (1991), 'Removing the Stigma: Fifteen Years of Progress', *American Psychologist* 46, 947–9.

Morss, J. (1995), *Growing Critical: Alternatives to Developmental Psychology* (London: Routledge).

Mosher, D.L. and O'Grady, K.E. (1979), 'Homosexual Threat, Negative Attitudes toward Masturbation, Sex Guilt, and Males' Sexual and Affective Reactions to Explicit Sexual Films', *Journal of Consulting and Clinical Psychology* 47, 860–73.

Parlee, M.B. (1996), 'Situated Knowledges of Personal Embodiment: Transgender Activists' and Psychological Theorists' Perspectives on "Sex" and "Gender"', *Theory and Psychology* 6, 625–45.

Patterson, C.J. (2006), 'Children of Lesbian and Gay Parents', *Current Directions in Psychological Science* 15, 241–5.

Pereira, K.L. (2006), 'Female Bonding: The Strange History of Wonder Woman', *Bitch* 33, 24–39.

Perry, H.S. (1982), *Psychiatrist of America: The Life of Harry Stack Sullivan* (Cambridge, MA: Harvard University Press).

Rhodes, M. (2000), 'Wonder Woman and Her Disciplinary Powers: The Queer Intersection of Scientific Authority and Mass Culture', in R. Reid and S. Traweek (eds), *Doing Science + Culture* (New York: Routledge).

Rieger, G., Chivers, M.L. and Bailey, J.M. (2005), 'Sexual Arousal Patterns of Bisexual Men', *Psychological Science* 16, 579–84.

Robbins, T. (1996), *The Great Women Super Heroes* (Northampton, MA: Kitchen Sink Press).

Robinson, L.S. (2004), *Wonder Women* (New York: Routledge).

Saffron, L. (1998), 'Raising Children in an Age of Diversity: Advantages of Having a Lesbian Mother', *Journal of Lesbian Studies* 2, 35–47.

Savic, I., Berglund, H. and Lindström, P. (17 May 2005), 'Brain Response to Putative Pheromones in Homosexual Men', *Proceedings of the National Academy of Science* 102, 7356–61.

Sedgwick, E.K. (1991), 'How to Bring Your Kids Up Gay: The War on Effeminate Boys', *Social Text* 29, 18–27.

Stacey, J. and Bilbarz, T.J. (2001), '(How) Does the Sexual Orientation of Parents Matter?', *American Sociological Review* 66, 159–83.

Sullivan, H.S. (1947), *Conceptions of Modern Psychiatry* (Washington, DC: William Alanson White Psychiatric Foundation).

—— (1954), *The Psychiatric Interview* (New York: W.W. Norton).

Terman, L.M. (1925), *Genetic Studies of Genius. Volume 1: Mental and Physical Traits of One Thousand Gifted Children* (New York).

—— and Miles, C.C. (1936), *Sex and Personality: Studies in Masculinity and Femininity* (New York: McGraw-Hill).

Terry, J. (1999), *An American Obsession* (Chicago, IL: University of Chicago Press).

Treichler, P.A. (1991), 'AIDS, Homophobia, and Biomedical Discourse: An Epidemic of Signification', in D. Crimp (ed.), *AIDS: Cultural Analysis, Cultural Activism* (Cambridge, MA: MIT Press).

Wake, N. (2006), '"The Full Story by No Means All Told": Harry Stack Sullivan at Shepperd-Pratt, 1922–1930', *History of Psychology* 9, 325–58.

Warner, M. (1999), *The Trouble With Normal* (New York: The Free Press).

'Nothing to Hide … Nothing to Fear': Discriminatory Surveillance and Queer Visibility in Great Britain and Northern Ireland

Kathryn Conrad

Surveillance has increasingly been part of the everyday experience of people throughout the world, whether it is through heightened security practices that have emerged through anxiety about the spread of global terrorism or the ever-increasing presence of commercial surveillance technologies, both licit and illicit. The significance of surveillance resonates with the history and politics of queer people, queer theory and queer methodologies, since surveillance is part of a system of power that, among other things, shapes subjectivity, as Michel Foucault (1979) has argued, and normalises, as Michael Warner (2000) has argued. Surveillance has been engaged, for instance, to monitor people with HIV and AIDS, to police the spaces in which dissident sexual behaviour occurs, and to expose the non-normative private sexual practices of those who have fought publicly against gay marriage. Surveillance also intersects with visibility/ exposure, simultaneously a goal of the minority-rights activism that has included queer sexualities as well as a fear of many who find themselves outside of the sexual mainstream. Brought together, each discipline has much to offer the other. The emerging discipline of surveillance studies has examined the relationship between theories (of, for example, vision, policing and subjectivity) and actual surveillance practices. Queer studies (or applied queer theory) has similarly investigated the relationship between theory and practice; queer geography, for instance, provides surveillance studies with a nuanced sense of the significance of the body and the subject in space (Duncan 1996; Bell and Valentine 1995; Boone et al. 2000). And queer theory itself offers challenging ways to reimagine the binary relationships – subject/object, private/public, visible/invisible, exposed/hidden – on which surveillance depends (Sedgwick 1990; 2003; Warner 2000; 2002). The conjunction of queer studies and surveillance studies has the potential to illuminate the relationship between the state and private forces that shape space, behaviour, subjectivity, consumerism and citizenship.

This chapter will 'queer' surveillance, interrogate the assumptions on which it is based and consider the uses to which it is put, by examining surveillance and policing practices in both the United Kingdom generally and, more specifically, in Northern Ireland, particularly as they have been directed at queer people. In the human crises engendered by surveillance, I will suggest, we also see a crisis in the meanings and value of the public, privacy, visibility and normalisation issues that have long resonated with queer theory and queer studies.

Surveillance Studies: Reading through the Gaps

Surveillance studies is an emerging interdisciplinary field that takes a critical position with regard to surveillance technologies and practice and their implications. Interestingly, there are at least two conspicuous absences in contemporary academic discussions of surveillance, including UK surveillance, studies of which have created some of the foundational works in the field. The first is surveillance in Northern Ireland (see the work of Armstrong and Norris, and the journal *Surveillance and Society*). The invisibility of Northern Ireland in surveillance studies is particularly ironic, given that Northern Ireland is clearly *not* invisible to surveillance technologies. The absence of studies of surveillance in Northern Ireland, however, is presumably at least in part due to the unavailability of official statistics on the subject, even in post-Agreement Northern Ireland, given the ongoing military and police surveillance of suspected paramilitary organisations and groups.[1] To some degree, the absence could also be part of the internalisation of the notion of Northern Irish 'exceptionalism' on the part of UK academics in particular – that is, the uncritical acceptance of Northern Ireland as a 'special case' in the UK. Surveillance of one sort or another has nonetheless shaped both public and private space in Northern Ireland since at least the emergency powers acts of the 1970s, and has reinforced the sense of Northern Ireland, both from within and without, as a peripheral colony in crisis rather than as an integral part of the United Kingdom. In contemporary Northern Ireland, the full extent of military surveillance operations is considered to be classified information. But as in the rest of the UK, surveillance for the purposes of thwarting paramilitary and terrorist activity is only part of the picture. Surveillance of commercial space and police surveillance for crime – that is, what might be considered 'normal' or 'non-political' surveillance – have been in place for at least as long as they have been in the rest of

---

1   Post-Agreement refers to the period after the institution of the 'Belfast Agreement', also known as the 'Good Friday Agreement', a document that emerged out of the 'peace process' and that includes provisions for governance of Northern Ireland. The Agreement was approved by referenda in Northern Ireland and the Republic of Ireland in 1998.

Great Britain. Norris and Armstrong note that, in the UK in general, the post-Cold War 'peace dividend' meant the transfer of technologies from the military realm into criminal justice and policing applications and also into commercial applications (1999, 32, 38–9). The equivalent move has been echoed in Northern Ireland since the ostensible end of violence there (that is, since the end of both open violence between paramilitary groups and organised paramilitary violence directed at state forces); there, the 'peace dividend' has been in the form of increasing commercial investment in the formerly conflict-torn region, and military technologies have found a similar niche in the rising Northern Ireland economy.

The second conspicuous absence in the academic analysis of surveillance and surveillance technologies is surveillance of sexual activity. Such analysis has been offered, but by those in queer studies rather than those in surveillance studies – as in, for instance, David Bell's analysis of the 'assemblage of bodies, technologies, and spaces' that constitutes the '(hetero)sexual practice and subculture known as "dogging"' (2006, 387). The absence is certainly not for the paucity of the subject matter. Sexual activity in public toilets, sexual voyeurism and sexual 'exposure' – regardless of the gender of the actors – is illegal in the UK under the Sexual Offences Act (2003). The Police Service of Northern Ireland (PSNI) reported, on request from several gay activist groups, that in 2005–2006 there were 59 surveillance operations directed at public sex, only some of which were direct violations of the Act. Of those operations, a significant proportion (in several communities, the only operations) were directed against homosexual sexual activity.[2] When asked, the PSNI has, unsurprisingly, been reticent about sharing the exact method of the surveillance activities.[3] Nonetheless, it is instructive to analyse how its enforcement is attempted, especially in Northern Ireland, and to think about this enforcement in light of the larger critiques raised by those who have analysed both surveillance activity and sexual culture more generally.

These absences in surveillance studies are themselves instructive. They suggest the challenges inherent in analysing a discourse that relies as much on containment and secrecy (e.g. military surveillance, informers, secret footage) as it does on visible signs (the surveillance camera, the CCTV warning sign) for its effectiveness. But one often under-analysed aspect of surveillance is the media

---

2   The language of Chief Constable J.A. Harris refers to surveillance of the 'homosexual community' and 'heterosexual community', perhaps reflecting the language of the activists who asked for statistics; however, it is worth noting that those arrested for homosexual public sex are often not men who identify with the 'homosexual community'.

3   Correspondence with PSNI Inspector Robin Dempsey suggested that in at least one instance, the arrests of 10–12 men in the public toilets in Coleraine, CCTV was not used, although newspaper reports continued to cite the use of CCTV in those arrests. Assistant Chief Constable J.A. Harris reported that graffiti set off the surveillance, and that the 'police observations of the car park ... revealed men meeting and going inside the toilets or meeting and driving off in cars'. Gay cruising sites also offer access to information about those planning to meet for sexual activity, although it is unclear whether the police have used these sites to target their surveillance.

itself. As Lee Edelman notes in his analysis of the US public reactions to the arrest of Walter Jenkins, President Lyndon Johnson's chief of staff, in a YMCA bathroom and the subsequent charges of 'indecent gestures', the media itself 'foster[s] an internalisation of the repressive supervisory mechanisms of the State' (1994, 156); in other words, the media is a technology of surveillance and, I would suggest, a technology that extends beyond the state, which, as many surveillance studies critics have noted, is by no means the only user of surveillance technologies. The significance of the media in surveillance is further supported by Bell, who notes that the media not only helps to create the fear of crime, terrorism and moral panic[4] that justifies the use of surveillance technologies, but constitutes part of the 'scene' of voyeurism itself (2006, 391); in this sense, I might suggest that the media as surveillance technology helps to perpetuate the conditions that justify its use, creating a kind of feedback loop or circuit of both desire and fear that embeds surveillance more completely into our culture.

The ubiquity of surveillance has led many writers in surveillance studies to evoke Foucault's influential *Discipline and Punish* (1979), particularly his use of 'panopticism'. The latter term arises from Jeremy Bentham's Panopticon, a model carceral structure in which the prisoner perceives himself to be under the constant threat of surveillance whether or not s/he actually is; Foucault uses the panopticon as a way of thinking about surveillance as a disciplinary mechanism, particularly the ways in which power is embedded in social structures and evokes self-regulation to create a carceral culture. Many practitioners of surveillance studies have been drawn to the Foucauldian model to suggest the ways in which surveillance technologies and practice potentially limit freedom through the internalisation of the disciplinary gaze. Some recent analysts, however, have suggested that the Foucauldian thesis is not applicable to the current surveillance *status quo*: the omnipresence of surveillance has not produced the self-regulation in its subjects promised by Foucault's theory.[5] Indeed, surveillance technologies seem to have become a commonplace for many who are regularly subjected to them, fading into the background and out of the consciousness of most people unless they are confronted with them directly (as when and if, for instance, they are arrested).

But the Foucauldian thesis, as I will suggest, may be more applicable to those for whom the notion of visibility is already charged: that is, those who fall outside

---

4   'Moral panic' is a term that gained popularity in the wake of Stanley Cohen's *Folk Devils and Moral Panics: The Creation of the Mods and Rockers*. He defines the process of moral panic thus: 'A condition, episode, person or group of persons emerges to become defined as a threat to societal values and interests; its nature is presented in a stylised and stereotypical fashion by the mass media; the moral barricades are manned by editors, bishops, politicians and other right-thinking people; socially accredited experts pronounce their diagnoses and solutions; ways of coping are evolved or (more often) resorted to; the condition then disappears, submerges or deteriorates and becomes more visible' (2002, 1).

5   For critiques of the Foucauldian perspective in surveillance studies, see especially Lyon (2003a); Yar (2003). For further discussions of Foucault and panopticism see also Fussey (2004); Hier (2004); Cole (2004); Goold (2004); Norris and Armstrong (1999).

the realm of the normative and who are thus more likely to be sensitive to the possibility of exposure. The practice of surveillance, as I will suggest, normalises visibility, which in turn helps to shape and reinforce the very narratives of normality and the spaces in which normative and non-normative behaviour is allowed; and participating in those narratives of normality can be, as Warner suggests in *The Trouble with Normal* (2000), particularly attractive to the already-marginalised – in this case, both queer and Northern Irish subjects more generally. Predictably, surveillance impacts the already-marginalised more heavily, as we will see; but I will also suggest that the self-regulation that emerges from surveillance, the pressure toward normalisation, creates a kind of cultural inertia that facilitates the shrinkage of the space – both literal and figurative – for challenges to surveillance practices.

Surveillance in Great Britain

Even before the West's preoccupation with terrorist activity in the new millennium, the United Kingdom had become the most surveilled state in Europe and, arguably, the world (Goold 2004, 1, 17). Benjamin Goold, following Stuart Hall and others, notes that the lead-up to the 1979 General Election saw an increase in anti-crime rhetoric, which set the terms for this as a central issue in the competition for votes over subsequent decades (2004, 28–34). The case of toddler James Bulger, whose 1993 abduction was caught on CCTV camera and broadcast throughout the world after his death at the hands of two ten-year-old boys, galvanised public opinion about the usefulness of CCTV surveillance in particular (2004, 34–5; Norris and Armstrong 1999, 37; Norris 2003, 255), even though the surveillance did not prevent the crime. Pete Fussey notes that 'crime control partnerships ... have empowered and incorporated a range of previously lay actors into crime and disorder policy forums (many of which were previously unconnected with crime control), thus increasing the influence of individual agency and preconceived ideas of crime and criminality' (2004, 258); even as the UK has decentralised its policing and involved communities and lay entities in its policing processes, in other words, the tendency toward surveillance has neither been diminished nor ensured more informed applications of the technologies. Clive Norris and Gary Armstrong note that any 'fears surrounding the increased use of surveillance could be dismissed by the simple sloganising of the then Prime Minister John Major: "If you've got nothing to hide you've got nothing to fear"' (1999, 32).

The increase in surveillance in the UK marks a change not only in criminology but in the larger society. In their compelling and detailed study of CCTV in the UK, Norris and Armstrong note that the rise of the use of surveillance technologies signals an orientation toward 'actuarial justice', focused on the prevention of future crimes (1999, 25–6). The shift towards 'actuarial justice' has meant mass surveillance and the 'legal abandonment of individualised suspicion' (1999, 26), marked less by a focus on known offenders than on classes of people deemed likely to commit crimes, a practice commonly referred to in the United States as 'profiling' and criticised widely there for its racist implications. Of course, such profiling is not limited to racial minorities, but is applied broadly: in the UK, for instance, Norris and Armstrong note that groups of people going to football matches can legally be stopped and searched (1999, 26). They suggest, following other scholars of urban studies, that this change in criminological practice has come with the rise of 'stranger society', in which the 'growth of individualism, autonomy and personal freedom' is accompanied by a move away from traditional community forms and more privatisation (1999, 20–23). The increase in the privileging of privacy over communal forms has meant, ironically enough, less privacy for individuals in practice – particularly in the UK, where privacy is not legally guaranteed.

Norris and Armstrong, Goold, and other critics have suggested a close connection between commercial interests and the focus of surveillance attention in Britain. Mass surveillance need not, according to David Lyon, always be read as 'sinister': it is, he suggests, 'appropriate to think of such surveillance as in some ways positive and beneficial, permitting new levels of efficiency, productivity, convenience, and comfort that many in the technologically advanced societies take for granted' (2003b, 18). Nonetheless, as Norris notes:

> ... privatised space increasingly contains the amenities previously located in the public or civic realm such as shops, banks, pharmacists and cinemas. But in this privatised space there is little commitment to democratic ideals of public access and assembly; the commitment is to commercial success. If people and their associated behaviours, whether legal or not, disrupt this entrepreneurial mission, they are to be excluded. (2003, 277)

Further, Norris and Armstrong observed in their study that 'the targeting of ... groups had less to do with their criminogenic potential but more to do with the capacity to portray a negative image of the city. In a sense targeting is as much about the commercial image of the city than crime ...' (1999, 141). This practice extends commercially-motivated surveillance activity from private spaces – that is, spaces owned by individuals and private organisations rather than by the government – into the realm of public or civic space, such as streets, public toilets, parks and other places, for the purposes of protecting commercial interests. As Norris and Armstrong put it, 'increasingly ... this public space is being reconstituted, not as an arena for democratic interaction, but as the site of mass consumption. Individuals are recast as consumers rather than citizens, as potential harbingers of profit, rather than bearers of rights' (1999, 8). This disturbing trend inevitably leads to the contraction of spaces in which contestation of the *status quo* is tolerated.

Certain people are more likely to be singled out for surveillance than others. Lyon notes that while 'probabilities play a greatly increased role in assessment of risk', the application of such probabilities 'also depends on stereotypes, whether to do with territory ... or social characteristics' (2003b, 16). Norris and Armstrong articulate this tendency in greater detail. The 'working rules' that they observed in their study of surveillance operators and police suggest that, given the vast data with which they are presented, operators must work with prior understandings of what might constitute a criminal behaviour or person and what might be indicative of a time or place in which a crime might occur. They suggest that 'for operators the normal ecology of an area is also a "normative ecology"' (1999, 140). The results of such understandings 'produced ... a highly differentiated pattern of surveillance leading to a massively disproportionate targeting of young males ... particularly ... if they are black or visibly identifiable as having subcultural affiliations' (1999, 150; see also Goold 2004, 153–63). As Norris writes, 'rather than promoting a democratic gaze, the reliance on categorical suspicion further intensifies the surveillance of those already marginalised and further increases their chance of official stigmatisation' (2003, 266). Moreover, if surveillance is seen as 'an extension of discriminatory and unjust policing, the consequential loss of legitimacy may have serious consequences for the social order' (Norris and Armstrong 1999, 151).

Perhaps the most striking analysis is their observation that 'it is almost as though operators construct a map of moral progress through the streets which is unidirectional. People of good moral character know where they are going and proceeded to their destination without signs of deviation' (1999, 144). This phrasing resonates with the notion of 'queer', particularly insofar as 'queer' invokes a path that is not straight, in several senses of the word. When seeking to engage in queer sexual behaviour, a person may not follow a straight path in the most literal sense as well, inviting surveillance regardless of the legality of the behaviour as s/he attempts to cruise, make eye contact and engage in other codes, often unspoken, that will enable a connection. Non-normative behaviour, however legal, is more visible than normative behaviour, and precipitates surveillance. Once begun, surveillance piques interest and fills the human need for story and, 'like all of us, operators like to know the end of the story – even if it has a happy ending' (1999, 132). But the story's beginning – the impetus for surveillance – is shaped by previous stories, and the necessarily incomplete nature of surveillance encourages the surveillers to draw on previous experiences and assumptions to complete the story. The comments Norris and Armstrong make about narrative highlight the fact that those who engage in and act on surveillance must fill in the epistemological gaps provided by surveillance, which only provides, often quite literally, part of the picture.[6] But as Irma van der Ploeg argues in her analysis of the ontology and epistemology of biometric surveillance, the virtual body created by information – whether it be the 'digital persona' created through biometric data collection or, as I would argue, the narrative of the person created through visual surveillance technologies – is as central to personhood and bodily integrity as the physical body (2003, 70–71), and the ways that information is manipulated has profound consequences for individuals and targeted groups, as we will see in the next section.

Nonetheless, for all of the difficulties posed by surveillance, it has the potential to be applied, in however imperfect a way, to safeguard marginalised and at-risk

---

6   For a discussion of the incomplete nature of CCTV data, for instance, see Cameron (2004, 136–9).

members of society. Significantly, however, Norris and Armstrong discovered that surveillance was rarely applied in a protectional way, although Goold's study found somewhat more protectional surveillance of women, even though women were still considerably less surveilled, and usually surveilled when they were known offenders. Norris and Armstrong found that even in cases where male-on-female violence was observed, there was no deployment of police, even though the 'domestic' violence took place in public. CCTV in particular 'fosters a male gaze' by allowing operators to use the cameras for voyeuristic reasons; with regard to the targeting of women, voyeuristic use of the cameras outnumbered protective use 'by five to one' (Norris and Armstrong 1999, 129). Significantly, Norris and Armstrong's study, following Brown, shows a tendency to use surveillance for 'public order' over 'private violence' even when such violence occurs in what is clearly public space. These findings suggest a very particular notion of public and private, one that suggests that public disorder is that which has the potential to disturb the greatest number of people, not that which is, strictly speaking, illegal. A man hitting his female companion on a public street, seen this way, poses less of a threat to public order than, say, a man kissing another man in a parked car. None of the studies engages with the issue of the protection of homosexuals or, more broadly, those who engage in sexual activity with those of the same gender. The absence is telling, as such people are often subject to harassment and violent 'gay-bashing', even in spaces normally considered 'safe'.[7] The gaze fostered by surveillance culture would appear to be a heterosexual, heteronormative and, quite simply, sexist male gaze.

When we consider the reasoning behind the Sexual Offences Act (2003), there would appear to be an impulse both to protect privacy, as in the prohibition against sexual voyeurism, and to protect 'public order', as in the prohibition against the use of public toilets as sites for sexual activity. Interestingly, Norris and Armstrong found that surveillance camera operators and police took advantage of 'the long understood relationship between cars and sex' (1999, 129) for their own voyeuristic purposes. Although the study never specifies that such voyeurism was directed at heterosexual encounters exclusively, the examples given are all of operators and officers watching men and women together. It is not clear whether such voyeuristic surveillance has continued in the wake of the Sexual Offences Act (2003), although the fact that such voyeurism was an unremarkable part of the surveillance culture suggests that there may be little impetus to change. The former practice at least

---

7 Dereka Rushbrook, in 'Cities, Queer Space, and the Cosmopolitan Tourist', examines the commodification of gay space in large metropolitan centres and notes that 'the increased visibility that facilitates tourists' identification of queer sites also marks them to the public at large' (2002, 10), leading, ironically, to the 'straightening' of some of these formerly safe spaces to ensure its inhabitants' safety (2002, 10–13). Rushbrook draws on Wayne Myclik's work in the United States, which notes that 'queer spaces, those areas in which gay men are known to congregate and have been designated as safe spaces, are, ironically, the most frequent settings for [anti-gay] violence, exceeding by 28 percent straight public areas' (1996, 162).

suggests a fine line between legitimate surveillance and voyeurism, and at most a fundamental hypocrisy visible in the intersection between the impetus behind the policing of public sexual activity and the culture of surveillance used to enforce it.

Surveillance in Northern Ireland

Given the practice of surveillance in the rest of the United Kingdom, then, we might ask whether surveillance in Northern Ireland is substantially different. In his analysis of Northern Ireland, sociologist Allen Feldman has examined the 'scopic regime of the state' (1997, 48). The state's gaze, according to Feldman, creates a 'surveillance grid' and the resulting 'scopic penetration contaminates private space and lives' (1997, 27) by shaping individual subjectivity and behaviour through fear and anxiety. Feldman's analysis places surveillance first in the hands of the state as a means of direct social control, an apt description of the state of surveillance during the height of the Northern Ireland conflict in the 1970s and 1980s. But Feldman's perspective, like that of many in surveillance studies, resonates with Foucault's panoptical model insofar as it also examines the complexity of the relationship between power, vision and visibility, by no means unidirectional phenomena. Certainly, citizens of Northern Ireland have been far more conscious of the presence of surveillance technologies for longer than those in the rest of the United Kingdom, as Nils Zurawski (2004, 499–500) has noted. And the resistance to surveillance is still quite ardent in some quarters: in the nationalist community there remains a deep suspicion of state surveillance for any reason, and police cameras have not been invited into Catholic West Belfast because of the association between police surveillance, collusion and abuse of power by forces of the state. Nonetheless, surveillance remains part of the arsenal of power in Northern Ireland, regardless of who wields it. The response by non-state entities to the tyranny of the 'scopic regime' has often been more surveillance, as Zurawski notes in his study of non-technological surveillance. Such surveillance can take many forms, whether it be photographs taken by paramilitaries 'considered equivalent to both the gun sight and the pointed rifle', as Feldman puts it (1997, 26); the CCTV cameras that abound in 'public' places and commercial establishments, particularly in urban areas; cameras aimed at protestors or paraders; or police surveillance operations focused on public parks. Surveillance, covert and overt, continues actively to shape Northern Irish space.

One might imagine, given the charged and partisan history of surveillance in Northern Ireland, that the resistance to it would be more widespread throughout the culture. Further, if we examine the history of surveillance of homosexual activity in Northern Ireland, one might expect an even more charged response within the queer/gay activist community. Homosexual activity was decriminalised in Great Britain in 1967 but remained illegal in Northern Ireland until 1982, carrying the threat of up to life imprisonment for those convicted. In 1976, the Royal Ulster Constabulary (the former name of the Northern Irish police force) made a series of arrests of gay men, begun on the basis of a complaint from a mother of one of the men who was concerned about her son's activities and tenuously justified as a search for illegal drugs. The membership rolls of the Northern Ireland Gay Rights Association (NIGRA)/Gay Liberation Society were seized in the raids, which led to the questioning and arrest of more than two dozen men. The subsequent outrage in the gay activist community sparked a concerted effort to secure the decriminalisation of homosexual activity in Northern Ireland, with Jeffrey Dudgeon, one of the gay activists harassed by the police, bringing a case against the United Kingdom. Fearing the success of this activism, the Reverend Ian Paisley, head of the Democratic Unionist Party and a minister of the Free Presbyterian Church in Ravenhill, Belfast, spearheaded a campaign against the extension of the 1967 Act. Thanks to Dudgeon's case with the European Court of Human Rights, homosexuality was eventually decriminalised.[8]

Activism is, of course, a way to bring visibility to a group or issue, a way of entering the public sphere of civil society. Visibility, however, is a double-edged sword. From the late 1970s until well into the new century and the rise of new, more inclusive policing initiatives, there was an increase in police activity against popular gay cruising and 'cottaging' spots in Northern Ireland.[9] Belfast gay newsletters like *Gay Star* and *Upstart* regularly ran articles warning men who had sex with men about police surveillance activities and informing them of their rights when arrested.[10] Decriminalisation was, in other words, not the end to the problems facing men who had sex with men: according to an autumn 1996 article in *Upstart*, there was a significant increase in murders of gay men,[11] from approximately one per year in the 1970s and 1980s to a startling four per year in the 1990s. Police surveillance was focused on men who had sex with men, in other words, not on violent gay-bashing.

For this reason, surveillance is a potentially charged issue in the gay community. Violence remains a risk as the gay community becomes even more visible, both through sanctioned channels (e.g. pride parades, which garner enthusiastic onlookers and some protest in Northern Ireland; the recent legalisation of civil partnerships for lesbians and gays; and the recent legalisation of adoption by lesbian and gay couples) and illicit channels (e.g. 'public' sex and the subsequent publicity of arrests). The out gay community in particular has a vexed relationship with the illicit practice of cottaging: although some out gay men participate in cottaging

---

8   For a further discussion of the politics of the Save Ulster from Sodomy campaign and its aftermath, see Conrad (2004, 41–7).

9   'Cottaging' is UK slang and refers to the practice of soliciting sex in public or semi-public places, such as public restrooms (also referred to as 'tearooms'). The practice can refer to simply soliciting sex in such places and then moving on to a private or semi-private space, or engaging in sex in the 'tearoom' itself.

10   See, for instance, 'The Ins and Outs of Cottaging' (Summer 1981, 4); 'When in Doubt Say Nowt' (1982, 1); '"Walkin" the Dog' (February 1989, 1); 'It's a Purge' (March 1989, 1); 'We Are Being Watched' (April 1993, 1).

11   It is not clear from the article whether the murdered men identified as gay; however, the article intends at least to identify the murder of men who had sex with men.

and other public sexual activity, it is also the site wherein men who might not be part of the gay community have sex with other men – men who often have access to less information and fewer resources about sex, and who may either choose to identify themselves sexually in ways that do not fit the 'normal' heterosexual/homosexual binary, or who engage in such activities through lack of access to more socially acceptable channels. These men are a group whose practices we might aptly term 'queer': sexually dissident and, intentionally or not, challenging the unspoken assumptions on which the current sexual culture is based. As Michael Warner notes, the gay community in the United States, particularly in New York, has not been eager to articulate and support a public sexual culture even if they participate in it: the push toward privatisation has been the norm (2000, 167–8). A celebration of the 'normality' of gay citizens has meant the marginalisation of any public discussion of a public sexual culture; instead, it has been abandoned, along with those who participate in it. Visibility, it seems, comes at a price.

In recent years, policing in Northern Ireland has been ostensibly liberalised, with the newly-named Police Service of Northern Ireland making a concerted attempt to encourage better reporting of hate crimes, particularly those motivated by religious affiliation, disability, race or homophobia (PSNI Hate Crimes website). Community policing initiatives have encouraged more dialogue between specific communities and the police. In the wake of such changes, during Pride Week 2004, the Belfast Pride organisers arranged a session called 'Meet the Police'. The majority of attendees were men – all adult men, ranging in age from early 20s to mid 60s. The police were there encouraging those present to report hate crimes against queer people under the new, more liberal reporting guidelines that allow both anonymous reporting and reporting by third parties. In the course of the meeting, several of the men present at the meeting noted some difficulty in getting a quick response to violent gay-bashing incidents in the centre of Belfast. Several men at the meeting requested increased police surveillance of known gay cruising areas, including the possibility of the use of CCTV, to protect men from gay-bashing and recommended that the police consider handing out information to men in cruising areas informing them of safety hazards and giving them contact information for gay support groups and services. The police responded by noting that men caught breaking the law would have to be arrested. Breaking the law, in this context, was having sex in public, not gay-bashing.

Gay-bashing remains a concern of the gay community, however, despite the relative lack of interest on the part of the police. In the spring of 2006, the Superintendent of the Coleraine PSNI, Dawson Cotton, stated, in a letter responding to queries from gay activists, that he became aware in January 2005 of a group of paramilitaries who were threatening to 'take action' over 'sexual acts between men in toilets in Coleraine'. This intelligence, according to the Superintendent, led to the PSNI informing the gay activist Rainbow Project, who put a warning about the threat on an internet bulletin board, and to the police visiting the toilets looking for 'known paramilitary suspects'; according to the Superintendent, 'nothing further came to light' (Cotton 2006, 1–2).

But indeed, something did come to light, albeit not the protection from gay-bashing the men from the Pride 'Meet the Police' session in Belfast clearly intended when they asked for more surveillance in their own city in 2004. In March 2006, twelve men were arrested and ten fined in Coleraine for violating Section 71 of the 2003 Sexual Offences Act after being caught having sex in a public toilet. The Act specifies that one is liable to arrest if one has sex 'in a lavatory to which the public or a section of the public has or is permitted to have access, whether on payment or otherwise'. The arrests were, in the language of Coleraine District Policing Partnership Manager Suzanne Crozier, who authorised the surveillance, the 'final phase of the surveillance operation'. This indicates that the toilets had been watched for some time. Several officials suggested that the offences were 'not appropriate for caution', meaning that arrest, rather than a warning, was somehow more appropriate in these cases. In no official documents, however, has it been made clear why these offences were more 'severe' than any other instance of public sex in the UK, many of which are dealt with through cautions. Except for one 29-year-old, all of the men were in their 40s; all were consenting. Investigating officer Constable Paul Creith said he was 'not aware of any of the accused approaching anyone outside of the cottaging ring' (Smyth 2006), and no specific complaints about the activity were revealed. The resident magistrate, Mr McNally, noted that the accused were 'all decent people, all law abiding apart from these activities, which would not have been illegal if they had occurred in private' (Smyth 2006). Although he had the power to imprison the men, he did not, and fined most of them less than a tenth of the maximum fine of £5,000. His one reason for not invoking a conditional discharge was the 'public aspect of the offences', presumably referring to his statement that 'people should be able to use public toilets without having to be confronted by such sexual activity' (Smyth 2006).

It is unclear, however, whether or how anyone was actually 'confronted' by 'such sexual activity'. The police clearly stated that no one else was approached. The codes and practices of 'cottaging' are such that discovery by non-participating men is avoided at all costs.[12] One can assume that this is no less true in Northern Ireland, where public acceptance of homosexual behaviour has lagged behind the UK. As Michael Warner notes, '"public sex" is public in the sense that it takes place outside the home, but it usually takes place in areas that have been chosen for their seclusion, and like all sex involves extremely intimate and private associations' (2000, 173). NIGRA, in its submission to the Department of Health on suicide prevention strategies in the gay community, refers to such sexual activity more accurately as 'semi-public'. The fact that lavatories are considered 'private' in Section 68 of the Act, the section that prohibits sexual voyeurism, points to the vagueness of the legal application of the terms 'public' and 'private'. Such terms seem to rely on a commonsense division between public and private that is neither common nor, given its inconsistent application, quite sensical.

---

12   For a detailed discussion of cottaging practices, see especially Laud Humphreys's classic sociological study of the US, *Tearoom Trade* (1975) and Hollister (1999). For a brief discussion of the practices in Northern Ireland, see NIGRA's (2006) submission to the Northern Ireland Government's Suicide Strategy (Department of Health).

The application of these vague terms and the surveillance technologies that enforce them have, however, had a profound effect on the lived experience of men who have sex with men in 'public' places in Northern Ireland. Lisa Smyth of the *Belfast Telegraph* reported on the arrests in an article entitled 'Flushed Out' (2006). The article noted that, since the raid and arrests, the men were subjected to threats and violent attacks. One man had his car set on fire and pushed into his home. While the surveillance was enacted by the police and authorised by the Policing Partnership Manager, it did not stop there: in the same article, Smyth published the names, addresses and photographs of the arrested men. The subtitle specified that the defendants included 'a church elder and an ex-police reservist'. And the *Belfast Telegraph* was not alone: papers in Coleraine and Derry published the names of the men upon their first appearance in court. Since then, according to Sean Morrin of the Rainbow Project, one man had to sell his home and leave his job, and another was 'seeking emergency shelter as his life is in real danger' (Morrin 2006). Paramilitary threats from the Ulster Volunteer Force (UVF) were apparently the source of a significant part of the harassment, as NIGRA has noted (NIGRA 2006). Nonetheless, the police surveillance activities continued after these arrests, focused in large part on the Lisburn area; some 48 operations have taken place in the course of a year (Harris 2006; NIGRA 2006). One man arrested in these sweeps committed suicide. As NIGRA has pointed out, the increase in the number of operations has meant that the support structure in the gay community has not been able to keep up with police operations (NIGRA 2006). Gay websites continue to report gay-bashing and harassment at cottaging sites. The visibility suffered by these men is hardly the emancipatory notion of visibility celebrated by liberal activism; indeed, it further reinforces the notion that the media itself is a formidable technology of surveillance.

The arrests and reaction to them are instructive. They show quite clearly that there is a culture of surveillance in Northern Ireland, as in the rest of the UK; but the surprising thing it tells us – surprising given the charged and relatively recent history of surveillance in Northern Ireland – is that this culture of surveillance seems to operate with the consent of the majority of the governed, including many gay men. The gay men at the 'Meet the Police' session in 2004 assumed that surveillance would and could work on their behalf and on the behalf of other men who have sex with men and who are threatened by violence. They assumed that they, as gay men, were part of civil society, and they assumed that the state could and should use surveillance to protect them from crime. In other words, they assumed that the police would focus on the clear crime of violent assault rather than the more ambiguous and victimless crime of 'public' sex. The age of some of these men is such that they would have been alive during the notorious RUC raids of the 1970s as well as of the regular sweeps of parks and cottaging sites in the 1980s and 1990s which focused on men who had sex with men even after the decriminalisation of sexual activity. Yet they had a faith in surveillance as a legitimate tool of policing.

This faith emerges out of a liberal activist context that Rob Kitchin and Karen Lysaght have termed 'sexual citizenship', 'concerned with the defining and administering of rights (civil, political, social, cultural) dependent on an individual being a "good" sexual citizen, that is, conforming to "appropriate" sexual acts, behaviours and identities as defined by the State and wider society' (2004, 84). While their own work is focused on mapping the history and context for sexual citizenship in Northern Ireland rather than with articulating a more radical critique, Kitchin and Lysaght note Carl Stychin's formulation of the division liberal politics enables between 'good gays' – those willing to compromise in order to be tolerated and win acceptance as citizens – and 'bad queers' unwilling to compromise (Kitchin and Lysaght 2004, 84; Stychin 1998, 200). This distinction is evident in the surveillance practices focused on queer men in Northern Ireland and, to some degree, in the responses to it. Although the gay community has expressed its outrage over recent police practices, the activist focus has nonetheless remained on finding ways to achieve sexual citizenship. As Kitchin and Lysaght suggest, 'while it might be tempting to use the data we have generated to envisage a radical vision of sexual citizenship it would not be representative of the views of the individuals we interviewed and it is [an] extremely unrealistic proposition given the present political situation in Northern Ireland' (2004, 100). In other words, the gay activist response to surveillance has ultimately been to accept the normalising pressures exerted by surveillance technology.

Surveillance in Northern Ireland is, perhaps, an indication both of the unquestioned acceptance of surveillance in the UK more generally and of the post-ceasefire, post-Agreement normalisation of Northern Irish society. In Northern Ireland, 'normalisation' is a term used by the government to describe the process of moving away from the infrastructure used to manage the conflict. More broadly, normalisation means reconceptualising Northern Irish political, governmental and social structures, generally to make them more like the rest of the UK. In the post-Agreement environment of normalisation, surveillance intended to prevent crime is acceptable, somehow different from the surveillance grid of Northern Ireland operating during the height of the conflict. The 'new' surveillance would seem to be a sign of things to come: a hopeful change in focus in the wake of the 'peace dividend' that holds the promise of increased commercial development and growth and an operating liberal democracy – the latter, as NIGRA has suggested, being something Northern Ireland currently lacks (NIGRA 2006). But it is unclear whether the ideals of a liberal democracy can be achieved with the use of surveillance or even whether a liberal democracy in practice offers protection to its most marginalised members, as both Stychin and Warner suggest. Normalisation, as the Northern Ireland examples indicate, is not necessarily progress. Normalisation can mean the acceptance, even the embrace, of surveillance that enables the protection of personal property or the selling of newspapers or the development of 'family-friendly' areas, even when that surveillance also impinges on privacy and bodily integrity as much as or more than the surveillance employed during the conflict. Normalisation can mean defaulting into other cultural patterns, such as the classist, sexist and racist norms that inform surveillance in the rest of the UK.

In post-Agreement Northern Ireland as elsewhere in Western culture, visibility has been celebrated as a way of entering into the civic realm. The Belfast Agreement in particular stresses 'parity of esteem' between 'communities', which has, in practice, meant balancing the demands of equal visibility and funding between nationalist and unionist communities; recently, there has been more of an effort to broaden this concept to ensure a visible representation by groups or 'communities' that do not fit those categories in the interests of diversity, however token.[13] But those who cannot or will not be visible, who do not engage in the politics of identitarian visibility, are just as likely to be exposed, to suffer from the architecture of surveillance, as they were before the conflict. And those who do engage, such as out gay men, may find that their rights to full citizenship cannot be taken for granted. Unlike during the Troubles, however, there seem to be fewer people to sympathise and challenge this state of affairs; and surveillance itself restricts the arenas in which such a challenge may occur. And this may be, to use Warner's phrase, the trouble with 'normal'.

Acknowledgements

My special thanks to Jeff Dudgeon and Brendan O'Connell; although they share no responsibility for any flaws in fact or argument herein, they provided information without which this chapter could not have been completed.

Suggested Further Reading

Ball, K., Green, N., Koskela, H. and Phillips, D.J. (eds) (forthcoming 2009), 'Gender, Sexuality and Surveillance', a special issue of *Surveillance and Society*, http://www.surveillance-and-society.org (accessed 30 August 2008).

Lyon, D. (ed.) (2003), *Surveillance as Social Sorting: Privacy, Risk and Digital Discrimination* (London and New York: Routledge).

Norris, C. and Armstrong, G. (1999), *The Maximum Surveillance Society: The Rise of CCTV* (Oxford: Berg).

Warner, M. (2000), *The Trouble with Normal: Sex, Politics, and the Ethics of Queer Life* (Cambridge, MA: Harvard University Press).

—— (2002), *Publics and Counterpublics* (Cambridge, MA: Zone Books).

---

13 See Conrad (2006) for a discussion of the impact of the Belfast Agreement's construction of 'community' on the Northern Ireland public sphere and on the queer counterpublic resistant to its simplistic applications. For an analysis of public sphere theory and counterpublics, particularly queer counterpublics see Warner (2002). For queer public sphere theory, see also Berlant (1997).

References

Bell, D. (2006), 'Bodies, Technologies, Spaces: On Dogging', *Sexualities* 9:4, 387–407.
—— and Valentine, G. (eds) (1995), *Mapping Desire: Geographies of Sexualities* (London and New York: Routledge).
Berlant, L. (1997), *The Queen Goes to Washington City: Essays on Sex and Citizenship* (Durham, NC: Duke University Press).
Boone, J., Dupuis, M., Meeker, M., Quimby, K., Sarver, C., Silverman, D. and Weatherston, R. (eds) (2000), *Queer Frontiers: Millennial Geographies, Genders, and Generations* (Madison, WI: University of Wisconsin Press).
Cameron, H. (2004), 'CCTV and (In)dividuation', *Surveillance and Society*: CCTV special issue, 2:2–3, 136–44, http://www.surveillance-and-society.org (accessed 1 July 2006).
Cohen, S. (2002 [1972]), *Folk Devils and Moral Panics: The Creation of the Mods and Rockers* (London: Routledge).
Cole, M. (2004), 'Signage and Surveillance: Interrogating the Textual Context of CCTV in the UK', *Surveillance and Society*: CCTV special issue, 2:2–3, 430–45, http://www.surveillance-and-society.org (accessed 1 July 2006).
Conrad, K. (2004), *Locked in the Family Cell: Gender, Sexuality, and Political Agency in Irish Nationalist Discourse* (Madison, WI: University of Wisconsin Press).
—— (2006), 'Queering Community: Reimagining the Public Sphere in Northern Ireland', *Critical Review of Social and Political Philosophy* 9:4, 589–602.
Cotton, D. (2 March 2006), Superintendent, Coleraine Police Service of Northern Ireland (PSNI). Letter to Andrew Muir, ref no. 00/2006/101/46.
Crozier, S. (28 February 2006), Coleraine District Policing Partnership Manager. Letter to Andrew Muir.
Duncan, N. (ed.) (1996), *BodySpace: Destabilizing Geographies of Gender and Sexuality* (London and New York: Routledge).
Edelman, L. (1994), *Homographesis: Essays in Gay Literary and Cultural Theory* (New York and London: Routledge).
Feldman, A. (1997), 'Violence and Vision: The Prosthetics and Aesthetics of Terror', *Public Culture* 10:1, 24–60.
Foucault, M. (1979), *Discipline and Punish: The Birth of the Prison*, trans. A. Sheridan. (New York: Vintage).
Fussey, P. (2004), 'New Labour and New Surveillance: Theoretical and Political Ramifications of CCTV Implementation in the UK', *Surveillance and Society*: CCTV special issue, 2:2–3, 251–69, http://www.surveillance-and-society.org (accessed 1 July 2006).
Gay Star (Serial). Belfast: Northern Ireland Gay Rights Association. Available as part of the NIGRA archive (D3762), Public Records Office Northern Ireland. Partial run available at the Linen Hall Library Northern Ireland Political Collection.
Goold, B. (2004), *CCTV and Policing: Public Area Surveillance and Police Practices in Britain* (Oxford and New York: Oxford University Press).
Harris, J.A. (31 May 2006), Assistant Chief Constable, PSNI. Written response to Coalition on Sexual Orientation. Belfast.

Hier, S.P. (2004), 'Probing the Surveillant Assemblage: On the Dialectics of Surveillance Practices as Processes of Social Control', *Surveillance and Society*: CCTV special issue, 2:2–3, 399–411, http://www.surveillance-and-society.org (accessed 1 July 2006).

Hollister, J. (1999), 'A Highway Rest Area as a Socially Reproducible Site', in W.L. Leap (ed.), *Public Sex/Gay Space* (New York: Columbia University Press).

Humphreys, L. (1975), *Tearoom Trade: Impersonal Sex in Public Places* (New York: Aldine De Gruyter).

'It's a Purge' (March 1989), *Upstart* 1:2, 1.

Kitchin, R. and Lysaght, K. (2004), 'Sexual Citizenship in Belfast, Northern Ireland', *Gender, Place and Culture* 11:1, 83–103.

Lyon, D. (ed.) (2001), *Surveillance Society: Monitoring Everyday Life* (Buckingham: Open University Press).

—— (2003a), *Surveillance as Social Sorting: Privacy, Risk and Digital Discrimination* (London and New York: Routledge).

—— (2003b), 'Surveillance as Social Sorting: Computer Codes and Mobile Bodies', in D. Lyon (ed.), *Surveillance as Social Sorting: Privacy, Risk and Digital Discrimination* (London and New York: Routledge).

Morrin, S. (2006), Rainbow Project. Letter to *Belfast Telegraph*, c. March 2006 (n.d.).

Myclik, W.D. (1996), 'Renegotiating the Social/Sexual Identity of Places: Gay Communities as Safe Havens or Sites of Resistance?', in N. Duncan (ed.), *BodySpace: Destabilizing Geographies of Gender and Sexuality* (London and New York: Routledge).

Norris, C. (2003), 'From Personal to Digital: CCTV, the Panopticon, and the Technological Mediation of Suspicion and Social Control', in D. Lyon (ed.), *Surveillance as Social Sorting: Privacy, Risk and Digital Discrimination* (London and New York: Routledge).

—— and Armstrong, G. (1999), *The Maximum Surveillance Society: The Rise of CCTV* (Oxford: Berg).

—— Moran, J. and Armstrong, G. (eds) (1998), *Surveillance, Closed Circuit Television, and Social Control* (Aldershot: Ashgate).

—— McCahill, M. and Wood, D. (2004), 'The Growth of CCTV: a Global Perspective on the International Diffusion of Video Surveillance in Publicly Accessible Space', *Surveillance and Society*: CCTV special issue 2:2–3, 110–35, http://www.surveillance-and-society.org (accessed 1 July 2006).

Northern Ireland Gay Rights Association (NIGRA) (23 June 2006), 'Self-Inflicted Fatalities in the Gay Community: History, Causes and Preventative Measures'. Submission in Response to the Northern Ireland Government's Suicide Strategy Published by the Department of Health.

Ploeg, I. van der (2003), 'Biometrics and the Body as Information: Normative Issues of the Socio-technical Coding of the Body', in D. Lyon (ed.), *Surveillance as Social Sorting: Privacy, Risk and Digital Discrimination* (London and New York: Routledge).

'Police Accused of Bias over CCTV' (15 November 2005), *BCC News* (Northern Ireland), http://news.bbc.co.uk/1/hi/uk_politics/northern_ireland/4438158.stm (accessed 1 July 2006).

Police Service of Northern Ireland. Hate Crimes website, http://www.psni.police. uk/index/hate_crimes.htm (accessed 1 July 2006).

Rushbrook, D. (2002), 'Cities, Queer Space, and the Cosmopolitan Tourist', *GLQ: A Journal of Lesbian and Gay Studies* 8:1–2, 183–206 [Online access through MUSE provided by the University of Kansas; in-text citations reflect online pagination].

Sedgwick, E.K. (1990), *Epistemology of the Closet* (Berkeley and Los Angeles, CA: University of California Press).

—— (2003), *Touching Feeling: Affect, Pedagogy, Performativity* (Durham, NC and London: Duke University Press).

Smyth, L. (29 March 2006), 'Flushed Out: Ten Men, Including a Church Elder and Ex-Police Reservist, Engaged in Sex Acts in a Public Toilet', *Belfast Telegraph*, http://www.belfasttelegraph.co.uk/news/story.jsp?story=684424 (accessed 1 July 2006).

Stychin, C. (1998), *A Nation by Rights: National Cultures, Sexual Identity Politics, and a Discourse of Rights* (Philadelphia, PA: Temple University Press).

'The Ins and Outs of Cottaging' (Summer 1981), *Gay Star* 4, 4.

United Kingdom (1998), *The Belfast Agreement: An Agreement Reached at the Multi-Party Talks on Northern Ireland* (London: HMSO).

—— (2003), Sexual Offences Act (2003), Chapter 42 (London: HMSO), http://www. opsi.gov.uk/ACTS/acts2003/20030042.htm (accessed 1 July 2006).

Upstart (Serial). Belfast. Available as part of the NIGRA archive (D3762), Public Records Office Northern Ireland. Partial run available at the Linen Hall Library Northern Ireland Political Collection (closed access).

'"Walkin" the Dog' (February 1989), *Upstart* 1:1, 1.

Warner, M. (2000), *The Trouble with Normal: Sex, Politics, and the Ethics of Queer Life* (Cambridge, MA: Harvard University Press).

—— (2002), *Publics and Counterpublics* (Cambridge, MA: Zone Books).

'We Are Being Watched' (April 1993), *Upstart* 5:4, 1.

'When in Doubt Say Nowt' (1982), *Gay Star* 7, 1.

Yar, M. (2003), 'Panoptic Power and the Pathologisation of Vision: Critical Reflections on the Foucauldian Thesis', *Surveillance and Society* 1:3, 254–71, http://www. surveillance-and-society.org (accessed 1 July 2006).

Zurawski, N. (2004), 'I Know Where You Live!: Aspects of Surveillance, Watching and Social Control in a Conflict Zone (Northern Ireland)', *Surveillance and Society*: People Watching People special issue 2:4, 498–512, http://www.surveillance-and-society.org (accessed 1 July 2006).

Biologically Queer

Myra J. Hird

*I still cringe at the memory of seeing old D-ram mount S-ram repeatedly …
True to form, and incapable of absorbing this realisation at once, I called these
actions of the rams aggressosexual behaviour, for to state that the males had
evolved a homosexual society was emotionally beyond me. To conceive of those
magnificent beasts as 'queers' – Oh God! I argued for two years that, in [wild
mountain] sheep, aggressive and sexual behaviour could not be separated … I
never published that drivel and am glad of it … Eventually I called the spade
a spade and admitted that rams lived in essentially a homosexual society.
(Geist 2002, 97-8, The Blackburn Press)*

*We are statistically molarly heterosexual, but personally homosexual, without
knowing it or being fully aware of it, and finally we are transsexual in an
elemental, molecular sense. (Deleuze and Guattari 1996/1972, 70)*

Introduction

Thus far, queer theory has analytically evolved as a largely socio-cultural enterprise, and the chapters in this reader attest to the variety of ways in which queer theory is both conceptualised and developed within this purview. That is, queer analyses largely emanate from the social sciences and humanities, and focus on social, political, economic and cultural aspects of queering theory and praxis. Such a focus implies a certain distillation of social from natural forces, as though little may be gleaned from the non-human living world. The aim of this chapter is to offer a short foray into what I argue is the very social, and very queer, non-human world. Particularly with regard to questions of sex and sexuality, I hope to show that non-human matter is engaged in very lively flows that incite questions about the parameters of queer theory, and indeed, the very constitution of 'queerness' itself. As a starting point, I begin by providing a few examples of the diversity of sex and sexuality amongst non-humans.[1] Once this diversity is established, I turn to a more theoretical exploration of the term 'queer' and how it might be enhanced by considering the non-human realm.

Not Suitable for Family Viewing: Sexuality in the Non-Human Living World

There is not enough space to document the almost countless instances of non-human living organisms paraded before the media to testify as to the 'naturalness' of conservative human 'family values'. These values consist of monogamous pair-bonding between 'opposite'-sex partners recognised by society (marriage), sexual behaviour for the purpose of reproduction (this precludes sex for pleasure and sex between same-sex partners and partners of different species – except in rare circumstances), the prohibition against incest, parental (and especially female) care of young, and celibacy in non-married individuals.

Yet the observation of non-human animal behaviour reveals these values to be distinctly human. Non-human animals engage in a very wide range of behaviours, only some of which would be recognised within a 'family values' rubric. With regard to monogamy, for instance, cultural norms heavily influence biological data.[2] Monogamy refers to having only one mate, usually through one or more breeding season. Monogamy also implies that each pair will only mate with each other, although this characteristic has yet to be proven to exist for most birds and mammals. Indeed, leading biologist E.O. Wilson notes that 'monogamy, and especially monogamy outside the breeding season, is the rare exception. Parent-offspring bonds usually last only to the weaning period and are then often terminated by a period of conflict' (2000, 315).[3] For those species that do exhibit monogamous behaviour this does not imply anything about the frequency of sexual or social interactions between mates (Kleinman 1977).

Thus, single parenting, or indeed no parental investment at all, is the *norm* in the non-human living world (only 5 percent of mammals form life-time heterosexual pair bonds). Yet, in human cultures, single parenting is seen as the antithesis of the 'natural' order of things. Amongst non-human living organisms, daycare, fostering

---

1   The distinction between human and nonhuman living organisms is, simultaneously, crucial to the history of politics, economics and culture, and notoriously difficult to define. Biologists define a species by the ability of members to sexually reproduce sexually reproductive offspring. Social scientists and humanities scholars are not so sure (see Grosz 1995; Haraway 1989; 1991; 1992; 2001; 2003; Wolfe 2003a; 2003b).

2   Interestingly, Kleinman (1977) notes that monogamy is among 'the more highly evolved forms of social organization' but then also concedes that monogamy is much more common in birds (90 percent) than mammals (less than 5 percent).

3   For a discussion of offspring abuse within nonhuman primates see Reite and Caine (1983).

and adoption are also common; as are infanticide (many parents eat their children) and incest. To take one example, a study of Spotted Sandpipers, Oring et al. (1992) found that fully half of the broods had been produced by more than two birds. Birth control is not restricted to humans either; many animals practise forms of birth control through vaginal plugs, defecation, abortion through the ingestion of certain plants, ejection of sperm and, in the case of chimpanzees, nipple stimulation. Embryos are also known to kill each other before birth.

Nor do many animals have sex solely or primarily in order to reproduce. There is a general lack of acknowledgement of pleasure as an organising force in relations between non-human animals, and evolutionary theory generally. E.O. Wilson (2000) notes that male house flies remain copulating with female house flies for a full hour after all of its sperm are transferred, despite the fact that this prolonged copulation decreases its ability to have sex with other flies (and thus produce more offspring). Wilson notes that some insects have sex for an entire day. Anne Fausto-Sterling (1997) critiques a number of studies of animal behaviour in order to demonstrate how selective behaviours are taken up and reinforced as common (and thus, normative) whilst other behaviours initially observed seem to vanish altogether in subsequent studies. For instance, Darling recounts masturbatory behaviour in stags:

> *He may masturbate several times during the day. I have seen a stag do this three times in the morning at approximately hourly intervals, even when he has had a harem of hinds. This act is accomplished by lowering the head and gently drawing the tips of the antlers to and fro through the herbage. Erection and extrusion of the penis ... follow in five to seven seconds ... Ejaculation follows about five seconds later. (Darling; quoted in Fausto-Sterling 1997, 51)*

The primary reason, according to Fausto-Sterling, that behaviours such as masturbation are often not reported is because animal behaviourists operating within a traditional evolutionary paradigm focus on reproduction at the population level, rather than sexual behaviour at the individual level. A focus on reproduction produces a skewed vision of animal life as not only exclusively heterosexual, but in a narrow 'functionalist' sense of sexual activity for the purpose of sexual reproduction only. Thus, sexual activities such as masturbation become difficult to account for in such paradigmatic circumstances, an important point I will return to at the end of this chapter.

Perhaps the single most popular debate about sexual diversity, however, concerns homosexual behaviour. Homosexual behaviour occurs in over 450 different species of animals, and is found in every geographic region of the world and in every major animal group (Bagemihl 1999; see also Roughgarden 2004). Homosexual behaviour in animals does not take any one form, but is enormously diverse, and in some species is more diverse than heterosexual behaviour (Pavelka 1995). Some behaviours are common in same- and 'opposite'-sex behaviour, such as anal stimulation. Lifetime pair-bondings that evince homosexual behaviour are not prevalent in mammal species, but nor are heterosexual lifetime pair-bondings. Bisexual behaviour is widespread as well, with more than half of mammals and bird species engaging in both heterosexual and homosexual activities. Studies also suggest that non-human animal homosexual behaviour varies in frequency within and between species from non-existence (that is, it has not been observed by zoologists) to levels that meet or surpass heterosexual behaviour. Homosexual behaviour has also been observed in all age groups. There is no evidence that homosexual interactions are more common amongst males than females. Finally, animals clearly learn sexual behaviours within their social groups and pass sexual behaviours down from generation to generation.

And as though homosexual non-human sexual behaviour did not disturb heteronormative theories of 'normal' reproduction and evolution, sex between different species has also been documented. People recognise that sexual intercourse between a horse and donkey might produce an ass, but, on the whole, transspecies sex is considered impossible. But emerging evidence suggests that sexual behaviour amongst non-human animals is again much more plastic and diverse than human culture allows. For instance, while sexual behaviour between flowers and various insects is so commonplace that it is rarely recognised as transspecies sexual activity, other examples have been found. Krizek (1992) observed and documented a sexual interaction between two different orders of insects, a butterfly and a rove beetle. The rove beetle was perched on a leaf with its abdomen elevated. The butterfly approached and for several seconds explored the beetle's anogenital organs with its proboscis. Krizek notes that other such interactions, between different orders of human and non-human animals, have been observed.

Non-Human Sex Diversity

Virtually all plant and many animal species are intersex. That is, living organisms are often both sexes simultaneously – which means that there are not really 'two sexes' at all. Robert Warner (1975; 1984) notes that new reports suggest that intersex in fish is much more common than once assumed (for a comprehensive study of intersex in animals see Reinboth 1975). Most fungi have thousands of sexes.

Many animal species routinely practice transsex, by changing from one sex to another, either once or several times (Hird 2004; 2006). We need to be clear here that we are not referring to some sort of sex 'role' change, but complete physical sex change. David Policansky (1982) documents some of the widely distributed, both geographically and taxonomically, sex changing species.[4] In some families of fish, transsex is so much the norm that biologists have created a term for those 'unusual' fish that do *not* change sex – *gonochoristic*. The coral goby, for instance, changes sex

---

4   Sex change here refers to an organism that functions as one sex during one breeding season and the 'other' sex during another breeding season. This definition excludes those organisms that can change sex within one breeding season.

both ways, between female and male, depending on a number of circumstances. When goby fish are placed together, the smaller of two males usually changes sex to become female and the larger of two females usually changes sex to become male (Nakashima, Kuwamura and Yogo 1995). Goby fish will also change sex rather than travel long distances to find an 'opposite' sex mating partner.

As a further example, earthworms and marine snails are male when young and female when they grow older. Chaetopod annelids show a similar development, but in certain environmental circumstances will change back into males. For instance, when two females are confined together, one female may kill the other female by biting her in half or eating all the available food. When this female has had sex with a male, the male might then turn into a female and bite her in two (Denniston 1980).

Other animals practice transvestism by visually, chemically or behaviourally resembling the 'opposite' sex.[5] Sometimes transvestism takes a physical form, when animals physically resemble the 'opposite' sex. Transvestism might also be behavioural, when a non-human animal behaves in ways associated with the 'opposite' sex of their species. Some entomologists, for instance, describe transvestism in various insect species. Denis Owen (1988) describes female *Papilio phorcas* (a type of butterfly) who take on 'male pattern' wings of other male butterflies that fly faster and are better able to avoid prey. And over 4,000 known species are parthenogenic; that is, all the individuals are female and they reproduce without sex – what we humans term 'virgin birth' (Margulis and Sagan 1997).

Human Sex Diversity

How might we make sense of these findings? Traditionally, the natural sciences have tended to interpret evidence within a heteronormative framework that privileges the division of species into two sexes, and within-species relationships structured by sexual reproduction. Perhaps worse, the social sciences have tended to unilaterally ignore research on non-human living organisms, even when these

---

5   Bruce Bagemihl (1999) notes that transvestism does not mean taking on activities or behaviours that are considered to be either typically 'female' or 'male'. For instance, the sexual reproduction of offspring is typically considered to be in the female domain. But for sea horses and pipe fish, the male bears and gives birth to offspring. So, male sea horses and male pipe fish are not practising transvestism when they produce offspring. Bagemihl notes this is also the case for behaviours involved in what biologists term 'courtship'. In many species, females are more aggressive than males in these behaviours. Should a female in these species behave passively, she would be practising transvestism. It is worth noting here that non-human animals who engage in transvestite behaviour, like their human counterparts, specifically avoid homosexual behaviour. The misconception that transvestites (usually male) attempt to be 'feminine' in order to attract sexual relationships with men is as erroneous for the non-human, as it is for the human animal world.

findings seem to have much to contribute to key debates such as sexual difference. For instance, even if we restrict our discussion (for a moment) to human beings, we must circumvent an enormous amount of evidence in order to maintain any notion that humans are sexually dimorphic and heterosexual.

Human bodies, like those of other living organisms, are only 'sexed' from a particularly narrow perspective (Hird 2002). The *vast* majority of cells in human bodies are intersex (and this category itself is only possible by maintaining a division between 'female' and 'male' chromosomes), with only egg and sperm cells counting as sexually dimorphic. *Most* of the reproduction that we undertake in our lifetimes has nothing to do with 'sex'. The cells in our bodies engage in constant, energetic reproduction in the form of *recombination* (cutting and patching of DNA strands), *merging* (fertilisation of cells), *meiosis* (cell division by halving chromosome number, for instance in making sperm and eggs) and *mitosis* (cell division with maintenance of cell number) (Margulis and Sagan 1997). Nor does reproduction take place between discrete 'selves', as many cultural analyses would have it. Indeed, only by taking our skin as a definitive impenetrable boundary are we able to see our bodies as discrete selves (see also Cohen 2003).[6] Our human bodies are more accurately 'built from a mass of interacting selves ... the self is not only corporeal but corporate' (Sagan 1992, 370). Our cells also provide asylum for a variety of bacteria, viruses and countless genetic fragments. And none of this reproduction requires any bodily contact with another human being. Indeed, what I would call our bodily state of sexual *indifference* is founded upon an entire evolutionary legacy, during which our ancestors reproduced without sex. That is, evolutionarily speaking, sex is a recent phenomenon. Lynn Margulis and Dorion Sagan argue that sexual reproduction evolved by accident as a necessary by-product of the evolution of multicellularity and cellular differentiation. In multicellular organisms, cells begin to specialise and carry out different functions: 'mixis ... becomes a consequence of the need to preserve differentiation ... mixis itself is dispensable and ... was never selected for directly' (Margulis and Sagan 1986, 180).[7] Put another way, 'multicellularity provided evolutionary advantages and sex came along for the ride' (Fausto-Sterling 1997, 53).

---

6   Lewis Thomas puts it more directly: from the point of view of the mitochrondria in our bodies (which occupy as much volume in themselves as the rest of us), we 'could be taken for a very large, motile colony of respiring bacteria, operating a complex system of nuclei, microtubules, and neurons for the pleasure and sustenance of their families, and running, at the moment, a typewriter' (1974, 72).

7   Mixis refers to the 'production of a single individual from two parents by way of fertilisation occurring at the level of fused cells or individuals' (Margulis and Sagan 1986, 232).

Becoming Heteronormative

So evidence may certainly be harnessed that problematises society's neat delineation of sex into two distinct, essential categories, and its correlative normatisation of heterosexuality. Why then do we continue to operate as though sex dimorphism materially exists? Well, it turns out that societies did not always operate with this assumption. A number of studies have begun to argue that, prior to the eighteenth century, women and men were considered to share one morphological body (Daston and Park 1998; Laqueur 1990; Oudshoorn 1994; Tuana 1989). Femininity and masculinity were determined more by close attention to signs of movement, temperament, voice and so on which indicated on which side of the one axis of 'sex' any individual gravitated – active/passive, hot/cold, formed/unformed, informing/formable. That is, individuals were thought to be positioned on a single axis of 'sex'. Interestingly, this single axis also applied to what, in contemporary society, has become the emblem of sexual difference: genitals. The Greek myth of Zeus depicts the father of all gods inventing interior reproduction by relocating the penis inside half of the human population. Thus, women's genitals were seen as simply male genitals displayed internally rather than externally.

This idea persisted throughout the pre-Enlightenment period. Being the superior form, male bodies contained the heat necessary to 'display' the penis and scrotum externally; lacking heat, female bodies bore their penis and scrota internally. The leading medical and philosophical scholars detailed the anatomical equivalence of vagina and penis, labia and foreskin, uterus and scrotum, ovaries and testicles (indeed, separate words for these body parts were only invented as a result of the two-sex model). Countless drawings, often produced from dissections, depicted the vagina as an internal penis. Only as a result of considerable controversy and political upheaval did the contemporary 'two-sex' model eventually dominate scientific discourse, and 'an anatomy and physiology of incommensurability replaced a metaphysics of hierarchy in the representation of woman in relation to man' (Laqueur 1990, 5–6).

Medical literature during this time is replete with accounts of individuals changing sex. For instance, Ambroise Paré details several stories of people's genitals changing from internal to external display. For instance, Marie became Manuel when her penis was expelled from her body when she began menstruating; a young man in Rheims who lived as a girl until at the age of 14 began 'frolicking' with a chambermaid and his penis was suddenly displayed outside of his body; a young man was once a girl until she jumped across a ditch and the exertion pushed her penis outside of her body: 'Marie, soon to be Marie no longer, hastened home to her/his mother, who consulted physicians and surgeons, all of whom assured the somewhat shaken woman that her daughter had become her son' (Laqueur 1990, 126; see also Daston and Park 1998; Schiebinger 1993). As Laqueur argues:

... the modern question, about the 'real' sex of a person, made no sense in this period, not because two sexes were mixed but because there was only one to pick from and it had to be shared by everyone, from the strongest warrior to the most effeminate courtier to the most aggressive virago to the gentlest maiden. (1990: 124)

By the nineteenth century, the understanding and practice of 'sex' based upon signs of temperament, behaviour, clothes and posture was usurped by a formulation of sex as fixed, essential and demonstrating sexual *difference*. For instance, Londa Schiebinger charts how eighteenth-, nineteenth- and twentieth-century European botanists attempted to find supporting evidence for the normative preference for heterosexuality, sexual reproduction and the theory of sex complementarity. The history of botany shows a remarkable insistence on the recreation of reassuringly familiar concepts such as sexual difference amongst plants (despite the fact that most flowers are intersex), marital bonds between plants (the term 'gamete' originates in the Greek *gamein*, 'to marry'), active male and passive female sexuality ('male' stamens were said to have visible orgasms as opposed to the 'female' pistils which showed little sexual excitement and modesty) and monogamy (even though plants reproduce through pollination which is transported via insects and air) (1993: 105).

How did our understanding of sex change over time? The answer may be found in the development of scientific disciplines, changes in approaches to bodies, as well as political changes. The study of anatomy led to emerging fields including molecular biology, biochemistry, endocrinology, neurobiology and histology. These subfields focused attention even more sharply on micro structures and functions: cells, hormones, neuro-transmitters and so on. Michel Foucault (1994/1963) points out that an important element of this epistemic shift was the emerging focus on the body revealing its secrets through visualisation. Dissection literally opened up the body to scrutiny and medical scientists were able to focus on the 'truth' revealed by the inside of the body rather than on the 'superficiality' of the outside of the body (Schiebinger 1993). Part of this 'truth' was 'sexual difference', and 'sex' began to permeate throughout the body, no longer in the form of seed, heat or humours, but in visible objects. For instance, the pre-modern view of the penis as anatomically expressed either inside or outside of the body, now gave way to a separate classificatory scheme: male penis and female vagina. Ovaries and testes, once considered the same organ, were also distinguished by their own names. And in an ironic twist of history repeating itself, in 1559 Renaldus Columbus claimed to have discovered the female clitoris (Schiebinger 1993; see also Traub 2002; Lochrie 2005). This was a significant declaration because it suggested the 'truth' of the body could be found visually and manually (through touch), and also because it further challenged the one-sex paradigm insofar as females could not have two penises – vagina and clitoris. The search for anatomical differences between women and men did not rest with the genitals and gonads. Anatomy books began to provide detailed pictorial descriptions of differences in skeletons, brains, skulls, hair, eyes, sweat, blood vessels and so on. In this way, 'sex' and 'sexual difference' began to permeate the entire body and 'by the 1790s, European anatomists presented the male and female body as each having a distinct telos – physical and intellectual strength for the man, motherhood for the woman' (Schiebinger 1989, 191).

As well as the increasing number of medical books detailing anatomical differences between women and men, politicians and social critics wrote treatises that emphasised 'sexual difference'. For instance, Jean-Jacques Rousseau's famous novel *Emile* sought to ground his arguments about the incommensurability of women and men through biological difference. Indeed, Rousseau maintained that 'a perfect woman and a perfect man ought not to resemble each other in mind any more than in looks' (Schiebinger 1993, 226). Rousseau's books, like those of his contemporaries, were particularly influential because they were able to bring apparently new evidence to old arguments. That is, this new politics sought to maintain old hierarchies, not through notions of the divine rights of men, but through the newly emerging biological foundation of sex complementarity. Specifically, sex complementarity held that women and men were, biologically, better suited to different roles, and that these roles complemented each other to form the optimum living, working system. Women were to maintain the family and household whilst men controlled the public political sphere. Sex complementarity maintained the gendered division of labour between private and public spheres by taking up the new sciences of biology and anatomy that were already at work on emphasising 'sexual difference'. In this vital way, biology, as the purveyor of stable, ahistorical and impartial 'facts' about 'sexual difference', became the foundation of political prescriptions about social order. Thus Geddes was able to pronounce to the British parliament in 1889 that 'what was decided among the pre-historic Protozoa cannot be annulled by an act of Parliament' (quoted in Laqueur 1990, 6).[8] So it was not a human-made political order that maintained women's subordination and disenfranchisement, but 'nature' itself that revealed social inequality.

Becoming Queer

If the Enlightenment was able to create and sustain the paradigm of sex dimorphism (and heteronormativity) by primarily relying upon scientific evidence, should queer theory then eschew evidence from biology and the study of animal behaviour? Not necessarily. In this final section I want to explain why I use evidence from biology and studies of animal behaviour in my explorations of queer. To do so I describe two paradigmatic approaches to understanding sex and sexuality. I argue that the first paradigm dominates research on sexual difference within both the natural and social sciences, while the second approach presents a way of understanding sex and sexuality that opens possibilities for queer research.

---

8   Lest we think this an outdated sentiment, note the statement by Allen Quist, Republican candidate for Minnesota governor in 1994: 'You have a political arrangement, and when push comes to shove, the higher level of political authority … should be in the hands of the husband. There's a genetic predisposition' (1994, 7).

In her path-breaking book, *Abstract Sex* (2004), Luciana Parisi outlines two mutually antagonistic approaches to the study of sex. The first approach (the historical context of which I have just outlined), is based upon the centrality of reproduction, both in terms of generating species variations and differences, and also in terms of within-species organisation (i.e. that the relations of organisms within any given species is organised around the need to sexually reproduce). As such, sex is inextricably linked with both genital sex and sexual reproduction. We may now see why studies of animal behaviour have tended to reinforce heteronormative expectations.

This approach is most strongly associated with neo-Darwinism, for instance in Richard Dawkins's popular theory of the 'selfish gene' (1976) in which organisms are determined by their genes' desire to reproduce. As Parisi notes, 'these hypotheses reiterate a binary system of identification of the sexes (male and female) that has enormous implications for the understanding of sexual and gender differences' (2004, 50). Parisi defines this approach as 'sadistic', insofar as it is based upon an economy of desire that emphasises climax (in a specifically sexual sense in terms of male ejaculation, and in a slightly more abstract sense in terms of the production of offspring from sexual reproduction) and the autonomy (singularity) of all organisms. Within this paradigm, Parisi locates Sigmund Freud's theory of the pleasure principle (1961/1920), which associates pleasure with the (nucleic) reproduction of life.

In contrast, what Parisi terms the 'masochistic' approach suggests an entirely different economy, one based not upon the positive cathexis of desire, but on negative (in the sense that they are not directed toward sexual reproduction) flows. This paradigm does not conceive of sex in terms of sexual reproduction, but in a much wider sense in terms of the associations within and between organisms. This means, in the first instance, that organisms are not autonomous entities in themselves, but rather exist through a meshwork of symbiotic relationships. In other words, human bodies, like those of other animals, live in necessary trans-species symbiotic relationships. As Alphonso Lingis recognises:

> ... *human animals live in symbiosis with thousands of anaerobic bacteria – six hundred species in our mouths, which neutralise the toxins all plants produce to ward off their enemies, four hundred species in our intestines, without which we could not digest and absorb the food we ingest ... The number of microbes that colonise our bodies exceed the number of cells in our bodies by up to a hundredfold.* (1994, 167)

Because organisms are not individuated in the way in which the first approach requires in order to emphasise the desire for (nucleic) sexual reproduction, this changes the ways in which we might understand the relationships between physical matter, organisms and the social organisations in which they are structured:

> *Abstract sex points to the non-linear coexistence of the biophysical (the cellular level of the body-sex defined by bacteria, viruses, mitochondrial organelles,*

eukaryotic cells); the biocultural (the anthropomorphic level of the human body-sex defined by psychoanalysis, thermodynamics, evolutionary biology and anatomy in industrial capitalism); and the biodigital (the engineering level of the body-sex defined by information science and technologies such as in vitro fertilisation, mammal and embryo cloning, transgenic manipulation and the human genome in cybernetic capitalism) layers of the virtual body-sex. (Parisi 2004, 12)[9]

'Masochistic' sex is not concerned with nucleic sexual reproduction, but encompasses the entire myriad other forms of sex: viral hijacking, contagion, mitosis, mutation, parthenogenesis and so on. For this reason, Parisi talks of sex as 'constituted by assemblages of microbodies that hyperlink the most divergent forms and functions of reproduction' (2004, 22), and Gilles Deleuze and Félix Guattari speak of 'rhizomes' (1987; see also Braidotti 2005; Hurley 2005/2006).

Indeed, Deleuze and Guattari call attention to the radical divergence of these two approaches in the quotation at the beginning of this chapter. What Parisi calls the 'sadistic' approach, Deleuze and Guattari refer to as 'molar'. For this reason, they write that we are statistically heterosexual (sadistic approach) but transsexual 'in a molecular sense' (masochistic approach). Deleuze and Guattari employ the example of the wasp and orchid: 'by pollinating the orchid, the wasp becomes part of its reproductive apparatus, which at the same time becomes a piece of the wasp' (Parisi 2004, 138). Deleuze and Guattari describe this relationship as an event, or a 'becoming-wasp of the orchid and a becoming-orchid of the wasp' (1987, 10). They might seem to offer a radical account, but this understanding of the wasp-orchid becoming is very familiar (albeit described using different terms) within the biology literature. For instance, microbiologist Lynn Margulis has spent her career documenting the sheer diversity of what queer theorists term 'becomings' (Margulis and Sagan 2003). Margulis's research primarily focuses on bacteria that she (amongst others; see Sonea and Mathieu 2000; Wallin 1927) has shown to be the origins of life on Earth. In other words, bacteria are our ancestors. Against the central tenet of neo-Darwinism – that inherited variation is mainly produced by random genetic mutation within individuated species (Mayr 1991; 2001) – Margulis argues that new tissues, organs and species evolved primarily through long-lasting relationships between different species (Margulis 1981). This challenges standard textbook and popularised accounts that emphasise competition and individualism as the major driving forces behind evolution. For Margulis, evolution has depended upon the 'intimacy of strangers', or symbiotic merger (Sapp 1994). She writes: 'our concept of the individual is totally warped. All of us are walking communities of microbes ... Every plant and animal today is a symbiont living in close contact with others' (quoted in Neimark 2005, 2). In other words, we evolved through symbiosis and symbiogenesis.

---

9   Parisi makes the further point that the 'body-sex' is a product of neither a given essence or socio-cultural conditions alone: 'a body is composed and decomposed by the activity of molecules and particles, forces and energies. It is not simply biological or cultural' (2004, 27).

Two aspects of 'becomings' are central from a biological perspective. First, individual beings do exist, but only 'as the outcome of becomings ... of irreversible processes of individuation' (DeLanda 2002, 84). That is, becomings are 'built-in' since individuation (of cells, tissues and so on) is itself defined as the very process of development from a range of possibilities. Second, symbiotic becomings involve innovation because the resultant long-term merger produces novel capabilities. For instance, the symbiotic merger of various bacteria in the hind guts of termites allows termites to digest food (wood). Margulis has shown that eukaryotic cells (cells with membrane bounded nuclei – humans are made up of eukaryotic cells) are a symbiotic merger of at least three different kinds of bacteria. For instance, these bacteria allow human cells to metabolise (through mitochondria). So innovation is another way of saying that symbiosis precipitates becomings. Using the insights of physicist Ilya Prigogine on becoming, DeLanda states:

> ... whereas embryogenesis is a process through which a yet unformed individual becomes what it is [individuation], acquiring a well-defined inside (the intrinsic properties defining its being), symbiosis represents a process through which a fully formed being may cease to be what it is to become something else, in association with something heterogeneous on the outside. (2002, 101–2; emphasis mine)

A growing literature (see for example Deleuze and Guattari 1987; Parisi 2004; Hird 2004; Margulis and Sagan 1986; 1991; 1995; 1997; DeLanda 1995; 1997a; 1997b; 1998) is directed by an interest in becomings in relation to sex and sexuality. Evidence generated within this paradigm stands to make a significant contribution to queer discussions of the constitution, boundaries and technologies of sex and sexuality. For instance, Donna Haraway is a well-known contributor to these discussions. Her early work questioned the human/primate/cyborg divide (1989; 1991: 1992) while her more recent work (2001; 2003) convincingly argues for the inter- and intra- relationships among species: indeed, Haraway's aim is to question the taxonomic species distinction. Recall the biological definition of species I gave at the beginning of this chapter and reflect upon Haraway's understanding of the fundamental symbiosis of species, or 'companion-species':

> Genes are not the point, and that surely is a relief. The point is companion-species making. It's all in the family, for better or worse, until death do us part. This is a family made up in the belly of the monster of inherited histories that have to be inhabited to be transformed. I always knew that if I turned up pregnant, I wanted the being in my womb to be a member of another species; maybe that turns out to be the general condition. It's not just mutts, in or out of the traffic of international adoption, who seek a category of one's own in significant otherness. (2003, 96)

Acknowledgement

Portions of this chapter appear in Hird, M. (2004), *Sex, Gender and Science* (Basingstoke: Palgrave Macmillan).

Suggested Further Reading

Bagemihl, B. (1999), *Biological Exuberance: Animal Homosexuality and Natural Diversity* (New York: St. Martin's Press).

Giffney, N. and Hird, M.J. (eds) (2008), *Queering the Non/Human* (Aldershot: Ashgate).

Haraway, D. (2003), *The Haraway Reader* (London and New York: Routledge).

Hird, M.J. (2004), *Sex, Gender and Science* (Basingstoke: Palgrave Macmillan).

Margulis, L. and Sagan, D. (1997), *What is Sex?* (New York: Simon and Schuster).

References

Bagemihl, B. (1999), *Biological Exuberance: Animal Homosexuality and Natural Diversity* (New York: St. Martin's Press).

Braidotti, R. (2005), 'Affirming the Affirmative: On Nomadic Affectivity', *Rhizomes: Cultural Studies in Emerging Knowledge* 11/12, http://www.rhizomes.net/issue11/hurley/index/html (accessed 10 August 2007).

Cohen, J.J. (2003), *Medieval Identity Machines* (Minneapolis, MN and London: University of Minnesota Press).

Daston, L. and Park, K. (1998), *Wonders and the Order of Nature* (New York: Zone Books).

Dawkins, R. (1976), *The Selfish Gene* (Oxford: Oxford University Press).

DeLanda, M. (1995), 'Uniformity and Variability: An Essay in the Philosophy of Matter', *Doors of Perception 3: On Matter Conference* (Amsterdam: Netherlands Design Institute).

—— (1997a), 'Immanence and Transcendence in the Genesis of Form', *The South Atlantic Quarterly* 96:3, 499–514.

—— (1997b), *A Thousand Years of Nonlinear History* (New York: Swerve Editions).

—— (1998), 'Deleuze and the Open-ended Becoming of the World', *diss.sense: Zeitschrift für Literatur and Kommunikation*, http://www.diss.sense.uni konstanz. de/virtualitaet/delanda.htm (accessed 20 November 2007).

—— (2002), *Intensive Science and Virtual Philosophy* (New York: Continuum).

Deleuze, G. and Guattari, F. (1987), *A Thousand Plateaus: Capitalism and Schizophrenia* (London: The Athlone Press).

—— (1996/1972), *Anti-Oedipus: Capitalism and Schizophrenia* (Minneapolis, MN: University of Minnesota Press).

Denniston, R.H. (1980), 'Ambisexuality in Animals', in J. Marmor (ed.), *Homosexual Behavior: A Modern Reappraisal* (New York: Basic Books).

Fausto-Sterling, A. (1997), 'Feminism and Behavioral Evolution: A Taxonomy', in P. Gowaty (ed.), *Feminism and Evolutionary Biology: Boundaries, Intersections, and Frontiers* (New York: Chapman and Hall).

Foucault, M. (1994/1963), *The Birth of the Clinic* (London: Vintage Books).

Freud, S. (1961/1920), *Beyond the Pleasure Principle*, ed. and trans. J. Strachey (New York and London: W.W. Norton).

Grosz, E. (1995), *Space, Time and Perversion* (London and New York: Routledge).

Haraway, D. (1989), *Primate Visions: Gender, Race and Nature in the World of Modern Science* (New York: Routledge).

—— (1991), *Simians, Cyborgs, and Women: The Reinvention of Nature* (London and New York: Routledge).

—— (1992), 'When Man™ is on the Menu', in J. Crary and S. Kwinter (eds), *Incorporations* (New York: Urzone Books).

—— (2001), 'More than Metaphor', in M. Mayberry, B. Subramaniam and L. Weasel (eds), *Feminist Science Studies* (New York: Routledge).

—— (2003), *The Companion Species Manifesto: Dogs, People, and Significant Otherness* (Chicago, IL: Prickly Paradigm Press).

Hird, M.J. (2002), 'Re(pro)ducing Sexual Difference', *Parallax* 8:4, 94–107.

—— (2003), 'From the Culture of Matter to the Matter of Culture', *Sociological Research Online* 8:1, http://www.socresonline.org.uk/8/1/hird.html (accessed 30 August 2007).

—— (2004), *Sex, Gender and Science* (Basingstoke: Palgrave Macmillan).

—— (2006), 'Animal Trans', *Australian Feminist Studies* 21:49, 35–48.

Hurley, P. (2005/2006) 'On a Series of Queer Becomings: Selected Becomings-invertebrate 2003–2005', *Rhizomes: Cultural Studies in Emerging Knowledge* 11/12, http://www.rhizomes.net/issue11/hurley/index/html (accessed 10 August 2007).

Kleinman, D.G. (1977), 'Monogamy in Mammals', *Quarterly Review of Biology* 52, 39–69.

Krizek, G.O. (1992), 'Unusual Interaction Between a Butterfly and a Beetle: "Sexual Paraphilia" in Insects?', *Tropical Lepidoptera* 3:2, 118.

Lingis, A. (1994), *Foreign Bodies* (New York: Routledge).

Laqueur, T. (1990), *Making Sex* (Cambridge, MA: Harvard University Press).

Lochrie, K. (2005), *Heterosyncracies: Female Sexuality When Normal Wasn't* (Minneapolis, MN and London: University of Minnesota Press).

Margulis, L. (1981), *Symbiosis in Cell Evolution*, 2nd edition (San Francisco, CA: W.H. Freeman).

—— and Sagan, D. (1986), *Origins of Sex: Three Billion Years of Genetic Recombination* (New Haven, CT: Yale University Press).

—— (1991), *Mystery Dance* (New York: Summit Books).

—— (1995), *What is Life?* (Berkeley, CA: University of California Press).

—— (1997), *What is Sex?* (New York: Simon and Schuster).

—— (2003), *Aquiring Genomes: A Theory of the Origin of Species* (New York: Basic Books).

Mayr, E. (1991), *One Long Argument: Charles Darwin and the Genesis of Modern Evolutionary Thought* (Cambridge, MA: Harvard University Press).

—— (2001), *What Evolution Is* (New York: Basic Books).

Nakashima, Y., Kuwanmura, T. and Yogo, Y. (1995), 'Why Be a Both-Ways Sex Changer', *Ethology* 101, 301–7.

Neimark, J. (2005), 'Lynn Margulis', http://www.nyu.edu/classes/neimark/margulis. html (accessed 5 August 2005).

Oring, L., Fleischer, R., Reed, J. and Marsden, K. (1992), 'Cuckoldry Through Stored Sperm in the Sequentially Polyandrous Spotted Sandpiper', *Nature* 359, 631–3.

Oudshoorn, N. (1994), *Beyond the Natural Body: And Archaeology of Sex Hormones* (London and New York: Routledge).

Ouist, A. (1994), *Los Angeles Times* 12 July, 7.

Owen, D.F. (1988), 'Mimicry and Transvestism in *Papilio phorcas*', *Journal of Entomological Society of Southern Africa* 51, 294–6.

Parisi, L. (2004), *Abstract Sex: Philosophy, Bio-Technology and the Mutations of Desire* (London and New York: Continuum).

Pavelka, M.M. (1995), 'Sexual Nature: What Can We Learn from a Cross-Species Perspective?', in P. Abramson and S. Pinkerton (eds), *Sexual Nature, Sexual Culture* (Chicago, IL: University of Chicago Press).

Policansky, D. (1982), 'Sex Change in Plants and Animals', *Annual Review of Ecology and Systematics* 13, 471–95.

Quist, Allen (1994), quoted in the *Los Angeles Times*, July 12, Part B, page 7 in a piece written by Linda R. Hirshman.

Reinboth, R. (ed.) (1975), *Intersexuality in the Animal Kingdom* (New York, Heidelberg, Berlin: Springer-Verlag).

Reite, M. and Caine, N. (eds) (1983), *Child Abuse: The Nonhuman Primate Data* (New York: Alan R. Liss).

Rothblatt, M. (1995), *The Apartheid of Sex* (New York: Crown).

Roughgarden, J. (2004), *Evolution's Rainbow* (Berkeley, CA: University of California Press).

Sagan, D. (1992), 'Metametazoa: Biology and Multiplicity', in J. Crary and S. Kwinter (eds), *Incorporations* (New York: Urzone Books).

Sapp, J. (1994), *Evolution by Association: A History of Symbiosis* (Oxford: Oxford University Press).

Schiebinger, L. (1989), *The Mind Has No Sex? Women in the Origins of Modern Science* (Cambridge, MA: Harvard University Press).

—— (1993), *Nature's Body* (London: Pandora).

Sonea, S. and Mathieu, L. (2000), *Prokarytology: A Coherent View* (Montreal: Les Presses de l'Université de Montréal).

Strain, L., Dean, J., Hamilton, M. and Bonthron, D. (1998), 'A True Hermaphrodite Chimera Resulting from Embryo Amalgamation after In Vitro Fertilization', *The New England Journal of Medicine* 338:3, 166–9.

Thomas, L. (1974), *The Lives of a Cell* (New York: Viking Press).

Traub, V. (2002), *The Renaissance of Lesbianism in Early Modern England* (Cambridge: Cambridge University Press).

Tuana, N. (1989), 'The Weaker Seed: The Sexist Bias of Reproductive Theory', in N. Tuana (ed.), *Feminism and Science* (Bloomington, IN: Indiana University Press).

Wallin, I. (1927), *Symbionticism and the Origin of Species* (Baltimore, MD: Williams and Wilkins).

Warner, R.R. (1975), 'The Adaptive Significance of Sequential Hermaphroditism in Animals', *American Naturalis* 109, 61–82.

—— (1984), 'Mating Behavior and Hermaphroditism in Coral Reef Fish', *American Scientist* 72, 128–36.

Wilson, E. (2000), *Sociobiology: The New Synthesis* (Cambridge, MA: Harvard University Press).

Wolfe, C. (ed.) (2003a), *Zoontologies: The Question of the Animal* (Minneapolis, MN: University of Minnesota Press).

—— (2003b), *Animal Rites: American Culture, the Discourse of Species, and Posthumanist Theory* (Chicago, IL: University of Chicago Press).

The New Queer Cartoon

Noreen Giffney

Who's That Slug in My Closet? The New Queer Cartoon

Monsters, Inc. (2001) employs signifiers of the factory, the corporation, the city and consumerism in its representation of Monstropolis, a city populated by monsters, which exists in a parallel universe to the human world (Freeman 2005). The company invoked by the cartoon's title is in the business of scaring: 'We scare because we care'. *Monsters, Inc.* takes as its premise the childhood fear that a monster might be lurking in one's bedroom closet to explore what it might mean for this fantasy to become reality. In this cartoon, monsters do not just lurk in closets they *work* in them, generating power for their city from the screams of frightened children. Power begets power here as the (destructive) might of the monster is transformed through the (affective) conduit of the child's terror into (productive) energy for the purposes of keeping Monstropolis in working order. James P. Sullivan (Sully), a giant blue, hairy, bear-like creature, and Mike Wazowski (Mikey), a large eye encased in a green head on legs, are the protagonists and together make up the company's top scaring team. While following their adventures in which they uncover a nasty plot literally to suck the screams out of children mechanically and make scarers redundant, we become privy to Sully and Mikey's homosocial bond, which is mediated paternally through their relationship with Boo, a human female child. While Mikey's heterosexuality is symbolised by his attraction to his snake-haired, 'schmoopsie-poo' Celia, Sully's hermetic lifestyle and bachelor's disinterest in dating suggest that he is a workaholic certainly but also potentially raise questions as to whether he can be read as straight. This is where Roz comes in – or out as the case might be.

Roz is a slug and is employed as the dispatch manager in Monsters, Inc. She wears a baggy cardigan, thick-rimmed spectacles, a severe haircut, a large mole on the right side of her chin and a permanent grimace on her face. A signpost situated above her desk spells out her motto: 'It's my way or the highway'. She is a castratrice, a demasculating presence who almost amputates Mikey's fingers with her office shutter when he tries to charm her into giving him a case file. She functions as a de-phallicising metaphor more generally in her interrupting of Mikey's speech in every encounter and thus the cutting off of his virility, manifested as it is in his flirtatious banter: 'Good morning, Roz, my succulent little garden snail'; 'Roz, my tender, oozing blossom, you're looking fabulous today'. If the central motif of this cartoon is the monster within the closet, Roz performs this role with aplomb (Benshoff 1997). While Roz does not self-identify as lesbian, a number of cultural signifiers are enacted in her figuration so that she is connotatively – if not denotatively – lesbian (Creed 1995; Doty 1993). She is lesbian, in other words, not by desire but by pastiche. While her physicality draws on stereotypes of the lesbian body – rotund, unfeminine, ugly and animalistic (Valentine 1998) – her voice gives her away as it were: there is something not quite womanly about her. This unwomanliness is literalised in the fact that Roz is voiced by Bob Peterson, a man. This is a further indication of, what Judith Halberstam terms, Roz's 'female masculinity' (1998), which Halberstam reminds us often correlates with lesbianism in the heteronormative imaginary: 'Lesbianism has long been associated with female masculinity and female masculinity in turn has been figured as undesirable by linking it in essential and unquestionable ways to female ugliness' (2002, 359). Roz's masculine vocal chords become significant and not merely coincidental when considered alongside Celia's vocalisation by Jennifer Tilly, an actress somewhat typecast due to her previous roles as 'ditsy' 'bimbos'.[1]

In a sense, Roz embodies the technologies of the closet and its attendant acts of passing, outing and coming out. She is a peripheral character, one who spends much of her time outside of the field of action looking in: she tells Mikey 'I'm watching you, Wazowski. Always watching ... Always'. As the company's dispatch manager, she works closeted away all day in an office booth, partitioned off from the main floor of the building. This role however, as we find out near the close of the cartoon, is a façade: Roz is an undercover agent of the Child Detection Agency (CDA), on a mission to expose (or 'out') the illegal activities of some of the company's employees. It is not until the outtakes – themselves the abjected coils of the 'real' film, the outside of the inside in other words (Fuss 1991) – that the implications of her being an exemplar of lesbianism become more explicit. '[Q]ueerness as outtake', in the words of Ellis Hanson, 'places in dialectical tension the excluded and the central, the untheorized and the transparent, the unwatchable and the transfixing' (1999, 18). The joke is now on us as we witness Roz emerging from a toilet cubicle ('Hello'), a shower curtain ('Ta da') and finally from Sully's closet ('Guess who?'). Roz, it appears, has been on the inside, hiding in plain sight all along. Roz's triple outing makes flesh the comments of Judith Butler on the act of coming out: 'For being "out" always depends to some extent on being "in"; it gains its meaning only within that polarity. Hence, being "out" must produce the closet again and again in order to maintain itself as "out"' (Butler 2004 [1991], 123). Despite the supposed displacement of any suspicions of homosexuality from Sully onto Roz, it seems that there remains a trace of something monstrous, something queer hidden unbeknownst to him in his closet.

---

1   A similar strategy is played for laughs in *Shrek 2* (2004) and *Shrek the Third* (2007), in which male talk show host Larry King provides the voice of Doris, one of Cinderella's ugly sisters, presented here as a transvestite.

This discussion of *Monsters, Inc.* raises a number of questions which in turn point to the concerns of those undertaking queer theoretical work on film and more particularly on the cartoon or animated feature. What are we looking at here? Is Roz the result of a conscious effort by the producers of *Monsters, Inc.*? Does she point to subtextual encodings buried within this cartoon? Is she an archetype of cultural assumptions of what it means to be 'lesbian', 'old', 'ugly', 'unwomanly'? Is her figuration a negative, homophobic one (is the joke on her)? Does she offer a critique of such negative, homophobic representations of female villains in other cartoons (is the joke on them)? Does she present a strategy for resisting normalising discourses of lesbianism (is the joke on viewers who fail to understand this message; viewers who are still laughing at Roz)? What is my relation to *Monsters, Inc.* as a spectator? What effects does my self-identification as 'non-heterosexual' – however ambivalent my attachment to that label might be – have on my response to this cartoon and specifically to the characterisation of Roz? As non-heterosexual am I more attuned to recognising the norms enacted by compulsory heterosexuality and the potential for lesbian representation via stereotyping? Does my non-heterosexual positioning move me to look for something within this animated text; to uncover hidden ciphers, to privilege moments that are significant for me as a viewer? Does my choice of identifier lead me to *do* something to *Monsters, Inc.*; to change this cartoon in some way, to insert myself into this text in order to identify with it projectively? In the viewing of this cartoon, is it *I* who am altered, remade through my relation with it? Is there something in *Monsters, Inc.* for me to see, interpret or identify with – am I taking something from it in other words – or am I putting something of myself into this cartoon; something which is not there in the first place?[2]

The term 'queer' is employed variously as a noun, adjective, verb and adverb. Queer as a noun (*queer/s* or *queerness* in a film) denotes an essence, thing, aspect or identity – something already existent within a film to be seen or uncovered by viewers. This can be either denotative as in a character clearly marked out as queer or connotative as in a bundle of signifiers to be interpreted by audiences 'in the know'. Queer as an adjective (a *queer* film) symbolises a property of a film; a category, descriptor or generic convention. In this, viewers ask what it is about a film that renders it queer. This can have a broader focus when writers discuss common themes, stylistic devices and concerns which a number of films share and thus mark them out as similar (New Queer Cinema, for example). Queer as a verb (to *queer* a film) refers to a methodological framework or technique of analysis. It loosely describes the strategies through which a viewer interprets a film or the changes enacted by a film on said viewer, as they occur, in the process of watching it. Queer as an adverb (to see or read a film *queerly*) points to the importance of the viewer's relation to a film. While queer as an adverb identifies the particularities

---

2   See the following for debates as to whether queer represents a methodological framework for examining films or something to be searched for and/or found within those same texts: Doty 1993; Whatling 1997; Hanson 1999; Doty 2000.

of the process through which a viewer impacts on a film and *vice versa*, queer as a verb signifies the process itself.

Queer theoretical engagements with film studies include a number of different approaches: the discursive examination of the representation of sexual and gender identity categories and those who sport them across a range of films (Wilton 1995; Phillips 2006), as well as how gender and sexuality intersect with other forms of identification such as race, ethnicity, nationality, class, age, religion and dis/ability (Patel 2002; McRuer 2006).[3] There is a concerted effort to attend to heteronormativity by discussing how particular films promote, make visible, challenge and subvert – sometimes simultaneously – compulsory heterosexuality (Diamond 2005; Sullivan 2003). These analyses treat films – either singly or in more broad-based studies – as texts and undertake close readings of, for example, characters, dialogue, particular scenes, intertextual elements as cues to latent themes and diagetic elements such as light and sound. They are based on the understanding that the viewer creates meaning in the text as much as those behind the camera.[4] The viewer after all is in relationship with the film.[5] This chapter is an example of such an approach. This particular style of analysis interests me because of my academic training in textual analysis and the way in which the close scrutiny of a single film represents an intimate act for me which allows me the pleasure of really engaging with that text on a number of levels and from a variety of vantage points. In this chapter, I will use *Shrek* (2001) to illustrate some of the characteristics of what I refer to here as the new queer cartoon.

Is it possible to read *Shrek* as part of New Queer Cinema? Coined by B. Ruby Rich in an article in *Sight and Sound Magazine* in 1992 and reproduced in Aaron's collection, New Queer Cinema functions loosely as an umbrella term to denote a set of films:

> ... *united by a common style. Call it 'Homo Pomo': there are traces in all of them of appropriation and pastiche, irony as well as a reworking of history with social constructionism very much in mind ... these works are irreverent, energetic, alternately minimalist and excessive. Above all, they're full of pleasure. They're here, they're queer, get hip with it. (2004 [1992], 16)*

Chief characteristics of films nestling under the New Queer Cinema banner include a flagrant disregard for and defiance of norms, conventions and rules and an unapologetic attitude towards representing the complexity of queer lives. In an article in *Sight and Sound Magazine* in 2000, Rich spoke of New Queer Cinema in the past tense;

---

3   A number of films concentrate, for example, on national cinema: Kuzniar 2000; Cestaro 2004; Griffiths 2006.

4   There have also been a few studies of the queer auteur, including Morrison 2000; Richardson 2008.

5   See MacCormack (2008) for an exploration of the viewer's relationship with cinema.

> *... from the beginning the New Queer Cinema was a more successful term for a moment than a movement. It was meant to catch the beat of a new kind of film- and video-making that was fresh, edgy, low-budget, inventive, unapologetic, sexy and stylistically daring.*

Michele Aaron and her fellow contributors to *New Queer Cinema: A Critical Reader* (2004) suggest that New Queer Cinema is a historical category, a moment that has now passed. Aaron's contributors, who also talk about New Queer Cinema in the past tense, seem to have taken their lead from Rich. For example, Monica B. Pearl comments in her chapter on HIV/AIDS that '*The Hours* is not New Queer Cinema. Chiefly because it was produced outside of the general timeframe of what has been designated New Queer Cinema' (2004, 32). Does Rich own the rights, as it were, to New Queer Cinema simply because she coined the term? Should she alone plot the trajectory and announce the end of a phenomenon simply because she was the first person to use such a term in writing?

New Queer Cinema has not taken account of the subversive potential of the cartoon. In this chapter I am proposing a subgenre of New Queer Cinema: the new queer cartoon to facilitate a discussion of *Shrek* within the context of New Queer Cinema while recognising how this particular animated feature differs from the generic conventions currently masquerading as New Queer Cinema.[6] Judith Halberstam has proposed the term Pixarvolt (2006; 2007; 2008), an amalgam of the animation company's moniker, Pixar, and revolt, for cartoons which:

> *... proceed by way of fairly conventional narratives about individual struggle but they mostly use the individual character only as a gateway to intricate stories of collective action, anti-capitalist critique, group bonding and alternative imaginings of community, space, embodiment and responsibility. (2008, 271)*

Pixarvolt productions are, according to Halberstam, in tune with their target audience: children. They eschew an interest in family and romance as she claims children are not interested in such states. While considering Pixarvolt a useful term for examining the underlying philosophy of films made by Pixar studios, I am not convinced of its translatability when exploring cartoons by other mainstream studios or independent production companies. The new queer cartoon is, for my purposes, a more flexible label for opening up a discussion of *Shrek*, in which the joke is on the norm rather than the outsider; postmodernism is the guiding philosophy, camp is the structuring aesthetic while intertextuality and pastiche are its organising principles. New queer cartoons expose cultural scripts for the constructions they are, subverting them by directly referencing norms governing sexuality and gender, and are littered with sexual innuendo and jokes about gender. They are often aimed more at adults than children so that there are multiple

---

6   There is much work to be done on queerly-produced independent animated films, which I do not have space to deal with in this chapter.

narratives operating simultaneously and in layers. Anthropomorphism, a staple of the animated feature, is again employed in new queer cartoons but is turned in on itself so that the analogy with humans becomes a critical lens through which societal norms are exposed to scrutiny and with the potential for change. New queer cartoons are collaborative creations: meaning is produced as much by the viewer as by the screenwriters, cartoonists, voiceover actors, directors, producers and advertisers.

New queer cartoons are concerned with making visible and making fun of heteronormativity. Heteronormativity refers to the institution of heterosexuality, in other words, the promotion of heterosexuality as the normal, natural, original way to be, live or behave. It is also the belief that everyone is or should be male or female and heterosexual. As a result anyone who does not identify as either male or female and heterosexual is considered to be a deviant and someone who is not normal. Heterosexuality's normalcy is constantly re-enforced by the churches, the state, the media, cultural products and the medical, legal and educational establishments. Heteronormativity also dictates that people should be heterosexual in certain ways, for example, to act masculine if a man, feminine if a woman and, in a 'perfect' world, to be married, monogamous and have children. This chapter analyses one such cultural product, the cartoon, supposedly the mainstay of (heteronormative) family values. Sporting G (general) and U (universal) certificates, the cartoon is suitable for all. Or is it? For readers who say 'leave it alone, it's only a cartoon and just for kids', I say by way of response: the cartoon as a cultural product is often used to indoctrinate children and re-institute adults in the (correct) ways of heteronormativity. This chapter offers, through a discussion of *Shrek*, a critique of the way in which some cartoons inscribe (human) heteronormative relations, morals and expectations on their nonhuman characters (Cokely 2005; Dennis 2003; Griffin 2004) by discussing how *Shrek* departs from, mocks and subverts heteronormativity at every turn. The focus here is not on the human body but on the nonhuman, for as Jeffrey Jerome Cohen puts it, 'The body is not human (or at least, it is not only human)' (2003, 41). When I say nonhuman I mean two things: firstly, my concern is with synthespians or virtual actors: 'computer-generated images enacting … parts … historically played by real-actors' (Creed 2000, 79). Secondly, I will examine the characterisation of and relations between, among others, an ogre, a donkey, a dragon and a human, Princess Fiona, who looked so photo-realistic at the commencement of the shoot, that she had to be 'de-humanised' a bit in order to fit in.

Is That Your Ass I'm Looking at, or Do You Have a Donkey Behind You? The Anal Erotics of Ass Humour

In a directorial debut by Andrew Adamson and Vicky Jensen and boasting Mike Myers, Eddie Murphy, Cameron Diaz and John Lithgow as cyber-stars, *Shrek* forms part of a postmodern corpus of cartoons, including *Antz* and *Toy Story* among others. These cartoons differ from earlier incarnations, such as *Sleeping Beauty,* *Snow White and the Seven Dwarves* and *Beauty and the Beast*, by being aimed, not just at children, but also and often more so at adults. Irreverent and satirical, these cartoons, while keeping some of the traditional formula – boy has adventure, meets/rescues girl, they fall in love, marry and live happily ever after – expose sometimes with hilarious results the traditional formula for the construction that it is. Intertextuality is tantamount to the success of these cartoons. For example, there are many references to other films and cultural forms in *Shrek*: Cameron Diaz's Princess Fiona expertly fights as she did in *Charlie's Angels*, Shrek pats Donkey while saying 'That'll do, donkey. That'll do' which mirrors the farmer and his pig in *Babe*, and the Gingerbread Man rounds off the film in the style of Tiny Tim in *A Christmas Carol*. Lauded as 'The Greatest Fairytale Never Told', *Shrek* is a camped-up serving of the fairytale thought otherwise – in effect, it is queer, right up to the so-called 'heterosexual' closing still: 'And They Lived Ugly Ever After'.

Shrek is an extended commentary on the absurdity of hegemonic masculinity. The male body and performances of masculinity come in for scrutiny in a cartoon that continuously serves up the essence of Jacques Lacan's dictum: the phallus is the penis plus lack. This is achieved through the employment of a camp aesthetic so that *Shrek* becomes a pantomime with masculinity as its central gag. *Shrek* is set up as a kind of drag show that takes to task heteronormative notions that sex, gender and sexuality should all line up perfectly, i.e. that men should be masculine and desire women (and *vice versa*). The first shot of Lord Farquaad is taken from his (apparently) big black boots up, so that he appears masculine and stately. He exhibits what one of my former students referred to as 'a phallic strut', i.e. 'that he appears to be led by his penis'.[7] The shot is accompanied by loud, boisterous music and we see Farquaad's face with a strong chin, hard expression and the shadow of stubble – an epiphany of manliness. The next shot shows him as he passes by two guards, at which point we realise that he only measures up to their elbows. Later on we are treated to a shot of Farquaad's hairy chest as he sits up in bed admiring Princess Fiona's image in the mirror. His masculine posturing makes him look ridiculous, especially when we witness the Gingerbread Man spitting milk into his eye, while screaming 'Eat me!' Farquaad is, in a sense, a perfect exemplification of kinging, which Judith Halberstam claims, 'reads dominant male masculinity and explodes its effects through exaggeration, parody, and earnest mimicry' (2005, 130).

Shrek makes a mockery of male bravado many times in the cartoon, when men quake in their boots, answering in high-pitched voices (sometimes screams) when he confronts them. When one of Farquaad's knights approaches Shrek in the forest and tells him that Farquaad has given him orders to arrest Shrek, Shrek retorts: 'you and what army?', at which point we see that all of the knight's peers have deserted him. Similarly, at the beginning of the cartoon, Shrek has to tell the terrified men with his saliva all over their faces that it is time to run. Robin Hood's band of merry men – merry in the gayest sense of the word – double up as dance troupes from

---

7   I am grateful to Catriona Corcoran for this insight.

West Side Story and *River Dance*. If that is not obvious enough, the karaoke session at the close of the cartoon features the lads singing a YMCA tune, while Robin Hood winks into the camera at us. The wink here stands in for the 'nudge, nudge' of the open secret. Robin confirms what we all suspect about his 'merry' men. At the end of the cartoon, the three little pigs look tough in their rapper outfits (we witness them break-dancing and beating out a rendition of 'Who Let The Dogs Out?' in the karaoke), but act and talk like gay men in their most-stereotypically queenly form. When one of them pipes up that Lord Farquaad 'huffed and he puffed ... and he signed an eviction notice', we are thinking of puff, more as a noun than as a verb.

Two body parts come in for special attention in *Shrek*: the penis and the arse. The phallus becomes a measuring tape for the shortcomings and failures of hegemonic masculinity. Viewers are treated to numerous jokes about Farquaad's stature, including pointed remarks at the size of his penis – or lack of it. When Shrek and Donkey arrive in Duloc, while looking up at one of the town's huge towers, Shrek bemusedly asks Donkey: 'Do you think he [Farquaad] is compensating for something?', a joke Donkey does not comprehend. Donkey later understands the joke, and when Fiona asks of Lord Farquaad, Shrek comments, 'Men of Farquaad's stature are in *short* supply', to which Donkey replies, 'There are those who think *little* of him'. As they laugh, Fiona retorts angrily, 'You're just jealous that you can't measure up to a great ruler like Lord Farquaad' to which Shrek replies, 'Maybe you're right Princess, but I'll let you do the *measuring*'. Later, as they near Duloc, its large white phallic tower in the centre, Princess Fiona asks (disappointedly), 'That's Duloc?', to which Donkey replies: 'Yeah, I know. You know Shrek thinks that Farquaad is compensating for something, which I think means that he has a really ...', at which point Shrek stamps on his neck so that we do not get to hear the presumably 'small dick' at the end of the sentence. The penis is continuously alluded to in phallic gestures that keep it present (in our minds) in its (material) absence. For example, Shrek damages his groin sliding down the staircase as he and his companions flee from Dragon's castle, while a tree trunk appears strategically between (a full-frontal nude) Shrek and viewers when he is washing himself in the swamp. The assumption that this tree is placed in such a position to protect Shrek's modesty is undermined when, in a supplementary DVD documentary on the making of the cartoon, we are treated to a full-frontal nude shot of Shrek without any genitals at all!

The arse as a site of eroticism and abjection, desire and disgust takes centre stage in *Shrek*. The cartoon is particularly concerned with the potential for penile-anal eroticism in jokes about Pinocchio, the wooden puppet and his growing nose (or woody standing in here for an erect penis). The karaoke session, for example, rounds off with Donkey calling back to Pinocchio: 'Hey Pinocchio, you wanna watch that nose man!' Celia Daileader is beautifully articulate in her analysis of:

> ... *our culture's fascination with the ass. We have the piece of ass, the smart ass, the asshole, the expression, 'my ass!' we have the pain in the ass, the dumbass, the jackass, the kick in the ass. Nobody loves a tightass. And in choosing a mate, many want a nice ass. The ass is the butt of invective and*

the aim (puns intended) of the erotic gaze. It seems the more we abject it the more it haunts us like our origins, it's always back there; it's a bodily thing of darkness that we must, ultimately, acknowledge as our own. (2002, 327)

Shrek opens with an ogre of the same name using a fairytale as toilet paper to wipe his arse, before flushing it into a swamp full of excrement and other waste products. Right from the beginning we can see that Shrek is not going to be bound by the strictures of the fairytale: he rips out numerous pages from the fairytale, scoffing, 'Like that's ever going to happen!' He continues, 'What a load of ...' before the flushing of the loo drowns out presumably (given Shrek's location) the word 'shit' or 'crap'. After the toilet door bursts open, Shrek walks out vigorously shaking the fairytale loo paper off his foot. He also picks his knickers (or perhaps his pantomime tights?) out of his arse, before we see him jumping nakedly into the swamp for a wash – receiving a quick flash of the top of (the crack of) his buttocks.

The male arse (or ass) is a constant site of scrutiny (punning and amusement) in *Shrek*, whether it is Shrek's arse defecating, farting, being wiped, bumped (by Donkey), kissed (by Dragon) or pierced (by the arrow of one of Robin Hood's men, which is subsequently dislodged by Fiona). In fact, in addition to providing a few laughs, bodily secretions (often perceived as the body's most abject possessions) are seen to have practical uses in *Shrek*, including Shrek using the entrails of a caterpillar-like bug to wash his teeth, using wax from his ear as a candle and belching into the fireplace to light the fire. Similarly, when Shrek burns his foot trying to put out a camp fire, Donkey urinates on it to put it out. The casting of a male Donkey as Shrek's companion provides a number of puns.[8] After rescuing Princess Fiona, Shrek tells her that he must return to 'rescue [his] ass' (which he does subsequently as he runs from the castle, the dragon's breathy flames licking up towards his own arse and that of Donkey). Indeed, we also see Dragon chasing her ass – both her own and Donkey's – as she runs in circles after Shrek and his fleeing companions. When Shrek tries to apologise to Donkey for his grumpy behaviour near the close of the film, Donkey tells him that 'no-one likes a kiss ass', no-one that is, unless you are a female Dragon who finds the idea of kissing (and eroticising) a donkey (ass) romantic. Elsewhere Shrek tells Donkey to behave or he'll give him 'a smacked bottom', and perhaps I am stretching all this arsing around too far here, but in answer to Shrek's question, 'Are you coming Donkey?', the ass played by Eddie Murphy replies 'I'm right behind you'. If *Shrek* is not pointing to the fleshy corporeality of the male arse or the ass as male, it is commenting on the male as arse (meaning fool or idiot) in the vertically-challenged (and tiny arsed, in fact, anal) Lord Farquaad. While Dragon might not fulfil her wish to kiss male ass (i.e. Donkey), she gets to eat a male arse (w)hole, when she gleefully consumes Farquaad and belches out his crown.

---

8   Readers should note the controversy raised by the casting of Eddie Murphy, a black man, to play a donkey, a beast of burden, who exercises a servile position. While a comedian seems an obvious choice 'to make an ass' of himself, the cartoon has received a torrent of criticisms for the potentially racist undertones involved in such a casting decision and representation.

From Hetero-Species to Homo-Species Desire in One Hour and a Half: Closet Anxiety, or When a Woman Loves an Ogre

Shrek's comments are not limited to masculinities; the cartoon has much to say about the performance of femininity. In her interview on the *Shrek* DVD, Princess Fiona insists that she took the part in *Shrek* because she 'got to kick some butt'. One example being the following: by the time they reach the forest, Shrek and Donkey are so used to Fiona playing the damsel in distress routine, that they stand open-mouthed as she beats Robin Hood's men single-handedly in a style that would make Bruce Lee or Jackie Chan envious. Astonished, Shrek asks Fiona, 'Where did that come from? Where did you learn that?' When asked about her future plans in an interview on the additional features on the DVD, Fiona answers: 'Snow White and I were planning on a re-make of *Thelma and Louise*'. Considering the lesbo-erotics of *Thelma and Louise* (attested to by one of its stars, Susan Sarandon, in *The Celluloid Closet*) and the dearth of women in this cartoon, this statement resounds clearly and queerly in the heteronormative landscape that is *Shrek*. Fiona possesses a straight mind in *Shrek* – a mimicry of the position of many viewers watching the cartoon. According to Monique Wittig, to live in society is to live in heterosexuality, for the straight mind sees nothing else: 'you-will-be-straight-or-you-will-not-be' (1992, 28). Wittig points to the existence within culture of:

> ... *a core of nature which resists examination, a relationship excluded from the social in the analysis – a relationship whose characteristic is ineluctably in culture, as well as in nature, and which is the heterosexual relationship ... the straight mind cannot conceive of a culture, a society where heterosexuality would not order not only all human relationships but also its very production of concepts and all the processes which escape consciousness.* (1992, 27, 28)

In opposition to Shrek who does not play by the rules (he rips pages out of the fairytale, while scoffing: 'Like that's ever going to happen!'), Princess Fiona adheres to the fairytale's regulations. She remains locked up in a tower, observing courtly rituals, while waiting for the first man who will rescue her so she can marry him. Particularly amusing are Fiona's flattening of her garments over her stomach and puckering of her lips as she awaits Shrek's kiss, which does not come. Instead, he shakes her roughly, telling her gruffly to 'wake up!' It does not cross Fiona's mind that her rescuer might be a woman or even a nonhuman creature such as an ogre – or what she might do in such instances. When Princess Fiona demands that Shrek remove his helmet so that she can 'look on the face of [her] rescuer', he retorts, 'I'm not your type', to which she replies, 'Of course you are, you're my rescuer'. Farquaad is the epitome of normativity who acts out of his insecurities and prejudices, especially in his attempts to abject the fairytale 'trash poisoning [his] perfect world'. He is concerned with creating and preserving, what he sees as his 'perfect kingdom'. He replies to the Gingerbread Man's calling him a monster, with the statement: 'I'm not a monster here, you are, you and the rest of that fairytale trash poisoning my perfect world'.

While we see lots of male homosociality in the film, the two main female leads, Dragon and Princess Fiona, have no lines to say to each other. *Shrek* debunks the myth of fairytale romance, showing that romance has little to do with love or even desire for another person. Karma Lochrie goes further still, 'heterosexually organized sexuality is exclusively masculine-centred ... heterosexuality excludes not only women but also women's pleasure' (2001, 89). Despite Fiona's talk of 'true love', she only wants to marry Farquaad to break the witch's spell. Similarly, Farquaad, has little interest in the three women, Cinderella, Snow White, Fiona, in the *Blind Date* scenario, he is only interested in marrying one of them – any one will do – so that Duloc can have the 'perfect king' – him. As the magic mirror puts it, 'all [he] has to do is marry a princess'. Shrek's remark to Fiona, 'he's just marrying you so he can be king. He's not your true love', is a precise appraisal of the situation. When Farquaad discovers that Princess Fiona is in love with Shrek, he screams: 'This marriage is binding! See! See!', despite the fact that they have not even kissed – never mind consummated it. He continues, 'I will have order! I will have perfection! I will have ...' at which point he is gobbled up by Dragon. Farquaad cares little about consummating the marriage, telling the ogress Fiona that he'll lock her in the attic.

There are two central cross-species (romantically-imbued) relationships in *Shrek*: Shrek and Princess Fiona, and Dragon and Donkey.[9] The burgeoning romantic attachment between Fiona and Shrek is played out as a kind of erotic awakening, more specifically, a homoerotic awakening. While Princess Fiona moves from hetero-species desire (human and ogre) to homo-species desire (ogre and ogre), her (painful) metamorphosis is enacted by means of her navigating a closet. When confiding in Donkey, Princess Fiona insists, 'You can't breathe a word, no-one must ever know', to which he retorts angrily, 'What's the point of being able to talk if you have to keep secrets?' Fiona desperately reiterates her request: 'Promise you won't tell, promise'. By day, she is human (i.e. normal), by night, an ogre (i.e. queer). The spell, Princess Fiona tells Donkey, says: 'By night one way, by day another. This shall be the norm until you find love's first kiss and then take love's true form.' She hides, what turns out to be, her real identity (and thus her homo-species desire) from all those around her, fearing she will be ostracised. Referring to her ogress state when speaking with Donkey, Princess Fiona insists that she is 'a princess and this is not how a princess is meant to look', later reiterating the point: 'princess and ugly don't go together'. When Princess Fiona transforms into her true form – that of an ogre – after kissing Shrek, she is confused, 'I don't understand, I was supposed to be beautiful', to which Shrek replies, 'But you *are* beautiful'. It is only when she accepts the ogre (i.e. the queer) within herself that she can be happy and

---

9   I do not have space in this chapter to discuss the homosocial triangle between Shrek, Donkey and Princess Fiona. For just one example, see the argument (reminiscent of a warring couple) between Donkey and Shrek over who owns the swamp. According to Shrek, the swamp is his and his alone. Donkey sees things differently: in his reckoning, he did half the work (of rescuing Princess Fiona) and so should get half the credit (i.e. the swamp).

stop hiding at night behind locked doors and boulders. The witch's spell signifies societal pressures to be normal, and Princess Fiona's repressive desire to fit in, which is broken, sundered forever when she 'comes out'. Farquaad's reaction to Fiona's transformation, so that he stands flanked by two ogres (Fiona and Shrek) on the Church's alter is reminiscent of the comments of homophobes who dislike the idea of same-sex couples: 'It's disgusting! Guards! Guards! I order you to get them out of my sight!' When Shrek first walks in and tries to tell Fiona he loves her, Farquaad begins making fun of him, to which Fiona asks Shrek, 'Is this true?' Farquaad's answer is typical of a homophobic response when confronted with same-sex desire: 'Who cares? It's preposterous!'[10]

While Dragon exploits every opportunity to blow smoke rings into Donkey's coughing face, flutter her huge eyelashes, and take his tale in her mouth, Donkey exhibits no visible attraction to Dragon, unless you count his 'I like big butts' statement in the karaoke. Donkey raps: 'I like big butts and I cannot lie, you other brothers can't deny. When a girl walks in with an itty bitty waste and a round thing in your face, you get', at which point he is cut off as Dragon hits him with her tail. Donkey flirts with Dragon in the castle in an attempt to save his life, even before he realises she's a 'girl Dragon', at which point he tells her that she 'reeks of feminine beauty'. Dragon's stalking of Donkey invokes much laughter, and perhaps more than a little puzzlement for those curious enough to mull over the logistics of a possible sexual encounter between the two. This certainly makes one rethink the heteronormative understanding that heterosexuality, in Karma Lochrie's words, 'is intercourse between penises and vaginas' (2001, 88). Michael O'Rourke's comment provides lots of possibilities when mulling over the Dragon–Donkey relationship: 'the erotic potential in a reterritorialized Deleuzian body, a griddable body with multiple sites of (hetero)erotic potential, where sexual pleasure covers multiple areas of/on/in the body' (2005, 113). What can we take from the apparent absurdity of their relationship? Perhaps something as simple (but with profound implications) as the following: if a donkey and a dragon can get together, why not two men, two women?

Karma Lochrie writes in a cross-temporal essay on the Bill Clinton–Monica Lewinsky affair and medieval notions of sexuality: 'in this time of heterosexual confusion, we are obligated to investigate queerness not only in deviant or excluded sexualities but in heteronormativity itself' (2001, 91). New queer cartoons pose a challenge for us as viewers. They encourage us to sit up and take note of what is passing as entertainment before us and our children. They confront us with normative assumptions and make us laugh at our own complicity in the proliferation of such assumptions when we are forced to question what we have just heard in the meaning-laden innuendo of their dialogue. Above all, they remind us why we enjoy watching fictional representations in the first place: not so that we can see the world as it is, but to help us imagine the world as it might be.

---

10   See Burger and Kruger (2001, xi) for a discussion of queer theory's forwarding of a 'logic of the preposterous'.

Acknowledgements

Earlier versions of this chapter were presented at University College Dublin, the University of London and King's College, London. I owe my thanks to the students in my 'Queer Readings of Film' undergraduate and postgraduate seminars in 2002, 2004 and 2006 for their helpful responses to my work in this chapter. I am especially grateful to Nicole Murray and Michael O'Rourke who have been subjected to multiple drafts and for their generous and constructive feedback.

Suggested Further Reading

Aaron, M. (ed.) (2004), *New Queer Cinema: A Critical Reader* (Edinburgh: Edinburgh University Press).

Cokely, C.L. (2005), '"Someday My Prince Will Come": Disney, the Heterosexual Imaginary and the Animated Film', in C. Ingraham (ed.), *Thinking Straight: The Power, the Promise and the Paradox of Heterosexuality* (New York and London: Routledge).

Freeman, E. (2005), '*Monsters, Inc.*: Notes on the Neoliberal Arts Education', *New Literary History*, 36:1, 83–95.

Halberstam, J. (2006), 'Boys Will Be … Bois? Or, Transgender Feminism and Forgetful Fish', in D. Richardson, J. McLaughlin and M.E. Casey (eds), *Intersections between Feminism and Queer Theory* (Basingstoke: Palgrave Macmillan).

—— (2008), 'Animating Revolt/Revolting Animation: Penguin Love, Doll Sex and the Spectacle of the Queer Non-Human', in N. Giffney and M.J. Hird (eds), *Queering the Non/Human* (Aldershot: Ashgate).

References

A Christmas Carol (1938), dir. E.L. Marin [feature film].

Aaron, M. (2004), 'New Queer Cinema: An Introduction', in M. Aaron (ed.), *New Queer Cinema: A Critical Reader* (Edinburgh: Edinburgh University Press).

Antz (1998), dirs. E. Darnell and T. Johnson [animated cartoon].

Babe (1995), dir. C. Noonan [feature film].

Beauty and the Beast (1991), dirs. G. Trousdale and K. Wise [animated cartoon].

Benshoff, H.M. (1997), 'Introduction: The Monster and the Homosexual', in *Monsters in the Closet: Homosexuality and the Horror Film* (Manchester and New York: Manchester University Press).

Burger, G. and Kruger, S.F. (2001), 'Introduction', in G. Burger and S.F. Kruger (eds), *Queering the Middle Ages* (Minneapolis, MN and London: University of Minnesota Press).

Butler, J. (2004 [1991]), 'Imitation and Gender Insubordination', in S. Salih with J. Butler (eds), *The Judith Butler Reader* (New York and London: Routledge).

Cestaro, G.P. (2004), *Queer Italia: Same-Sex Desire in Italian Literature and Film* (New York and Basingstoke: Palgrave Macmillan).

Charlie's Angels (2000), dir. McG [feature film].

Cohen, J.J. (2003), *Medieval Identity Machines* (Minneapolis, MN and London: University of Minnesota Press).

Cokely, C.L. (2005), '"Someday My Prince Will Come": Disney, the Heterosexual Imaginary and the Animated Film', in C. Ingraham (ed.), *Thinking Straight: The Power, the Promise and the Paradox of Heterosexuality* (New York and London: Routledge).

Creed, B. (1995), 'Lesbian Bodies: Tribades, Tomboys and Tarts', in E. Grosz and E. Probyn (eds), *Sexy Bodies: On the Strange Carnalities of Feminism* (New York and London: Routledge).

—— (2000), 'The Cyberstar: Digital Pleasures and the End of the Unconscious', *Screen* 41:1, 79–86.

Daileader, C.R. (2002), 'Back Door Sex: Renaissance Gynosodomy, Aretino, and the Exotic', *English Literary History* 69:2, 303–34.

Dennis, J.P. (2003), 'Queertoons: The Dynamics of Same-Sex Desire in the Animated Cartoon', *Soundscapes: Online Journal on Media Culture* 6, http://www.iccerug.nl/~soundscapes/VOLUME06/Queertoons.shtml (accessed 14 November 2007).

Diamond, L.M. (2005), '"I'm Straight, But I Kissed a Girl": The Trouble with American Representations of Female-Female Sexuality', *Feminism and Psychology* 15:1, 104–10.

Doty, A. (1993), *Making Things Perfectly Queer: Interpreting Mass Culture* (Minneapolis, MN and London: University of Minnesota Press).

—— (2000), *Flaming Classics: Queering the Film Canon* (New York and London: Routledge).

Freeman, E. (2005), '*Monsters, Inc.*: Notes on the Neoliberal Arts Education', *New Literary History*, 36:1, 83–95.

Fuss, D. (1991), 'Inside/Out', in D. Fuss (ed.), *Inside/Out: Lesbian Theories, Gay Theories* (New York and London: Routledge).

Griffin, S. (2004), 'Pronoun Trouble: The Queerness of Animation', in H. Benshoff and S. Griffin (eds), *Queer Cinema: The Film Reader* (New York and London: Routledge).

Griffiths, R. (ed.) (2006), *Queer Cinema in Europe* (Bristol and Chicago, IL: Intellect Books).

Halberstam, J. (1998), *Female Masculinity* (Durham, NC: Duke University Press).

—— (2002), 'The Good, the Bad, and the Ugly: Men, Women, and Masculinity', in J. Kegan Gardiner (ed.), *Masculinity Studies and Feminist Theory* (New York: Columbia University Press).

—— (2005), *In a Queer Time and Place: Transgender Bodies, Subcultural Lives* (New York and London: New York University Press).

—— (2006), 'Boys Will Be … Bois? Or, Transgender Feminism and Forgetful Fish', in D. Richardson, J. McLaughlin and M.E. Casey (eds), *Intersections between Feminism and Queer Theory* (Basingstoke: Palgrave Macmillan).

—— (2007), 'Forgetting Family: Queer Alternatives to Oedipal Relations', in G.E. Haggerty and M. McGarry (eds), *A Companion to Lesbian, Gay, Bisexual, Transgender and Queer Studies* (Oxford: Blackwell).

—— (2008), 'Animating Revolt/Revolting Animation: Penguin Love, Doll Sex and the Spectacle of the Queer Non-Human', in N. Giffney and M.J. Hird (eds), *Queering the Non/Human* (Aldershot: Ashgate).

Hanson, E. (1999), 'Introduction: Out Takes', in E. Hanson (ed.), *Out Takes: Essays on Queer Theory and Film* (Durham, NC and London: Duke University Press).

Kuzniar, A.A. (ed.) (2000), *The Queer German Cinema* (Stanford, CA: Stanford University Press).

Lochrie, K. (2001), 'Presidential Improprieties and Medieval Categories: The Absurdity of Heterosexuality', in G. Burger and S.F. Kruger (eds), *Queering the Middle Ages* (Minneapolis, MN and London: University of Minnesota Press).

MacCormack, P. (2008), *Cinesexuality* (Aldershot: Ashgate).

McRuer (2006), 'Introduction: Compulsory Able-Bodiedness and Queer/Disabled Existence', in *Crip Theory: Cultural Signs of Queerness and Disability* (New York and London: New York University Press).

Monsters Inc. (2001), dirs. Pete Docter and David Silverman [animated cartoon].

Morrison, J. (ed.) (2000), *The Cinema of Todd Haynes: All that Heaven Allows* (London: Wallflower Press).

O'Rourke, M. (2005), 'On the Eve of a Queer-Straight Future: Notes Toward an Antinormative Heteroerotic', *Feminism and Psychology* 15:1, 111–15.

Patel, G. (2002), 'On Fire: Sexuality and Its Incitements', in R. Vanita (ed.), *Queering India: Same-Sex Love and Eroticism in Indian Culture and Society* (New York and London: Routledge).

Pearl, M.B. (2004), 'AIDS and New Queer Cinema', in M. Aaron (ed.), *New Queer Cinema: A Critical Introduction* (Edinburgh: Edinburgh University Press).

Phillips, J. (2006), *Transgender on Screen* (Basingstoke: Palgrave Macmillan).

Rich, B.R. (2000), 'Queer and Present Danger', *Sight and Sound Magazine* 10:3, http://www.bfi.org.uk/sightandsound/feature/80/ (accessed 1 September 2008).

—— (2004 [1992]), 'New Queer Cinema', in M. Aaron (ed.), *New Queer Cinema: A Critical Reader* (Edinburgh: Edinburgh University Press).

Richardson, N. (2008), *The Queer Cinema of Derek Jarman* (London: I.B. Tauris).

Riverdance: The Show (1995), dir. J. McColgan [dance show].

Shrek (2001), dirs. Andrew Adamson and Vicky Jensen [animated cartoon].

Shrek 2 (2004), dirs. Andrew Adamson and Kelly Asbury [animated cartoon].

Shrek the Third (2007), dirs. Chris Miller and Raman Hui [animated cartoon].

Sleeping Beauty (1959), dir. C. Geronimi [animated cartoon].

Snow White and the Seven Dwarves (1937), dir. D. Hand [animated cartoon].

Sullivan, N. (2003), 'Queer: A Question of Being or a Question of Doing?', in *A Critical Introduction to Queer Theory* (Edinburgh: Edinburgh University Press).

Toy Story (1995), dir. J. Lasseter [animated cartoon].

Valentine, G. (1998), '"Sticks and Stones May Break My Bones": A Personal Geography of Harassment', *Antipode: A Radical Journal of Geography* 30:4, 305–32.

West Side Story (1961), dirs. J. Robbins and R. Wise [feature film].

Whatling, C. (1997), *Screen Dreams: Fantasising Lesbians in Film* (Manchester and New York: Manchester University Press).

Wilton, T. (ed.) (1995), *Immortal, Invisible: Lesbians and the Moving Image* (New York and London: Routledge).

Wittig, M. (1992), 'The Straight Mind', in *The Straight Mind and Other Essays* (New York and London: Beacon Press).

Post-Queer Considerations

David V. Ruffolo

What are the possibilities and potentialities for rethinking queer studies? Are there distinctions to be made between *possibilities* and *potentialities* that can reimagine the politics of queer and the queering of politics? This chapter takes this distinction into critical examination by linking *queer* to possibilities and *post-queer* to potentialities. Queer theory's emergence in the latter part of the twentieth century transformed our understandings of the body by fostering new ways to explore the relationships amongst bodies, identities and culture. 'The body' became a central point of critique and quite often an essential point of departure for identity politics. Although important shifts from identity politics to a politics of identity have transpired through queer theory's commitment to exposing the injustices attributed to fixed and stable bodies, queer bodies (often cited as mobile and fluid materialities) maintain their proximity as fundamental entry points of analysis. In this chapter's exploration of a post-queer time and space, I am not suggesting a ridding of queer *per se* but an eradication of 'bodies' in relation to contemporary queer studies and theories. I am arguing for a radical reinvigoration of queer theory's body politics by challenging current conceptualisations of bodies in queer studies and theories through the creation of new spaces to think about bodies in a post-queer time and space. What follows confronts the inherent positions, utilisations and overall conceptions of 'the body' as a predominant lens of analysis in various queer theories that have surfaced in the late twentieth century and continue to materialise well into the new millennium. This assertion is not implying that the body has in some way become less significant to the politics of queer. In contrast, there is no better time than now for queer theory to critically reexamine (queer) bodies and to develop a vital resurgence capable of engaging the present and future politics of our world.

From Queer Possibilities to Post-Queer Potentialities

My critique of queer stems out of what I consider to be the limitations of thinking about queer bodies through subjectivity; bodies that are taken up in significations, representations and identifications. The body's relationship to subjectivity is a key site of interrogation for this post-queer analysis of contemporary queer studies. In what follows, I argue that many of the developments in queer theories and studies over the past 20 years have largely been facilitated through a commitment to subjectivity. Although these progressions are unquestionably imperative to the politics of queer and the queering of politics, I believe that the relationship between bodies and subjectivity is limiting because it reiterates the past and can only imagine a future through prior emergences. This is what I refer to as the realm of the possible: exploring bodies through subjectivity, signification, representation and identification. Post-queer considerations, on the other hand, are attracted to disrupting the link between bodies and subjectivity so as to introduce more creative ways of thinking about bodies. I am therefore calling for a shift from queer possibilities – what I read as subjugated subjectivities – to post-queer potentialities – what can be regarded as becomings. To put it another way, post-queer considerations make the critical shift from subjugated bodies of possibility that work within the realm of the *real* to post-queer bodies of potentiality working in the realm of the *virtual*.[1]

Potentialities are virtualities that are directed towards the future which become actualised in the present – actualisations that ultimately inform future virtualities. Deleuzian virtualities are experiences that are deeply marked by difference: events that play out in the future in order to form the present that informs that future. In other words, the potentiality of virtualities are not known in actual experiences but are realised through these experiences. It is, if you will, a game that is played in the future while being directed through the present that informs that future. This offers a stark differentiation from subjectivity that represents the past through present re/significations. The Deleuzian virtual is therefore not a 'virtual reality' that represents reality in images. The virtual always surpasses the actual and it is through the unknown potentiality of the virtual that difference is produced. This offers important implications for thinking about post-queer bodies because although the world is made up of actual bodies, the potentiality for difference is not determined by what precedes bodies (this being what I refer to as the possibilities of queer when they are related to subjectivity). Post-queer difference, rather than being limited to what has already emerged (subjectivity), is a potentiality where virtualities not only actualise bodies but are also influenced by these actualisations. I am therefore putting forth the notion that post-queer is directed towards the open future (virtualities) while queer is confined to what has already emerged in the past (realities). Becoming is therefore the process in which virtualities are actualised and is therefore not confined to the limitations of subjectivity.

My use of 'post-queer', rather than postqueer, post/queer or (post)queer is strategic: I understand 'post-queer' to be a Deleuzian plateau between queer and a time and space that might follow current conceptions of queer (in contrast to 'postqueer' that might suggest a definitive time after queer; post/queer that could insist on leaving queer behind; or (post)queer that might privilege either post

---

1   This shift is informed by the Deleuzian differentiation between the real/possible and the actual/virtual. See Deleuze (1994).

or queer). I consider post-queer to be a Deleuzo-Guattarian line of flight: a new direction where post-queer differs from queer by breaking connections with queer in order to produce new becomings (Deleuze and Guattari 1987). The relationship between queer and post-queer can also be considered a Bakhtinian dialogic relation (Bakhtin 1981). Bakhtinian dialogism insists on a level of openness where dialogic relations are not reduced to their dialogic contributions. Queer and post-queer are concurrently created and altered through their dialogic encounters and are therefore not placed in hierarchies (queer does not take precedence over post-queer, and *vice versa*). The differences created through these dialogisms – the lines of flight – suggest that there is always the potential to create something new through the dialogic relations of queer and post-queer. I argue that these dialogic relations can produce new and creative ways for thinking about the relationship amongst bodies, identities and culture. Consequently, my critique of queer is intended not only to reimagine queer but also to take into consideration the future *potentialities* of queer. To further situate the division I am setting up between queer and post-queer, I want to clarify my use of *bodies* in this chapter. When queer theories and studies conceptualise 'the body' through subjectivity, differentiation and movement, it is often marked by the resignification of physical bodies and as a result, I argue, the body becomes limited by its material dimensions. Post-queer bodies, in contrast, are not strictly material or corporeal. My discussion of post-queer bodies is therefore not limited to a physical realm. My use of bodies in the post-queer sense, particularly when read through virtualities, extends to bodies of theoretical work, bodies of knowledge, knowledge of bodies, institutional bodies, bodies of thought, systemic bodies and cultural bodies. Post-queer is therefore not to be read as a time and space that comes after queer. I read it as a plateau – a permanent in-between state – that negotiates the tension I am raising between subjectivity (the real) and becoming (the virtual).

Post-Queering Queer Theory

Queer theory's exercise of subjectivity has largely painted a particular representation of bodies as subjects implicated in identity norms. These representations have been and continue to be challenged by many queer theorists and activists by revealing the heteronormative organisations of bodies, identities and culture. Identity norms that situate fixed bodies in binary identity categories have largely been the focus of early queer theorising. These important contributions highlight the hierarchical, patriarchal and systemic processes of organisation that attempt to stabilise the body as a unified whole. Exposing and disrupting these oversimplifications of the body has led to realisations that bodies are *normatively essentialised*. *The History of Sexuality* volumes by Michel Foucault (1978; 1985; 1986) along with his *Discipline and Punish* (1977) and other writings that see intersections between bodies, power and subjectivity made a significant impact on early queer theorising (For Foucault 1980a; 1980b; 1997a; 1997b; 1997c; 1998; 2000). I consider these genealogical investigations to have bridged significantly the link between bodies and subjectivity in many queer studies and theories. In particular, notions of subjection, discipline, confession, observation, examination and biopower are heightened through these examinations and are inevitably brought to the forefront of queer theory's concern with disturbing normative identity politics. From this, bodies are taken up as disciplined subjects that emerge through power as a relational force. These subjects of power are deeply implicated in socio-political practices that work to discipline (i.e. normalise) bodies as closed materialities and thus further reinforce understandings of bodies through significations and representations. For instance, arguing against the repressive hypothesis of sex in *The History of Sexuality, Volume I*, Foucault exposes how sex became a discourse (*scientia sexualis*). Here, the body is continuously subjected to sexual discourses and is therefore represented by and signified through these ideologies. This suggests that there is nothing essential or natural about sex but instead, 'sex' is produced as a discourse through the subjugation of body-subjects. Foucault's genealogical investigation of sexuality links the body to subjectivity because the representations and significations of sex always precede the body as power relations in the form of sexual discourses. The Foucauldian notion of *inscription* is central to the fashioning of subjugated subjectivities. For example, we see here that bodies are inscribed by the discursive initiatives of sex that produce subjects of sex and therefore sexed-bodies. The various levels of bodily inscriptions working to normalise the body as a stable, whole and fully knowable materiality arise through queer theory's interest in decentring collective identity categories. I argue that this adds force to queer theory's interest in travelling along the terrain of possibilities (rather than potentialities). This is specifically noted in queer theory's work on identity politics that seeks to exercise a disturbance of 'natural' categories that essentially precede the body – examinations that rely on significations and representations to expose the complexity of inscriptive techniques and technologies that produce seemingly fixed bodies.

Judith Butler's work in the early 1990s – predominantly *Gender Trouble* (1990) and *Bodies that Matter* (1993) – had, and in many ways still has, a considerable impact on queer theorisations. Butler, in a lot of respects, follows a similar trajectory to Foucault by linking the body to subjectivity in her analysis of gender's discursive production. By arguing that gender is not an essential category that is strictly equated to biological sex, Butler resignifies the body by positioning gender as a fundamentally discursive category. Although Butler breaks new ground through this assertion, I argue that the body maintains its proximity to subjectivity as it is reiterated in the discursive realm. As a result, I consider this a limited reading because the body is restricted to the possibilities of re/signification and re/presentation that are in relation to that which precedes the body. Butler's theory of performativity concretises this claim. Performativity is arguably her most influential and cited contribution to queer theory and has been adopted by many queer theorists interested in exposing the normative productions of identity categories. Gender performativity identifies how the category 'gender' becomes materialised over time through the continuous reiteration of gendered norms:

how the body becomes a gendered subject by reiterating specific gender norms that precede and circulate through the body. Although Butler works within a Foucauldian framework of subjectivity and discursivity, she establishes a critical differentiation from Foucault in her work on performativity (Butler 1989; 2002). Whereas the Foucauldian notion of inscription implies that something is done *to* the body, Butler's performativity claims that something is done *through* the body. The distinction I am making here suggests that the Foucauldian body is produced *by* discourse and the Butlerian body is produced *through* discourse. Queer studies strengthens the body's relationship to subjectivity by utilising performativity to facilitate the shift from fixed and stable bodies to mobile and fluid subjects that become intelligible through identifications, representations and significations.

This is, of course, not to suggest that Foucault's work on subjugation and Butler's theory of performativity are the only means by which bodies have become significantly tied to subjectivity. And I am certainly not implying that Butler solely influences how queer studies and theories conceptualise the body. A great deal of important queer work on the body has surfaced over the past couple of decades. Much of which, I argue, has added to what I am calling the possibilities of queer bodies. Some examples being Eve Kosofsky Sedgwick's move from essentialism and constructivism to 'minoritising' and 'universalising' accounts of identities (1990); Diana Fuss's take on sexual difference through psychoanalytic identifications (1991; 1995); Judith Halberstam's shaping of 'female masculinity' (1998); Viviane Namaste's critique of 'queer theory's erasure of transgender subjectivity' (2000); David Eng's investigation of race's relation to masculinity and the politics of sexuality (2001); and José Esteban Muñoz's 'disidentifications' from conventional norms attributed to race and sex (1999). These are, again, a sample of how queer studies and theories intersect physical, material and/or corporeal bodies with subjectivity. I am arguing that the possibility for change is limited here because the body is always in relation to preceding identifications, representations and significations. The use of queer as a noun, verb and adjective has established a variety of views on how queer can be defined, used, politicised, personalised, appropriated, exploited and challenged. My critique of queer comes out of these definitions, explorations and examinations. This is, again, not to suggest that these assertions have lost their political effectiveness. In fact, there is much work to be done in the areas of queer theories and studies and I am putting forth the notion that *post-queer* is one way to move forward.

Movement: Virtual/Actual vs Real/Possible

Gilles Deleuze, in *Difference and Repetition* (1994), draws on the work of Henri Bergson to introduce the virtual/actual and real/possible. I equate the distinctions between the virtual/actual and real/possible to the dialogical relations between post-queer and queer, respectively. As I suggested above, the virtual/actual is the potential of becoming (post-queer) while the real/possible is limited to past/present significations and representations (queer). Brian Massumi, in *Parables for the Virtual*, articulates the difference between the virtual/actual and real/possible using Bergson's infamous bow and arrow analogy ('Zeno's paradoxes of movement'; Massumi 2002, 6). To think in terms of the real/possible is to work within a framework of positionality where movement, after an arrow is launched, can be traced along a 'linear trajectory made up of a sequence of points or positions that the arrow occupies one after the other' (2002, 6). Real/possible movement is highly determinable because it is traceable: the arrow's movement can be determined by tracing its linear pathway along specific points. I argue that considerations of the body through significations, representations and identifications (subjectivity) are conceptualisations of the body through the real/possible. The real/possible body is an ongoing reemergence where mobility is determined by the possibilities of the present that are informed by the reiterations of the past. Movement is therefore halted in subjectivity because the body is calculated through positionality. For example, the identification of bodies in and through identities stops the movement of bodies and positions them on the linear trajectory of identity categories. As a consequence, bodies are not only limited to the possibilities attributed to identity categories but are also bound to the overall constraints of representation where movement stops as a result of signification's positionality – the resulting 'divisibilities' and 'measurabilities' of bodies that are translated into specific positions (what Massumi refers to as 'back-formations').

The virtual/actual, in contrast, is not reducible to significations, representations and identifications (possibilities) because it works within the realm of the *potential*. The virtual is a reality in and of itself where virtual potentialities go through processes of actualisation. Movement, as a becoming, is an immanent process. Immanence implies that the actualisations of the virtual do not become specific points that can be signified or represented: the actualisations always inform future virtualities where, for example, the arrow is never fully registered on specific points throughout its flight. Massumi identifies the following differentiation between the potential (virtual/actual) and the possible (real/possible):

> *Potential is unprescribed. It only feeds forward, unfolding toward the registering of an event: bull's-eye. Possibility is a variation implicit in what a thing can be said to be when it is on target. Potential is the immanence of a thing to its still indeterminate variation, under way ... Implication is a code word. Immanence is process.* (2002, 9)

I consider the real/possible to be a question of *being* and the virtual/actual to be one of *becoming*. Deleuze makes the following assertions about the virtual/actual:

> *The actualisation of the virtual ... always takes place by difference, divergence or differenciation. Actualisation breaks with resemblance as a process no less than it does with identity as a principle. Actual terms never resemble the singularities they incarnate. It does not result from any limitation of a pre-existing possibility ... For a potential or virtual object, to be actualised is to create divergent lines which correspond to – without resembling – a virtual*

multiplicity. The virtual possesses the reality of a task to be performed or a problem to be solved: it is the problem which orientates, conditions and engenders solutions, but these do not resemble the conditions of the problem. (1994, 212)

The virtual potentialities of the body articulate a politics of becoming where the actualised body always has the potential to virtually *become*.

The creativity of post-queer bodies lies in the ability of the virtual/actual to take into consideration the future potentialities of the body that have yet to be actualised. This is, once again, in contrast to subjugated bodies that, in agreement with Massumi, result in a 'cultural freeze-frame' where the body ultimately reaches 'gridlock' (2002, 3). Movement for the real/possible is a 'displacement' where the body moves from position to position. Movement for the virtual/actual, on the other hand, is transformative because the body does not refer to itself or the specific points of dis/re-placement but is instead engaged with the *transition itself* as a 'real-material-but-incorporeal' body (2002, 5). Massumi describes the relationship between corporeality and incorporeality by making a comparison to energy's connection to matter:

> *Energy and matter are mutually convertible modes of the same reality. This would make the incorporeal something like a phase-shift of the body in the usual sense, but not one that comes after it in time. It would be a conversion or unfolding of the body contemporary to its every move. Always accompanying. Fellow-traveling dimension of the same reality. (2002, 5)*

Energy speaks to the potentiality of matter in the same way that virtuality marks the potentiality of actualised bodies. These transformations mark an affected body whose future is comprised of virtual potentialities that have yet to actualise – virtualities that are not predetermined and actualities that are not reducible to positionality. Virtualities and actualities are Bakhtinian dialogic relations that are constantly producing new connections – *contractions* and *dilations*, as Massumi puts it, where one contracts while the other dilates (1992, 65). This is similar to Manuel DeLanda's (2002; 2006) work on the spatiotemporal aspects of life where the radical potential of the virtual lies in its ability to actualise new forms of life that could not be determined prior to the actualisation of specific virtualities. This is, again, in contrast to the real/possible that 'does not add anything to a predefined form, except reality' (DeLanda 1999, 34). Consequently, despite the calls for mobile and fluid bodies in contemporary queer studies, the body maintains a cohesive stability when it is ultimately represented and resignified through processes of subjectivity. These bodies, in many ways, are mobile-stabilities that constantly shift, yet never get anywhere because they are limited to the realm of the possible. Post-queer bodies, on the flip side, become an assemblage of creativities that continuously make and break connections through the actualisations of virtualities.

Desiring-Machines, Rhizomes, Flows, Thresholds

I am arguing for the need to think about bodies in terms of virtual connections. The bodily connections I am referring to are what Gilles Deleuze and Félix Guattari term *desiring-machines*. Desiring-machines are comprised of breaks and flows where movement is a process of becoming rather than a site of re/signification:

> *Every machine functions as a break in the flow in relation to the machine to which it is connected, but at the same time is also a flow itself, or the production of a flow, in relation to the machine connected to it. This is the law of the production of production. That is why, at the limit point of all the transverse or transfinite connections, the partial object and the continuous flux, the interruption and the connection, fuse into one: everywhere there are breaks-flows out of which desire wells up, thereby constituting its productivity and continually grafting the process of production onto the product. (1983, 36–7)*

Conceptualising bodies as desiring-machines implies that they are rhizomatic materialities that continuously make (connect) and break (disconnect) connections with other desiring-machines to produce flows of production: 'Everywhere *it* is machines – real ones, not figurative ones: machines driving other machines, machines being driven by other machines, with all the necessary couplings and connections' (1983, 1). Rhizomatic bodies are assemblages of desiring-machines that are in a constant state of becoming: 'Nothing here is representative; rather, it is all life and lived experience … Nothing but bands of intensity, potentials, thresholds, and gradients' (1983, 19). Post-queer rhizomatic bodies are in contrast to what Deleuze and Guattari term arborescence. I equate arborescence to physical, material and corporeal bodies that are linked to subjectivity. Arborescence is a hierarchical way of conceptualising materiality: the body is considered to be a sum of parts where each part only becomes intelligible through its relation to the entire structure. Desiring-machines are rhizomatic because the connections that are created and broken do not refer back to an existing state – what I consider to be the subjugating practices of the real/possible. Post-queer bodies are thresholds of becoming where the body is always in a state of negotiation between two multiplicities.[2] The becoming-body of desiring-machines, rhizomatics, flows and thresholds never reiterates the past and does not refer back to existing states because it is always directed towards the future by making and breaking connections with other becoming-bodies. Focusing

---

2   'A multiplicity is defined not by its elements, nor by a center of unification or comprehension. It is defined by the number of dimensions it has; it is not divisible, it cannot lose or gain a dimension *without changing its nature*. Since its variations and dimensions are immanent to it, *it amounts to the same thing to say that each multiplicity is already composed of heterogeneous terms in symbiosis, and that a multiplicity is continually transforming itself into a string of other multiplicities, according to its thresholds and doors'* (Deleuze and Guattari 1987, 249).

on the virtual/actual, rather than the real/possible, removes the inclination to stabilise the body using essentialist discourse because the body is always moving forward as a becoming-body concerned with creating new dialogical connections with other desiring-machines.

Assemblages, Spatial-Temporalities and Incoherences

Post-queer is interested in the objectivities of bodily connections rather than the subjective acts of representation and signification. These objective connections, however, are not situated as polarisations to subjective acts. They expose bodies as creative becomings where multiple forms of assemblages are produced through material flows. The material assemblages spoken about here exceed the flows of material 'bodies': Deleuze's posthumanist affirmations encompass all flows of production including 'nonhuman agencies' (DeLanda 1999, 41). This is, again, why my conceptualisation of bodies is not limited to physical, material or corporeal bodies but is extended to, for instance, bodies of theoretical work, bodies of knowledge, knowledge of bodies, institutional bodies, bodies of thought, systemic bodies and cultural bodies. Although there is no explicit access to the virtual realm, the actualisations of the virtual expose the future potentialities of bodies where change is inevitable. Elizabeth Grosz (1994; 1995; 1999; 2005) takes on many of these assertions in her work concerning the spatio-temporality of bodies. In *Time Travels* (2005), Grosz compliments these post-queer considerations by exploring the potentialities, multiplicities and connections of bodies. Grosz's Deleuzian critique of feminism contributes to my critique of queer by exposing how bodies are limited when they are attached to specific forms of representation and signification. For example, Grosz explains how feminist politics founded on representations are restricted when they work towards political, social and/or economic ends that can be predetermined (2005, 162). Once more, these are possibilities rather than potentialities. Grosz's call for a feminist future interested in the virtualities of bodies marks a critical shift in contemporary feminism by focusing on the potentialities of sexual difference – a future that is not yet known (2005, 164). What makes Grosz's assertions so provocative are the potentialities for bodies to become in a time and space that is not definitively known but can be imagined through the virtual present of the actual. Grosz's virtual imaginings of sexual difference offer important implications for contemporary queer studies because they draw attention to the limitations of politics working towards a future that can be known and can be visualised through the tools that are presently available. Grosz's critique of subjugated subjectivity, her call for a politics of the imperceptible, her interest in creating new problems and experiments, and concern with the investigation of unactualised virtualities are all critical to post-queer considerations (2005, 167–8). Although I cannot fully account for these advancements in this chapter, it is important to note that Grosz's virtualities work from the inside-out rather than the outside-in (what I have attributed to discursivity and inscription). The inside-out of the virtual/actual is interested in what the body *can do* (rather than what the body *is* as seen through the real/possible). In agreement with Grosz, space and time are not 'neutral or transparent media whose passivity enables the specificity of matter to reveal itself' but are 'active ingredients in the making of matter (2005, 174). Conceptualising post-queer bodies through the active forces of time and space can expose the *unactualised virtualities of the past* and the *potential actualities of the future*.

J. Bobby Noble's *Sons of the Movement* (2006) accounts for the unactualised virtualities of the past and the potential actualities of the future that I am speaking of here. This book identifies the limitations of queer as well as the future potentialities of queer by taking a socio-political look at the female-to-male (FtM) transition process. By focusing on the cultural aspects of trans movement, Noble embarks on a theoretical and political journey that is not restricted by the realm of subjectivity. For example, Noble does not limit trans movement to medicalised practices that can quite often normalise, collectivise and particularise the body. Noble's political embodiment of a 'pre-man space of boy/boi' articulates a virtuality of *incoherence* where the body cannot be reduced to, or resignified in, specific categories and norms. A politics of incoherence challenges the limitations of queer theory's investment in subjectivity by advancing a political project directed towards the future potentialities of bodies rather than the reiteration of existing bodily forms. I find Noble's critique of Halberstam to be particularly relevant to my assertion that the body's relation to subjectivity is limiting: although Halberstam's 'female masculinity' challenges masculinity's immediate association with maleness, it fundamentally resignifies the body using terms that precede the body (i.e. female and masculinity). I agree with Noble's claim that Halberstam's 'solution to the problem of categorical thinking is to come up with still more categories' (2006, 25). I consider Noble's claim that 'queer' is beginning to become an 'unusable term' by claiming that queer 'has the potential to be centripetal or stabilising the space it marks, or centrifugal, that is, destabilising the spaces it flags' (2006, 9) to be directly equated with queer's relationship to subjectivity. I read Noble's politics of incoherence as a politics of becoming (post-queer) rather than a politics of representation, signification and identification (queer).

Post-Queer Virtualities and Actualities: Neoliberal Capitalism, Globalisation, Neocolonialism

In order to further conceptualise my call for a post-queer time and space, I want to focus on the virtualities and actualities of bodies in relation to contemporary politics, globalisation and economics. I argue that the virtualities of contemporary neoliberal capitalism can offer new directions for contemporary queer studies and theories to think about bodily actualisations. The turn of the century offered a heightened interest in global politics among various scholars and activists. The events marking 9/11 and the creation of a 'post-9/11' world is arguably a defining moment of a new global era: terror, security, fear and privacy (or lack thereof) have become the global marketing tools of contemporary politics – this is, at the very least, the ideology of politics in the West. The interest in global politics among queer scholars and activists is most definitely not new. The events of 9/11, however, stimulate new ways of thinking about globalisation in relation to economics, terrorism and (inter)nationalism. This new world order that is conceptualised through a post-9/11 era has concretised a new stage of analysis for scholars and activists interested in the intersections of bodies, identities and culture. For instance, in a special issue of *Social Text*, edited by David Eng, Judith Halberstam and José Esteban Muñoz, appears one collection that grasps the reality of contemporary queer politics on a global scale. The question 'What's Queer about Queer Studies Now?' – also the title of the issue – compliments their call for a 'renewed queer studies'. The contributors challenge the thresholds of contemporary queer studies and question its future by researching how globalisation, terrorism, immigration, citizenship and human rights are reimagining global politics and how global politics are redefining queer. The collection makes monumental leaps for contemporary queer studies and theories because it begins to take into account the virtualities of body politics: how bodies are played in the future of global politics while being directed by current neoliberal actualisations that ultimately inform this future.

In this last section, I want to concretise the post-queer considerations of this chapter by discussing how bodies are virtually produced and ultimately actualised through neoliberal control mechanisms of innovation, movement and access. A post-queer time and space embodies the Deleuzian shift from disciplinary societies (Foucault) to control societies: 'We're moving toward control societies that no longer operate by confining people but through continuous control and instant communication' (Deleuze 1995a, 174).[3] Deleuzian control societies are used here to explain how bodies are continuously produced and monitored through open systems of information and communication. I want to expose how the virtualities of 'selling services' and 'buying activities' actualise what I refer to as *info-material knowledges* that can control social processes through global markets. One way of exploring the present and future actualities of post-queer bodies is by examining the virtualities of biotechnologies. Nikolas Rose's *The Politics of Life Itself* (2007) uncovers the relationships between biopolitics, biomedicine and knowledge economies. Rose demonstrates how pharmaceutical initiatives in conjunction with medical research produce new ways of thinking about bodies: how biomedicine develops new technologies for thinking about the identification, treatment and circulation of bodies. For example, locating anxiety and depression at the molecular level individualises the body through genetics. In doing so, biology is no longer read as a limit but a limitless materiality. These new ways of articulating the body are in essence establishing a new ontology of the body that is directly implicated in psychopharmacology. Rose uses a Foucauldian lens to think about the relationships

---

3   See Deleuze's 'Control and Becoming' (1995a) and 'Postscript on Control Societies' (1995b) for a thorough reading of control societies, specifically in contrast to disciplinary societies.

amongst bodies, identities and culture. Despite his important advancements, Rose's examination of *the politics of life itself* is limited because it works within a framework of subjectivity (power, subjection and discipline inform his assertions). Although Rose identifies the emergence of new techniques/technologies of the self (Foucault), his analysis becomes restricted when the body is inextricably linked to the Foucauldian subject. For instance, Rose identifies how bodies attain various levels of 'biovalue' that are highly racialised, classed and gendered: in an example, Rose explains how biomedicine is one tool for targeting specific groups through the search for a 'criminal gene' (see Chapter 8). The 'biological criminology' that Rose is speaking of here produces bodies as subjects of the disciplinary practices of biotechnologies. Bodily signification, subjectivity and representation are implicated here as new biosocial groups are created through the intersection of psychopharmacology and biomedicine. Although Rose identifies new forms of subjection that are integral to this new era of biological citizenship, I argue that 'the body' and 'the politics of life itself' are limited when emphasis is placed on the *effects* of biotechnologies. Consequently, I assert the need to explore biotechnological innovations through the Deleuzian virtual/actual. In doing so, bodies are no longer subjects of biotechnologies – bodies that are subjected to the disciplinary practices of biotechnological innovations – but are open entities that virtually become through the actualisations of biomedicine and knowledge economics.

I want to concentrate on the ways in which biotechnologies and knowledge economics virtually *innovate the body*. Kaushik Sunder Rajan identifies how the expansion of genomic research in the United States and India virtually produces new ways to think about bodies – more particularly, how 'one can now *represent* life in informational terms that can be packaged, turned into a commodity, and sold as a database' (2006, 16). I want to centre on Sunder Rajan's reading of biological materiality, biological information and innovative knowledges to explain how bodies are actualised through virtual processes and how these actualisations inform future virtualities that are eventually actualised: the virtualities of researching biological materiality are actualised through the creation of biological information that is then translated into innovative knowledges that inform future research on biological materiality. In other words, the virtualities and actualities of biotechnological innovations produce new ways for thinking about bodies through the dialogic relations of biological materiality and biological information. As I mentioned in the introduction to this chapter, my use of bodies is not limited to the physical realm. This is most evident here where biotechnological innovations not only produce new ways for conceptualising bodies but also function to control social processes through what Nitzan and Bichler refer to as 'differential accumulation' (2002): procedures utilised by systems of control societies to control capital through production. I consider bioethics to be at the forefront of this discussion and I argue that contemporary queer studies should be concerned with these conceptualisations of bodies because new forms of social control are established in this age of biological citizenship. My interest here is not to return the body to a pre-psychopharmaceutical state. My concern resides in the production of new bodies *vis-à-vis* the virtual potentialities of biotechnologies.

Gargi Bhattacharyya offers an important reading of contemporary biopolitics through her critique of neoliberalism and globalisation as a form of neocolonialism in *Traffick: The Illicit Movement of People and Things* (2005). I draw on Bhattacharyya here to critically think about the virtualities and actualities of post-queer bodies in a post-9/11 world. I read her work as infused with a politics of becoming, rather than subjectivity, because she exposes the virtualities of the present in her discussion of globalisation's 'underbelly': the illegal distribution of money, drugs, people and arms. These connections are important for a post-queer time and space because they offer new ways of thinking about bodies as affects rather than effects. *Traffick* exemplifies how the illicit movement of people and things – organised crimes, illegal drug trades, circulation of small arms, human trafficking, forced labour, sex trades – has given rise to, rather than resulted from, globalisation. The underbelly of capitalisation and globalisation that Bhattacharyya identifies makes the important shift from subjectivity (i.e. subjected bodies as the *effects* of capitalism) to a politics of becoming where the illegal movement of people and things marks the virtualities of contemporary citizenship discourse. For example, the actualisations of human trafficking expose the virtualities of neocolonialism, globalisation and neoliberalism: trafficked bodies are not the effects of globalisation and neoliberalism but are instead affected bodies that are integral to the circulation of neocolonialism. This paints a vital contrast to the promotion of globalisation as the seemingly 'free' movement of people and things. Bhattacharyya shows how 'the alternative routes to economic participation that emerge in the nooks and crannies of globalisation' are points of access where 'many regions of the world enter the realm of international trade' even though these affiliations are often deemed 'unorthodox and half-acknowledged practices' (2005, 26). The virtualities and actualities of neocolonialism and globalisation in this work offer new and important ways for thinking about bodies where it becomes evident that the illicit movement of people and things is not a consequence of capitalism but is instead the driving force of global politics. I believe that the virtualities and actualities of biopolitics, biotechnologies and knowledge economics chart creative territories for contemporary queer studies – potentialities interested in exposing the 'underbelly' of body politics. A post-queer politics of becoming can expose the rhizomatic networks, flows of production and potential thresholds produced through the virtualities of biotechnological innovations, biopolitical initiatives and global infrastructures that actualise bodies.

The post-queer considerations of this chapter are intended to map a new terrain for contemporary queer studies and theories to think about bodies through virtualities and actualities. A politics of becoming is a creative process that imagines an open future where the virtual/actual divorces bodies from the limitations of subjectivity, representation and signification. Post-queer offers new directions that pay critical attention to the virtualities of the present and actualities of the future. They account for the complexities of our world by creatively thinking about bodies as potentialities and becomings.

Suggested Further Reading

Deleuze, G. (1994), *Difference and Repetition* (New York: Columbia University Press).
Grosz, E. (2004), *In the Nick of Time: Politics, Evolution, and the Untimely* (Durham, NC: Duke University Press).
Massumi, B. (2002), *Parables for the Virtual: Movement, Affect, Sensation* (Durham, NC: Duke University Press).
Noble, J.B. (2006), *Sons of the Movement: FtMs Risking Incoherence on a Post-Queer Cultural Landscape* (Toronto: Women's Press).
O'Rourke, M. (2005/2006) (ed.), 'The Becoming-Deleuzoguattarian of Queer Studies', Special issue of *Rhizomes: Cultural Studies in Emerging Knowledge*, 11/12.

References

Bakhtin, M.M. (1981), 'Discourse in the Novel', in M. Holquist (ed.), *The Dialogic Imagination: Four Essays by M.M. Bakhtin* (Austin, TX: University of Texas Press).
Bhattacharyya, G. (2005), *Traffic: The Illicit Movement of People and Things* (London: Pluto Press).
Butler, J. (1989), 'Foucault and the Paradox of Bodily Inscriptions', *The Journal of Philosophy* 86:1, 601–7.
—— (1990), *Gender Trouble: Feminism and the Subversion of Identity* (New York and London: Routledge).
—— (1993), *Bodies That Matter: On the Discursive Limits of 'Sex'* (New York and London: Routledge).
—— (2002), 'Bodies and Power, Revisited', *Radical Philosophy* 114, 3–9.
DeLanda, M. (1999), 'Deleuze, Diagrams, and the Open-Ended Becoming of the World', in E. Grosz (ed.), *Becomings: Explorations in Time, Memory, and the Future* (Ithaca, NY: Cornell University Press).
—— (2002), *Intensive Science and Virtual Philosophy* (New York: Continuum).
—— (2006), *A New Philosophy of Society: Assemblage Theory and Social Complexity* (New York: Continuum).
Deleuze, G. (1994), *Difference and Repetition* (New York: Columbia University Press).
—— (1995a), 'Control and Becoming', in *Negotiations* (New York: Columbia University Press).
—— (1995b), 'Postscript on Control Societies', in *Negotiations* (New York: Columbia University Press).
—— and Guattari, F. (1983), *Anti-Oedipus: Capitalism and Schizophrenia* (Minneapolis, MN: University of Minnesota Press).
—— (1987), *A Thousand Plateaus: Capitalism and Schizophrenia* (Minneapolis, MN: University of Minnesota Press).

Eng, D. (2001), *Racial Castration: Managing Masculinity in Asian America* (Durham, NC: Duke University Press).

—— Halberstam, J. and Muñoz, J.E. (2005), 'Introduction: What's Queer about Queer Studies Now?', *Social Text* 23:3–4, 1–17.

Foucault, M. (1977), *Discipline and Punish: The Birth of the Prison*, trans. A. Sheridan (New York: Random House).

—— (1978), *The History of Sexuality: An Introduction, Volume One*, trans. R. Hurley (New York: Random House).

—— (1980a), 'Body/Power', in C. Gordon (ed.), *Power/Knowledge: Selected Interviews and Other Writings 1972–1977* (New York: Pantheon).

—— (1980b), 'The Confession of the Flesh', in C. Gordon (ed.), *Power/Knowledge: Selected Interviews and Other Writings 1972–1977* (New York: Pantheon).

—— (1985), *The History of Sexuality: The Use of Pleasure, Volume Two*, trans. R. Hurley (New York: Random House).

—— (1986), *The History of Sexuality: The Care of the Self, Volume Three*, trans. R. Hurley (New York: Random House).

—— (1997a), 'The Birth of Biopolitics', in J. Faubion (ed.), *Michel Foucault: Ethics* (New York: The New Press).

—— (1997b), 'Subjectivity and Truth', in J. Faubion (ed.), *Michel Foucault: Ethics* (New York: The New Press).

—— (1997c), 'Technologies of the Self', in J. Faubion (ed.), *Michel Foucault: Ethics* (New York: The New Press).

—— (1998), 'Nietzsche, Genealogy, History', in J. Faubion (ed.), *Michel Foucault: Aesthetics, Method, and Epistemology* (New York: The New Press).

—— (2000), 'The Subject and Power', in J. Faubion (ed.), *Michel Foucault: Power* (New York: The New Press).

Fuss, D. (1991), 'Inside/Out', in D. Fuss (ed.), *Inside/Out: Lesbian Theories, Gay Theories* (New York: Routledge).

—— (1995), *Identification Papers* (New York: Routledge).

Grosz, E. (1994), *Volatile Bodies: Toward a Corporeal Feminism* (Bloomington, IN: Indiana University Press).

—— (1995), *Space, Time, and Perversion* (New York: Routledge).

—— (1999), 'Thinking the New: Of Futures Yet Unthought', in E. Grosz (ed.), *Becomings: Explorations in Time, Memory, and the Future* (Ithaca, NY: Cornell University Press).

—— (2005), *Time Travels: Feminism, Nature, Power* (Durham, NC: Duke University Press).

Halberstam, J. (1998), *Female Masculinity* (Durham, NC: Duke University Press).

Massumi, B. (1992), *A User's Guide to Capitalism and Schizophrenia: Deviations from Deleuze and Guattari* (Cambridge, MA: MIT Press).

—— (2002), *Parables for the Virtual: Movement, Affect, Sensation* (Durham, NC: Duke University Press).

Muñoz, J.E. (1999), *Disidentifications: Queers of Color and the Performance of Politics* (Minneapolis, MN: University of Minnesota Press).

Namaste, V. (2000), *Invisible Lives: The Erasure of Transsexual and Transgendered People* (Chicago, IL: University of Chicago Press).

Nitzan, J. and Bichler, S. (2002), *The Global Political Economy of Israel* (Sterling, VA: Pluto Press).

Noble, J.B. (2006), *Sons of the Movement: FtMs Risking Incoherence on a Post-Queer Cultural Landscape* (Toronto: Women's Press).

Rose, N. (2007), *The Politics of Life Itself: Biomedicine, Power, and Subjectivity in the Twenty-First Century* (Princeton, NJ: Princeton University Press).

Sedgwick, E.K. (1990), *Epistemology of the Closet* (Berkeley and Los Angeles, CA: University of California Press).

Sunder Rajan, K. (2006), *Biocapital: The Constitution of Postgenomic Life* (Durham, NC: Duke University Press).

PART IV

RELATIONALITY

Intimate Counter-Normativities: A Queer Analysis of Personal Life in the Early Twenty-First Century[1]

Sasha Roseneil

Foreword

In what has come to be seen as one of the earliest announcements of the project of queer theory, Diana Fuss declared its 'urgent' work to be 'call[ing] into question the stability and ineradicability of the hetero/homosexual hierarchy, suggesting that new (and old) sexual possibilities are no longer thinkable in terms of a simple inside/outside dialectic' (1991, 1). The move enacted by queer theory from the focus of lesbian and gay studies on 'lesbian' and 'gay' identities, actors and movements, to a broader concern with the constitution, and fracturing, of the heterosexual/ homosexual binary, forms the backdrop to this chapter. My exploration of the organisation of contemporary personal life is not specifically concerned with those who carry the identities of 'lesbian' or 'gay', although the research I report included lesbians and gay men amongst its sample. Rather the chapter enacts a queer analysis of personal life in the sense that it explores how the salience of the heterosexual/ homosexual binary is being transformed at the start of the twenty-first century. It also reports the finding of queer social processes: its central argument is that there is a process of queering underway – a destabilisation of the heterosexual/ homosexual binary, and a challenging of heteronormativity – amongst those who are living at the cutting edge of changes in the organisation of personal life. The chapter, therefore, makes a sociological intervention in the field of queer studies, which, in its orientation to the cultural, the textual and the historical, has tended to lack analysis of social change and contemporary social formations.

---

1   This chapter draws on Roseneil and Budgeon (2004) and Roseneil (2005).

There is something queer afoot in the organisation of personal life in the West at the start of the twenty-first century. More and more people are spending longer periods of their lives outside heteronormative intimacies. Practices of personal life which have historically been socially and culturally marginal to the heterosexual order are becoming more widespread and increasingly socially significant. Processes of individualisation are challenging the romantic heterosexual couple and the modern family formation it has supported, and the normative grip of the sexual and gender order which has underpinned the modern family is weakening. Whilst the idea of 'family' retains an almost unparalleled ability to move people, both emotionally and politically, much that matters to people in their personal lives increasingly takes place beyond 'the family', between partners who are experimenting with new forms of sexual/love relationship which challenge heteronormativity, and within networks of friends which de-centre the conjugal couple. These intimate counter-normativities are not the exclusive terrain of lesbians, gay men and sex radicals; rather, they are the practice of a growing sector of the population, across the spectrum of sexual identification and orientation.

This chapter develops a queer analytic for the study of personal life in the twenty-first century which is grounded in an appreciation of the variety of ways people live their lives outside the heteronorm. The first section of the chapter offers a queer critique of sociology for the heteronormative frameworks within which it has studied personal life. The second section then proposes an extension of existing frameworks for the analysis of transformations in personal life, arguing for the importance of a queer analysis of social change, and suggests that there is a need for research focusing on those who are at the cutting edge of social change. The chapter ends with an overview of the findings of my research on those who are living and loving beyond the heteronorm.

Thinking Beyond the Heteronormative Family

Over the past decade a plethora of television series across the Anglophone West – *Friends*, *Seinfeld* and *Will and Grace* from the United States, *Queer as Folk* and *This Life* from the UK, *The Secret Life of Us* from Australia – has recognised the increasing significance of lives led beyond the family. In each of these programmes it is the sociability of a group of friends, rather than a conventional family, that provides the love, intimacy, care and support essential to everyday life in the city. The global popularity of these programmes suggests that they speak to the lives of their viewers. Yet if we were to seek our understanding of practices of love, intimacy and care from the sociological literature, we would assume that they still took place almost solely under the auspices of the heteronormative 'family'.

This is not to say that sociologists have ignored changes within the family. On the contrary, much has been written in recent years about the meaning of the dramatic rise in divorce rates,[2] the increase of births outside marriage[3] (and to a lesser extent outside any lasting heterosexual relationship), the rise in lone parenthood,[4] the decline in the popularity of marriage,[5] the expansion of cohabitation[6] and solo living, and the climbing proportion of women who are not having children.[7] Sociologists have sought to meet both the empirical challenge of changes in family and gender relations, and the theoretical challenge of anti-essentialist, postmodern, black and minority ethnic feminist, and lesbian and gay emphases on difference in personal life. Indeed many British and US family sociologists have engaged with the problem of the concept of 'family', in a time of increasing levels of family breakdown and re-formation. David Morgan (1996), for instance, suggests that we should use 'family' not as a noun, but as an adjective, and proposes a notion of 'family practices' to counter the reification of the concept. Others have sought to deal with social change and the challenges posed by lesbian and gay movements and theorists by pluralising the notion of 'family', so that they now always speak of 'families'. The approach currently dominant in Anglo-American family sociology emphasises the diversity of family forms and experiences, and how the membership of families changes over time, as they breakdown and re-form. In its more liberal-minded incarnations, this approach welcomes lesbian and gay 'families of choice' into the 'family tent' (Stacey 2002). This shift has been important in countering the explicitly anti-gay and anti-feminist political discourse of 'family values', which developed in the United States and the UK during the 1980s and 1990s, and which still has such a strong grip on US public culture (Roseneil and Mann 1996; Stacey 1996; Weeks 1995; Wright and Jagger 1999). However, from a perspective informed by queer theory, these moves to pluralise notions of 'family' are insufficient to the task of understanding contemporary personal life, because they leave unchanged the heteronormativity of the sociological imaginary,[8] and because they fail to consider the meaning of these changes for the wider organisation of the sexual.

---

2   Between 1958 and 1969 the number of divorces in the UK doubled, and doubled again by 1972, peaking in 1993. After a slight drop between 1993 and 2000, the number of divorces has risen again annually (Social Trends 2006).

3   Between 1980 and 2004 the proportion of births outside marriage in the UK rose from 12 percent to 42 percent (Social Trends 2006).

4   Between 1972 and 2005 the proportion of children living in lone-parent families rose from 7 percent to 24 percent (Social Trends 2006).

5   The proportion of women (aged 18–49) who are married has declined from 74 percent in 1979 to 49 percent in 2002, and the proportion who are single has risen from 18 percent to 38 percent (General Household Survey 2002). (Comparable data is not available for men).

6   The proportion of single (never married) women (aged 18–49) who are cohabiting increased from 8 percent in 1979 to 31 percent in 2002 (General Household Survey 2002). (Comparable data is not available for men).

7   The proportion of women reaching the end of their child-bearing years who are childless has increased from 13 percent of those born in 1949 to 18 percent of those born in 1959 (Social Trends 2006).

8   Ingraham (1996) argues that feminist sociology and the sociology of gender, and their studies of marriage, family and sexual violence, in particular, depend on a

Sociology continues to marginalise the study of love, intimacy and care beyond the 'family', even though it has expanded the scope covered by this term to include a wider range of 'families of choice'. The discipline is undergirded by heteronormative assumptions; in other words by 'institutions, structures of understanding, and practical orientations that make heterosexuality seem not only coherent – that is, organized as a sexuality – but also privileged' (Berlant and Warner 2000, 312). Researchers still produce analyses which are almost exclusively concerned with monogamous, dyadic, co-residential (and primarily hetero) sexual relationships, particularly those which have produced children, and on changes within these relationships, and the tendency to fuse the study of (hetero)sex and intimacy means that the discipline fails to accord real attention to non-sexual intimacies or to sexual relationships outside the conjugal couple model. Jo Van Every's (1999) systematic survey of British sociological research and writing on families and households published in 1993 found 'an overwhelming focus on the "modern nuclear family"' consisting of married couples who lived together in households only with their children. She argues convincingly that:

> ... despite all the sociological talk about the difficulty of defining families and the plurality and diversity of family forms in contemporary (postmodern?) societies, sociologists were helping to construct a 'normal' family which looked remarkably similar to that which an earlier generation of sociologists felt confident to define. (1999, 167)

In other words, researchers remain firmly constrained within the boundaries of heteronormativity.

The 'non-standard intimacies' (Berlant and Warner 2000) created by those living non-normative sexualities pose a particular challenge to a discipline which has studied personal life primarily through the study of families. Some lesbians and gay men refer to their emotional networks quite consciously – often with a knowing irony – as 'family' (Weston 1991; Nardi 1992; 1999; Preston with Lowenthal 1996; Weeks, Heaphy and Donovan 2001).[9] However, when writers such as Kath Weston (1991), Jeffrey Weeks et al. (2001) and Judith Stacey (2004) adopt the term 'families of choice' to refer to lesbian and gay relationships and friendship networks, this may actually direct attention away from the extra-familial, radically counter-heteronormative nature of many of these relationships.

Considerable evidence from lesbian and gay studies suggests that friendship, as both a practice and an ethic, is particularly important in the lives of lesbians and gay men (Altman 1982; Weston 1991; Nardi 1992; 1999; Weeks 1995; Preston with Lowenthal 1996; Roseneil 2000a; Weeks, Heaphy and Donovan 2001; Weinstock and

---

heterosexual imaginary, and argues for a shift from the study of gender to the study of heterogender.

9 Weeks, Heaphy and Donovan (2001) discuss the differences between their interviewees in relation to the adoption of the term 'family' to describe their intimate relationships, and acknowledge that many reject the term.

Rothblum 1996).[10] Networks of friends form the context within which lesbians and gay men lead their personal lives, offering emotional continuity, companionship, pleasure and practical assistance. Sometimes problematised, marginalised or rejected by their families of origin, lesbians and gay men build and maintain lives outside the framework of the heterosexual nuclear family, grounding their emotional security and daily lives in their friendship groups. Hite (1988), Weeks, Heaphy and Donovan (2001), Weinstock and Rothblum (1996), as well as my own research (Roseneil 2000a), draw attention to the blurring of the boundaries, and movement between, friendship and sexual relationships which often characterises lesbian and/or gay intimacies. Friends become lovers, lovers become friends, and many have multiple sexual partners of varying degrees of commitment. And, as became all too apparent in the context of AIDS, an individual's 'significant other' – the person who takes primary responsibility at times of illness and need – is often not a sexual partner (Preston with Lowenthal 1996). Relationships which are hard to define within the language of 'family' – between friends, non-monogamous lovers, ex-lovers, partners who do not live together, partners who do not have sex together, those which do not easily fit the 'friend'/'lover' binary classification system – and the wider networks within which these relationships are sustained, de-centre the primary significance that is commonly granted to sexual partnerships, and mount a challenge to the privileging of conjugal relationships in research on personal life.

Yet practices, relationships and networks such as these reported in the lesbian and gay studies literature largely fail to be registered in the discipline of sociology which retains an imaginary which, without ever explicitly acknowledging it, sees the heterosexual couple as the heart of the social formation, as that which pumps the life-blood of social reproduction. In this context, the question prompted by a queer perspective, with its concern to interrogate rather than assume the stability and salience of sexual identity categories, is to what extent might similar practices, relationships and networks exist more widely, beyond those who self-identify as lesbian or gay? I return to this question later in the chapter.

Queer Social Change and the Analysis of Contemporary Personal Life

It is widely believed by sociologists that we are living through a period of profound social change in the organisation of personal life. For example, as part of an argument about the undoing of patriarchalism, Manuel Castells (1997) suggests that the patriarchal family is under intense challenge, and that lesbian, gay and feminist movements around the world are key to understanding this challenge. And Anthony Giddens's (1992) argument about the 'transformation of intimacy', and Ulrich Beck and Elisabeth Beck-Gernsheim's (1995; 2002) work on the changing

---

10   For a discussion of feminist thinking about friendship see Roseneil (2006a).

meanings and practices of love and family relationships, suggest that in the contemporary world processes of individualisation and de-traditionalisation and increased self-reflexivity are opening up new possibilities and expectations in heterosexual relationships.[11]

With a (rather cursory) nod in the direction of feminist scholarship and activism, such work recognises the significance of the shifts in gender relations mainly due to the changed consciousness and identities which women have developed in the wake of the women's liberation movement. Giddens considers that the transformation of intimacy currently in train is of 'great, and generalisable, importance' (1992, 2). He charts changes in the nature of marriage such as the emergence of the 'pure relationship' characterised by 'confluent love', a relationship of sexual and emotional equality between men and women. He links this with the development of 'plastic sexuality' freed from 'the needs of reproduction' (1992, 2). He identifies lesbians and gay men as 'pioneers' in the pure relationship and plastic sexuality, and hence at the forefront of processes of individualisation and de-traditionalisation.[12] Beck and Beck-Gernsheim argue that 'the ethic of individual self-fulfilment and achievement is the most powerful current in modern society' (2002, 22). They believe that the desire to be 'a deciding, shaping human being who aspires to be the author of his/her life' is giving rise to unprecedented changes in the shape of family life. Family membership shifts from being a given, to a matter of choice. As social ties become reflexive, and individualisation increasingly characterises relations among members of the same family, we are moving into a world of the 'post-familial family' (Beck-Gernsheim 1999).

Whilst some have argued that this body of work over-states the degree of change, and underplays the continuance of gender inequalities and class differences in intimate life (Jamieson 1998; Duncan and Edwards 1999; Langford 1999; Silva and Smart 1999; Smart 2000; Ribbens, McCarthy and Edwards 2002), it undoubtedly maps the theoretical terrain from which investigations of contemporary personal life must proceed. However, from a queer perspective, it is important that we also consider how the wider sexual organisation of the social is undergoing transformation.

I want to suggest that we are currently witnessing a significant destabilisation of the homosexual/heterosexual binary which has characterised the modern sexual order. The hierarchical relationship between the two sides of the binary, and its mapping onto an inside/out (Fuss 1991) opposition is undergoing intense challenge. There are a number of 'queer tendencies'[13] at work in the contemporary

---

11   The research of Finch (1989) and Finch and Mason (1993) on family obligations suggests that family ties are now understood less in terms of obligations constituted by fixed ties of blood, and more in terms of negotiated commitments, which are less clearly differentiated from other relationships.

12   In this acknowledgement of non-heterosexual identities and practices, Giddens's work differs from that of Beck and Beck-Gernsheim whose discussion fails to acknowledge its exclusive concern with heterosexuality.

13   For a more detailed exposition see Roseneil (2000b; 2002). These queer tendencies

world which are contributing to this fracturing of the binary. For example, there is a trend towards the 'normalisation' of the homosexual (Bech 1999) in most Western nations, as there are progressive moves towards the equalisation of legal and social conditions for lesbians and gay men (Adam 2001).[14] The passing in the UK of the Civil Partnerships Act in 2004 is one of the most obvious examples of this, granting as it does a legal status close to marriage for lesbian and gay couples who choose to register their partnership. This brings some lesbians and gay men institutionally much closer to the heteronorm, and marks a significant shift in public understandings of the notion of a conjugal couple. Homosexual and heterosexual ways of life thus become less marked as different by law, social policy and in public culture.[15]

Most significant, for my argument here, there is a tendency towards the de-centring of hetero-relations, both socially and at the level of the individual. The heterosexual couple, and particularly the married, co-resident heterosexual couple with children, no longer occupies the centre-ground of Western societies, and cannot be taken for granted as the basic unit in society. This is a result of the social changes outlined earlier, particularly the rise in divorce, births outside marriage, lone parenthood, solo living, and not having children. Individuals are being released from traditional heterosexual scripts and the patterns of hetero-relationality which accompany them. Across Europe, North America and Australia, the conventional family is now very much a minority practice. For instance in Great Britain, between 1971 and 2005 the proportion of households that were composed of a heterosexual couple with dependent children fell from 35 to 22 percent, and the percentage of the population living as part of such a household fell from 52 to 37 (Social Trends 2006). The proportion of lone parent households more than doubled, from 3 to 7 percent,[16] and one-person households soared from 18 to 29 percent, with the greatest increase, from 6 to 15 percent, amongst those under retirement age, and particularly amongst those between 25 and 44, the age group most expected to be settled into a reproductive heterosexual couple (Social Trends 2006).[17] All this

---

are: queer auto-critique, the decentring of hetero-relations, the emergence of hetero-reflexivity, and the cultural valorising of the queer. The word 'tendency' is used deliberately to suggest the still provisional nature of these shifts, and with the existence of countervailing tendencies in mind. The use of the term is indebted to Sedgwick (1993).

14 On US exceptionalism see Adam (2003).

15 For a critique of the limitations of the Civil Partnership Act from a queer perspective see Roseneil (2004).

16 This figure is for lone parents with dependent children.

17 I acknowledge that the majority of births outside marriage are to co-habiting couples, and, in general, I acknowledge the increase in the prevalence (Ermisch and Francesconi 2000; Lewis 2001) and the social acceptability of co-habitation amongst heterosexual couples (Barlow, Duncan, James and Park 2001). This does not, however, diminish the argument about the significance of the social de-centring of, firstly, the married heterosexual couple and, secondly, the heterosexual couple, *per se*.

means that contemporary living arrangements are diverse, fluid and unresolved, and that hetero-relations are no longer as hegemonic as once they were.

A few sociologists have started to recognise the significance of these changes in the sexual organisation of the social. Judith Stacey (1996) understands them in terms of the 'queering of the family': meanings of family are undergoing radical challenge, as more and more kinship groups have to come to terms with the diverse sexual practices and living arrangements chosen by their own family members. She suggests that there can be now few families which do not include at least some members who diverge from traditional, normative heterorelational practice, whether as divorcees, unmarried mothers and fathers, lesbians, gay men or bisexuals. Anthony Giddens's remark that lesbians and gay men are forging new paths for heterosexuals as well as for themselves is picked up by Jeffrey Weeks, Brian Heaphy and Catherine Donovan who suggest that 'one of the most remarkable features of domestic change over recent years is … the emergence of common patterns in both homosexual and heterosexual ways of life as a result of these long-term shifts in relationship patterns' (1999, 85). They see both homosexuals and heterosexuals increasingly yearning for a 'pure relationship', experiencing love as contingent, and confluent, and seeking to live their sexual relationships in terms of a friendship ethic (Weeks, Heaphy and Donovan 2001).

What this suggests is that there is a need for more research exploring the personal lives of those who are in the avant-garde of these processes of social change. The 'Care, Friendship and Non-Conventional Partnership Project' set out to do just that.

Intimate Counter-Normativities

The de-centring of hetero-relations pointed to by aggregate level statistics provides the backdrop to my own qualitative research into contemporary practices of personal life. The 'Care, Friendship and Non-Conventional Partnership Project'[18] started from the recognition that more and more people are living outside conventional hetero-relations, and focused on those who might be considered the most 'individualised' in our society – people who do not live with a partner. The research explored who matters to people who are living outside the conventional heteronormative couple, what they value about their personal relationships, how they care for those who matter to them, and how they care for themselves.

In-depth interviews were carried out with 53 people aged between 25 and 60 in three locations in northern England – a former mining town that is relatively conventional in terms of gender and family relations; a small town in which

---

18   This project was led by Sasha Roseneil, with Shelley Budgeon and Jacqui Gabb as research fellows. For a more detailed discussion of the methodology and findings see Roseneil and Budgeon (2004). For other work on intimacy and care beyond the conventional family, see contributions to Budgeon and Roseneil (2004).

alternative, middle-class, 'downshifted' lifestyles and sexual nonconformity are common; and a multi-ethnic inner-city area characterised by a range of gender and family practices, a higher-than-average proportion of women in the labour force and a large number of single-person and non-couple households. The sample included men and women, with and without children, of a range of ages, ethnic and socio-economic backgrounds, occupations and sexual orientations, and with varying household living arrangements. This gave detailed insight into the contours and textures of the personal lives of a sample of individuals who do not live in the queer metropolis, and very few of whom identify in any way as gender or sexual radicals. Yet the research found evidence of some decidedly counter-heteronormative practices of intimacy. These were: the prioritising of friendship, the de-centring of sexual/love relationships within individuals' life narratives, and experimenting beyond heteronormative conjugality.

Across the sample men and women from all three localities, of a range of ages, lifestyles, occupations and sexualities placed a high value on their friends and their friendships. Friendship occupied a central place in their personal lives. There was a strong discourse about the importance of and need for friendship in a changing and insecure world. Friends appeared more often than parents or siblings in the innermost circle of the relationship maps we asked interviewees to draw, and there was little difference between those who were in couple relationships and those who were single in terms of the importance of friends. It was friends who provided most of the emotional care and support the interviewees received, particularly when sexual/love relationships ended, and much of the practical day-to-day assistance and support as well. Most interviewees had a combination of long-established and more recent friendships in their 'personal community' (Pahl and Spencer 2004), and most had a range of more and less close friends. Many had an elective community, a cluster of friends, who lived locally, and some had been involved in actively constructing a neighbourhood community of friends, either by moving to be near to friends, or encouraging friends to move nearer to them. These local friendship networks socialised together and engaged in reciprocal childcare and other forms of support.[19] The physical space of the home, culturally associated in Britain since the rise of the companionate marriage model with the conjugal couple and the nuclear family, became a much less privatised place, open to the visits of friends, who would 'hang out', and sometimes stay for extended periods, particularly during times of personal crisis. A number of interviewees considered ex-lovers/partners/spouses to be close friends, and there was a notable degree of movement between the categories of friend and lover.

In parallel with the importance accorded to friendship came a de-centring of sexual/love relationships in the narratives of the interviewees. There was a clear tendency to de-emphasise the couple relationship, both amongst those in relationships and those who were single. Only one of the interviewees saw her partner as the most important person in her life, to the exclusion of others. She

---

19   There are similarities here with Stack's (1974) classic work on the importance of friendship in survival strategies in a black community.

was a recent migrant to Britain whose family lived overseas. For everyone else, the people who mattered were either friends or a combination of friends, partner, children and family. What this meant was that the sexual/love relationship was rarely constructed as the exclusive space of intimacy, and indeed for many it was not even the primary space of intimacy. This de-centring of the sexual/love relationship was understood self-reflexively by many interviewees as consequent on the experience of divorce or the ending of a long-term cohabiting relationship; the pain and disruption this caused was seen as giving rise to a new orientation to relationships – the linked downplaying of sexual/love relationships and the increased valuing of friendships. This was not a temporary phase and people did not return to conventional couple relationships as soon as an opportunity arose. Re-interviewing people between a year and a half and two years later, there was a remarkably consistent prioritisation of friendship.

The heteronormative companionate conjugal couple model,[20] which determines the sexual/love relationship to be co-residential (if no longer married), the primary (if not exclusive) space of intimacy, and to be moving in this direction, if not yet achieved, was, therefore, overwhelmingly not the practice of the people interviewed in this research.[21] Very few expressed a conscious yearning to be part of a conventional co-habiting couple or family. In not conforming to the dominant heteronormative relationship teleology, which posits that a relationship should be 'going somewhere' – that somewhere being shared residence and long-term commitment – sexual/love relationships were described instead as being about the construction of mutual pleasure in the present. As such they involved a significant degree of conscious, reflexive thought, and discussion and negotiation. Of the interviewees with partners, almost all had *chosen* not to live together. Very few saw cohabitation as the inevitable and desirable next stage of their relationship, and were thus implicitly challenging the expectation that sexual relationships logically and inexorably should move towards cohabitation and 'settling down'. Across differences of socio-economic class, gender and sexuality, and with only a few exceptions, cohabitation was not constructed as an unequivocally desired goal by the interviewees. They were overwhelmingly positive about not living with their partner, and almost all regarded non-residential relationships as valid ways of living in their own right, not as a stepping stone on the journey towards a 'proper' relationship. Many of these relationships also shared a rejection of the romance narrative, clearly separating sex from romance, with a small number of heterosexual relationships offering clear parallels to the 'fuck buddies' of several of the gay men who were interviewed.

Underlying these orientations was a widespread and profound ambivalence about the cohabiting couple form. Many of the interviewees' sexual/love relationships were being conducted outside a paradigm of 'settling', and were very

---

20 On the rise of the 'companionate marriage' model as a dominant ideal in the post war era see Finch and Mansfield (1991).

21 For a more detailed discussion of non-cohabitation amongst the interviewees see Roseneil (2006b).

much works in progress – understood and accepted as contingent, unresolved and fluid. This description has resonance with Giddens's (1992) notion of the 'pure relationship' and Bauman's (2003) metaphor of 'liquid love'. Whilst I have been critical elsewhere of what I have called the 'patriarchal pessimism' (Roseneil 2004) of Bauman's account of contemporary intimate life, with its nostalgia for bygone days of stable families and secure communities, the processual, undecided character of many of the sexual/love relationships in this study echoes some of the themes of Bauman's analysis.

Concluding Remarks

This chapter has engaged with the notion of queer in two ways. It has cast a queer lens on contemporary processes of social change, expanding sociological understandings of transformations in personal life beyond their focus on the family and heterosexual intimacies, in order that non-heteronormative practices could be registered that rarely enter the sociological agenda. It has also identified processes of queering – social transformations which are destabilising the heterosexual/homosexual binary and challenging heteronormative formations of personal life.

The practices of personal life of the people in my research – the prioritising of friendship, the related de-prioritising of sexual/love relationships, and experimentation with sexual/love relationships beyond the conventional couple form – are potentially of great significance for queer studies. Although it was a relatively small-scale study, because this group of people is at the forefront of processes of individualisation and is a fast growing sector of the population, the findings of my research point to an important emerging social trend, the queering of personal life. More and more people are living lives which challenge the division of the social into heterosexual and homosexual ways of being, and which contest the normativities of heterosexuality and hetero-relationality. Practices which might previously have been regarded as distinctively 'homosexual', such as making friendship central in life, and rejecting the conventional cohabiting conjugality are becoming more widespread, as intimate life increasingly exceeds not just the category of 'family' but also the couple form.

This convergence between homosexual and heterosexual ways of life amongst people at one end of the spectrum of individualisation is happening in parallel to a similar convergence at the other end of the spectrum, amongst those choosing coupledom, cohabitation and often children, as civil/domestic partnership, or marriage, becomes available to same-sex partners on similar terms to traditional heterosexual marriage in many countries. To return to Diana Fuss's delineation of the project of queer theory, cited at the start of the chapter, whilst it might be too early to declare the end of the heterosexual/homosexual hierarchy, the binary is becoming increasingly unstable, and its mapping onto an inside/outside relation less and less straightforward.

Suggested Further Reading

Bech, H. (1999), 'After the Closet', *Sexualities* 2:3, 343–9.
Berlant, L. and Warner, M. (2000), 'Sex in Public', in L. Berlant (ed.), *Intimacy* (Chicago, IL: Chicago University Press).
Roseneil, S. (2007), *Sociability, Sexuality, Self: Relationality and Individualization* (London and New York: Routledge).
Stacey, J. (1996), *In the Name of the Family: Rethinking Family Values in the Postmodern Age* (Boston, MA: Beacon Press).
Weeks, J., Heaphy, B. and Donovan, C. (2001), *Same Sex Intimacies: Families of Choice and Other Life Experiments* (London and New York: Routledge).

References

Adam, B. (2001), 'Families without Heterosexuality: Challenges of Same-Sex Partnership Recognition', paper presented to ESRC Research Group for the Study of Care, Values and the Future of Welfare International Seminar 4, January 2002, http://www.leeds.ac.uk/cava (accessed 20 May 2008).
—— (2003), 'The Defense of Marriage Act and American Exceptionalism: The "Gay Marriage" Panic in the United States', *Journal of History of Sexuality* 12:2, 259–76.
Altman, D. (1982), *The Homosexualization of America* (New York: St. Martin's Press).
Barlow, A., Duncan, S., James, G. and Park, A. (2001), 'Just a Piece of Paper? Marriage and Cohabitation in Britain', in A. Park, J. Curtice, K. Thomson, L. Jarvis and C. Bromley (eds), *British Social Attitudes: The 18th Report* (London: Sage).
Bauman, Z. (2003), *Liquid Love* (Cambridge: Polity).
Bech, H. (1999), 'After the Closet', *Sexualities* 2:3, 343–9.
Beck, U. and Beck-Gernsheim, E. (1995), *The Normal Chaos of Love* (Cambridge: Polity).
—— (2002), *Individualization* (London: Sage).
Berlant, L. and Warner, M. (2000), 'Sex in Public', in L. Berlant (ed.), *Intimacy* (Chicago, IL: Chicago University Press).
Budgeon, S. and Roseneil, S. (2004), 'Beyond the Conventional Family: Intimacy, Care and Community in the 21st Century', a special issue of *Current Sociology* 52:2.
Castells, M. (1997), *The Power of Identity* (Oxford: Blackwell).
Duncan, S. and Edwards, R. (1999), *Lone Mothers, Paid Work and Gendered Moral Rationalities* (Basingstoke: Macmillan).
Ermisch, J. and Francesconi, M. (2000), 'Patterns of Household and Family Formation', in R. Berthoud and J. Gershuny (eds), *Seven Years in the Lives of British Families* (Bristol: The Policy Press).
Finch, J. (1989), *Family Obligations and Social Change* (Cambridge: Polity).

—— and Mansfield, P. (1991), 'Social Reconstruction and Companionate Marriage', in D. Clark (ed.), *Marriage, Domestic Life and Social Change* (London and New York: Routledge).

—— and Mason, J. (1993), *Negotiating Family Responsibilities* (London and New York: Routledge).

Fuss, D. (1991), *Inside/Out: Lesbian Theories, Gay Theories* (New York and London: Routledge).

General Household Survey (2002), http://www.statistics.gov.uk/LIB2002/default.asp (accessed 20 May 2008).

Giddens, A. (1992), *The Transformation of Intimacy: Sexuality, Love and Eroticism in Modern Societies* (Cambridge: Polity).

Hite, S. (1988), *The Hite Report: Women and Love – A Cultural Revolution in Progress* (London: Viking).

Ingraham, C. (1996), 'The Heterosexual Imaginary: Feminist Sociology and Theories of Gender', in S. Seidman (ed.), *Queer Theory/Sociology* (Oxford: Blackwell).

Jamieson, L. (1998), *Intimacy: Personal Relationships in Modern Societies* (Cambridge: Polity).

Langford, W. (1999), *Revolutions of the Heart: Gender, Power and the Delusions of Love* (London: Routledge).

Lewis, J. (2001), *The End of Marriage? Individualism and Intimate Relations* (Cheltenham: Edward Elgar).

Morgan, D.H.J. (1996), *Family Connections* (Cambridge: Polity).

Nardi, P. (1992), 'That's What Friends Are For: Friends as Family in the Gay and Lesbian Community', in K. Plummer (ed.), *Modern Homosexualities: Fragments of Lesbian and Gay Experience* (London and New York: Routledge).

—— (1999), *Gay Men's Friendships: Invincible Communities* (Chicago, IL: Chicago University Press).

Pahl, R. and Spencer, L. (2004), 'Personal Communities: Not Simply Families of "Fate" or "Choice"', *Current Sociology* 52:2, 199–222.

Preston, J. with M. Lowenthal (1996) *Friends and Lovers: Gay Men Write About the Families They Create* (New York: Plume).

Ribbens McCarthy, J. and Edwards, R. (2002), 'The Individual in Public and Private: The Significance of Mothers and Children', in A. Carling, S. Duncan and R. Edwards (eds), *Analysing Families: Morality and Rationality in Policy and Practice* (London and New York: Routledge).

Roseneil, S. (2000a), *Common Women, Uncommon Practices: The Queer Feminisms of Greenham* (London: Cassell).

—— (2000b), 'Queer Frameworks and Queer Tendencies: Towards an Understanding of Postmodern Transformations of Sexuality', *Sociological Research Online* 5:3, http://www.socresonline.org.uk/5/3/roseneil.html (accessed 20 May 2008).

—— (2002) 'The Heterosexual/Homosexual Binary: Past, Present and Future', in D. Richardson and S. Seidman (eds), *The Lesbian and Gay Studies Handbook* (London: Sage).

—— (2004), 'Why We Should Care about Friends: An Argument for the Queering of the Care Imaginary in Social Policy', *Social Policy and Society* 3:4, 409–19.

—— (2005), 'Living and Loving beyond the Boundaries of the Heteronorm: Personal Relationships in the 21st Century', in L. Mackie, S. Cunningham-Burley and J. McKendrick (eds), *Families in Society: Boundaries and Relationships* (Cambridge: Policy Press).

—— (2006a), 'Foregrounding Friendship: Feminist Pasts, Feminist Futures', in M. Evans and J. Lorber (eds), *The Gender and Women's Studies Handbook* (London: Sage).

—— (2006b), 'On Not Living with a Partner: Unpicking Coupledom and Cohabitation', *Sociological Research Online* 11:3, http://www.socresonline.org. uk/11/3/roseneil.html (accessed 20 May 2008).

—— and S. Budgeon (2004), 'Cultures of Intimacy and Care Beyond the Family: Personal Life and Social Change in the Early Twenty-First Century', *Current Sociology* 52:2, 135–59.

—— and K. Mann (1996), 'Backlash, Moral Panics and the Lone Mother', in E. Silva (ed.), *Good Enough Mothering? Feminist Perspectives on Lone Motherhood* (London: Routledge).

Sedgwick, E.K. (1993), *Tendencies* (Durham, NC and London: Duke University Press).

Silva, E. and Smart, C. (eds) (1999), *The 'New' Family?* (London: Sage).

Smart, C. (2000), 'Stories of Family Life: Cohabitation, Marriage and Social Change', *Canadian Journal of Family Law* 17:1, 20–53.

—— and Neale, B. (1999), *Family Fragments* (Cambridge: Polity).

Social Trends (2006), http://www.statistics.gov.uk/socialtrends36/ (accessed 20 May 2008).

Stacey, J. (1996), *In the Name of the Family: Rethinking Family Values in the Postmodern Age* (Boston, MA: Beacon Press).

—— (2002), 'Fellow Families? Genres of Gay Male Intimacy and Kinship in a Global Metropolis', CAVA International Seminar Paper, http://www.leeds.ac.uk/cava/papers/intseminar3stacey.htm (accessed 20 May 2008).

—— (2004), 'Cruising to Familyland: Gay Hypergamy and Rainbow Kinship', *Current Sociology* 52:2, 181–98.

Stack, C. (1974), *All Our Kin: Strategies for Survival in a Black Community* (New York: Harper and Row).

Van Every, J. (1999), 'From Modern Nuclear Family Households to Postmodern Diversity? The Sociological Construction of "Families"', in G. Jagger and C. Wright (eds), *Changing Family Values* (London and New York: Routledge).

Weeks, J. (1995), *Invented Moralities: Sexual Values in an Age of Uncertainty* (Cambridge: Polity).

——, Donovan, C. and Heaphy, B. (1999), 'Everyday Experiments: Narratives of Non- Heterosexual Relationships', in E. Silva and C. Smart (eds), *The 'New' Family?* (London: Sage).

——, Heaphy, B. and Donovan, C. (2001), *Same Sex Intimacies: Families of Choice and Other Life Experiments* (London and New York: Routledge).

Weinstock, J.S. and E.D. Rothblum (1996) (eds), *Lesbian Friendships: For Ourselves and Each Other* (New York: New York University Press).

Weston, K. (1991), *Families We Choose: Lesbians, Gay Men and Kinship* (New York: Columbia University Press).

Wright, C. and Jagger, G. (eds) (1999), *Changing Family Values* (London and New York: Routledge).

Queer Middle Ages

Steven F. Kruger

The European Middle Ages – as that era over against which Western modernity has most insistently constructed itself – is always already queer, imagined as primitive, exotic, dangerous, chaotic. At the same time, and contradictorily, we conceive this outmoded era as a time of stability and conservatism, dominated by an all-powerful Church and a rigidly hierarchical sociopolitical system antithetical to modernity and its characteristic values of 'democracy', 'secularity' and 'progress'. This too makes the era, from a modern perspective, queer, if in ways dissonant with contemporary uses of the term to suggest sexualities challenging to settled norms and dominant ideologies. The question for a queer medieval studies then becomes how to bring queer theory to bear on an era that is already, in popular but also often in academic imaginings, doubly and contradictorily queer?[1]

As Glenn Burger and I have suggested elsewhere, queer theory provides us with a way to call into question a periodisation that would firmly divide the modern from the medieval or premodern (whether that division marks the premodern other as chaotic and uncontrolled or as stable and staid). One of queer theory's crucial moves is to show how 'normative logic[s]' depend 'not on some natural law but instead on the performative citation of a norm, constructed as a *cause* or natural origin, that is nonetheless an *effect* of its very citation' (Burger and Kruger 2001, xi). That is, in what we have called a 'logic of the preposterous' (literally, the preposterous is that which confuses or queers the difference between pre- and post-), queer work disrupts stabilised notions of identity and normality that present themselves as unchanging and unchangeable *causes* in the world, showing these instead to be *effects*.[2] My gender is readable as feminine or masculine not because I am, in my essence, female or male, feminine or masculine, but because I faithfully, performatively cite a set of gender norms: such citation has as its result the projection of a gendered core of selfhood that then is (mis)understood as the *cause* of my successful performance of gender even though it is in fact the *effect* of a set of (largely unconscious) acts and ways of being in the world. Gender and

---

1   For a recent useful overview of and reflection on queer medievalist work, see O'Rourke (2003).
2   See, for instance, Butler (1990; 1993); Edelman (1994); Dollimore (1991).

sexuality are given their cultural power by being normalised as deriving 'naturally', 'essentially' from a given core of self thought to determine who we are as subjects and as social agents; queer theory denaturalises gender and sexuality, showing that such a core of self does not exist as an essence but is instead a projection that helps prop up social understandings and norms, and helps maintain the *status quo*.

Turning this queer argument to the question of periodisation, then, we might recognise that the attempt to stabilise the Middle Ages as something essentially other to modernity is a construction analogous to attempts to stabilise and essentialise gender or sexuality. That is, the Middle Ages is not an essence that exists prior to modernity but instead an after-the-fact construction occasioned by modernity's definition of itself over against that which preceded it. The Middle Ages is an effect of the coming into being of a regime that exists by virtue of its ability to distance itself from its predecessor: that predecessor is imagined, on the one hand, as a chaotic primitivity superseded by modern orderliness and, on the other, as a highly structured, inflexible conservatism superseded by modern progress. Mounting challenges to notions of stable periodisation – where one era inexorably supersedes another – can be integral to queer rethinkings of sexuality, since normalising constructions of sexuality tend to depend (if often tacitly) on an unquestioned historical thinking in which 'primitive' sexual and social forms are replaced by modern marriage and family, which direct a 'natural' heterosexuality into 'proper', socially stable channels. As Valerie Rohy has recently argued, '[r]esistance to phobic definitions of homosexuality ... might mean a turn away from the discipline of straight time, away from the notions of historical propriety that, like notions of sexual propriety, function as regulatory fictions' (2006, 70). A recent book like Carla Freccero's *Queer/Early/Modern* develops 'analyses proceed[ing] otherwise than according to a presumed logic of cause and effect, anticipation and result; and otherwise than according to a presumed logic of the "done-ness" of the past, since queer time is haunted by the persistence of affect and ethical imperatives in and across time' (2006, 5).

One first place that queer theory might lead us in relation to the Middle Ages, then, is to a questioning of the understandings that would make the medieval essentially prior to and other than the modern. I do not mean to suggest, of course, that there are no differences between social or cultural regimes in, say, fourteenth-century and twenty-first-century England; there certainly are. But a queer understanding would lead us to question assumptions about what those differences are, and to recognise that there is no single, absolute point of demarcation separating modern ideologies or cultural phenomena or social structures from 'essentially' medieval ones. What we think of as medieval and try to keep at a distance inhabits modernity in significant ways; conversely, what we have come to believe to be purely modern (the 'individual', for instance, or 'sexuality' as Michel Foucault defines it) may be found – if, again, with significant differences – within the medieval.[3] The idea of the *post*modern, or even the post-postmodern, further complicates such a historical

---

3   For additional challenges to traditional periodisation, also see Biddick (2003); Fradenburg and Freccero (1996); Latour (1993).

rethinking. As we enter, or construct, any new era, we must consider what is at stake in defining the new. What in modernity or postmodernity do we disavow, and why? And as we move 'post-', is there something 'pre-' – something characteristic of modernity's, or postmodernity's, supposed predecessor and other – that we also move to embrace?[4]

In the chapter that follows, I look at several of the most important and influential ways in which scholars have approached the study of medieval sexuality and brought queer constructions into play in their work. This is not meant as an exhaustive survey of the field, but instead suggests how a queer engagement with the medieval past has reshaped medieval studies especially by reconfiguring the relationship between past and present, modern and medieval. I also hope to suggest some productive avenues for future scholarship, and some ways in which queer medievalist work might be productive not only for medieval studies but also for queer studies concerned with periods other than the Middle Ages.

'Gay People' in the Middle Ages

A crucial starting point for work on medieval sexuality was the 1980 publication of John Boswell's scholarly, and popular, *Christianity, Social Tolerance, and Homosexuality: Gay People in Western Europe from the Beginning of the Christian Era to the Fourteenth Century*.[5] Here, Boswell reassessed a wealth of Christian European material to suggest that the Church's intolerance of 'homosexuality' was a relatively late development: 'social tolerance' characterised the late antique and early and high medieval periods, with intolerance growing especially after the twelfth century. Boswell also identified – using, for instance, Latin homoerotic poetry exchanged between male clerics as evidence – what he thought of as a flourishing gay subculture in the twelfth century.[6] Michael Rocke, in his *Forbidden Friendships: Homosexuality and Male Culture in Renaissance Florence* (1996), has more recently argued for the centrality of a male homoerotic sexual culture in late-medieval/Renaissance Florence.[7]

In many ways, Boswell's work is decidedly un-queer, fitting instead a model of historical research in gay/lesbian studies that predates queer theory by a couple of decades. Following the Foucault of the first volume of the *History of Sexuality* (1978/1976), and the argument that it is only in the nineteenth century that a sexuality

---

4   For recent reflections on the medieval's relation to the postmodern, see Dinshaw (1999); Kruger (2001).

5   Other important early work includes that of Goodich (1979); Brundage (1987); Bullough and Brundage (1982); but it was Boswell's book that made the biggest initial impression and that has continued to be most influential.

6   This has probably been the most controversial part of Boswell's argument. For different readings of some of the material treated by Boswell, see McGuire (1988; 1994).

7   Also see Mormando (1999) on the 'social underworld' of early Renaissance Italy.

emerges based on *identity* (rather than juridical regimes of sexually transgressive *acts*), it has been axiomatic in most queer work that gay and lesbian identities are modern, largely late-nineteenth- and twentieth-century, phenomena.[8] To speak, as Boswell does, of 'gay people' in the Middle Ages (even with the elaborate rationale he gives, in his second chapter) rubs against the grain of queer theory's anti-essentialising impulse: if there is no stable, essential gay or lesbian self, to speak of gay or lesbian people, and homosexuality as such, centuries before the invention of such identity categories, is deeply problematic. Indeed, soon after its appearance, Boswell's work was strongly critiqued by scholars who argued that sexuality must be understood as socially constructed rather than essential.[9]

Such critiques are no doubt warranted: Boswell's work sometimes threatens to erase the differences between contemporary 'gayness' and specifically medieval constructions of desire, affection, homosocial friendship and official celibacy. Later reconsiderations of the source material Boswell used develop nuances that his large historical sweep and overarching argument about the early Church's tolerant attitude toward homosexuality pass over; they also focus attention on significant gaps in Boswell's account, especially his lack of attention to women's sexuality.[10] One might nonetheless identify a certain queer impulse in Boswell's work insofar as it pushes towards a significant reconfiguration of existing assumptions about the history of sexuality and the relationship between the past and the present. If we assume (as is often the case in the ongoing debate over gay marriage in the United Sates) that Christianity has *always*, from the Bible on, failed to tolerate homosexuality, then Boswell is intent on showing that such a view is, from the Bible on, demonstrably incorrect – historically inattentive and philologically over-simple. In other words, Boswell intervenes in a dominant construction of the Christian European Middle Ages as inherently and monolithically conservative, instead arguing that strong intolerance of homosexuality is a *late* medieval development. We could say that Boswell risks essentialising 'gay people' in order to deessentialise and historicise Christianity. Boswell also thus implicitly connects twentieth-century gay liberationist movements to a historically older, tolerant Christianity that he suggests stands closer than a homophobic (fifteenth- or twentieth-century) Church to the original meanings and impulses of the religion.

Boswell's historical work (careful and impressively erudite though it may be) thus emerges with a clear political agenda: it uses history to help provide space, in its contemporary, post-Stonewall moment, for gay and lesbian Christians. Such

---

8   For an important reading of Foucault on acts and identities, see Halperin (1998), which now appears in revised form in Halperin (2002). On Foucault from a medievalist perspective, see Lochrie (1997a).

9   See the dialogue among Padgug (1989); Halperin (1989); Boswell (1989). See also the immediate response of gay academic activists concerned that Boswell's work was too conciliatory to a longstanding Western Christian homophobic tradition, Gay Academic Union (1981).

10   For some examples, more and less critical of Boswell, see Jordan (1997); Brooten (1996); Jaeger (1999); Murray and Eisenbichler (1996); Holsinger and Townsend (2002); Kuefler (2006).

an agenda seems clear, too, in Boswell's later (and last) book *Same-Sex Unions* (1994), where he works to demonstrate a long tradition of marriage-like same-sex relationships within Christian Europe. The historical scholarship here is clearly intended to bolster an argument in Boswell's own moment for recognising gay and lesbian marriages. Later historical work like Mark Jordan's *The Invention of Sodomy in Christian Theology* (1997), though not relying on a transhistorical category like Boswell's 'gay people', shares in the impulse to rethink the Christian past in order to make the present more livable for gay and lesbian Christians. Jordan in fact follows up his excavation of the medieval development of discourses on sodomy with more explicit work on the modern after-effects of those discourses in *The Silence of Sodom: Homosexuality in Modern Catholicism* (2000); his most recent work – *Blessing Same-Sex Unions: The Perils of Queer Romance and the Confusions of Christian Marriage* (2005) – pursues a project again akin to Boswell's.[11] A recent book like Alan Bray's *The Friend* (2003) does similar work, arguing that – for a long period of time, both in the Middle Ages and into modernity – the Church respected and even celebrated intense male-male friendships; although Bray argues that these should not be thought of as necessarily or primarily homoerotic, his work nonetheless contributes to a collective scholarly argument that Western Christianity has not been so insistently condemning of non-heteronormative relationships as we now tend to think.

From more radical queer perspectives, the attempt to make Christianity (and such long-standing institutions as marriage) more welcoming places for lesbians and gay men appears conservative, part of a normalising impulse that writers like Michael Warner (1999) have recognised within mainstream gay/lesbian movements. But it does shake up our sense of history to find – as Boswell does – echoes of late-twentieth-century gay culture and politics in a Middle Ages long thought antithetical to sexual expressions of many kinds. And later work on sodomy like Jordan's, William Burgwinkle's, and Larry Scanlon's, which insists on a rigorous historicisation of the medieval category, often suggests ways in which that category – though 'moved beyond' as modern sexuality becomes a discourse not of sexual acts but instead of sexual identities – remains significant for the current moment. As Eve Kosofsky Sedgwick emphasises, older sexual constructions like the sodomitical continue (if uncomfortably) to inhabit newer (late-nineteenth-, early-twentieth-century) definitions of sexuality (1990, 44–8). Boswell's work, and the medievalist work that follows from Boswell, emphasises that, while there are certainly breaks between medieval understandings of sexuality and our own, the medieval might nonetheless sometimes surprisingly shed light on the contemporary. As David Halperin has emphasised in his *How to Do the History of Homosexuality* (in part, a response to Sedgwick), we must find ways to grapple simultaneously with historical continuities (for example, the ways in which sodomy does not simply disappear from modern sexuality) and change (for example, how sodomy necessarily means differently within new historical circumstances):

---

11   For other important recent work on medieval sodomy, see Burgwinkle (2004); Scanlon (in progress); on a somewhat later period, see Puff (2003).

> ... *if earlier historical forms of sexual discourse are not superseded by later ones, if notions of sodomy or inversion continue to appear within the discourses of homosexuality and to assert their definitional authority, there are good historical reasons for that, and those reasons remain to be explored.* (2002, 12)

It is instructive that Foucault – whose work has been used to bolster the critique of Boswell – found *Christianity, Social Tolerance, and Homosexuality* an important historical work. He provided a blurb for the publication of Boswell's book, calling it 'A truly groundbreaking work'. As Didier Eribon has recently pointed out, Foucault emphasised *both* that 'homosexuality is not a natural given, that it is not unchanging throughout the centuries, that it is something that appeared in the nineteenth century' (2004, 314–15) *and* that 'throughout history there have been conscious identities, both individual and collective, that formed around the fact that certain individuals practiced a particular or a minority sexuality' (2004, 315). And Eribon emphasises, in making the latter point, that 'Foucault mentioned his agreement with Boswell many times' (2004, 315; full discussion 314–18). We might indeed think of the later volumes of Foucault's *History of Sexuality* (1985/1984; 1986/1984), which move to consider premodern (classical) sexual constructions at some length, as in part a response to Boswell, a recognition that the fuller story of Western sexual discourses and constructions necessitates looking much further back in history than did Volume One of the *History*.[12] And Carolyn Dinshaw, in her *Getting Medieval*, recognises Boswell's work – and its impact on lesbians and gay men (revealed, for instance, in letters written to Boswell following the publication of his book) – as participating in *queer* history: 'A queer tracing a history', she suggests, 'is engaged in a process of building a self', forging 'queer subjectivity ... through cross-identifications in the realm of sexuality and gender' (1999, 170). This certainly seems to describe at least part of what historians like Boswell and Jordan are up to in their work, which if not always avowedly queer nonetheless does participate in and further a queer historical critique.

The Touch of the Queer and Radical Alterity

As we have just seen, Dinshaw's *Getting Medieval* explicitly foregrounds the ways in which thinking about medieval sexualities might inflect contemporary (postmodern) lives. For Dinshaw, as for Louise Fradenburg and Carla Freccero, history itself is an 'erogenous zone', a place where different moments in time might rub up against each other with a mixture of desire and (dis)identification (Fradenburg and Freccero 1996, viii).[13] Dinshaw's queer history is not the substitution of one

---

12   Foucault makes explicit use of Boswell in Volume Three of *The History of Sexuality* (1986/1984, 74, 190). Also see Foucault's comments on Boswell (1988, 286–7).

13   For a similarly suggestive, pre-queer treatment of history, see Benjamin (1969).

historical moment for another: the medieval past does not clarify our present analogically or allegorically. Rather, by excavating a medieval past, bringing it back into our thinking, we 'make new relations, new identifications, new communities with past figures who elude resemblance to us but with whom we can be connected partially by virtue of shared marginality, queer positionality' (1999, 39). The queer figures of the past do not 'resemble' us (as metaphors), but they might *touch* us (metonymically).

In looking at medieval moments, too, Dinshaw emphasises 'the touch of the queer' in an attempt to understand how dissonant bodies, performances or sexualities might disrupt and reshape medieval communities. Thus, for instance, she argues that Margery Kempe – in the way she dresses and in her socially disruptive behaviour – brings a queer touch to bear on her surroundings, 'undoing proper Christian identity and destabilising generally recognised authority' (1999, 153). Although Kempe's sexual behaviour is not queer in a contemporary sense – she is not a modern lesbian[14] – that behaviour is decidedly challenging to social expectations: a married woman with a large number of children, she negotiates an agreement to live celibately with her husband, at the same time that her claims to a religious life free her up to travel (on pilgrimage) and to become a more public person than would otherwise be allowed.[15] Dinshaw's analysis of Kempe's queerness depends, then, not on a specific sexual identity ('lesbian') or on discrete sexual acts, but instead on a being in the world that challenges, 'undoes', and 'destabilises' conventions and norms.

Such work insists, at one and the same time, on treating the Middle Ages in its own terms – not importing modern identities or sexualities into the past – and on making the medieval resonate with the contemporary. But any bringing to the past of contemporary formulations – including a queerness reconceived as not solely sexual in its significance, but instead, in Dinshaw's words, as a 'relation of unfittingness, disjunctiveness … uncategorisability … being-left-out' (1999, 158) – runs the risk of seeming to flatten out the differences between our own time and those previous moments. Some scholars working on medieval sexuality have emphasised a more radical otherness or 'alterity' to medieval sexual acts and understandings. Thus, for instance, Allen Frantzen, in *Before the Closet: Same-Sex Love from Beowulf to Angels in America*, insists that contemporary constructions of sexual identity (like those dependent on the figure of the closet) do violence to the medieval record when they are brought uncritically to bear upon it: 'the thesis of this book is that the existence of the closet was not recognised by the men and women of Anglo-Saxon England' (1998, 3). Frantzen insists that the figure of 'the shadow' better describes medieval ways of thinking about sexual otherness: 'same-sex relations are as closely attached to heterosexual relations as shadows are to their objects, and indeed … same-sex relations are indispensable to culture' (1998, 15). In a very different register, Karma Lochrie's recent book, *Heterosyncrasies: Female Sexuality When Normal Wasn't*, argues that work (like Dinshaw's) that assumes the operation of something like

14   For another queer approach to Kempe, see Lavezzo (1996).
15   On the practice of chaste marriage, see Elliott (1993).

'heteronormativity' against which queer presences define themselves distorts the medieval evidence: Lochrie shows how the very idea of the 'normal' is a modern (nineteenth- and twentieth-century) one, dependent upon the development of a statistical thinking about human phenomena that is distinctly non-medieval, and could not be the way in which the Middle Ages organised social understandings.

> [Whereas d]esire for someone of the opposite sex in modern norm-speak is natural or normal because it is the most widespread sexual practice ... Desire for someone of the opposite sex in medieval nature-speak is natural in the corrupted sense of resulting from the Fall, but it is not in any sense legitimated by its widespread practice or idealised as a personal or cultural goal. (2005, xxiii)

Rereading a variety of medieval texts that foreground female sexuality, Lochrie demonstrates that these reveal very different sexual constructions than ones dependent on the idea of norms and normality.[16]

Even as scholars like Frantzen and Lochrie emphasise the gap between our own understandings of sexuality and medieval ones, drawing a stronger line of demarcation between the modern and the premodern than does Dinshaw (or Boswell), their work does do something queer with the relations between modernity and its medieval predecessor. Despite his insistence that constructions like the closet do not work for medieval material, Frantzen recognises that the differences of medieval sexuality might speak powerfully to contemporary formulations, and what we tend to leave out of these. Looking, in an autobiographical afterword, at his own twentieth-century experiences – growing up in the rural Midwest, serving in the US army and stationed in the Republic of Korea – Frantzen argues that this world 'still bore some resemblance to same-sex relations in premodern Europe' (1998, 27).[17] Lochrie's concern with denormalising medieval sexuality interlocks with her insistence that queer work turn from its concentration on men's sexuality (and specifically male sodomy) to women – a concern clearly in part motivated by contemporary feminist commitments. And Lochrie's insistence on historicising the normal results not only in a reconceptualisation of medieval sexuality but also in a refocusing on the sexualities of the twentieth century produced under the regime of the normal: as Lochrie insists in a chapter concerned with the development of 'modern norm-speak' by scientists and sexologists like Alfred Kinsey, to realise that our ideas of normality are recent innovations results in a significantly different way of looking at contemporary sexuality. If the very idea of a normal (hetero)sexuality is a recent construction, then we might imagine future sexualities, like their medieval predecessors, as structured in radically different ways.

---

16   See also Lochrie (1999). For further important work that looks specifically at medieval female same-sex relations, see Sautman and Sheingorn (2001).

17   For a reading of Frantzen's autobiographical move, see Cohen (2003, 35–7).

Social/Sexual Reconfigurations

Queer medievalists have brought their gaze to a rethinking of medieval bodies, sexualities and communities in a variety of social spaces. Boswell and Jordan focus largely on the Church and on religious/theological formulations.[18] Others such as Lochrie (1997b), E. Ann Matter (1986), Jacqueline Murray (2004), Bruce Venarde (1997), Dyan Elliott (1999) (and, again, Boswell [1980]) have considered especially the lives of religious men and women. Sexual queerness – if not anything precisely like gay and lesbian identities – strikes the contemporary eye in particularly strong ways when it comes to all-male and all-female religious communities that do not privilege male-female relations or secular families based on these but instead celibacy and often intense affective connections among their members. V.A. Kolve considers, in an extraordinarily full and subtle way, how the 'anxiety … concerning same-sex desire' in such an institutional setting might be 'control[led]' and 'rechannel[led] into acceptable forms' (1998, 1018) through literary/cultural works such as the late-twelfth-century play *The Son of Getron*.

Literary representations of queer (or even perhaps proto-gay/lesbian) characters, or literary texts that explicitly thematise 'unnatural' sex, have also gathered a significant amount of critical and scholarly attention, as in recent discussions of the circle of the sodomites in Dante's *Inferno*;[19] treatment of the scenes in which men are accused of homosexual inclinations in such works as the *Roman d'Eneas* and Marie de France's *Lanval*;[20] the discussions that, since Monica McAlpine's 1980 article 'The Pardoner's Homosexuality and How It Matters', have circulated around Chaucer's Canterbury Pardoner (and also, more recently, other pilgrims like the Summoner);[21] and the line of thinking that reads Alain de Lille's depiction of 'the plaint of Nature' concerning sexual deviance.[22] Tison Pugh has recently proposed an approach to medieval literary genres that 'typically foreground heterosexual desire and heteronormativity', highlighting how these 'risk being high-jacked by queer and queering sensibilities' (2004, 2).[23] And in a discussion that makes impressive use of queer, psychoanalytic and poststructuralist theory, Anna Kłosowska (2005) queers a number of more and less canonical medieval French texts – the *Romance of the Rose*, *Perceval*, *Yde and Olive*.

---

18 Individual writers like Peter Damian (author of the *Liber Gomorrhianus*, which addresses the 'prevalence' of sodomy among cloistered religious men) have received particular attention; see, in addition to Boswell (1980, 210–13), Jordan (1997, 45–66); Burgwinkle (2004, 53–65); Scanlon (1998); Kruger (2006, 90–96).
19 See, for example, Holsinger (1996); Camille (2001).
20 See Gaunt (1992); Burgwinkle (1993; 2004); Guynn (2000); Kłosowska (2005, 117–44).
21 On the Pardoner, in addition to McAlpine (1980), see Dinshaw (1989, 156–86); Burger (1992; 2003, 140–59); Kruger (1994); Sturges (2000); Zeikowitz (2002); Calabrese (1993); Minnis (2003). On the Summoner, see Bowers (2001); Cox (1995). For a queer reading of Chaucer's contemporary, John Gower, see Watt (2003).
22 Ziolkowski (1985); Leupin (1989); Pittenger (1996); Schibanoff (2001); Burgwinkle (2004, 170–99); Scanlon (1995). See Schibanoff (2006) for a fuller development of her argument.
23 For a different consideration of gender and sexuality in relation to medieval literary genre, see Gaunt (1995).

Scholars have also begun to recognise that medieval secular society contained significant and sometimes quite capacious queer spaces – spaces outside kin relations, spaces with their own distinctive homoaffective and erotic charge. Judith Bennett (2000), reflecting on medieval 'lesbian-like' institutions and ways of life, draws our attention not only to orthodox same-sex religious communities for women and to beguinages, but also to the significant populations of women living singly, outside marriage and separate from their natal families, especially in late-medieval urban situations.[24] Claire Sponsler (2001) analyses the political discourses that pit the marital relationship of a king (like England's Edward II) against his strong, intimate, even explicitly erotic relations with male advisers and confidants. Richard Zeikowitz (2003) (using especially Sedgwick's theoretical work on homosociality in *Between Men* [1985]) makes the argument that chivalric/ aristocratic culture is intensively shaped by male-male homosocial bonds – by knights' identification with each other and by strong desires that accompany such identifications. Medieval chivalry sanctioned, even produced powerful, erotically charged connections between men at the same time at which it policed those connections with the threat that *too* close a male-male attachment might stray into a disallowed effeminacy or sodomy (as in the case of Edward II or, later, Richard II). In Zeikowitz's reading, indeed, male homosociality structures what we retrospectively identify most strongly with the 'heterosexuality' of medieval culture, 'courtly love'; it would be impossible, for instance, to read the love relation between Chaucer's *Troilus and Criseyde* without attending to the equally strongly cathected relationship between Troilus and Pandarus.[25]

Glenn Burger's recent book, *Chaucer's Queer Nation* (2003), is the fullest recognition to date of how late-medieval social institutions and the changes and reconfigurations they go through appear thoroughly different when we look at them through queer eyes. Often the *Canterbury Tales* is read as Chaucer's prescient envisioning of an emergent modernity – revealing a developing Englishness and English nation; a nascent middle class; marriage on its way to a fully modern, 'companionate' model; social institutions taking on newly secular forms; even a proto-Protestantism more than a century before the Reformation. Looking back on the *Canterbury Tales*, critics read back into the text such modern formations, making Chaucer the author ('father') of an English tradition that breaks definitively with the 'superstition' and 'benightedness' of the medieval. Alternatively, we can follow a critic like D.W. Robertson (1962) in reading Chaucer as wholly medieval, judging 'modernising' readings of the Chaucerian text as distortive projections back onto a medieval past understandable only in non-modern terms. What Burger's queer revisioning enables, however, is a disruption of the confident periodising judgements that would make Chaucer either quintessentially medieval or modern *avant la lettre*. A performance like that of Chaucer's Miller, working through bodies

---

24   Also see Bennett and Froide (1998).
25   For another queer reading of *Troilus and Criseyde*, see Pugh (2004, 81–106). And for additional work on 'courtly love' and the history of sexuality, see Jaeger (1999) and Schultz (2006).

set in motion, undercuts gender hierarchy, foregrounds the violence inherent in male-male relations of rivalry and injects the affect of *shame* into the text, and into the text's relation to its audience, so as to suggest identities standing in a shameful (unsanctioned, queer) relation to recognised social structures and order, whether the stabilised 'medieval' structures of the *Knight's Tale* or the emergent 'modern' ones in which the Miller himself (as a traditional 'peasant' moving out of the peasant class) participates. Burger here recognises a similarity to the ways in which twentieth-century gay pornography like John Preston's calls out to and helps call into being contemporary queer positions. In Burger's reading, too, Chaucer's Pardoner figures not by occupying an established gay or homosexual identity (or an older identity like that of eunuch or sodomite) but instead by introducing a disruptive queer presence. And where the 'Marriage Group' of the *Canterbury Tales* has often been read as working ultimately to sanction a 'new' kind of modern, bourgeois marriage (represented most fully in the marriage of Dorigen and Arveragus in the *Franklin's Tale*), Burger restores the uncertainties and tensions to Chaucer's extended engagement with *conjugality*, showing how the treatment of marriage operates not to stabilise a model of companionate, love-based, modern 'heterosexual' marriage but instead to use the partial emergence of that model of marriage (beginning as early as the twelfth century) to think through major social changes occurring in Chaucer's day but not yet by any means settled. Marriage becomes in these tales a way to consider dissonant gender and sexual positions – Burger suggests, for instance, that we think the Wife of Bath through Judith Halberstam's (1998) category of 'female masculinity' – and the not yet fully established, still endangered, dangerous and unstable, 'middle' class ('gentil') identities of the pilgrims who tell tales of marriage (the Wife of Bath, Clerk, Merchant and Franklin). *Conjugality* allows an examination of various social structures that are in the process of being shaped but whose final form – and acceptability – remains undetermined. If the *Canterbury Tales* moves toward modernity, toward a kind of closure that allows new social groups to voice their newness, it also remains enmeshed in its own uncertain, late-medieval moment, exploring not-yet-modern/not-only-medieval configurations pregnant with all kinds of future possibilities. Burger suggests that even the explicitly penitential movement of the end of the *Canterbury Tales* – usually read as enabling closure, through a move back into Christian discourses of sin, penitence and redemption – in fact opens up more possibilities than it closes down.

If we read back onto the past a certainty based on what in fact has emerged historically – if we see, for instance, in the formations and imaginations of the past only that kind of heterosexual relation that has become dominant in modernity and remains so in our own moment – then we do violence to the past. Work like Burger's (and the other queer scholarship surveyed here) repositions such 'proto-modern' formations in their fuller, more undecided moment, and this work thus disturbs a sense of the settledness of modernity itself. When we recognise the many things in the medieval moment that did *not* lead to modernity, we realise that things might have emerged differently; Chaucer gestures in directions that weren't taken up and that might provide us with material for reimagining (and working to change) what did happen to come into being *as* 'the modern'. Further, things that we find in Chaucer (and the Middle Ages more generally) that seem to have disappeared in modernity might be recognised, as we rethink the past, not truly to have disappeared. Alongside the dominant, alongside what we call modern, can we not recognise the survival, the marginal thriving, of other, distinctly non-modern possibilities?

For these reasons, it is particularly important that queer medievalists find ways to touch the queer work happening in other periods and (sub)disciplines. Rather than lament that 'modernists' pay no attention to the premodern, medievalists need to reach into modern material to suggest the ways in which our work might matter beyond the strict borders of the Middle Ages. One example of such a productive transgression of period and disciplinary boundaries is Bruce Holsinger's provocative argument that modern/postmodern French critical theory operates on the basis of a 'premodern condition': 'the critical discourse of postwar France [should] be reconceived in part as a brilliantly defamiliarising amalgamation of medievalisms that together constitute the domain of the avant-garde premodern' (2005, 4). If, as Holsinger argues, what we call contemporary theory is itself shaped – in clear but often unacknowledged ways – by an engagement with the Middle Ages, then to ignore the medieval as we continue to theorise (post)modernity is misguided.

Indeed, all the queer medievalist work so far reviewed argues – more or less explicitly – that the Middle Ages matter (as alterity, as proximity, as difference, as continuity) for what happens after them, and for us now. The medievalist's ability to make evident the importance of the medieval for (post)modernity depends in part on a receptivity among non-medievalists to hearing how the medieval might matter to them – and such a receptivity is not necessarily always present. But the way in which Boswell's work, or Dinshaw's more recently, has resonated for at least some whose major concern is not the Middle Ages might give us hope for a future dialogue between medievalists and those concerned with more modern or contemporary questions about sexuality. To enable that dialogue, queer medievalists need to make clearer the ways in which the medieval is pertinent to its successors, not simply an exotic (queer) other that doesn't matter once we enter the modern world. All the queer medievalist work that I've discussed here argues (though in quite disparate, sometimes contradictory ways) that the simple division of medieval and modern can't be easily maintained. And much of this work takes up questions – about marriage, life outside 'traditional' families, the religious shaping of sexuality – that continue to be of urgent importance well into modernity. In addressing such questions, queer medievalism engages explicitly with material that those working on modernity have claimed as distinctly their own, and thus calls for a reconception of the historical limits that have bounded much work on (post)modern sexuality.

In the concluding section of this chapter, I will briefly examine one additional area of intense concern within contemporary queer studies – that of intersectionality, the ways in which sexuality is interarticulated with such other categories as gender, race, ethnicity, class, age, religion – in order to suggest that here, too, medievalists might make an important intervention into concerns of urgent interest to those working to understand modern sexual constructions.

Multiple Differences

Burger's project in *Chaucer's Queer Nation* insistently points out how the limits of sexuality as a category of analysis are impossible to determine in advance. If Chaucer's Pardoner seems most easily subject to a queer analysis, why not also the bodily disruptions of the *Miller's Tale*? Why not, too, the seemingly 'heterosexual' relations of the tales of the 'Marriage Group', which upon analysis show a whole series of social reconfigurations and dissonances working in and through the relations of conjugality? Why not also the orthodox, Christian movement to penitence at the conclusion of the *Canterbury Tales*, which refocuses attention on the uncertain movements of history as much as it brings the Christian pilgrimage of the *Tales* back into focus?

One of the things queer theory has recently insisted – following a feminist recognition that gender can never be simply conceived on its own, independent from such forces as class, race and sexuality – is that sexuality is not separable from age, gender, race, ethnicity, class, religion.[26] Queer medievalist work has begun to think through such intersecting and mutually informing differences in ways that again act to reconfigure both how we understand medieval culture and how we conceive the relations between past and present. The essays in Josiah Blackmore and Gregory Hutcheson's *Queer Iberia* (1999) attend closely to the ways in which the racially and religiously complex situation of medieval Iberia – as meeting ground of Christianity, Islam and Judaism; Europe and Africa – is inflected by, and inflects, discourses of sexuality. The same is true in Hutcheson's (2001) own treatment of the ways in which, in Iberian Christian discourses, 'Moors' come to be associated with sodomy ('Sodomitic Moor'). Noreen Giffney (2003; 2004) has argued forcefully for the usefulness of queer theory (and monster theory) in reading European constructions of a newly emergent Mongol threat to Eastern Europe during the thirteenth century. In *Medieval Identity Machines* (2003), Jeffrey J. Cohen uses the theorising of Deleuze and Guattari to consider a variety of complex identity constructions – knights' intimate connections to their horses; Margery Kempe's gendered 'becoming Jewish'; the inflection of Christian–Saracen relations by discourses of enjoyment (sexual and gustatory). Geraldine Heng's *Empire of Magic* (2003) considers how, in medieval romance, fantasies about cultural others operate simultaneously in terms of racial, class, and sexual difference.[27] My own recent work in *The Spectral Jew: Conversion and Embodiment in Medieval Europe* (2006) operates in similar ways: looking at medieval Jewish–Christian relations, I argue that these are consistently dependent upon ideas about the body that are – implicitly or explicitly – gendered and sexualised.

Rigid periodisations around categories like race, which make race a modern invention that emerged out of the experience of Western colonialism, like those that

---

26 For important queer work in this area, see Butler (1993); Muñoz (1999); Pellegrini (1997); Somerville (2000); Reid-Pharr (2001); Eng (2001).

27 For other important recent work on romance that resonates with queer readings, see Burns (2002); Ingham (2001); McCracken (2003).

would insist that sexual identity is only conceivable within modernity, cordon off the Middle Ages from a whole range of modern and contemporary concerns.[28] But recognising that there are proto- or quasi-racial complexities in the Middle Ages that, while not modern, nonetheless reflect on modern constructions (superseded by and/or surviving into later forms) might enable us to see contemporary race, modern colonialism and a postcolonial world (our own globalising space) in new ways. To recognise, for instance, the consistent ways in which medieval Jewish–Islamic–Christian religious difference was connected to a gendered and sexualised body might speak to contemporary constructions of Muslim–Christian difference – a difference relying in part on religious, doctrinal distinctions but also having a racialised, gendered and sexualised force, as we see when, in the West, Muslim men are made particularly violent or Muslim women particularly vulnerable. Attending to medievalist work on intersectionality like that briefly sketched above might enable a rethinking of how constructions of racial otherness, superiority and inferiority, depend on interimplications with gender, sexuality and religious belief – both in the past and in the contemporary moment.

My own recent work, for instance, asks what happens – in relation to categories like race, gender, sexuality, the body – when (as we often see in medieval Christian texts) someone converts from one religion to another. Is this conversion only about religion, or are other aspects of an embodied self implicated? Considering the possibility of religious conversion means grappling with complex identity constructions in which religion is not easily extricable from gender, sexuality, race, age, a body conceived of in particular stereotyped ways. Thus, medieval Christianity most often thinks Jewishness in strongly essentialising ways, as an unchanging and unchangeable, 'stiff-necked'ness; to imagine such rigidified Jews as subject to conversion is to imagine a paradox or even an impossibility (which, of course, does not mean that such imaginations are uncommon).[29] More particularly, if Jewish men are conceived – as they are in certain medieval Christian discourses – as bleeding every month (like women); or if Muslim men are depicted as monstrous or demonic in the colour and form of their bodies, what is thought to happen to those wrongly shaped, devilish or feminine male bodies if and when Jewish or Muslim men convert? Does the religious conversion serve as a kind of 'master switch' for identity that brings the new religious identity, and something like a raced and sexed body, into 'proper' alignment? Alternatively, does convert identity entail dissonances, failures of alignment, identity at cross-purposes with itself (as is strongly suggested when converts are renamed not so much as Christians but as Christian*ised* – Hermannus quondam Judaeus [the sometime Jew]; Pablo Christiani; Petrus Alphonsi 'ex Judeo Christiani')? In thinking such questions through, some recent work in gender and sexuality has remarkable resonance. Thus, Jay Prosser's

---

28   For consideration of whether and how the category of race functioned in the European Middle Ages, see Hahn (2001). For medievalist work that engages with postcolonial theory, see Cohen (2001).

29   For a more extended reflection on the paradoxical construction of Jewish conversion in medieval Christian texts, see Kruger (1997; 2006).

Second Skins: The Body Narratives of Transsexuality (1998) shows persuasively how transsexuality might be productively conceived as, paradoxically, an identity of non-self-identity, an identity in which the experience of *transition* is as crucial as any starting or ending point. The religious convert's post-conversion identity might productively be thought in similar ways. But just as contemporary theoretical work like Prosser's might be productively brought to our consideration of medieval material, so medievalist work might speak to contemporary gender and sexuality studies: recognising the ways in which medieval religious conversion entails a certain crisis of identity in relation to gender and sexuality, we might ask whether the transitions of transsexuality are themselves limited to the realms of gender and sexuality. How do these 'conversions' of identity affect one's status in relation, for instance, to racial or ethnic identifications? Do these remain stable, or does a radical change in one's sex/gender destabilise too one's sense of having a particular ethnic or racial or national identity?

Recognising the complex interimplications of religion with other identity categories suggests, like queer medievalist work more generally, a different kind of Middle Ages than does most traditional historicising work – a Middle Ages for which, in writing the history of medieval religion and religious conflict, we do a disservice to the historical record if we ignore gender, sexuality, race, age. At the same time, we should recognise that a queer reading of this history is motivated not by some 'pure' historicist impulse (as though that were possible) but by a desire to think the Middle Ages in a way that might also bring something useful to our thinking about contemporary questions. The medieval evidence should call our attention to the ways in which religious differences still work not just in terms of 'themselves' but through such culturally charged categories as gender, sexuality, age, race, the body. Rereading the history of *medieval* Christian European engagements with Islam, Judaism, the Mongols, the 'East' might provide us with different ways of looking at and thinking about early modern moments of exploration and intercultural contact, European exploitation of Africa, Asia and the 'New World', later moments of colonialism and imperialism and contemporary, twenty-first century, interreligious, interracial, geopolitical contacts and conflicts of great moment – when we turn back from the queer Middle Ages to examine, again, the world in which we live.

Acknowledgements

For their careful readings of earlier versions of this chapter, I thank Noreen Giffney, Michael O'Rourke and Glenn Burger.

Suggested Further Reading

Burger, G. (2003), *Chaucer's Queer Nation* (Minneapolis, MN: University of Minnesota Press).
—— and Kruger, S.F. (eds) (2001), *Queering the Middle Ages* (Minneapolis, MN and London: University of Minnesota Press).
Burgwinkle, W.E. (2004), *Sodomy, Masculinity, and Law in Medieval Literature: France and England, 1050–1230* (Cambridge: Cambridge University Press).
Dinshaw, C. (1999), *Getting Medieval: Sexualities and Communities, Pre- and Postmodern* (Durham, NC: Duke University Press).
Lochrie, K. (2005), *Heterosyncrasies: Female Sexuality When Normal Wasn't* (Minneapolis, MN: University of Minnesota Press).

References

Benjamin, W. (1969), 'Theses on the Philosophy of History', in H. Arendt (ed.), *Illuminations*, trans. H. Zohn (New York: Schocken).
Bennett, J.M. (2000), '"Lesbian-Like" and the Social History of Lesbianisms', *Journal of the History of Sexuality* 9, 1–24.
—— and Froide, A.M. (eds) (1998), *Singlewomen in the European Past, 1250–1800* (Philadelphia, PA: University of Pennsylvania Press).
Biddick, K. (2003), *The Typological Imaginary: Circumcision, Technology, History* (Philadelphia, PA: University of Pennsylvania Press).
Blackmore, J. and Hutcheson, G.S. (eds) (1999), *Queer Iberia: Sexualities, Cultures, and Crossings from the Middle Ages to the Renaissance* (Durham, NC: Duke University Press).
Boswell, J. (1980), *Christianity, Social Tolerance, and Homosexuality: Gay People in Western Europe from the Beginning of the Christian Era to the Fourteenth Century* (Chicago, IL: University of Chicago Press).
—— (1989), 'Revolutions, Universals, and Sexual Categories', in M. Duberman, M. Vicinus and G. Chauncey, Jr. (eds), *Hidden from History: Reclaiming the Gay Past* (New York: New American Library).
—— (1994), *Same-Sex Unions in Premodern Europe* (New York: Villard Books).
Bowers, J. (2001), 'Queering the Summoner: Same-Sex Union in Chaucer's *Canterbury Tales*', in R.F. Yeager and C.C. Morse (eds), *Speaking Images: Essays in Honor of V.A. Kolve* (Asheville, NC: Pegasus Press).
Bray, A. (2003), *The Friend* (Chicago, IL: University of Chicago Press).
Brooten, B.J. (1996), *Love between Women: Early Christian Responses to Female Homoeroticism* (Chicago, IL: University of Chicago Press).
Brundage, J.A. (1987), *Law, Sex, and Christian Society in Medieval Europe* (Chicago, IL: University of Chicago Press).
Bullough, V.L., and J.A. Brundage (eds) (1982), *Sexual Practices and the Medieval Church* (Buffalo, NY: Prometheus Books).

Burger, G. (1992), 'Kissing the Pardoner', *PMLA* 107, 1143–56.

—— (2003), *Chaucer's Queer Nation* (Minneapolis, MN: University of Minnesota Press).

—— and Kruger, S.F. (eds) (2001), *Queering the Middle Ages* (Minneapolis, MN: University of Minnesota Press).

Burgwinkle, W.E. (1993), 'Knighting the Classical Hero: Homo/Hetero Affectivity in *Eneas*', *Exemplaria* 5, 1–43.

—— (2004), *Sodomy, Masculinity, and Law in Medieval Literature: France and England, 1050–1230* (Cambridge: Cambridge University Press).

Burns, E.J. (2002), *Courtly Love Undressed: Reading through Clothes in Medieval French Culture* (Philadelphia, PA: University of Pennsylvania Press).

Butler, J. (1990), *Gender Trouble: Feminism and the Subversion of Identity* (New York: Routledge).

—— (1993), *Bodies That Matter: On the Discursive Limits of 'Sex'* (New York and London: Routledge).

Calabrese, M.A. (1993), '"Make a Mark That Shows": Orphean Song, Orphean Sexuality, and the Exile of Chaucer's Pardoner', *Viator* 24, 269–86.

Camille, M. (2001), 'The Pose of the Queer: Dante's Gaze, Brunetto Latini's Body', in G. Burger and S.F. Kruger (eds), *Queering the Middle Ages* (Minneapolis, MN: University of Minnesota Press).

Cohen, J.J. (ed.) (2001), *The Postcolonial Middle Ages* (Basingstoke: Palgrave Macmillan).

—— (2003), *Medieval Identity Machines* (Minneapolis, MN: University of Minnesota Press).

Cox, C.S. (1995), '"Grope Wel Bihynde": The Subversive Erotics of Chaucer's Summoner', *Exemplaria* 7, 145–77.

Dinshaw, C. (1989), *Chaucer's Sexual Poetics* (Madison, WI: University of Wisconsin Press).

—— (1999), *Getting Medieval: Sexualities and Communities, Pre- and Postmodern* (Durham, NC: Duke University Press).

Dollimore, J. (1991), *Sexual Dissidence: Augustine to Wilde, Freud to Foucault* (Oxford: Clarendon Press).

Edelman, L. (1994), *Homographesis: Essays in Gay Literary and Cultural Theory* (New York: Routledge).

Elliott, D. (1993), *Spiritual Marriage: Sexual Abstinence in Medieval Wedlock* (Princeton, NJ: Princeton University Press).

—— (1999), *Fallen Bodies: Pollution, Sexuality, and Demonology in the Middle Ages* (Philadelphia, PA: University of Pennsylvania Press).

Eng, D. (2001), *Racial Castration: Managing Masculinity in Asian America* (Durham, NC: Duke University Press).

Eribon, D. (2004), *Insult and the Making of the Gay Self*, trans. M. Lucey (Durham, NC: Duke University Press).

Foucault, M. (1978/1976) *The History of Sexuality, Vol. 1: An Introduction*, trans. R. Hurley (New York: Pantheon/Random House).

—— (1985/1984), *The History of Sexuality, Vol. 2: The Use of Pleasure*, trans. R. Hurley (New York: Pantheon/Random House).

—— (1986/1984), *The History of Sexuality, Vol. 3: The Care of the Self*, trans. R. Hurley (New York: Pantheon/Random House).

—— (1988), 'Sexual Choice, Sexual Act: Foucault and Homosexuality' (interview with J. O'Higgins), in L.D. Kritzman (ed.), *Politics, Philosophy, Culture: Interviews and Other Writings 1977–1984* (New York: Routledge).

Fradenburg, L. and Freccero, C. (eds) (1996), *Premodern Sexualities* (New York and London: Routledge).

Frantzen, A.J. (1998), *Before the Closet: Same-Sex Love from Beowulf to Angels in America* (Chicago, IL: University of Chicago Press).

Freccero, C. (2006), *Queer/Early/Modern* (Durham, NC: Duke University Press).

Gaunt, S. (1992), 'From Epic to Romance: Gender and Sexuality in the *Roman d'Eneas*', *Romanic Review* 83, 1–27.

—— (1995), *Gender and Genre in Medieval French Literature* (Cambridge: Cambridge University Press).

Gay Academic Union (1981), *Homosexuality, Intolerance, and Christianity: A Critical Examination of John Boswell's Work* (New York: Scholarship Committee, Gay Academic Union).

Giffney, N. (2003), 'Qu(e)erying Mongols', *Medieval Feminist Forum* 36, 15–21.

—— (2004), '"The Age Is Drowned in Blood": Reading Anti-Mongol Propaganda, 1236–55', unpublished PhD Diss., University College Dublin.

Goodich, M. (1979), *The Unmentionable Vice: Homosexuality in the Later Medieval Period* (Santa Barbara, CA: ABC-Clio).

Guynn, N.D. (2000), 'Eternal Flame: State Formation, Deviant Architecture, and the Monumentality of Same-Sex Eroticism in the *Roman d'Eneas*', *GLQ: A Journal of Lesbian and Gay Studies* 6, 287–319.

Hahn, T. (ed.) (2001), 'Race and Ethnicity in the Middle Ages', a special issue of *Journal of Medieval and Early Modern Studies* 31.

Halberstam, J. (1998), *Female Masculinity* (Durham, NC: Duke University Press).

Halperin, D.M. (1989), 'Sex before Sexuality: Pederasty, Politics, and Power in Classical Athens', in M. Duberman, M. Vicinus and G. Chauncey, Jr. (eds), *Hidden From History: Reclaiming the Gay Past* (New York: New American Library).

—— (1998), 'Forgetting Foucault: Acts, Identities and the History of Sexuality', *Representations* 63, 93–120.

—— (2002), *How to Do the History of Homosexuality* (Chicago, IL: University of Chicago Press).

Heng, G. (2003), *Empire of Magic: Medieval Romance and the Politics of Cultural Fantasy* (New York: Columbia University Press).

Holsinger, B. (1996), 'Sodomy and Resurrection: The Homoerotic Subject of the *Divine Comedy*', in L. Fradenburg and C. Freccero (eds), *Premodern Sexualities* (New York and London: Routledge).

—— (2005), *The Premodern Condition: Medievalism and the Making of Theory* (Chicago, IL: University of Chicago Press).

—— and Townsend, D. (2002), 'Ovidian Homoerotics in Twelfth-Century Paris: The Letters of Leoninus, Poet and Polyphone', *GLQ: A Journal of Lesbian and Gay Studies* 8, 389–423.

Hutcheson, G.S. (2001), 'The Sodomitic Moor: Queerness in the Narrative of *Reconquista*', in G. Burger and S.F. Kruger (eds), *Queering the Middle Ages* (Minneapolis, MN: University of Minnesota Press).

Ingham, P.C. (2001), *Sovereign Fantasies: Arthurian Romance and the Making of Britain* (Philadelphia, PA: University of Pennsylvania Press).

Jaeger, C.S. (1999), *Ennobling Love: In Search of a Lost Sensibility* (Philadelphia, PA: University of Pennsylvania Press).

Jordan, M.D. (1997), *The Invention of Sodomy in Christian Theology* (Chicago, IL: University of Chicago Press).

—— (2000), *The Silence of Sodom: Homosexuality in Modern Catholicism* (Chicago, IL: University of Chicago Press).

—— (2005), *Blessing Same-Sex Unions: The Perils of Queer Romance and the Confusions of Christian Marriage* (Chicago, IL: University of Chicago Press).

Kłosowska, A. (2005), *Queer Love in the Middle Ages* (New York: Palgrave Macmillan).

Kolve, V.A. (1998), 'Ganymede/Son of Getron: Medieval Monasticism and the Drama of Same-Sex Desire', *Speculum* 73, 1014–67.

Kruger, S.F. (1994), 'Claiming the Pardoner: Toward a Gay Reading of Chaucer's *Pardoner's Tale*', *Exemplaria* 6, 115–39.

—— (1997), 'Conversion and Medieval Sexual, Religious, and Racial Categories', in K. Lochrie, P. McCracken and J. Schultz (eds), *Constructing Medieval Sexuality* (Minneapolis, MN: University of Minnesota Press).

—— (2001), 'Medieval/Postmodern: HIV/AIDS and the Temporality of Crisis', in G. Burger and S.F. Kruger (eds), *Queering the Middle Ages* (Minneapolis, MN: University of Minnesota Press).

—— (2006), *The Spectral Jew: Conversion and Embodiment in Medieval Europe* (Minneapolis, MN: University of Minnesota Press).

Kuefler, M. (ed.) (2006), *The Boswell Thesis: Essays on Christianity, Social Tolerance, and Homosexuality* (Chicago, IL: University of Chicago Press).

Latour, B. (1993), *We Have Never Been Modern*, trans. C. Porter (Cambridge, MA: Harvard University Press).

Lavezzo, K. (1996), 'Sobs and Sighs between Women: The Homoerotics of Compassion in the *Book of Margery Kempe*', in L. Fradenburg and C. Freccero (eds), *Premodern Sexualities* (New York and London: Routledge).

Leupin, A. (1989), *Barbarolexis: Medieval Writing and Sexuality*, trans. K.M. Cooper (Cambridge, MA: Harvard University Press).

Lochrie, K. (1997a), 'Desiring Foucault', *Journal of Medieval and Early Modern Studies* 27, 3–16.

—— (1997b), 'Mystical Acts, Queer Tendencies', in K. Lochrie, P. McCracken and J. Schultz (eds), *Constructing Medieval Sexuality* (Minneapolis, MN: University of Minnesota Press).

—— (1999), *Covert Operations: The Medieval Uses of Secrecy* (Philadelphia, PA: University of Pennsylvania Press).

—— (2005), *Heterosyncrasies: Female Sexuality When Normal Wasn't* (Minneapolis, MN: University of Minnesota Press).

Matter, E.A. (1986), 'My Sister, My Spouse: Woman-Identified Women in Medieval Christianity', *Journal of Feminist Studies in Religion* 2, 81–93.

McAlpine, M. (1980), 'The Pardoner's Homosexuality and How It Matters', *PMLA* 95, 8–22.

McCracken, P. (2003), *The Curse of Eve, the Wound of the Hero: Blood, Gender, and Medieval Literature* (Philadelphia, PA: University of Pennsylvania Press).

McGuire, B.P. (1988), *Friendship and Community: The Monastic Experience, 350–1250* (Kalamazoo, MI: Cistercian Publications).

—— (1994), *Brother and Lover: Aelred of Rievaulx* (New York: Crossroad).

Minnis, A. (2003), 'Chaucer and the Queering Eunuch', *New Medieval Literatures* 6, 107–28.

Mormando, F. (1999), *Bernardino of Siena and the Social Underworld of Early Renaissance Italy* (Chicago, IL: University of Chicago Press).

Muñoz, J.E. (1999), *Disidentifications: Queers of Color and the Performance of Politics* (Minneapolis, MN: University of Minnesota Press).

Murray, J. (1996), 'Twice Marginal and Twice Invisible: Lesbians in the Middle Ages', in V.L. Bullough and J.A. Brundage (eds), *The Handbook of Medieval Sexuality* (New York: Garland).

—— (2004), 'Masculinizing Religious Life: Sexual Prowess, the Battle for Chastity, and Monastic Identity', in P.H. Cullum and K.J. Lewis (eds), *Holiness and Masculinity in the Middle Ages* (Cardiff: University of Wales Press).

—— and Eisenbichler, K. (eds) (1996), *Desire and Discipline: Sex and Sexuality in the Premodern West* (Toronto: University of Toronto Press).

O'Rourke, M. (2003), 'Becoming (Queer) Medieval', *Medieval Feminist Forum* 36, 9–14.

Padgug, R. (1989), 'Sexual Matters: Rethinking Sexuality in History', in M. Duberman, M. Vicinus and G. Chauncey, Jr. (eds), *Hidden from History: Reclaiming the Gay Past* (New York: New American Library).

Pellegrini, A. (1997), *Performance Anxieties: Staging Psychoanalysis, Staging Race* (New York: Routledge).

Pittenger, E. (1996), 'Explicit Ink', in L. Fradenburg and C. Freccero (eds), *Premodern Sexualities* (New York and London: Routledge).

Preston, J. (ed.) (1992), *Flesh and the Word*, vol. 1 (New York: Dutton).

Prosser, J. (1998), *Second Skins: The Body Narratives of Transsexuality* (New York: Columbia University Press).

Puff, H. (2003), *Sodomy in Reformation Germany and Switzerland, 1400–1600* (Chicago, IL: University of Chicago Press).

Pugh, T. (2004), *Queering Medieval Genres* (New York and Basingstoke: Palgrave Macmillan).

Reid-Pharr, R. (2001), *Black Gay Man* (New York: New York University Press).

Robertson, D.W. Jr. (1962), *A Preface to Chaucer: Studies in Medieval Perspectives* (Princeton, NJ: Princeton University Press).

Rocke, M. (1996), *Forbidden Friendships: Homosexuality and Male Culture in Renaissance Florence* (New York: Oxford University Press).

Rohy, V. (2006), 'Ahistorical', *GLQ: A Journal of Lesbian and Gay Studies* 12, 61–83.

Sautman, F.C. and Sheingorn, P. (eds) (2001), *Same Sex Love and Desire among Women in the Middle Ages* (New York: Palgrave).

Scanlon, L. (1995), 'Unspeakable Pleasures: Alain de Lille, Sexual Regulation, and the Priesthood of Genius', *Romanic Review* 86, 213–42.

—— (1998), 'Unmanned Men and Eunuchs of God: Peter Damian's *Liber Gomorrhianus* and the Sexual Politics of Papal Reform', *New Medieval Literatures* 2, 37–46.

—— (in progress), *At Sodom's Gate: Medieval Writing, Postmodern Theory, and the Regulation of Desire*.

Schibanoff, S. (2001), 'Sodomy's Mark: Alan of Lille, Jean de Meun, and the Medieval Theory of Authorship', in G. Burger and S.F. Kruger (eds), *Queering the Middle Ages* (Minneapolis, MN: University of Minnesota Press).

—— (2006), *Chaucer's Queer Poetics: Rereading the Dream Trio* (Toronto: University of Toronto Press).

Schultz, J.A. (2006), *Courtly Love, the Love of Courtliness, and the History of Sexuality* (Chicago, IL: University of Chicago Press).

Sedgwick, E.K. (1985), *Between Men: English Literature and Male Homosocial Desire* (New York: Columbia University Press, 1985).

—— (1990), *Epistemology of the Closet* (Berkeley and Los Angeles, CA: University of California Press).

Somerville, S. (2000), *Queering the Color Line: Race and the Invention of Homosexuality in American Culture* (Durham, NC: Duke University Press).

Sponsler, C. (2001), 'The King's Boyfriend: Froissart's Political Theater of 1326', in G. Burger and S.F. Kruger (eds), *Queering the Middle Ages* (Minneapolis, MN: University of Minnesota Press).

Sturges, R. (2000), *Chaucer's Pardoner and Gender Theory: Bodies of Discourse* (New York: Palgrave Macmillan).

Venarde, B. (1997), *Women's Monasticism and Medieval Society: Nunneries in France and England, 890–1215* (Ithaca, NY: Cornell University Press).

Warner, M. (1999), *The Trouble with Normal: Sex, Politics, and the Ethics of Queer Life* (New York: Free Press).

Watt, D. (2003), *Amoral Gower: Language, Sex, and Politics* (Minneapolis, MN: University of Minnesota Press).

Zeikowitz, R. (2002), 'Silenced but Not Stifled: The Disruptive Queer Power of Chaucer's Pardoner', *Dalhousie Review* 82, 55–73.

—— (2003), *Homoeroticism and Chivalry: Discourses of Male Same-Sex Desire in the Fourteenth Century* (New York: Palgrave Macmillan).

Ziolkowski, J. (1985), *Alan of Lille's Grammar of Sex: The Meaning of Grammar to a Twelfth-Century Intellectual* (Cambridge, MA: Medieval Academy of America).

Smacking My Bitch Up:
Queer or What?

Nikki Sullivan

When the music video for The Prodigy's *Smack My Bitch Up* was first released in 1997 it quickly became a point of sometimes heated debate amongst my peers. What most interested me about the varying opinions expressed over drinks and dinners, in powder rooms and classrooms, on street corners and buses, was that they reflected not only my own ambivalent and contradictory feelings about the video but also those of the public more generally. Whilst in a British poll the video, directed by Swedish filmmaker Jonas Åkerlund, was voted the sixty-first best pop video of all time, it was simultaneously condemned for its alleged advocating of violent and/or sexist behaviour, and either banned from being screened or relegated to late-night time spots. So what is it about the video that has provoked such strong responses? Whilst I'm unable to offer a definitive answer to this question, my own viewing experience may shed some light on the issue.

The video, shot on a hand-held camera from the point of view of the protagonist, consists of an evening in which the anonymous person behind the viewfinder gets showered and dressed, snorts some cocaine, goes to a bar, gets drunk, gets involved in a fight, feels-up some topless dancers who are showered in champagne, vomits in a seedy public toilet, and has a casual sexual encounter with a gorgeous lusty woman: all this to the accompaniment of a relentless grungy techno-beat and the words 'change my pitch up, smack my bitch up' repeated over and over. It's not surprising, then, that on first viewing I regarded the video as portraying fairly typical 'masculinist' behaviour, and as such, as at best uninteresting, and at worst offensive.

Having unquestioningly formed this opinion I was unprepared for the now infamous denouement in which the camera tracks the protagonist's play-partner leaving the apartment and then turns towards a full-length mirror that reflects back the figure of the protagonist. The reflection which, contrary to (my) expectation, brings the viewer eye-to-eye with an attractive, feminine, white woman, is revelatory not only at the level of denotation, but also in as much as it reflects back the heteronormative assumptions informing the/this viewer's gaze. Stunned, and somewhat confused, I was forced to ponder why it was that I had so readily assumed the protagonist to be male and what the subjective affects of such an assumption might be. Perhaps more confronting still was the fact that whilst under the illusion that the protagonist was male I had felt little more than mildly annoyed at the actions that took place, once it was revealed that it was a woman who was confidently and without apology taking recreational drugs, behaving 'aggressively', feeling-up half naked women and having casual sex, I couldn't help but feel aroused. Did this mean that I had internalised heterosexist fantasies or that I identified with masculinist values and was therefore taking up a phallocentric subject position? Was I colluding with heteropatriarchy? I didn't think so, but then again, the ensuing conversations I had with others made it clear that not everyone agreed.

The (partial) explanation I want to offer for my ambivalent feelings about this video – the vomiting in particular did little for me,[1] as did the fracas with the DJ, but the lyrics, the lust and the sense of euphoria excited me – is that it engenders queer affects. What I mean by this is that the clip could be said to challenge, to denaturalise, to render unstable, heteronormative ideas about gender and gendered behaviour, and, as I've noted, has the capacity to reveal the ways in which such assumptions inform, at a less than conscious level, the perceptions and self-identity of even those of us who like to think of ourselves as well versed in postmodernism and in the politics of gender and sexuality. Let me explain this by returning to the question of why I had so readily assumed the protagonist to be male. Clearly, whilst viewing the unfolding events, I had, without thinking about it, assumed an almost intrinsic connection between the deployment and the eroticisation of power and (controlled) 'violence', and heterosexual masculinity. Hence my surprise when I found that the protagonist was not only a woman, but a 'feminine' woman at that: had the woman been 'butch' the challenge may well have proved less provocative.[2] Without attempting to explain and excuse the assumptions I initially made, I want to suggest that such a response is, in part, an effect of the paucity of images – in mainstream, and traditionally in feminist texts – of (feminine) women actively involved in the eroticisation of power, in the use of controlled violence, and, more particularly, in the foregrounding of a woman's pleasure *as her own*.

Whilst getting-off on the defiant foregrounding of the eroticisation of power-play in this particular production of (a) woman's pleasure *as her own*,[3] I simultaneously

---

1   For an interesting account of the erotics of vomiting see Berlant and Warner (1998).

2   This may also have been the case if the protagonist's race, class, age, physical ability and so on had been other than what they seemingly were. For a discussion of the relation between race and/or ethnicity and S/M, see Duncan (1996).

3   I'm aware that pornography aimed at a straight audience often contains the kinds of images found in the video under discussion, but the important difference, for me at least, is that the latter appears to foreground an example of female pleasure that is not ultimately structured around and for male pleasure. This is not, however, to suggest that its affects are, or can be, circumscribed: the clip may well be a turn on for some straight white male fans of mainstream porn. Neither am I suggesting that what I am identifying here as the queer potential of the clip is simply a product or reflection of the director's intent.

felt guilty for doing so. Like the cock-sucking lesbian protagonist of Patrick Califia-Rice's[4] 'The Surprise Party',[5] I was worried that pleasure not structured by guilt, by force, by reciprocity, by a bid for freedom, by contractual obligations, by the needs of another, was perhaps perverse, 'violent', unfemini(ne)st. 'Well of course it is', I imagine Califia saying with a wink and a deep-throated laugh, it's queer – hence the dis-ease, the ambivalence. But whilst I agree with this (imagined) claim I remain aware of, and value, the inevitable existence of other possible interpretations of *Smack My Bitch Up* and of the eroticisation of power-play that it seems to endorse.[6] I imagine, for example, that Mary Daly (1979) might argue that the video constitutes a gratuitous illustration and effect of what she calls 'sadosociety', and following on from this, that feminists such as Sheila Jeffreys might propose that both the video and the lyrics are sadomasochistic, antifeminist and politically conservative, that they reproduce, rather than challenge, mainstream values, practices and identities.

I'll return to these kinds of claims and the assumptions that inform them in due course, but for the moment I want to suggest that, for me at least, *Smack My Bitch Up*, and the strong responses it has evoked, raise a whole range of questions about sadomasochism and the affects it could be said to produce, particularly in regard to heteronormative constructions of identity, gender and sexuality. Such a suggestion clearly presumes that *Smack My Bitch Up* can be regarded as sadomasochistic despite the fact that the video does not contain images of the accoutrements often associated with sadomasochism, that is, whips, paddles, shackles, ropes, leather, latex and so on. My framing of the text (both audio and visual) in this way is informed by my understanding of sadomasochism as a set of diverse practices loosely connected by the exploration and eroticisation of power-play,[7] and by my desire to open up this term beyond the definitions by which it is all too often constrained. In other words, rather than simply claiming that sadomasochism (and by association *Smack My Bitch Up*) is queer – and thus transgressive – I want to queer sadomasochism and in turn my own ambivalent position in relation to it.

Queer is, Queer Does

Before I turn my attention to a discussion of sadomasochism it may be pertinent to say a few things about the term queer, its possible uses and the way in which queer critical practice is intended to function in this chapter. So, let me begin with

---

4   Patrick Califia-Rice was, at the time of publication of *Macho Sluts*, known as Pat Califia.

5   This is one of a number of stories in Califia's *Macho Sluts* (1988).

6   The claim that the video is explicitly concerned with the eroticisation of power-play is clearly supported by The Simpsons' *Smack My Bitch Up* (2005).

7   Langdridge and Butt (2005) note an increasing tendency to replace the term sadomasochism with 'erotic power exchange' in order to avoid the common and somewhat limiting association of S/M with pain.

a few oft-cited definitions. According to David Halperin 'queer is by definition, *whatever* is at odds with the normal, the legitimate, the dominant' (1995, 62). It is, as Cherry Smyth explains, 'a strategy, an attitude … a radical questioning of social and cultural norms' (1996, 280). Queer, as Annamarie Jagose puts it, 'is less an identity than a *critique* of identity' (1996b) which is not, I would argue, quite the same as the claim made by Halperin, that queer 'is an identity without an essence' (1995, 62). Such understandings, however, seem to exist in direct contrast to the popular use of the term as shorthand for, and interchangeable with, 'gay, lesbian, bisexual, transgender' (GLBT), and/or to the assumption that queer practice has a consistent, definable set of characteristics.

Taking the latter position one could argue that *Smack My Bitch Up* – and/or sadomasochism more generally – is queer because it features singular definably queer subjects (for example 'lesbians') involved in definably queer practices (recreational drug taking,[8] casual 'rough' sex, and so on), which produce singular definably queer (oppositional) effects. However, if, as poststructuralist theorists have argued, meaning and identity are polysemic constructs that are complex, contradictory, in process, ultimately undecidable and, at the same time, contextually specific, then no action, no identity, no text can be *intrinsically* counter-normative (or otherwise). A practice may, as Clare Whatling notes, 'be oppositional under certain conditions, but is never always so'. Sadomasochistic practices, she writes, are 'likely to play into, as well as out of, the dominant structures of the society in which [they are] practiced' (1993, 194).

One way of avoiding the problems associated with the notion of queer as a noun, is, as Janet R. Jakobsen suggests, to 'complete the Foucauldian move from human being to human doing' (1998, 516). What Jakobsen means by this is that it may be more productive to think of queer as a verb (a set of actions), rather than as a noun (an identity, or even a nameable positionality formed in and through the practice of particular actions). Queer, in this sense, is something like a deconstructive practice; one that cannot have 'a consistent set of characteristics' (Jagose 1996b, 96), but nevertheless ceaselessly interrogates both the preconditions and effects of specific identities, discourses, relations, actions, events and so on. So, rather than reproducing the kind of heteronormative logic that informs the construction of being in terms of binary oppositions – queer/straight, sadomasochist/vanilla, power/powerlessness, good/bad, queer theory/identity politics, presence/absence, pure/impure – this chapter will attempt to approach the issue of sadomasochism queerly.

---

8   According to Halperin, Foucault advocated the use of what he called 'good drugs' in order to intensify experiences of pleasure (1995, 94). Halperin reproduces this move, including 'recreational drugs' in a list of 'illicit' practices which intensify pleasure, affording what Foucault refers to as 'an exceptional possibility of desubjectivization' (1988, 36), and thus contributing to the queering of heteronormative practices and identities.

Sadomasochism: A Term with a History

Since their discursive constitution[9] in 1890, when Richard von Krafft-Ebing first named them in the fifth edition of *Psychopathia Sexualis* (1965/1886), sadism and masochism have been regarded as different, but connected phenomena. Sadism, which Krafft-Ebing described as 'the impulse to cruel and violent treatment of [another] … and the colouring of the idea of such acts with lustful feeling' (cited in Crozier 2004, 277), was named after the Marquis de Sade, author of *120 Days of Sodom, Justine* and *Philosophy in the Bedroom*. Unlike the more common notion of masochism as the enjoyment of pain, Krafft-Ebing, drawing on the writing of Leopold von Sacher-Masoch, author of, amongst other things, *Venus in Furs* and *The Master Masochist*, associated masochism with the drama of subjection and thus, as Nick Mansfield notes, with theatre.[10] In response to Krafft-Ebing's analysis, a number of European writers developed a range of ideas about sadism and masochism,[11] but like Sigmund Freud, whose work is perhaps the most readily available to a contemporary audience, most regarded these practices as perversions or 'sexual aberrations'.[12] From the outset, then, sadism and masochism have been discursively constructed according to two dominant (and related) paradigms. On the one hand, for writers such as Sade and Sacher-Masoch sadistic and/or masochistic practices function to repudiate supposedly universal moral truths and the subjectivity(ies) to which they give rise, on the other, theorists such as Krafft-Ebing and Freud have argued that sadism and masochism are more properly forms of psychopathology. Those who have followed in the footsteps of the former have gone on to claim that sadism and masochism should be regarded as potentially positive forms of subversion, whereas those who regard such phenomena as aberrations seek, in various ways, to overcome them.

Versions of these polarised positions prevail in contemporary writings on what has now come to be known as sadomasochism – a term which implies the inextricability of sadism and masochism. I will examine pro- and anti-sadomasochism discourses in due course, but for the moment I want to focus briefly on the conceptualisation of the relationship between sadism and masochism that informs such positions. There are those who, like Freud, claim that sadism and masochism are separate sides of the same coin, that 'a sadist is always at the same time a masochist' (Freud 1977, 50), and, as we shall see, there are those who believe that sadism and masochism are polar opposites and that therefore people are inclined to one position or the other. The problem with both conceptualisations

---

9　This does not mean that prior to this time what we might now think of as sadomasochistic practices did not exist, but rather, that up until this time such practices had not been constituted in medicalised terms as identifiable pathologies that could be regarded as expressive of particular personality types.

10　For a detailed discussion of the literary, aesthetic and/or theatrical elements of masochism, see Mansfield (1997).

11　See Crozier (2004).

12　See Freud (1955; 1977; 1984).

is that they are informed by, and reproduce, what Luce Irigaray (1985) has critically referred to as an Economy of the Same: the first conflates sadism and masochism thus making impossible an analysis of the specificities of each in any given context, and the latter implies the existence of two fixed (id)entities, again obfuscating the complex, contradictory, contextually specific and therefore contingent meaning and character of sadism, masochism and the relation between them. Queering this oppositional logic, Mandy Merck proposes the use of the sign s/m in which the slash foregrounds Roland Barthes's understanding of semiological indeterminacy. Sadomasochism, she writes, is '[p]erhaps ... best expressed here by the familiar abbreviation "s/m". Like Barthes's S/Z ... s/m suggest opposition without fixed content, content which the appropriately termed 'slash' both stands in for and cuts out' (1993, 237). Since this configuration implies the necessary intertwining of terms that are always, as Jacques Derrida (1976) might put it, 'under erasure', it seems to me to enable the kind of critical interrogation that this chapter aims to undertake. Given this, I will use the term S/M (where appropriate).

Recent Definitions and Debates

Before examining the debates surrounding and informing S/M it is important to note that this term has been used to cover a diverse range of practices some of which may not necessarily be regarded as sexual *per se*. S/M may involve fantasising about or participating in spanking, flagellation, biting, marking, slapping, burning, cutting, pain, fisting, cannibalism, role-play, water-sports, various forms of restraint or bondage, domination and submission, humiliation, discipline, the use of sex-toys, pornography, uniforms and so on.[13] S/M fantasies and/or play can include one or more participants of any age, ethnicity, race, class, occupation, body type, religious inclination, gender and sexuality, and can be participated in to varying degrees and frequencies. What this suggests is that S/M is less a singular definable entity, than a heterogeneous set of practices, the meaning and experience of which is contingent on a range of contextual (historico-cultural and personal) factors and the relations between them. This is perhaps what Mark Thompson means when he says that 'S/M is a topic infused with ambiguity and contradiction (1994, xi). Taking this as a starting point, then, one may begin to develop a critical analysis of the diverse and sometimes queer affects of specific S/M scenarios. However, for the most part, this is not what has occurred in contemporary writings on S/M, many of which attempt to define S/M as either exemplifying resistance to heteronormativity – that is, as nameably queer – or as in collusion with it.

Critics of S/M generally argue that S/M 'impulses are created and sustained by events and images within our society, and ... sadomasochistic behaviour reproduces and therefore condones many of the power imbalances and destructive features of our lives' (cited in Whatling 1993, 193). John Rechy takes this position

---

13   See Antiniou (1995). This list is necessarily far from definitive.

arguing that participation in S/M is symptomatic of guilt and self-loathing. The gay male sadist, he writes, 'is transferring his feelings of self-contempt for his own homosexuality onto the cowering "M", who turns himself willingly into what gayhaters have called him' (1979, 261). Thus, Rechy concludes, 'Gay S&M is the straight world's most despicable legacy' (1979, 262). In a comparable critique Diana Russell states that 'sadomasochism among lesbians involves ... the internalisation of a homophobic heterosexual view of lesbian' (1982, 176), and as such is anti-lesbian, anti-woman and anti-feminist. In keeping with Russell's position is Sheila Jeffreys' claim that S/M exemplifies what she refers to as 'heterosexual desire', that is, 'desire that is organised around eroticised dominance and submission' (1998, 76); desire in which one participant is 'othered'. For these critics and others like them, then, S/M reflects and reproduces dominant relations of power, and power *per se* is intrinsically problematic.

Such a position is informed by a top-down model of power in which the ruling elite alone possesses and employs power to the detriment of all those who do not or cannot inhabit the position of the norm. Power, on this model, is repressive; it is negative and dis-enabling. However, in his landmark critique of what he refers to as 'the repressive hypothesis', Foucault (1980) has argued that power is productive rather than simply oppressive, that it constitutes rather than curtails (pre-discursive) meanings, identities, practices, forms of social relations. Moreover, like poststructuralist theorists more generally, Foucault is critical of dichotomous logic and its essentialising effects – of, for example, the (heteronormative) understanding of power and powerlessness as singular, definable, polarised entities. Emphasising the heterogeneous, contingent, contradictory and shifting character of social life he argues:

> ... *where there is power, there is resistance, and yet, or rather consequently, this resistance is never in a position of exteriority in relation to power ... The existence [of power relations] depends on a multiplicity of points of resistance: these play the role of adversary, target, support, or handle in power relations. These points of resistance are present everywhere in the power network. Hence there is no single locus of great Refusal ... or pure law of the revolutionary. Instead there is a plurality or resistances ... [which] by definition ... can only exist in the strategic field of power relations.* (1980/1976, 95–6)

In other words, for Foucault resistance is inextricable from power rather than being opposed to it. And since resistance is not, and cannot be, external to systems of power/knowledge then an oppositional politics which attempts to replace dominant ideologies with counter-hegemonic truths is inherently self-defeating because insofar as it enables 'one side to maintain its political purity at the expense of the other' (Whatling 1993, 194) it ultimately reproduces an Economy of the Same. This being the case, it follows that political goals or strategies that claim to be universally applicable need to give way to a plurality of heterogeneous and localised practices, the effects of which will never be singular nor entirely predictable in advance.

Rather than imagining – as some critics of S/M do – the existence of (pure revolutionary) sexual relations outside of and untouched by heteropatriarchy, Patrick Califia-Rice, one of S/M's most well-known proponents, argues that insofar as all sexuality is culturally shaped, it is impossible to posit an absolute distinction between the dichotomous logic that is a powerful part of S/M, and that of social relations more generally, informed as they are by a humanist epistemology. Hence, he asserts, there is no grounds for the claim that S/M 'is the result of institutionalised injustice to a greater extent than heterosexual marriage' (1996, 233). Rather than denying a connection between power and S/M, writers such as Califia argue that S/M's strength, its political potential, lies in its foregrounding of the constructedness of sexuality and its highly negotiated strategic re-enactment and re-inscription of dominant power relations. Patrick D. Hopkins takes a similar position, suggesting that S/M might be conceived as a simulation rather than a replication of heteropatriarchal values and relations. He writes:

> *SM participants do not rape, they do rape scenes ... do not enslave, they do slave scenes ... do not kidnap, they do capture and bondage scenes ... As with other kinds of ... simulations, there appear to be many similarities between the 'real' activity and the staged activity ... But similarity is not sufficient for replication. Core features of real patriarchal violence, coercive violence, are absent ... The interpretive context is different. The material conditions are different. (1994, 123–4)*

So, what does such simulation (have the potential to) achieve, and how does it achieve it? Writers such as Hopkins and Califia would argue that in some cases at least, S/M constitutes a working of sexuality and/or pleasure *against* identity, that it engenders queer affects. This kind of claim is founded on the conceptualisation of S/M roles as something other than the expression of an innate self – that in fact the performative character of such roles foregrounds the ways in which acts and gestures create the illusion of an innate core – and on the connected assumption that roles are therefore reversible or at least not as sedimented as social roles more generally seem to be. As Califia puts it, 'If you don't like being ... a bottom switch your keys. Try doing that with your biological sex or your race or your socioeconomic status' (1996, 233). Similarly, in keeping with his critique of the individualising effects of humanist discourses and discursive practices that surround and inform heteronormative conceptions of sexuality, Foucault states, 'the S&M game is very interesting because ... it is always fluid. Of course, there are roles, but everybody knows very well that those roles can be reversed' (1997, 169).[14]

---

14   One may well ask, as Leo Bersani does, whether or to what extent the reversal of roles, or the taking up of a position denied one in one's daily life, challenges the logic that informs hegemonic social relations. Bersani writes: 'in sadomasochism everyone gets a chance to put his or her boot in someone else's face – but why not question the value of putting on boots for that purpose in the first place?' (1995a, 18). Bersani also makes an insightful intervention into debates about power(lessness), erotic life and 'queer' politics in *Homos* (1995b).

Despite claims such as these, evidence suggests that not all S/M practitioners embrace the fluidity of roles, nor are they all interested in performing parodic deconstructions of heteronormative logic. Califia himself notes that unlike the San Francisco fisting community of the 1970s in which:

> ... *exclusive tops were thought to be brittle and pretentious; exclusive bottoms ... to be sexually boring and greedy ... The S/M community tends to be polarised with people identifying themselves as tops/sadists/dominants/ masters/mistresses or bottoms/masochists/submissives/slaves.* (1991, 231)

Even a brief look at S/M websites such as www.collarme.com tends to support this, with few members identifying as switches and the vast majority describing themselves as, for example, 'bisexual sissyboy *sub*', 'rubber *master*', 'straight male *bottom*', 'true *Dominant* Female' (my emphases). This tendency to conceive of one's self in fixed, singular, definable terms, to 'interpret ... performative experiences in terms of ... "SM souls" or "SM natures"' (Hopkins 1994, 136) is nowhere more apparent than in 'Submission', the first story in the 1991 BBC documentary *Pleasure and Pain*[15] in which we meet John and Sable, a submissive and a dominant respectively, who live their polarised identities in essentialised and essentialising ways. Whilst John is not always to be found suspended from the ceiling in a leather harness, tied to a crucifix clad only in the tiniest of leather briefs, or literally relegated to the doghouse, he nevertheless performs the role of submissive in almost every scene of the documentary – whilst washing the dishes, discussing films, going for walks, eating in restaurants and so on. In other words, John and Sable are what you might call 'hardcore', or '24/7' S/Mists for whom S/M is regarded as a reflection of their true selves rather than as something they indulge in now and again and/or in a variety of ways. Sable, for example, says 'I do not play out my role and neither does he [John]. It's got to be utterly real for both of us.' Similarly, of the 13 couples interviewed in Ted Polhemus's *Rituals of Love: Sexual Experiments, Erotic Possibilities* (1994) only two consider themselves to be switches. Of the others, four couples have reversed roles occasionally, but not, it seems, with much success. The remaining five couples are uninterested in, or even turned off by the thought of, role reversal.

Perhaps we can conclude from this that some people live their roles as an expression of what they believe to be their innate identities whereas others treat S/M as something more like a game in which it is possible to take up a variety of positions. The latter approach presupposes a level of flexibility, experimentation, malleability and agency not apparent in the former: it suggests that S/M is a game in which, to some extent at least, participants create their 'selves' at will.[16] This is the – somewhat optimistic, in my opinion – picture of S/M that Foucault paints in

---

15 *Pleasure and Pain* (1991) is part 2 of a series on masculinity entitled *From Wimps to Warriors*, a BBC production directed by Marc Munden and Penny Woolcock.

16 Clearly this process is not entirely open-ended since it is dictated, in often complex ways, by one's embodied history. See, for example, Duncan (1996); Wadiwel (this volume).

'Sex, Power, and the Politics of Identity' (1997), in which he characterises S/M as a subversive form of self-fashioning, or self-(trans)formation through the use of pleasure. Pleasure is of particular interest to Foucault because unlike the notion of desire, its discursive or conceptual history is such that it has not, he argues, become imbricated in hermeneutic logic. In an interview in a 1981 edition of *Mec* magazine Foucault claims that the term pleasure:

> ... escapes the medical and naturalistic connotations inherent in the notion of desire. That term [desire] has been used as a tool ... a calibration in terms of normality. Tell me what your desire is and I will tell you who you are, whether you are normal or not, and then I can qualify or disqualify your desire. The term pleasure on the other hand is virgin territory, almost devoid of meaning. There is no pathology of pleasure, no 'abnormal' pleasure. It is an event 'outside of the subject' or on the edge of the subject, within something that is neither body nor soul, which is neither inside nor outside, in short a notion which is neither ascribed nor ascribable. (cited in Macey 1993, 365)

Drawing on Foucault's work on the use of pleasure in Greco-Roman culture, David Halperin agrees, suggesting that the pleasures produced by practices such as fisting, anonymous sex, bondage and so on, function – however briefly – to 'shatter identity, and dissolve the subject' (1995, 95). In other words, such practices (can) work against the logic of heteronormative sex which ultimately serves to reproduce subjects (in the humanist sense).[17] Halperin substantiates this claim by arguing that unlike heterosexual coitus which tends to be end-driven, practices such as fisting or bondage do not necessarily lead to orgasm, reproduction and so on, but instead focus on the process of pleasure as something which occurs between bodies and/or body parts, and thus 'is not secreted by identity' (1995, 95). Further, illustrating Foucault's claim that S/M is 'a creative enterprise which has as one of its main features ... the *desexualisation* of pleasure' (1997, 165), Halperin notes that rather than being fixated on the genitals (as heteronormative sex is) and thus reaffirming sexual categorisations founded on object choice, S/M practices and pleasures are differentiated along 'dimensions that include preference for certain acts, certain zones or sensations, certain physical types ... certain symbolic investments, certain relations of age or power ... a certain number of participants, and so on' (Sedgwick

---

17   Calvin Thomas defines heteronormative sex as 'sex which ultimately serves to reproduce subjects' (2000, 33), that is, either off-spring, or hegemonic identities, or personages as Foucault might say. However, the question of what kinds of sex produce (solely) these effects, and what kinds of sex undermine this logic is, as this chapter argues, open to debate. For example, despite Halperin's claim that practices such as bondage can function to 'shatter identity and dissolve the subject' (1995, 95), Mansfield argues that 'the dispersal of the subject [in and through masochistic practices] does not preclude its centering ... The subject maintains a consistency of agency and intention that preserves a centred authoritarian subject at the same time ... [that it disperses itself]. It constantly initiates its own destruction with the reassertion of itself as goal, remaining consistently present throughout, at least as its throbbing narrative core' (1997, 19).

1990, 8). In this way, one could argue, S/M queers heteronormative identities and the practices and institutions that support them and are supported by them.

However, claiming that S/M can produce queer affects is not the same as saying that S/M is queer. The important difference here is that the former claim avoids reproducing universalising essentialist logic by acknowledging that S/M practices can and do engender heterogeneous affects. So, for example, whilst S/M practices performed by particular people in a particular context may not, as Halperin suggests, be fixated on the genitals, they may nevertheless reproduce heteronormative gender(ed) values. Evidence of such can be found in Califia's experience of the S/M community[18] in which it is 'still assume[d] that being penetrated is a submissive act and sticking it in is dominant' (1991, 230). Despite appearances to the contrary, this association of penetration with submission, inferiority and 'femininity' informs (and is reproduced by) Robert Hopcke's claim that S/M is a politically powerful practice for gay men, a poignant way to 'give a patriarchal, heterosexist society a stinging slap in the face by calling upon the masculine power of men's connection to men to break the boxes of immaturity and effeminacy into which gay men have been put' (1991, 71). What Hopcke implies, then, is that gay male S/M constitutes an 'unadulterated reclamation of masculinity' (1991, 71) in as much as it breaks the heteronormative association of submission and/or penetration with femininity: it gives gay men – even those who are submissive and/or penetrated – back their masculinity. In other words, bottoms need no longer feel inferior because they are, after all, masculine (at least, one presumes, if they are men). Employing the same sort of argument – which at one level may appear to be playing with and/or deconstructing dichotomous logic – Franko B., a self-identified top, questions the traditional association of powerlessness with submission, arguing that his partner Philip, a self-identified bottom, 'has more power because he's the one who allows me to do things to him' (cited in Polhemus 1994, 91). What is interesting, and perhaps telling, about these particular claims is the emphasis on autonomy, agency, maturity, power – characteristics or ideals traditionally associated with the humanist subject and thus with the Masculine. Ultimately, then, one might argue that such an emphasis sidesteps rather than critically interrogates the (negative) value of terms such as passivity, penetrability, objectivity, immaturity, inferiority and femininity, and as such (re)produces (amongst other things) affects that could be considered other than queer.

Rather than suggesting, then, as some critics have, that S/M either is or isn't queer, what I want to argue is first, that any attempt to furnish S/M with a definable, singular identity is inherently problematic, and second, that given this, the question(s) that drives queer critical practice should be what S/M – as a heterogeneous and open-ended set of historically and culturally situated practices – *does*, how it functions, what affects it produces, rather than what it is or what it means. S/M does not, and cannot, I would suggest, have a coherent identity, nor, despite characterisations to the contrary, do its advocates or its critics. Any attempt

---

18   Califia is referring to a particular community that existed in San Francisco in the 1990s.

to claim the opposite, to define a unified identity (for S/M and, by association, for oneself as an advocate or critic of S/M), to separate 'the pure' from 'the impure', to displace the 'impure' onto the outside, the other, necessarily fails, as Lynda Hart notes, to 'recognise the inherent contradiction of "epistemological resolution"' (1998, 60). Ironically – at least for those who object to S/M on the grounds that it is violent – such an approach, founded as it is on the 'metaphysics of presence', does violence to the other insofar as it constitutes the other as an isolated, one-dimensional, entirely knowable object whose value can without question, and in accordance with normative/normalising criteria that the one who judges assumes, be established. According to Derrida, metaphysics involves the construction of hierarchies and orders of subordination and the prioritisation of presence and purity at the expense of the contingent and the complicated. Metaphysical thought, or, if you prefer, heteronormative logic, always privileges one side of an opposition, and ignores or marginalises the alternative term of that opposition. In *Margins of Philosophy*, Derrida writes:

> *An opposition of metaphysical concept ... is never the face-to-face of two terms, but a hierarchy and an order of subordination. Deconstruction ... must, by means of a double gesture, a double science, a double writing, practise an overturning of the classical opposition, and a general displacement of the system. It is on that condition alone that deconstruction will provide the means of intervening in the field of oppositions it criticises. (1982, 195)*

As I understand it, then, queer practice, like deconstruction which 'bends all its efforts to cracking nutshells' (Caputo 1997, 32), is concerned with doing violence to the discursive mechanisms that are informed by and inform heteronormative logic and the forms of social life to which it gives rise. But in heeding Derrida's words we might remember that queer practice must involve a 'double gesture' rather than simply being an oppositional mode of engagement intentionally employed by an already constituted subject who is then reproduced in and through such a move. This double gesture is less a gesture of the subject than an affect which queers, 'break[s] open, shatter[s], stretch[es], expand[s], seduce[s], coerce[s], force[s] – if necessary – one's *own* ability to imagine alternatives to the rigid, limited, and impoverished sites of desire to which we have constrained ourselves' (Hart 1998, 68). For me, *Smack My Bitch Up* performs this double gesture, although never in the same way twice: each encounter with *Smack My Bitch Up* is different (for me), and yet each time I find myself *exposed* to something beyond the horizon of the 'same'. Each exposure affects and is affected by what Derrida refers to as *l'invention de l'autre* (the in-coming of the other): I am thrown up against myself, against the limits of my own imagination, I find myself constrained, bound, and at the same time, called to come/cum(?) – '*viens, oui, oui*' as Derrida (1995, 65) puts it. And this call is less an invitation than an interruption, a breaking open, a stretching, an expanding, a seduction, a coercion that performs, in one sense at least, the (potentially) queer affects of S/M that this chapter has attempted to articulate.

Acknowledgement

The author would like to thank Edinburgh University Press for granting permission to reprint material from Sullivan, N. (2003) 'Sadomasochism as Resistance?', in *A Critical Introduction to Queer Theory* (Edinburgh: Edinburgh University Press).

Suggested Further Reading

Foucault, M. (1988), 'Le Gai Savoir (I)', *Mec Magazine* 5 June, 32–6.
Halperin, D. (1996), 'The Queer Politics of Michel Foucault', in D. Morton (ed.), *The Material Queer: A Lesbigay Cultural Studies Reader* (Boulder, CO: Westview Press).
Hart, L. (1998), *Between the Body and the Flesh: Performing Sadomasochism* (New York: Columbia University Press).
Linden, R. et al. (eds) (1982), *Against Sadomasochism: A Radical Feminist Analysis* (San Francisco, CA: Frog in the Well).
Samois (eds) (1981), *Coming to Power* (Boston, MA: Alyson).

References

Antoniou, L. (1995), *Some Women* (New York: Masquerade Books).
Barthes, R. (1995/1970), *S/Z*, trans. R. Miller (New York: Hill and Wang).
Berlant, L. and M. Warner (1998) 'Sex in Public', *Critical Inquiry* 24:2, 547–66.
Bersani, L. (1995a), 'Foucault, Freud, Fantasy and Power', *GLQ: A Journal of Lesbian and Gay Studies* 2:1–2, 11–33.
—— (1995b), *Homos* (Cambridge, MA: Harvard University Press).
Califia, P. (1983), 'A Secret Side of Lesbian Sexuality', in T. Weinberg and G.W. Levi Kameli (eds), *S and M: Studies in Sadomasochism* (Buffalo, NY: Prometheus).
—— (1988), *Macho Sluts* (Boston, MA: Alyson).
—— (1991), 'The Limits of the S/M Relationship, or Mr Benson Doesn't Live Here Anymore', in M. Thompson (ed.), *Leather Folk: Radical Sex, People, Politics, and Practice* (Boston, MA: Alyson).
—— (1996), 'Feminism and Sadomasochism', in S. Jackson and S. Scott (eds), *Feminism and Sexuality: A Reader* (New York: Columbia University Press).
Caputo, J. (ed.) (1997), *Deconstruction in a Nutshell: A Conversation with Jacques Derrida* (New York: Fordham University Press).
Collarme.com, http://www.collarme.com (accessed 1 March 2006).
Crozier, I. (2004), 'Philosophy in the English Boudoir: Havelock Ellis, *Love and Pain*, and Sexological Discourses on Algophilia', *Journal of the History of Sexuality* 13:3, 275–305.

Daly, M. (1979), *Gyn/Ecology: The Metaethics of Radical Feminism* (London: The Women's Press).

Deleuze, G. (1989), *Masochism: Coldness and Cruelty and Venus in Furs*, trans. J. McNeil (New York: Zone Books).

Derrida, J. (1976), *Of Grammatology*, trans. G. Spivak (Baltimore, MD: The Johns Hopkins University Press).

—— (1982), *Margins of Philosophy*, trans. A. Bass (Chicago, IL: University of Chicago Press).

—— (1995), 'Passages: From Traumatism to Promise', in E. Weber (ed.), *Points ... Interviews, 1974–1994* (Stanford, CA: Stanford University Press).

Duncan, P.L. (1996), 'Identity, Power, and Difference: Negotiating Conflict in an S/M Dyke Community', in B. Beemyn and M. Eliason (eds), *Queer Studies: A Lesbian, Gay, Bisexual and Transgender Anthology* (New York: New York University Press).

Foucault, M. (1980/1976), *The History of Sexuality, Volume I: An Introduction*, trans. R. Hurley (New York: Vintage).

—— (1988), 'Le Gai Savoir (I)', *Mec Magazine* 5 (June), 32–6.

—— (1997), 'Sex, Power, and the Politics of Identity', in *Michel Foucault: Ethics, Subjectivity, and Truth*, (ed.), P. Rabinow (New York: The New Press).

Freud, S. (1955/1919), 'Child is Being Beaten: A Contribution to the Study of the Origin of Sexual Perversions', in *The Standard Edition of the Complete Psychological Works of Sigmund Freud*, ed. and trans. J. Strachey (London: Hogarth).

—— (1977/1905), 'Three Essays on the Theory of Sexuality', in *On Sexuality*, ed. and trans. A. Richards (Harmondsworth: Penguin Books).

—— (1984/1924), 'The Economic Problem of Masochism', in *On Metapsychology* (ed.), A. Richards, trans. J. Strachey (Harmondsworth: Penguin Books).

Halperin, D.M. (1995), *Saint Foucault: Towards A Gay Hagiography* (Oxford: Oxford University Press).

—— (1996), 'The Queer Politics of Michel Foucault', in D. Morton (ed.), *The Material Queer: A Lesbigay Cultural Studies Reader* (Boulder, CO: Westview Press).

Hart, L. (1998), *Between the Body and the Flesh: Performing Sadomasochism* (New York: Columbia University Press).

Hopcke, R.H. (1991), 'S/M and the Psychology of Male Initiation: An Archetypal Perspective', in M. Thompson (ed.), *Leatherfolk: Radical Sex, People, Politics, and Practice* (Boston, MA: Alyson).

Hopkins, P.D. (1994), 'Rethinking Sadomasochism: Feminism, Interpretation, and Simulation', *Hypatia* 9:1, 116–39.

Irigaray, L. (1985), *This Sex Which Is Not One* (Ithaca, NY: Cornell University Press).

Jagose, A. (1996a), *Queer Theory* (Melbourne: Melbourne University Press).

—— (1996b), 'Queer Theory', *Australian Humanities Review* 4 http://www.lib.latrobe.edu.au/AHR/archive/Issue-Dec-1996/jagose.html (accessed 1 March 2002).

Jakobsen, J.R. (1998), 'Queer Is? Queer Does?: Normativity and the Problem of Resistance', *GLQ: A Journal of Gay and Lesbian Studies* 4:4, 511–36.

Jeffreys, S. (1986), 'Sado-Masochism: The Erotic Cult of Fascism', *Lesbian Ethics* 2:1, 65–82.

—— (1993), *The Lesbian Heresy: A Feminist Perspective on the Lesbian Sexual Revolution* (Melbourne: Spinifex Press).

—— (1994), 'Sadomasochism, Art and the Lesbian Sexual Revolution', *Artlink* 14:1, 19–21.

—— (1998), 'Heterosexuality and the Desire for Gender', in D. Richardson (ed.), *Theorising Heterosexuality: Telling it Straight* (Buckingham: Open University Press).

Krafft-Ebing, R. von. (1965/1886), *Psychopathia Sexualis*, trans. F.S. Klaf (London: Staples Press).

Langdridge, D. and Butt, T. (2005), 'The Erotic Construction of Power Exchange', *Journal of Constructivist Psychology* 18, 65–73.

Macey, D. (1993), *The Lives of Michel Foucault* (New York: Pantheon Books).

Mansfield, N. (1997), *Masochism: The Art of Power* (Westport, CT: Praeger).

Merk, M. (1993), *Perversions: Deviant Readings* (New York and London: Routledge).

Pleasure and Pain (1991), dirs. M. Munden and P. Woolcock [documentary film].

Polhemus, T. and Randall, H. (1994), *Rituals of Love: Sexual Experiments, Erotic Possibilities* (London: Picador).

Prodigy, The (1997), 'Smack My Bitch Up', *The Fat of the Land* [music track].

Rechy, J. (1979), *The Sexual Outlaw* (London: Futura).

Russell, D. (1982), 'Sadomasochism: A Contra-Feminist Activity', in R. Linden et al. (eds), *Against Sadomasochism: A Radical Feminist Analysis* (San Francisco, CA: Frog in the Well).

Sacher-Masoch, L. von (1989/1869), *Venus in Furs*, trans. U. Moeller and L. Lindgren (New York: Blast Books).

—— (1996/1907), *The Master Masochist: Tales of Sadistic Mistresses*, trans. E.L. Randell and V. Howarth (London: Senate).

Sade, Marquis de (1965/1801), *The Complete Justine, Philosophy in the Bedroom, and Other Writings*, trans. R. Seaver and A. Wainhouse (New York: Grove Press).

—— (1966/1795), *The 120 Days of Sodom and Other Writings*, trans. R. Seaver and A. Wainhouse (New York: Grove Press).

Samois (eds) (1981), *Coming to Power: Writings and Graphics on Lesbian S/M* (Berkeley, CA: Samois).

Sedgwick, E.K. (1990), *The Epistemology of the Closet* (Berkeley, CA: University of California Press).

Simpsons, the (2006), 'Smack My Bitch Up', http://media-putfile.com/TheSimpsons--Smack-My-Bitch-Up (accessed 1 January 2005).

'Smack My Bitch Up' (1997), dir. Jonas Åkerlund [music video].

Smyth, C. (1996), 'What Is This Thing Called Queer?', in D. Morton (ed.), *The Material Queer: A LesBiGay Cultural Studies Reader* (Boulder, CO: Westview Press).

Sullivan, N. (1997), 'Fleshing Out Pleasure: Canonisation or Crucifixion?', *Australian Feminist Studies* 12:26, 283–92.

—— (1999), 'Queer Pleasure(s): Some Thoughts', *Social Semiotics* 9:2, 251–5.

——(2003), *A Critical Introduction to Queer Theory* (Edinburgh: Edinburgh University Press).

Thomas, C. (ed.) (2000), *Straight with a Twist: Queer Theory and the Subject of Heterosexuality* (Chicago, IL: University of Illinois Press).

Thompson, B. (1994), *Sadomasochism: Painful Perversion or Pleasurable Play?* (London: Cassell).

Whatling, C. (1993), 'Who's Read *Macho Sluts*?', in J. Still and M. Worton (eds), *Textuality and Sexuality: Reading Theories and Practices* (Manchester: Manchester University Press).

'Quare' Studies, or (Almost) Everything I Know about Queer Studies I Learned from My Grandmother[1]

E. Patrick Johnson

The following comments indicate something of the nuanced nature of the term queer:

> I'm more inclined to use the words 'black lesbian,' because when I hear the word queer I think of white, gay men. (Isling Mack-Nataf; quoted in Smyth 1996, 280)

> I define myself as gay mostly. I will not use queer because it is not part of my vernacular – but I have nothing against its use. The same debates around naming occur in the 'black community.' Naming is powerful. Black people and gay people constantly renaming ourselves is a way to shift power from whites and hets respectively. (Inge Blackman; quoted in Smyth 1996, 280)

> Personally speaking, I do not consider myself a 'queer' activist or, for that matter, a 'queer' anything. This is not because I do not consider myself an activist; in fact I hold my political work to be one of my most important contributions to all of my communities. But like other lesbian, gay, bisexual, and transgendered activists of colour, I find the label 'queer' fraught with unspoken assumptions which inhibit the radical political potential of this category. (Cohen 1997, 451)

---

1   A longer version of this chapter appeared in *Text and Performance Quarterly* 21:1 (January 2001) and in E.P. Johnson and M.G. Henderson (eds), *Black Queer Studies: A Critical Anthology*, edited by E. Patrick Johnson and Mae G. Henderson (Durham, NC: Duke University Press, 2005). It appears here with a new postscript.

Quare Etymology (With Apologies to Alice Walker [1983])

Quare (Kwâr), [adj.] 1. meaning queer; also, opp. of straight; odd or slightly off kilter; from the African American vernacular for queer; sometimes homophobic in usage, but always denotes excess incapable of being contained within conventional categories of being; curiously equivalent to the Anglo-Irish (and sometimes 'Black' Irish) variant of queer, as in Brendan Behan's famous play The Quare Fellow.

— n. 2. a lesbian, gay, bisexual, or transgendered person of colour who loves other men or women, sexually and/or nonsexually, and appreciates black culture and community.

— n. 3. One who thinks and feels and acts (and, sometimes, 'acts up'); committed to struggle against all forms of oppression – racial, sexual, gender, class, religious, etc.

— n. 4. One for whom sexual and gender identities always already intersect with racial subjectivity.

— n. 5. Quare is to Queer as 'reading' is to 'throwing shade'. (Johnson 1995)

I am going out on a limb. This is a precarious position, but the stakes are high enough to warrant risky business. The business to which I refer is reconceptualising the still incubating discipline called 'queer' studies. Now, what's in a name? This is an important question when, as James Baldwin proclaims, I have 'no name in the street' or, worse still, 'nobody *knows* my name' (1993; 1972). I used to answer to 'queer', but when I was hailed by that naming, interpellated in that moment, I felt as if I was being called 'out of my name'. I needed something with more 'soul', more 'bang', something closer to 'home'. It is my name after all!

Then I remembered how 'queer' is used in my family. My grandmother, for example, used it often when I was a child and still uses it today.[2] When she says the word, she does so in a thick, black, southern dialect: 'That sho'll is a "quare" chile.' Her use of 'queer' is almost always nuanced. Still, one might wonder, what, if anything, could a poor, black, 80-something, southern, homophobic woman teach her educated, middle-class, thirty-something, gay grandson about queer studies? Everything. Or *almost* everything. On the one hand, my grandmother uses 'quare' to denote something or someone who is odd, irregular or slightly off kilter – definitions in keeping with traditional understandings and uses of 'queer'. On the other hand, she also deploys 'quare' to connote something excessive – something that might philosophically translate into an excess of discursive and epistemological meanings grounded in African American cultural rituals and lived experience. Her knowing

---

2   My grandmother made her transition on 12 July 2004, before the publication of this
     volume. I dedicate this contribution in her memory.

or not knowing *vis-à-vis* 'quare' is predicated on her own 'multiple and complex social, historical, and cultural positionality' (Henderson 1992, 147). It is this culture-specific positionality that I find absent from the dominant and more conventional usage of 'queer', particularly in its most recent theoretical reappropriation in the academy.

I knew there was something to 'quare', that its implications reached far beyond my grandmother's front porch. Little did I know, however, that it would extend from her porch across the Atlantic. Then, I found 'quare' in Ireland.[3] In his *Quare Joyce*, Joseph Valente writes:

> ... *I have elected to use the Anglo-Irish epithet* quare *in the title as a kind of transnational/transidiomatic pun.* Quare, *meaning odd or strange, as in Brendan Behan's famous play,* The Quare Fellow, *has lately been appropriated as a distinctively Irish variant of* queer, *as in the recent prose collection* Quare Fellas, *whose editor, Brian Finnegan, reinterprets Behan's own usage of the term as having 'covertly alluded to his own sexuality'. (1998, 4; emphasis added)*

Valente's appropriation of the Irish epithet 'quare' to 'queerly' read James Joyce establishes a connection between race and ethnicity in relation to queer identity. Indeed, Valente's 'quare' reading of Joyce, when conjoined with my grandmother's 'quare' reading of those who are 'slightly off kilter', provides a strategy for reading racial and ethnic sexuality. Where the two uses of 'quare' diverge is in their deployment. Valente deploys quare to devise a queer literary exegesis of Joyce. Rather than drawing on 'quare' as a *literary* mode of reading/theorising, however, I draw upon the *vernacular* roots implicit in my grandmother's use of the word to devise a strategy for theorising racialised sexuality.

Because much of queer theory critically interrogates notions of selfhood, agency and experience, it is often unable to accommodate the issues faced by gays and lesbians of colour who come from 'raced' communities. Gloria Anzaldúa explicitly addresses this limitation when she warns that 'queer is used as a false unifying umbrella which all "queers" of all races, ethnicities and classes are shored under' (1991, 250). While acknowledging that 'at times we need this umbrella to solidify our ranks against outsiders', Anzaldúa nevertheless urges that 'even when we seek shelter under it ["queer"], we must not forget that it homogenises, erases our differences' (1991, 250).

'Quare', on the other hand, not only speaks across identities, it *articulates* identities as well. 'Quare' offers a way to critique stable notions of identity and, at the same time, to locate racialised and class knowledges. My project is one of recapitulation and recuperation. I want to maintain the inclusivity and playful

---

3   I have long known about the connection between African Americans and the Irish. As noted in the film *The Commitments* (1991): 'The Irish are the blacks of Europe'. The connection is there – that is, at least until the Irish became 'white'. For a sustained discussion of how Irish emigrants obtained 'white' racial privilege, see Ignatiev (1995).

spirit of 'queer' that animates much of queer theory, but I also want to jettison its homogenising tendencies. As a disciplinary expansion, then, I wish to 'quare' 'queer' such that ways of knowing are viewed both as discursively mediated and as historically situated and materially conditioned. This reconceptualisation foregrounds the ways in which LGBT people of colour come to sexual and racial knowledge. Moreover, quare studies acknowledges the different 'standpoints' found among lesbian, bisexual, gay and transgendered people of colour differences – differences that are also conditioned by class and gender (Collins 1995).

Quare studies is a theory of/for gays and lesbians of colour. Thus, I acknowledge that in my attempt to advance 'quare' studies, I run the risk of advancing another version of identity politics. Despite this, I find it necessary to traverse this political minefield in order to illuminate the ways in which some strands of queer theory fail to incorporate racialised sexuality. The theory that I advance is a 'theory in the flesh' (Moraga and Anzaldúa 1983, 23). Theories in the flesh emphasise the diversity within and among gays, bisexuals, lesbians and transgendered people of colour while simultaneously accounting for how racism and classism affect how we experience and theorise the world. Theories in the flesh also conjoin theory and practice through an embodied politic of resistance. This politics of resistance is manifest in vernacular traditions such as performance, folklore, literature and verbal art.

This chapter offers an extended meditation on and an intervention in queer theory and practice. I begin by mapping out a general history of queer theory's deployment in contemporary academic discourse, focusing on the lack of discourse on race and class within the queer theoretical paradigm. Following this, I offer an analysis of one queer theorist's (mis)reading of two black gay performances. Next, I propose an intervention in queer theory by outlining the components of quare theory, a theory that incorporates race and class as categories of analysis in the study of sexuality. Quare theory is then operationalised in the following section where I offer a quare reading of Marlon Riggs's film *Black Is ... Black Ain't*. The final section calls for a conjoining of academic praxis with political praxis.

'Race Trouble': Queer Studies or the Study of White Queers

At the moment when queer studies has gained momentum in the academy and forged a space as a legitimate disciplinary subject, much of the scholarship produced in its name elides issues of race and class. While the epigraphs that open this chapter suggest that 'queer' sometimes speaks across (homo)sexualities, they also suggest that 'queer' is not necessarily embraced by gays, bisexuals, lesbians and transgendered people of colour. Indeed, the statements of Mack-Nataf, Blackman and Cohen reflect a general suspicion of the term 'queer', that the term often displaces and rarely addresses their concerns.[4]

---

4   In *Bodies That Matter*, Judith Butler anticipates the contestability of 'queer', noting that it excludes as much as it includes but that such a contested term may energise a new

Indeed, some theorists identify 'queer' as a site of indeterminate possibility, a site where sexual practice does not necessarily determine one's status as queer. Lauren Berlant and Michael Warner argue that queer is 'more a matter of aspiration than it is the expression of an identity or a history' (1995, 344). Accordingly, straight-identified critic Calvin Thomas appropriates Judith Butler's notion of 'critical queerness' to suggest that 'just as there is more than one way to be "critical", there may be more than one (or two or three) to be "queer"' (1997, 83). But to riff off the now popular phrase 'gender trouble', *there is some 'race' trouble here with queer theory*. More particularly, in its 'race for theory' (Christian 1985, 51–63), queer theory has often failed to address the material realities of gays and lesbians of colour. As black British activist Helen (Charles) asks:

> *What happens to the definition of 'queer' when you're washing up or having a wank? When you're aware of misplacement or displacement in your colour, gender, identity? Do they get subsumed … into a homogeneous category, where class and other things that make up a cultural identity are ignored? (1993, 101–2)*

Beyond queer theory's failure to focus on materiality, it has also failed to acknowledge consistently and critically the intellectual, aesthetic and political contributions of non-white, non-middle-class LGBT people in the struggle against homophobia and oppression. Moreover, even when white queer theorists acknowledge these contributions, rarely do they self-consciously and overtly reflect on the ways in which their own whiteness informs their own critical queer position, and this is occurring at a time when naming one's positionality has become almost standard protocol in other areas of scholarship. Although there are exceptions, most often white queer theorists fail to acknowledge and address racial privilege.[5]

---

kind of political activism (1993, 228–9). Moreover, there are LGBT people of colour who embrace 'queer'. In my experience, however, those who embrace the term represent a small minority.

5   While it is true that many white queer theorists are self-reflexive about their own privilege and indeed incorporate the works and experiences of gays, bisexuals, lesbians and transgendered people of colour into their work, this is not the norm. Paula Moya calls attention to how the theorising of women of colour is appropriated by postmodernist theorists: '[Judith] Butler extracts one sentence from [Cherríe] Moraga, buries it in a footnote, and then misreads it in order to justify her own inability to account for the complex interrelations that structure various forms of human identity' (1997, 133). David Bergman (1991, 163–87) also offers a problematic reading of black gay fiction when he reads James Baldwin through the homophobic rhetoric of Eldridge Cleaver and theorises that black communities are more homophobic than whites ones. For other critiques of simplistic or dismissive readings of the works of gays, bisexuals, lesbians and transgendered people of colour see Helen (Charles) (1994); Vivian Namaste (2000) and Vivien Ng (1997). One notable exception is Ruth Goldman's 'Who is That *Queer* Queer', in which she, as a white bisexual, calls other white queer theorists to task for their failure to theorise their whiteness: 'those of us

Because LGBT people of colour often ground their theorising in a politics of identity, they frequently fall prey to accusations of 'essentialism' or 'anti-intellectualism'. Galvanising around identity, however, is not always an unintentional 'essentialist' move. Many times, it is an intentional strategic choice.[6] Cathy Cohen, for example, suggests that 'queer theorising which calls for the elimination of fixed categories seems to ignore the ways in which some traditional social identities and communal ties can, in fact, be important to one's survival' (1997 450). The 'communal ties' to which Cohen refers are those which exist in communities of colour across boundaries of sexuality. For example, my grandmother, who is homophobic, nonetheless must be included in the struggle against oppression in spite of her bigotry. While her homophobia must be critiqued, her feminist and race struggles over the course of her life have enabled me and others in my family to enact strategies of resistance against a number of oppressions, including homophobia. Some queer activist groups, however, have argued fervently for the disavowal of any alliance with heterosexuals, a disavowal that those of us who belong to communities of colour cannot necessarily afford to make.[7]

'Your Blues Ain't Like Mine': The Invalidation of 'Experience'

As a specific example of how some queer theorists (mis)read or minimise the work, lives and cultural production of gays, lesbians, bisexuals and transgendered people of colour and to lay the groundwork for a return to a focus on embodied performance as a critical praxis, I offer an analysis of one queer theorist's reading of black gay performance. In *The Ethics of Marginality*, for example, queer theorist John Champagne uses black gay theorists' objections to the photographs of Robert Mapplethorpe to call attention to the trouble with deploying 'experience' as evidentiary. Specifically, Champagne focuses on a speech delivered by Essex Hemphill, a black gay writer and activist, at the 1990 OUTWRITE conference of gay and lesbian writers. In his speech, Hemphill critiqued Mapplethorpe's photographs of black men.[8] Champagne takes exception to Hemphill's critique,

---

who are white tend not to dwell on our race, perhaps because this would only serve to normalise us – reduce our queerness, if you will' (1996, 169–82).

6   For more on 'strategic' essentialism, see Case (1996); de Lauretis (1989); Fuss (1989, 1–21).

7   For a sustained discussion of queer activists' disavowal of heterosexual political alliances, see Cohen (1997).

8   Robert Mapplethorpe's photographs of black gay men have been and continue to be the source of great controversy in the black gay community. The reactions to the photos range from outrage to ambivalence to appreciation. I believe the most complex reading of Mapplethorpe is found in Isaac Julien and Kobena Mercer's essay 'True Confessions: A Discourse on Images of Black Male Sexuality', in which they write: 'While we recognise

arguing that Hemphill's reading is 'monolithic' and bespeaks 'a largely untheorised relation between desire, representation, and the political' (1995, 59). What I wish to interrogate, however, is Champagne's reading of Hemphill's apparent 'emotionality' during the speech.

In Champagne's account, Hemphill began to cry during his speech, to which there were two responses: one of sympathy/empathy and one of protest. Commenting on an overheard conversation between two whites in the audience, Champagne writes, 'Although I agreed with much of the substance of this person's comments concerning race relations in the gay and lesbian community, I was suspicious of the almost masochistic pleasure released in and through this public declaration of white culpability' (1995, 58). I find it surprising that Champagne would characterise what appears to be white *reflexivity* about racial and class privilege as 'masochistic' given how rare such self-reflexivity is in the academy and elsewhere. After characterising as masochistic the two whites who sympathetically align themselves with Hemphill, Champagne aligns himself with the one person who displayed vocal disapproval by booing at Hemphill's speech:

> *I have to admit that I admired the bravura of the lone booer. I disagreed with Hemphill's readings of the photographs, and felt that his tears were an attempt to shame the audience into refusing to interrogate the terms of his address. If, as Gayatri Spivak has suggested, we might term the politics of an explanation the means by which it secures its particular mode of being in the world, the politics of Hemphill's reading of Mapplethorpe might be described as the politics of tears, a politics that assures the validity of its produced explanation by appealing to some kind of 'authentic', universal, and (thus) uninterrogated 'human' emotion of experience. (1995, 58–9)*

Champagne's own 'bravura' in *his* reading of Hemphill's tears illuminates the ways in which many queer theorists, in their quest to move beyond the body, ground their critique in the discursive rather than the corporeal. I suggest that the two terrains are not mutually exclusive, but rather stand in a dialogical/dialectical relationship to one another. What about the authenticity of pain, for example, that may supersede the cognitive and emerges from the heart – not *for* display but *despite* display? What is the significance of a black *man* crying in public? We must grant each other time and space not only to talk *of* the body, but through it as well.[9] In Champagne's formulation, however, bodily 'experience' is anti-intellectual and Hemphill's 'black' bodily experience is manipulative. This seems to be an

---

the oppressive dimension of these images of black men as Other, we are also attracted: We want to look but don't always find the images we want to see. This ambivalent mixture of attraction and repulsion goes for images of black gay men in porn generally, but the inscribed or preferred meanings of these images are not fixed; they can at times, be pried apart into alternative readings when different experiences are brought to bear on their interpretation' (1991, 170).

9 I thank Soyini Madison for raising this issue.

unself-reflexive, if not unfair, assumption to make when, for the most part, white bodies are discursively and corporeally naturalised as universal. Historically, white bodies have not been trafficked, violated, burned and dragged behind trucks because they embody racialised identities. In Champagne's analysis of 'blackness', bodily 'whiteness' goes uninterrogated.[10]

In order to posit an alternative reading of Hemphill's tears, I turn to bell hooks's insights regarding the ways in which whites often misread emotionality elicited through black cultural aesthetics. 'In the context of white institutions, particularly universities', hooks writes, 'that mode of address is questionable precisely because it moves people. Style is equated in such a setting with a lack of substance' (1990, 21). hooks believes that this transformation of cultural space requires an 'audience [to] shift … paradigms' and, in that way, 'a marginal aspect of black cultural identity [is] centralised' (1990, 22). Unlike Champagne's own diminution of the 'subversive powers [and politics] of style' (1995, 127–8), hooks affirms the transgressive and transformative potential of style, citing it as 'one example of counter-hegemonic cultural practice' as well as 'an insertion of radical black subjectivity' (1990, 22) Despite Champagne's statements to the contrary, his own reading of Hemphill constitutes himself as a 'sovereign subject' within his theory of anti-subjectivity, a positionality that renders him 'overseer' of black cultural practices and discourse. On the other hand, Hemphill's tears, as a performance of black style that draws upon emotionality, may be read as more than simply a wilful act of manipulation to substantiate the black gay 'experience' of subjugation and objectification. More complexly, it may be read as a 'confrontation with difference which takes place on new ground, in that counter-hegemonic marginal space where radical black subjectivity is *seen*, not overseen by any authoritative Other claiming to know us better than we know ourselves' (hooks 1990, 22) In his 'reading' of Hemphill, Champagne positions himself as 'authoritative Other', assuming, as he does, the motivation behind Hemphill's tears.[11]

Unlike Champagne's deployment of queer theory, the model of quare studies that I propose would not only critique the concept of 'race' as historically contingent and socially and culturally constructed/performed, it would also address the material effects of race in a white supremacist society. Quare studies requires an acknowledgement by the critic of her position within an oppressive system.

---

10 I am speaking specifically about the historical devaluing of black bodies. In no way do I mean to deny that white gay, lesbian, bisexual and transgendered people have been emotionally, psychologically and physically harmed. The recent murder of Matthew Shepard is a sad testament to this fact. Indeed, given the ways in which his attackers killed him (tying him to a post, beating him and leaving him for dead), there is a way in which we may read Shepard's murder through a racial lens. What I am suggesting, however, is that racial violence (or the threat of it) is enacted upon 'black' bodies in different ways and for different reasons than it is on 'white' bodies.

11 'Emotionality' as manipulative or putatively repugnant may also be read through the lens of gender. Generally understood as a weak (read feminine) gender performance, emotional display among men of any race or sexual orientation represents a threat to heteronormativity and therefore is usually met with disapproval.

To fail to do so would, as Ruth Goldman argues, '[leave] the burden of dealing with difference on the people who are themselves different, while simultaneously allowing white academics to construct a discourse of silence around race and other queer perspectives' (1996, 173). One's 'experience' within that system, however discursively mediated, is also materially conditioned. A critic cannot ethically and responsibly speak from a privileged place, as Champagne does, and not own up to that privilege. To do so is to maintain the force of hegemonic whiteness, which, until very recently, has gone uninterrogated.[12]

Seeing Through Quare Eyes: Reading Marlon Riggs's *Black Is ... Black Ain't*

In Riggs's documentary, *Black Is ... Black Ain't*, we find an example of quare theory operationalised. Thus, in order to demonstrate the possibilities of quare, I turn now to an analysis of this film. Completed after Riggs's death in 1994, this documentary chronicles Riggs's battle with AIDS and also serves as a meditation on the embattled status of black identity. *Black Is ... Black Ain't* 'quares' 'queer' by suggesting that identity, although highly contested, manifests itself in the flesh and, therefore, has social and political consequences for those who live in that flesh. Further 'quaring' queer, the film also allows for agency and authority by visually privileging Riggs's AIDS experience narrative. Indeed, the film's documentation of Riggs's declining health suggests an identity and a body in the process of *being* and *becoming*. Quare theory elucidates the mechanics of this both/and identity formation, and, in so doing, it challenges a static reading of identity as only performativity or only performance.

Initially, I focus on how the film engages performativity, focusing as it does on problematising notions of essential blackness. One of the ways in which the film engages this critique is by pointing out how, at the very least, gender, class, sexuality and region all impact the construction of blackness. Indeed, the title of the film points to the ways in which race defines, as well as confines, African Americans. The recurrent trope used by Riggs to illuminate the multiplicity of blackness is gumbo, a dish that consists of whatever the cook wishes. It has, Riggs remarks, 'everything you can imagine in it'. This trope also underscores the multiplicity of blackness insofar as gumbo is a dish associated with New Orleans, a city confounded by its mixed raced progeny and the identity politics that mixing creates. The gumbo trope is apropos because, like 'blackness', gumbo is a site of possibilities. The film argues that when African Americans attempt to define what it means to be black, they delimit the possibilities of what blackness can be. But Riggs's film does more than just stir things up. In many ways it reduces the heat of the pot, allowing everything

---

12 For examples of white critics who interrogate 'whiteness' as an obligatory and universalising trope, see Frankenberg (1997); Hill (1997); Roediger (1994).

in the gumbo to mix and mesh, yet maintain its own distinct flavour. Chicken is distinct from andouille sausage, rice from peas, bay leaves from thyme, cayenne from paprika. Thus, Riggs's film suggests that African Americans cannot begin to ask dominant culture to accept their difference as 'others' nor their humanity until African Americans accept the differences that exist among themselves.

Class represents a significant axis of divisiveness within black communities. As Martin Favor (1999) persuasively argues, 'authentic' blackness is most often associated with the 'folk' or, working-class blacks. Moreover, art forms such as the blues and folklore that are associated with the black working class are also viewed as more genuinely black. This association of the folk with black authenticity necessarily renders the black middle class as inauthentic and apolitical. In *Black Is ... Black Ain't*, Riggs intervenes in this construction of the black middle class as 'less black', by featuring a potpourri of blacks from various backgrounds. Importantly, those who might be considered a part of the 'folk' questionably offer some of the most anti-black sentiments, while those black figures most celebrated in the film – Angela Davis, Barbara Smith, Michele Wallace and Cornel West – are of the baby boomer generation. Riggs undermines the idea that 'authentic' blackness belongs to the black working class by prominently displaying interviews with Angela Davis, Michelle Wallace and Barbara Smith. While ostracised for attending integrated schools and speaking Standard English or another language altogether, these women deny that their blackness was ever compromised. The film critiques hegemonic notions of blackness based on class status by locating the founding moment of black pride and radical black activism within black middle-class communities in the 1960s, thereby reminding us that 'middle-class' is also an ideological construct as contingently constituted as other social and subject positionalities.

Riggs also unhinges the link between hegemonic masculinity and authentic blackness. By excerpting misogynist speeches by Louis Farrakhan, a southern black preacher, and the leader of an 'African' village located in South Carolina, and by juxtaposing them with the personal narratives of bell hooks and Angela Davis, Riggs undermines the historical equation of 'real' blackness with black masculinity. The narrative hooks relates regarding her mother's spousal abuse is intercut with and undercuts Farrakhan's sexist and misogynist justification of Mike Tyson's sexual advances that eventually led to his being accused of and convicted for raping Desiree Washington. The narrative set forth by hooks story also brackets the sexism inherent in the black preacher's and African leader's justification of the subjugation of women based on biblical and African mythology. Musically framing this montage of narratives is rap artist Queen Latifah's performance of 'U-N-I-T-Y', a song that urges black women to 'let black men know you ain't a bitch or a "ho"'. Riggs's decision to use Latifah's song to administer this critique is interesting on a number of levels. Namely, Latifah's own public persona, as well as her television and motion picture roles, embody a highly masculinised femininity or, alternatively what Judith Halberstam might call 'female masculinity' (1998, 1–42). Riggs uses Latifah's song and the invocation of her persona, then, in the service of further disrupting hegemonic constructions of black masculinity, as well as illuminating the sexism found within the black community.

While I find the film's critique of essentialised blackness persuasive, I find its critique of homophobia in the black community and its demand for a space for homosexual identity within constructions of blackness even more compelling. As a rhetorical strategy, Riggs first points to those signifiers of blackness that build community (e.g. language, music, food and religion). Indeed, the opening of the film with the chant-like call and response of black folk preaching references a communal cultural site instantly recognisable to many African Americans. But just as the black church has been a political and social force in the struggle for the racial freedom of its constituents, it has also, to a large extent, occluded sexual freedom for many of its practitioners, namely gays and lesbians. Thus, in those opening scenes, Riggs calls attention to the double standard found within the black church by exemplifying how blackness can 'build you up, or bring you down', hold you in high esteem or hold you in contempt. Riggs not only calls attention to the racism of whites, he also calls attention to homophobia in the black community and particularly in the black church. Throughout the film, however, Riggs challenges the traditional construction of the black church by featuring a black gay and lesbian church service. Given the black church's typical stance on homosexuality, some might view this avowal of Christianity as an instance of false consciousness. I argue, however, that these black gay men and lesbians are employing disidentification insofar as they value the cultural rituals of the black worship service yet resist the fundamentalism of its message. In the end, the film intervenes in the construction of black homosexuality as anti-black by propagating gay Christianity as a legitimate signifier of blackness.

Riggs's film implicitly employs performativity to suggest that we dismantle hierarchies that privilege particular black positionalities at the expense of others, that we recognise that darker hue does not give us any more cultural capital or claim to blackness than does a dashiki, braids or a southern accent. Masculinity is no more a signifier of blackness than femininity; heterosexuality is no blacker than homosexuality; and living in the projects makes you no more authentically black than owning a house in the suburbs. Indeed, what Riggs suggests is that we move beyond these categories, these hierarchies that define and confine in order to realise that, depending on where you are from and where you are going, black is and black ain't.

While the film critically interrogates cleavages among blacks, it also exposes the social, political, economic and psychological effects of racism, and the role it has played in defining blackness. By adopting this dual focus rather than exclusively interrogating black discursivity, Riggs offers a perspective that is decidedly quare. He calls attention to differences among blacks and between blacks and their 'others';[13] he grounds blackness in lived experience; and he calls attention to the consequences of embodied blackness. The montage of footage from the LA riots and

---

13   Paul Gilroy's construction of the 'Diaspora' functions similarly to what I mean here in that he propagates that 'Diaspora' 'allows for a complex conception of sameness and an idea of solidarity that does not repress the differences within in order to maximise the differences between one "essential" community and others' (1995, 24).

interviews with young black men who characterise themselves as 'gang bangers' bring into clear focus the material reality of black America and how the black body has historically been the site of violence and trauma.

Nowhere in the film is a black body historicised more pointedly and powerfully, however, than in the scenes where Riggs is featured walking through the forest naked or narrating from his hospital bed from which his t-cell count is constantly announced. According to Riggs, these scenes are important because he wants to make the point that not until we expose ourselves to one another will we be able to communicate effectively across our differences. Riggs's intentions notwithstanding, his naked black body serves another function within the context of the film. It is simultaneously in a state of being *and* becoming. I intend here to disrupt both these terms by refusing to privilege identity as either solely performance or solely performativity and by demonstrating the dialogic/dialectic relationship of these two tropes.

Paul Gilroy's theory of diaspora is useful in clarifying the difference between being and becoming. According to Gilroy, 'Diaspora accentuates *becoming* rather than *being* and identity conceived diasporically, along these lines, resists reification' (1995, 24). Here, Gilroy associates 'being' with the transhistorical and transcendental subject and 'becoming' with historical situatedness and contingency. In what follows, I supplement Gilroy's use of both terms by suggesting that 'being' and 'becoming' are sites of performance *and* performativity. I construe 'being' as a site of infinite signification *as well as* bodily and material presence. 'Being' calls the viewer's attention not only to 'blackness' as discourse, but also to embodied blackness in that moment where discourse and flesh conjoin in performance. If we look beyond Riggs's intent to 'expose' himself to encourage cross-difference communication, we find that his nakedness in the woods functions ideologically in ways that he may not wish. For example, his nakedness may conjure up the racist stereotype of the lurking, bestial, and virile black male that became popular in the eighteenth- and nineteenth-century American imaginary. On the other hand, his embodied blackness in the woods and in his hospital bed also indicate a diseased body that is fragile, vulnerable, and a site of trauma, a site that grounds black discursivity materially in the flesh. At the literal level, Riggs's black male body is exposed as fragile and vulnerable, but it also synecdochically stands in for a larger body of racist discourse on the black male body in motion. This trope of black bodily kinaesthetics is manifest in various forms (e.g. the vernacular expression 'keep the nigger running', the image of the fugitive slave, and contemporary, hypermasculinised images of black athletes). Racist readings of Riggs's black male body are made possible by the context in which Riggs's body appears, the woods. Within this setting, blackness becomes problematically aligned with nature, reinscribing the black body as bestial and primal. This imagery works against Riggs's intentions – namely, running naked in the woods as a way to work through the tangled and knotty web that is identity. Indeed, the images of Riggs running naked through the woods signify in multiple troubling ways that, once let loose, cannot be contained by either Riggs's authorial intentions or the viewer's gaze. The beauty of *being*, however, is that where it crumbles under the weight of deconstruction, it reemerges in all its bodily facticity. Although Riggs's body signifies in ways that constrain his agency, his embodied blackness also enlivens a discussion of a 'fleshy' nature. Whatever his body signifies, the viewer cannot escape its material presence.

Riggs's body is also a site of *becoming*. He dies before the film is completed. Riggs's body physically 'fades away', but its phantom is reconstituted in our current discourse on AIDS, race, gender, class and sexuality. Thus, Riggs's body discursively rematerialises and intervenes in hegemonic formulations of blackness, homosexuality and the HIV-infected person. As a filmic performance, *Black Is ... Black Ain't* resurrects Riggs's body such that when the film is screened in universities, shown to health care providers, viewed in black communities or rebroadcast on PBS where it debuted, the terms and the stakes for how we think about identity and its relation to HIV/AIDS are altered. Like Toni Morrison's character Sula, Riggs dreams of water carrying him over that liminal threshold where the water 'would envelop [him], carry [him], and wash [his] tired flesh always' (1973, 149). After her death, Sula promises to tell her best friend Nel, that death did not hurt, ironically announcing her physical death alongside her spiritual rebirthing. Her rebirthing is symbolised by her assuming a foetal position and travelling 'over and down the tunnels, just missing the dark walls, down, down until she met a rain scent and would know the water was near' (1973, 149). Riggs dreams of a similar journey through water. In his dream, Harriet Tubman serves as a midwife cradling his head at the tunnel's opening and helps him make the journey. Once on the other side, Riggs, like Sula, lives on and also makes good on his promise to return through his living spirit captured in the film. The residual traces of Riggs's body become embedded in the ideological battle over identity claims and the discourse surrounding the disproportionate number of AIDS-infected people of colour. His becoming, then, belies our being.

Ultimately, *Black Is ... Black Ain't* performs what its title announces: the simultaneity of bodily presence and absence, being and becoming. Although Riggs offers his own gumbo recipe that stands in for blackness, he does so only to demonstrate that, like blackness, the recipe can be altered, expanded, reduced, watered down. At the same time, Riggs also asks that we not forget that the gumbo (blackness) is contained within a sturdy pot (the body) that has weathered abuse, that has been scorched, scoured and scraped, a pot/body that is in the process of becoming, but nonetheless *is*.

Unlike queer theory, quare theory fixes our attention on the discursive constitution of the recipe even as it celebrates the improvisational aspects of the gumbo and the materiality of the pot. While queer theory has opened up new possibilities for theorising gender and sexuality, like a pot of gumbo cooked too quickly, it has failed to live up to its critical potential by refusing *all* the queer ingredients contained inside its theoretical pot. Quare theory, on the other hand, promises to reduce the spillage, allowing the various and multiple flavours to co-exist – those different flavours that make it spicy, hot, unique and sumptuously brown.

Unconvinced that queer studies, theory and activism are soon to change, I summon quare studies as an interventionist disciplinary project. Quare studies addresses the concerns and needs of gay, lesbian, bisexual and transgendered people across issues of race, gender, class as well as other identities and subject positions. While attending to discursive fields of knowledge, quare studies is also committed to theorising the practice of everyday life. Because we exist in discursive as well as material bodies, we need a theory that speaks to that reality. Indeed, quare studies may breathe new life into our 'dead' (or deadly) stratagems of survival.

Postscript (20 December 2006)

I began writing 'Quare Studies' out of a sense of urgency. It was the late 1990s and queer theory was all the rage. The work of Judith Butler, David Halperin, Eve Sedgwick, Michael Warner and others had intervened in the academy's myopic focus on gender and directed our attention to ways that sexuality provided yet another rich site from which to theorise power relations and identity politics. The reappropriation of the term 'queer' as a signifier of indeterminacy became the salvo for theorists who wanted to avoid the essentialist/anti-essentialist trappings of identity politics debates. Thus, the term made it possible to theorise sexuality in ways that revolutionised our thinking about sexuality and gender, specifically, and identity in general. This theorising then became codified as a field of study as it gained momentum in the academy and claimed its space as a legitimate disciplinary subject. Many of us who identified as queer finally felt that the academy was going to take seriously the study of sexuality in ways that expanded rather than foreclosed the ways that it intersected with other identity markers and fields of study.

Not only were we wrong, but also we had underestimated the extent to which queer studies would calcify into a homogenous rather heterogeneous signifier of sexuality – a move, incidentally, Judith Butler herself foretold when she wrote: 'The term [queer] will be revised, dispelled, rendered obsolete to the extent that it yields to the demands which resist the term precisely because of the exclusions by which it is mobilised' (1993, 229). The latter part of Butler's statement – 'the exclusions by which it is mobilised' – turned out to be more than just a premonition as it soon became apparent to queer scholars of colour, including myself, that queer theory and the attendant field of enquiry, queer studies, was a one trick pony. That is, sexuality and sexuality alone would be the sign under which queer was mobilised. Moreover, queer studies was merely a euphemism for the study of white queers in general, and more specifically, white queer men.

The realisation that queer studies as a praxis was not going to account for race and class was hard to swallow, especially given the fact that so many queers of colour had produced work demonstrative of the spirit of the term's boundarylessness and political efficacy. Moreover, those of us who grew up in black, brown and working-class neighbourhoods understood that the history of race relations in the United States demanded from its disenfranchised a coalitional political agenda that reached across various identity markers that did not necessarily transcend difference from within. Rather, the demand was to grapple with that difference –

identitarian, ideological and political – to productive ends with the knowledge that sometimes the coalition would fail. After all, people of colour are also perpetuators of sexism, classism and homophobia. Nonetheless, historically, the political, social, cultural and economic return on an investment in coalitional movements has been worth the investment.

The urgency in writing 'Quare' then, emerged from my desire to speak truth to power. Indeed, I wanted the piece to serve as a prolegomenon to a broader conversation about the politics of queer studies and queer theory and to raise the question: who does this new field of study benefit – inside and outside of the academy? In the midst of writing the essay (and submitting it to several journals that rejected it), another idea came to me. I decided that an essay would not be enough – that there should be a national conference on the topic of queer studies that focused on race and class. Thus, Mae Henderson and I convened the Black Queer Studies in the Millennium Conference on 4–7 April 2000 at the University of North Carolina at Chapel Hill. This interdisciplinary conference brought together scholars from English, film studies, black studies, public policy, legal studies, cultural studies, performance studies, creative writing and pedagogical studies and proved a historic moment at the *fin de siècle*.

Since the 2000 conference, the scholarship in queer studies that accounts for race and class has increased exponentially, including my own co-edited volume with Mae Henderson, *Black Queer Studies: A Critical Anthology*, published by Duke University Press in 2005 and based on the conference.[14] In the spring of 2008 in Chicago, a conference on black and Latino/a sexuality was hosted by various institutions in Chicago and funded in part by the Ford Foundation. The production of books, essays, journal issues and conferences on this topic is a hopeful indication that – at least in the academy – the call for inclusion and for a discussion of race and class within sexuality studies has been heard.

My manifesto in 'Quare Studies', however, was not just a call for a paradigm shift within the academy, but outside it as well. I call for a critical quare *praxis* that would disavow bourgeois and esoteric understandings of racialised and classed sexualities in favour of pragmatic and material solutions to issues facing queer communities of colour. This is an area in which I still see a lack of commitment. The resurgence of AIDS/HIV infections among black Americans – both men and women – indicates that not enough work is being done by academics to deploy their knowledge beyond the ivory tower. The 'Down Low' phenomenon, for instance, was a missed opportunity for queer academics to intervene in the discourse about how men who have sex with men but who do not identify as gay complicate

---

14   In addition to our volume, Dwight McBride and Jennifer Brody co-edited a special issue of *Callaloo* entitled, 'Plum Nelly' (2000), which features essays solely devoted to black queer studies. There are other monographs and essays published over the past seven years, but are too numerous to mention all of them. Some of them include Quiroga (2000); Reid-Pharr (2001); Manalansan IV (2003); Ferguson (2005); McBride (2005); Stockton (2006). The noticeable absences in this list of course are texts by lesbians of colour.

rigid notions about sexual identity because of their race and class. Instead, the media hijacked the public discourse and self-serving opportunists like J.L. King, a 'recovering' down low brother, profited from the media frenzy by disseminating simplistic and sensational discourse about this community of sexual dissidents.[15] This is but one example of the ways in which academics failed to be on the frontlines of issues on the outside of the academy.

My grandmother passed away on 12 July 2004 at the age of 90. Her life was no less quare than her death. After a prolonged illness and having outlived all of her children except for one – my mother – my grandmother waited until my sister, with whom she was living in her final days, left her bedside before taking her last breath. She told my sister, 'Go check the mail for your sweepstakes check'. This was a running joke in my family because we were always hoping that somehow a miracle visit from Ed McMahon would deliver us from poverty. We knew that this was merely a pipe dream, but we half jokingly held onto it throughout my childhood. In the time it took my sister to walk to the mailbox and back, my grandmother made her transition. I do not believe that this was a coincidence. My grandmother wanted to die the way she had lived – with pride and on her own terms. My hope is that queer/quare studies follows the example of my grandmother by maintaining a sense of hope in the midst of despair, while also keeping one foot grounded in the work that must be done.

Suggested Further Reading

Charles, H. (1993), 'Queer Nigger: Theorizing "White" Activism', in J. Bistow and A. Wilson (eds), *Activating Theory: Lesbian, Gay, Bisexual Politics* (London: Lawrence and Wishart).

Cohen, C. (1997), 'Punks, Bulldaggers, and Welfare Queens: The Radical Potential of Queer Politics?', *GLQ: A Journal of Lesbian and Gay Studies* 3, 437–65.

Ferguson, R. (2005), *Aberrations in Black: Toward a Queer of Color Critique* (Minneapolis, MN: University of Minnesota Press).

Johnson, E.P. and Henderson, M.G. (eds) (2005), *Black Queer Studies: A Critical Anthology* (Durham, NC: Duke University Press).

McBride, D.A. (2005), *Why I Hate Abercrombie and Fitch: Essays on Race and Sexuality* (New York: New York University Press).

---

15   For media coverage of the down low phenomenon, see Venable (2001); Denizet-Lewis (2003); Smith (2004); King (2005; 2006). See also Raimondo (this volume).

References

Anzaldúa, G. (1991), 'To(o) Queer the Writer: Loca, escrita y chicana', in B. Warland (ed.), *Inversions: Writings by Dykes, Queers and Lesbians* (Vancouver: Press Gang).

Baldwin, J. (1972), *No Name in the Street* (New York: Dial).

—— (1993), *Nobody Knows My Name: More Notes of a Native Son* (New York: Vintage).

Bergman, D. (1991), *Gaiety Transfigured: Gay Self-Representation in American Literature* (Madison, WI: University of Wisconsin Press).

Berlant, L. and Warner, M. (1995), 'What Does Queer Theory Teach Us about "X"?', *PMLA* 110:3, 343–9.

Black Is ... Black Ain't (1995), dir. M. Riggs [documentary film].

Brody, J.D. and McBride, D.A. (eds) (2000), 'Plum Nelly: New Writings in Black Queer Studies', a special issue of *Callaloo* 23.1.

Burke, K. (1967), *Philosophy of Literary Form* (Baton Rouge, LA: Louisiana State University Press).

Butler, J. (1993), *Bodies That Matter: On the Discursive Limits of 'Sex'* (New York: Routledge).

Case, S-E. (1996), *The Domain Matrix: Performing Lesbian at the End of Print Culture* (Bloomington, IN: Indiana University Press).

Champagne, J. (1995), *The Ethics of Marginality: A New Approach to Gay Studies* (Minneapolis, MN: University of Minnesota Press).

Charles, H. (1993), 'Queer Nigger: Theorizing "White" Activism', in J. Bistow and A. Wilson (eds), *Activating Theory: Lesbian, Gay, Bisexual Politics* (London: Lawrence and Wishart).

Christian, B. (1985), 'The Race for Theory', *Cultural Critique* 6, 51–63.

Clarke, C. (1983), 'The Failure to Transform: Homophobia in the Black Community', in B. Smith (ed.), *Home Girls: A Black Feminist Anthology* (New York: Kitchen Table).

Cohen, C. (1997), 'Punks, Bulldaggers, and Welfare Queens: The Radical Potential of Queer Politics?', *GLQ: A Journal of Lesbian and Gay Studies* 3, 437–65.

—— (1999), *Boundaries of Blackness: AIDS and the Breakdown of Black Politics* (Chicago, IL: University of Chicago Press).

Collins, P.H. (1995), 'The Social Construction of Black Feminist Thought', B. Guy-Sheftall (ed.), *Words of Fire: An Anthology of African-American Feminist Thought* (New York: New Press).

Commitments, The (1991), dir. A. Parker [feature film].

Crenshaw, K.W. (1991), 'Mapping the Margins: Intersectionality, Identity Politics, and Violence Against Women of Color', *Stanford Law Review* 43, 1241–99.

De Lauretis, T. (1989), 'The Essence of the Triangle, or Taking the Risk of Essentialism Seriously: Feminist Theory in Italy, the U.S. and Britain', *differences: A Journal of Feminist Cultural Studies* 1:2, 3–37.

Denizet-Lewis, B. (3 August 2003), 'Double Lives on the Down Low', *New York Times Magazine*, 28–33, 48, 52–3.

Favor, M. (1999), *Authentic Blackness: The Folk in the New Negro Renaissance* (Durham, NC: Duke University Press).

Ferguson, R. (2005), *Aberrations in Black: Toward a Queer of Color Critique* (Minneapolis, MN: University of Minnesota Press).

Frankenberg, R. (ed.) (1997), *Displacing Whiteness: Essay in Social and Cultural Criticism* (Durham, NC: Duke University Press).

Fuss, D. (1989), *Essentially Speaking: Feminism, Nature and Difference* (New York: Routledge).

Gilroy, P. (1995), 'To Be Real: The Dissident Forms of Black Expressive Culture', in C. Ugwu (ed.), *Let's Get It On: The Politics of Black Performance* (Seattle, WA: Bay Press).

Goldman, R. (1996), 'Who Is That Queer Queer?', in B. Beemyn and M. Eliason (eds), *Queer Studies: A Lesbian, Gay, Bisexual and Transgender Anthology* (New York: New York University Press).

Halberstam, J. (1998), *Female Masculinity* (Durham, NC: Duke University Press).

Henderson, M.G. (1992), 'Speaking in Tongues', in J. Butler and J.W. Scott (eds), *Feminists Theorize the Political* (New York: Routledge).

Hill, M. (ed.) (1997), *Whiteness: A Critical Reader* (New York: New York University Press).

hooks, b. (1990), *Yearning* (Boston, MA: South End Press).

Ignatiev, N. (1995), *How the Irish Became White* (New York: Routledge).

Johnson, E.P. (1995), 'Snap! Culture: A Different Kind of Reading', *Text and Performance Quarterly* 3, 121–42.

—— and Henderson, M.G. (eds) (2005), *Black Queer Studies: A Critical Anthology*, (Durham, NC: Duke University Press).

Julien, I. and Mercer, K. (1991), 'True Confessions: A Discourse on Images of Black Male Sexuality', in E. Hemphill (ed.), *Brother to Brother: New Writings by Black Gay Men* (Boston, MA: Alyson).

King, J.L. (2005), *On the Down Low: A Journey into the Lives of 'Straight' Black Men* (New York: Harlem Moon).

—— (2006), *Coming up from the Down Low: The Journey to Acceptance, Healing, and Honest Love* (New York: Three Rivers Press).

Latifah, Q. (1993), 'U.N.I.T.Y.', on *Black Reign* [music album].

Manalansan IV, M. (2003), *Global Divas: Filipino Gay Men in the Diaspora* (Durham, NC: Duke University Press).

McBride, D.A. (2005), *Why I Hate Abercrombie and Fitch: Essays on Race and Sexuality* (New York: New York University Press).

Moraga, C. and Anzaldúa, G. (1983), *This Bridge Called My Back: Writings by Radical Women of Color* (New York: Kitchen Table Press).

Morrison, T. (1973), *Sula* (New York: Knopf).

Moya. P. (1997), 'Postmodernism, "Realism", and the Politics of Identity Cherríe Moraga and Chicano Feminism', in M.J. Alexander and C.T. Mohanty (eds), *Feminist Genealogies, Colonial Legacies, Democratic Futures* (New York: Routledge).

Namaste, V. (2000), *Invisible Lives: The Erasure of Transsexual and Transgendered People* (Chicago, IL: University of Chicago Press).

Ng, V. (1997) 'Race Matters', in A. Medhurst and S.R. Munt (eds), *Lesbian and Gay Studies: A Critical Introduction* (London: Cassell).

Quiroga, J. (2000), *Tropics of Desire: Interventions from Queer Latino America* (New York: New York University Press).

Reid-Pharr, R. (2001), *Black Gay Man: Essays* (New York: New York University Press).

Roediger, D. (1994), *Towards the Abolition of Whiteness* (London: Verso).

Scott, J.W. (1992), 'Experience', in J. Butler and J.W. Scott (eds), *Feminists Theorize the Political* (New York: Routledge).

Simmons, R. (1991), 'Some Thoughts on the Issues Facing Black Gay Intellectuals', in E. Hemphill (ed.), *Brother to Brother: New Writings by Black Gay Men* (Boston, MA: Alyson).

Smith, B. (1983), 'Home', in B. Smith (ed.), *Home Girls: A Black Feminist Anthology* (New York: Kitchen Table).

Smith, T. (August 2004), 'Deadly Deception: Men on the Down Low View Dishonesty as Survival', *Essence*, 148–51.

Smyth, C. (1996), 'What Is This Thing Called Queer?', in D. Morton (ed.), *Material Queer: A LesBiGay Cultural Studies Reader* (Boulder, CO: Westview).

Stockton, K.B. (2006), *Beautiful Bottom, Beautiful Shame: Where 'Black' Meets 'Queer'* (Durham, NC: Duke University Press).

Thomas, C. (1997), 'Straight with a Twist: Queer Theory and the Subject of Heterosexuality', in T. Foster, C. Siegel, and E.E. Berry (eds), *The Gay '90's: Disciplinary and Interdisciplinary Formations in Queer Studies* (New York: New York University Press).

Valente, J. (1998), 'Joyce's (Sexual) Choices: A Historical Overview', in J. Valente (ed.), *Quare Joyce* (Ann Arbor, MI: University of Michigan Press).

Venable, M. (July 2001), 'A Question of Identity', *Vibe*, 98–108.

Walker, A. (1983), *In Search of Our Mother's Gardens: Womanist Prose* (San Diego, CA: Harcourt Brace Jovanich).

'A Strange Perversity': Bringing Out Desire between Women in *Frankenstein*

Mair Rigby

Paying attention to the women in Mary Shelley's *Frankenstein* opens a space for demonstrating a productive relationship between queer theory and lesbian-feminist critical approaches. Despite the theoretical tensions that mark this encounter, I contend that the insistence upon creating radically different, disruptive and perverse readings, which is characteristic of both fields of enquiry, can pave the way towards a newly constructive alliance. A queer and lesbian reading makes it possible to foreground the significance of relations between women in a text which initially appears to be dominated by powerful male desires. There is also scope to twist existing feminist perspectives in exciting new directions and show how queer critical practices work to unravel the heteronormative interpretative paradigms that so often silently govern acceptable ways of reading.[1] Offering close readings of the relationships between Victor Frankenstein's mother, Caroline, his adopted sister and sweetheart, Elizabeth Lavenza, and the family servant, Justine Moritz, my approach works with a series of perceptual shifts. Reading the novel from off-centre lesbian and queer angles, I explore moments at which it is possible to perceive a slippage between friendship, female identification and ambiguous but dynamic same-sex desires.

Frann Michel's illuminating essay, 'Lesbian Panic in Mary Shelley's *Frankenstein*' (1999), provides a point of departure for this discussion. Reading the novel in relation to 'cultural representations of horror associated with the late eighteenth- and early nineteenth-century's newly constructed role of the sapphist' (1999, 239–40), Michel brings back into view the 'horror of sapphic agency' (1999, 241) that surrounds and informs the text. I will expand upon the ramifications of her claim that the novel

---

1   I use the term 'heteronormativity' here to refer to the network of norms which make 'heterosex the normal term, the commonsensical position, unremarkable and everyday, in relation to which nonheterosex is queer, odd, to be commented on and policed' (Jakobsen 1998, 518).

'reveals a triangulated and mediated relationship – a relation of difference and, potentially, of desire – among Elizabeth, Justine, and Caroline' (1999, 244). I will also engage more fully with her final observation that the text opens up 'specular questions about how relations between women are and are not to be seen, and how they are (not) seen by critics' (1999, 250). This point raises further important questions about the relationship between queer and lesbian reading, for queer scholarship has not always 'seen' lesbian possibilities.

Queer criticism has been attracted to *Frankenstein* for the text's representation of monstrosity and excess, as well as its interest in desire, power and transgression. The novel was first published in 1818 and revised for the 1831 third edition.[2] On the surface it does appear to be very much 'a novel about men' (Michel 1999, 238). Opening with the explorer Captain Walton finding Victor Frankenstein in the Arctic Circle, the story is ostensibly presented as a warning against overreaching ambition. Victor recounts the obsession with creating life that leads to the birth of a monster from whom he flees in horror. The vengeful Monster returns, murders Victor's younger brother, frames Justine for the crime and threatens more destruction if Victor will not provide him with a companion. When Victor fails to complete this task the Monster murders Victor's closest friend and Elizabeth. Victor then pursues the Monster into the Arctic where, on Walton's ship, Victor dies, following which, the repentant Monster decides to burn himself to death. In terms of queer readings, recent *Frankenstein* scholarship has drawn largely upon the work of Eve Kosofsky Sedgwick, developing her analysis of male homosocial culture, homoerotic desire, homosexual panic and homophobia within the nineteenth-century 'paranoid Gothic'.[3] While this work has been tremendously productive, it has enacted a tendency to privilege male narratives, a trend which lesbian-feminist critics, such as Terry Castle, have identified and critiqued in queer theory more generally.[4]

---

2   In this chapter, I use the 1831 revised edition as the base text because I think it is the one with which most general readers will be familiar, but where relevant I will also refer to differences in the 1818 first edition. In recent years, there has been debate concerning the advantages of the 1818 version. Nora Crook (2003) explores the debate and challenges some assumptions.

3   It has become relatively common to read *Frankenstein* in the light of the 'paranoid Gothic': the 'literary genre' in which Sedgwick argues that 'homophobia found its most apt and ramified embodiment' (1991, 186). In *The Coherence of Gothic Conventions* (1986), Sedgwick goes so far as to call the nineteenth century the 'Age of Frankenstein', a period 'distinctly and rhetorically marked by the absolute omnipresence of homophobic paranoid tableaus such as that of Victor and the Monster pursuing each other across the Arctic Ice' (1986, x). See also the chapter 'Toward the Gothic' in her book *Between Men* (1985). For further discussions along these lines, see McGavran (1999); Daffron (1999). Eberle-Sinatra (2005) is helpful in illustrating why this text has been so productive in relation to readings of male homosexuality.

4   Castle argues that the term 'queer' 'makes it easy to enfold female homosexuality back "into" male homosexuality and disembody the lesbian once again'. She finds herself at odds with queer theory which, in her view, 'in its Sedgwickian incarnation' seems to 'denote primarily the study of male homosexuality' (1993, 12, 13).

Queer theory and lesbian studies have often been at odds with each other. While lesbian-feminist theorists have been accused of holding essentialist notions of female and lesbian subjectivity and adhering to an outmoded identity politics, they have argued that queer theory has misrepresented the complexities of their earlier work, demonstrated a generally masculinist bias and elided the specificity of lesbian experience. In response, I situate this chapter within a growing body of work challenging the either/or model and arguing that queer and lesbian approaches can inform and play off one another in more productive ways.[5] I conceptualise queer reading as a position of strategic critical resistance to 'the normal, the legitimate, the dominant', which is never conceptualised only in negative terms because, as David Halperin insists, it is vital that resistance to heteronormativity remain 'positive and dynamic and creative' (1995, 62, 66). Without losing sight of queer theory's interrogation of sexual identity, its power to expose the heterosexual matrix, its interest in performativity and emphasis upon creating alternative readings, I want to offer a 'queer-lesbian' reading which privileges a focus on female relations and puts the term 'lesbian' back at the forefront of the analysis.[6] For the purposes of this chapter, I conceive queer-lesbian reading as an approach that re-deploys queer and lesbian theories in order to perform a different kind of resistant, creative reading.

An alliance between queer theory's interest in the discursive and historical production of sexual identity and lesbian theory's focus on female subjectivity and women's relationships could extend both fields of enquiry. With respect to female desire, *Frankenstein* also raises queer theoretical and lesbian-feminist concerns about reading and visibility in relation to the discourses through which desire between women has been made culturally intelligible. It is important to consider how this text engages with what Valerie Traub calls 'the historical production of lesbian possibility (and impossibility)', and how it provides opportunities for examining 'the conditions of intelligibility whereby female-female intimacies gain, or fail to gain, cultural signification' (2002, 34, 28). There is more to be said on the subject of 'lesbian panic'. Misha Kavka identifies a discernible 'lesbian register' in the Gothic, at least since Samuel Taylor Coleridge's 1816 poem *Christabel* (2002, 223). The threat of sapphic monstrosity and the panic it elicits may be more strongly foregrounded

---

5   Linda Garber discusses the history of this debate in her book *Identity Poetics* and argues that 'the lesbian feminism/Queer Theory polarisation is overwrought and unproductive' (2001, 1). Instead, she proposes an approach which 'refuses the either/or choice of lesbian feminism versus queer theory, in favour of a both/and option that asserts the right to a healthy skepticism in both directions' (2001, 6). As Noreen Giffney and Katherine O'Donnell explain, this kind of approach places 'the term lesbian at the center of analysis, whether as a materiality, concept, category of investigation, identity, political position or object choice' and regards past lesbian feminist work as 'something to be cherished and not denigrated' (2007, 7, 9). See also Halberstam (1996); Malinowitz (1996).

6   I take up the term 'queer lesbian' from Judith Halberstam who argues for a 'queer-lesbian studies' in which the term 'lesbian' modifies and qualifies 'queer', while the term 'queer' challenges 'the stability of identities subsumed by the label "lesbian"' (1996, 259).

in *Christabel*, but a discourse of anxiety about relations between women also lurks at the margins of *Frankenstein*. This text, in which there are no identifiable modern 'lesbians', actually has much to reveal about the way in which desire between women has been historically constructed as both something that should not be seen and a monstrous threat to the male-dominated world.

So Much Do I Esteem and Value Her

Due to the fact that is so often asserted that women are marginalised in *Frankenstein*, my proposed intention to excavate evidence of desire between them might initially appear to be a strange and perverse critical aim. If such desire is discernible, it is certainly more elusive than that which is readable between the men because the women clearly occupy more circumscribed positions. In *Frankenstein* criticism, it is not uncommon to read statements such as 'Shelley had rendered women absent from her novel' (Eberle-Sinatra 1998, 262). Since some of the most influential work on the text tends towards variations on this theme, to reiterate the exclusion of women yet again would not contribute anything new to the discussion. Moreover, the charge of *who* renders women absent from the novel should not, I think, be laid entirely at Mary Shelley's door. As Michel observes, feminist readings often repeat 'the novel's evasions', and a radical 'optical shift' will therefore be necessary 'to perceive even the (foreclosed) possibility of erotic relations between women … marginalised as they are by the homophobic and heterosexist paradigms both critiqued and constructed in the novel' (1999, 243, 241). She refers here not only to the text itself, but also to the heterosexist paradigms underscoring critical responses which 'replicate' and 'exacerbate those patterns' (1999, 241). We might ask, then, whether questions of female same-sex desire have been ignored in feminist and psychoanalytic readings of *Frankenstein* because there is nothing to be seen in the text, or because such readings have replicated, consciously or unconsciously, the cultural 'ghosting' which has long constituted desire between women as that which is not to be seen.[7]

For this reason, it is important to remember that literary criticism is itself *performative*, insofar as it is a discursive *practice* that creates, reiterates and conceals certain norms and normal ways of reading.[8] For instance, the repeated claim

---

7   In *The Apparitional Lesbian* Terry Castle explores the various ways in which lesbians and lesbian possibilities have been '"ghosted" – or made to seem invisible by the culture itself' (1993, 4).

8   Judith Butler describes performativity as the 'reiterative and citational practice by which discourse produces the effects that it names' (1993a, 2). In speech/act theory, a performative is a form of speech that enacts or *does* something. A useful way to think about the performativity of literary criticism might be to keep in mind the questions posed by Eve Kosofsky Sedgwick and Andrew Parker at the very beginning of their book on the subject: 'When is saying something doing something? And how is saying something doing something?' (Parker and Sedgwick 1995, 1).

that women are excluded in *Frankenstein* to some extent produces that sense of exclusion and reiterates (performs) what has become a critical norm. From a queer perspective, the performative reiteration of female marginalisation needs to be challenged if it discourages readers from interpreting the text on any other terms and occludes alternative reading possibilities. We should be aware that, as Michel implies above, criticism has itself tended to perform, replicate and normalise heteronormative and lesbophobic ways of reading. But queer theory, with its own performative masculinist bias, has also often allowed women to drop out of the picture.[9] Lesbian reading possibilities are therefore trebly marginalised by heteronormative *and* queer reading conventions, not to mention all the other 'well-established precepts, practices, and discursive conventions ... devoted to the supervision and confinement of women' (Hunt; quoted in Lochrie 1999, 304). When it comes to reading relations between women, we can therefore expect to be confronted with many voices informing us, directly and indirectly, that there is nothing of significance to be seen in the text.

The performativity of queer-lesbian reading should be emphasised because it is in the self-reflexive act of rendering the performance of queer-lesbian reading *visible* that it becomes possible to 'out' the often occluded performance of heteronormative and lesbophobic reading. In this respect, it can be called an 'ethical' approach, in terms of J. Hillis Miller's understanding of ethical reading as reading that takes responsibility for what it is attempting to *do* and the changes it is trying to effect.[10] I think 'perverse' is an appropriate term with which to describe my performative ethical reading strategy, drawing as I do upon lesbian theorist Bonnie Zimmerman's concept of 'perverse reading'. Zimmerman reclaims a word 'defined by the dictionary as "wilfully determined not to do what is expected or desired" ... a perverse reader is one highly conscious of her own agency' (1993, 139). To call a methodology 'perverse', in this sense, provides us with a way to think about queer-lesbian reading as a conscious and necessary determination to perform 'unexpected' readings which push beyond the sexually normalising strategies, and male-centred narratives, that can be found within the text and responses to the text. Appropriately, to claim a 'perverse' position also has connotations of being 'difficult', for the performance of queer-lesbian reading should not make people comfortable. As an approach, or set of approaches, it offers challenges to heterosexual, feminist, lesbian and queer reading.

---

9   In discussing how 'sodomy' has come to be understood as 'male same-sex acts and desires' (1999, 296), Karma Lochrie's raises significant points about why and how women tend to drop out of male-centred queer analysis.

10   By the 'ethics of reading', Hillis Miller means 'that aspect of the act of reading in which there is a response to the text that is both necessitated, in the sense that it is a response to an irresistible demand, and free, in the sense that I must take responsibility for my response and for the further effects, "interpersonal", institutional, social, political or historical, of my act of reading, for example as that act takes the form of teaching or of published commentary on a given text. What happens when I read *must* happen, but I must acknowledge it as *my* act of reading' (1987, 43).

To perform a queer-lesbian reading of *Frankenstein* is not to attempt to discover modern 'lesbians' in the text; it is rather to consider how historical discourses about desire between women inform the novel and shape reading possibilities. Queer-lesbian reading does therefore necessitate a 'woman seeing' perspective (Zimmerman 1993, 137) which values female relationships. Adrienne Rich's theory of 'woman identification' within the 'lesbian continuum' is useful in this instance, for it is possible to trace a story of female-identified-experience in *Frankenstein* when we focus upon narrative instances of 'primary intensity' between and among women.[11] The women in the novel can be placed within Rich's – admittedly broad – lesbian continuum in terms of sharing an emotional life, giving and receiving practical support and, to an extent, bonding against male tyranny. Caroline Frankenstein constructs a supportive group of women in the family, adopting Elizabeth because she 'had much desire to have a daughter' (33), and later including Justine as a privileged servant. She becomes mother, aunt and protectoress for Elizabeth and Justine, who are sisters and friends to each other. The text certainly contains a powerful representation of courageous female friendship when Elizabeth defends Justine after she is accused of murdering William. This lone act of defence can be read as an instance of female resistance to heteropatriarchal power relations. In court, she bases her assumption of Justine's innocence upon the quality of her relationships with other women: 'She nursed Madame Frankenstein, my aunt, in her last illness, with the greatest affection and care, and afterwards attended her own mother during a tedious illness' (82). Her argument that Justine cannot be a murderer because she cares for women opens a point in the narrative where it is possible to glimpse an alternative story in which women are defined by their relations to one another, rather than to men. At this moment, the text briefly reveals what might be called a 'lesbosocial' narrative in which relations between women are privileged, although sublimated by a male narrative. Whether or not these relationships are ultimately read as encompassing a charge of desire, they do appear to constitute a largely engulfed, but just visible, alternative story about the attachments between three women.

Yet, until recently, the significance of the women's story has been largely ignored. For instance, feminist critic Kate Ellis argues that the character of Safie, who runs away from her tyrannical father in search of her lover Felix, displays an independence that 'would be unthinkable to Elizabeth' (1979, 126). Her conclusion is a good example of performative heterocentrism within literary criticism. To identify female agency and independence only in the context of heterosexual romance is to perform a heteronormative reading of the text, replicating the larger, and not at all innocent, cultural tendency to trivialise and silence relations between women. It

---

11 Rich uses the phrase 'lesbian continuum' to denote a wide range of woman-identified experience, while 'woman identification' is understood as 'a source of energy, a potential springhead of female power, curtailed and contained under the institution of heterosexuality' (1993, 244). She refers to lesbian possibility as 'an engulfed continent which rises fragmentally into view from time to time only to become submerged again' (1993, 238).

is important to remember that, as Michel Foucault observes, silence 'is an element that functions alongside the things said, with them and in relation to them within over-all strategies' (1998, 27). It is imperative that queer-lesbian approaches attempt to expose the 'over-all strategies' and knowledge/power relations informing critical decisions about the significance, or lack of significance, of female relationships in texts. Consciously or unconsciously, Ellis performs a silencing strategy, replicating the dominant view that, when it comes to relations between women, there is probably nothing to be seen. But, from a queer-lesbian counter perspective, we could argue that Elizabeth actually displays a radical independence which would be unthinkable to Safie.

Although Adrienne Rich's work has been very influential within lesbian studies, she has been critiqued within queer studies for her perceived essentialism, as well as for collapsing lesbian sexual specificity into more generalised forms of female homosocial bonding.[12] However, in the interests of esteeming and valuing, rather than denigrating, the work of lesbian theorists, I want to reassert the radically queer implications of her refusal to draw a firm line between erotic and non-erotic female relationships. Rich's refusal is radical because women's relationships have historically been made intelligible in relation to a conceptual division between non-sexual friendship and proscribed sexual relations.[13] In *The Renaissance of Lesbianism*, Traub describes the genealogy of female same-sex desire, from the early modern period onwards, as being fashioned out of two rhetorics: 'a medico-satiric discourse of the [sexually active] tribade, and a literary-philosophical discourse of idealized [chaste] friendship' (2002, 8). The notion of such a divide has allowed 'lesbian' possibilities to be subsumed and contained but, at the same time, has haunted the representation of supposedly chaste friendships with a construction of same-sex desire as a monstrous possibility. Viewing the division itself as a disciplinary practice, queer-lesbian reading should expose the effects of this performative discourse by attending to textual moments where the lines are blurred and anxieties surrounding female bonding feed into fears about sapphic monstrosity.

'Lesbian panic' can be described as women's phobic responses to the possibility or actuality of female same-sex desire.[14] Expressions of 'horror, dismay, and

---

12   Essentialism can be described as 'a belief in a naturalised identity, a self that exists prior to socialisation, springing from an internal core into the social world', whereas for poststructuralist queer theorists, 'the social world constructs through language, the categories within which we make ourselves intelligible to ourselves' (Malinowitz 1996, 267). Linda Garber challenges the view that lesbian writers like Rich are as essentialist as they have been perceived to be. See especially her first chapter, 'The Social Construction of Lesbian Feminism', in *Identity Poetics* (2001, 10–30).

13   In her book *Surpassing the Love of Men* (1985), Lillian Faderman was the first critic to offer an in-depth historical analysis of the ways in which relations between women have been imagined, constructed and categorised into acceptable and unacceptable forms of behaviour.

14   Patricia Juliana Smith offers a more detailed definition: 'In terms of narrative, lesbian panic is, quite simply, the disruptive action or reaction that occurs when a character – or conceivably, an author – is either unable or unwilling to confront or reveal her own

embarrassment' at 'legibly sapphic engagements' (Michel 1999, 239) represent visibly phobic responses to the possibility of sexual relations between women. However, it is important to take into account the more covert and insidious effects of lesbian panic, especially within the kind of disavowing responses that tend to be set up as commonsensical positions. For instance, in her literary biography of Mary Shelley, Muriel Spark writes, 'It should be recognised that Mary was a little in love with Jane, if that phrase can be used about two women without implication of abnormal behaviour' (1987, 116). From a queer-lesbian perspective, the resistance to sex between women implied in Spark's disavowal of 'abnormal behaviour' causes the biographical text to reveal its performance in 'lesbian panic'. Spark's comment is also striking in the context of Traub's argument that the conditions for modern lesbian possibilities have been created through an encounter between discourses of 'harmless friendship' and ideologies 'interpreting female intimacy as a problem in need of social discipline' (2002, 19). For as Shelley's relationship with Jane Williams is read as a chaste friendship haunted by 'abnormal' behaviours, we see lesbian possibilities and impossibilities constructed in relation to the conventions of this ideological encounter. Unless we cultivate an awareness of the various ways in which lesbian panic and more generally phobic discourses about relations between women continue to inform the way we read, we will not be able to appreciate fully the way such discourses work within the text.

In *Frankenstein*, representations of heterosexualised feminine submissiveness can actually be de-stabilised when close attention is paid to subtextual undercurrents in relations between women. The death of Caroline is one such pressure point in the text. This statement might appear unlikely because Caroline is also represented as a feminine stereotype and her death seems a conventional case of self-sacrifice, but close examination reveals another, or perhaps an *othered*, story within Victor's narrative. In one of several scenes in which male authorities are presented trying to block female relations, Elizabeth contracts scarlet fever and the men of the family try to prevent Caroline from nursing her. At first she 'yielded to our intreaties', but there is a limit to her obedience: 'when she heard that the life of her favourite was menaced, she could no longer control her anxiety' (42). Caroline saves Elizabeth and 'the consequences of this imprudence were fatal to her preserver' (42). This incident is altered from the 1818 version, which reads, 'when she heard that her favourite was recovering, she could no longer debar herself from her society, and entered her chamber long before the danger of infection was past' (26). Depending on the reader's response, the 1818 version could cause Caroline's death to appear somewhat frivolous. But it could also enhance a reading of love between women, if it suggests she cannot bear to be out of Elizabeth's company for long. Still, in both versions, Victor tells a story about over-emotional femininity causing unnecessary death through irrational behaviour. If we read 'perversely' beyond the terms of his

lesbianism or lesbian desire ... In any instance, the character is led by her sense of panic to commit irrational or illogical acts that inevitably work to the disadvantage or harm of herself or others' (1995, 569).

blinkered and blinkering narrative, not only does this moment appear instead as a case of intense love between women, it hints at more troubling possibilities.

In a culture in which lesbian possibility has long been discursively produced as a form of resistance to men, the bonds between women suggest a deeper threat to the male-dominated world lurking in the textual background.[15] Caroline's death has the potential to fracture the assumption of female submission because the crucial male element is missing from the heteronormative equation: she does *not* sacrifice herself for a man, but for a woman. I want to emphasise the important sentence which slips past almost unnoticed: 'the life of *her favourite* was menaced' (42; my emphasis). The problem, in heteropatriarchal terms, is not that Caroline is not devoted and self-sacrificial, but rather that she sacrifices herself for the wrong person, abandoning the male members of her family in the saving of her *favourite* – her much desired 'daughter'. Implicitly accusing Elizabeth of stealing Caroline's affections and life from the family, Victor really hints at his own anxiety when he says 'she could no longer control her anxiety' and labels her action as 'imprudence'. Out of control, imprudent, blinded by her attachment to Elizabeth, perhaps Caroline manipulates the stereotypical role, only to deviate from the male imperative; her feminine performance could then mask a primary attachment to another woman. Once such cultural anxieties are brought back into view, Victor's comments appear symptomatic of a wider fear that the 'primary threat' of female bonding is 'the elimination of the male' (Straayer; quoted in Berenstein 1995, 255). Although this possibility cannot be spoken directly, the performative language of avoidance, the reiterative sublimating and trivialising of relations between women, can be read as the unacknowledged language of lesbian phobia.

In the context of silencing strategies, it is intriguing to note the way the text is altered in Kenneth Branagh's film adaptation *Mary Shelley's Frankenstein* (1992). Presenting a heteropatriarchal fantasy in which Caroline (Cherie Lunghi) dies in childbirth begging Alphonse (Ian Holm) to kill her in order that the baby son might live, the film shifts her death from a female-identified tragedy to male-identified maternal sacrifice. Eberle-Sinatra observes that this film demonstrates a 'strict heterosexual agenda' (1998, 253). In this case, it is appropriate that it also works to render relationships between women unimportant, except insofar as they serve male-dominated narratives. Of course one might argue that the filmmakers simply could not see far enough beyond heterosexual cinematic paradigms to ascribe importance to the details of Caroline's death in the novel. Then again, perhaps the alteration from novel to film can be placed within a spectrum of phobic responses, inasmuch as the drive to sublimate or erase the disruptive potential of female bonding is an aspect of a more general lesbian phobia. But, while Branagh's film circumvents the issue, the novel can be read, at least in part, as a story about the problems involved in representing and reading love between women.

---

15   Terry Castle observes, 'It would be putting it mildly to say that the lesbian represents a threat to patriarchal protocol: Western civilization has for centuries been haunted by a fear of "women without men" – of women indifferent or resistant to male desire' (1993, 4–5).

Remembering Justine Moritz

In the 1818 edition of *Frankenstein*, Elizabeth writes to Victor, 'Do you not remember Justine Moritz? Probably you do not' (46). Her answer to her own question serves as a reminder that Justine is not only one of the most marginalised figures in the novel, but also one whose significance is often passed over in critical readings.[16] She should not be so easily dismissed and I want to emphasise the importance of remembering and re-negotiating Justine's position. From a queer-lesbian perspective, she is actually one of the more intriguing figures in *Frankenstein*, not least because both queer and lesbian readings have always regarded marginality as a source of productive possibilities. It is worth noting that the power of a perceptual shift is emphasised more than once in relation to Justine. Elizabeth tells us that 'through a strange perversity, her mother could not endure her' (63). Here it seems the reader is meant to understand that her bad mother's 'strange perversity' has led to her rejection, but from the rejecting mother's point of view, it is Justine who embodies the 'strange perversity' or, in other words, the alarming 'queerness'. By calling attention to the fact that there is another way of reading – a 'perverse' perspective – not only does Justine's story illustrate possibilities for perverse reading, she also has something to reveal about the dangers of being read queerly.

Although she is undeniably feminine and submissive, Justine is positioned as a site of potential sex and gender trouble in the text and, as such, it is not in fact surprising when she is touched by the Monster, condemned and executed. Judith Butler notes that in a culture in which gender is a '*compulsory* performance ... acting out of line with heterosexual norms brings with it ostracism, punishment, and violence' (1991, 24). The fact that Justine suffers 'ostracism, punishment, and violence' suggests that there is indeed something 'out of line' about her 'performance'. Like the Monster, she is a marginal member of the Frankenstein family. Neither really a servant, nor truly a family member, she occupies an oddly liminal precarious position that leaves her open to being read as a 'monstrous simulacrum' of a family member (Hirsch 1996, 128–9). The fact that she is the only woman in the text with no living male attachments is also important, for to be fatherless and unmarried implies exclusion from patriarchal protection and a state of dangerous freedom. As Tania Modleski observes, 'nothing could be *more* "historically and ideologically significant" than the existence of the single woman in patriarchy' (quoted in White 1995, 102). Up to a point, then, the trouble emerges from how and where Justine is positioned in the text, but if Michel is correct in arguing that her 'primary attachments are to other women' (1999, 244), Justine represents a threat to stable sexual definitions no matter how submissive she appears. What is suggested, and what I want to emphasise here, is what Patricia

---

16   Ann Frank Wake's argument that Justine's trial illuminates the necessity of 'female communities that supported women's emotional survival within the patriarchal construct' and opens a space for women's subculture in the text (2001, 493) is a notable exception to the critical norm. Although she does not approach the question of same-sex desire, she emphasises something often overlooked in *Frankenstein* criticism.

White calls 'a deviation from heterosexualized femininity' (1995, 94). In terms of this 'deviation', it becomes easy for the Monster to ensure she will be accused of the crime he has committed because she is already positioned as a site of 'difference' and potential, if not actual, perversity. Moreover, although she clearly does not inhabit a modern lesbian identity, her deviant position does include a number of markers that have since become associated with lesbianism.

The trouble with Justine also has its source in her propensity to challenge the *idea* of a clear boundary between erotic and non-erotic female bonding. Caroline conceives 'a great attachment' for Justine, and Elizabeth notes that although she did not make any 'professions', you could see by Justine's eyes that 'she almost adored her protectoress' (63). Her love for Caroline is expressed through the gaze and imitation of her object and she goes so far as to perform this identification: 'she paid the greatest attention to every gesture of my aunt. She thought her the model of all excellence ... so that even now she often reminds me of her' (63–4). This is clearly a 'performance' in the theatrical sense of the word, but it is also 'performative', in the sense that Justine repetitively enacts, embodies and comes to visibly represent the bonds between women in the text. Elizabeth reminds Victor that Justine attended Caroline 'with the most anxious affection' and, like her friends, became 'very ill' (64). The fact that she nurses Caroline gives more weight to the subtle hints of lesboeroticism in the text, for as Ashley Tauchert notes, the tropes of illness and nursing have often been used to encode 'unspeakable' sexual intimacies in literature (2000, n. 11).

Of course it is also possible to read Justine's response to Caroline as an instance of non-desiring female identification. As Butler explains, in the context of some psychoanalytic theories, identification and desire are constructed as mutually exclusive relations, in which case Justine cannot want both to *be* Caroline and to *have* Caroline at the same time. However, 'It is important to consider that desire and identification can coexist, and that their formulation in terms of mutually exclusive oppositions serves a heterosexual matrix' (1991, 26). Michel notes that readings of *Frankenstein* have indeed avoided seeing the possibility of a 'lesbian subtext' by subsuming 'relations between women under the rubric of identification' (1999, 240), thus replicating the lesbian panic and proscription of desire between women in the novel. In relation to queer-lesbian reading, this refusal to see certain possibilities raises further questions about power/knowledge relations: who gets to decide what counts as erotic and non-erotic and, further, who gets to decide that female identification and desire are mutually exclusive relations? I agree with Michel's conclusion that 'the crime of which Justine is convicted' is not so much murder, as it is 'her raising the possibility of a relation between women that is *not* constituted by identification' (1999, 248). But, to push the point a little harder, we could also say Justine raises the possibility that 'woman identification' and desire *can* coexist in a text. Perhaps the real danger to epistemological (un)certainties, and the source of disruptive queer-lesbian reading in the text, is to be found in the way Justine's relationships with Elizabeth and Caroline threaten to collapse the conventional opposition between desire and identification by suggesting that sometimes female identification can actually represent desire.

Once the Monster places the miniature portrait of Caroline upon Justine's body, the community reads her body as monstrous. Not only does his touch reveal a potential for strangeness that already underlies her position; he also 'outs' a society poised and ever ready to read certain female subjects as monsters. The Monster has already been read as an embodiment of displaced male homoerotic desire and homosexual panic (McGavran 1999, 49), but he can stand for a great deal more than tensions within homosocial society. The fact that feminist critics have read 'his' position as female has interesting implications for a reading of desire between 'women' in the text. After all, the Monster is denied phallic privilege, cut out of the male homosocial structure of the exchange of women and, in some respects, positioned as a 'wife' to Victor.[17] Robert Anderson argues that 'he' occupies a space neither quite masculine, nor quite feminine, while transgender theorist Susan Stryker points out that the Monster 'problematizes' gender through 'his' unnatural construction and 'failure as a viable subject in the visual field' (1995, 241). If the Monster occupies a non-gender specific position, perhaps he can embody the unruly power of gender deviance and same-sex desire for women as well as for men, and in terms of 'lesbian panic', as well as 'homosexual panic'. Initially it appears that there is no lesbian panic in the relationships between Justine, Caroline and Elizabeth, which might lead one to conclude that there is no potential desire. But, perhaps it has not been evaded. Perhaps the destructive power of lesbian panic has been displaced, and is enacted by the Monster in his attack upon Justine who represents the potential for love between women in the text. From a queer-lesbian reading position, the Monster's contaminating touch might even be experienced as the touch of the 'tribade', a figure which, according to Traub, became a metaphor for the 'excessive and unruly female desire' that threatened to contaminate female friendship in the phobic cultural imagination from the Renaissance onwards.[18] The queer touch of the monstrous tribade precipitates the perceptual shift from 'harmless' friendship to erotic relations, just as the Monster precipitates the reading of Justine as monstrous and enacts the panic which disrupts lesbian possibilities in the text.

Michel concludes that the Monster points to the 'crime' of which Justine really *is* guilty: primary attachment to women and raising the spectre of same-sex desire. The placing of Caroline's portrait upon her body therefore signifies more than transference of the Monster's guilt and punishment. As a sign of a possible breach in erotic/non-erotic female relations it does indeed become a sign of monstrous

---

17   See Anderson on the Monster's failure as a properly gendered male subject and exclusion from the homosocial structure of exchange. From feminist perspectives, Gilbert and Gubar (1984) discuss the Monster's 'femaleness', while Jaqueline M. Labbe (1999) considers his position as a 'wife'.

18   In the classical period, 'tribadism' was understood as 'the sexual penetration of women (and men) by other women, by means of either a dildo or a fantastically large clitoris' (Halperin; quoted in Traub 2002, 17). Traub argues that the 'dissemination of classical literature and medical texts, concurrent with the anatomical rediscovery of the clitoris in the mid-sixteenth century, reintroduced the tribade to Western Europe' and 'inaugurated a crisis in the representation of female bodies and bonds' (2002, 16–17).

potential. If a horror of sapphic agency informs *Frankenstein*, the Monster's touch also warns us that the perceptual shift also carries a dangerous performative power, insofar as it does something to the way women's bodies and behaviours are read. In Coleridge's *Christabel*, Michel notes that Geraldine's panic-inducing 'hideousness appears to be revealed only by an optical shift, a difference in view' (1999, 241). Although she seems far removed from the monstrous Geraldine, Justine also appears as a beautiful feminine girl who, with an optical shift, becomes a monster. With another shift in perspective, it is possible to see that in her intense female friendships, detachment from patriarchy and heterosexuality, tendency to occupy marginal spaces, and identification with 'monsters', Justine, like Geraldine, can take a place within nascent discourses about the positions, identities and desires we now call 'lesbian'.

My Beloved and Only Friend

The final scene in which Justine and Elizabeth are together expands the continuum of female bonding in *Frankenstein* and the possibilities for queer-lesbian reading. When Elizabeth enters the dungeon to visit her innocently monstrous friend, it is possible for her to express more than she normally might, and it may be the very marginality of the space that makes an expression of unorthodox desire possible. Michel proposes that, in this scene, the representation shifts from supportive relations to something more subversive, 'almost, but not quite' sliding over into a representation of desire between women (1999, 239). However, Victor's control of the narrative threatens to break down any sapphic potential between the women as their declarations become increasingly ardent: 'Farewell, sweet lady, dearest Elizabeth, my beloved and only friend' (85). Sedgwick argues that in male homosocial culture a woman often appears in scenes where two men are represented together in order to divert the threat of homosexual possibility (1991, 15). If women function in male homosocial culture as mediums of exchange between men, it may be possible to theorise a necessary reversal in which men function as sexual barriers against desire between women. In other words, male homosocial culture not only routes male desire through triangular relations involving a woman; it also blocks women's desire for each other through triangular relations involving a man.

Victor *is* literally, as well as figuratively, the 'block' preventing any further progress in their story, because it is he, through the actions of his monster, who has caused Justine's death. This is apt because while phobic discourse has constructed love between women as a source of horror, it has also tried to render it invisible by refusing to ascribe it any significance. Evidently, it is important to remember that such containment strategies are actually indicative of the power, rather than the insignificance, of love between women. Queer-lesbian reading should therefore be alert to moments where the significance of female relations is blocked, and not only by the men in the text. In *Mary Shelley's Frankenstein*, for example, Justine (Trevyn McDowell) is 'heterosexualised'. She is represented as being in love with Victor

(Kenneth Branagh) and tells Elizabeth (Helena Bonham Carter) to go to Ingoldstadt because if he belonged to her, she would have already gone. This alteration repositions her not only as a 'normal' woman who expresses desire for a man, but also as a self-sacrificing facilitator of the heterosexual romance which this film champions.

With another shift in perspective, we might ask if Victor's presence in the cell simply affirms male dominance, or whether the discourse coding desire between women as that which is not to be seen actually endows it with subversive potential. After all, Victor is in fact excluded while Justine and Elizabeth say their farewells, retiring 'to the corner of the prison room' (84–5). Ignoring him, Justine throws 'herself at the feet of Elizabeth, weeping bitterly' (83). She defines herself as belonging to Elizabeth: 'your Justine' (84) and, when she does notice Victor, defines him in relation to Elizabeth as 'your cousin' (85). Her only concern about her false confession is that Elizabeth might think ill of her. It would appear that Justine responds to a world of female-centred power relations and expects women to protect her. Again this suggests that, encoded within the male homosocial narrative, there is a female homosocial or, as I prefer, lesbosocial narrative which men cannot perceive except as an unspeakable threat to be sublimated. Michel notes that contemporary representations tend to eroticise 'social-structural differences between women' (1999, 245). In *Frankenstein*, female sameness is emphasised, but important differences of age and class preclude the possibility of subsuming the relationships to 'romantic friendship'. In this respect, Elizabeth and Justine's relationship again meets a representational condition for threatening to collapse the (imaginary) opposition between erotic and non-erotic female bonds.

A further reading of desiring possibility between Elizabeth and Justine is produced from an attention to fantasy in the narrative. Elizabeth fantasises herself into the role of a hero who will save Justine from death at the last moment, although it is already too late to do so: 'Do not fear', she says, 'I will proclaim, I will prove your innocence. I will melt the stony hearts of your enemies by my tears and prayers.' Then, she goes on to insist, 'You shall not die! You, my playfellow, my companion, my sister, perish on the scaffold! No! No! I never could survive so horrible a misfortune' (84). Positioning herself as the 'lover' and Justine as her 'beloved', her rescue fantasy constructs an imagined feminine stance so assertive as to become heroic. This scene might be experienced as what Zimmerman calls a 'what if' moment (1993, 139), a fissure in the dominant narrative where an alternative story can be glimpsed. Moreover, if Elizabeth and Justine can be said to express desire for each other from 'feminine' positions, their relationship lacks the constituting presence of the 'masculine identification', which is presumed necessary for desire to exist within what Butler calls, the '*imaginary* logic' of the 'heterosexual matrix' (1993b, 28). It is precisely moments such as these that are of interest in queer readings, moments where the accepted representational relationship between gender intelligibility and desire begins to break down.

Elizabeth's final statement ruptures heteronormative representation: '"I wish", cried she, "that I were to die with you; I cannot live in this world of misery"' (85). Her (correct) construction of her future life as 'a world of misery' expresses a profound sense of female disillusion, as well as desire for ultimate union in death with a beloved of the same sex. Momentarily defamiliarising the 'normal' world, she imagines an alternative narrative in which same-sex love is primary – women might rescue each other from patriarchal authorities and, if that fails, die together. Evidently, the possibility for an expression of same-sex desire is here predicated upon its foreclosure in the imminent execution of Justine. Reading the text in relation to phobic discourses about female relations, we can therefore finally place the death of Justine within a long tradition of 'strategies' employed to maintain the status of female same-sex desire as 'impossible' (Traub 2002, 6). Figuring as the site of crisis at which the proscribed possibility of desire threatens idealised non-erotic female identification and friendship, she is also the point at which such possibilities must be killed off. Yet, at the same time, her death brings to 'life' the critical space in which queer-lesbian reading can begin re-reading and, in a sense, re-creating the text.

In 1835 Mary Shelley wrote, 'ten years ago I was so ready to give myself away – and being afraid of men, I was apt to get *tousy-mousy* for women … I am now proof as Hamlet says both against man & woman' (Bennett 1983, 255–6). Not only does Shelley's playful remembrance of her youthful tendency to get 'tousy-mousy' for women unravel the tidy weave of heteronormative presumption surrounding her life, it also serves as a nicely queer concluding point to this discussion concerning the performative politics of reading, and not reading, desire between women (see Friedman 2001). Geraldine Friedman traced the etymology of the phrase 'tousy-mousy' and found that it meant 'to pull around roughly' with connotations of roughing up, disturbance and dishevelment (2001, n. 41). Since a variant, 'towsy-mowsy', was used as slang for the female pudendum, the phrase becomes a rather appropriate frame for this discussion. After all, to disturb, 'rough up', 'tousle about' and pull a text around, in the aim of producing new reading possibilities, is an important objective for queer-lesbian reading. This is not to suggest that queer-lesbian reading can do whatever it likes with the text: on the contrary, Shelley's comment demands and necessitates queer-lesbian reading; it makes such a 'disturbing' response ethically *imperative*.[19] The phrase 'tousy-mousy' also brings into play that sense of the tactile in the disruptive, arresting power of the 'queer touch' articulated by Carolyn Dinshaw. The queer touch of Shelley's 'tousy mousy' desire draws attention to the construction of 'normal' female sexual desire by reminding the reader that Shelley's heterosexuality is presumed until her relationship with Jane Williams suggests otherwise. While Shelley's statement does not prove her 'lesbianism', as we would now understand that modern sexual category, it does 'rough up' the biographical text, representing a point at which queer and lesbian reading possibilities become not only imaginable, but also

---

19 I am here again drawing upon Hillis Miller's understanding of the ethical moment in reading as 'a response to something, responsible to it, respectful of it. In any ethical moment there is an imperative, some "I must" … On the other hand, the ethical moment in reading leads to an act. It enters into the social, institutional and political realms' (1987, 4).

necessary, even imperative. Perhaps, then, to perform queer-lesbian reading is, in a sense, to get 'tousy-mousy' for women, to tousle up the way we have come to read female relations and to make available self-reflexive, playful, challenging performative approaches which take queer and lesbian reading in new directions.

Suggested Further Reading

Friedman, G. (2001), 'Pseudonymity, Passing and Queer Biography: The Case of Mary Diana Dods', *Romanticism on the Net* 23, http://www.erudit.org/revue/ ron/2001/v/n23/005985ar.html (accessed 30 May 2008).
Haggerty, G. (2006), *Queer Gothic* (Chicago, IL: University of Illinois Press).
O' Rourke, M. and Collings, D. (2004), 'Introduction: Queer Romanticisms: Past, Present and Future', *Romanticism on the Net: Queer Romanticism* 36–7, http://www. erudit.org/revue/ron/2004/v/n36-37/011132ar.html (accessed 30 May 2008).
Stryker, S. (1995), 'My Words to Victor Frankenstein above the Village of Chaminoux: Performing Transgender Rage', *GLQ: A Journal of Lesbian and Gay Studies* 1:3, 237–54.
Tauchert, A. (2000), 'Escaping Discussion: Liminality and the Female-Embodied Couple in Mary Wollstonecraft's *Mary, A Fiction*', *Romanticism on the Net* 18, http://www.erudit.org/revue/ron/2000/v/n18/005923ar.html (accessed 30 May 2008).

References

Anderson, R. (1999), 'Body Parts That Matter: *Frankenstein*, or the Modern Cyborg?', http://www.womenwriters.net/editorials/anderson1.htm (accessed 5 July 2006).
Bennett, B.T. (ed.), (1983), *The Letters of Mary Wollstonecraft Shelley: Volume 11* (Baltimore, MD and London: Johns Hopkins University Press).
Berenstein. R.J. (1995), '"I'm Not the Sort of Person Men Marry": Monsters, Queers, and Hitchcock's *Rebecca*', in C.J. Creekmur and A. Doty (eds), *Out in Culture: Gay, Lesbian and Queer Essays on Popular Culture* (Durham, NC; London: Duke University Press).
Butler, J. (1991), 'Imitation and Gender Insubordination', in D. Fuss (ed.), *Inside/ Out: Lesbian Theories, Gay Theories* (New York; London: Routledge).
—— (1993a), *Bodies That Matter: On the Discursive Limits of 'Sex'* (New York and London: Routledge).
—— (1993b), 'Critically Queer', *GLQ: A Journal of Lesbian and Gay Studies* 1:1, 17– 32.
Castle, T. (1993), *The Apparitional Lesbian: Female Homosexuality and Modern Culture* (New York: Columbia University Press).

Coleridge, S.T. (2000), *Christabel. Samuel Taylor Coleridge: The Major Works* (ed.), H.J. Jackson (Oxford: Oxford University Press).

Crook, N. (2003), 'In Defence of the 1831 *Frankenstein*', in E. Schor (ed.), *The Cambridge Companion to Mary Shelley* (Cambridge: Cambridge University Press).

Daffron, E. (1999), 'Male Bonding: Sympathy and Shelley's *Frankenstein*', *Nineteenth Century Contexts* 21, 415–35.

Dinshaw, C. (1995), 'Chaucer's Queer Touches/A Queer Touches Chaucer', *Exemplaria* 7:1, 75–92.

Eberle-Sinatra, M. (1998), 'Science, Gender and Otherness in Shelley's *Frankenstein* and Kenneth Branagh's Film Adaptation', *European Romantic Review* 9, 253–70.

—— (2005), 'Readings of Homosexuality in Mary Shelley's *Frankenstein* and Four Film Adaptations', *Gothic Studies* 7:2, 185–202.

Ellis, K. (1979), 'Monsters in the Garden: Mary Shelley and the Bourgeois Family', in G. Levine (ed.), *The Endurance of Frankenstein: Essays on Mary Shelley's Novel* (Berkeley, CA and London: University of California Press).

Faderman, L. (1985), *Surpassing the Love of Men: Romantic Friendship and Love between Women from the Renaissance to the Present* (London: The Women's Press).

Foucault, M. (1998 [1976]), *The History of Sexuality, Volume 1: The Will to Knowledge*, trans. R. Hurley (London: Penguin).

Friedman, G. (2001), 'Pseudonymity, Passing and Queer Biography: The Case of Mary Diana Dods', *Romanticism on the Net* 23, http://www.erudit.org/revue/ron/2001/v/n23/005985ar.html (accessed 30 May 2008).

Garber, L. (2001), *Identity Poetics: Race, Class and the Lesbian-Feminist Roots of Queer Theory* (New York: Columbia University Press).

Giffney, N. and O'Donnell, K. (2007), 'Introduction: Twenty-First Century Lesbian Studies', in N. Giffney and K. O'Donnell (eds), *Twenty-First Century Lesbian Studies* (Binghampton, NY: Taylor and Francis).

Gilbert, S.M. and Gubar, S. (1984), *The Madwoman in the Attic: The Woman Writer and the Nineteenth-Century Literary Imagination* (New Haven, CT and London: Yale University Press).

Halberstam, J. (1996), 'Queering Lesbian Studies', in B. Zimmerman and T.A.H. McNaron (eds), *The New Lesbian Studies: Into the Twenty-First Century* (New York: The Feminist Press).

Halperin, D.M. (1995), *Saint Foucault: Towards a Gay Hagiography* (New York and Oxford: Oxford University Press).

Hirsch, D.A. (1996), 'Liberty, Equality, Monstrosity: Revolutionising the Family in Mary Shelley's *Frankenstein*', in J.J. Cohen (ed.), *Monster Theory: Reading Culture* (Minneapolis, MN: University of Minnesota Press).

Jakobsen, J.R. (1998), 'Queer Is? Queer Does? Normativity and the Problem of Resistance', *GLQ: A Journal of Lesbian and Gay Studies* 4:4, 511–36.

Kavka, M. (2002) 'The Gothic on Screen', in J.E. Hogle (ed.), *The Cambridge Companion to Gothic Fiction* (Cambridge: Cambridge University Press).

Labbe, J.M. (1999), 'A Monstrous Fiction: *Frankenstein* and the Wifely Ideal', *Women's Writing* 6:3, 345–65.

Lochrie, K. (1999), 'Presumptive Sodomy and its Exclusions', *Textual Practice* 13:2, 295–310.

MacCormack, P. (2004), 'Perversion: Transgressive Sexuality and Becoming Monster', *Thirdspace: A Journal of Feminist Theory and Culture* 3:2, http://www.thirdspace.ca/articles/3_2_maccormack.htm (accessed 8 November 2004).

Malinowitz, H. (1996), 'Lesbian Studies and Postmodern Queer Theory', in B. Zimmerman and T.A.H. McNaron (eds), *The New Lesbian Studies: Into the Twenty-First Century* (New York: The Feminist Press).

Mary Shelley's Frankenstein (1992), dir. Kenneth Branagh [feature film].

McGavran, J.H. (1999), '"Insurmountable Barriers to Our Union": Homosocial Male Bonding, Homosexual Panic, and Death on the Ice in *Frankenstein*', *European Romantic Review* 10, 46–67.

Michel, F. (1999), 'Lesbian Panic and Mary Shelley's *Frankenstein*', *GLQ: A Journal of Lesbian and Gay Studies* 2:3, 237–52.

Miller, J.H. (1987), *The Ethics of Reading* (New York: Columbia University Press).

Parker, A. and Sedgwick E.K. (eds) (1995), *Performativity and Performance* (New York: Routledge).

Rich, A. (1993), 'Compulsory Heterosexuality and Lesbian Existence', in H. Abelove, M.A. Barale and D.M. Halperin (eds), *The Lesbian and Gay Studies Reader* (New York and London: Routledge).

Savoy, E. (1999), '"That Ain't All She Ain't": Doris Day and Queer Performativity', in E. Hanson (ed.), *Out Takes: Essays on Queer Theory and Film* (Durham, NC and London: Duke University Press).

Sedgwick, E.K. (1985), *Between Men: English Literature and Male Homosocial Desire* (New York: Columbia University Press).

—— (1986), *The Coherence of Gothic Conventions* (London and New York: Methuen).

—— (1991), *Epistemology of the Closet* (London: Harvester Wheatsheaf).

Shelley, M. (1992), *Frankenstein or The Modern Prometheus* (ed.), M. Hindle (London: Penguin).

—— (1998), *Frankenstein or The Modern Prometheus: The 1818 Text* (ed.), M. Butler (Oxford: Oxford University Press).

Smith, P.J. (1995), '"And I Wondered if She Might Kiss Me": Lesbian Panic as Narrative Strategy in British Women's Fictions', *Modern Fiction Studies* 41:3–4, 567–607.

Spark, M. (1987), *Mary Shelley* (London: Penguin).

Stryker, S. (1995), 'My Words to Victor Frankenstein above the Village of Chamounix: Performing Transgender Rage', *GLQ: A Journal of Lesbian and Gay Studies* 1:3, 237–54.

Tauchert, A. (2000), 'Escaping Discussion: Liminality and the Female-Embodied Couple in Mary Wollstonecraft's *Mary, A Fiction*', *Romanticism on the Net* 18, http://www.erudit.org/revue/ron/2000/v/n18/005923ar.html (accessed 30 May 2008).

Traub, V. (2002), *The Renaissance of Lesbianism in Early Modern England* (Cambridge: Cambridge University Press).

Wake, A.F. (2001), 'Justine's Trial Revisited: A Space for Women's Subculture in Mary Shelley's *Frankenstein*', *European Romantic Review* 12:4, 493–516.

White, P. (1995), 'Supporting Character: The Queer Career of Agnes Morehead', in C.J. Creekmur and A. Doty (eds), *Out in Culture: Gay, Lesbian and Queer Essays on Popular Culture* (Durham, NC and London: Duke University Press).

Zimmermann, B. (1993), 'Perverse Reading: The Lesbian Appropriation of Literature', in S.T. Wolfe and J. Penelope (eds), *Sexual Practice, Textual Theory: Lesbian Cultural Criticism* (Cambridge, MA and Oxford: Blackwell).

Sex and the Lubricative Ethic

Dinesh Wadiwel

In his provocatively titled article, 'Is the Rectum a Grave?' (1988/1987), Leo Bersani asks an important question of sexuality, namely: why would one desire to be penetrated? Bersani's paper was authored amidst the wave of the AIDS crisis, reflecting all of the anxiety and doubt that this crisis placed over sexual practices (particularly, but not exclusively, between men), and hence these questions possessed a poignancy and urgency that today seems lacking in the West. Nevertheless I believe this question is still relevant, not only because the AIDS crisis continues on a path of untold devastation through Asia and Africa, but also because I believe a satisfactory answer remains, so far, fundamentally lacking. Bersani's answer is stridently unapologetic, although I believe ultimately incorrect. He argues that sexuality aims to oscillate between sensations that solidify our sense of self and those which lose or 'rupture' the self (1988/1987, 218; 1986, 38). While I don't take issue necessarily with this portrayal of sexuality – particularly as so much of the potency of sexuality appears to revolve around the loss of control over the self – I am less satisfied with the way in which Bersani interprets the relationships of power that correlate to this dynamic. Bersani argues that sex almost inevitably moves towards domination. In his words the 'effects of power ... can perhaps most easily be exacerbated and polarised into relations of mastery and subordination, in sex' (1988/1987, 216) ... 'as soon as persons are posited, the war begins' (1988/87, 218). This assumes that sex involves a struggle for domination over the other, and unsurprisingly this leads to an unchallenged assumption in Bersani's article that the specific pleasure of being penetrated is associated with a loss of power or control: 'to be penetrated is to abdicate power' (1988/87, 212).

In this chapter I do some thinking around lubricants, erotic practices and sphincters. I challenge the idea that being penetrated has anything to do with passivity or the loss of power; indeed I question whether the relations of power that compose sexuality have any essential relationship to positions of mastery and subordination. I must, first of all, confess to being unsure where I stand in relation to queer theory. This may in part be due to the well documented 'slipperiness' in defining this form of theoretical engagement. Nikki Sullivan neatly summarises the useful yet indeterminate nature of this area: queer 'is constructed as a sort of vague and indefinite set of practices and (political) positions that has the potential to challenge normative knowledges and identities' (2003, 43–4). The lack of ground for defining queer theory can be problematic, not only because it is not clear exactly on what grounds queer theory poses its challenge, but *who* queer theory seeks to represent, promoting 'a sense of inclusivity that is misleading, and worse still, enables exclusory praxis to go unchecked' (2003, 47). What interests me about queer theory is its capacity to act as a radical from of theoretical praxis, what Michael Warner describes as a 'thorough resistance to regimes of the normal' (1993, xxvi). In this sense, queer theory is valuable as a methodology that critiques heterosexuality and mainstream gay and lesbian culture. If we follow this course of investigation, we must ask questions of gender, sex and the cultural and political coding of bodies. Although discussions of sexuality inevitably invoke the human body in its most intimate sense, this chapter begins its exploration through the nonhuman actors that facilitate erotic scenes, starting with the fluid lubricant. This poses a challenge to how we are to think about sex between humans: how are we to think about nonhuman things and how they interact with erotic production?

'Actor Network' accounts of power provide one way of thinking about how nonhuman actors relate to human agents (Haraway 1991; Law 1986; Latour 1999; Sofia 2000). These accounts emphasise the need to examine the involvement of various entities and forces within networks of activity, including nonhuman actors such as technologies, discourses and contingencies. Nonhuman entities are inseparable parts of productive networks, and inevitably human activity finds itself formed around these nonhuman elements: our actions are intimately addressed to a multiplicity of nonhuman actors, ranging from computers to furniture, alarm clocks to lifts, motor vehicles and utensils. Bruno Latour argues that nonhuman delegates exercise agency within a network by 'standing in' for human actors (1999, 189). For example, Latour suggests that the speed hump, or 'sleeping policeman', is a nonhuman entity which quite literally acts as a delegate for a real policeman to slow traffic (1999, 188).

Nonhuman material objects are also important entities within networks of erotic production (Graham 2004). A sling, a piece of lingerie, a whip or a vibrator may all play significant if not indispensable roles in enabling an erotic scene to happen. These objects are agents: human participants must grapple with the possibilities and potentialities of the nonhuman in much the same way as humans grapple with other humans. As much as we would like to turn the nonhuman object to our own ends – to simply use it as a 'tool' or 'instrument' – the nonhuman organises our own actions around its needs. Nonhuman objects within networks of erotic production are necessarily unruly and headstrong. The vibrator, for example, requires a certain degree of care on behalf of its human partners in order to ensure its functionality within networks of erotic production: a fresh supply of batteries or the close proximity of the device to electric power; an attentiveness to ensure that its sensitive internal workings are safeguarded from the potentially damaging intervention of bodily fluids and lubricants; a willingness to attune the variability of one's own sexual pleasure to the potentiality of the machine, its size, its contours, the speed and variability of its vibrations. In this case, the vibrator is the actor: it is a lover that demands our respect, and asks us to pay heed to the potential it brings to the erotic scene, and like any lover (human or otherwise), it holds within it mysteries that are yet to be revealed, waiting to surprise us with pleasures (or frustrations) within the context of the erotic assemblage.

Gilles Deleuze and Félix Guattari's conception of 'desiring machines', as outlined in *Anti-Oedipus* (1994/1972), also offers a useful way to think about the ways in which nonhuman entities interact with human bodies (and human body parts) within erotic scenes. *Anti-Oedipus* was an important work because it provided an alternative way to approach analysis that did not carry with it an overdetermination of familial relationships in the formation of the self, since, as Deleuze and Guattari argue, the immense social symbolic value that is placed upon the figures within the 'Oedipal triangle' (1994/1972, 51–137) inevitably underpins the logic of social repression. In traditional psychoanalytic accounts, the unconscious is constructed as a set of drives which produces a relation of attachment between the self and one's parental figures. In opposition to the Oedipal focus of the unconscious drives, Deleuze and Guattari argue that the relations which are formed between the self, objects and organs need not relate to a symbolic and repressed libidinal attachment to the mother or the father, but to a creative assembly of a machinic relation in the world:

> *The satisfaction the handyman experiences when he plugs something into an electrical socket or diverts a stream of water can scarcely be explained in terms of 'playing mommy and daddy', or by the pleasure of violating a taboo. The rule of continually producing production, of grafting producing onto the product, is a characteristic of desiring machines or of primary production: the production of production. (1994/1972, 7)*

This approach is valuable for a number of reasons. Firstly, it suggests that the erotic scene is an active creation of its participants: Deleuze and Guattari suggest that production involves the continuous arrangement of 'desiring machines', that is assemblies of objects and parts coupled together (1994/1972, 36). Secondly, it makes it possible to consider a range of other components as part of the erotic assemblage, including objects that physically interact with bodies at play (a dildo, a carrot, a whip, a bed) and other incidental objects and events that make an erotic scene (wallpaper, a smooth Marvin Gaye record, a thunder storm). The erotic relation, like any relation, is contextual: it is a theatre of actors, supporting actors, props, dialogue and scenery. Thirdly, this model is capable of shifting discussion of the erotic away from so-called traditional concerns (the penis) and oppositions (male/female) which dominate many analyses of sexual relations, particularly those invested in psychoanalytic accounts of desire and eroticism.

Actor Network Theory and the work of Deleuze and Guattari offer us the opportunity to rethink our connections to nonhuman objects and reinscribe them productively within fields of power. Nevertheless, it is important to note that the two approaches have their differences in focus. Actor Network Theory provides an opportunity to examine the 'agency' of different interconnected nonhuman entities within the context of a broader field of production. It becomes possible, therefore, to give 'voice' to nonhuman entities that may usually be overlooked when examining a productive process. Deleuze and Guattari's concern, on the other hand, is not so much to articulate the role of nonhuman agents within a productive process, but to break apart entities within fields of production – human or otherwise – into micro elements. Deleuze and Guattari's approach is, in other words, fundamentally dehumanising (Cohen and Ramlow 2006; Anderson 2006). Human interactions become exchanges between organs: cunnilingus, for example, is not simply one person 'going down' on another, but a mechanic assembly between tongue and genitals.

Combining these approaches allows us to appreciate the significant role of nonhuman entities, but also helps us to break apart the human body and assess the 'agency' of human bit parts (for example, the hand, the arse and the eyes). The body may be conceptualised in this sense as a network, involving a complex interplay of flesh and nerves, an assemblage that the mind only imagines itself as commanding. This is not to evoke the age-old split between the mind and body, but merely to observe a phenomenology of the self as a tussle between the flesh, organs and nerves that compose us. The self is a grappling with our own flesh, in much the same way we grapple with the flesh of the world we find ourselves imbricated within (Merleau-Ponty 1992/1968). The importance of such an approach will become apparent in my discussion of the sphincter muscle.

Lubricants and Fisting

The lubricant is an important component in erotic practices. The lubricant is a substance that eases the passage of objects in relation with each other, which accords with our everyday mechanical conceptions of the way in which things move. The fluid lubricant is a substance that flows between surfaces in motion against each other, whether this is in the form of grease within a hinge, motor oil in an engine or saliva between bodies. The lubricant does not erase friction, rather it alters frictional effects through the substitution of a dry frictional condition with a lubricous fluid condition (Nunney 1975, 110). Given the capacity of the lubricant to ease the tangential movements of bodies, it is no surprise that many sexual practices involve the deployment of lubricative mediums to enable smoothed encounters. These fluids may be auto-manufactured by the erotic bodies, gently flowing from the passages and ducts of bodies at play, or may be deployed by erotic participants in the form of manufactured products (such as jellies or oils) which either aim to lubricate areas where there is no 'natural' lubricant, or to supplement an existing supply of lubricative fluids. Wherever the sexual relation involves touch, then the lubricant is an agent that renders possible the pleasurable embrace, by altering the frictional passage of sensitive skins over each other. Indeed, as eroticism may be considered an art of managing intensities of sensation, lubricants can be said to lie at the heart of erotic practice given their capacity to alter frictional effects. In the physical world the lubricant has a transformative capacity, in that it has an ability to make work what would otherwise fail to work. The merest hint of grease in a hinge, for example, may mean the difference between the ability of a door to open or, in the absence of such lubrication, the failure of that same door to budge.

The lubricant, in other words, makes possible what would otherwise be impossible. This is most graphically portrayed in erotic situations that stretch and contort the body beyond imagined physical boundaries. The erotic practice of fisting (or 'fist-f***ing') is an example of such an art. Fisting involves the insertion of a hand(s)/forearm, into one of the bodily orifices (usually vaginal and anal, but may also include the mouth/throat). The practice is by nature gentle and despite the implications of the name, fisting requires care and skill on the part of its practitioners. A lubricative function is essential to making this practice physically possible, and practitioners of fisting almost inevitably make use of large quantities of fluid lubricant in order to ease the passage of the hand into the bodily orifice. In the case of both vaginal and anal fisting, lubricant is liberally applied as it is literally splashed into the orifice before the hand is inserted, and is continually reapplied during the unfolding of the erotic act. Clubs dedicated to fisting incorporate lubricant containers within their design, such as the famous San Francisco sex club, the 'Catacombs', operating during the 1970s and early 1980s, which was famed for the large pots of lubricant which hung from the ceiling, adjacent to every sling (Rubin 1991, 127, 135).

While lubricants are central to successful and pleasurable fisting, it would be a mistake to say that this practice is reducible merely to a science of good lubrication. Apart from fluid lubricants, fisting also involves an elaborate web of communication strategies, as well as the often painstaking process of 'coaxing' the body into a position of comfort where this practice may become possible. Fisting involves an in-depth dialogue, which needs to be entered into between body organs before this practice becomes possible. As Gayle Rubin notes with reference to anal fisting: it 'is an art that involves seducing one of the jumpiest and tightest muscles in the body' (1991, 126). The erotic space has to be carefully constructed by the participants to facilitate this 'seduction': a process that may require a great deal of preparation and patience. One of Gary Dowsett's interviewees in his study, *Practicing Desire*, reported that his initiation into fisting took four days: 'It was done slowly, It was done properly' (1996, 180). These slow, patient practices that aim to coax and open the body to pleasure can themselves be described as lubricative even if they do not involve the deployment of fluid lubricants. In this sense, our understanding of the 'lubricative practice' may be broadened conceptually to include a whole range of objects and relations that are active in facilitating the operation of the erotic assemblage.

There are a number of erotic practices that could be described as conceptually lubricative in this manner. For example, the use of Amyl Nitrate by some fisting practitioners, as a sexual aid to loosen muscles, could count as a lubricant in its ability to ease the passage of objects moving in relation to one another. The use of props and devices, such a slings, music and uniforms may also facilitate the enactment of the erotic practice. A whole range of physical and non-physical markers, which construct the erotic scene and facilitate the erotic relation can also be included among examples of non-physical manifestations of the lubricative act. For example, one fistee notes that behind the tough black leather façade of the fister and amidst hard slaps and rough talk, he only needs to look into his lover's warm eyes for reassurance: 'His eyes say "I want you to feel real good, you can trust me buddy. I want to love your soul where I can really grab onto it"' (Mains 1991, 235). It is these eyes and a range of lubricative devices that transform an otherwise painfully impossible situation into an act of reciprocal pleasure.

Fisting is an example of how the body, mind and meaning of the erotic act can be altered through a well-lubricated facilitative practice. It is perhaps the latter point that emphasises the transformative capacity of the lubricative act most prominently, since fisting is a contemporary product of advanced collaborative experimentation with the body and its limits and pleasures. Thus Dowsett observes that to 'attain [the] skill [of being fisted] is no simple matter of drive or instinct. Fisting is a very clear example of the progress of sexual practice and the transformation of desire and pleasure again through a social process' (1996, 178).

Sphincters

The practice of fisting emphasises not so much a dialogue between the minds of the participants, but a connection and synergy between body organs. Lines of communication need to proliferate between coupled body parts. The anal sphincter or vaginal muscles need to be relaxed by the hand so that they are wide open enough to allow passage. Pat Califia,[1] in her collection of erotic stories, *Macho Sluts* (1988), describes this as if one were sending messages to the sphincter in some form of muscle dialect:

> *Little messages ran up those busy, delicately searching fingers, through forearm and bicep, to the shoulder, jogging it, keeping up a minute series of rhythmic movements designed to coax the arsehole, the mouth of the great snake, to unlock its jaws and swallow its meal, Kay's folded over, pointed, pared down, and slicked up hand. (1988, 132)*

The sphincter, that is, the bound muscular surrounds of the orifice, are spoken to by the hand that couples with it: their production rests upon the dialogue that ensues. Muscles converse delicately to each other enabling a speaking of the body (Chisholm 1995).

The practice of fisting challenges the ways in which body parts such as the sphincter, usually treated as a somewhat inane or superfluous participant in the erotic exchange, are considered. The sphincter is a headstrong muscle – not the closure to a passive receptacle – but the entrance to a dynamic, active space. Sphincters are the sensitive, sensual, pleasured and pleasuring, muscular openings

---

1   Califia now identifies as Patrick Califia-Rice (1997; 2002).

to the body. These organs actively negotiate the erotic, physically and conceptually represented as a flowing, arousing, slippery space, both renowned as 'tight and narrow' and 'loose and wide' (Astley-Schofield 1999). The 'coaxing' of the sphincter – described vividly by Califia – further suggests that this organ is an agent of erotic production, one that is demanding and actively negotiates the outcome of erotic encounters. Here we can extend the thesis – as advanced by Actor Network theorists – that the nonhuman entity may exert agency to include the organs of the body which, like the technological artefacts of the world, shape their human users actions with as much zeal as the human users claim to control the actions of the technology at their 'command'. Erotic production involves a negotiation between various entities which inevitably configures the actions/movements of bit-parts of assemblies in relation to one another. Like the traffic signal, which demands, within a particular social and juridical context, the attention of the motor vehicle operator, the sphincter requests its own forms of action, its own dialogue. Bodies and organs must be moved in relation to it: operators must respond to its demands (trim finger nails, exercise care and stealth, be ready to feed it more at its devouring request). Like many technologies, the pleasurably fisted sphincter may be said to command the actions of its human operators.[2] Califia is not engaging in a metaphoric displacement when she says that Kay is 'coaxing the asshole': it is the sphincter which is being talked to, a communication that occurs intimately with the muscle, away from the seemingly inquisitive and authoritarian gaze of the mind. It is possible to suggest that the act of fisting is pleasurable precisely because it defies the belief of the brain. That is, in some senses, the success of the practice is only guaranteed by the successful disconnection of the mind from the relay between the fist and the anal sphincter.

The sphincter has the potential to embody the lubricative principle, since, by its dilations, and its contractions, it invites creative possibility. The sphincter emulates the operation of a fluid lubricant, both easing the movements of those objects with which it moves in touch relations while opening the possibility of that which would not otherwise be possible. The dilations of the sphincter, in concert with the operation of other lubricative devices, make possible and pleasurable an act which would otherwise only be painful and/or violent. It is through variations in frictional dynamics, between the walls of the sphincter, that the intense sensations of pleasure and pain are produced. If the lubricative/frictional device is that mechanism which regulates the production of sensation, then the sphincter is the perfect, semi-autonomous, flexible embodiment of this technology. The sphincter can intensify friction to such a degree that the passage becomes dry, hard and bloody or ease itself to such a degree that it becomes possible to accommodate a human fist.

Traditional images of heterosexual eroticism have defined gender in terms of the perceived positioning and action of genitals. Luce Irigaray, in particular, has forcefully argued that the effect of the symbolic relationship is the formation of

---

2   The interrelationship between human and nonhuman elements is emphasised by Actor Network theorists, for example, see Mike Michael's discussion of the relation of body and body part movement to technological 'co(a)gents' (2000, 99–100).

feminine sexuality only through the lens of masculinity: for example, the clitoris is seen merely as a 'little penis' (1985a/1974, 26) while the vagina is attributed a functionality of only offering a 'lodging' space for the penis (1985a/1974, 23). This same symbolic economy of sexuality generates associations of activity and passivity, where masculinity is understood as the subjectivity that appropriates a feminised object (1985a/1974, 133–46). The penis is defined as active, as the penetrator, as deriving pleasure through its use in this mode. The vagina is, by implication, defined as its opposite: a passive receptacle for the penetrating male organ.

Yet there is no imperative for the relations of penetrated/penetrator to be cast into the seemingly auto-categories of passive/active, nor any reason to assume, following Bersani, that to 'be penetrated is to abdicate power'. On the contrary, it is possible to render the penetrated/penetrator scenario outside of the confines of this economy. Certainly Catherine Waldby suggests, for example, that heterosexual penetrative sex:

> ... need not be fantasised ... as powerful male penetration of soft womanly interior space, but rather as the vagina's embrace or grasp of the penis ... The penis does not act the phallus in sex unless it is lived by one or both partners as the phallus. If mutual erotic fantasy involved the penis' surrender or engulfment, then this counts also as a description. (1995, 270)

Such re-designations of the body are useful because they challenge the traditional assumption that to be penetrated means to surrender to domination or passivity, whether in heteroerotic or homoerotic assemblies (Jackson 1999, 167–73; Segal 1994; Dowsett 1996, 9). 'Receiving' from or 'giving' to others both involve activity, neither need involve 'the negation of power'. The sphincter is oblivious to the active/passive, powerful/powerless categorisation. This is not to suggest that the sphincter is inherently resistant to domination or that by extension the sphincter is not impervious to the categorisation of passivity. The sphincter occupies a dubious position within this logic, as well as within this eroticism. The sphincter may be open to penetration, but it is as unconvincing to suggest that it is a passive receptacle as it is to suggest that the function of the vagina is simply to offer 'lodging' for the penis. The sphincter gives as much as it takes. Pleasure is gained, not simply through lodgement but through the micro-dynamics of the relation that occurs between the ring muscle and the objects it seeks. Production occurs on many levels, facilitated by the activity of the sphincter: the local production of sensation, the renegotiation of the terms of operation of the lubricative device, the regulation of friction, the production of pleasure. Symbolically one may want to ask: what threat will the sphincter pose to our traditional logic? This organ is both hard and soft (like the penis), capable of giving and taking, is wilfully self-motivated, a thinking muscle, both tight and narrow and loose and wide, found both [in] male and female.

Foucault, Power and Lubricity

How do the sphincter and the lubricant inform our understanding of power? Can we speak of the lubricative act or gesture within the context of ethics? Michel Foucault provides perhaps the most significant contribution to our contemporary understanding of power and the relationship between sexual practice and ethics. Foucault argues that power is always characterised by a relational struggle, that it involves tactics, pursuit and resistance. The contexts within which the struggles that constitute power come about are also their productive element. Not only do lines of contestation produce the constraining forces that limit movement, they also – almost inevitability – produce avenues for 'liberation'. Foucault's stance on power strongly influences his approach to questions of sexuality. For example, the medical categorisation of homosexuality, while arguably functioning to ultimately repress homosexual relations, also formed the basis for its legitimation:

> ... in the gay movement the medical definition of homosexuality was a very important tool against the oppression of homosexuality in the last part of the nineteenth century and in the early twentieth century. This medicalisation, which was a means of oppression, has always been a means of resistance as well – since people could say, 'If we are sick, then why do you condemn us, why do you despise us?' And so on. (2000c/1984, 168)

According to Foucault, power does not just offer avenues for resistance, but also opens new possibilities for pleasure. He noted for example that sadomasochism was one form of sexual experimentation in which resistance to dominant forms of sexuality was capable of creatively exploring forms of pleasure that had not previously been conceived. In particular, some of these new practices shifted the focus of pleasure away from the sexual organs through the eroticisation of parts of the body other than the genitalia, thus 'inventing new possibilities of pleasure with strange parts of ... [the] ... body' (Foucault quoted in Miller, 1973, 165). The inventiveness that springs from the resistance to norms touches upon the distinctly 'ethical' stance of Foucault's later writing on sexuality and the relationship of pleasure to the body. This, in part, is influenced by his philosophical readings on the classical period, during which a discourse around the 'cultivation of self' emerged (1990/1984, 45–50). While Foucault suggests that this care of the self is the precursor to the latter Christian association of sexuality with a certain danger (1990/1984, 68), there is an element of this ethics of self that is unashamedly devoted to the development of self as a locus of pleasure.

For it is through a contemplation of the self and an exploration of the self's potentialities, that an ongoing pleasure can be attained by the self. In this process the self does not uncover its hitherto hidden identity, as a pleasure locked away to be brought to the surface by an external agent, but brings into being its own potentiality as an active creation. In Foucault's words, 'what we must work on, it seems to me, is not so much to liberate our pleasures but to make ourselves infinitely more susceptible to pleasure' (2000b/1989, 137). According to Foucault, we should not aim merely to discover what is innately pleasurable to the body, but constitute the ground of new pleasures: that is, seek an ascetic regulation of self in order to discover the unthought of pleasures (Halperin 1997, 76–9). This may involve a reorganisation of pleasure away from the genitals, what David Halperin describes as a process of 'devirilisation' (1997, 89–90). Practices, such as fisting, are particularly interesting in this regard because they involve parts of the body – such as the fist, forearm, anus – which are not subject to a traditional overcoding by gender (Massumi 1998). It is perhaps no surprise that this erotic practice should have caught Foucault's attention: 'Physical practices like fist f***ing … make of one's body a place for the production of polymorphic pleasures, while simultaneously detaching it from the valorisation of the genitalia' (Foucault quoted in Miller 1973, 266–7). What appears most impressive about fisting is the 'ethics' of its practice: in cultivating the sphincter to enjoy the pleasure of fisting, it is necessary to engender a simultaneous 'cultivation of the self'.

Like many accounts of power, Foucault relies on the analogy of physical force in his understanding of the dynamics of power. The effectiveness of this analogy rests upon the capacity of physical force to enable entities to move in ways they would not, if not compelled. To take the example of sovereign power as described by the English philosopher Thomas Hobbes: it is the ability of the sovereign to mobilise legitimised violence and compel its subjects by force to act, which characterises its distinctive power (1998/1651, 114). The Hobbesian sovereign delegates power, but maintains absolute control over his or her delegates. In Hobbes's words, civil laws may be described as 'artificial chains … fastened at one end, to the lips of that man, or assembly, to whom they have given the sovereign power; and at the other end … to … their own ears' (1998/1651, 140). This model of sovereignty, and the fundamental relationships of force inherent to it, is arguably still a defining feature of power today (Agamben 1998, 109).

Although Foucault's model lacks the overarching presence of the sovereign (1991/1978; 1998/1976, 135–59), force remains central to the account of power provided by Foucault, which involves a constantly evolving site of contestation: 'the moving substrate of force relations which, by virtue of their inequality, constantly engender states of power, but the latter are always local and unstable' (1998/1976, 93). Foucault saw power as involving tactics, strategy, covert operation and, in his words, 'warfare' (1998/1976, 102). As in the Hobbesian model, force relationships shape behaviour – for Foucault, 'the situation when you're not doing what you want' (2000c/1984, 167) – but as a result only register due to the resistance to force. In this respect, Foucault presents a largely 'frictional' model of power. While it is possible to imagine how this field of frictional force effects provides a useful analogy for some movements of power, it is not so clear that it translates entirely to the interpersonal field of erotic relations. The facilitative gesture functions to mediate relations of touch enabling participants to control the distribution of lubricative devices within the erotic scene, by placing the sensual dynamics of the erotic assembly within the control of its participants.

The physical dynamics of touch are important here, as it is sensitive flesh that does the business of delicately negotiating lubricative explorations. Irigaray draws a symbolic opposition between sight – as the privileged form of appropriation by the 'subject' under phallocentrism – and touch, as a less objective, seemingly feminine engagement with the other (1985a, 133–46; 1985b). The lubricative engagement is too slippery to be captured by the vision of the appropriating subject that finds sexuality only through the knowledge provided by what it sees. Touch must take precedence over vision. Erotic operators come to negotiate with each other's potentiality through a sensual exploration of dark erotic spaces, caverns that have no need of sight. This does not mean that vision does not play a role, rather vision is compelled to move as a caress. One should be reminded of the 'warm eyes' of the fister here: the warm eyes do not grasp or appropriate, on the contrary they are the open door by which a union of flesh occurs. Maurice Merleau-Ponty's work on vision and the role attributed to sight in positing the very flesh we are composed of provides a way to conceptualise this touching, lubricated gaze: 'it is that the thickness of the flesh between the seer and the thing is constitutive for the thing of its visibility as for the seer of his corporeity; it is not an obstacle between them, it is their means of communication' (1992/1968, 135).

The lubricant intimately touches and is touched, it becomes part of the continuous and uninterruptible flesh of the world within the erotic scene. Sight does not need to operate outside of this economy. The warm eyes caress the other, they arouse and comfort, their touch is as fleshy and inviting as a warm lubricated hand. Consent in this sense can never be approximated by submission to a contractual agreement (which some theorists of masochism, for example, argue). Rather it involves an intersubjective relay between different erotic participants, that is ongoing, always negotiable, each gesture to the other lacking necessity and refusable. Eroticism is essentially more lubricative than it is frictional. Erotic love presupposes the consensual management of that which would otherwise be experienced as frictional. Erotic practice, as we understand it, involves precisely the successive laying down of lubricative devices.

How then can we describe a lubricative power? If, following Foucault, we define frictional power as a field of contesting force effects, then lubricative power could be described as a delta of facilitative gestures and assemblies. Applying this to the intersubjective sphere, lubricative or facilitative power can be identified as involving the investment of the self, the arrangement of the body organs and other objects in the world, with respect to the other. It is the act of making possible through the deployment of the lubricative gesture. It invites the other to enter into and share its world. These openings are not only the result of active resistance to relations of force – that is the product of contestation – but are the consequence of actively facilitative practices that emerge from collaboration and reciprocity. This process occurs not merely between humans in erotic play, but is a grappling between human body parts (skin, organs, hair, eyes) and nonhuman parts (whips, dildos, satin sheets, fluid lubricants). Consent in this context, is the way in which we open and transport ourselves in relation to others – both human and nonhuman entities – who are situationally positioned in the world. Consent is represented by the gestures made by the self, the positioning and assembly of the self, the arrangement of the scene around the self, which create the ground of potentiality and pleasure. Consent is the process of distribution of lubricative devices which through their deployment indicate the investment of the self in the scene. In this sense, consent cannot be understood as being signified by a simple 'yes' or 'no', for consent involves the incremental folding out of the self into practices, through successive deployments.

This view of consent resonates with the concept of the cultivation of the self, in so far as erotic practices provide a praxis for understanding the potentialities of the self which open up an ethical relationship with others (Foucault 2000a/1989, 287). A 'lubricative' ethic then is the ongoing project of self in which we cultivate our hearts, bodies, minds and souls to engage openly with others; the desire to lay ourselves open. And although this is a work on the self, it intimately evokes the other by seeking what could be described as an unconditioned hospitality (Derrida 2000/1997) towards the erotic engagements of others. There is a place for the sphincter here, for it represents the work that is done on the body to make it more responsive to pleasure, to generate and regulate frictional effects, to open and narrow, to allow passage. For some this organ is merely mechanical: it opens; it closes, its dilations are functional and benign. For others this is a site of contemplation, development and exploration. It represents a way of thinking about how we encounter others and operates as an invitation to future pleasures and an ongoing project of training and cultivating ourselves to grapple more delicately with others, to dialogue more intensively. It can facilitate, invite, explore, it can transform. Perhaps the most seductive aspect of a lubricative ethic is the invitation into the unknown, the possibility of a leap into a clouded infinity of potentiality. This step forward into the dark points to the potentially vast, possibly dangerous, yet also perhaps pleasurable expanse that may be opened through the well-oiled, lubricative gesture. Power is as lubricative as it is frictional. And arguably the most fantastical and pleasurable projects begin with the lubricative act.

Does the lubricative ethic provide a way forward for queer theory? Certainly queer praxis, in so far as it aims to resist the normal and through this process open itself to new pleasures, might belong to a worldly *askēsis* that reflects an ethical lubricity. Similarly, queer theory may also be said to embody a lubricative ethic in its aim to facilitate radical transformation through an active negotiation with an object of 'enquiry'. This would suggest that the 'slipperiness' of queer theory is an essential aspect of its methodology: certainly, as a form of radical critique it has been required to be as malleable as possible in order to challenge the boundaries of the cultures it analyses. And though some may long for the arrival of 'solidity' in order for queer theorising to say something of 'force', arguably its explorations are only possible as a result of an ever-flowing and abundant fluidity. There is, of course an inherent risk in a theoretical project that seeks a pure lubricity: it is always in danger of succumbing to solidification, becoming well respected and institutionalised in order to speak with any authority. Perhaps queer theory may – to paraphrase Martin Heidegger (1990/1927) – be defined as that lubricant for which its own lubricity is persistently at issue.[3]

---

3   'Dasein is an entity which does not just occur among other entities. Rather it is ontically distinguished by the fact that, in its very Being, that Being is an issue for it' (Heidegger, 1990/1927, 32).

Suggested Further Reading

Astley-Schofield, S. (1999), 'Newly Desiring and Desired: Queer Man-Fisting Women', *M/C: A Journal of Media and Culture* 2:5, http://www.uq.edu.au/mc/9907/queer.html (accessed 1 January 2008).

Bersani, L. (1988/1987), 'Is the Rectum a Grave?', in D. Crimp (ed.), *AIDS: Cultural Analysis: Cultural Activism* (Cambridge, MA: MIT Press).

Califia, P. (1988), *Macho Sluts* (New York: Alyson).

Foucault, M. (2000/1984), 'Sex, Power and the Politics of Identity', interview by B. Gallagher and A. Wilson, in P. Rabinow (ed.), *Ethics: Subjectivity and Truth, Essential Works of Foucault 1954–1984 Volume One* (London: Penguin).

Thompson, M. (ed.) (1991), *Leatherfolk: Radical Sex, People, Politics and Practice* (New York: Alyson).

References

Agamben, G. (1998/1995), *Homo Sacer: Sovereign Power and Bare Life*, trans. D. Heller-Roazen, (Stanford, CA: Stanford University Press).

Anderson, D., (2006), 'The Force That Through the Wall Drives the Penis: The Becomings and Desiring-Machines of Glory Hole Sex', *Rhizomes* 11/12 (Fall 2005/Spring 2006), http://www.rhizomes.net/issue11/anderson/index.html.

Astley-Schofield, S. (1999), 'Newly Desiring and Desired: Queer Man-Fisting Women', *M/C: A Journal of Media and Culture* 2:5, http://www.uq.edu.au/mc/9907/queer.html (accessed 1 January 2008).

Bersani, L. (1986), *The Freudian Body: Psychoanalysis and Art* (New York: Columbia University Press).

—— (1988/1987), 'Is the Rectum a Grave?', in D. Crimp (ed.), *AIDS: Cultural Analysis: Cultural Activism* (Cambridge, MA: MIT Press).

Califia, P. (1988), *Macho Sluts* (Los Angeles, CA: Alyson).

Califia-Rice, P. (1997), *Sex Changes: The Politics of Transgenderism* (San Francisco, CA: Cleis).

—— (2002), *Speaking Sex to Power: The Politics of Queer Sex* (San Francisco, CA: Cleis).

Chisholm, D. (1995), 'The "Cunning Lingua" of Desire: Bodies-Language and Perverse Performativity', in E. Grosz and E. Probyn (eds), *Sexy Bodies: The Strange Carnalities of Feminism* (London and New York: Routledge).

Cohen, J.J. and Ramlow, T.R. (2006), 'Pink Vectors of Deleuze: Queer Theory and Inhumanism', *Rhizomes* 11/12 (Fall 2005/Spring 2006), http://www.rhizomes.net/issue11/cohenramlow.html.

Deleuze G. and Guattari, F. (1994/1972), *Anti-Oedipus: Capitalism and Schizophrenia*, trans. R. Hurley, M. Seem, H.R. Lane (Minneapolis, MN and London: University of Minnesota Press).

Derrida, J. (2000/1997), *Of Hospitality*, trans. R. Bowlby (Stanford, CA: Stanford University Press).

Dowsett, G. (1996), *Practicing Desire: Homosexual Sex in the Era of Aids* (Stanford, CA: Stanford University Press).

Foucault, M. (1990/1984), *The History of Sexuality, Volume 3: The Care of Self*, trans. R. Hurley (London: Penguin).

—— (1991/1978), 'Governmentality', in *The Foucault Effect: Studies in Governmentality* (eds), G. Burchell, C. Gordon and P. Miller (London: Harvester Wheatsheaf).

—— (1998/1976), *The History of Sexuality, Volume 1: An Introduction*, trans. R. Hurley (London: Penguin).

—— (2000a/1989), 'The Ethics of the Concern of the Self as a Practice of Freedom', in P. Rabinow (ed.), *Ethics: Subjectivity and Truth, Essential Works of Foucault 1954–1984, Volume One* (London: Penguin).

—— (2000b/1989), 'Friendship as a Way of Life', in P. Rabinow (ed.), *Ethics: Subjectivity and Truth, Essential Works of Foucault 1954–1984, Volume One* (London: Penguin).

—— (2000c/1984), 'Sex, Power and the Politics of Identity', interview by B. Gallagher and A. Wilson, in P. Rabinow (ed.), *Ethics: Subjectivity and Truth, Essential Works of Foucault 1954–1984, Volume One* (London: Penguin).

Graham, M. (2004), 'Sexual Things', *GLQ: A Journal of Lesbian and Gay Studies* 10:2, 299–303.

Halperin, D.M. (1997), *Saint Foucault: Towards a Gay Hagiography* (New York: Oxford University Press).

Haraway, D.J. (1991), 'A Cyborg Manifesto: Science, Technology, and Socialist-Feminism in the Late Twentieth Century', in *Simians, Cyborgs and Women: The Reinvention of Nature* (London: Free Association Books).

Heidegger, M. (1990/1927), *Being and Time*, trans. J. Macquarrie and E. Robinson (Carlton: Blackwell).

Hobbes, T. (1998/1651), *Leviathan* (Oxford: Oxford University Press).

Irigaray, L. (1985a/1974), *Speculum of the Other Woman*, trans. G.C. Gill (Ithaca, NY: Cornell University Press).

—— (1985b/1977), 'This Sex Which is Not One', in *This Sex Which is Not One*, trans. C. Porter and C. Burke (Ithaca, NY: Cornell University Press).

Jackson, S. (1999), *Heterosexuality in Question* (London: Sage).

Latour, B. (1999), *Pandora's Hope: Essays on the Reality of Science Studies* (Cambridge, MA: Harvard University Press).

Law, J. (1986), 'On the Methods of Long-distance Control: Vessels, Navigation and the Portuguese Route to India', in J. Law (ed.), *Power, Action and Belief: A New Sociology of Knowledge?* (London: Routledge and Kegan Paul).

Mains, G. (1991), 'The View from a Sling', in M. Thompson (ed.), *Leatherfolk: Radical Sex, People, Politics and Practice* (Boston, MA: Alyson).

Massumi, B. (1998), 'Involutionary Afterword', http://www.anu.edu.au/HRC/first_ and_last/works/crclintro.htm (accessed 1 January 2008).

Merleau-Ponty, M. (1992/1968), *The Visible and the Invisible*, trans. A. Lingis (Evanston, IL: Northwestern University Press).

Michael, M. (2000), *Reconnecting Culture, Technology and Nature: From Society to Heterogeneity* (London and New York: Routledge).

Miller, J. (1973), *The Passion of Michel Foucault* (London: HarperCollins).

Nunney, M.J. (1975), *The Automotive Engine* (London: Newnes-Butterworths).

Rubin, G.S. (1991), 'The Catacombs: A Temple of the Butthole', in M. Thompson (ed.), *Leatherfolk: Radical Sex, People, Politics and Practice* (Boston, MA: Alyson).

Segal, L. (1994), *Straight Sex: The Politics of Pleasure* (London: Virago).

Sofia, Z. (2000), 'Container Technologies', *Hypatia: A Journal of Feminist Philosophy* 15:2, 181–201.

Sullivan, N. (2003), *A Critical Introduction to Queer Theory* (Edinburgh: Edinburgh University Press).

Waldby, C. (1995), 'Destruction: Boundary Erotics and Refigurations of the Heterosexual Male Body', in E. Grosz and E. Probyn (eds), *Sexy Bodies: The Strange Carnalities of Feminism* (London: Routledge).

Warner, M. (1993), 'Introduction', in M. Warner (ed.), *Fear of a Queer Planet: Queer Politics and Social Theory* (Minneapolis, MN and London: University of Minnesota Press).

All Foucault and No Knickers: Assessing Claims for a Queer-Political Erotics

Tamsin Wilton

Queer is quite a distinctive academic project and only partly because it is predicated upon a reverse discourse of discreditable desires. What we are engaged with, we dykes, faggots, fairies, queens, trannies, bulldaggers, bisexuals, polysexuals, sodomites, cunnilinguists and queer-straights, is not only what people do in bed – and researchers have always found that challenging enough – we are engaged with what *we* do in bed. Our scholarship partakes of the marginalised and abject nature of our own bodies, selves and desires. That we are prepared to do this is, of course, powerful and empowering. As feminists discovered in the 1960s, researching and theorising your own oppression may itself be emancipatory (Collins 1990; Stanley 1990).

Queer has, however, taken a radical step beyond both of its intellectual progenitors – feminism and LGBT studies – by insisting that it is possible to perturb the entire field of the erotic and of gender by establishing a theoretical location, eccentric to heteronormativity that is amenable to occupation by *anyone who wishes to position themselves as queer*. Such acts of self-location as queer, unlike the self-naming women, gays or lesbians under the pre-queer rubric of identity politics, do not depend on gender affiliation or allegiance to specific perverse pleasures. They are produced rather by pronouncing and enacting counter-hegemonic interventions in the realm of heteroerotics, and persist for the duration of any such intervention. This potential for a kind of transubstantiation of desires endows queer theory with real intellectual and social potency. It also enables the robust playfulness that is queer performativity. Set against anxious mainstream heteronormativity, the hedonistic pluralism of queer counterculture is, truly, power play.

I want to outline my understanding of the genealogy of queer theory here, to outline its intellectual parameters and to assess its effectiveness in theorising the current political economy of the erotic by examining what I believe to be the key intellectual problems confronting us. These are: the organisation of gender regimes around heterosexualised relations of looking, the corporealities of reproductivity and what I call, *pace* Michel Foucault, *pornopticism*. What I hope to assess is the usefulness of queer theory in one of the most significant and complex enterprises in postmodern Western culture – the deconstruction and disaggregation of gender and sexuality.

Sex, in the sense of all things erotic, is overburdened with significance. In addition, there is the small matter of its altogether different meaning – that of being male or female. These two sets of meanings are, of course, neither separate nor separable, rather, they are mutually co-dependent, such that to be 'properly' male or female is to experience and perform one's sexuality as gendered in specific and restricted ways (Lacqueur 1992). This paradigm, in fact, moves beyond the social organisation of sexuality to saturate and structure much of modern thinking. What are sometimes referred to as the binaries of a particular European worldview are, in fact, polarities. The cultural forms produced by the hegemonic bloc and disseminated around the world by various imperialist projects – first nation-state colonialism, latterly globalising free-market capitalism – are radically, profoundly heteronormalising (Ware 1992).

Queer theory, then, identifies gender and the erotic as sites of contestation. Indeed, it is possible to put forward a persuasive argument that the dynamics of hegemony in the modern era have been characterised by an almost obsessive attention to sex, in all its many and proliferating meanings. As Elizabeth Young-Bruehl concludes in her analysis of the nature of prejudice, 'all types of prejudice can appear in homophobic forms' (1996, 137). This has been the case whatever the putative axis around which particular hegemonic contestations have coalesced. Thus, struggles around race, secularism, dis/ability or various forms of nationalism have all incorporated and, in some cases, been driven by, ideologies of masculinity and femininity (Davis 1982; Collins 1990; Ware 1992; McClintock 1995; Lewis 1996; Young 1996) and have all made, albeit obliquely in some cases, sets of claims about the erotic. Groups organised around human or civil rights claims have pointed to the ways in which particular discourses of the erotic have been produced by and in the interests of the class-group which has oppressed them. In addition, some, pre-eminently the disability rights movement, have demanded recognition of rights relating specifically to sex (hooks 1990; Hevey 1992; Shakespeare et al. 1996).

There is, then, a hegemonic form of the erotic, produced alongside other hegemonic processes, which asserts its dominance through inclusions, exclusions and various sanctions. This being so, counter-hegemonic activism of whatever kind must at least pay attention to sexualities. Far from being a frivolous or titillating distraction from 'serious' politics or 'serious' scholarship, I understand the erotic to be that arena of human interaction which is most intimately implicated in processes of social, cultural and historical transformation. To engage in queering theory is, therefore, no small responsibility.

Groping for Peace and Muff-Diving against the Patriarchy: Radical Sex

Sex radicalism is neither new nor confined to queers. Many counter-cultural or counter-hegemonic groups have found it tempting to suggest that to engage in prohibited forms of sexual activity may itself constitute a resistant or revolutionary act. It is important to acknowledge that 'revolutionary sexual activity' has, to date, largely been noteworthy for its profoundly negative impact on the human and civil rights of those – mostly, not exclusively women – on whose bodies such acts have been perpetrated. Feminists have joined human rights activists in exposing and condemning the almost universal practice of rape as a weapon of war (French 1992), and it seems that the great cruelties and abuses which accompany political upheaval often include an element of sexual sadism (Dowd Hall 1984). While it is not unknown for men to be victimised in this way, it is overwhelmingly women who experience sexual violence, not only during periods of social conflict but as a routine part of daily life (Muthien 2003; International Committee of the Red Cross 2004). Although I do not have space here to detail this distressing history, any claims for a politically radical erotics is obliged to recognise and to engage with it. I am, however, concerned here with the happier, albeit briefer, history of the various recent manifestations of liberatory erotic radicalism, ludic celebrations of *jouissance*, in the interests of different struggles of emancipation. My overview – tentative, exploratory, a kind of intellectual foreplay – starts with that exemplary moment, the 1960s, when the early seeds of queer were sown.

The so-called 'sexual revolution' of the 1960s has been widely critiqued by feminists among others (Jeffreys 1991). It is said that if you remember the 1960s, you can't have been there, which, if you think about it, is a remarkably clever way of silencing testimony. I remember the 1960s, I promise I was there and, since my archival tendencies were strong even in adolescence, I have boxes of documentary evidence from underground counter-culture. The erotic played a complex and subtle part in that counter-culture. A generation of young people who sat around the television every evening to watch horrific scenes of wholesale slaughter from Vietnam turned to the theories of Sigmund Freud, Wilhelm Reich and Aleister Crowley to construct a radical discourse of erotic affiliation. Baffled and traumatised by the daily diet of real-life violence, this was a generation which set *eros* against *thanatos* and developed a radical politics of the erotic (Greer 1970).

The availability of effective and apparently safe contraception, and moreover contraception controlled by women, cut heterosex away from reproduction more dramatically than ever before (Jaffe 1961). This was, within both religious and medical paradigms, to deracinate sex (Hubback 1957). In terms of the policing of women's sexuality, the pill threatened to extinguish altogether the traditional consequences of engaging in extramarital sex. The newly hedonistic heterodox moreover made nonsense of the discourse of reproductive normativity which was (and continues to be) the chief justification for homophobia (Rich 1986/1980; Pharr 1988). The political and moral structuration of the erotic was transformed.

The sexual freedoms of the 1960s were, inevitably, gendered. A political slogan of the times, 'F*** the system; never f*** the same woman twice', suggests to contemporary feminists that 1960s radicalism was shackled by resolutely patriarchal constructs of gender. The texts and iconography of the underground suggest a political consciousness that was struggling to engage with the complexities of gender politics.

Queer was seeded in the underground counter-culture of the time. The Stonewall Riots (1969) are generally identified as the originary moment of the kind of anti-assimilationist gay radicalism which eventually produced Queer Nation, HOMOCULT and the like. However, I think we need to acknowledge that queer theory can also be traced back to the sex radicalism of the 1960s and 1970s. As long ago as 1970, the famous 'c*** power' issue of *Oz* carried the following pronouncement under the heading: 'Beware the lavender menace ... gay is good ... lady gay is best'.

The engagement of feminism with the erotic began in the 1960s. Feminist claims for sexual radicalism were, however, more problematic. In particular, the attention of the women's liberation movement was obliged to turn away from relatively straightforward issues to do with discovering one's clitoris, learning about orgasms and teaching men about cunnilingus (Greer 1970). It became difficult to argue for sexual exploration as liberatory once feminist researchers had exposed the extent to which sex itself was deployed by men against women in a kind of gender terrorism. Germaine Greer who, up until then had cheerfully appropriated the erstwhile male privilege of sexual agency by bedding any man who took her fancy, acknowledged the 'male sexist piggery' of the movement. She continued to insist however that women would only relinquish their status as victims of male sexuality by developing sexual assertiveness on their own account.

This has proved to be a major stumbling block for feminist theory and activism around sexuality. In particular, the simple fact that sexual activity between women is unarguably safer for women than sexual activity with men presented feminists with a dilemma. The eventual outcome was that the movement schismed around the erotic. Lesbians were produced by this schism as both the virgin and the whore of feminism. The revolutionary lesbian feminism of Sheila Jeffreys and others defined the term 'lesbian' as 'a woman-identified woman who does not f*** men', stressing that, 'it does not mean compulsory sexual activism with a woman' (1991). This evacuation of the erotic from 'lesbian' required the demonisation of sexual libertarianism, as represented by dukes such as Pat Califia, Dorothy Allison, Gayle Rubin and Joan Nestle, all of whom were engaged in commandeering for lesbians erotic pleasures – such as sadomasochism, cruising and pornography – that were previously inaccessible to women (Rubin 1984; Nestle 1987; Califia 1988; Wilton 1996). These 'sex wars' made it impossible for lesbians to function effectively within the parameters of feminism and dealt a fatal blow to feminist interventions in the erotic. While mainstream feminism remained stalled in the face of this impasse, lesbian theorists working within the feminist paradigm went on to develop a creative and proactive approach to the deconstruction of genders and erotic subjectivities which became queer theory. The intellectual groundwork of queer was laid firmly within radical feminism (Garber 2001).

Julia Kristeva is typical of the French materialist feminists in her proposal that:

> The belief that 'one is a woman' is almost as absurd and obscurantist as the belief that 'one is a man' ... a woman cannot 'be'; it is something that does not even belong in the order of being. (Kristeva quoted in Tong 1989, 230)

Just as radical as this erasure of the categories 'woman' and 'man' from the ontological order is Monique Wittig's insistence that lesbians are external to gender altogether:

> Lesbian is the only concept I know which is beyond the categories of sex (woman and man), because the designated subject (lesbian) is not a woman ... what makes a woman is a specific relation to a man ... a relation which lesbians escape by refusing to become or to stay heterosexual. (Wittig 1981)

Luce Irigaray, adopting a different strategy, prefigures the disruptive radicality of queer in her notion of 'hommosexuality', by which she means *all* sexuality organised in and expressive of the interests of phallocentric masculinity, whether performed within or outside a presumptively heterosexual pairing. Such a radical investment in deconstruction has its origins in an early moment in twentieth-century feminism. In 1969 the US-based Radicalesbians, a breakaway group from the National Organisation of Women, wrote:

> Lesbianism ... is a category of behaviour possible only in a sexist society characterised by rigid sex roles and dominated by male supremacy ... In a society in which men do not oppress women ... the categories of homosexuality and heterosexuality would disappear. 'Lesbian' is one of the sexual categories by which men have divided up humanity. (quoted in Wilton 1995, 37)

It is no coincidence that the most stringent and radical feminist interventions into the intersections between gender and the erotic should have been developed by lesbians, since heterosexual feminism has been intellectually hampered by its refusal or inability to think beyond the heteropolar paradigm. It is, moreover, as Judith Butler points out, an inevitable and intrinsic characteristic of feminism to end by reifying and reinforcing the institution which it opposes, precisely by reason of that opposition: 'the feminist subject turns out to be discursively constituted by the very political system that is supposed to facilitate its emancipation' (1990, 12–13). According to Butler's reading of the feminist subject, it seems to me that the intellectual project of disassembling the regime of gender must travel through and beyond feminism. The positioning of 'lesbian' within a cultural-feminist paradigm would seem to bear this out, as Esther Newton recognised when she cautioned against the restrictions of the women's movement that 'swears it is the enemy of traditional gender categories and yet validates lesbianism as the ultimate form of femaleness' (quoted in de Lauretis 1994, 146). Thus, the most potent and exciting thrust of nascent queer theory appears in the work of lesbians who have come from and moved through feminism: Butler, Teresa de Lauretis, Elizabeth Grosz, Judith Halberstam and others.

The radical feminist roots of queer theory are rarely acknowledged. Indeed, feminism and queer are more usually seen as mutually antagonistic. Mary McIntosh (1993) has stated that queer fails to address gender, both theoretically and within the lesbian and gay community.[1] Much as Gayle Rubin (1984) asserted that feminism could be looked to for theories of gender but not the erotic, McIntosh concludes: 'on the one side, queer theory provides a critique of the heterosexual assumptions of some feminist theory and, on the other, feminists must agitate for an awareness of gender in queer thinking' (1993, 49). This is a strange misrepresentation of queer theory which has concerned itself with gender on a profound level, although not quite in the way McIntosh implies. In fact, queer theory has usurped feminism at the cutting edge of gender studies.

To propose that radical feminism is a lone parent and queer theory its love child is, of course, wholly inaccurate. In the best traditions of queer families, it is the offspring of many parents. I have named the counter-culture of the 1960s and Foucault's name must go on the birth certificate too. There is an additional ancestor responsible for queer's focus on corporeality and embodiment: the HIV/AIDS pandemic. The nervous adherence to the homo/hetero binary was exposed by the imperatives of safer sex promotions as naïve, presumptuous and dangerous (Doyal et al. 1994). We have been obliged to develop new ways of speaking about sexual couplings: referring to 'men who have sex with men' rather than 'homosexuals' or 'gay men', and to recognise that a lesbian 'identity' does not automatically imply abstinence from sexual activity with men (Wilton 1997). The only address to sexual actors that 'works' in safe sex terms is Cindy Patton's 'don't get semen in your anus or vagina', a reinscription of the binarism that cuts between the semensexuals and non-semensexuals, thus forcefully queering the entire social field of sexual behaviours. The safe sex promotional slogan, 'It's not who you do, it's what you do', forces us to disengage acts and desires from identities and makes it instead a matter of life and death.

Intellectual Activism of the Erotic

I have named the parents and now I turn to the characteristics of this lovechild. Its counter-assimilationist pungency makes 'queer' the sign *par excellence* of a reverse discourse of self-conscious sexual deviance, as does its seeming effortless ability to incorporate the relentlessly proliferating genders and sexualities of the

---

1   McIntosh's groundbreaking paper, 'The Homosexual Role' (1968), predates Foucault's work on the invention of the homosexual by almost a decade and must therefore be seen as one of the first queer texts.

postmodern. This should not be taken at face value. Within the general relations of hegemony which both mandate and institutionalise what Elizabeth Grosz (1995) calls 'heterocentricity', heterosexual privilege is not something you can renounce simply by widening your potential cohort of sexual partners or your repertoire of sexual pleasures.

There is a general tendency to understand oppositional political energies as reactive, standing against the proactivity of a hegemonic regime which – literally 'by definition' – sets the terms of engagement. Yet, by regrouping under the sign of queer, queers may be better understood as active, rather than reactive. As Elizabeth Grosz argues, in her engagement with Gilles Deleuze's reading of Friedrich Nietzsche:

> ... both active and reactive are equally effects or products of the will to power ... Reactive forces do not steal the energy from active forces; rather, they convert active forces into the forces of reaction, they separate a force from its effects, through the creation of myth, symbolism, fantasy, and falsification. (1995, 215)

This all sits very neatly with the fantastic, mendacious symbology of queer. Yet Grosz insists that queers are not reactive, but active. She writes: 'It can just as readily be claimed ... that homophobia, heterosexism, racism, and so on are reactive forces, which function in part to *prevent* alternatives, to negate them and ruminate on how to destroy them' (1995, 216). For Grosz, it appears to be a property of lesbian and gay sexualities to occupy the place of activity in this queered Nietzschean paradigm:

> ... it is plausible to suggest that ... gay and lesbian sexual practices and lifestyles, insofar as they risk a certain stability, a certain social security and ease, insofar as they refuse these imperatives, can and should be seen as a triumph of active and productive forces. (1995, 216)

Of course, such 'active and productive forces' are not inherent in lesbian and gay 'sexual practices and lifestyles'. Indeed, from a radical feminist perspective it is relatively easy to argue, for example, that certain characteristics of gay male sexual lifestyles collude with and act to reinforce gender stratification within the realm of the erotic. By declaring ourselves queer, however, that is in political opposition to systematic structures of gendered erotic regulation exposed as political precisely by means of our opposition, we seize the place of active productivity. The semantics moreover is strategically important. Just as the word 'homosexual' was obliged to follow the invention of the term 'homosexual', so in our own time there is a silence, a space confronting us when we speak of 'queer'.

Gender Semiotics in the Postmodern: Radical Unintelligibility?

That was then, this is now. What are the 'futural imaginings' of queer at the beginning of the twenty-first century? We need to explore strategies for queering three distinct, although related, discursive sites of hegemonic assertion: the gendered gaze, heteronormative reproductivity and our own location in what I think of as the pornopticon. I want to revisit early queer rhetoric and reassert that 'queer means to f*** with gender'. I want to unpick this playful little *double entendre* and assess its political implications. What does it mean to 'f*** with' gender, to mess it up, to trouble it? Just as important, does it mean to 'f***' *with gender*? Is it politically radical, culturally transformative, socially and psychologically significant to do sex as a self-aware, explicitly gender-conscious act? Is it even possible?

It is well established that the gaze is gendered and that the gendering of relations of looking is implicated in the political economy of heterosex (Berger 1972; Mulvey 1989). It seems to be that the semiotics of gender are shifting and becoming blurred and insubstantial. The carnal beauties of Calvin Klein's loveliest boy-model, Travis Fimmel, provoking us to crave aftershave (2003–2004), have resisted containment with the homoerotic. The many websites dedicated to celebrating his beauty are overwhelmingly run by and for women, as even the most cursory internet search reveals.

A remarkably queercore lesbian iconography has moved swiftly from Madonna's *Sex* (1992) via the pages of *The Face* into the safe domesticity of the *Radio Times*. The mainstreaming of queer is not the same thing as queering the mainstream of course, and this iconography is driven by capital. It is important to ask to what extent reading such iconographic shifts as evidence of 'queering' is justified and to what extent it is the familiar appropriative act of 'reading against the grain'.

The recuperative powers of capital being what they are, it now seems indisputable that a purportedly transgressive semiotics of queer performativity has been co-opted in the interests of the market. It is not so much that queers are now a target market, it is rather that postmodern capital routinely appropriates counter-cultural signifiers as part of the project of branding. As Naomi Klein points out, the proliferating forms of counter-cultural style on the street are commandeered in the interests of brand cool as soon as they take recognisable form (2000, 14).

The representation of lesbianism in popular culture is an important barometer of gender relations and their deployment via the erotic. The history of this representational praxis has, until very recently, demonstrated the extent to which the sexualised gaze is gendered as male. Many lesbian scholars have complained about the relative scarcity of an iconography of lesbian erotics within the historical record. Female same-sex encounters are far less commonly represented than are male. This situation only changes with the development of the concept of the pornographic in the eighteenth century and with the advent of technologies for mass-producing relatively cheap erotica. It goes without saying that the market for such imagery was exclusively male, the materiality of gender relations being such that women lacked any form of access to them. In short, where the paradigmatic consumer of the erotic is male and the commodity female, representations of same-sex encounters between women are not representations of lesbians at all, rather they represent 'girl on girl action', a spurious form of behaviour driven by and in the interests of male fantasy. This is, then, a stubbornly heteroscopic construct of the figure of the lesbian.

Mainstream culture is, indeed, exposed as phallocratic by the fact that it lacks any space for the representation of 'lesbian' desires and activities, whilst constructing and maintaining a substantial space for 'girl on girl' iconographies. Moreover, there is an intriguing stratum of this cultural praxis occupied by fashion iconography, whose putative audience is female. Of course, the *über*audience for women's fashion is male. The gaze turned by the female consumer on fashion pages in women's magazines is paradigmatically Bergeresque:

> *Men act and women appear. Men look at women. Women watch themselves being looked at. This determines not only most relations between men and women but also the relation of women to themselves. (Berger 1972, 47)*

Thus, the female consumer of such publications is engaged in learning how to manage her own sexualised gender-performativity in order to enhance her market value in the system of heterosexual political economy. Examining recent representations of 'lesbians', there is little evidence of any challenge to heterosexual relations of looking until the publication, in 1992, of Madonna's coffee-table book, *Sex*. Here, 'real' lesbians are assigned mass-market representational space for the first time. But, the book did not produce anything like the kinds of iconographic leakage into the mainstream that might have been expected. Glossy magazines continued to reproduce an iconography of girl-on-girl 'lesbianism' addressed to the phallocentric gaze of the heterosexual female reader. Such images did take on the ubiquitous semiotic of postmodern irony, as exemplified by *The Face*, which drew on cheesy retro imagery from that soft-porn art-house classic *Vampyros Lesbos* for a 1997 fashion spread. However, it was not until, of all things, a car manufacturer splashed cropped and tattooed dykes on the pages of the *Radio Times* that anything remotely resembling queer female sexuality penetrated the representational mainstream.

It remains the case that queer persons' lives and desires are permitted only within strictly delineated cultural parameters. The fashion spread sapphists are ignored – nobody wants to appear naïve enough to think that they are 'real'. This is in contrast to the kinds of punishment meted out to women who are, or who may be, real lesbians. For example, the Russian girl-pop duo tATu (This Girl Loves That Girl) caused something of a minor earthquake in the pop cultural scene having had a number one hit in the UK. Knowingly exploited by mass-market men's magazines, they were trashed by music magazine *Q*, whilst lesbian glossy *Diva* refused to believe that they might, actually, be lesbians. Perhaps most tellingly, daytime television presenters Richard Madely and Judy Finnegan launched a vitriolic attack on their act, not for promoting lesbianism but for appealing to paedophiles. Such strategies tellingly expose the sophisticated cultural strategies that maintain lesbian invisibility. Faced with the alarming possibility that two sexy young women might *prefer each other* and be sexually independent of men, they were effectively heterosexualised. Not only was there a flurry of media activity to 'out' them as having boyfriends, but also a complete silence was maintained about the possibility that other young women might find them attractive. Rather, their attractiveness to men (and adult men at that) was both exploited and condemned. The fate of tATu should make us wary of celebrating what appear to be traces of the queer in the mainstream.

How Queer Is Perversion? The Politics of the Pornopticon

Foucault claimed, in the first volume of *The History of Sexuality* (1990/1976), that the repressive hypothesis was a misperception, that sexuality, far from being a natural force repressed by the imposition of power in the interests of social order, was *deployed* through various micro-political processes. He spoke of the importance of the confessional and, according to Foucault, we are everywhere impelled to confess the truth of our sex, which we have been taught to see as the truth of ourselves. In a different context, Foucault drew upon Jeremy Bentham's design for the Panopticon, a specific architectural manifestation of the correctional institution, in order to demonstrate the imperative towards self-surveillance which he thought characterised contemporary forms of social control.

I am going to combine these two Foucauldian notions, and suggest that we now inhabit the pornopticon. The drive to confess a specifically sexual truth-of-self has, at the cusp of the millennium, intersected with the uncontainable proliferation of pornographies through new forms of technology to produce new forms of policing the erotic. The imperative to confess the truth of one's sex spares no one. However, the ever-increasing impact of the new technologies of surveillance mean that such confessions must increasingly take place under the voyeuristic public gaze. In short, confession has been replaced by scrutiny and surveillance, and the imperative on us all now is to make visible, to perform, our sexual truths. Such truth-telling increasingly appears as one among many new forms of pornography, and the extent to which these new pornographies have saturated mainstream popular culture – fracturing the semiotic boundary demarcating the pornographic zone – marks the neopornographic as an enterprise of anxiety, rather than *jouissance*. Everywhere can be seen hysterical, anxious attempts to reinscribe the discursive parameters of heteronormativity on a realm of the erotic which threatens everywhere to explode out of intelligibility and containment. There are, of course, two sides to this phenomenon. It may yet be that what I see as a recuperative hegemonic strategy turns out to be the cultural expression of new forms of resistance. Or, of course, both these things may be true at the same time. The question here is whether queer sexual practices continue to be queer once co-opted by the cultural mainstream. What difference will it make if straight men get sodomised? If women use strap-ons to penetrate their male partners? The American TV show *Will and Grace* once featured a scene where Grace's boyfriend confessed to her that he had been hunting for a birthday present she had hidden, and he had looked in her underwear drawer. 'I found where you keep my competition', he remarked. This line (which got a shocked pause and then a hearty laugh from the studio audience) effectively 'castrated' Grace, by implying that, whatever phallic object might have been secreted in this most feminine of places, it was used by Grace on herself, not her boyfriend. In short, it indicated her need for phallic penetration, not a possible appropriation of phallic power.

There is not space here fully to delineate what I mean by the fracturing of the pornographic zone. I shall simply offer some examples. Firstly, there has been what appears to be a hysterical re-heterosexualisation of female performativities, which has appropriated the bodies of celebrities in order to police and re-heterosexualise all women. This seems to me to have three elements: compulsory exposure of fetishised body parts, the expectation of sexual confession by all celebrities and a remorseless scrutiny of celebrity bodies and their failure to live up to what has become a *de facto* state of grace – unattainable norms of female attractiveness. Another marker of the fracturing of the boundary of the pornographic zone may be seen in the extent to which the iconographic lexicon of the perverse has leaked into the mainstream. Piercings, body shaving, elements of a perverse semiotics from sadomasochism, all of these now routinely circulate in open-access media, in a vocal discourse of sexual display. It is no longer the case that we must confess our sexualities. Rather, we are impelled to display them. Moreover, there is an expectation of perversion. Explicit images of masturbation – male as well as female – are now routine in popular culture. Androgyny, girl-on-girl action, bondage and sadomasochism are iconographic elements of the mainstream. Rock continues to be a relatively safe space for alternative forms of masculine performativities, although it protects its machismo by mocking those who stray too far. A little deconstruction makes it clear that the dominant address continues primarily to be towards straight men – there is little boy-on-boy action, the bondage almost always involves women tying up men, and the sadomasochism eulogises the dominatrix setting to work on her male client.

I suspect that there may be genuine opportunities for queering gender and the erotic in the context of the pornopticon – simply because the pace, fluidity and responsiveness of the new pornographies makes hegemonic recuperation difficult. It is, for example, far from straightforward to assess the implications of an act like that of the female rock star Peaches. Her stage show has all the trappings of dykely queer – but the delighted and titillated audience is full of straight guys. Her lyrics proclaim 'I like girls and I like boys/I don't need to make the choice', and the CD itself looks like one of Judy Chicago's vaginas from *The Dinner Party*. However, there was no outcry, and her record company – admittedly a small independent label – seems to have been quite happy to send a vagina-enhanced CD out into the marketplace.

A Brief Note on Reproduction

It seems likely that the existential significance of sex puts in place ontological and epistemological parameters fundamentally resistant to deconstruction. The whole business of reproduction is saturated with lusts, desires and pleasures – the lust for the extreme physicality of bearing a child, the unmanageable and excessive pleasures of having a small and naked body thrashing about, crammed among your internal organs, the lechery of breastfeeding, with its sopping T-shirts, tooth-marked nipples and the heady odour of regurgitated milk – such is the stuff of an erotics about which stands a profound and deeply uneasy silence. It is a silence as noticeable in the queer arena as anywhere else. Any adequate theory of gendered, sexed corporeality *must* engage with reproductivity. Neither feminism nor (yet) queer have been able to incorporate the business of sexual reproduction into a sophisticated oppositional theoretical framework. Yet such a task is urgent. The heterosexual imperative is, above all, structured around reproductivity. The entire doctrine of heteropolarity, of 'opposite sexes' set in some kind of natural, biologically driven complementarity, has the biologistics of reproduction as its keystone. And it is precisely the non-reproductive nature of homosex which, within the terms of a reproductive heteropolarity discursively produced in religious, scientific and juridical terms, *requires* its extermination. Let us not forget, for example, Anita Bryant's poisonous assertion that, because we are unable to breed, we recruit children.

Carry on Queering

These, then, are the tasks confronting queer theorists. Complex, mutually interwoven, they have proved (so far) beyond the resources of feminism and gender studies. I would like to conclude with some observations by Michel Foucault which seem to me to be appropriate. As he sets out to demolish the repressive hypothesis, Foucault utters a warning that reads, at the same time, like a eulogy. Few warnings can ever have quite so clearly expressed the seductive nature of that which the reader is being warned against:

> … *there may be another reason that makes it so gratifying for us to define the relationship between sex and power in terms of repression: something that one might call the speaker's benefit. If sex is repressed, that is, condemned to prohibition, non-existence and silence, then the mere fact that one is speaking about it has the appearance of a deliberate transgression. A person who holds forth in such language places himself [sic] to a certain extent outside the reach of power, he upsets established law, he somehow anticipates the coming freedom … Something that smacks of revolt, of promised freedom, of the coming of age of a different law, slips easily into this discourse of sexual oppression. Some of the ancient functions of prophecy are reactivated therein. Tomorrow sex will be good again. (1990/1976, 6–7)*

Acknowledgement

Sadly and suddenly on 30 April 2006 Tamsin Wilton died shortly after delivering the text of this chapter to us. We are enormously grateful to her son Tom Coveney for permitting us to include it in the collection. We have silently emended cultural references which would now appear dated, corrected grammatical and syntactical errors and added five suggested readings. Otherwise the text is as Professor Wilton left it.

Suggested Further Reading

Berlant, L. and M. Warner (1998), 'Sex in Public', *Critical Inquiry* 24:2, 547–66.

Foucault, M. (1991/1975), *Discipline and Punish*, trans. A. Sheridan (Harmondsworth: Penguin).

Fuss, D. (1992),'Fashion and the Homospectatorial Look', *Critical Inquiry* 18, 713–37.

Garber, L. (2001), *Identity Poetics: Race, Class and the Lesbian-Feminist Roots of Queer Theory* (New York: Columbia University Press).

Wilton, T. (1996), *Finger-Licking Good: The Ins and Outs of Lesbian Sex* (London: Cassell).

References

Berger, J. (1972), *Ways of Seeing* (Harmondsworth: Penguin).

Butler, J. (1990), *Gender Trouble: Feminism and the Subversion of Identity* (London: Routledge).

Califia, P. (1988), *Macho Sluts* (Boston, MA: Alyson).

Collins, P.H. (1990), *Black Feminist Thought: Knowledge, Consciousness and the Politics of Empowerment* (London: HarperCollins).

Davis, A. (1982), *Women, Race and Class* (London: The Women's Press).

De Lauretis, T. (1994), *The Practice of Love: Lesbian Sexuality and Perverse Desire* (Bloomington, IN: Indiana University Press).

Dowd Hall, J. (1984), '"The Mind That Burns in Each Body": Women, Rape and Racial Violence', in A. Snitow, C. Stansell and S. Thompson (eds), *Desire: The Politics of Sexuality* (London: Virago).

Doyal, L., Naidoo, J. and Wilton, T. (eds) (1994), *AIDS: Setting a Feminist Agenda* (London: Taylor and Francis).

Foucault, M. (1990/1976), *The History of Sexuality, Volume 1: The Will to Knowledge*, trans. R. Hurley (Harmondsworth: Penguin).

French, M. (1992), *The War against Women* (London: Hamish Hamilton).

Garber, L. (2001), *Identity Poetics: Race, Class and the Lesbian-Feminist Roots of Queer Theory* (New York: Columbia University Press).

Greer, G. (1970), *The Female Eunuch* (London: Paladin).

Grosz, E. (1995), *Space, Time and Perversion: Essays on the Politics of Bodies* (London: Routledge).

Hevey, D. (1992), *The Creatures Time Forgot: Photography and Disability Imagery* (London: Routledge).

hooks, b. (1990), *Yearning: Race, Gender and Cultural Politics* (Boston, MA: South End Press).

Hubback, J. (1957), *Wives Who Went to College* (London: Heinemann).

International Committee of the Red Cross (2004), *Addressing the Needs of Women Affected by Armed Conflict* (Geneva: The Red Cross).

Jaffe, G. (1961), *The Life Pill: Its Effect on You and Society* (London: Consul).

Jeffreys, S. (1991), *Anticlimax: A Feminist Perspective on the Sexual Revolution* (London: The Women's Press).

Klein, N. (2000), *No Logo* (Toronto: Knopf).

Lacqueur, T. (1992), *Making Sex: Body and Gender from the Greeks to Freud* (New York: Harvard University Press).

Lewis, R. (1996), *Gendering Orientalism: Race, Femininity and Representation* (London: Routledge).

Madonna (1992), *Sex* (Warner Books).

McClintock, A. (1995), *Imperial Leather: Race, Gender and Sexuality in the Colonial Contest* (London: Routledge).

McIntosh, M. (1968), 'The Homosexual Role', in K. Plummer (ed.), *The Making of the Modern Homosexual* (London: Hutchinson).

—— (1993), 'Queer Theory and the War of the Sexes', in J. Bristow and A. Wilson (eds), *Activating Theory: Lesbian, Gay, Bisexual Politics* (London: Lawrence and Wishart).

Mulvey, L. (1989), *Visual and Other Pleasures* (London: Macmillan).

Muthien, B. (2003), *Strategic Interventions: Intersections between Gender-Based Violence and HIV/AIDS* (Cape Town: Community Law Centre at the University of Western Cape).

Nestle, J. (1987), *A Restricted Country: Essays and Short Stories* (London: Sheba).

Pharr, S. (1988), *Homophobia: A Weapon of Sexism* (Little Rock, AR: Chardon Press).

Rich, A. (1986/1980), 'Compulsory Heterosexuality and Lesbian Existence', in *Blood, Bread and Poetry: Selected Prose 1979–1985* (London: Virago).

Rubin, G.S. (1984), 'Thinking Sex: Notes for a Radical Theory of the Politics of Sexuality', in C. Vance (ed.), *Pleasure and Danger* (London: Routledge and Kegan Paul).

Shakespeare, T., Gillespie-Sells, K. and Davies, D. (eds) (1996), *The Sexual Politics of Disability: Untold Desires* (London: Cassell).

Stanley, L. (1990), *Feminist Praxis: Research, Theory and Epistemology in Feminist Sociology* (London: Routledge).

Tong, R. (1989), *Feminist Thought: A Comprehensive Introduction* (London: HarperCollins).

Ware, V. (1992), *Beyond the Pale: White Women, Racism and History* (London: Verso).

Wilton, T. (1995), *Lesbian Studies: Setting an Agenda* (London: Routledge).

—— (1996), *Finger-Licking Good: The Ins and Outs of Lesbian Sex* (London: Cassell).

—— (1997), *EnGendering AIDS: Deconstructing Sex, Text and Epidemic* (London: Sage).

Wittig, M. (1981), 'One Is Not Born a Woman', in H. Abelove, M.A. Barale and D.M. Halperin (eds), *The Lesbian and Gay Studies Reader* (London: Routledge).

Young, L. (1996), *Fear of the Dark: 'Race', Gender and Sexuality in the Cinema* (London: Routledge).

Young-Bruehl, E. (1996), *The Anatomy of Prejudices* (New York: Harvard University Press).

Index

Printed in Great Britain
by Amazon